P9-BZQ-604

THE MARVEL COMICS ENCYCLOPEDIA

A COMPLETE GUIDE TO THE CHARACTERS OF THE MARVEL UNIVERSE

LONDON, NEW YORK, MUNICH,
MELBOURNE, and DELHI

Senior Editor Alastair Dougall
Senior Art Editor Nick Avery
Senior Designer Jill Bunyan
Editor Julia March
Design Manager Robert Perry
Publishing Manager Simon Beecroft
Category Publisher Alex Allan
Production Rochelle Talary
DTP Designer Hanna Ländin

First American Edition, 2006

06 07 08 09 10 10 9 8 7 6 5 4 3 2

Publlished in the United States by DK Publishing, Inc.
375 Hudson Street, New York, New York 10014

DK Publishing, Inc. offers special discounts for bulk purchases for sales promotions or premiums.
Specific, large-quantity needs can be met with special editions, including personalized covers, excerpts
of existing guides, and corporate imprints. For more information, contact Special Markets Department,
DK Publishing, Inc., 375 Hudson Street, New York, New York, NY 10014 Fax: 800-600-9098

Published in Great Britain by Dorling Kindersley Limited.

Library of Congress Cataloging-in-Publication Data

The Marvel Comics encyclopedia : the complete guide to the characters
of the Marvel universe. -- 1st American ed.
p. cm.

ISBN-13 978-0-7566-2358-6

1. Comic strip characters--United States--Encyclopedias. 2. Marvel
Comics Group--Encyclopedias. I. DK Publishing, Inc.
PN6725.M37 2006
741.5'697303--dc22

2006010470

Colour reproduction by Media Development and Printing Ltd., UK
Printed and bound in China by HungHing.

Discover more at
www.dk.com

THE MARVEL COMICS ENCYCLOPEDIA

A COMPLETE GUIDE TO THE CHARACTERS OF THE MARVEL UNIVERSE

Contents

The Contributors

TOM DEFALCO is also the Consultant Editor for the *Marvel Encyclopedia*. He is a best-selling author and a former editor-in-chief of Marvel. He is also the author of several Dorling Kindersley Ultimate guides to Marvel Super Heroes: *Avengers: The Ultimate Guide*, *Fantastic Four: The Ultimate Guide*, *Hulk: The Incredible Guide*, and *Spider-Man: The Ultimate Guide*.

PETER SANDERSON is a comics historian and critic, who was Marvel's first official archivist. He is the author of Dorling Kindersley's best selling *X-Men: The Ultimate Guide*. Mr. Sanderson was also one of the main writers of the first four versions of *The Official Handbook of the Marvel Universe*.

TOM BREVOORT is an Executive Editor for Marvel Comics, where he oversees titles such as *Avengers*, *Fantastic Four*, *Captain America*, *Iron Man*, and others. This also puts him in the unique position of being able to change any details of any Encyclopedia entry for which he couldn't locate the correct answer!

MICHAEL TEITELBAUM has been a writer, editor, and packager of children's books, comic books, and magazines for more than 20 years. Some of Michael's more recent writing includes *X-Men School*, *Story of the X-Men*, *Story of the Hulk*, *Story of Spider-Man*, and *Batman's Guide to Crime and Detection* for Dorling Kindersley.

DANIEL WALLACE is the author or co-author of more than a dozen books, including *Superman Returns: the Visual Guide* and the *DC Comics Encyclopedia* for Dorling Kindersley, *The Art of Superman Returns*, and the *New York Times*-best-selling *Star Wars: The New Essential Guide to Characters*.

ANDREW DARLING is a film, television and comics journalist, and the author of Dorling Kindersley's forthcoming *Ghost Rider: The Ultimate Guide* and *Thunderbirds: The Making of the Movie*. Andrew also writes for *SFX* and *Dreamwatch* magazines, the *Daily Mail* and contributed to *Star Wars* and *Prisoner* Fact Files.

Introduction

by Stan Lee

What a great idea!

It ranks way up there with the discovery of fire and the invention of the wheel. Just like them, it represents an epic milestone in the history of the human race. That's why I'm so incredibly proud to be writing this intro for a book that mankind has been hungering for, a book that is—now and forever—a shining beacon of wonder, a titanic tribute to talent unleashed, with the simple but awesome title of—"The Marvel Encyclopedia." Just imagine, within these colorful pages you'll find more than a thousand of Marvels' most classic characters, all brilliantly illustrated, with their lives and vital statistics laid bare for your closest scrutiny and your browsing delight.

On a personal note, I must confess, when I first dreamed up some of the more prominent characters you'll find in this great collectors' edition, I never dreamed that decades later they would have achieved the fame and popularity which they now enjoy. It's almost impossible to describe the feeling of pride, almost mixed with disbelief, that I feel when I realize how many great movies, video games, DVDs, toys and books are based on these heroes, villains and far-out stories which we, in the mighty Marvel bullpen, had so much fun creating. None of us could have suspected that our creations would become so famous throughout the world that we'd one day find ourselves featured in a prestigious encyclopedia.

And, speaking of this extraordinary volume, when it comes to finding the hero or villain you may be seeking, the publishers, out of the goodness of their fan-loving hearts, have made it as easy for you as recognizing the Hulk in a crowd. They've put the names of each and every one—of more than a thousand characters—in convenient alphabetical order.

Just imagine, starting with the creation of the "Fantastic Four," the world's greatest comic book (as we so modestly called it), you'll be able to find decade-by-decade highlights from Marvel's fabulous comic book history. If you want to know about any of the more than one thousand characters featured in this magnificent tome, you've only to turn to the right letter.

But what about the artwork? Glad you asked! You'll find illustrations from the very best of Marvel's amazing army of artists, pencilers and inkers who have made their indelible marks on the consciousness of comic book fans worldwide.

And, naturally, the accompanying texts are written by the most acclaimed scriptwriters in Marvel's galaxy of gifted scriveners. Every sentence is a tribute to the greatest Super Hero creations this side of Asgard.

But that's not all. Realizing that some of the spectacular characters in our Super Hero stable have actually achieved such status and fame that they are now truly worldwide legends, the editors have wisely decided to accord these special heroes and villains full-page, or even double-page layouts, plus a brief guide to their essential storylines.

There's so much more that I could say, but if I do it'll keep me from leaving my computer and reaching for my beautiful, brand-new Marvel Encyclopedia which is proudly sitting on my corner table. It might be my imagination, but I seem to see a glow around that voluminous volume, as though it's illuminated by some supernatural aura, some mystic radiance emanating from the combined power of the fantastic characters within its pages.

I know I must be fantasizing, and yet—as I slowly reach out to touch the cover of this magnificent book, I wonder—as you may wonder, too—what magic lies within?

Excelsior!

Stan

Abomination

FACTFILE

REAL NAME
Emil Blonsky

OCCUPATION
Criminal

BASE
Mobile

HEIGHT 6 ft 8 in
WEIGHT 980 lbs
EYES Green
HAIR None

FIRST APPEARANCE
Tales to Astonish #90 (April 1967)

POWERS
Superhuman strength enables leaps of two miles; tough skin withstands small arms fire. Unlike Hulk, the Abomination's strength does not increase with rage, and he rarely returns to human form; however he retains all Blonsky's mental faculties.

Born in Zagreb, Yugoslavia, Emil Blonsky became a spy and infiltrated the US Air Force base where scientist Bruce Banner (*see* HULK) was stationed. Blonsky discovered gamma-radiation equipment with which Banner intended to commit suicide. Testing the device on himself, Blonsky became the monstrous Abomination.

The Abomination fought the Hulk for domination of the Earth. Their first battles ended when he was kidnapped by the STRANGER. The crew of the starship Andromeda rescued him, and he served as their first mate until his return to Earth.

Further defeats by the Hulk eroded the Abomination's courage and he retreated to the New York sewers. Envious of Bruce Banner's apparent happiness, Blonsky poisoned his wife Betty (see BANNER, BETTY). The Hulk brought Blonsky to justice and the Abomination was imprisoned in a military installation. **AD**

The Abomination is even stronger than the Hulk. His body is covered with reptilian scales.

The Hulk and the Abomination have never got on.

Absorbing Man

FACTFILE

REAL NAME
Carl "Crusher" Creel

OCCUPATION
Criminal

BASE
Mobile

HEIGHT 6 ft 4 in
WEIGHT 365 lbs
EYES Blue
HAIR None

FIRST APPEARANCE
Journey Into Mystery #114 (March 1965)

POWERS
Can magically duplicate within himself the physical and mystical properties of anything he physically contacts, including various forms of energy. If his body is broken into pieces while he is in a non-human state, he can mentally reassemble it.

Seeking a pawn to use against his nemesis THOR, the Asgardian god LOKI endowed brutal prisoner "Crusher" Creel and his ball and chain with the power to "absorb" the physical properties of anything he touched. Creel broke out of prison and battled Thor, as Loki intended. However, Creel overreached himself by trying to absorb the power of the whole Earth and exploded. Thanks to his new powers, however, Creel was not truly dead, and Loki magically reassembled his body. Loki then enlisted the Absorbing Man as his ally in an attempt to overthrow Odin, monarch of Asgard (*see* GODS OF ASGARD), but Odin banished Creel into outer space.

Over the years the Absorbing Man has repeatedly battled his archfoe Thor and his other leading adversary, the HULK. Among the Absorbing Man's other main opponents are SPIDER-MAN and the AVENGERS. During the first "Secret War" staged by the BEYONDER, Creel met another super-villain, Mary "Skeeter" MacPherran, the second TITANIA. Together they served in BARON ZEMO'S MASTERS OF EVIL when that team took over Avengers Mansion. Creel and MacPherran became partners in crime, and eventually got married. They have since divorced and Creel has resumed his criminal career. **PS**

The Absorbing Man's body can even duplicate the unknown alloy of Captain America's shield.

Acolytes

FIRST APPEARANCE X-Men #1 (October 1991)
BASE Formerly Genosha, Avalon, Asteroid M
FOUNDER MEMBERS **Fabian Cortez** Increases mutants' powers; **Exodus** Psionic powers; **Anne-Marie Cortez** Mind control; **Chrome** Alters matter; **Marco Delgado** Increases size, strength; **Rusty Collins** Pyrokinetic; **Joanna Cargill** Strength; **Skids** Creates force-field; **Colossus** Becomes organic steel; **Spoor** Super-senses; mood-altering pheromones.

When he formed the Acolytes, Fabian Cortez claimed they were dedicated to MAGNETO'S dream of a world ruled by mutants. However, Cortez betrayed Magneto and vied with him for control of the group. Appointing Exodus as leader, Magneto often sent the Acolytes to do his dirty work. When the SCARLET WITCH used her reality-altering powers against mutantkind, most of the Acolytes lost their powers. **TD**

Mutant telepath Rogue of the X-Men attracts the unwelcome attentions of Magneto's Acolytes team.

Adversary

FIRST APPEARANCE Uncanny X-Men #188 (Dec. 1984)
REAL NAME Unknown (alias Naze, the great trickster)
OCCUPATION Ancient deity **BASE** An unknown dimension
HEIGHT/WEIGHT/EYES/HAIR Not applicable
SPECIAL POWERS/ABILITIES Can assume any form he desires; may be fought successfully through magic, but not though most forms of physical force; vulnerable to iron, steel, and adamantium.

The Cheyenne believe that the Adversary is a demonic god that toys with the fate of the universe, heedless of the deaths he causes. Forge was trained to be a shaman and combat him. After his teacher, Naze, was murdered and replaced by the Adversary, Forge joined the X-Men in an attempt to stop the monster. The Adversary is imprisoned by mystical spells, but may one day escape confinement. **TD**

Agamemnon

FIRST APPEARANCE Incredible Hulk Vol. 2 #381 (May 1991)
REAL NAME Vali Halfling **OCCUPATION** Godlike observer
BASE The Mount, a mountain base in Arizona
HEIGHT 5 ft 7 in **WEIGHT** 140 lbs **EYES** Brown **HAIR** Brown
SPECIAL POWERS/ABILITIES Virtually immortal; projects a holograph of himself as an old, bearded man [*below*] so that no one suspects that he truly looks like a teenaged boy.

The son of an Asgardian god and a mortal mother, Vali traded the pick of his future offspring with the alien Troyjan race in exchange for knowledge of immortality. He wished to improve the human condition by bringing an end to war, famine and disease and so he founded the Pantheon, an interventionist think-tank, whose members include many of the children he has sired over the years, and others he has adopted. However, when Agamemnon's betrayal of his children became known to the Pantheon, he attempted to slay them all! He seemingly died trying to escape Pantheon members when his rocket was shot down. **TB**

Agent Zero

FIRST APPEARANCE (as Maverick) X-Men Vol. 2 #5 (Feb. 1992)
REAL NAME Christopher Nord (changed to David North)
OCCUPATION Secret agent, mercenary **BASE** Berlin, Germany
HEIGHT 6 ft 3 in **WEIGHT** 230 lbs **EYES** Blue **HAIR** Brown
SPECIAL POWERS/ABILITIES Can absorb kinetic energy and utilize it for superhuman strength or release it as concussive blasts. Possesses aging suppression and enhanced healing factors.

Born in East Germany, Christopher Nord became a freedom fighter against the oppressive, postwar Communist regime. He was recruited by the Central Intelligence Agency for its Weapon X project and he changed his name to David North. By the early 1960s, North was partnered with Logan and Victor Creed, the future Wolverine and Sabretooth, in the CIA's "Team X." Later, North became a mercenary under the code name Maverick. After nearly being killed by Sabretooth, Maverick reluctantly rejoined the Weapon X project, which saved his life. Nord subsequently became the project's leading special operative taking the new identity of Agent Zero. **PS**

Agent X

FIRST APPEARANCE Agent X #1 (September 2002)
REAL NAME Nijo (aka Alex Hayden)
OCCUPATION Mercenary **BASE** Mobile
HEIGHT 6 ft 2 in **WEIGHT** 210 lbs **EYES** Brown **HAIR** None
SPECIAL POWERS/ABILITIES Augmented strength, agility, and dexterity; superhuman regenerative abilities; certain advanced mental abilities; enhanced skill as a marksman.

Agent X's real name is Nijo, but during a bout of amnesia he adopted the name Alex Hayden. Agent X is a combined consciousness which resides in the body of Nijo but which also contains the mental powers of Deadpool and Black Swan. Agent X was created when the corpse of Nijo was revived and given Deadpool's healing power by Black Swan, who has the ability to enter a person's mind and unleash viruses similar to computer viruses into their brain. Agent X subsequently founded a team of mercenaries known as Agency X with his girlfriend Outlaw, Taskmaster, Sandi Brandenberg, and the mutant Mary Zero. **MT**

Aguila, El

FIRST APPEARANCE Power Man/Iron Fist #58 (August 1977)
REAL NAME Alejandro Montoya
OCCUPATION Wealthy swashbuckler **BASE** New York City
HEIGHT 6ft **WEIGHT** 190 lbs **EYES** Brown **HAIR** Black
SPECIAL POWERS/ABILITIES Can discharge electrostatic blast over 30-ft (9-meter) range, of up to 10,000 volts; highly skilled swordfighter; above-average strength; great agility.

Born in Madrid, Spain, Alejandro Montoya developed the mutant ability to discharge bursts of electricity through metal conductors; such as his steel sword. Making his way to New York City he joined other costumed vigilantes, branded himself "El Aguila" (the Eagle) and fought those who preyed on the poor and needy—drug dealers, slumlords and the like. His exploits brought him into conflict with the police as well as those famed heroes for hire Power Man (see Cage, Luke) and Iron Fist. **AD**

Ahab

FIRST APPEARANCE Fantastic Four Annual #23 (1990)
REAL NAME Dr. Roderick Campbell
OCCUPATION Geneticist **BASE** Mobile
HEIGHT 6 ft 1in **WEIGHT** (as Campbell) 166 lbs (as Ahab) 222lbs
EYES Brown **HAIR** Brown **SPECIAL POWERS/ABILITIES** Ahab possesses a robotic body, and wields psionic lances which cause those struck to feel pain, to be enslaved to his will, or to perish.

In a future era which may or may not come to pass, Ahab was the creator of a process by which captured mutants were turned into Hounds, slaves to their master's will, and used to hunt down their fellow mutants. Ahab's body was rebuilt cybernetically after he was critically injured during the escape of his best Hound, Rachel SUMMERS, into the past. Once rebuilt, he pursued her back to the present, where he became a foe of the assorted X-MEN family of teams. **TB**

Ajak

FIRST APPEARANCE The Eternals Vol. 1 #2 (August 1976)
REAL NAME Ajak **OCCUPATION** Adventurer
BASE The City of the Space Gods, Andes Mountains
HEIGHT 6 ft 1 in **WEIGHT** 220 lbs **EYES** Gray **HAIR** Black
SPECIAL POWERS/ABILITIES Superhuman strength, virtual immortality and invulnerability; could psionically levitate, rearrange the molecular structure of objects, and project cosmic energy.

One of the Polar ETERNALS, Ajak was the spokesman for the Third and the Fourth Host of the CELESTIALS on Earth. Ajak befriended archaeologist Dr. Daniel Damian. When his daughter Margo was killed, the vengeful Damian used Celestial technology to turn Ajak into a murderous monster. Ajak disintegrated himself and Damian out of guilt. Ajak is survived by his brother, Arex. **PS**

Alliance of Evil

FIRST APPEARANCE X-Factor #5 (June 1985) **BASE** Mobile
MEMBERS AND POWERS
Frenzy Superhuman strength and endurance; steel-hard skin.
Tower Alters size, strength, resilience, and density.
Timeshadow Slips in and out of dimensional sync to travel at superspeed and create phase-form duplicates of himself.
Stinger Fires electricity through her fingers.

One of the least impressive Super Villain teams to threaten Earth, the Alliance of Evil was recruited by APOCALYPSE. Seeking to further his diabolical plot to change reality, Apocalypse commanded them to capture Michael Nowlan, a mutant with the ability to magnify their powers. Forced to do battle with X-FACTOR, the Alliance's initial victory was quickly turned on its head, much to Apocalypse's disgust. Abandoned by their master, the Alliance is thought to have disbanded. **AD**

Air-Walker

FACTFILE
REAL NAME
Gabriel Lan
OCCUPATION
Herald of Galactus
BASE
Various

HEIGHT 6 ft 1 in
WEIGHT 210 lbs
EYES Blue
HAIR White

FIRST APPEARANCE
Fantastic Four #120 (March 1972)

POWERS
Command of the Power Cosmic, the fundamental force of the universe, enables a variety of powers, including force blasts, interstellar flight, and ability to walk on air.

Chosen by the planet-devouring GALACTUS to become his latest Herald after the betrayal of the SILVER SURFER, Xandarian starship captain Gabriel Lan was similarly endowed with the Power Cosmic, becoming Gabriel, the Air Walker. As the Air Walker, Gabriel served his newfound master faithfully for several years, seeking out worlds teeming with the life energies that Galactus needed to consume to survive. But when their interstellar travels led them to the home system of the mysterious Ovoids, Gabriel fell into a trap intended to slay Galactus, and was struck down.

Sensing a spark of life still remaining within his fallen Herald, Galactus transferred the Air Walker's essence into a robotic copy of his original form. However, a vital element was lost in the transference, and the Air Walker thereafter was as emotionless as the machine into which his consciousness had been transplanted—and was soon replaced as Galactus' herald. **TB**

The robotic Air-Walker was eventually destroyed in a battle with the Silver Surfer.

All-Winners Squad

FIRST APPEARANCE All-Winners Comics #19 (Fall 1946)
MEMBERS AND POWERS
Captain America Superior strength, speed, agility, and endurance.
Human Torch Can control fire and can fly.
Namor Increased strength, can fly, can breath in air or water.
Whizzer Can run at super speed.
Miss America Superhuman strength, can fly.

Following World War II, the heroes of the All-Winners Squad decided to stay together to fight crime in the US rather than foreign enemies. They battled and stopped Adam-2, an android who designed a robot army. Later they faced Future Man, a time traveler from the year 1,000,000 who hoped to destroy humanity in order to allow his race to inhabit the Earth. The Squad also battled the SHE-HULK who had traveled back in time to help some gangsters acquire an atomic bomb. **MT**

THE ALL-WINNERS SQUAD
1 Miss America ***2*** Captain America ***3*** The Human Torch ***4*** Namor, the Sub-Mariner ***5*** Whizzer

Alpha Flight

Canada's foremost Super Hero team

The Alpha Flight team roar into action.

Conceived as the Canadian government's answer to the recent spate of superhuman activity within the United States, Alpha Flight was the brainchild of James MacDonald Hudson, soon to be known first as Vindicator, then as GUARDIAN. Inspired by the FANTASTIC FOUR, Hudson and his wife Heather convinced the Canadian government to found Department H, which would be tasked with assembling a team of superhumans indigenous to the Great White North.

ESSENTIAL STORYLINES

- ***Uncanny X-Men #120–121***
Alpha Flight ambushes the X-Men in an attempt to recover the AWOL Wolverine for the Canadian government.
- ***Alpha Flight #12***
Guardian is seemingly killed during Alpha's battle with Omega Flight.
- ***Alpha Flight Vol. 3 #1–6***
With the real Alpha Flight missing, Sasquatch assembles a new team of off-beat heroes.

FACTFILE

ORIGINAL MEMBERS

GUARDIAN
Electromagnetic battlesuit allows him to fly, surrounds him with a powerful force-field, and permits him to throw bolts of electromagnetic force.

VINDICATOR
Geothermic battlesuit allows her to fly, cause the earth to erupt volcanically, and blast a lavalike substance from her hands.

SHAMAN
Withdraws needed objects from enchanted medicine pouch.

SASQUATCH
Superhuman strength and imperviousness to harm.

PUCK
Trained fighter, skilled acrobat.

SNOWBIRD
Transforms into various Canadian animal forms.

BASE
Tamarind Island, British Columbia

FIRST APPEARANCE
Uncanny X-Men #120 (April 1979)

ALPHA FLIGHT (2006)
1 Centennial ***2*** Sasquatch
3 Yukon Jack ***4*** Puck II
5 Nemesis ***6*** Major Mapleleaf

WANTED: A LEADER

The project was implemented using a three-tiered training system: new recruits or those whose powers proved unstable would be assigned to Gamma Flight. Those whose command of their abilities required further training formed the basis of Beta Flight. The front line, the active members whose job it would be to rout any superhuman threats to the nation, were Alpha Flight.

Hudson intended that the man known as Logan (*see* WOLVERINE) or WEAPON X, whom he and his wife had nursed back to sanity after years living in the Canadian wilderness, would lead Alpha Flight. However, that task fell to Hudson himself when Logan was recruited by PROFESSOR X to become a member of his X-MEN team.

Alpha Flight endured a rocky relationship with the Canadian government, being cast aside, then drafted back into military service. And while the Beta and Gamma Flight units produced some heroes who went on to serve with Alpha Flight, such as PUCK, the programs were perverted for evil purposes, forming the nucleus of the sinister Omega Flight, Alpha's opposite number. Still, the members of Alpha Flight soldiered on, through deaths and resurrections, strange transformations and sudden reversals—loyal to their mission of protecting their homeland.

When the rest of Alpha Flight had been abducted by the alien Plodex, SASQUATCH assembled a new, oddball squad. This team included the 97-year-old Centennial, Major Mapleleaf, the son of a World War II-era hero, the deadly Nemesis, Puck II (PUCK's daughter), and the mysterious Yukon Jack. Whether these heroes will stay in Alpha Flight remains to be seen. **TB**

The original team battled Wendigo and other villains in a story that featured Canadian PM Pierre Trudeau!

Alraune, Marlene

FIRST APPEARANCE The Hulk #11 (October 1978)
REAL NAME Marlene Alraune **OCCUPATION** Art history student, archaeologist, social worker **BASE** Spector Mansion, Long Island
HEIGHT 6ft 2in **WEIGHT** 130 lbs **EYES** Blue **HAIR** Blonde
SPECIAL POWERS/ABILITIES Marlene has the strength and agility of a normal woman; she is a skilled markswoman, gymnast, and hand-to-hand combatant and a resourceful crimefighter.

Marlene was in the Sudan with her father, archaeologist Dr. Peter Alraune, Sr., when he was murdered by mercenary Raoul Bushman. Another mercenary, Marc Spector, saved Marlene's life, but Bushman left him to die in the desert. Dr. Alraune's workers brought Spector's inert body to the tomb of Pharaoh Seti III. Spector miraculously revived, and he and Marlene returned to the US, where he became the crimefighter Moon Knight. Marlene is his confidante, girlfriend, and ally. PS

American Eagle

FIRST APPEARANCE Marvel Two-In-One Annual #6 (1981)
REAL NAME Jason Strongbow
OCCUPATION Champion of the Navaho Tribe
BASE Navaho Reservation, Arizona
HEIGHT 6 ft **WEIGHT** 200 lbs **EYES** Brown **HAIR** Black
SPECIAL POWERS/ABILITIES Superstrength, speed and endurance; shoots a crossbow with specialized bolts.

While leading a protest against the mining of a mountain sacred to the Navaho tribe, Jason Strongbow and his brother, Ward, encountered Klaw inside the mine. The ensuing confrontation led to Klaw releasing a sonic blast that reacted with uranium in the rock and mutagenically enhanced both brothers. Adopting the mantle American Eagle, Jason tracked Klaw to the Savage Land where he defeated the villain with the aid of the Thing, Ka-Zar and Wyatt Wingfoot, but at the cost of Ward's life. Jason returned to his tribe, and has since fought evil alongside the Fantastic Four. AD

A-Next

In one possible timeline the Avengers decide to disband, and Avengers Mansion becomes a tourist attraction. Ten years pass and Kevin Masterson, son of Thunderstrike, visits Avengers Compound and learns that Jarvis has been holding his father's enchanted mace for him! Loki decides to steal the mace and accidentally sets in train a series of events that culminate in the formation of a brand new, young team of Avengers, related in various ways to the former members. TD

FACTFILE

FOUNDING MEMBERS

THUNDERSTRIKE
Super-strong, generates thunder blasts of concussive force.

MAINFRAME
Program that lives within mobile armored, multi-weaponed, super-strong robot body.

STINGER
Flies, shrinks, generates bio-electric blasts.

J2
Super-strong, nearly unstoppable and indestructible.

EDWIN JARVIS
Director of operations.

ADDITIONAL MEMBERS
American Dream; Bluestreak; Jubilee; Freebooter; Scarlet Witch; Speedball.

BASE
Avengers Compound

FIRST APPEARANCE
A-Next #1 (October 1998)

A-NEXT
1 Stinger
2 J2
3 Jubilee
4 Speedball
5 Mainframe
6 Thunderstrike

Anaconda

FIRST APPEARANCE Marvel Two-In-One #1 (June 1980)
REAL NAME Blanche "Blondie" Sitznski
OCCUPATION Freelance criminal **BASE** Mobile
HEIGHT 6 ft 2 in **WEIGHT** 220 lbs **EYES** Green **HAIR** Blonde
SPECIAL POWERS/ABILITIES Able to stretch her limbs, wrap them around people or objects, and exert enough power to crush one-inch thick steel. Few humans can break free from her grasp.

Former Steelworker Blanche Sitznski underwent bioengineering changes at the mutagenics lab of a now defunct Roxxon subsidiary called the Brand Corporation, and became Anaconda. She used her new snakelike powers as a member of the Serpent Squad, retrieving the Serpent Crown, an ancient power object. After a spell as a freelance mercenary, Anaconda joined Sidewinder in a new criminal organization called the Serpent Society. MT

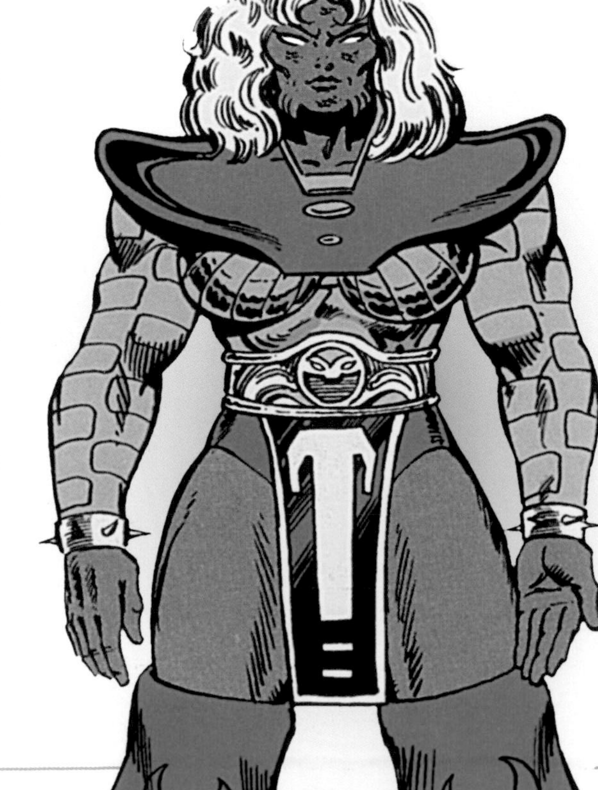

Ancient One

Five centuries ago the master sorcerer called the Ancient One was a young farmer in the Himalayan village of Kamar-Taj. He studied sorcery with another villager, KALUU. When Kaluu sought to use his powers for conquest, the youth thwarted him, and henceforth dedicated his life to opposing evil sorcerers. He eventually became Sorcerer Supreme of Earth's dimension.

Though magic greatly extended his life, the Ancient One knew that his death was inevitable and sought to train a successor. He accepted BARON MORDO as a pupil, although he was aware of Mordo's potential for evil. Then the American surgeon Stephen Strange arrived, hoping that the Ancient One could cure his injured hands. Instead Strange found a new vocation and asked to become the Ancient One's pupil. Under the Ancient One's tutelage, DOCTOR STRANGE ultimately became the new sorcerer supreme of the Earth dimension.

Later, to prevent the demon Shuma-Gorath from entering the Earth dimension through his mind, the Ancient One persuaded Strange to shut down the elderly sorcerer's brain. Thus the Ancient One died in mortal form, but his astral form became "one with the universe." **PS**

In the retelling of Doctor Strange's origin in the 2004 series *Strange*, the Ancient One has a more contemporary look.

FACTFILE

REAL NAME
Unrevealed

OCCUPATION
Sorcerer Supreme

BASE
Kamar-Taj, Tibet, China

HEIGHT 5 ft 11 in
WEIGHT 160 lbs
EYES Brown
HAIR Bald, with white beard

FIRST APPEARANCE
Strange Tales Vol. 1 #110 (July 1963)

ANCIENT ONE

POWERS

Vast natural talent allied to years of training made him the greatest sorcerer in Earth's dimension, capable of astral projection, mesmerism, illusion-casting etc; able to hurl bolts of energy and possessed of extraordinary longevity.

Andromeda

FIRST APPEARANCE Defenders #143 (May 1985)
REAL NAME Andromeda **OCCUPATION** Warrior **BASE** Atlantis
HEIGHT 5 ft 8 in **WEIGHT** 180 lbs **EYES** Green **HAIR** Auburn
SPECIAL POWERS/ABILITIES Her physiology is suited to survival beneath the ocean; unusually strong for an Atlantean woman; highly skilled combatant, expert with a trident; on land, special serum allows her to breathe unaided for 12 hours.

Inspired by tales of NAMOR the Sub-Mariner's adventures among the humans of the surface world, the Atlantean soldier called Andromeda (a corruption of her true Atlantean name) used a serum that allowed her to breathe air and also changed the color of her skin to allow her to survive above the waves. Now resembling a normal human being, she called herself Andrea McPhee and set out to follow in Namor's footsteps. For a time, she adventured with the Defenders, a team to which Namor once belonged. After the group disbanded, she eventually returned to her duties in Atlantis. **TB**

Angar

FIRST APPEARANCE Daredevil #100 (June 1973)
REAL NAME David Alan Angar
OCCUPATION Criminal **BASE** San Francisco
HEIGHT 6ft 10in **WEIGHT** 155lbs **EYES** Brown **HAIR** Brown
SPECIAL POWERS/ABILITIES His scream creates chemical toxins in the brains of his victims, causing short-term memory loss and nightmarish hallucinations.

Disillusioned social activist David Angar volunteered for an experiment that would give him superpowers. Exposed to technology brought to Earth by the priestess MOONDRAGON, Angar developed a hallucination-inducing scream. Engaged by Moondragon's malevolent partner, Kerwin J Broderick, to kill DAREDEVIL and BLACK WIDOW, only Daredevil's persuasive skills stayed Angar's voice. Becoming a criminal for hire, Angar spent time in prison and lost his powers. MASTER KHAN, who wanted Angar to brainwash prisoners to perform terrorist acts, later reinstated them. Angar was eventually gunned down by police during a robbery. **AD**

Ani-Mator

FIRST APPEARANCE New Mutants # 59 (January 1988)
REAL NAME Dr. Fredrick Animus **OCCUPATION** Geneticist
BASE Formerly "Paradise", island in North Atlantic **HEIGHT** 5ft 6in
WEIGHT 127 lbs **EYES** Brown **HAIR** Nearly bald
SPECIAL POWERS/ABILITIES Has a vast knowledge of genetics, beyond that of most scientists. Creates new species of life with humanoid characteristics by the genetic manipulation of animals.

Brilliant geneticist Fredrick Animus was obsessed with the genetics of mutation. He was contacted by Cameron HODGE, commander of the anti-mutant group known as THE RIGHT. Hodge set Animus up on an island and supplied him with animals to use as test subjects. There, Animus created "Ani-Mates" by splicing together animal and human genes, and began calling himself the Ani-Mator. Even though some of his Ani-Mates had human levels of intelligence, Ani-Mator treated them cruelly. When one, BIRD-BRAIN, escaped and returned with members of the NEW MUTANTS, they freed the Ani-Mates and MAGIK exiled Ani-Mator to the dimension called Limbo. **MT**

Annihilus

FIRST APPEARANCE Fantastic Four Annual #6 (1968)
REAL NAME Annihilus **OCCUPATION** Conqueror; destroyer
BASE Sector 17A of the Negative Zone
HEIGHT 5 ft 11 in **WEIGHT** 200 lbs **EYES** Green **HAIR** None
SPECIAL POWERS/ABILITIES Exoskeleton can withstand vast external pressure (up to 1,500 psi). He can breathe in the vacuum of space. His wings enable him to fly at up to 150 mph.

In the Negative Zone, spores were released on the barren planet Arthros by the dying crew of a Tyannan ship which crashed on the planet. One of those spores grew into an insect-like being called Annihilus. Wielding the Cosmic Control Rod, which gives him great power and cunning, he became master of the life forms that grew from the other spores released on Arthros. He set out to conquer the other worlds of the Negative Zone, and his later attempt to conquer Earth put him in conflict with the Fantastic Four. MT

Anya

FIRST APPEARANCE Amazing Fantasy Vol. 1 #1 (July 2004)
REAL NAME Anya Corazón
OCCUPATION Adventurer; student **BASE** New York City
HEIGHT 5 ft 2 in **WEIGHT** 105 lbs **EYES** Brown **HAIR** Brown
SPECIAL POWERS/ABILITIES Anya can stick to walls, climb up buildings, shoot webs, and has a "Spidey" sense that warns her of impending danger.

Quick-tempered high-school student Anya Corazón lived with her father in Brooklyn, New York. Her father was an investigative reporter and also the landlord of their apartment building. Caught in the crossfire between two warring mystical clans, the Spider Society and the Sisterhood of the Wasp, Anya was mortally wounded. Miguel, an agent of the Spider Society, performed an ancient ritual upon her and gave her a spider-shaped tatoo, thereby unlocking her spider-like powers, and Anya learned that she was the last in a 900-year-old line of Hunters, charged with saving the world. Confused and unsure about her new abilities—which are similar to the powers that Spider-Man possesses—Anya took the name Araña (which means "spider" in Spanish) and set about her quest. MT

Ant-Man II

Ant-Man II

FACTFILE

REAL NAME
Scott Edward Lang

OCCUPATION
Adventurer; former burglar, electronics technician

BASE
Avengers Mansion

HEIGHT 6 ft
WEIGHT 190 lbs
EYES Blue
HAIR Blond

FIRST APPEARANCE
Avengers Vol. 1 #181 (March 1979)

POWERS
Possesses ability to shrink himself and other objects and people, usually to ant size, but also to microscopic levels. Cybernetic helmet allows him telepathic control of ants. Helmet amplifies his voice so that he can be heard by normal-sized humans.

Lang was an electronics expert who briefly turned to crime to help support his family. He was eventually arrested and sent to prison. After being paroled for good behavior, he worked at Stark Industries. His wife divorced him, but gave him custody of their daughter Cassie. Scott learned that Cassie needed an expensive heart operation, but her surgeon had been kidnapped. He resorted to burglary, breaking into the home of Dr. Hank Pym and stealing his old Ant-Man costume and shrinking formula. After rescuing the surgeon and saving Cassie, Scott turned himself in, but Pym decided to allow him to continue as Ant-Man. Scott often aided the Avengers and eventually joined the team. When his ex-wife learned that he was the new Ant-Man, she sued and won custody of Cassie. Scott was later killed in action when the Scarlet Witch disassembled the Avengers. TD

As Ant Man, Scott was just ½ in tall and weighed little more than 1 lb.

Scott frequently clashed with the volatile Jack of Hearts, who thought Scott was not powerful enough to be a member of the Avengers.

Apalla the Sun Queen

FIRST APPEARANCE Doctor Strange Vol. 2 #22 (April 1977)
REAL NAME Apalla **OCCUPATION** Embodiment of the Sun
BASE Earth's solar system **HEIGHT** Variable **WEIGHT** Variable
EYES Variable **HAIR** Flaming orange
SPECIAL POWERS/ABILITIES Possesses all the powers of the Sun: able to generate heat, light etc; it is likely her abilities are restricted by her physical form.

Apalla is the corporeal manifestation of the Sun. Although thought to walk upon the Earth, sightings of her are few. When the league of sorcerers, the Creators, wished to take over the stars and transform them into humans, Apalla helped Doctor Strange oppose them. A further encounter involved Captain Mar-Vell. Due to a radioactive overdose, Mar-Vell was draining her energies each time he used his powers. The pair rectified the situation before lasting damage could be done. **AD**

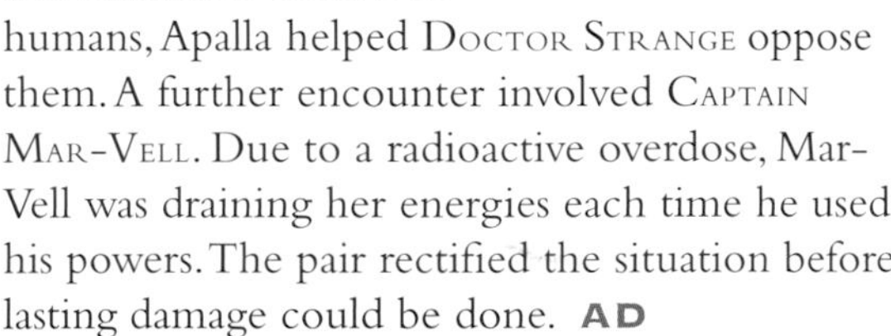

Aquarian

FIRST APPEARANCE Adventure Into Fear #17 (October 1973)
REAL NAME Wundarr **OCCUPATION** Adventurer
BASE Commune on southern California coast
HEIGHT 5 ft 10in **WEIGHT** 165 lbs **EYES** Brown **HAIR** Brown
SPECIAL POWERS/ABILITIES Surrounded by null-field that neutralizes other superhumans' kinetic and electromagnetic energies; walks on air.

When Wundarr's father thought their homeworld of Dakkam was about to explode, he sent his young son into space. Wundarr landed on Earth, where the Sun's energy endowed him with superhuman powers. An encounter with a Cosmic Cube augmented these powers and gave him great knowledge and a sense of purpose. Restyling himself Aquarian, he is now a self-professed prophet. **AD**

Arabian Knight

FIRST APPEARANCE Incredible Hulk #250 (August 1980)
REAL NAME Abdul Qamar
OCCUPATION Bedouin chieftain **BASE** Saudi Arabia
HEIGHT 5 ft 10 in **WEIGHT** 170 lbs **EYES** Brown **HAIR** Black
SPECIAL POWERS/ABILITIES Scimitar fires force bolts and penetrates almost any material; rides magic carpet, which could also convert into battering ram or envelop enemies.

Having uncovered the tomb of his ancestor, who had been a hero to his people, Abdul Qamar acquired his three mystic weapons, and set out to carry on his tradition as the modern Arabian Knight. He fought for justice for many years, but eventually perished when his life force was randomly and remotely sucked away from him by the life-draining Humus Sapien—leaving him a casualty of a conflict which had nothing to do with him directly. **TB**

Apocalypse

FACTFILE
REAL NAME
En Sabah Nur
OCCUPATION
Conqueror
BASE
Mobile

HEIGHT Variable, usually 7 ft
WEIGHT Variable
EYES Blue
HAIR Black

FIRST APPEARANCE
(In shadow) X-Factor #5 (June 1986), (fully shown) X-Factor #6 (July 1986)

POWERS
Can alter the atomic structure of his body to change shape. Can increase his size by absorbing additional mass. Possesses superhuman strength, stamina and durability.

Born nearly 5,000 years ago in ancient Egypt, Apocalypse is one of the earliest known mutant humans. Left to die, the infant was found by outlaw leader Baal, who named him "En Sabah Nur," or "The First One." Baal taught Nur his philosophy of the survival of the fittest and told him he was fated to be a conqueror. Nur traveled the world for thousands of years, instigating wars to test which nations were "fittest," and was worshipped as a god by ancient civilizations. In the 20th century Nur, now called Apocalypse, decided that the emerging superhuman mutants were destined to supplant "unfit" ordinary humans. Hence he often battled the original X-Factor and the X-Men, who were dedicated to peaceful coexistence between mutants and other humans. Though extraordinarily long-lived, Apocalypse's physical body eventually wore out, but he survives by projecting his consciousness into host bodies. In an alternate timeline, the "Age of Apocalypse," Apocalypse conquered North America and enslaved humanity; he was killed by Magneto. **PS**

Apocalypse's first modern team of Horsemen, his warrior servants, included Famine, War, Pestilence, (from left to right) and Archangel as Death (not shown).

ARCADE

ARCADE

FACTFILE

REAL NAME
Unknown

OCCUPATION
Assassin; playboy

BASE
Various Murderworlds in undisclosed locations

HEIGHT 5 ft 6 in
WEIGHT 140 lbs
EYES Blue
HAIR Red

FIRST APPEARANCE
Marvel Team-Up Vol. 1 #65 (January 1978)

POWERS
Genius at engineering, electronics, and robotics; habitual liar, using deceit to confuse opponents.

An engineering genius and a ruthless hitman, Arcade came by his fortune after allegedly murdering his billionaire father. He is obsessed with traps and games, and executes his victims in secret, amusement-park-style complexes he designs himself and dubs "Murderworlds." He charges $1 million per hit, but the money barely covers his expenses; he kills for sheer enjoyment.

Arcade is assisted by two henchmen, Miss Locke and Mr. Chambers. His victims include business tycoons and Super Heroes such as the X-MEN, SPIDER-MAN, and CAPTAIN BRITAIN, whom he kidnaps and then releases inside Murderworld. He studies victims' weaknesses, chooses an appropriate killing method, and then looks on gleefully as they fight for their lives against his killing machines, which are often modeled on arcade games. Super Villains pay to use Murderworld as a training ground, or purchase Arcade's robots, which are virtually indistinguishable from real people. **DW**

--THE X-MEN ARE AS GOOD AS DEAD!

Arcade is delighted when his victims express terror and panic. Recently, Arcade kidnapped the Thing and a roomful of party guests, and tormented them on remote Murder Island.

ARCANNA

FIRST APPEARANCE Defenders #112 (October 1982)
REAL NAME Arcanna Jones
OCCUPATION Adventurer **BASE** Squadron City
HEIGHT 5 ft 8 in **WEIGHT** 115 lbs **EYES** Blue **HAIR** Blonde
SPECIAL POWERS/ABILITIES Arcanna possesses extensive magical powers, especially over natural forces, such as wind and water; able to levitate and ride the wind, sometimes on a pole.

A former medium who spent years developing her natural affinity for magic, Arcanna was encouraged to use her mystic powers in the service of mankind by her husband. Arcanna joined the ranks of the SQUADRON SUPREME, the foremost costumed champions of her home reality, and became one of its staunchest members—eventually using her magic powers to hollow out the enormous crater in which they built their upgraded headquarters, Squadron City. **TB**

ARCHANGEL *SEE OPPOSITE PAGE*

ARKON

FIRST APPEARANCE Avengers #75 (April 1970)
REAL NAME Arkon ("The Magnificent")
OCCUPATION Ruler ("Imperion") **BASE** The planet Polemachus
HEIGHT 6 ft **WEIGHT** 400 lbs **EYES** Brown **HAIR** Brown
SPECIAL POWERS/ABILITIES Superhuman strength, speed, agility, and stamina; skin and muscles are more dense than that of humans; recovers from injury at a much faster rate than humans.

Arkon is a great leader and warrior on the planet Polemachus. The culture of Polemachus glorifies war and Arkon became his world's greatest warrior. As Imperion of the largest country on Polemachus, Arkon attempted to conquer the other nations of his world. But when Polemachus was faced with planet-wide annihilation, Arkon came to Earth believing that its destruction could save his homeworld. On Earth, IRON MAN teamed with THOR in a plan which saved Polemachus and stopped Arkon's aggression. **MT**

ARMADILLO

FIRST APPEARANCE Captain America Vol. 1 #308 (August 1985)
REAL NAME Antonio Rodriguez
OCCUPATION Professional wrestler **BASE** Mobile
HEIGHT 7 ft 6 in **WEIGHT** 540 lbs **EYES** Brown **HAIR** None
SPECIAL POWERS/ABILITIES Body resembles that of a gigantic humanoid armadillo, with sharp claws and armor plating; possesses superhuman strength and durability.

When his wife became mortally ill, Antonio Rodriguez turned to Dr. Karl Malus, who promised to try to cure her if Antonio worked for him and submitted to his experiments. Malus combined genes from an armadillo with Rodriguez's genes, transforming him into a super-powerful being resembling a humanoid armadillo. Malus assigned the Armadillo to invade the West Coast Avengers Compound. There Captain America defeated the Armadillo but realized he was not a criminal at heart. Though the Armadillo has sometimes run foul of the law, he prefers to earn his living in wrestling matches against super-strong opponents. **PS**

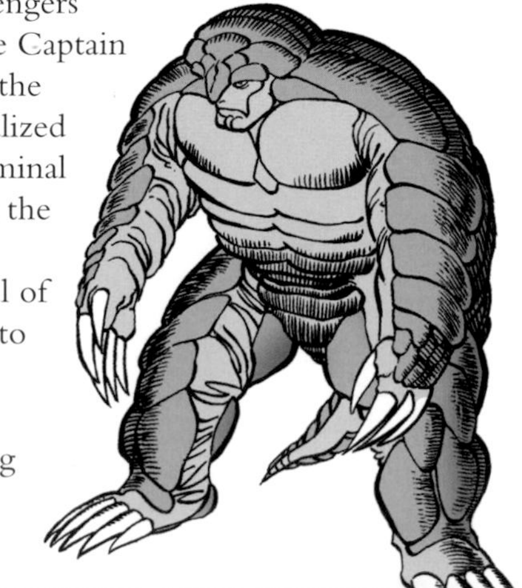

Archangel

The Avenging Angel

Warren's skin gained a blue pigment during his time working for Apocalypse.

Warren Worthington was born into a wealthy family. At private school, during his late teens, Warren noticed wings budding from his shoulder blades. Fearful of attracting attention, he strapped them to his body but secretly began experimenting with flying. When a fire started in his school, Warren flew to the rescue of his schoolmates disguised in a nightshirt and blond wig. He was mistaken for an angel and so, when he headed to New York City to become a costumed crime fighter, he took the moniker Avenging Angel.

ITINERANT X-MAN

Warren soon came to the attention of PROFESSOR X and joined the Professor's fledgling band of X-MEN. At first, Warren disguised his face with a mask, but he later discarded it, believing that his handsome, telegenic features would help gain the team public support. Such vanity, combined with a certain flightiness, has been a hallmark of Warren's life as a mutant. With his vast, inherited wealth it was perhaps inevitable that he would become a media playboy. Similarly, although he remained loyal to Professor X's

Having lost both his parents, the X-Men have become a surrogate family to Archangel, bickering and fighting but also protecting and defending each other.

broad ideals, he drifted between various superpowered teams, using his fortune to provide backing to the Champions of Los Angeles, the DEFENDERS and later X-FACTOR. While with X-Factor Warren's wings were damaged battling the MARAUDERS. The wings became infected and had to be amputated. The loss of his wings so depressed Warren that he attempted suicide. Saved by the mutant warlord APOCALYPSE, Warren was offered the chance to grow new wings of steel if he became one of Apocalypse's Horsemen—Death. Confused and still depressed, Warren agreed, but this Faustian pact brought him into direct conflict with his X-Men friends. Only the apparent death of his old friend ICEMAN brought Warren to his senses. Following this epiphany, Warren's metal wings molted to reveal feathers beneath. He rededicated himself to the X-Men's cause and rejoined the group. To mark this new beginning Warren rechristened himself Archangel. **AD**

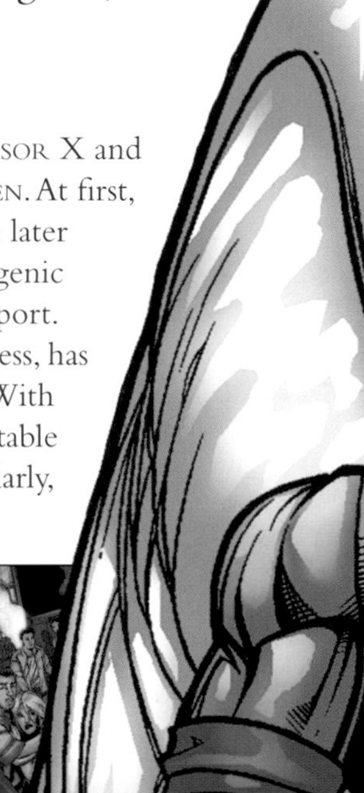

When his wings are pinned to his body, Warren can pass as a non-mutant.

ESSENTIAL STORYLINES

- ***X-Men Vol. 1 #54–6*** Warren Worthington's origins are shown—from a public schoolboy who grows wings to a member of the X-Men.
- ***X-Factor #10–15, Thor #373–4*** Angel's wings are amputated and he is driven to suicide.
- ***X-Factor #21–25*** Apocalypse appoints Angel as his Fourth Horseman, Death.

FACTFILE

REAL NAME
Warren Kenneth Worthington III

OCCUPATION
Hero and Chairman of Worthington Industries

BASE
New York State ("Avengers Tower"), Manhattan, New York

HEIGHT 6ft
WEIGHT 150lbs
EYES Blue
HAIR Blond

FIRST APPEARANCE
X-Men #1 (September 1963)

POWERS

Feathered wings can carry up to twice his weight and bear him to 29,000 feet; able to fly up to 150mph; enhanced lungs enable him to breath at high altitudes; possesses extraordinary eyesight and blood has healing qualities.

During his recent stay in Genosha as part of the Excalibur team, Archangel battled the high-tech soldiers known as the Weaponeers.

Aries

Born under the sign of the Ram

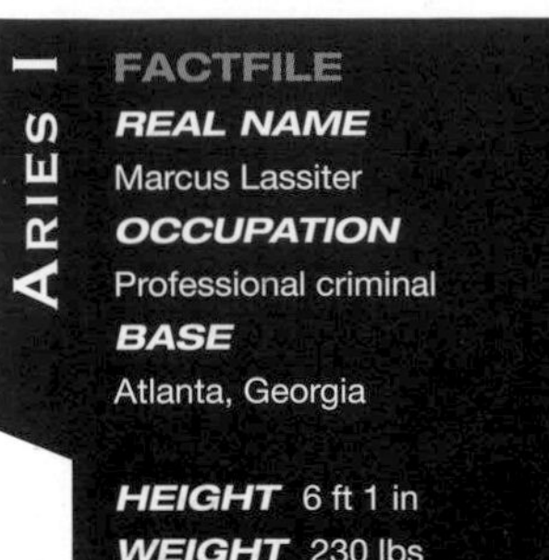

Aries I

FACTFILE

REAL NAME
Marcus Lassiter

OCCUPATION
Professional criminal

BASE
Atlanta, Georgia

HEIGHT 6 ft 1 in
WEIGHT 230 lbs
EYES Brown
HAIR Unknown

FIRST APPEARANCE
Avengers Vol. I #72 (January 1970)

Aries II

FACTFILE

REAL NAME
Grover Raymond

OCCUPATION
Professional criminal

BASE
Chicago, Illinois

HEIGHT 6 ft
WEIGHT 225 lbs
EYES Brown
HAIR Black

FIRST APPEARANCE
Avengers Vol. I #120 (February 1974)

POWERS

The horns of Aries' costume were made of an incredibly hard, unknown material. He used them as a weapon, charging into opponents. Aries also wielded the Zodiac Key, an otherdimensional, sentient power object capable of firing energy bolts and transporting people across dimensions.

Aries II's first appearance, in *Avengers* #120.

The first Aries, the human known as Marcus Lassiter, takes Manhattan.

Aries was a member of the criminal organization known as Zodiac. Founded by Cornelius van Lunt was comprised of 12 human criminals, of which Marcus Lassiter (Aries), was one. Each member of the organization was based in a particular city in the US and took their codename from the astrological sign under which he or she was born.

Aries I prepares to unleash his power against Avengers leader Captain America.

The Zodiac Key

The original human Aries, Marcus Lassiter took possession of the powerful interdimensional Zodiac Key. He then led a small army and succeeded in capturing Manhattan Island and sealing it off from the rest of the world with a force field. He tried to hold the island for ransom but this plan was stopped by the Avengers and Daredevil. The first Aries died in an explosion. The Zodiac Key was apparently destroyed (though this turned out to be untrue).

Aries I

Aries II

As Daredevil looks on, Aries I threatens to execute the Avengers team using the Zodiac Key. But though he sets the chamber ablaze, it is his own plans for conquest that will shortly go up in smoke.

Horned Villains

The second human Aries, Grover Raymond, physically merged with the alien Lucifer and died as a result. The third human Aries, whose real name is unknown, battled Iron Man II (James Rhodes) and was killed by a member of the android Zodiac organization.

A second criminal group called Zodiac, led by Jacob Fury, was made up of android versions of the original human Zodiac members. The first android Aries (Aries IV) possessed superhuman strength. The second android Aries (Aries V) could shoot fire from his horns, although this might have simply been a power of his costume, not of the android himself. **MT**

ESSENTIAL STORYLINES

- ***Avengers #82*** Marcus Lassiter (Aries I) places a force field around the island of Manhattan and attempts to hold it for ransom. He is unsuccessful and is killed trying to escape.
- ***Avengers #120*** Grover Raymond (Aries II) is recruited into the Zodiac Cartel to replace Marcus Lassiter, but finds himself in conflict with Taurus.

FACTFILE

ARMAGEDDON

REAL NAME
Arm'Chedon

OCCUPATION
Warlord of the Troyjan

BASE
Troyjan-controlled space

HEIGHT 9 ft
WEIGHT 2,528 lbs
EYES Inapplicable; Troyjans have no pupils.
HAIR Gray

FIRST APPEARANCE
Incredible Hulk Vol. 2 #413 (January 1994)

POWERS
Superhuman strength and energy manipulation; enhanced durability and resistance to injury; warlike temperament; great leadership qualities.

Armageddon

Leader of the long-lived intergalactic race known as the Troyjan, the teen who would one day be known as Armageddon almost single-handedly reversed the fortunes of his race's declining empire. Under his leadership, the Troyjan expanded their galactic power base, and became a force to be reckoned with. Armageddon's attentions first turned to Earth after his son Trauma abducted ATALANTA of the PANTHEON in order to make her his mate. Trauma was subsequently killed in battle with the incredible HULK. Vowing revenge, Armageddon used a resurrection device created by the gamma-enhanced genius known as the LEADER to reincarnate the then-deceased Thunderbolt ROSS, in order to lure the Hulk into his clutches. Once the Hulk had been captured, Armageddon intended to use his life-force to restore Trauma to life. But the Hulk's energy proved too powerful, and it incinerated the remains of the deceased Troyjan warrior—leaving Armageddon with an even greater desire for revenge! **TB**

Armageddon's son, Trauma, lost his life in battle with the Hulk after trying to abduct Atalanta of the Pantheon.

To avenge his son's death, Armageddon launched attacks against the Pantheon and the Earth.

Armbruster, Col. John

FIRST APPEARANCE Incredible Hulk Vol. 1 #164 (June 1973)
REAL NAME Colonel John D. "Jack" Armbruster
OCCUPATION Colonel in US Air Force **BASE** Mobile
HEIGHT 6 ft 1 in **WEIGHT** 225 lbs **EYES** Blue **HAIR** Gray
SPECIAL POWERS/ABILITIES Military strategist, resourceful, honorable, and heroically loyal; inveterate pipe-smoker.

Colonel Armbruster led a force to rescue General ROSS from the Russians. Although Ross' son-in-law, Major TALBOT, was lost during the mission, it was deemed successful and Armbruster was given control of Project Greenskin, an attempt to study the effects of gamma-radiation on the human body. Armbruster's main objective was to capture the HULK, which he succeeded in doing. When Talbot eventually returned, apparently having escaped from the Russians, Armbruster suspected foul play: when he shook hands with Talbot, his watch stopped. Armbruster discovered that there was a bomb in Talbot's body and dragged the Major into a pit. The bomb exploded, killing them both, but preventing the assassination of the US President. **AD**

Aron, the Rogue Watcher

FIRST APPEARANCE Captain Marvel #39 (July 1975)
REAL NAME Aron **OCCUPATION** Cosmic meddler
BASE Mobile; intergalactic **HEIGHT** Variable **WEIGHT** Variable
EYES White; yellow when angry **HAIR** None
SPECIAL POWERS/ABILITIES Vast cosmic abilities; changed appearance at will; able to move between dimensions; subdued enemies with psionic blasts, or teleported them.

A young Watcher, as such temporal matters as age are measured by that intergalactic race, Aron eschewed his people's pledge of non-interference in all things, choosing instead to use his great cosmic abilities for his evil enjoyment. He toyed with the lives of the FANTASTIC FOUR, replacing them with corrupt duplicates, and later engineered a civil war within his own Watcher race. As Aron was about to destroy the Fantastic Four, UATU THE WATCHER, who was responsible for our section of the cosmos, reluctantly killed him. **TB**

Atalanta

FIRST APPEARANCE The Incredible Hulk #376 (December 1990)
REAL NAME Unrevealed **OCCUPATION** Pantheon operative
BASE The Mount, southwestern United States
HEIGHT 5 ft 10 in **WEIGHT** Unknown **EYES** Blue **HAIR** Black
SPECIAL POWERS/ABILITIES Wields a bow and arrows composed of an unknown form of energy that turns matter into super-heated plasma.

Named after the huntress of Greek mythology, Atalanta is a member of the PANTHEON, a covert organization of superhumans which intervenes in world affairs to prevent disasters. A deadly shot with her flaming bow, Atalanta's skin, body tissue and skeleton are denser than a normal human's, affording her greater resistance to injury. She also possesses a fast healing factor and an extended lifespan. A psychic power enables her to mentally perceive her target even if she is unable to see it.

Virtually nothing is known about the origin of Atalanta, except that she is related to other members of the Pantheon. She has been the lover of fellow Pantheon member Achilles. **PS**

ATLANTEANS

Undersea warrior race

ATLANTEANS

FACTFILE

NOTABLE ATLANTEANS

PRINCE NAMOR
LADY DORMA (Namor's first royal consort, deceased),
ATTUMA (barbarian warlord)
KRANG (usurper),
VASHTI (Namor's Grand Vizier),
PRINCE BYRRAH
LADY FEN (Namor's mother, deceased),
NAMORA (Namor's cousin, deceased),
NAMORITA
BEEMER (would-be usurper).

FIRST APPEARANCE
Fantastic Four Annual #1 (1963)

POWERS
Atlanteans' gills allow them to breathe underwater; they only survive five minutes out of water. They are about ten times stronger and faster than "surface dwellers." They easily withstand the crushing pressure and freezing temperatures at the bottom of the ocean.

Atlantis was once a small continent in the Atlantic Ocean. The cradle of an advanced civilization, Atlantis was torn apart by earthquakes and sank into the sea some 20,000 years ago. About 10,000 years ago, a genetic offshoot of Man, *Homo Mermanus* evolved the ability to live underwater. These mermen discovered the ruins left by the ancient Atlanteans and settled in them.

The current emperor of Atlantis, Namor has often battled outside invaders and faced treachery from traitorous relatives—like his cousin Beemer—who have attempted to steal his throne.

FIRST CONTACT

The new undersea kingdom of Atlantis often fell prey to natural disasters and attacks from barbarians. About 150 years ago, to protect his people, Emperor Thakorr moved the capital near to Antarctica. The Atlanteans remained undisturbed until an American research ship commanded by Captain Leonard McKenzie set off explosive charges to break up some icebergs, sending shockwaves down into Atlantis. Fearing his city was under attack, Thakorr sent his daughter to investigate. Princess Fen fell in love with Captain McKenzie and married him. When she failed to return, her father sent a war party to rescue her and McKenzie fell in the attack. Fen returned to Atlantis and gave birth to Prince NAMOR, the Sub-Mariner.

Unique Atlantean architecture employs submerged coral reefs.

LIFE UNDER WATER

The Atlanteans' skin is usually light blue and their eyes tend to be blue or grey. They live on a diet of raw fish and seaweed and dwell in caves and coral reefs. Atlanteans communicate by high-pitched vocal sounds and elaborate gestures. Their government is a coalition of tribes, ruled by an emperor. A Council of Elders advises the emperor and serves as lawmakers, statesmen and judges. Most Atlanteans worship Neptune, the Greek god of the sea. They live in a rigid warlike society and each citizen joins a guild to become a hunter, farmer, tradesman, craftsman, entertainer, or warrior. No one knows how many Atlanteans exist, but their population is believed to be fewer than 10,000. **TD**

The ancient Atlanteans consisted of several warring barbarian tribes, each led by warlord. The tribes formed alliances over the years, eventually uniting under a single emperor.

Key Atlanteans
1 Namora ***2*** Beemer
3 Namor, the Sub-Mariner
4 Lady Dorma

Atlas

FIRST APPEARANCE Thunderbolts #1 (April 1997)
REAL NAME Erik Josten
OCCUPATION Adventurer; former criminal **BASE** Mobile
HEIGHT 6 ft **WEIGHT** 225 lbs **EYES** None; replaced by containment spheres for unknown energy **HAIR** Red
SPECIAL POWERS/ABILITIES Atlas can grow in size from 6 ft to 60 ft; superhumanly strong and durable.

Having used the identity Power Man and Goliath, Erik Josten joined Baron Zemo and his Masters of Evil as Atlas. The group later changed its name to the Thunderbolts. While battling the criminal Count Nefaria, Atlas was exposed to Nefaria's ionic bomb and became a being composed of pure ionic energy. He later managed to place his ionic energy into the body of his love Dallas Riordan, and the combined being returned to the Thunderbolts to battle Graviton. **MT**

Attuma

FIRST APPEARANCE Fantastic Four #33 (December 1964)
REAL NAME Attuma **OCCUPATION** Barbarian chieftain; former ruler of Atlantis **BASE** Atlantic Ocean
HEIGHT 6 ft 8 in **WEIGHT** 196 lbs **EYES** Brown **HAIR** Black
SPECIAL POWERS/ABILITIES Superhuman strength and stamina; can breathe underwater and see clearly in the depths; expert hand-to-hand combatant and with most Atlantean weapons.

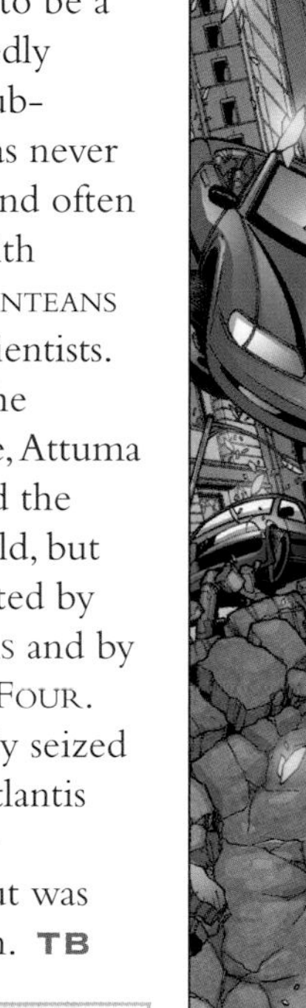

Born to the blue-skinned race of underwater dwellers *Homo Mermanus*, Attuma belongs to a tribe of nomadic barbarians and trained to be a warrior. He has repeatedly fought Namor the Sub-Mariner, but has never defeated him, and often allies himself with renegade Atlanteans or human scientists. Despising the human race, Attuma has attacked the surface world, but been thwarted by the Avengers and by the Fantastic Four. Attuma briefly seized control of Atlantis after Namor abdicated, but was overthrown. **TB**

Avalanche

FIRST APPEARANCE X-Men 141 (January 1981)
REAL NAME Dominic Szilard Janos Petros
OCCUPATION Member of the Brotherhood of Evil Mutants
BASE Mobile **HEIGHT** 5 ft 7 in **WEIGHT** 195 lbs
EYES Brown **HAIR** Brown
SPECIAL POWERS/ABILITIES Vibrations generated from his hands can bring down buildings and cause earthquakes.

Dominic Petros was a Greek immigrant to the US with mutant powers. Calling himself Avalanche, he was recruited into the Brotherhood of Evil Mutants by the shape-shifting mutant Mystique and participated in the Brotherhood's first attempted assassination of Senator Robert Kelly. Although Avalanche left the Brotherhood for a time to blackmail California with the threat of an earthquake, he had returned to the group when it turned itself over to the US government and began working as a military strike force. Avalanche's whereabouts are presently unknown—he was battling with the Brotherhood once again when they were sucked into the black hole inside the head of the mutant, Xorn. **AD**

Aurora

Aurora

FACTFILE
REAL NAME
Jeanne-Marie Beaubier
OCCUPATION
Adventurer, special operative of the Canadian government
BASE
Canada

HEIGHT 5 ft 11 in
WEIGHT 125 lbs
EYES Blue
HAIR Black

FIRST APPEARANCE
The Uncanny X-Men #120 (April 1979)

POWERS
Can run and fly at superhuman speed. Can project bright white light.

Orphans Jeanne-Marie Beaubier and her twin brother Jean-Paul were separated, and Jeanne-Marie was raised in a strict religious school for girls.

Jeanne-Marie was so unhappy she threw herself off a roof—and found herself flying. This was the first manifestation of her mutant powers, but Jeanne-Marie thought a miracle had taken place. She told the headmistress, but was punished for blasphemy. Jeanne-Marie developed a personality disorder: her everyday self was introverted, but her repressed side was uninhibited. Five years later, Jeanne-Marie became a teacher at the school. One night, Wolverine saw her use super-speed to defend herself from a mugger. Wolverine introduced her to James MacDonald Hudson, who reunited Jeanne-Marie with her brother. Taking the code names Aurora and Northstar, Jeanne-Marie and Jean-Paul joined Hudson's team of Canadian heroes, Alpha Flight. Since then Aurora's psyche has continued to change, even manifesting a third personality. **PS**

AVENGERS

Earth's mightiest heroes

AVENGERS

FACTFILE

KEY MEMBERS
(see individual entries for powers)
THOR; IRON MAN; ANT-MAN I (Dr. Hank Pym aka Giant-Man, Goliath, Yellowjacket); **WASP; HULK; CAPTAIN AMERICA; WONDER MAN; HAWKEYE; VISION; SCARLET WITCH; QUICKSILVER; BLACK PANTHER; BLACK WIDOW; HERCULES; BLACK KNIGHT; SHE-HULK; PULSAR** (Monica Rambeau aka Captain Marvel, Photon); **QUASAR; CRYSTAL; SERSI; ANT-MAN II** (Scott Lang).

BASE
Stark Tower, Manhattan; formerly Avengers Mansion (aka Avengers Embassy) Manhattan, and Avengers Compound, Palos Verdes, California

FIRST APPEARANCE
Avengers #1 (September 1963)

ALLIES/FOES

ALLIES Rick Jones, Edwin Jarvis, the Fantastic Four.

FOES Space Phantom, the Lava Men, the Mole Man, Baron Zemo, his Masters of Evil, Kang, Ultron, Collector, Grandmaster, Electro, Sauron, Madame Hydra.

ISSUE #1

Written by Stan Lee, penciled by Jack Kirby and inked by Dick Ayers, the first issue of *The Avengers* guest-starred Rick Jones, the Teen Brigade and the Fantastic Four.

The Avengers are dedicated to safeguarding the planet from super-menaces too powerful for a single hero or the armed forces of any one country to combat. Formed shortly after the first public appearance of the FANTASTIC FOUR, the Avengers immediately won government approval from the National Security Council of the United States and the General Assembly of the United Nations. Unlike the FF, the Avengers' roster is always changing. Members join, leave and return—a precedent set by the Hulk, who left the team weeks after it was first formed.

Loki tried to escape by casting a spell that made his body radioactive. However, the heroes soon trapped him within a lead-lined tank.

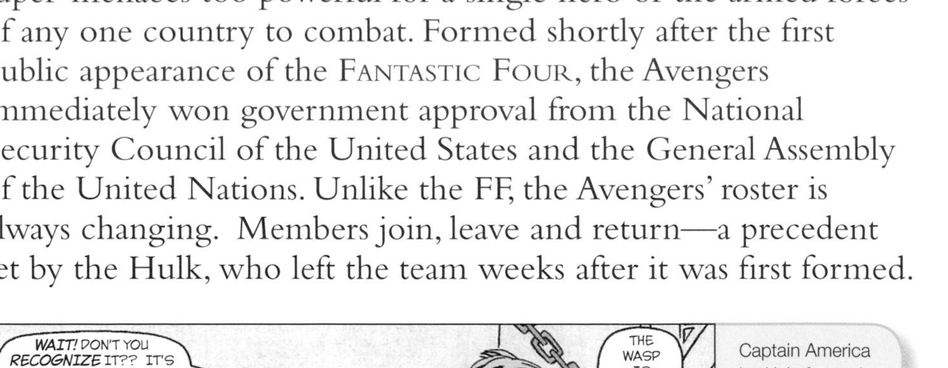

Captain America had lain frozen in the Arctic ice since the end of World War II. Decades later, he was discovered and revived by the Avengers.

HERO TEAM

The Avengers were formed by accident. LOKI, Asgardian God of Evil, wanted revenge on his half-brother Thor. After searching for a menace powerful enough to challenge Thor, he selected the Hulk and tricked him into causing a train wreck. When the Hulk's former partner Rick JONES heard this news, he attempted to alert the Fantastic Four, but Loki diverted his radio signal and sent it to Thor. But the thunder god wasn't the only one to answer the call. The astonishing Ant-Man (see PYM, Dr. Henry), the WASP and IRON MAN also responded. While the other heroes battled the Hulk, Thor tracked down Loki and captured him. After learning that the Hulk was innocent, Ant-Man suggested that the heroes form a team. The Wasp suggested they call themselves "something colorful and dramatic, like ...the Avengers."

AVENGERS MANSION

Tony Stark donated his three-story townhouse to the team who renamed it Avengers Mansion and later significantly modified it to fit their needs. Stark also funded the new team and provided them with most of their high-tech

THE AVENGERS (2004)
1 The Wasp ***2*** Hawkeye ***3*** Scarlet Witch ***4*** Captain America ***5*** The Vision ***6*** Iron Man

For most of its history, the Avengers employed a rotating chairmanship that allowed different acting members to chair meetings and make administrative decisions. Captain America usually served as team leader in the field.

equipment, weaponry, security countermeasures and computer systems. He also used his government contacts to lobby for A-1 or Avengers Priority security clearance to aid the team's operations.

The Avengers began to establish themselves by fighting foes like the Space Phantom, the Lava Men, the Mole Man, Baron Zemo, his Masters of Evil and Kang. The team also met Wonder Man who later sacrificed himself to save them. All of the founding members eventually left the team, leaving Captain America in charge with a band that first consisted of Hawkeye, the Scarlet Witch and Quicksilver. The Wasp and Hank Pym, who had exchanged his Ant-Man to become the first Goliath, returned to the team. The Olympian demigod Hercules also became a member. Serving as an agent for the Mandarin, the first Swordsman even attempted to join.

The Old Order Changeth

Accidentally created by Hank Pym, the robot Ultron tried to kill the Avengers. He even built the android Vision, who betrayed him and served as an Avenger for many years. Haunted by guilt, Pym's marriage to the Wasp deteriorated and he left the team.

The Avengers fought alongside the alien Captain Mar-Vell in a cosmic battle that came to be known as the Kree-Skrull War. The membership continued to change as the Black Widow, the Beast, the now-reformed Swordsman, Mantis, and Hellcat all became members. A romance developed between the Vision and the Scarlet Witch and they married.

The National Security Council began to take an active interest in the team and appointed Henry Peter Gyrich liaison officer. He tried to control team membership by recruiting Falcon and Ms. Marvel (*see* Warbird). In recent years, Justice, Firestar, Triathlon, Silverclaw, Jack of Hearts, Ant-Man and a new female Captain Britain served as members.

Dissassembled/Reassembled

A victim of her own reality-altering powers, the Scarlet Witch had a nervous breakdown and brought about the deaths of Jack of Hearts, Ant-Man and her former husband the Vision, and also caused the destruction of Avengers Mansion. After she was defeated, her former teammates were so traumatized that they disbanded the team. However, the mass jailbreak of 87 of the most dangerous criminals on Earth convinced Captain America to reform the Avengers. Before long, the new Avengers team found themselves battling major threats to global security once more. **TD**

THE ULTIMATES

On a parallel Earth, government scientists created a super-soldier formula, but lost it when Captain America disappeared during World War II. Many years later, Dr. Bruce Banner was hired to recreate it. Working out of a rundown research facility in Pittsburgh, he engaged in secret superhuman trials on civilians and even tested the formula on himself, transforming himself into the rampaging Hulk. General Nick Fury took custody of Banner and ordered him to complete his research in order to create a new super-team called the Ultimates. This team included Dr. Hank Pym, a cybertronics expert and a world authority on super-genetics.

THE ULTIMATES (2004)
1 Giant-Man ***2*** Iron Man ***3*** Hawkeye ***4*** Wasp ***5*** Captain America ***6*** Black Widow ***7*** Thor

When Kang the Conqueror and his son Marcus waged all-out war against the Earth, the Avengers led the planet's defensive effort. Although Kang temporarily succeeded in subduing the entire world, the Avengers led a resistance movement that eventually overthrew his new dynasty.

THE AVENGERS (2005)
1 Ronin (aka Echo) ***2*** Iron Man ***3*** Spider-Man ***4*** Wolverine ***5*** Captain America ***6*** Spider-Woman (Jessica Drew) ***7*** Cage

ESSENTIAL STORYLINES

- ***Avengers #4*** The Avengers rescue Captain America from an icy tomb and invite him to join the team.
- ***The Greatest Battles of the Avengers (tpb)*** The Avengers fight many of their most deadly foes.
- ***Avengers: The Korvac Saga (tpb)*** The Guardians of the Galaxy help the Avengers battle Michael Korvac.
- ***Avengers: Under Siege (tpb)*** The new Baron Zemo and his Masters of Evil launch an assault on Avengers Mansion
- ***Avengers: Disassembled*** The Scarlet Witch warps reality and attacks her former teammates.

Avengers, West Coast

The Avengers' West Coast "branch office"

Avengers, West Coast

FACTFILE

FOUNDING MEMBERS
HAWKEYE
MOCKINGBIRD
IRON MAN
TIGRA
WONDER MAN

FINAL MEMBERS
SCARLET WITCH
SPIDER-WOMAN II
(Julia Carpenter)
WAR MACHINE
U.S. AGENT

ADDITIONAL MEMBERS
HUMAN TORCH I
(James Hammond)
LIVING LIGHTNING
MOON KNIGHT

BASE
Avengers Compound, 1800 Palos Verdes Drive, California

FIRST APPEARANCE
West Coast Avengers #1 (September 1984)

ALLIES/FOES

ALLIES Hank Pym (resident scientist), The Thing.

FOES Graviton, Ultron, The Grim Reaper, Master Pandemonium, Mephisto, Lethal Legion.

While chairman of the Avengers, the Vision decided to expand the team and sent Hawkeye and his new wife Mockingbird to Los Angeles to establish a second headquarters on the West Coast. Hawkeye purchased a 15-acre estate on the Pacific coast. It consisted of a main building, surrounded by several guest cottages that housed various Avengers over the years. The mountainside beneath the main building accommodated the high-security Avengers Assembly Room, a hospital, laboratories and a hanger for Avengers' Quinjets.

Most of the West Coast Avengers had served on the East Coast team and returned to New York after this branch office closed.

GROWING PAINS

The team faced its first crisis when Mockingbird and Hawkeye argued over whether the Avengers had the right to use lethal force. Hawkeye later resigned when the government assigned the US Agent to the team and he temporarily joined the Great Lakes Avengers. The Wasp moved to the West Coast to join her former husband Dr. Pym and the team aided their East Coast counterparts in the Kree-Shi'ar war known as Operation: Galactic Storm. After falling under the control of Magneto and Immortus, the Scarlet Witch used her reality-altering powers against the West Coast Avengers.

Hawkeye and Mockingbird eventually reconciled and rejoined the team, and the Scarlet Witch (now cured) became the team's chairperson. During an attack by the demon Mephisto and the Lethal Legion, Mockingbird was killed and the Compound severely damaged. Hawkeye resigned to mourn his wife's death and Captain America and the Black Widow decided to close the West Coast branch. **TD**

ESSENTIAL STORYLINES
- ***West Coast Avengers #1–4*** Hawkeye and Mockingbird establish the new team.
- ***West Coast Avengers #17–23*** Dr. Pym contemplates suicide, the team is transported into the past, and Mockingbird is captured by the Phantom Rider.
- ***Avengers West Coast #55–57, 59–62*** The Scarlet Witch falls victim to Magneto and Immortus.

CHARACTER KEY
1 *Spider-Woman II* ***2*** *US Agent* ***3*** *Living Lightning* ***4*** *Hawkeye* ***5*** *Iron Man* ***6*** *Scarlet Witch* ***7*** *Wonder Man*

Trapped by the X-Men and the Fantastic Four, the Mad Thinker and the Puppet Master turn the Awesome Android loose in a last attempt to escape justice.

Awesome Android

FIRST APPEARANCE Fantastic Four #15 (June 1963)
REAL NAME Answers to "Awesome Andy"
OCCUPATION Legal aide **BASE** New York City
HEIGHT 15 ft **WEIGHT** 1421 lbs **EYES** None **HAIR** None
SPECIAL POWERS/ABILITIES Possessed the ability to duplicate any special powers directed against it.

The Awesome Android was the creation of the evil MAD THINKER, constructed using research notes that once belonged to scientist Reed Richards (*see* MISTER FANTASTIC). The Mad Thinker intended to use the Awesome Android as a weapon to destroy the FANTASTIC FOUR. However, as time went by, the android developed a personality of its own and freed itself from the Thinker's villainous thrall.

"Awesome Andy" now works peacefully as an aide in the legal offices of Goodman, Lieber, Kurtzburg & Holliway. **TB**

Ayesha (Her)

FIRST APPEARANCE Marvel Two-In-One #61 (March 1980)
REAL NAME Paragon
OCCUPATION None **BASE** Outer space
HEIGHT 6 ft 6 in **WEIGHT** 390 lbs **EYES** White **HAIR** Blonde
SPECIAL POWERS/ABILITIES Controls cosmic energy which prevents aging; uses this energy to rearrange matter, project concussive blasts, to fly, and to open cosmic rifts into warp-space.

Formerly known as Paragon and Her, Ayesha was created by a group of scientists calling themselves the ENCLAVE. Hoping to create a perfect life form, they created a being called Him. But Him (later known as Adam WARLOCK) refused to be controlled. They then tried to create a perfect female they called Paragon, but she also rebelled, destroying the Enclave's base. After meditating in a cocoon, she emerged as Her, able to tap into pure cosmic energy. She hoped to mate with Warlock but, following his death, set off to find a suitable companion. **MT**

Azazel

FIRST APPEARANCE The Uncanny X-Men #428 (October 2003)
REAL NAME Azazel **OCCUPATION** Conqueror
BASE La Isla de Demonas, off the coast of Florida; the *Brimstone*
HEIGHT 5 ft 11 in **WEIGHT** Unknown **EYES** Black **HAIR** Gray
SPECIAL POWERS/ABILITIES The full extent of his powers is unknown; can teleport himself, take on human form, and mentally influence his offspring.

Azazel is the leader of the Neyaphem, a race of mutants who resemble demons. In ancient times Azazel was thought to be the devil. Azazel claims that he once ruled the Earth until he and the Neyaphem were banished to another dimension by the Cheyarafim, a race of mutants who resembled angels. As part of his plan to reconquer Earth, Azazel mated with various women, fathering mutants with teleportational powers. Among the women he seduced was the mutant MYSTIQUE, who gave birth to their son Kurt Wagner, alias NIGHTCRAWLER. When Nightcrawler learned that Azazel was his father, he not only rejected him, but helped defeat him. **PS**

AZAZEL AND HIS CREW
1 Azazel ***2*** Ginniyeh
3 Minion of Azazel ***4*** Ydrazil ***5*** Jillian

BANNER, BETTY

The Hulk's beloved

BETTY BANNER

FACTFILE

REAL NAME
Elizabeth Ross Banner

OCCUPATION
None

BASE
Mobile

HEIGHT 5 ft 6 in
WEIGHT 110 lbs
EYES Blue
HAIR Brown

FIRST APPEARANCE
Incredible Hulk #1
(May 1962)

POWERS
No superhuman powers, but courageous and resourceful; steadfastly loyal to her husband Bruce Banner through many shared tribulations.

The only daughter of renowned military general Thaddeus "Thunderbolt" Ross, Betty spent her formative years firmly under her father's thumb. Thunderbolt Ross had wanted a son, and had no use for his unfortunate daughter; after her mother died during Betty's teenage years, she was sent away to boarding school. After graduating, she returned to her father's side, a repressed wallflower. Thunderbolt Ross was then in charge of a top-secret project to create a new type of weapon, employing the limitless power of gamma radiation. The head scientist on the project was the quiet, bookish Bruce Banner, and an attraction between Betty and Banner soon developed.

Betty Banner met her future husband Bruce when she came to live on a New Mexico military base with her father, Thunderbolt Ross.

ESSENTIAL STORYLINES
- ***Hulk Vol. 2 #168–169***
MODOK transforms Betty into the Harpy.
- ***Hulk Vol. 2 #319***
After years of courtship and chaos, Bruce Banner finally marries Betty.
- ***Hulk Vol. 2 #465–469***
Betty is exposed to radiation poisoning; Bruce desperately tries to save her.

TRAGIC LOVE

Their relationship was forever changed when, during the gamma-bomb test, Banner was struck by the full force of the detonation, and its radiations transformed him into the Hulk whenever he grew angry. Banner tried to keep his condition secret from Betty, which only served to alienate them. Betty was then ardently pursued by Major Glenn Talbot (see TALBOT, Col. Glenn), the new aide attached to her father's Hulkbuster task force. Eventually, the secret of Banner's dual identity became public knowledge, and his transformations and rampages created a rift between Betty and himself. With no one else to turn to, Betty married Major Talbot. Their union soon ended in divorce, however, and Talbot died attempting to destroy the Hulk.

HARPY HORROR

Betty continued to find herself entangled in the lives of Bruce Banner and the Hulk. At one point she was transformed by the villainous MODOK into a gamma-empowered flying menace known as the Harpy. But even these trials could not destroy her love for hapless Bruce Banner, and eventually, despite her father's objections, she married him.

However lasting happiness was not to be theirs. After spending years living as fugitives, Betty was poisoned by the Hulk's long-time enemy the ABOMINATION, who used his own gamma-irradiated blood to do the deed hoping to incriminate Banner. Placed in cryonic suspension, Betty was thereafter revived by the LEADER, and for a time aided her fugitive husband as his shadowy contact, Mr. Blue. Her present whereabouts are unknown, but it is a virtual certainty that she will re-enter the life of the Hulk before too long. **TB**

Bruce Banner's transformation into the rampaging Hulk has brought Betty a lot of strife, yet she remains devoted to her husband.

Balder the Brave

Prophecy has it that the death of Norse God Balder will result in Ragnarok—the destruction of Asgard, the home of the Norse Gods (*see* Gods of Asgard). For this reason Odin commanded his wife Frigga to make Balder (his son) invulnerable to physical injury and so she cast spells that protected him from everything except mistletoe.

The God of mischief, Loki, Thor's adopted brother, learned of this and tricked the blind God Hoder to fire an arrow, tipped with mistletoe wood, at Balder. Only Odin's intervention saved him, but before his recovery, Balder's soul was to travel through the underworld where it encountered the spirits of those he had killed.

Balder's return to the land of the living was not without difficulties: he fell into a deep depression after Nanna, his beloved, sacrificed herself to save him from marrying the Norn sorceress Kamilla. Roving the desert, determined to kill himself, Balder gained hope from a vision of the future. Since then, he has come to love Kamilla, with whom he fought against Surtur and the legions of the Muspelheim. He also ruled Asgard when Odin was believed dead, but following the God-ruler's return Balder went back to his new love, Kamilla. **AD**

A natural leader, Balder the Brave has led his people on countless campaigns.

FACTFILE

REAL NAME
Balder

OCCUPATION
Norse God of Light

BASE
Asgard

HEIGHT 6 ft 4 in
WEIGHT 320 lbs
EYES Blue
HAIR White

FIRST APPEARANCE
Journey into Mystery #85 (October, 1962)

POWERS
Charismatic leader; formidable swordsman, horseman, and hand-to-hand combatant; in Asgard dimension, only weapons tipped with mistletoe can cause him harm; able to produce and emit light; possesses superhuman strength, endurance, and longevity.

Banner, Betty *see opposite*

Banner, Dr. Brian

FIRST APPEARANCE The Incredible Hulk Vol. 2 #312 (Oct. 1985)
REAL NAME Brian Banner
OCCUPATION Atomic physicist **BASE** Dayton, Ohio
HEIGHT 5 ft 10in **WEIGHT** 145 lbs **EYES** Brown **HAIR** Brown
SPECIAL POWERS/ABILITIES Scientific genius.

Married to his childhood sweetheart, Rebecca, Dr. Banner worked as an atomic physicist for the US government and helped develop the country's first atomic weapons. The more he studied atomic radiation, the more he feared it. Suspecting that he had been exposed to trace amounts of radiation, Banner was horrified when he learned that his young wife was pregnant. When she began to suffer complications, he became convinced that the child would be mutant and grow up to become a monster. His paranoia increased when his son Bruce showed signs of great intelligence. Banner began to drink heavily and often exploded in fits of temper. After striking and accidentally killing his wife, he was convicted of manslaughter and confined to a mental institution. His son Bruce (see Hulk) would be profoundly affected by this family trauma. **TD**

Banshee

After his wife's death, Irish Interpol agent and mutant Sean Cassidy was forced to join Factor Three, a organization of evil mutants, by the evil Changeling. The group gave him the name Banshee and controlled him by fitting him with an explosive headband. Professor X, leader of the X-Men, used his telepathic powers to remove the band and Banshee then defeated Factor Three. Later, Banshee joined the X-Men and became co-head—with Emma Frost—of Xavier's Academy, where he taught the young mutants of Generation X. Following the tragic death of his beloved, Dr. Moira MacTaggart, Banshee suffered a breakdown. He then formed X-Corps, which came into conflict with his former X-Men colleagues. **MT**

FACTFILE

REAL NAME
Sean Cassidy

OCCUPATION
Director of X-Corps

BASE
Cassidy Keep, Ireland

HEIGHT 6 ft
WEIGHT 170 lbs
EYES Blue-green
HAIR Blond

FIRST APPEARANCE
Uncanny X-Men #28 (January 1967)

POWERS
Banshee's "sonic scream" can propel him into flight, shatter solid objects, and fire percussive blasts, which can place others into trances or knock them unconscious.

Banshee unleashes a devastating sonic scream at Cyclops and his fellow X-Men.

Baron Blood

FIRST APPEARANCE The Invaders Vol. 1 #7 (June 1976)
REAL NAME Lord John Falsworth
OCCUPATION Former German assassin **BASE** London
HEIGHT 5 ft 10 in **WEIGHT** 180 lbs **EYES** Red **HAIR** Black
SPECIAL POWERS/ABILITIES Vampiric powers, including superhuman strength, hypnotic abilities, and invulnerability to conventional weaponry; could fly without transforming into a bat.

The younger son of a British aristocrat, John Falsworth was killed and vampirized by Dracula. As Baron Blood, Falsworth served German intelligence during World War I and II. During World War II Baron Blood battled Union Jack (who was secretly his brother, Montgomery) and the Invaders. Decades later, Blood was beheaded by Captain America. Two later vampires took the name Baron Blood: Doctor Strange's brother Victor and Montgomery's grandson Kenneth Crichton. **PS**

Baron Von Strucker

FIRST APPEARANCE Sgt. Fury And His Howling Commandos #5 (January 1964) **REAL NAME** Baron Wolfgang Von Strucker
OCCUPATION Terrorist leader **BASE** Mobile
HEIGHT 6 ft 2 in **WEIGHT** 225 lbs **EYES** Blue **HAIR** None
SPECIAL POWERS/ABILITIES Can release the virulent Death Spore Virus from within his body at will. He wears the Satan Claw, capable of discharging electrical shocks, upon his right hand.

Baron Von Strucker fought for the Nazis during World War II as the leader of the Blitzkrieg Squad, Germany's answer to the Howling Commandos led by Sgt. Nick Fury. After the war, Strucker took control of a Japanese secret society and evolved it into the worldwide terror group Hydra. Kept alive and vigorous by the Death Spore virus within his body, Von Strucker's goal is total world domination. **TB**

Baron Mordo

Doctor Strange and Baron Mordo battle in astral form before their mentor, the Ancient One.

As a child, Karl Mordo gained an interest in the occult from his grandfather, Viscount Crowler. As an adult Mordo sought out a mystic master known as the Ancient One in Tibet. The Ancient One recognized that Mordo had great potential as a sorcerer, but he also saw that Mordo was motivated only by a desire to gain power for his own ends.

Mordo plotted to destroy the Ancient One by sending his spirit image to hypnotise the Ancient One's servant into poisoning his food. Mordo threatened to let the Ancient One die if he did not reveal all his knowledge of black magic. In the nick of time, Mordo's plot was discovered by Dr. Stephen Strange, another of the Ancient One's pupils. Strange sent *his* spirit image to Tibet and the two spirit images fought, as the old man lay in a coma. Strange managed to use his amulet to revive the old man.

SWORN ENEMIES

Mordo swore revenge on his former master and Strange and allied himself with a being with vast power, the dread entity Dormammu, in several failed attempts to destroy Strange. Evenly-matched adversaries, Baron Mordo and Dr. Strange remain bitter enemies. **MT**

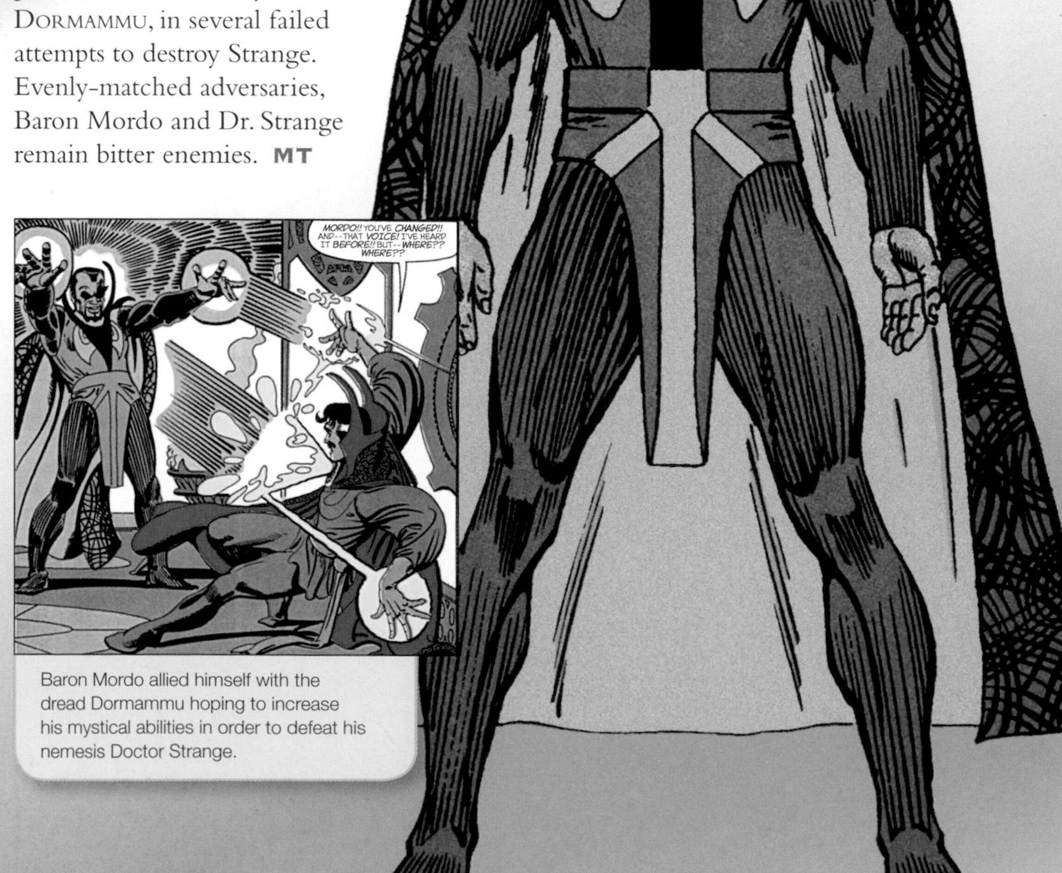

Baron Mordo allied himself with the dread Dormammu hoping to increase his mystical abilities in order to defeat his nemesis Doctor Strange.

FACTFILE
REAL NAME
Karl Amadeus Mordo
OCCUPATION
Sorcerer
BASE
Castle Mordo, Varf Mandra, Transylvania

HEIGHT 6 ft
WEIGHT 250 lbs
EYES Brown
HAIR Black

FIRST APPEARANCE
Strange Tales #111 (August 1963)

POWERS
Mordo can separate his spirit self from his physical body and travel through space unaffected by physical laws. He can mentally control others and can hurl magical energy bolts.

Baron Zemo

Like father, like son

After the accident that bonded his mask to his face, the original Baron Zemo became obsessed with destroying Captain America

Helmut Zemo is the son of Baron Heinrich Zemo, a Nazi scientist during World War II who designed super-weapons. Heinrich Zemo was working on a glue, "Adhesive X," that could never be dissolved, hoping it could be used to immobilize Allied troops. CAPTAIN AMERICA broke into his lab and, in the fight, Cap's shield shattered the vat containing the adhesive and Zemo's mask was glued to his head.

FACTFILE

REAL NAME
Helmut Zemo

OCCUPATION
Criminal entrepreneur

BASE
Mobile

HEIGHT 5 ft 11 in
WEIGHT 183 lbs
EYES Blue
HAIR Blond

FIRST APPEARANCE
Captain America #168 (June 1971)

POWERS
Master strategist, extensive training in hand-to-hand combat, and excellent marksman; lacks his father's scientific genius.

MASTER OF EVIL

Zemo later went to London to steal an experimental drone plane. Captain America and his teenage partner Bucky BARNES attempted to stop him, but Bucky was killed and Captain America was flung into the ocean, where he fell into a state of suspended animation. When the Nazis lost the war, Zemo fled to the jungles of South America where he conquered a small kingdom.

Decades later, he came out of hiding after learning that Captain America had been revived by the Avengers. Zemo formed the first MASTERS OF EVIL and later transformed Simon Williams into WONDER MAN, but failed in all his attempts to destroy the Avengers. He was accidentally crushed by a landslide during a battle with Captain America.

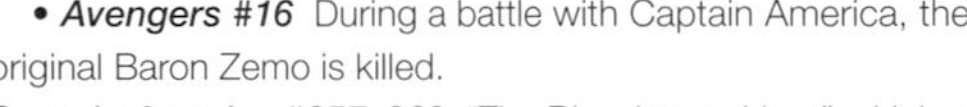

Zemo's hatred of Captain America ultimately led to the rock fall that killed him.

ESSENTIAL STORYLINES

- ***Avengers #16*** During a battle with Captain America, the original Baron Zemo is killed.
- ***Captain America #357–362*** "The Bloodstone Hunt"—Helmut Zemo tries to resurrect his father.
- ***The Avengers: Under Siege, tpb*** Helmut's new Masters of Evil invade the Avengers' Mansion and take Edwin Jarvis hostage.
- ***Thunderbolts: Justice Like Lightning, tpb*** Helmut Zemo repositions the Masters of Evil into seeming heroes.

FROM VILLAIN TO HERO

The Baron's son Helmut vowed to get revenge on Cap. Calling himself Phoenix, he attempted to drown Cap and his partner FALCON in a boiling vat of Adhesive X. The searing liquid splashed Helmut, horribly scarring his face and giving it the appearance of melted wax. Zemo then sent an army of mutates after Cap and attempted to locate the five fragments of the Bloodstone hoping to restore his father to life. Zemo also organized a new Masters of Evil and invaded Avengers Mansion.

When the Avengers temporarily disappeared from this reality, Zemo gathered his Masters of Evil. They became the THUNDERBOLTS, Super Villains masquerading as heroes. Helmut assumed the identity of Citizen V, a British costumed hero murdered by the original Baron Zemo. However, like most of the Thunderbolts team, Zemo seemed to grow into the role of being a *real* hero and now claims that he just wants to protect the Earth. **TD**

MASTERS OF EVIL
1 Absorbing Man ***2*** Baron Zemo
3 Screaming Mimi ***4*** Mr. Hyde ***5*** Moonstone
6 The Fixer ***7*** Power Man

Helmut Zemo claims that he wants to atone for his past misdeeds.

BUCKY BARNES

FACTFILE
REAL NAME
James Buchanan Barnes
OCCUPATION
Adventurer; army camp mascot
BASE
Mobile

HEIGHT 5 ft 7 in
WEIGHT 140 lbs
EYES Brown
HAIR Red-brown

FIRST APPEARANCE
Captain America #1
(March 1941)

POWERS
Excellent hand-to-hand combatant, skilled marksman, Olympic-level athlete, acrobat and gymnast.

Bucky discovers that Steve Rogers has a secret—he's the superpowered costumed war hero Captain America.

BARNES, BUCKY

Orphan James Buchanan "Bucky" Barnes was a mascot for the soldiers at Camp Lehigh, Virginia, where Steve Rogers was stationed. After learning that Steve was CAPTAIN AMERICA, Barnes began helping him on his missions, and eventually became his official partner. Captain America and Bucky were in London when they discovered that their old enemy BARON ZEMO was attempting to steal a bomb-filled drone plane. As the plane took off, Bucky leaped aboard and was apparently killed trying to defuse it. Captain America was hurled into the English Channel. Decades later Cap was revived by the AVENGERS. He has learned that Bucky might have also survived and is a super-agent known as the Winter Soldier. **TD**

Personally trained by Captain America, Bucky learned Cap's unique fighting style that employed acrobatics and gymnastics in combat situations.

BASILISK

FACTFILE
REAL NAME
Basil Elks
OCCUPATION
Criminal; terrorist
BASE
Mobile

HEIGHT 5 ft 11 in
WEIGHT 210 lbs
EYES Red
HAIR None

FIRST APPEARANCE
Marvel Team-Up #16
(December 1973)

POWERS
Generated microwave-related energy, which he could project from his eyes as force blasts, to heat or freeze things, or to levitate himself. Possessed superhuman strength and durability and could teleport himself.

BASILISK

When burglar Basil Elks tried to steal a gem from a museum, a guard fired his gun, striking the gem. The "gem" was the Alpha-Stone of the KREE, which exploded, giving Elks superhuman powers. Elks dubbed himself Basilisk after the mythological serpent. Basilisk tried to destroy civilization, only to be thwarted by SPIDER-MAN and the THING. Elks was assassinated by SCOURGE.

The second Basilisk was a mutant who could shoot a paralysis beam from his single eye. He was killed by Kuan-Yin Xorn, who impersonated Magneto and led a new mutant Brotherhood. **PS**

XORN'S BROTHERHOOD
1 Angel's child holding No-Girl ***2*** Martha Johansson the living brain ***3*** Ernst ***4*** Basilisk ***5*** Xorn as Magneto ***6*** Esme (Stepford Cuckoo) ***7*** Baby of Angel and Beak ***8*** Beak ***9*** Angel ***10*** Toad

BASTION

FIRST APPEARANCE Uncanny X-Men #333 (June 1996)
REAL NAME Sebastion Gilberti
OCCUPATION Anti-Mutant crusader **BASE** Mobile
HEIGHT 6 ft 3 in **WEIGHT** 375 lbs **EYES** Red **HAIR** White
SPECIAL POWERS/ABILITIES Enhanced strength, speed, physical stamina, and resistance to injury; also immune to telepathic probes.

The being known as Bastion is a human/SENTINEL hybrid, possessed of elements of the Sentinel robot known as Master Mold and the advanced Sentinel prototype from the future called Nimrod. Adopted by a human woman named Rose Gilberti, the human-looking Bastion at first had no memory of his origin. Later, the Sentinel-influenced Master Mold and Nimrod parts of his being reawakened, and he set about assembling the international anti-mutant strike force known as Operation: Zero Tolerance. Using Prime Sentinels, Bastion captured CYCLOPS, WOLVERINE, STORM, PHOENIX, and CANNONBALL and took over the Xavier Institute. Bastion was eventually stopped by SHIELD. **MT**

Batroc the Leaper

Batroc

FACTFILE

REAL NAME
Georges Batroc

OCCUPATION
Mercenary

BASE
Mobile

HEIGHT 6 ft
WEIGHT 225 lbs
EYES Brown
HAIR Black

FIRST APPEARANCE
Tales of Suspense #75 (March 1966)

POWERS
Self-professed master of Savate, the French form of kickboxing; allegedly an expert hand-to-hand combatant; does not have any superhuman abilities but describes self as Olympic-standard weight lifter with ability to leap vast distances; devises military tactics that serve to bewilder opponents.

Describing himself as the world's greatest mercenary and master of Savate, Marseilles-born Georges Batroc trained himself in this Gallic martial art while serving in the French Foreign Legion. Since embarking on a life of crime, Batroc has fought some of the world's greatest Super Heroes, including Captain America and the Punisher. Sadly, he has rarely survived these confrontations with more than the smallest degree of dignity.

Batroc is the eponymous leader of Batroc's Brigade, a motley collection of martial artists, assassins, and mercenaries whose membership is fluid. In the Brigade's early days, Batroc hired members for specific jobs, but most of the missions were unsuccessful. Employed to obtain the "seismo-bomb" from a foreign power, Batroc teamed with the Swordsman and the Living Laser, but they did not succeed. Later, the Red Skull hired him to attack Captain America. Although banded with Porcupine and Whirlwind, the mission failed.

Batroc has only scored significant victories with the British weapon master Zaran and South American revolutionary Machete. During their first mission the three triumphed, snatching Captain America's shield for Obadiah Stane. **AD**

Battlestar

FIRST APPEARANCE Captain America #341 (May 1988)
REAL NAME Lemar Hoskins
OCCUPATION Government agent **BASE** Chicago,
HEIGHT 6 ft 2 in **WEIGHT** 196 lbs **EYES** Blue **HAIR** Black
SPECIAL POWERS/ABILITIES Superhuman strength and stamina; can lift 10 tons; excels at hand-to-hand combat, gymnastics, and acrobatics; carries an indestructible adamantium shield.

Wrestler Lemar Hoskins was given treatments by the Power Broker which gave him superhuman strength. He joined the Bold Urban Commandos or Buckies, a group who supported Captain America's rival John Walker, the Super-Patriot (*see* US Agent). The Commission on Superhuman Activities asked Walker to replace Steve Rogers as Captain America, and Hoskins teamed up with him, adopting the name Bucky. He later set out on his own as Battlestar. **MT**

Beak

FIRST APPEARANCE New X-Men #117 (October 2001)
STATUS Hero **REAL NAME** Barnell Bohusk
OCCUPATION Member of the Exiles
BASE The Multiverse
HEIGHT 5 ft 9 in **WEIGHT** 140 lbs
EYES Black **HAIR** White
SPECIAL POWERS/ABILITIES
Agile with enhanced endurance; hollow bones and befeathered arms allow him to glide for short distances.

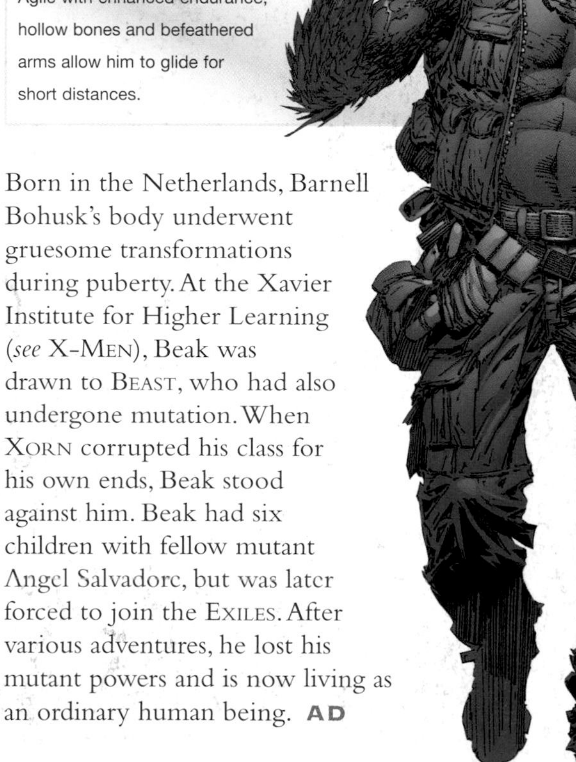

Born in the Netherlands, Barnell Bohusk's body underwent gruesome transformations during puberty. At the Xavier Institute for Higher Learning (*see* X-Men), Beak was drawn to Beast, who had also undergone mutation. When Xorn corrupted his class for his own ends, Beak stood against him. Beak had six children with fellow mutant Angel Salvadore, but was later forced to join the Exiles. After various adventures, he lost his mutant powers and is now living as an ordinary human being. **AD**

Beast

Mind of a genius, body of a wild thing!

Beast

FACTFILE

REAL NAME
Henry P. "Hank" McCoy

OCCUPATION
Adventurer, biochemist

BASE
The Xavier institute, Salem Center, New York

HEIGHT 5 ft 11 in
WEIGHT 402 lbs
EYES Blue
HAIR Brown (originally); blue-black (currently)

FIRST APPEARANCE
X-Men Vol. 1 #1 (September 1963)

POWERS

The Beast possesses superhuman strength, agility, durability, and enhanced senses, including catlike night vision. He is able to recover with superhuman swiftness from minor wounds. He also possesses genius-level IQ, with extraordinary expertise in genetics, biochemistry and other subjects.

Dr. McCoy recklessly drank his own serum, which gave him a more bestial form and increased superpowers.

Nuclear-power-plant worker Norton McCoy was exposed to intense radiation, and his son Henry was born a mutant, with unusually large hands and feet. Henry's schoolmates called him "Beast," but his mutant physique enabled him to become a star football player. When a criminal called the Conquistador abducted Henry's parents to force Henry to work for him, the X-Men came to the rescue. The team's founder, Professor X, recruited Henry and, codenamed the Beast, he thus became one of the X-Men's original members.

BEAST WITH THE X-MEN
1 Wolverine ***2*** Jean Grey ***3*** Beast (wearing reading glasses) ***4*** Professor X ***5*** Emma Frost ***6*** Cyclops

UNCHAINED

Under Xavier's tutelage McCoy earned his Ph.D. and went on to become a genetic researcher at the Brand Corporation. There he developed a serum that further mutated him: he grew fur all over his body, as well as fangs and pointed ears.

Initially McCoy attempted to masquerade as a normal human by using a latex mask and gloves. However, the Beast abandoned this disguise, joined the Avengers, and publicly revealed his true identity. Later, the Beast reorganized another team, the Defenders. After this incarnation of the Defenders collapsed, the Beast rejoined Xavier's other four original X-Men in a new mutant team, X-Factor. Soon afterwards, the Beast was captured by former Brand scientist Dr. Carl Maddicks, who used a serum to cause the Beast to revert to his previous, more human appearance. Still later, the mutant Infectia's powers returned the Beast to his fur-covered form.

The Beast has grown more massive and more feline in appearance: his face now resembles a lion's.

Though the Beast can be fierce in battle, paradoxically he is also a man of high intellect, sharp wit, and great kindness.

The Appliance of Science

The original members of X-Factor rejoined the X-Men, and McCoy succeeded in creating a cure for the Legacy Virus, drawing on research by Dr. Moira MacTaggart. The Beast thereafter briefly served in the spinoff team, the X-Treme X-Men. After the Beast was nearly killed in combat, fellow member Tessa saved his life by using her powers to mutate him even further. The Beast remains an active combatant, the X-Men's resident scientist, and a teacher at the Xavier Institute. **PS**

ESSENTIAL STORYLINES

- ***X-Men Vol. 1 #49–53***
The extraordinary origin of the Beast explained for the first time.
- ***Amazing Adventures Vol. 2 #11–16***
the Beast mutates into his furry ape-like form and combats the Secret Empire.
- ***X-Treme X-Men #3***
The Beast mutates into his leonine form.

Belladonna

FIRST APPEARANCE Spectacular Spider-Man Vol. 1 #43 (June 1980)
REAL NAME Narda Ravanna
OCCUPATION Criminal **BASE** New York City
HEIGHT 5 ft 5 in **WEIGHT** 120 lbs **EYES** Blue-gray **HAIR** Brown
SPECIAL POWERS/ABILITIES Extensive knowledge of chemistry enables development of sinister chemical weapons.

With her sister, Desiree Vaughan-Pope, Narda Ravanna was the founder of Vaughan-Pope Cosmetics and responsible for product development. When they refused to sell the company to Roderick Kingsley (*see* HOBGOBLIN), he used the media to smear their products, driving them out of business. Hungry for revenge, Narda returned to the US, her home country. As Belladonna, Narda developed weapons from stolen neo-atropine and attacked Kingsley with the help of several allies. When SPIDER-MAN intervened, she attempted to kill the web-slinger but he thwarted her efforts and handed her over to the police. **MT**

Bereet

FIRST APPEARANCE Rampaging Hulk #1 (January 1977)
REAL NAME Bereet
OCCUPATION Krylorian Techno-Artist **BASE** The planet Krylor
HEIGHT/WEIGHT Unrevealed **EYES** Brown **HAIR** Unrevealed
SPECIAL POWERS/ABILITIES Carried the tools of her trade with her in a special distortion pouch. Accompanied by a hovering device called Sturky that could convert matter.

A renowned Techno-Artist from the planet Krylor, Bereet first came to prominence among her race when she created a series of adventure films depicting the earliest version of the HULK combating a fictitious invasion of Earth by the Krylorians.

After several attempts to duplicate this early success, she journeyed to Earth intending to document the ongoing exploits of the true Hulk, and became embroiled in a number of his adventures. She remained on Earth and became a movie director in Hollywood. **TB**

Berengetti, Michael

FIRST APPEARANCE Incredible Hulk Vol. 2 #347 (Sept.1988)
REAL NAME Michael Berengetti
OCCUPATION Casino owner **BASE** Las Vegas
HEIGHT 5 ft 10 in **WEIGHT** 170 lbs **EYES** Brown **HAIR** Black
SPECIAL POWERS/ABILITIES Highly skilled businessman, with a deep knowledge of underworld politics. Skilled with firearms, and had a talent for mathematics relating to games of chance.

Michael Berengetti owned Las Vegas's Coliseum casino, and hired the HULK as a bodyguard and leg-breaker during the period when the Hulk sported gray skin and a cunning intellect. Berengetti, who called the Hulk "Joe Fixit," ensured that the Hulk had steady access to tailored suits and Las Vegas's more sensual pleasures. After the Hulk left Vegas, the android Frost (employed by the gangster Sam Striker) killed Berengetti. **DW**

An honorable employer, Berengetti treated the loyal members of his staff as members of his family.

Beta Ray Thor

Beta Ray Bill was a guardian-warrior of an extraterrestrial race whose galaxy was destroyed by the ancient demon Surtur. He was created when scientists transferred his life force into a bioengineered carnivorous beast, with increased strength, speed and agility. While traveling in suspended animation, Beta Ray Bill's starship entered the Milky Way Galaxy, where THOR was sent to investigate. They battled and Thor was separated from his enchanted hammer, Mjolnir, which changed back into Donald Blake's cane. When Beta Ray Bill struck the cane on a wall he suddenly possessed Thor's power and a variation of the Thunder God's costume.

After a battle on Asgard in which Beta Ray Thor spared Thor's life, Odin (*see* GODS OF ASGARD) commissioned the creation of new enchanted hammer, called Storm Breaker, possessing the same powers as Mjolnir, Thor's hammer. Odin gave Storm Breaker to Beta Ray Thor. Since then he has used his great powers to protect both his race's fleet and the Asgardians. **MT**

Beta Ray Thor and Hercules battle fire demons from the Asgardian world of Muspelheim.

FACTFILE

REAL NAME
Beta Ray Bill

OCCUPATION
Warrior

BASE
Mobile; his alien race's space fleet, his own warship Skuttlebutt

HEIGHT 6 ft 7 in
WEIGHT 480 lbs
EYES None visible
HAIR None

FIRST APPEARANCE
Thor # 337 (November 1983)

BETA RAY THOR

POWERS

Beta Ray Thor has the same powers as Thor himself. He has superhuman strength, and is immune to all disease and injury. His Asgardian metabolism gives him far greater endurance at all physical activities than humans.

Beyonder

Observer of worlds

FACTFILE
REAL NAME
Beyonder
OCCUPATION
Criminal/hero
BASE
Kyln prison

HEIGHT 6 ft 2 in (variable)
WEIGHT 240 lbs
EYES Blue
HAIR Black

FIRST APPEARANCE
Secret Wars #1
(May 1984)

POWERS
Virtually omnipotent; the Beyonder can change reality just by thinking; has assumed various physical forms, created planets, destroyed galaxies, and taken control of every mind on Earth.

The infinite energies of a Cosmic Cube experimented on by scientist Owen Reece transformed Reece into Molecule Man and also formed the Beyonder. At first the Beyonder was a non-corporeal entity. As he acquired consciousness he began observing the activities of humans. Intrigued by what he saw, he created a planet, combining elements from various worlds including a small part of Detroit. He christened it Battleworld and gathered together a clutch of Super Heroes and Villains, in order to watch them fight. However, the Beyonder grew tired of just looking on...

The Beyonder created Battleworld—a single planet orbiting a lonely star.

Everything in the Beyonder's dimension was part of him. All matter—planets, suns, people—were aspects of his being, and he could alter and restructure it on the merest whim.

ENDLESS QUEST

The Beyonder arrived on Earth, and took the appearance of Molecule Man, Captain America, and finally a square-jawed alpha male with bad dress sense. He traveled the world learning about humanity. He was toilet-trained by Spider-Man, learned about money from a homeless woman, and had a fling with the musician Dazzler.

The Beyonder still felt unfulfilled and became increasingly unstable—a threat to the entire multiverse. He decided that he needed to be fully human and tried to transplant himself into the body of a baby, which was gestating in a machine he had built. Before the child could be born, Molecule Man destroyed the birth tank to save the multiverse, channelling the resulting explosive energies into a new and empty universe.

Kosmic Union

The Beyonder was rediscovered by the Fantastic Four who were led to this new universe by Dr Doom. In time, the Beyonder and Molecule Man fused to become a new Cosmic Cube. Then this Cube expelled the Molecule Man and became the female entity Kosmos (above) who now exists in mortal form as a being called the Maker. **AD**

Returning to Earth after the Secret War, the Thing had some scores to settle with the Beyonder. The Thing's stay on Battleworld had caused terrible heartache and he was not happy.

ESSENTIAL STORYLINES
- ***Secret Wars #1–12*** The Beyonder creates Battleworld and gets the Earth's Super Heroes to fight there.
- ***Secret Wars Vol. 2 #1–9*** The Beyonder arrives on Earth and learns about humanity.
- ***Fantastic Four Annual #23*** The Beyonder and Molecule Man merge to form a new entity named Kosmos.

The twin cranium of the Bi-Beast gives it double intelligence as well as two distinct personalities.

Bi-Beast

Created to be the guardian of the Avian race at a time when they were forced to go into hibernation in order to survive, the android Bi-Beast patrolled their now silent Sky Island, maintaining its security and keeping it from harm. But after years of loneliness, the twin persona of the Bi-Beast went mad, and they attempted to kidnap Betty Ross (see Banner, Betty), who had been transformed into a winged, gamma-powered monster called the Harpy. But the Hulk pursued the Bi-Beast, and after a savage battle, Bruce Banner used the scientific apparatus found in Sky Island to cure Betty's condition, much to the displeasure of the Bi-Beast.

Thereafter, the Bi-Beast continued its lonely vigil, attacking any and all who came within reach. Eventually, however, the Avians were revived, and so the savage Bi-Beast is no longer alone. **TB**

FACTFILE

REAL NAME
Bi-Beast

OCCUPATION
Guardian of the Avian race

BASE
Sky Island of the Avian race

HEIGHT 7 ft 8 in (variable)
WEIGHT 360 lbs (variable)
EYES Black
HAIR None

FIRST APPEARANCE
Incredible Hulk #169 (November 1973)

POWERS

Bi-Beast's artificial minds contain the accumulated knowledge of the Avian race–the top head specializes in knowledge related to warfare and combat, while the lower head is the repository of information pertaining to history and culture.

Big Hero 6

FIRST APPEARANCE Sunfire And Big Hero 6 #1 (Sept. 1998)
MEMBERS AND POWERS
Sunfire Projects heat and flame and can fly.
Silver Samurai Projects energy through his sword.
Gogo Tomago Turns into an explosive ball of energy.
Honey Lemon Obtains almost any object from her "Power Purse"
Hiro Takachiho 13-year-old scientific genius.
Baymax "Synthformer" robot that can change into a dragon.

Big Hero 6 is Japan's official team of superhuman agents. The Japanese government first formed the Giri, a group of officials and businessmen, to find and train superhuman recruits and to oversee their activities. The initial lineup of Big Hero 6 included Sunfire, formerly of the X-Men; and Wolverine's old adversary the Silver Samurai. Sunfire and the Silver Samurai were replaced by Sunfire's sister Sunpyre, who possesses similar powers, and the mysterious Ebon Samurai. **PS**

Big Hero 6
1 Hiro Takachiho
2 Baymax
3 Honey Lemon
4 Go Go Tomago
5 Silver Samurai
6 Sunfire

Big Man

FIRST APPEARANCE Amazing Spider-Man #10 (March 1964)
REAL NAME Frederick Foswell **OCCUPATION** Reporter, criminal
BASE New York City **HEIGHT** 5 ft 10 in; (Big Man) 6 ft 1 in
WEIGHT 185 lbs **EYES** Blue **HAIR** Gray
SPECIAL POWERS/ABILITIES Brilliant criminal mind, master of disguise and crack shot. Padded costume to appear more robust and taller; wore mask and used a device that deepened voice.

Daily Bugle reporter Foswell tried to organize New York's gangs under his leadership as the Big Man, employing the Enforcers as his henchmen. After clashing with Spider-Man, the police learned the Big Man's identity and arrested Foswell. He served his time in prison and, thanks to the generosity of publisher J. Jonah Jameson, returned to the *Bugle*. Foswell adopted the identity of Patch to spy on the underworld and aided in the capture of the Crime-Master. Foswell later returned to crime and worked for the Kingpin. He sacrificed himself to save his former employer J. Jonah Jameson. **TD**

Bird-Brain

FIRST APPEARANCE New Mutants #56 (October 1987)
REAL NAME Bird-Brain **OCCUPATION** None
BASE Paradise, an island in the North Atlantic **HEIGHT** 6 ft
WEIGHT 125 lbs **EYES** Red **HAIR** Vari-colored feathers
SPECIAL POWERS/ABILITIES Wings enable flight; entire body is hollow-boned, like a bird's; able to breathe at high altitudes; eyes are specially adapted to withstand high winds during flight.

Bird-Brain is a half-human, half-animal creature known as an Ani-Mate. He was created through genetic engineering by Dr. Frederick Animus, the Ani-Mator. Although Bird-Brain and his fellow Ani-Mates possessed human-level intelligence, the Ani-Mator treated them like slaves.

After being subjected to a number of cruel tests, Bird-Brain used his wings to fly away from the Ani-Mator's Paradise Island. He was placed in quarantine by the US authorities in preparation for being sent to a research laboratory for further testing, when he escaped. Bird-Brain was then recruited by the New Mutants, who returned with him to Paradise Island in order to help free his fellow Ani-Mates from the Ani-Mator's cruel thrall. **MT**

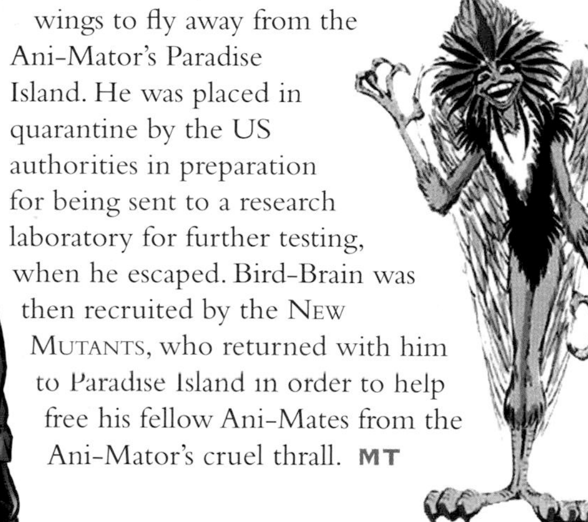

BISHOP

FACTFILE
REAL NAME
Lucas Bishop
OCCUPATION
Adventurer; law enforcement officer
BASE
The Xavier institute, New York; "District X," New York City

HEIGHT 6 ft 6 in
WEIGHT 275 lbs
EYES Brown
HAIR Black

FIRST APPEARANCE
The Uncanny X-Men #282 (November 1991)

POWERS
Can absorb energy directed against him and project it from his body as concussive force or utilize it to enhance his strength, resistance to injury, and recuperative ability. Expert with a samurai sword and firearms.

Bishop and his partner, Ishmael Ortega, patrol Manhattan's mutant ghetto, Mutant Town, alias District X.

Bishop

Bishop comes from an alternate future in which the robot SENTINELS had taken control of North America and most of the X-MEN had been killed. Born in a "mutant relocation camp," Bishop was branded with an "M" to identify him as a member of that race. In time, mutants and humans joined in the Summers Rebellion that overthrew the Sentinels. Bishop and his sister Shard were taught by their grandmother about the X-Men and PROFESSOR X's vision of peaceful coexistence between mutants and people. Bishop later joined Xavier's Security Enforcers (XSE), a mutant police force combating criminal mutants. Bishop pursued one such mutant criminal, Trevor Fitzroy, to the time period of his heroes, the X-Men, and was invited to join the team. Subsequently, Bishop became the partner of NYPD cop Ismael Ortega, fighting crime in "District X," Manhattan's mutant ghetto. **PS**

Black Bolt

FIRST APPEARANCE Fantastic Four #1 (December 1965)
REAL NAME Blackagar Boltagon **OCCUPATION** Monarch of the Inhumans **BASE** Blue Area of Moon **HEIGHT** 6 ft 2 in
WEIGHT 210 lbs **EYES** Blue **HAIR** Black
SPECIAL POWERS/ABILITIES Harnesses electrons; power linked to vocal chords, which trigger shockwaves; antenna channels power, giving superhuman strength, speed; fires concussive blasts; creates force fields; flight.

Black Bolt was born in Attilan, secret refuge of the INHUMANS. He was the son of Agon, head of the ruling Council of Genetics. His infant cries created massive destruction, forcing his parents to place him in a sound-proof chamber. An energy-harnessing suit was designed for him and he was trained to use his powers. After he was released, aged 19, Black Bolt learned that his younger brother Maximus was about to betray the Inhumans to the alien KREE race. Black Bolt shouted, creating a shockwave that blasted the Kree ship out of the sky. It crashed into the parliament building, killing his parents. Black Bolt became the ruler of the Inhumans; however the two brothers have often battled for the throne. Black Bolt is married to MEDUSA. **TD**

Black Cat

BLACK CAT

FACTFILE
REAL NAME
Felicia Hardy
OCCUPATION
Cat-burglar; adventurer
BASE
New York City

HEIGHT 5 ft 10 in
WEIGHT 120 lbs
EYES Green
HAIR Platinum blonde

FIRST APPEARANCE
Amazing Spider-Man #194 (July 1979)

POWERS
Devices in costume give far greater strength, speed, and agility than a normal woman.

Peter Parker adored Felicia but, unfortunately, she preferred his amazing alter ego.

The daughter of a famous cat burglar, Felicia Hardy was determined to follow in her father's footsteps. And so she devised the costumed identity of the Black Cat, setting up pre-arranged "accidents" so as to make it appear as though she possessed the ability to cause bad luck to befall others. But the Cat herself was a victim of bad luck when she ran afoul of the amazing SPIDER-MAN.

Becoming smitten with the Wall-Crawler, the Black Cat pursued him amorously, and for a time became one of his closest confidantes, one of the very few people who knew he was really Peter Parker. After she was savagely beaten by the mutant SABRETOOTH, the Cat obtained mystical bad luck powers through the machinations of the KINGPIN. These abilities faded away, as did her romance with Spider-Man, who couldn't reconcile spending the rest of his life with a compulsive thief who wasn't interested in him as Peter Parker. But though Peter eventually married Mary Jane Watson (*see* PARKER, Mary Jane), the Black Cat remains one of his closest friends and allies—despite the fact that she works the shady side of the street more often than not. **TB**

Black Knight

Knight of the Ebony Blade

The first Black Knight, Sir Percy of Scandia, was born in the 6th Century and became one of the bravest knights at the court of King Arthur Pendragon at Camelot. Here he led a double life, posing as a mild-mannered fop while secretly fighting evil as the Black Knight, armed with the Ebony Blade, a sword fashioned by Merlin the Magician from the Starstone meteorite. Centuries later, Sir Percy's spirit returned to converse with his ancestors, Professor Nathan Garrett and Dane Whitman, each of whom would take up his mantle.

Raised in Scandinavia, Sir Percy was a new face to the people of Camelot.

FACTFILE
REAL NAME
Dane Whitman
OCCUPATION
Adventurer
BASE
New York City

HEIGHT 6 ft
WEIGHT 190 lbs
EYES Brown
HAIR Brown

FIRST APPEARANCE
Avengers Vol. 1 #47 (December 1967)

POWERS
An able scientist, Whitman built on discoveries of his uncle, Nathan Garrett; rides a winged horse and has power lance that fires heat and force beams; also wields Ebony Blade, sometimes more curse than blessing.

VILLAINOUS KNIGHT

Nathan Garrett met the spirit of Sir Percy during a visit to the family home of Garrett Castle, and was offered the chance to become a latter-day Black Knight. However, Garrett failed to draw the Ebony Blade from its scabbard thereby proving himself unworthy. Determined to become the Black Knight by other means, Garrett developed a lance that fired energy bolts, and embarked on a criminal career mounted upon a genetically engineered winged horse. Garrett battled the Avengers with the Masters of Evil, dying in a fight with Iron Man. Before passing away, Garrett confessed his crimes to his nephew, Dane Whitman, and begged him to restore his honor.

A brilliant scientist, Garrett used his knowledge to create a winged steed.

The dark sorcerer Kalmari battled Dane Whitman with a dragon, but this version of the Black Knight proved victorious.

THE GOOD KNIGHT

Adopting his uncle's Black Knight persona, Dane Whitman vowed to fight for the forces of good. Although initially mistaken as the previous Black Knight and attacked by the Avengers, Whitman gradually won his spurs and became one of their number. Blessed with a noble spirit, Whitman was able to draw the Ebony Blade once wielded by his ancestor Sir Percy. Unfortunately, the sword had been cursed with the blood of those felled by Sir Percy, all those years before. This curse dogged Whitman throughout the many battles that he was to fight until, that is, Dr. Strange finally recognized what it was. In order to cleanse it, Whitman was instructed to plunge the sword into the Brazier of Truth, located in Garrett Castle. Whitman's effort shattered the Brazier. Since it was this mystical object that held Sir Percy's spirit in this world, its destruction finally allowed him to rest. **AD**

ESSENTIAL STORYLINES
- ***The Black Knight #1-3*** Sir Percy begins his adventures as the Black Knight.
- ***Avengers Vol.1 #71*** Dane Whitman helps the Avengers beat Kang and becomes a member.
- ***Dr Strange Vol. 2 #68*** Whitman cleanses the Ebony Blade of evil and frees Sir Percy's ghost.

The Ebony Blade renders its user invulnerable but, if it tastes blood, will eventually corrupt him.

Black Panther

FACTFILE

REAL NAME
T'Challa

OCCUPATION
Monarch of Wakanda

BASE
Wakanda

HEIGHT 6 ft
WEIGHT 200 lbs
EYES Brown
HAIR Black

FIRST APPEARANCE
Fantastic Four #52
(July 1966)

POWERS
Olympic-level athlete, acrobat and gymnast; combat specialist. Mask enhances night vision; gloves expel gases; vibranium boots enable him to land from great heights; vibranium in costume makes bullets or punches lose power.

The "Black Panther" is an honorary title bestowed on the reigning monarch of the jungle kingdom of Wakanda. T'Challa was only a child when he succeeded his father, who had been murdered by KLAW, the master of sound. Before T'Challa assumed the Wakandan throne, he was educated in the finest schools in Europe and America. He then embarked on a series of grueling tests to prove that he was worthy of donning the mantle of the Black Panther, the sacred totem of his people. After passing each test, he gained possession of a special heart-shaped herb found only in Wakanda, which enhanced his five senses and physical prowess to the peak of human perfection.

Although Black Panther has often allied himself with the FANTASTIC FOUR and the AVENGERS, the Black Panther is still the king of Wakanda and his people are always his highest priority. Realizing that the time had come for him to have an heir, he asked Ororo Munroe, STORM of the X-MEN, to marry him. **TD**

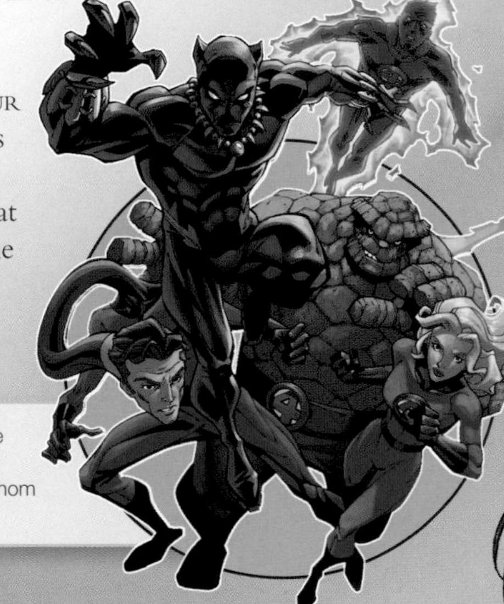

Ally from Africa: claws at the ready, the resourceful Black Panther springs into action alongside the Fantastic Four, whom he has aided on several occasions.

Black Mamba

FIRST APPEARANCE Marvel Two-In-One #64 (June 1980)
REAL NAME Tanya Sealy
OCCUPATION Mercenary **BASE** Mobile
HEIGHT 5 ft 7 in **WEIGHT** 115 lbs **EYES** Green **HAIR** Black
SPECIAL POWERS/ABILITIES Projects Darkforce energy, which suffocates opponents; hypnotic powers trick targets into thinking that Darkforce is a loved one, allowing it to ensnare them.

A former call girl, Tanya Sealy was one of a group of people who were surgically altered by the Roxxon Oil Company in order to become a covert special agent. A surgical implant allowed Sealy to tap into her brain's energy in a way that gave her control of the Darkforce, an inky cloud of energy, and also some hypnotic powers. Joining the ruthless Serpent Squad, Black Mamba and her fellow operatives set out to find an ancient power object known as the Serpent Crown. Later, Black Mamba joined with ANACONDA and Sidewinder as a freelance mercenary in a new team called the SERPENT SOCIETY. **MT**

Black Talon

FIRST APPEARANCE Avengers #152 (October 1976)
REAL NAME Unrevealed
OCCUPATION Houngan (voodoo priest) **BASE** Louisiana
HEIGHT 6 ft 2 in **WEIGHT** 240 lbs **EYES** Brown **HAIR** Black
SPECIAL POWERS/ABILITIES Supernatural voodoo powers, including the ability to create and control zombies, human corpses that can be reanimated through voodoo magic.

Black Talon is a Creole with true voodoo powers. This man, whose real name is unknown, is actually the second to wear the Black Talon costume. The first was a fake voodoo priest who was killed by his own cult when they found out he was a fraud. The true houngan Black Talon formed his own cult and was then contacted by the GRIM REAPER, who wanted his dead brother WONDER MAN brought back to life as a zombie. When Black Talon did this, the Reaper's brother attacked the AVENGERS, who subdued him and then defeated Black Talon himself. **MT**

Black Tom

FIRST APPEARANCE X-Men Vol. 1 #99 (June 1976)
REAL NAME Thomas Samuel Eamon Cassidy
OCCUPATION Criminal **BASE** Mobile
HEIGHT 6 ft **WEIGHT** 200 lbs **EYES** Blue **HAIR** Black
SPECIAL POWERS/ABILITIES In human form, Tom could project blasts of heat and concussive force, focused through his shillelagh. In plant form, Black Tom can mentally control other plant life.

Like his brother Sean Cassidy, the BANSHEE, Black Tom Cassidy is an Irish-born mutant. Losing both the Cassidy fortune and the woman he loved, Maeve Rourke, to Sean, Black Tom turned to crime. Partnered by the JUGGERNAUT, Black Tom has fought the X-MEN and other Super Heroes. After he was shot, doctors grafted a wood-like material onto his wounds, transforming Tom into a sentient humanoid plant who can control other plants. **PS**

Black Widow

Uncompromising and deadly

Natasha has assumed many roles, including surrogate mother, field agent, and implacable opponent of a rival Black Widow.

Shortly after Russia's World War II victory at Stalingrad, a lady, trapped in a burning building, threw her baby to a stranger below—a soldier named Ivan Petrovich. He raised the baby, named Natasha, who turned out to be a superb student, athlete, and ballerina. She married test pilot Alexei Shostakov, but their happiness was cut short. Faking Shostakov's death and leaving Natasha to grieve, the KGB trained him to become the Red Guardian—a Russian super-soldier. The KGB then manipulated Natasha into becoming a spy codenamed Black Widow.

While they don't always see eye-to-eye, Black Widow remains loyal to her old lover, Daredevil.

HARD TIME

Two espionage missions against Stark Industries brought her into contact with the adventurer Hawkeye, and it was ultimately he that inspired Natasha to claim her freedom and join SHIELD. A romance between the pair proved short-lived.

Encountering the Red Guardian on a mission, she had only just learned his true identity when he was shot and killed, the double shock causing Natasha to withdraw from her relationship with Hawkeye.

In the years that followed, Natasha became romantically involved with Daredevil and founded the Champions team of Super Heroes. She also led the Avengers during one of its most testing periods, when several members lost their lives.

During her career, Natasha has had to assume many different roles: she has been the surrogate mother to a small baby and the implacable opponent to a rival Black Widow–Yelena Belova. Despite the many emotional hardships she has suffered, Natasha Romanova essentially remains the same woman—a morally uncompromising and deadly combatant. AD

KEY STORYLINES

- ***Daredevil #87–90*** Black Widow and Daredevil move to San Francisco; Black Widow's history is explained.
- ***Pale Little Spider #1–3*** The origins of Yelena Belova are explained for the first time.
- ***Black Widow Vol. I #1–3*** The two Black Widows, Natasha Romanova and Yelena Belova, go head-to-head and their bitter enmity begins.

BLACK WIDOW I

FACTFILE

REAL NAME
Natalia (Natasha) Alianovna Romanova

OCCUPATION
Intelligence agent

BASE New York City

HEIGHT 5 ft 7 in
WEIGHT 125 lbs
EYES Blue
HAIR Red/auburn

FIRST APPEARANCE
Tales of Suspense Vol. 1 #52 (April 1964)

POWERS

Martial artist; Olympic-level gymnast; trained spy; cartridges on wrist house various devices: tear-gas, spring-loaded cable, radio transmitter.

BLACK WIDOW II

FACTFILE

REAL NAME
Yelena Belova

OCCUPATION
Intelligence agent

BASE Russia

HEIGHT 5 ft 7 in
WEIGHT 135 lbs
EYES Blue
HAIR Blonde

FIRST APPEARANCE
Inhumans Vol. 2 #5 (March 1999)

POWERS

Only experience and gadgets separate Belova from the first Black Widow: Belova achieved even higher marks in training; she is also a martial-arts expert and Olympic-level gymnast.

YELENA BELOVA

Like Natasha, Yelena Belova was trained at the KGB's notorious Red Room. The two Black Widows soon clashed; however Natasha's experience gave her the edge. Antipathy between the pair continues to fester.

Blade

Born a half-vampire (dhampir) when his mother was fatally bitten by vampire Deacon Frost while giving birth, Blade was brought up by vampire hunter Jamal Afari. DRACULA later transformed Afari, and Blade was forced to kill his foster father. Now nursing two grudges, Blade set out for revenge against both Dracula and Deacon Frost. During his quest he allied with Quincy HARKER, Rachel VAN HELSING, and Frank DRAKE against Dracula, while "vampire detective" Hannibal KING assisted him against Frost.

Blade, King, Drake, and DOCTOR STRANGE helped unleash the Montesi Formula, a mystical incantation that temporarily destroyed all the vampires on Earth. Blade opened a detective agency with King, named Borderline Inc., and battled occult threats with King and Drake under the name Nightstalkers. DW

Blade doesn't take orders well and is difficult to work with in large team settings.

FACTFILE

REAL NAME
Eric Brooks

OCCUPATION
Vampire hunter

BASE
Mobile

HEIGHT 6 ft 2 in
WEIGHT 180 lbs
EYES Brown
HAIR Black

FIRST APPEARANCE
Tomb of Dracula Vol. 1 #10 (July 1973)

POWERS
Immune to vampire bites and vampiric hypnosis; enhanced strength, speed, senses, and healing. Immune to vampire's susceptibility to sunlight. Carries arsenal of anti-vampire weapons; guns fire garlic-filled, silver bullets; trademark blade is titanium; martial-arts expert.

Blade remains committed to his mission to rid the world of vampires. He now possesses the abilities of a pseudo-vampire due to a bite from Morbius. Part vampire himself, he suppresses his inherited and incurable thirst for blood with a special serum, and immense willpower.

Blacklash

FIRST APPEARANCE Tales of Suspense #97 (January 1968)
REAL NAME Mark Scarlotti (aka Mark Scott)
OCCUPATION Assassin-for-hire **BASE** Mobile
HEIGHT 6 ft 1 in **WEIGHT** 196 lbs **EYES** Blue **HAIR** Blond
SPECIAL POWERS/ABILITIES Expert with whip and nunchakus. Possesses two cybernetically-controlled whips, anti-gravity bolas and a necro-lash releasing electrical energy generated by gauntlets

A talented engineer, Scarlotti joined the MAGGIA crime organization. He developed super-weapons, such as a steel-fiber whip that cut through metal. First calling himself Whiplash, he made his name by battling IRON MAN to a draw. As Mark Scott, he worked undercover as head of research at Stark International's Cincinnati factory and became a costume operative for Justin HAMMER. Scarlotti upgraded his arsenal and changed his name to Blacklash. He now works as a mercenary and contract assassin. TD

Blackout

FIRST APPEARANCE: Nova #19 (May 1976)
REAL NAME Marcus Daniels
OCCUPATION: Criminal **BASE** New York City
HEIGHT 5ft 10in **WEIGHT** 180 lbs **EYES** Gray **HAIR** Brown
SPECIAL POWERS/ABILITIES: Projects and manipulates semi-solid black energy known as the Darkforce; has the strength and agility of a normal human being.

Exposed to "black star" rays by the physicist Dr. Abner Croit, Daniels gained the ability to control this cosmic radiation. He adopted the moniker "Blackout" and embarked on a series of robberies. Over time, exposure to this dark energy led to creeping insanity. Although his ally MOONSTONE helped him to direct and extend his powers, she also sought to control his mind, as did their joint master, BARON ZEMO. During an attack on the Avenger's Mansion, Blackout endeavoured to resist Zemo's mental commands, but these efforts led to a brain hemorrhage and Blackout's death. AD

Blink

FIRST APPEARANCE Uncanny X-men #317 (October 1994)
REAL NAME: Clarice Ferguson **OCCUPATION** Adventurer
BASE Mobile **HEIGHT** 5 ft 5 in **WEIGHT** 125 lbs
EYES Green **HAIR** Magenta
SPECIAL POWERS/ABILITIES Blink is a mutant with the ability to create teleportational warps; carries a dagger and a set of javelins.

Having been brought up in the brutal Age of Apocalypse by her world's version of SABRETOOTH, Blink eventually became "unstuck in time"—exiled from her home reality. Recruited by the Timebroker and entrusted with the Tallus, a wrist-worn device that provides mission info, she and a team of fellow EXILES were charged with repairing the broken links in the chain of realities across the multiverse. Since that time, she has traveled from Earth to Earth, doing what must be done to put the multiverse back on the proper path. TB

Blizzard

The story of Blizzard begins and ends with the name Stark. Employed by Stark Industries, Dr Gregor Shapanka became obsessed with his own mortality and attempted to steal and sell Stark transistor technology in order to fund research into longevity.

After being sacked for his misdemeanours, Shapanka developed a suit capable of generating immense cold. Using it to perform acts of villainy, he came to be known as Jack Frost or Blizzard and became a nemesis of Iron Man, battling him time and again. Shapanka's life came to an end when he was killed by Arno Stark, an Iron Man from the year 2020 who had travelled back in time to retrieve Shapanka's retina patterns to disarm a bomb.

Shapanka's successor as Blizzard was Donny Gill, an employee of Justin Hammer. Having employed the original Blizzard to undertake various questionable schemes in the past it is likely that it was Hammer who provided Gill with his Blizzard suit. His work for Hammer was to lead to his imprisonment, but when released Iron Man persuaded Gill to leave Hammer's employ and Tony Stark took him under his wing. **AD**

Suit contains tiny cryogenic units called micro-cryostats.

The more water there is in the air, the more powerful is Blizzard's suit. In arid conditions it is useless.

FACTFILE

REAL NAME
Dr. Gregor Shapanka

OCCUPATION
Former scientist; criminal

BASE New York City

HEIGHT 5 ft 6 in
WEIGHT 165 lbs
EYES Brown
HAIR Brown

FIRST APPEARANCE
Tales of Suspense Vol. 1 #45 (September 1963)

POWERS
Gloves on Blizzard's battlesuit could project intense cold, generate freezing mist, mini-blizzards of snow, sleet, and darts of ice that could pierce metal; he could freeze people by covering them in frost; escaped capture by creating an ice slide. He has no superhuman powers.

Blob

Once a lowly carnival freak in a traveling circus, life changed for Fred J. Dukes when he was visited by the uncanny X-Men, who revealed to him that, like themselves, he was a mutant. Rather than accept their offer of membership in their school, Dukes became drunk on his newfound status, and attempted to destroy them as the Blob. Recruited thereafter by Magneto to become a member of his Brotherhood of Evil Mutants, the Blob entered into a life of crime, coming into conflict not only with the X-Men, but the Avengers and the Defenders as well. For a time, the Blob worked with the government-sponsored incarnation of the brotherhood known as Freedom Force, but more recently he has renewed his lawless career as a genetic terrorist, albeit more muscle than brains. **TB**

When the Blob sets himself in one position, his mutant ability makes it almost impossible for an outside force to dislodge him.

FACTFILE

REAL NAME
Fred J. Dukes

OCCUPATION
Criminal; former circus performer

BASE
Mobile

HEIGHT 8 ft
WEIGHT 976 lbs
EYES Brown
HAIR Brown

FIRST APPEARANCE
UNCANNY X-MEN #3 (January 1964)

POWERS
Superhuman strength and durability. Fatty body can absorb bullets, even artillery shells, and is impervious to injury; however eyes, ears, nose, and mouth are not as injury-resistant. When he plants himself firmly, the Blob bonds with the ground beneath him and cannot be moved.

Bloodhawk

FIRST APPEARANCE Avengers #179 (January 1979)
REAL NAME Bloodhawk **OCCUPATION** Adventurer
BASE Muara, an island in the Atlantic Ocean **HEIGHT** 6 ft 3 in
WEIGHT 150 lbs **EYES** Black **FEATHERS** Reddish-brown
SPECIAL POWERS/ABILITIES Superhuman strength and stamina; able to fly and communicate with birds; possesses razor-sharp claws.

Bloodhawk is the only son of a geneticist who experimented on his own wife. The poor woman died giving birth to a mutant of hawklike appearance and characteristics. Unable to accept the horror he had created, Bloodhawk's father turned his son over to his best friend, who removed the child from civilization. Plagued by bouts of insanity, Bloodhawk grew to adulthood in the South Seas. When a powerful totem was stolen from his island home, he journeyed to the US and battled the AVENGERS to recover it. Bloodhawk later gave his life to save Thor. **TB**

Bloodscream

FIRST APPEARANCE Wolverine Vol. 2 #4 (February 1989)
REAL NAME Unknown **OCCUPATION** Enforcer
BASE Madripoor, Southeast Asia **HEIGHT** 6 ft 5 in
WEIGHT Unknown **EYES** Unknown **HAIR** Gray
SPECIAL POWERS/ABILITIES Although not a true vampire, has many vampire powers: superhuman strength, agility, accelerated healing, hypnotic ability; can also kill or cause bleeding by touch.

Bloodscream was once a 16th-century sailor, whom a necromancer turned into a pseudo-vampire—a condition that could only be cured by drinking an immortal's blood. Centuries later, Bloodscream, now a Nazi soldier, encountered WOLVERINE. Meeting Wolverine decades later, Bloodscream saw the mutant hadn't aged. Assuming Wolverine was immortal, Bloodscream has hounded him ever since. **MT**

Bloodstone, Ulysses

Ulysses meets his nemesis, Ulluxy'l, for the first time.

Born in the Hyborian Age over 10,000 years ago, the man now known as Ulysses Bloodstone originally belonged to a Scandinavian tribe of hunter-gatherers, from which he was lured away by Ulluxy'l Kwan Tae Syn. This alien being was the guardian of a crystal entity called the Hellfire Helix, a being that was seeking to dominate the Earth. To fulfil its goal, the Helix needed a human servant, so it endowed the tribe's foremost hunter with superhuman powers. However, when it went on to kill his tribe members, the hunter grabbed at it, causing the Helix crystal to shatter into hundreds of pieces, one of which embedded itself in his chest. The crystal fragment saved his life and made him immortal, but the rest of his tribe were wiped out. The reddish crystal and his wandering existence led him to adopt the name Ulysses Bloodstone. The other pieces of the Helix were scattered all over the world.

FACTFILE
REAL NAME
Unknown; took the name Ulysses Bloodstone
OCCUPATION
Soldier of fortune
BASE
Bloodstone Island

HEIGHT 6 ft 2 in
WEIGHT 255 lbs
EYES Blue
HAIR Blond

FIRST APPEARANCE
Marvel Presents #1 (October 1975)

POWERS
Superhuman strength; blood-red Helix crystal endowed him with immortality and regenerative ability: could even regrow limbs; also had invisible third eye in forehead giving him psychic powers; expert with all kinds of weapons, though favored a customized sawn-off shotgun firing explosive shells.

Island Base

Vowing vengeance on Ulluxy'l, Ulysses spent the rest of his life searching for the alien, while Ulluxy'l devoted his existence to piecing the Helix back together.

During his quest, Ulysses earned a fortune through mercenary work and shrewd investments, establishing six headquarters across the world and a base on what became known as Bloodstone Island.

Inheriting her father's fortune and powers, 18-year-old Elsa battles evil across the world. Dracula and the Egyptian necromancer Rakses are just some of her foes.

Inevitably, Ulysses' fate was bound up with that of the Helix. In one final, climactic confrontation, a dying Ulysses managed to destroy the crystal altogether and so achieved vengeance for his tribe. Ulysses left behind his ex-wife and his daughter, Elsa. Wearing a bloodstone choker that endowed her with superhuman powers, she vowed to continue her father's fight against evil. **AD**

Bloodstorm

FIRST APPEARANCE Mutant X #1 (October 1998)
REAL NAME Ororo Munroe
OCCUPATION Adventurer **BASE** Earth of Mutant X universe
HEIGHT 5 ft 11 in **WEIGHT** 196 lbs **EYES** Blue **HAIR** White
SPECIAL POWERS/ABILITIES Possessed vampiric powers, including hypnotic abilities and the power to transform into mist, a bat, or a wolf; can control the weather over limited areas.

Years ago DRACULA bit STORM of the X-MEN, who began transforming into a vampire. In the main Marvel Universe, Storm was cured. But on the alternate Earth where the "Mutant X" series was set, Storm completed her metamorphosis, becoming the vampiress known as Bloodstorm. She nevertheless refused to turn villainess, and fed only on the blood of that reality's FORGE, with his consent. Bloodstorm joined the Six, a team mostly comprised of former members of that reality's X-Men. For aiding the people of yet another alternate Earth, Earth X, Bloodstorm was rewarded by receiving a blood transfusion which cured her vampirism. **PS**

Blue Shield

FIRST APPEARANCE Dazzler #5 (July 1981)
REAL NAME Joseph Cartelli **OCCUPATION** Security Director for Project: Pegasus **BASE** Mount Athena, New York
HEIGHT 6 ft **WEIGHT** 180 lbs **EYES** Blue **HAIR** Brown
SPECIAL POWERS/ABILITIES Formerly wore microcircuitry-lined belt which increased strength and generated force field around body; now, owing to prolonged exposure, no longer needs belt.

Even as a boy, Joseph Cartelli seemed destined for a jail cell. He was always cutting school, running errands for local gangsters, or committing petty crimes. A boyhood friend of his was an inventor who borrowed money from loan sharks to build a personal force field. When this friend was murdered by the Barrigan crime family for failing to repay the debt, Cartelli decided to use the force field to help get his revenge. He went undercover, joining the Barrigans' gang with the intention of destroying it from within. After accomplishing this goal, Cartelli tried to join the AVENGERS as the Blue Shield. He later replaced QUASAR as the Security Director for Project: Pegasus. **TD**

Bluebird

FIRST APPEARANCE Untold Tales of Spider-Man #11
REAL NAME Sally Avril **OCCUPATION** Student; adventurer
BASE Midtown High School, New York **HEIGHT** 5 ft 2 in
WEIGHT 110 lbs **EYES** Brown **HAIR** Black (blonde wig)
SPECIAL POWERS/ABILITIES Stolen technology from the Vulture enabled her to fly using power pack and wings; also had a device that emitted an ultrasonic, ear-splitting scream.

A classmate of Peter Parker's at Midtown High, Sally Avril adopted the costumed identity of Bluebird after being inspired by the exploits of SPIDER-MAN. Possessing no superhuman abilities or even proper training, Bluebird proved to be a danger to herself and to others, until Spider-Man eventually convinced her to put aside her costumed identity and return to life as a student. Tragically, she was killed shortly thereafter in an automobile accident. **TB**

Boomerang

FIRST APPEARANCE Tales to Astonish #81 (July 1966)
REAL NAME Frederick Myers
OCCUPATION Assassin for hire **BASE** Mobile
HEIGHT 5 ft 11 in **WEIGHT** 175 lbs **EYES** Brown **HAIR** Black
SPECIAL POWERS/ABILITIES Brilliant baseball pitcher; famed for customized boomerangs, such as explosive "shatterangs," poisonous "gasarangs," diamond sharp "razorangs."

Australian Fred Myers moved to the US as a child and became a major league baseball player renowned for his amazing accuracy. Suspended for taking bribes, a bitter Myers turned to crime full-time. The criminal organization known as the Secret Empire gave him the codename Boomerang and, mindful of his throwing skills, equipped him with a range of specialized projectile weaponry. Boomerang later obtained financial backing from Justin HAMMER and became an assassin, working for HAMMERHEAD and alongside the SINISTER SYNDICATE. Boomerang has battled SHIELD, DAREDEVIL and SPIDER-MAN and, although these heroes have been victorious, they know that they can't relax—after all, boomerangs nearly always come back. **AD**

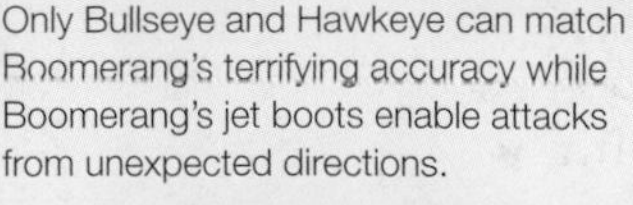
Only Bullseye and Hawkeye can match Boomerang's terrifying accuracy while Boomerang's jet boots enable attacks from unexpected directions.

Box

Robotic armored crimefighter

Box

FACTFILE

REAL NAME
Roger Bochs

OCCUPATION
Alpha Flight member

BASE
Tamarind Island, British Columbia

HEIGHT 7 ft
WEIGHT 465 lbs
EYES Blue
HAIR Red

FIRST APPEARANCE
Alpha Flight #1
(August 1983)

POWERS

An engineering genius, Bochs built the first Box robot to serve as a bipedal robotic transportation for himself; the Box robot possessed vast strength and durability; Bochs was able to "phase" in and out of robot at will.

Box IV

FACTFILE

REAL NAME
Madison Jeffries

OCCUPATION
Alpha Flight member

BASE
Tamarind Island, British Columbia

HEIGHT 10 ft (variable)
WEIGHT 195 lbs (variable)
EYES Blue
HAIR Black

FIRST APPEARANCE
Alpha Flight #10
(May 1984)

Mutant power to manipulate metal, plastic and glass allows Jeffries to extend capability of Box; robot armor now much lighter and able to increase its size and weight seemingly without limit.

Roger Bochs' life was pitted by sadness. It is unclear why he had no legs, but for much of his early life he defined himself by his paraplegic status. Eventually, he stepped beyond these limitations, building a giant humanoid robot—Box—in which he could travel, gaining the freedom that so many others took for granted.

Wheelchair-user Roger Bochs' early life was sad and lonely.

JOINING ALPHA FLIGHT

With his robotic chariot, Roger came to the attention of James McDonald Hudson who was recruiting for Alpha Flight. Hudson recruited Roger into Alpha Flight's training programme and he was progressing well when the Canadian government withdrew funding. Out of a job, Roger returned to his native Saskatchewan.

Hudson kept the team going but Roger's return to it was a long time coming. Hired by Jerome Jaxon to join the nefarious Omega Flight, Roger was expected to help them destroy Alpha Flight. He opposed this but was helpless when Jaxon took control of Box and sent it into battle. By the end of the struggle, both Jaxon and Hudson were dead and Box was seriously mangled. Roger was invited to rejoin the exhausted Alpha Flight, but first he needed to rebuild his robot.

With the help of fellow team member, Madison Jefferies, Roger constructed a superior Box model, but when he became unlucky in love, his life began a downward spiral. Manipulated into merging his being with Madison's unbalanced brother, Roger became part of a new entity—Omega. His endeavors to limit Omega's sinister activities led to him being effectively lobotomized and when Omega was defeated and died, Roger passed away, too.

ESSENTIAL STORYLINES

- *Alpha Flight #41–49*
  Charts Roger Bochs' physical and mental decline, and his death as part of Omega.
- *Alpha Flight #102–105*
  Madison Jeffries helps Alpha Flight battle Diablo... and then there's the small matter of getting married to Lillian Crawley.

The new improved Box allowed Roger to phase in and out of it.

MADISON JEFFRIES

When Roger Bochs died, his friend Madison Jeffries became the next man to wear the Box armor. A mutant capable of manipulating metal, Madison used his abilities to augment the machine.

Madison's life had been defined by his experiences in Vietnam, where he served with his brother, Lionel. The pair suffered deep emotional scarring when an explosion wiped out their squad: Lionel was driven insane by this event while Madison was left feeling alienated from the world. His work as a machinist for Alpha Flight helped give some meaning to his life and the Box armor allowed him to make a more significant contribution to the team. AD

With his intuitive grasp of all things mechanical, Madison Jeffries made great strides in enhancing Box.

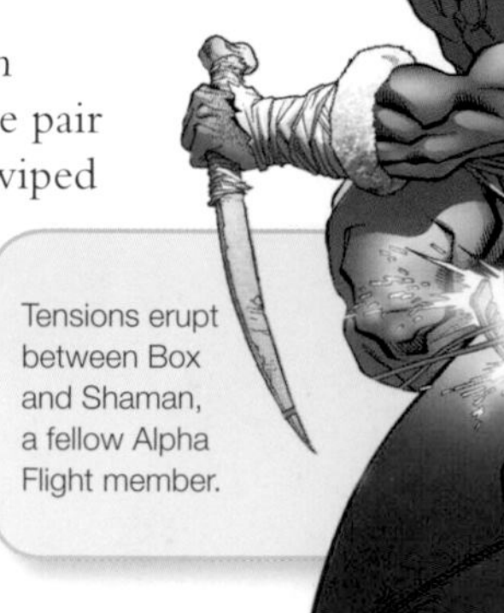

Tensions erupt between Box and Shaman, a fellow Alpha Flight member.

Braddock, Jamie

FIRST APPEARANCE Captain Britain Weekly #9 (December 1976)
REAL NAME James Braddock
OCCUPATION Ex-racing driver, slave-trafficker **BASE** London
HEIGHT 6 ft 1 in **WEIGHT** 151 lbs **EYES** Blue **HAIR** Black
SPECIAL POWERS/ABILITIES Possesses the ability to warp reality, which he perceives as made of string; he can thus twist objects, such as people's bodies, into grotesque, agonizing shapes.

The brother of Captain Britain and the X-Man called Psylocke, sleazy playboy Jamie Braddock was captured by the insane criminal mastermind known as Doctor Crocodile. Tortured by Crocodile, Jamie's latent mutant ability to reshape reality around him manifested itself at the same moment that he lost his grip on sanity. Now, he has become one of the most dangerous beings in the universe—capable of turning the world around him upside down, and thoroughly out of his mind. **TB**

Brand, Lucas

FIRST APPEARANCE Tomb of Dracula #9 (June 1973)
REAL NAME Lucas Brand
OCCUPATION Gang leader; assassin **BASE** London
HEIGHT 6 ft 4 in **WEIGHT** 210 lbs **EYES** Red **HAIR** Brown
SPECIAL POWERS/ABILITIES Standard vampiric powers, including superhuman strength and invulnerability to most weapons. Strong willpower enabled him to resist Dracula's mental control.

Lucas Brand and the members of the British motorcycle gang he led came across a weakened Dracula, beat him up and attempted to drown him. In retaliation, Dracula bit and killed Brand, who thereby became a vampire himself. Later Brand was recruited by Doctor Sun, a criminal mastermind who existed as a bodiless, living brain. On Sun's behalf, Brand overcame Dracula, but when Brand then turned against Doctor Sun, Sun destroyed the would-be rebel. **PS**

Lucas Brand was one of the very few vampires in the world who was able to resist the mental control of that lord of vampires, Count Dracula.

Brood

Brood, The

The Brood are a race of alien insectoids that spread across the universe like a cancer by injecting their eggs into other living beings. As the eggs hatch, the host is physically consumed and transformed into a member of the Brood. The Insectoids use a race of sentient space whales called the Acandi as living starships. Native to the Shi'ar Galaxy, the Brood often aided Deathbird in her attempts to overthrow her sister Lilandra Neramani as the Shi'ar Majestrix.

The Brood infected the X-Men and planted the egg of a Bloodqueen into Professor X, but the team was saved by Wolverine who was able to resist the transformation process. Although their home planet Broodworld has been destroyed, many of the Brood have survived and have begun to rebuild their race. **TD**

Wolverine's healing factor let him resist the Brood egg that was deposited in his body.

FACTFILE

OCCUPATION
Extraterrestrial mercenaries

BASE
Shi'ar Galaxy

HEIGHT 8 ft
WEIGHT 825 lbs
EYES Red
HAIR None
SCALES Green

FIRST APPEARANCE
Uncanny X-Men #155 (March 1982)

POWERS

Individuals possess six legs, transparent wings, razor-sharp teeth, armor-plated scales and long tails that are divided into two deadly stingers. The Brood are extremely durable, very hard to destroy, and vicious fighters, determined that their malignant race will survive.

The alien Brood eventually found their way to Earth and injected a team of mutants; however they were defeated by the X-Men.

Brother Voodoo

FIRST APPEARANCE Strange Tales #169 (September 1973)
REAL NAME Jericho Drumm
OCCUPATION Houngan (voodoo priest) **BASE** Port-au-Prince, Haiti
HEIGHT 6 ft **WEIGHT** 220 lbs **EYES** Brown **HAIR** Brown
SPECIAL POWERS/ABILITIES Summoning brother's spirit from within own body doubles his strength; can send this spirit forth to possess other people; can create fire and smoke; hypnotic control over animals.

After years practicing as a psychologist in the US, Jericho Drumm returned to his native Haiti. There, his brother Daniel, the local houngan (voodoo priest) was dying following a battle with a sorcerer possessed by the spirit of the serpent-god Damballah. Drumm studied the voodoo arts and proved a powerful houngan, made even stronger when he merged with the spirit of his dead brother. As Brother Voodoo, he vanquished Damballah and his evil cult. **MT**

Brotherhood Of Evil Mutants

Mutant terrorist organization

Brotherhood of Evil Mutants

FACTFILE

MEMBERS/POWERS

MAGNETO (LEADER)
Manipulates magnetic forces.

ASTRA
Varies her molecular density.

TOAD
Tongue stretches 25 ft; leaps great heights; super-strong.

QUICKSILVER
Superhuman speed.

SCARLET WITCH
Chaos magician.

MASTERMIND
Illusion-caster.

BLOB
Immovable; impervious to injury.

UNUS
Impenetrable force-field.

LORELEI
Hypersonic, paralysing scream.

BASE
Mobile

FIRST APPEARANCE
Uncanny X-Men #4 (March 1964)

ALLIES/FOES

ALLIES Magneto

FOES Professor X, The X-Men, New Mutants, X-Factor, X-Force, the Avengers, Cable, all non-mutant human beings.

THE FIRST BROTHERHOOD
1 The Toad ***2*** Mastermind ***3*** Magneto ***4*** Quicksilver ***5*** The Scarlet Witch

Founded by Magneto, the Brotherhood of Evil Mutants has remained, through its various incarnations, the opposite number of the X-Men; while the X-men's mission has always been to promote tolerance and co-existence between mutants and normal humans, the Brotherhood's goal has been nothing less than total domination over mankind, and quite possibly the eradication of normal humans entirely.

MUTANT MENACE

Originally, Magneto formed the Brotherhood as a strike force, helping him to oppose Professor X's X-Men, who had foiled his takeover of the Cape Citadel rocket base. This initial assemblage included the high-leaping Toad, Mastermind, creator of perfect illusions, the super-swift Quicksilver, and his sister, the hex-casting Scarlet Witch. Time and again they struck against their X-Men foes and against humanity, never scoring a true victory. And eventually, with the defeat of Magneto, this incarnation of the Brotherhood was no more—and the misguided Quicksilver and the Scarlet Witch went on to become members of the Avengers.

Some years later, the mysterious, shape-shifting mutant terrorist Mystique formed a new Brotherhood of Evil Mutants under her command. This grouping was comprised of the immovable Blob, the earth-shaking Avalanche, the flame-wielding Pyro, and the future-predicting Destiny. This incarnation of the Brotherhood eventually transformed into Freedom Force when it was offered amnesty by the US Government in exchange for becoming government operatives. But Freedom Force was at its heart corrupt, and after assorted clashes with the X-Men and other hero groups such as the Avengers, the program was quietly disbanded.

ESSENTIAL STORYLINES

- ***X-Men #4***
The newly-formed Brotherhood has its first clash with the X-Men.
- ***Uncanny X-Men #141–142***
Mystique's Brotherhood attempts to assassinate Senator Robert Kelly and prevent the passing of the Mutant Registration Act.
- ***The Brotherhood #1***
X's agents are assembled for covert terrorist missions against humankind.

MYSTIQUE'S BROTHERHOOD
1 Avalanche ***2*** Blob ***3*** Pyro ***4*** Mystique

Bad Brothers

Since then, a number of other individuals have attempted to form their own permutations of the team. The Toad created his own Brotherhood in an attempt to destroy the mutant soldier from the future known as Cable. Havok of the X-Men assembled a Brotherhood of his own as a combat unit against humanity at a point when his faith in Professor X's dream was at a low. And the mysterious mutant operative known only as X created a many-celled version of the Brotherhood in his ongoing terror campaign against the human race. It remains to be seen what form this ever-changing assembly will take in the future. **TB**

CURRENT BROTHERHOOD
1 Black Tom Cassidy
2 Juggernaut
3 Avalanche
4 Exodus
5 Sabretooth
6 Mammomax

Brutacus

FIRST APPEARANCE Fantastic Four Vol. 1 #186 (September 1977)
REAL NAME Unrevealed **OCCUPATION** Warlock
BASE New Salem, Colorado **HEIGHT** 6 ft 5 in
WEIGHT 310 lbs **EYES** Brown **HAIR** Orange
SPECIAL POWERS/ABILITIES Enhanced strength and reflexes, damage resistance, ability to change into lion form, other unrevealed powers of sorcery.

Brutacus was born the son of warlock Nicholas Scratch in the supernatural village of New Salem, along with six siblings. When Scratch ordered his mother, Agatha Harkness, to stand trial for abandoning New Salem for a life in the outside world of ordinary folk, he transformed Brutacus and his other children into inhuman creatures so the Fantastic Four could not interfere. Calling themselves Salem's Seven, the group engaged in countless acts of wickedness. In a final battle with the Vision and the Scarlet Witch, an explosion of magical energy killed Brutacus and wiped out the entire population of New Salem. **DW**

Buchanan, Sam

FIRST APPEARANCE Ghost Rider Vol. 3 #28 (August 1992)
REAL NAME Samuel Buchanan
OCCUPATION Agent for Paranormal Law Enforcement Team
BASE Mobile **HEIGHT** Unrevealed **WEIGHT** Unrevealed
EYES Brown **HAIR** Brown
SPECIAL POWERS/ABILITIES Highly trained marksman and expert hand-to-hand combatant.

A special agent for Interpol, Sam Buchanan was a level-headed, no nonsense sort of chap who didn't believe in magic. Following the release of Lilith, the demon-queen, from imprisonment, there was a steady increase in demonic activity and Sam was assigned to protect human-demon hybrid, Victoria Montesi. For a long time, while continuing to protect Victoria, he insisted that the mystical events that he witnessed had a rational explanation; eventually he was persuaded to believe what he was seeing. When this assignment finally ended, Sam Buchanan joined the Paranormal Law Enforcement Team, where it is thought he still works. **AD**

Bushmaster

FIRST APPEARANCE Captain America #310 (October 1985)
REAL NAME Quincy McIver **OCCUPATION** Professional criminal
BASE Mobile **HEIGHT** 18 ft 6 in from head to tail
WEIGHT Unknown **EYES** Brown **HAIR** Black
SPECIAL POWERS/ABILITIES Cyborg tail enables him to travel and attack at speeds of up to 40 mph; retractable poison fangs on backs of hands.

Bushmaster's serpentine tail both supports his body and is a formidable weapon, being strong enough to crush a 6-inch-thick steel pipe.

Quincy McIver's limbs were amputated by a ship's propeller and he was rebuilt as a cyborg with a snakelike tail by the Brand Corporation. Shortly after this transformation, Bushmaster accepted Sidewinder's invitation to join the Serpent Society. While battling Modok, Bushmaster's mechanical arms were severed, but they were later reattached. As well as his powerful tail, Bushmaster has six-inch fangs on the back of his hands that deliver a fast-acting poison created from snake venom. **MT**

Bullseye

Bullseye's origins remain mysterious. A notorious assassin, he first clashed with his archenemy, Daredevil, while trying to extort money from the rich. The New York crimelord the Kingpin then hired him to be his chief assassin. But while Bullseye was imprisoned, the Kingpin replaced him with the ninja Elektra. To reclaim his position, Bullseye killed Elektra. She and Daredevil had once been lovers, and Daredevil came after Bullseye. In the battle, Bullseye fell from a great height, leaving him paralyzed.

The Japanese scientist Lord Dark Wind repaired Bullseye's broken bones with adamantium, and Bullseye resumed his criminal career and his war with Daredevil. He also murdered Karen Page, whom Daredevil had loved for many years.

Bullseye has also had other costumed adversaries, including the Punisher, Deadpool and Gambit. **PS**

FACTFILE

REAL NAME
Lester (last name unrevealed)

OCCUPATION
Assassin

BASE
New York City

HEIGHT 6 ft
WEIGHT 200 lbs
EYES Blue
HAIR Blond

FIRST APPEARANCE
Daredevil Vol. 1 #131 (March 1976)

POWERS
Can use almost any object as a weapon and throw it with deadly aim; spine and other bones are reinforced with adamantium, making them unbreakable; highly formidable hand-to-hand combatant..

Bullseye's temporarily gets the better of his greatest enemy, the blind costumed crimefighter Daredevil.

CABLE

A living link between present and future

The warrior from the future known as Nathan Dayspring Askani'son, alias Cable, was actually born in modern times as Nathan Christopher Summers. He is the son of Scott Summers, CYCLOPS of the X-MEN, and his first wife Madelyne PRYOR, a clone of Jean GREY, alias Phoenix.

Cable has spent his life as a warrior, but longs for peace. He once established the airborne city of Providence as a futuristic utopia.

LIFE-SAVER

APOCALYPSE infected Nathan with a "techno-organic" virus, which would have killed him by turning his body to organic metal. A woman from the Clan Askani brought the child to her own time, an alternate 40th-century future. There Mother Askani, a version of Rachel Summers, halted the virus' spread. She also had Nathan cloned. Apocalypse, who ruled this era, abducted the clone, who grew to become Cable's evil twin, STRYFE. Mother Askani transported the souls of Scott Summers and Jean Grey into the future and, as "Slym" and "Redd", they raised young Nathan. After the boy had destroyed Apocalypse, Scott and Jean returned to their own time.

Next to Apocalypse, Cable's greatest enemy is literally himself: the terrorist Stryfe is Cable's clone. Stryfe framed Cable for an assassination attempt on Charles Xavier. Stryfe's mind once even took possession of Cable's body.

Nathan became the Clan Askani's foremost freedom fighter against the New Caananites, led by Stryfe. Nathan married a fellow warrior, Aliya, and they had a son, Tyler, but she was murdered by Stryfe. When Stryfe traveled back to the 20th century, Cable pursued him. There Cable founded the mercenary team SIX PACK, which included his lover DOMINO. Later, Cable took command of the NEW MUTANTS, and reorganized them into X-FORCE. Eventually Cable seemingly destroyed the modern day Apocalypse; he then traveled the world as the mercenary Soldier X.

In time, Cable came to believe that his powers were killing him. DEADPOOL and the Fixer removed part of his brain and replaced the techno-organic matter in Cable's body, saving his life, but greatly reducing his powers. **PS**

In the "House of M" storyline, Cable devolved into an infant. Deadpool rescued the baby from Mister Sinister, and Cable soon returned to his true age.

FACTFILE

REAL NAME
Nathan Christopher Summers

OCCUPATION
Adventurer; former freedom fighter and US government agent

BASE
Mobile

HEIGHT 6 ft 8 in
WEIGHT 350 lbs
EYES Blue
HAIR White

FIRST APPEARANCE
Uncanny X-Men #201 (January 1986)

POWERS
Mutant with telepathic and telekinetic abilities. Possesses superhuman strength.

ESSENTIAL STORYLINES
- ***Adventures of Cyclops and Phoenix #1–4***
Scott Summers and Jean Grey raise young Nathan Summers in a distant future.
- ***The New Mutants #86–100***
Cable remolds the New Mutants into X-Force.
- ***Uncanny X-Men #294–296***
"The X-Cutioner's Song" storyline, featuring Cable's showdown with his nemesis Stryfe, which also crossed over into other Marvel titles.

CALLISTO

FIRST APPEARANCE Uncanny X-Men #169 (May 1983)
REAL NAME Unrevealed **OCCUPATION** Former leader of the Morlocks, former model, former bodyguard **BASE** Formerly the Alley (tunnel beneath Manhattan); Mobile
HEIGHT 5 ft 9 in **WEIGHT** 130 lbs **EYES** Blue **HAIR** Black
SPECIAL POWERS/ABILITIES Superhumanly keen senses, including night vision.

Callisto acted as leader of the MORLOCKS, mutant outcasts who lived beneath the Manhattan streets. When MISTER SINISTER'S MARAUDERS massacred the Morlocks, Callisto was one of the survivors. She and most of the remaining Morlocks were taken to another dimension by Mikhail RASPUTIN. There Callisto and Mikhail organized the young Morlocks into the terrorist group Gene Nation. The Morlock Masque transformed Callisto's arms into tentacles. Callisto became a gladiator in the underground organization the Arena, and then journeyed to Genosha and led a band of mutants there. PS

CALYPSO

FIRST APPEARANCE New Mutants Vol. I #16 (June 1984)
STATUS Villain (deceased) **REAL NAME** Calypso Ezili
OCCUPATION Witch; troublemaker **BASE** New York City
HEIGHT 5 ft 8 in **WEIGHT** 120 lbs **EYES** Brown **HAIR** Black
SPECIAL POWERS/ABILITIES Skilled in Voodoo magic; combines potions and spells to confuse enemies; controls enemies with Yorumba spirit drum; can revive dead and resurrect herself.

Born and raised in Haiti, Calypso was initiated into the arts of Voodoo. Meeting KRAVEN THE HUNTER shortly after his first defeat by SPIDER-MAN, Calypso formed a love-hate attachment to him. She enjoyed seeing Kraven enraged and tricked him into attacking the Wallcrawler again. After Kraven's death, Calypso became unhinged, killing her sister to obtain her supernatural powers. Although killed by the LIZARD, Calypso resurrected herself and clashed with DAREDEVIL, before dying once more, at the hands of Alyosha Kravinoff. AD

Powered by a thermo-chemical reaction, Cannonball slams into Wolverine. A force field protects him from the impact.

CANNONBALL

Sam Guthrie's mutant abilities first revealed themselves while he was trapped in a coal mine with a group of co-workers. The stress triggered his powers of propulsion, which helped free Guthrie and his partners. Later, Donald Pierce, a renegade member of the HELLFIRE CLUB, found Guthrie using a device he had built from stolen plans for PROFESSOR X's mutant-locating device, Cerebro. Pierce recruited Guthrie to help him battle Professor X and his NEW MUTANTS. Pierce ordered Guthrie to kill the New Mutants, but he refused. Pierce tried to kill Guthrie, but Professor X saved Guthrie's life and defeated Pierce. Xavier invited Guthrie to join the New Mutants as Cannonball. He became one of the team's leaders, and later a member of the X-MEN. MT

FACTFILE
REAL NAME
Samuel Guthrie
OCCUPATION
Adventurer; student, ex-coal miner
BASE
Professor Xavier's School for Gifted Youngsters, Salem Center, New York

HEIGHT 6 ft
WEIGHT 150 lbs
EYES Blue-gray
HAIR Blond

FIRST APPEARANCE:
Marvel Graphic Novel #4 (1982)

POWERS
Possesses the mutant power to create thermo-chemical energy and release it from his body in a powerful burst. Force field surrounding body gives superhuman durability.

Cannonball explodes into action, teaming up with fellow X-Men Bishop, Storm, and Sage.

The equal and opposite reaction to the thermo-chemical energy Cannonball generates propels his body into the air like a human rocket.

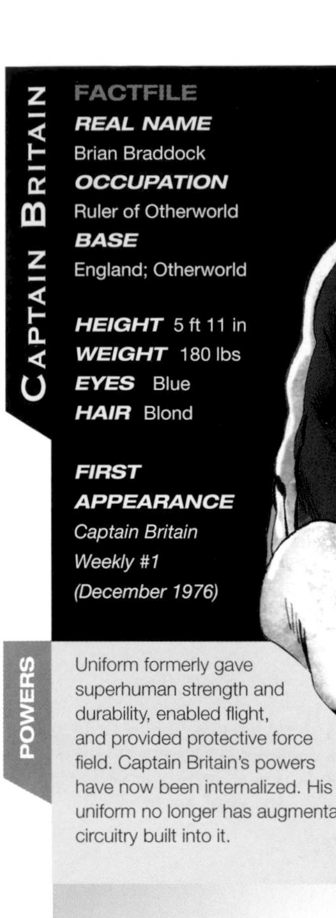

CAPTAIN BRITAIN

FACTFILE
REAL NAME
Brian Braddock
OCCUPATION
Ruler of Otherworld
BASE
England; Otherworld

HEIGHT 5 ft 11 in
WEIGHT 180 lbs
EYES Blue
HAIR Blond

FIRST APPEARANCE
Captain Britain Weekly #1 (December 1976)

POWERS
Uniform formerly gave superhuman strength and durability, enabled flight, and provided protective force field. Captain Britain's powers have now been internalized. His uniform no longer has augmentation circuitry built into it.

CAPTAIN BRITAIN

Chosen to become the champion of the nation of Great Britain by MERLIN and his daughter ROMA, Brian Braddock was gifted with the title and powers of Captain Britain. Both alone and as a member of EXCALIBUR, Captain Britain strove to be worthy of his new role. Eventually, he discovered that he was one of an almost infinite number of Captains created by Merlin and Roma and positioned throughout the multiverse to safeguard existence, and that his father had once been a denizen of the Otherworld, where they resided. When Roma and the Otherworld were threatened by Mastermind, the sentient computer created by James BRADDOCK, Captain Britain, wielding the sword Excalibur, defeated his foe. He later succeeded Roma as ruler of the Otherworld and commander of the CAPTAIN BRITAIN CORPS. **TB**

Captain Britain married Meggan, a fellow member of the team Excalibur.

Captain Britain saves Alice from the Crazy Gang, dressed as characters from the pages of Lewis Carroll's *Alice in Wonderland*.

CAPTAIN BRITAIN CORPS

FACTFILE
MEMBERS
Assorted interdimensional incarnations of **CAPTAIN BRITAIN,** including **CAPTAIN UK, CAPTAIN ANGLETERRE, CAPTAIN COMMONWEALTH, CAPTAIN EMPIRE, CAPTAIN ENGLAND, CAPTAIN MARSHALL, KAPTAIN BRITON, HAUPTMANN ENGLANDE, BROTHER BRIT-MAN** and others.
BASE
Otherworld; various Earths across the multiverse.

FIRST APPEARANCE
Mighty World of Marvel #13

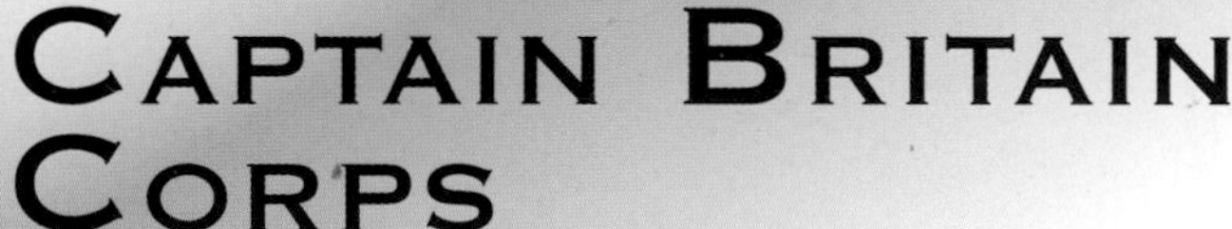

CAPTAIN BRITAIN CORPS

The Captain Britain Corps is an alliance of interdimensional champions, all empowered by MERLIN and his daughter Roma, and charged with protecting their home realities from dimensional incursions. Based out of the central nexus realm known as Otherworld, which has connection points to all of the other realms of the multiverse, the many members of the Captain Britain Corps—each an analogue of the mainstream Captain Britain—are stationed so as to be able to detect threats to all of existence, and intercept them—as well as protecting their members' Earths from home-grown menaces. With Merlin having perished, and Roma no longer ruler of Otherworld, the Captain Britain Corps is now led by the Captain Britain of Earth-616, the mainstream reality of the Marvel Universe. **TB**

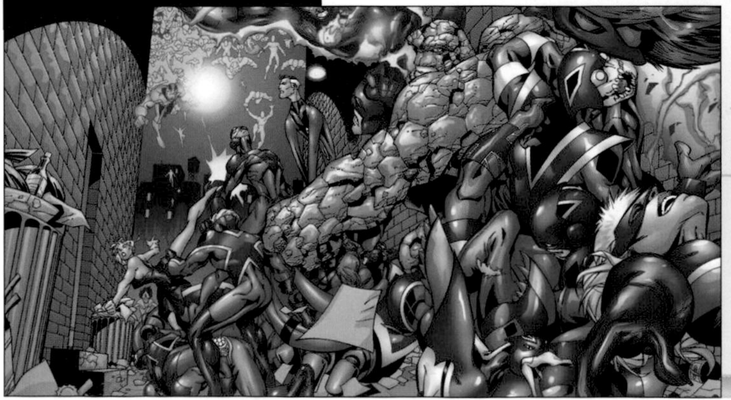

The Captain Britain Corps interceded when it was feared that the mutant powers once possessed by Franklin Richards, son of the Fantastic Four's Mr. Fantastic and the Invisible Woman, might destroy the multiverse.

CAPTAIN FATE

FIRST APPEARANCE Man-Thing Vol. 1 #13 (January 1975)
REAL NAME Captain Jebediah Fate
OCCUPATION Pirate **BASE** The ship *Serpent's Crown* in the Bermuda Triangle, Atlantic Ocean
HEIGHT 6 ft 3 in **WEIGHT** Unknown **EYES** Gray **HAIR** Gray
SPECIAL POWERS/ABILITIES No longer ages, and is invulnerable to certain forms of injury.

In 1795, Jebediah Fate was the first mate to the pirate queen Maura Hawke when they encountered the satyr Khordes, who desired a mate. The traitorous Fate and his men turned Hawke over to Khordes in exchange for treasure. Hawke cursed Fate and his accomplices to sail the seas for eternity, and Khordes' magic made her curse come true. Centuries later, Fate again encountered Khordes and Hawke, now reincarnated as oceanographer Maura Spinner, as well as the monstrous MAN-THING. Though Fate was killed by gunfire, the demon Thog resurrected him, and Fate clashed with the Man-Thing, Maura and Khordes yet again. **PS**

Captain America

Living Legend of World War II

CAPTAIN AMERICA

FACTFILE
REAL NAME
Steve Rogers
OCCUPATION
Adventurer
BASE
Brooklyn, New York; Stark Tower ("Avengers Tower"), Manhattan, New York

HEIGHT 6 ft 2 in
WEIGHT 240 lbs
EYES Blue
HAIR Blond

FIRST APPEARANCE
Captain America Comics #1 (March 1941)

POWERS

The Super-Soldier Serum brought Rogers to the peak of physical perfection; able to lift twice his own body weight; expert military strategist; Olympic-level martial artist and gymnast; resistant to disease and fatigue.

ALLIES/FOES

ALLIES Bucky Barnes, Nick Fury, Sharon Carter, Rick Jones, The Falcon, Nomad (Jack Monroe), The Avengers

FOES The Red Skull, Baron Zemo, MODOK, the terrorist organizations AIM and Hydra, Crossbones

ISSUE #1

Captain America burst into action battling Hitler in his first issue. Cap's shield changed shape to circular in forthcoming issues because of objections from the creators of another hero called the Shield.

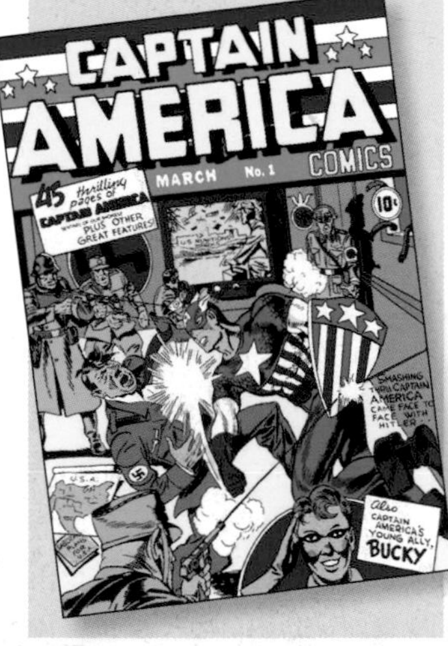

In the late 1930s, with the threat of world war looming in Europe, the American high command embarked upon a program to create the perfect soldier. Project: Rebirth, spearheaded by Dr. Abraham Erskine, was intended to create a battalion of supreme fighting men, stronger and more resilient than normal soldiers, expertly trained and equipped —a bulwark against Nazi aggression. The first test subject for Erskine's revolutionary Super-Soldier Serum was a young, would-be artist named Steve Rogers, who had attempted to enlist, but had been turned away, classified 4-F, because of his physical frailty.

Abraham Erskine, operating under the codename Professor Reinstein, created the Super-Soldier Serum. It turned frail Steve Rogers into a perfect specimen of humanity.

THE SUPER SOLDIER

Subjected to Erskine's process, Rogers' body virtually doubled in size, as millions of healthy cells were created almost instantaneously. His physique was accelerated to the pinnacle of human perfection, all weakness and deficiency drained out of it.

However the secret test area had been infiltrated by Nazi sympathizers, who slew Dr. Erskine, the only person who knew how the process worked. Although Rogers quickly captured the saboteurs, it was clear that there would be no battalion of super-soldiers now—Steve Rogers would be the only one.

Captain America arrives in the nick of time to prevent Sharon Carter being blasted into the blue, courtesy of Nazi menace Red Skull.

Equipped with a virtually unbreakable red, white and blue shield, the product of a metallurgical accident, and trained in combat, tactics, espionage, and the fighting arts, Rogers was rechristened Captain America. Clad in a striking star-spangled uniform, he became a symbol for the US fighting forces and a dread nemesis of the Axis powers.

In his many battles against Nazi aggression, Captain America was joined by a sidekick, the worldly James "Bucky" Barnes, who had discovered the secret of Rogers' true identity.

The result of a metallurgical accident, Captain America's shield is the most durable object known to man.

Among the foes combated by Cap in the present day is MODOK, the Mental Organism Designed Only for Killing. MODOK was the result of an experiment by the sinister think-tank known as Advanced Idea Mechanics, or AIM.

BUCKY'S DEATH

Toward the end of World War II, Cap and Bucky Barnes set out to foil Baron Zemo's scheme to steal a drone plane laden with a bomb. As the plane took off, Bucky and Cap leaped aboard. Cap fell into the sea, but Bucky clung on trying to defuse the bomb. The bomb exploded, Bucky was killed, and Cap has been haunted by the memory ever since.

Together, Cap and Bucky tore a swath through the ranks of the enemy forces, vanquishing such Nazi menaces as the RED SKULL, Agent Axis, and the Iron Cross. The duo were often joined by their allies in the INVADERS team, including the original HUMAN TORCH and NAMOR, the Sub-Mariner.

In 1945, Cap and Bucky were on a mission to apprehend the German scientist BARON ZEMO, who planned to steal an experimental long-range Drone Plane developed by the British. As the plane took off, Cap and Bucky made a desperate leap to catch it. Cap couldn't maintain his hold, and plummeted earthward... seconds later the plane self-destructed, ending the life of Bucky Barnes. Cap's body plunged into the icy waters below, where he was frozen into a state of suspended animation, a condition he would remain in for decades to come.

To safeguard morale, the Allied high command kept the deaths of Cap and Bucky secret and recruited other heroes to play the role of Captain America. Meanwhile, the true Captain America slumbered within the ice.

THE RETURN

Eventually, while searching for their foe Namor (the same person who had fought alongside Steve Rogers in the INVADERS), the AVENGERS came across Captain America's body floating in the icy waters, and revived him. Now Captain America was a man out of time, a soldier whose war was long over. Attempting to find a place for himself in this strange new society, Cap accepted an offer of Avengers membership, and swiftly became the binding glue that held the team together.

Reformed criminal Sam Wilson, alias Harlem's guardian the Falcon, has been one of Captain America's closest friends and most frequent crime-fighting partners.

THE AVENGERS
1 Hawkeye ***2*** The Wasp ***3*** Falcon ***4*** Captain America, team leader ***5*** Iron Man ***6*** Vision ***7*** Scarlet Witch

Cap also offered his services to his old war buddy Nick FURY, now head of the worldwide peacekeeping organization SHIELD. It was while operating as a SHIELD agent that Cap first encountered Sharon CARTER, SHIELD's Agent 13, who would become his paramour.

Today, hailed as the most trusted costumed champion of them all, Captain America fights on, struggling to uphold freedom and democracy, both alone and with the Avengers. **TB**

ESSENTIAL STORYLINES

- ***Captain America & The Falcon #153-156*** Cap and his partner the Falcon must combat the replacement Captain America and Bucky of the 1950s, who have been driven mad by the flawed serum that gave them their abilities.
- ***Captain America Vol. 4 #1-6*** Captain America reveals his true identity as Steve Rogers to the world after he is forced to take the life of a terrorist leader.
- ***Captain America Vol. 5 #1-14*** Cap is on the trail of the Winter Soldier, a legendary assassin from the pages of history who may actually be his former sidekick Bucky Barnes!

Over the years, Cap has battled with numerous opponents intent on taking up his mantle. One of his challengers was the "Anti-Cap", a modern day counterpart created by Naval Intelligence as an extreme anti-terrorist operative. Eventually facing defeat by Captain America for a second time, the Anti-Cap chose death rather than capture.

Captain Mar-Vell

Protector of the Universe

FACTFILE
REAL NAME
Mar-Vell
OCCUPATION
Captain in Kree space fleet
BASE
Mobile

HEIGHT 6 ft 2 in
WEIGHT 240 lbs
EYES Blue
HAIR White; transformed to blond by Eon, a cosmic caretaker

FIRST APPEARANCE
Marvel Super Heroes #18 (January 1968)

Captain Mar-Vell

POWERS
Thanks to his Kree "nega-bands," Mar-vell possessed great strength (he could lift 10 tons), a high degree of imperviousness to harm, and the ability to fly. He could also exist in outer space without having to breathe.

Mar-Vell gained the ability to fire bolts of solar energy after his ailing psionic partner Rick Jones was treated with life-saving electromagnetic radiation by Professor Benjamin Savannah.

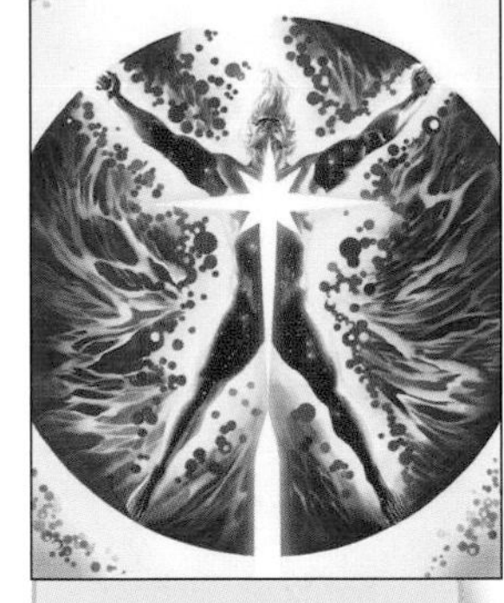
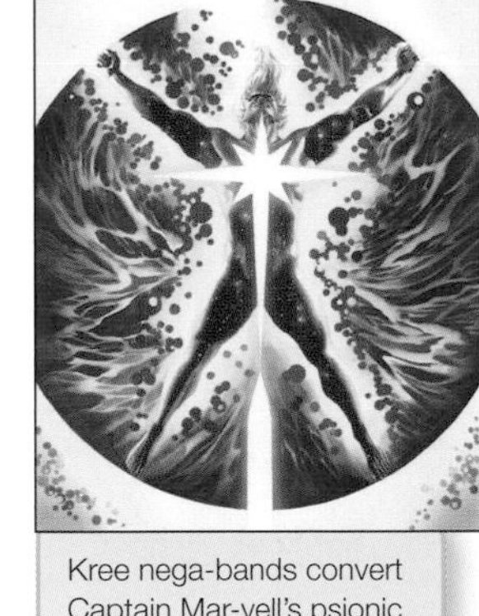
Kree nega-bands convert Captain Mar-vell's psionic energy into incredible power.

Captain Mar-Vell was a member of the Kree, an alien humanoid race who built an empire known as the Greater Magellanic Cloud. Captain Mar-Vell was a "White Kree," who have the same skin color as Caucasian Earth humans and similar physiology. (Most members of the Kree race have blue skin.) As captain of a Kree space fleet, Mar-Vell distinguished himself in battles against the shape-changing Skrulls, the Krees' age-old foes.

ESSENTIAL STORYLINES
- ***The Life of Captain Mar-Vell 1991 (tpb)*** Marv-Vell battles Thanos and performs other feats of cosmic heroism.
- ***Avengers #89–#97*** The Avengers aid Mar-Vell during the epic Kree-Skrull War.
- ***The Death of Captain Mar-Vell (tpb)*** Captain Mar-Vell succumbs to cancer, but achieves a hero's death.

Mar-Vell impersonated a dead scientist named Dr. Walter Lawson when he first came to Earth.

In delirium while dying from cancer, Captain Mar-Vell is haunted by terrifying phantoms of the enemies he fought and defeated during his career as a Super Hero.

PROTECTOR

Captain Mar-Vell's qualities did not go unremarked by the Supreme Intelligence, the force that governed the Kree. Wary of mankind's growing scientific abilities, the Intelligence sent Mar-Vell to sabotage the planet's space programs. However Mar-Vell grew to respect the people of Earth and helped them, earning the soubriquet "Captain Marvel."

The Supreme Intelligence then used Mar-Vell to forge a telepathic link with a human being. The Intelligence believed that humans possessed vast psionic potential, which it longed to possess. It would then destroy humanity. The Intelligence secretly enabled Mar-Vell to bond with Rick Jones by means of a pair of Kree "nega-bands. "

The Intelligence used the psionic link with Jones to nullify the Skrull space fleet. The effort almost cost Jones his life, and Mar-Vell used his own life force to bring back Jones from the brink of death. Mar-Vell then defeated the death-worshipping would-be conqueror Thanos who wished to destroy all life in the universe. Around this time, Mar-Vell also met with the mysterious, ancient alien being Eon, who gave him "cosmic awareness," persuaded him to renounce the Kree's warmongering ways, and designated him "Protector of the Universe."

Death of a Hero

During a battle with the Nitro of the Lunatic Legion, an alien-criminal organization formed by a band of renegade Kree scientists, Mar-Vell was exposed to a carcinogenic gas. Mar-Vell subsequently developed cancer and died on Saturn's moon, Titan, surrounded by his lover, Elysius, Rick Jones, the Avengers (who posthumously made him an honary member), and many Super Hero friends. Mar-Vell's son, Genis-Vell, eventually took over his mantle. MT

FACTFILE

REAL NAME
Genis-Vell

OCCUPATION
Adventurer

BASE
Mobile throughout the universe

HEIGHT 6 ft 2 in
WEIGHT 195 lbs
EYES Blue
HAIR Blond (becomes white when "cosmically aware")

FIRST APPEARANCE
Silver Surfer Annual #6 (1993)

POWERS
Kree Nega-bands confer superhuman strength and durability, the ability to fly, the power to project concussive energy blasts; Genis-Vell possesses "cosmic awareness", allowing him to perceive cosmic threats or dangers.

CAPTAIN MARVEL

The Kree nega-bands enabled Genis to fly through outer space without oxygen or protection.

Following the tragic death from cancer of the Kree warrior CAPTAIN MAR-VELL, his lover Elysius, an ETERNAL of Titan, used cell samples taken from his body to conceive a son she named Genis-Vell. To help keep the child safe from harm, Titanian science accelerated Genis-Vell's aging so that he rapidly reached physical maturity. As soon as he discovered his heroic lineage, Genis-Vell donned his father's nega-bands and became an adventurer, fittingly called Legacy. Genis-Vell later adopted his father's name, "Captain Marvel."

In order to save the life of his father's long-time friend Rick Jones, the new Captain Marvel's atomic structure was bonded to his. This meant that whenever Captain Marvel was in the Earth dimension, Rick Jones was cast into a microverse, and vice versa. In mental contact with each other, Jones acted as Genis-Vell's advisor.

After battling Atlas, Genis absorbed the Kree nega-bands (shown on his wrists) into his body.

THE BROKEN BOND

Genis-Vell subsequently went insane and helped the conceptual beings Entropy and Epiphany to destroy the universe. However, Genis then triggered a new "Big Bang," recreating the cosmos. Once more insane, Genis became a menace to the universe. Elysius and another Titan, Eros, successfully returned Genis to sanity. The bonding between Jones and Genis was undone, allowing them to exist on Earth separately.

After Atlas beat Genis nearly to death, BARON ZEMO utilized moonstones to help Genis heal his body. Genis took the name Photon and joined the THUNDERBOLTS. Zemo learned that the moonstones' effect on Genis would cause the universe's destruction. Zemo therefore killed Genis and scattered his body through the Darkforce Dimension.

The name "Captain Marvel" was briefly used by Phyla-Vell, Genis's sister, who had been similarly created by Elysius. **PS**

Monica Rambeau was known first as Captain Marvel and then Photon. When Genis took the name Photon (right), Rambeau renamed herself Pulsar.

CAPTAIN UNIVERSE

FIRST APPEARANCE Micronauts #8 (August 1979)
REAL NAME Various, including Ray and Steve Coffin, Monty Walsh
OCCUPATION Not applicable **BASE** Mobile
HEIGHT Various **WEIGHT** Various **EYES** Various **HAIR** Various
SPECIAL POWERS/ABILITIES Captain Universe is any person endowed with the Uni-Power; abilities include superstrength, flight, and ability to alter an object's molecular structure.

The Uni-Power is energy emanating from the Microverse that appears as a clot of energy. Uni-Power bestows upon an individual the powers and knowledge of Captain Universe, as well as a special costume. The Uni-Power only stays with an individual for a short period before moving on. The transfer from one person to the next is almost instantaneous—the cosmos is never without a Captain Universe. In recent years, the might of the Uni-Power has been borne by ex-astronauts, cat burglars and individuals as notable as Bruce Banner (*see* HULK) and DOCTOR STRANGE. **AD**

CAPTAIN ULTRA

FIRST APPEARANCE Fantastic Four #177 (December 1976)
REAL NAME Griffin Gogol
OCCUPATION Stand-up comedian, former plumber
BASE Chicago, Illinois **HEIGHT** 5 ft 11 in **WEIGHT** 175 lbs
EYES Unknown **HAIR** Unknown
SPECIAL POWERS/ABILITIES Captain Ultra is superhumanly strong and durable, and can fly; also has a great sense of humor.

Captain Ultra began his superhuman career as a would-be super-villain, who hoped to join the FRIGHTFUL FOUR. The Four were impressed by his strength, but not by his vulnerability—he passed out in the presence of any open flame. His bid rejected, Captain Ultra went into therapy with DOC SAMSON, the psychiatrist, who helped him to overcome his aversion to fire. This didn't improve Captain Ultra's fortunes as a hero, but it did give him the confidence to move into a new line of work—as a stand-up comedian. **TB**

Cardiac

FIRST APPEARANCE (Dr. Wirtham) Amazing Spider-Man #342 (December 1990), (Cardiac) Amazing Spider-Man #343 (January 1991)
REAL NAME Dr. Elias "Eli" Wirtham
OCCUPATION Surgeon, researcher, vigilante **BASE** New York City
HEIGHT 6 ft 5 in **WEIGHT** 300 lbs **EYES** Brown **HAIR** Black
SPECIAL POWERS/ABILITIES Superhuman strength, speed and stamina, bulletproof skin, can project beta particle-force blasts.

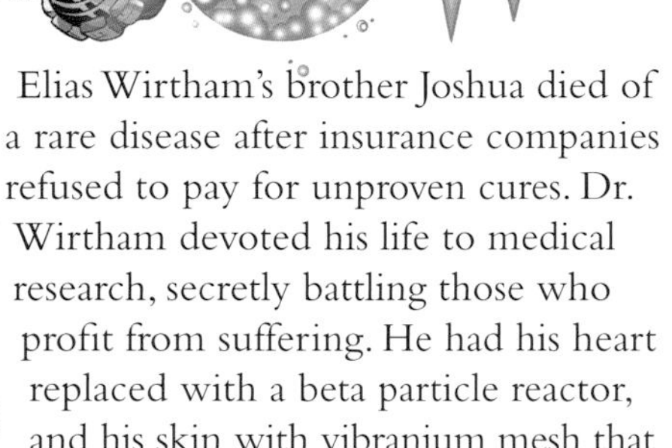

Elias Wirtham's brother Joshua died of a rare disease after insurance companies refused to pay for unproven cures. Dr. Wirtham devoted his life to medical research, secretly battling those who profit from suffering. He had his heart replaced with a beta particle reactor, and his skin with vibranium mesh that transmits the particles to his muscles, giving him amazing strength. As Cardiac, he has clashed with SPIDER-MAN. **PS**

Carrion

The first Carrion was a clone of Miles Warren who was SPIDER-MAN's enemy, the JACKAL. Before his death, Warren left a clone of himself in a capsule, but something went wrong and the creature that emerged was like a living corpse. Carrion died in a fire following a battle with Spider-Man. Many years later, a fellow research student of Peter Parker's named Malcolm McBride discovered a test tube containing a genetic creation of Warren's, the "Carrion virus." The virus consumed McBride and turned him into a second incarnation of Carrion. When Miles Warren's body was examined by Dr. William Allen, he was infected by the virus, and became the third and most powerful incarnation of Carrion. **MT**

FACTFILE
REAL NAME
"Miles Warren" (actually a clone of the original Miles Warren)
OCCUPATION
None
BASE
New York City

HEIGHT 5 ft 11 in
WEIGHT 175 lbs
EYES Yellow
HAIR None

FIRST APPEARANCE
Spectacular Spider-Man #25 (December 1978)

CARRION

POWERS
Carrion could repel living matter, levitate, destroy living matter with his touch, reduce the density of his body to become almost intangible, and teleport.

Carnage

FACTFILE
REAL NAME
Cletus Kasady
OCCUPATION
Spreader of Chaos
BASE
New York City

HEIGHT 6 ft 1 in
WEIGHT 190 lbs
EYES Green
HAIR Red

FIRST APPEARANCE
Amazing Spider-Man #244 (February 1991)

CARNAGE

POWERS
Superhuman strength; can generate swing lines and bladed weapons; able to neutralize Spider-Man's spider-sense.

Imprisoned for multiple murders, Cletus Kasady was sharing a cell with Eddie Brock, parasitical VENOM's host, when that symbiote arrived to attempt a jailbreak. Venom left behind its spawn, which bonded with Kasady resulting in a new symbiote, the creature now known as Carnage. The bond between Carnage and Kasady is more profound than that between Brock and Venom—the fact that they refer to themselves as "I" rather than "we" is testament to this. Carnage is also far more powerful, violent and deadly than its parent—following his first encounter with the creature, SPIDER-MAN was forced to enlist the help of the HUMAN TORCH and even VENOM to defeat it. It has fought alongside DEMOGOBLIN, DOPPELGANGER, SHRIEK, and CARRION, and has bonded with BEN REILLY, the SILVER SURFER and JOHN JAMESON. Once, Carnage was even reabsorbed into Venom but Kasady bonded with a version of the creature that had previously inhabited the negative Zone. Carnage is incarcerated at present but with its record of frequent escapes from Ravencroft Institute, it still poses a very real danger. **AD**

Like its parent, Venom, Carnage quickly came to regard Spider-Man as its arch nemesis.

Carter, Sharon

FIRST APPEARANCE Tales of Suspense Vol. 1 #75 (March 1966)
STATUS Active **REAL NAME** Sharon Carter
OCCUPATION SHIELD liaison officer **BASE** Mobile
HEIGHT 5 ft 8 in **WEIGHT** 135 lbs **EYES** Blue **HAIR** Blonde
SPECIAL POWERS/ABILITIES Highly trained field agent; martial-arts expert and weapons expert; special talent for disguise, infiltration, and undercover work.

Sharon Carter grew up inspired by her relative Peggy Carter's tales of heroism from World War II. During the war Peggy had been Captain America's lover and a member of the French Resistance. Her stories of bravery inspired Sharon to take part in international espionage and law enforcement. Sharon decided to become a SHIELD operative. She worked under the codename Agent 13 and was also a member of SHIELD's "Femme Force." Captain America reawakened in the modern era and Carter formed her own relationship with him. They worked together on many missions and became both allies and lovers. She was believed to have been killed while under the mind-control of Doctor Faustus, however, Carter returned to SHIELD for a brief stint as its executive director. She currently serves as Captain America's SHIELD liaison officer. **DW**

Cat People

FIRST APPEARANCE Giant-Size Creatures #1 (May 1974)
BASE The Land Within, an otherdimensional netherworld
SPECIAL POWERS/ABILITIES Mystical abilities; enhanced strength, speed, and agility, similar to those of a human-sized cat.

The Cat People were brought into existence thousands of years ago when a kindly human sorcerer named Ebrok enchanted two ordinary cats called Flavius and Helene into humanoid form. He then instructed these first two Cat People in the magical arts.

In time, the numbers of the Cat People grew, to the displeasure of Ebrok's fellows in the Sorcerer's Guild. The Cat people were subsequently exiled to the limbolike realm they call the Land Within, whose properties caused them and their descendents to become demons. The Sorcerer's Guild also decreed that a member of the Cat People, given the title the Balkatar, must always answer if summoned. The current Balkatar is named Grigar.

The legendary heroine of the Cat People is known as Tigra, a human woman who was transformed into a catlike warrior by the Cat People's sorcery. Today, Greer Nelson has similarly been transformed into the heroine Tigra by a combination of the Cat People's magic and human science, and she serves as their emissary to the outside world and as a member of the mighty Avengers. **TB**

Cat & Mouse

FIRST APPEARANCE Marvel Preview #21 (May 1980)
REAL NAMES (Cat) Mark Grant, (Mouse) Stephanie Wald
OCCUPATION (Cat) Musician, Shroud operative; (Mouse) Shroud operative **BASE** New York City **HEIGHT** (Cat) 6ft 1in, (Mouse) 5 ft 10 in **WEIGHT** (Cat) 195 lbs; (Mouse) 135 lbs. **EYES** (Cat) Brown; (Mouse) Blue **HAIR** (Cat) Black; (Mouse) Blonde
SPECIAL POWERS/ABILITIES Cat is a cat burglar and electronics expert. Mouse is a pickpocket and getaway driver.

Daring cat burglar Cat was recruited into a gang run by a criminal known as the Crooked Man. He met Mouse, a singer and small-time crook. They became close friends and joined the Shroud to help take down their former employer.

Deciding to join the Shroud's crusade to destroy crime from within, they opened and began performing at the Cat's Jazz Club, which became the Shroud's unofficial base. Before the Club was destroyed, Cat & Mouse played host to such adventurers as Spider-Man, Tatterdemalion, Dansen Macabre and the West Coast Avengers. They later aided the Shroud against the Scorpion and various other crimelords. **TD**

Catseye

FIRST APPEARANCE New Mutants Vol. I #16 (June 1984)
STATUS Villain (deceased) **REAL NAME** Sharon Smith
OCCUPATION ex-Hellion team member **BASE** Mobile
HEIGHT 6 ft **WEIGHT** 140 lbs **EYES** Lavender **HAIR** Lavender
SPECIAL POWERS/ABILITIES Transformed into a cat and a human-panther hybrid with increased strength, agility, reflexes, and senses; hybrid also boasted razor-sharp claws and prehensile tail.

The abilities of most mutants are only manifested at puberty. Not so with Sharon Smith—her capacity to change into a cat was revealed when she was very young. Abandoned by her parents, Sharon was raised feral by a stray cat. She was a teenager before she came to the attention of Emma Frost, the White Queen. Under her guidance the highly intelligent Sharon received an accelerated education; within a year she gained high-school literacy and joined the Hellions. Her time with them was tragically short, an attack on the Hellfire Club leading to her death. **AD**

Celestials

FACTFILE

KNOWN CELESTIALS
ARISHEM THE JUDGE, JEMIAH THE ANALYZER, TEFRAL THE SURVEYOr, GAMMENON THE GATHERER, NEZARR THE CALCULATOR, ONEG THE PROBER, HARGEN THE MEASURER, ESON THE SEARCHER, ZIRAN THE TESTER, ONE ABOVE ALl, EXITAR THE EXECUTIONER.

HEIGHT (average) 2,000 ft
WEIGHT (average) 260 tons

FIRST APPEARANCE
Eternals #1 (July 1976)

POWERS
Cosmic power on a scale immeasurable by Earth standards; have visited Earth, but eradicated all evidence and memory of their existence.

The Celestials are a race of virtually immortal space gods whose conscious minds gestate in the form of living galaxies for more than a million years. Once the Celestial is deemed worthy, this mind is encased by a full suit of virtually indestructible body armor that is "dimensionally transcendental," (far larger on the inside than it appears to be on the outside). Each Celestial appears to have a specific purpose. Barely a dozen and a half are known by their names and function, but many more are believed to exist. For reasons of their own, the Celestials travel throughout the Universe, performing genetic experiments. They later return a million years later to judge the results of their experiments. If the world is judged favorably, it is allowed continue. If not, it is cleansed of life. **TD**

Though the Celestials have visited Earth on four different occasions, they have erased all physical evidence of their existence. They have also purged the memories of all the humans who saw them.

Centurius

FACTFILE

REAL NAME
Dr. Noah Black

OCCUPATION
Geneticist

BASE
Mobile

HEIGHT 6 ft
WEIGHT 225 lbs
EYES Brown
HAIR None

FIRST APPEARANCE
Nick Fury, Agent of SHIELD #2 (July 1968)

POWERS
Scientific genius specializing in genetics; evolved himself into a perfect human specimen, with attendant strength, agility, and durability; high-tech body armor incorporates an array of weapons; experiments with his Evolutionizer device have increased his lifespan.

The ridicule of the scientific community led brilliant scientist Dr. Noah Black to hide himself away on Valhalla Island, where he began to experiment on himself with his Evolutionizer. His experiments led him to become super-evolved, but also increased his mania, and he came to believe that humanity should be wiped out and started afresh. Calling himself Centurius, Black intended to gather up superior specimens of life around the world, shepherd them to an ark, then destroy human civilization while he and his recruits waited in the skies above the Earth. A century later they would land and reclaim the world. His initial plot was thwarted by Nick Fury and SHIELD, but Centurius continued to threaten world security. He is now in SHIELD custody, in the maximum security prison known as the Raft. **TB**

Centurius attempted to turn the world into a new Garden of Eden.

Century

FIRST APPEARANCE Force Works #1 (July 1994)
REAL NAME Century **OCCUPATION** Adventurer
BASE/HEIGHT/WEIGHT/EYES Unknown **HAIR** White
SPECIAL POWERS/ABILITIES Combines memories, skills and abilities of one hundred Hodomur; projects energy from hands; wields the Parallax, a bladed weapon that binds his multiple personalities together and enables interdimensional travel.

Following the destruction of their world Hodomur by the extradimensional entity, Lore, the survivors created a new being from one hundred of their number.

Named Century, this creature was compelled to track down and destroy Lore, and given a lifespan of a hundred years to attain this goal. During this quest, the pirate, Broker, enslaved Century, blanking his mind—only Century's desire to find Lore remained. This desire led him to Earth where he served on the Super Hero team Force Works until it disbanded.

Lore is now dead—destroyed by the Scarlet Witch—and Century's whereabouts are unknown. **AD**

Cabe, Bethany

FIRST APPEARANCE Iron Man #117 (December 1978)
REAL NAME Bethany Cabe
OCCUPATION Bodyguard **BASE** Mobile
HEIGHT 5 ft 7 in **WEIGHT** 125 lbs **EYES** Green **HAIR** Red
SPECIAL POWERS/ABILITIES Bethany Cabe is a trained investigator, an expert markswoman, and extensively trained in self-defense techniques.

After the apparent death of her ex-husband, a West German diplomat whose life was ruined by drugs, Bethany Cabe swore she would never be dependent on anyone again. She trained extensively, and became a highly respected bodyguard. Bethany's path soon crossed that of Anthony Stark, the millionaire industrialist who is also Iron Man, and they became romantically involved. When Stark's alcoholism threatened to destroy him, Bethany convinced him to get help. The romance ended, however, when Cabe's ex-husband turned out to be still alive, though in a comatose state. Bethany felt honor-bound to nurse him back to health. **TB**

Cable *see opposite page*

Caledonia

FIRST APPEARANCE Fantastic Four Vol. 3 #9 (September 1998)
REAL NAME Alysande Stuart
OCCUPATION Champion **BASE** New York City
HEIGHT 5 ft 6 in **WEIGHT** 130 lbs **EYES** Blue **HAIR** Blonde
SPECIAL POWERS/ABILITIES Wore a warrior's armor and a long red cloak; wielded an enormous sword with the skill and courage of a great warrior of old; accomplished athlete.

In another world, Alysande Stuart was descended from a long line of ancient Scottish warrior champions. Her warrior name was Caledonia, and she also served as Captain Britain. Freed from captivity in her world, Caledonia arrived in New York City. She worked as a nanny to Franklin Richards, son of Reed Richards and Sue Storm (Mr Fantastic and Invisible Woman), and thus came under the protection of the Fantastic Four.

Caledonia was eventually killed by the insane, murderous Jamie Braddock. **MT**

Caliban

FIRST APPEARANCE Uncanny X-Men #148 (August 1981)
REAL NAME Unrevealed **OCCUPATION** Adventurer; Apocalypse's Horseman Pestilence; X-Force's ally. **BASE** Mobile
HEIGHT 6 ft 8 in **WEIGHT** 275 lbs **EYES** Black **HAIR** None
SPECIAL POWERS/ABILITIES Psionic ability to detect presence of other mutants; psionically intensifies others' fear; creates a psychoactive virus that attacks the mind; superhuman strength.

Named after the character in Shakespeare's *The Tempest,* Caliban used his mental powers to detect mutants to help Callisto assemble the underground society of mutant outcasts called the Morlocks. The X-Factor team saved Caliban from death when the Marauders massacred most of the Morlocks. The childlike Caliban agreed to serve Apocalypse in exchange for enhanced powers to take his revenge. **PS**

Cage, Luke

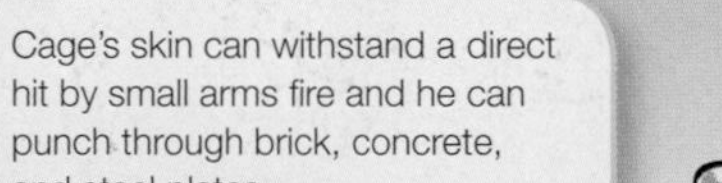

Cage's skin can withstand a direct hit by small arms fire and he can punch through brick, concrete, and steel plates.

The man who would someday call himself Luke Cage grew up on the streets of Harlem. While he often committed petty crimes as a youth, Luke realized the error of his ways as he grew older. A rivalry over a woman turned bitter and the other man, a criminal named Willis Stryker, framed him for possessing heroin. After being sent to prison, he volunteered to be a test subject for an experimental chemical in order to obtain an early parole. An angry guard tried to kill him by giving him an overdose. Instead of killing him, the drug reacted with his unique body chemistry and gave him superhuman strength. He escaped prison, faked his death and adopted the name Luke Cage. He made a name for himself as a solo hero for hire sometimes using the name Power Man. He then formed a partnership with Danny Rand (Iron Fist). He joined the New Avengers and began a relationship with a woman named Jessica Jones. Luke and Jessica had a daughter and have since married. **TD**

FACTFILE

REAL NAME
Carl Lucas

OCCUPATION
Bodyguard; investigator

BASE
Stark Tower, New York

HEIGHT 6 ft 6 in
WEIGHT 425 lbs
EYES Brown
HAIR Black

FIRST APPEARANCE
Luke Cage, Hero For Hire #1 (July 1972)

POWERS

Cage possesses superhuman strength, very dense muscle and bone tissue and steel-hard skin. He recovers three times faster from injury than a normal person and is an experienced and skilled street fighter.

After preventing a robbery at a diner, the owner gave Cage a reward and the idea to go into business as a hero for hire.

AMAZING FANTASY #15 (1962)

Marvel's most popular Super Hero—the always amazing Spider-Man—premieres in the last issue of a suspense comic. Peter Parker, Aunt May, Uncle Ben, and Flash Thompson all make their first appearances as Spider-Man learns that, "with great power there must also come great responsibility.

AVENGERS #4 (1964)

Stan Lee and Jack Kirby resurrect the original Captain America from the 1940s and reintroduce him to the modern age of comics.

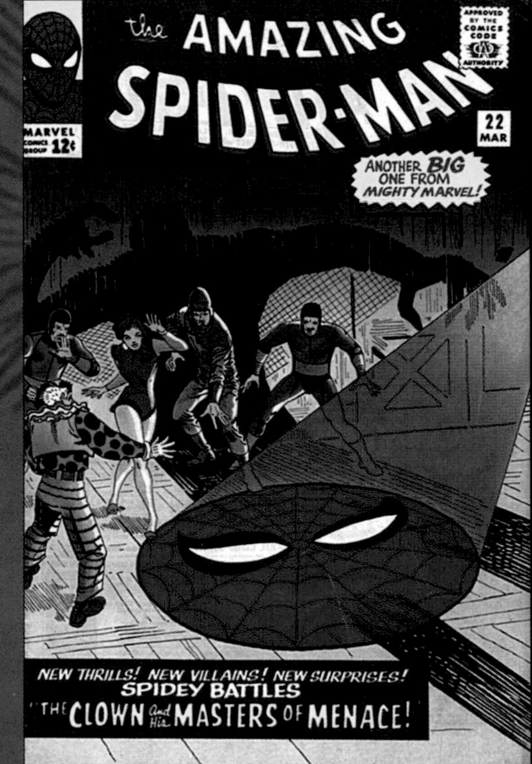

AMAZING SPIDER-MAN #22 (1964)

The Webhead meets the Circus of Crime for the second time and battles the Ringmaster, the Clown, and Princess Python.

AMAZING SPIDER-MAN #39 (1966)

John Romita takes over the Wall-Crawler's art chores when Peter Parker is unmasked and captured by his greatest enemy: Norman Osborn, the original Green Goblin!

MARVEL TALES #3 (1966)

As Marvel Comics became more popular, the company began to publish reprints of their earlier work so that readers could catch up on the histories of their favorite characters.

THE MIGHTY THOR #145 (1967)

As punishment for disobeying his father, Thor is stripped of his immortality and powers and abandoned on Earth. He lands a job working for the Ringmaster and his Circus of Crime.

MARVEL IN THE 1960s

Although it had published characters like Captain America, the Human Torch and the Sub-Mariner in the 1930s, 40s and 50s, the company that would become Marvel Comics had given up on Super Heroes when the 1960s began, and was only publishing monster comics, westerns and teenage romances. According to comic book legend, publisher Martin Goodman heard that the competition had launched a team of Super Heroes that was selling well. He asked his editor, Stan Lee, to come up with a new super-team. Stan developed the Fantastic Four and hired Jack Kirby as illustrator.

Launched as a bimonthly in 1961, *Fantastic Four #1* was followed by *The Incredible Hulk #1* in 1962. The same year saw the first appearance of Spider-Man in *Amazing Fantasy #15* and Thor in *Journey Into Mystery #83*. Spider-Man received his own title in 1963, the year that also premiered *Avengers #1*, *X-Men #1*, *Sgt. Fury And His Howling Commandos #1* and Iron Man in *Tales of Suspense #39*. *Daredevil #1* appeared in 1964. With the launch of *Nick Fury, Agent of SHIELD* in 1968, Nick became the first character to simultaneously star in two series set during different time periods: World War II and the modern era!

FANTASTIC FOUR #1 (1961)

The Marvel Universe is born with a bimonthly title that introduces Mr. Fantastic, the Thing, the Invisible Girl and the Human Torch to the world.

TALES TO ASTONISH #44 (1963)

The Ant-Man gains a partner and meets his future wife when Janet Van Dyne becomes the Wasp and joins his series.

SGT. FURY AND HIS HOWLING COMMANDOS #13 (1964)

In a story set during World War II, Captain America and Bucky join Sgt. Nick Fury to foil a typically fiendish Nazi plot.

FANTASTIC FOUR ANNUAL #3(1965)

Almost every Super Hero and Villain in the then Marvel Universe appears on the scene to celebrate the wedding of Reed Richards and Sue Storm. The guest list even includes a brief appearance by Stan Lee and Jack Kirby.

Cerise

FIRST APPEARANCE Excalibur #47 (March 1992)
REAL NAME Cerise
OCCUPATION Soldier **BASE** Shi'ar Empire
HEIGHT 5 ft 10 in **WEIGHT** 130 lbs **EYES** Brown **HAIR** Black
SPECIAL POWERS/ABILITIES Uses the energy of the red light spectrum to create weapons, force fields, vortexes, and shields. She can fly, direct energy blasts, and hold her breath for 7 minutes.

Cerise is an alien of the extra-terrestrial Shi'ar race, which absorbs other cultures into their vast interplanetary empire through violent conquest. Disillusioned with the brutal tactics of the Shi'ar war machine, Cerise deserted from their army and fled to Earth. There, she became a member of Excalibur, a mutant team that was an offshoot of the X-Men. Cerise fell in love with Nightcrawler, at the time a member of Excalibur.

In time, the Shi'ar empress Lilandra pardoned Cerise for her act of desertion, and brought her back into the Empire as an operative to investigate reports of Shi'ar brutality. **MT**

Chamber

FIRST APPEARANCE Generation X #1 (November 1994)
REAL NAME Jonothon Starsmore
OCCUPATION Weapon X field agent **BASE** Mobile
HEIGHT 5 ft 9 in **WEIGHT** 140 lbs **EYES** Brown **HAIR** Auburn
SPECIAL POWERS/ABILITIES Can manipulate the furnace of psionic energy in his chest to fire concussive blasts or cause objects to explode; possesses short-range telepathy.

Jonothon "Jono" Starsmore's mutant power manifested itself when an explosion of psionic energy inside his chest disintegrated the lower half of his face. Able to communicate only through telepathy, Jono became moody and withdrawn. He helped found the Generation X team as Chamber, and later joined the X-Men. A longtime relationship with his teammate Husk ended badly when she struck up a romance with Archangel. Agents from the Weapon X program recently made Chamber a field agent, and their scientists have apparently restored his face. **DW**

Chameleon

Dmitri Smerdyakov grew up in Russia as the half-brother and servant of Sergei Kravinoff, who later became known as the original Kraven the Hunter. Smerdyakov eventually became the mercenary spy known as the Chameleon, who was renowned as a master of disguise. Originally Chameleon relied on makeup, costumes, and his acting skill; he now uses a special serum and clothing to impersonate others.

The Chameleon first clashed with his nemesis, Spider-Man, when he attempted to frame the crimefighter for the theft of classified plans for a missile defense system. However, Spider-Man captured the Chameleon and exposed him as the real thief. The Chameleon has also contended against other Super Heroes, including the Hulk and Daredevil.

After the original Kraven committed suicide, the Chameleon lost his sanity, and jumped from a bridge. However, he turned up alive in an insane asylum, and resumed his criminal career. **PS**

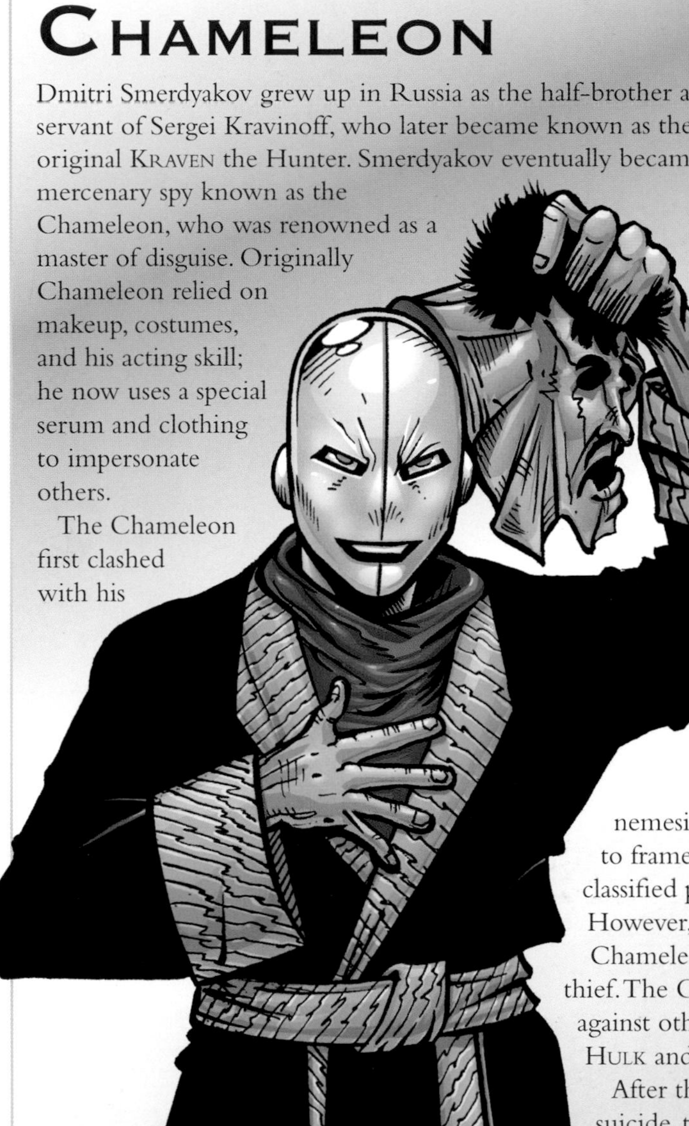

FACTFILE
REAL NAME
Dmitri Smerdyakov
OCCUPATION
Professional spy and criminal
BASE
Mobile

HEIGHT Unrevealed
WEIGHT Unrevealed
EYES Unrevealed
HAIR Unrevealed

FIRST APPEARANCE
Amazing Spider-Man #1 (March 1963)

POWERS
Experimental serum renders his flesh malleable, so that he can alter his appearance without makeup or prosthetics. Clothing contains "memory material" that responds to his nerve impulses, and change appearance at will.

Champion of the Universe

FIRST APPEARANCE Marvel Two-In-One Annual #7 (1982) **REAL NAME** Tryco Slatterus **OCCUPATION** Competitor **BASE** Mobile **HEIGHT** 9 ft 2 in **WEIGHT** 5,050 lbs **EYES** Silver **HAIR** Red **SPECIAL POWERS/ABILITIES** Has channeled the power primordial, the energy derived from the Big Bang, into his physical form, making his body a perfect fighting machine. Has also mastered thousands of different martial arts from across the universe.

Like many of the Elders of the Universe, the Champion's origin has been lost in antiquity. A true immortal, he devotes himself to physical self-perfection to avoid boredom. He considers himself the living spirit of competition and the eternal challenger striving for greatness. After training for millennia, he travels the universe, challenging the champions of each planet to personal combat. If he finds them unworthy, he exterminates all life on their planets. The winner of over 50,000 bouts, the Champion has never lost a fight. He once challenged the great heroes of Earth to a match and he was especially impressed with the Thing's courage. **TD**

Champions of Xandar

FIRST APPEARANCE Fantastic Four #208 (July 1979)
BASE The planet Xandar; Nova-Prime starship
KEY MEMBERS AND POWERS
Nova-Prime Flight; superhuman strength, invulnerability.
Protector Psionic ability.
Powerhouse Siphons energy from any power source, including living beings.
Comet Flight; can project electrical energy.
Crimebuster No superhuman powers.

THE CHAMPIONS OF XANDAR
1 Comet **2** Nova-Prime **3** Powerhouse
4 Protector **5** Crimebuster

The Champions of Xandar was a team of superhumanoid beings who formed to protect the planet Xandar. Xandar suffered three huge alien invasions. In the first, the Luphoms shattered Xandar into pieces. Survivors on the four largest fragments connected the four planetoids with huge bridges and rebuilt their civilization.

The second invasion was by the shape-shifting Skrulls, who hoped to bring Xandar into their empire. Having kept an active militia, Nova Corps, since the first invasion, the Xandarians resisted. They were aided by the Fantastic Four, and then by a group of Xandarians and Earth heroes, who banded together as the Champions of Xandar. Together, Nova Corps and the Champions repelled the Skrull invasion, though Crimebuster was killed. The third invasion, by Nebula, wiped out the entire population, including the remaining Champions. MT

Chance

FIRST APPEARANCE Web of Spider-Man #15 (June 1986)
REAL NAME Nicholas Powell
OCCUPATION Mercenary; gambler **BASE** New York City
HEIGHT 6 ft **WEIGHT** 185 lbs **EYES** Blue **HAIR** Brown
SPECIAL POWERS/ABILITIES Chance's armored costume contains wrist-blasters, boot-jets for flight, and assorted other weapons and paraphernalia.

A chronic gambler and inveterate risk-taker, Nicholas Powell took the name Chance and sought work as a mercenary to satisfy his craving for thrills. Chance's standard modus operandi is to wager his fee at double-or-nothing odds against his success—if he fails, he receives nothing. Chances's assignments have brought him into conflict with numerous Super Heroes, including Spider-Man and Daredevil. Chance is thoroughly immoral—but he prides himself on his ability to beat the odds. TB

Chandler

FIRST APPEARANCE Incredible Hulk #347 (September 1988)
REAL NAME Marlo Chandler Jones **OCCUPATION** Former actress, aerobics instructor, talk show host, comic shop co-owner **BASE** Los Angeles, California **HEIGHT** Over 6 ft
WEIGHT Unknown **EYES** Green **HAIR** Black
SPECIAL POWERS/ABILITIES Has the strength of a normal woman who exercises regularly.

Marlo Chandler was the Hulk's girlfriend when he was "Joe Fixit," an enforcer for organized crime. Later, she became the girlfriend of the Hulk's friend Rick Jones. A madwoman, Jacqueline Shorr, who claimed to be Rick's mother, murdered Marlo, but she was resurrected by the Leader. Marlo and Rick married and had their own TV talk show, *Keeping Up With the Joneses.* The couple separated for a while and Marlo had a fling with Moondragon before returning to Rick. PS

Changeling

A one-time member of the terrorist organization Factor Three, the Changeling changed sides when he learned that its leader, the alien Mutant Master, was seeking to eradicate humanity. When the Changeling discovered that he had contracted a terminal illness, he decided to make amends for his past misdeeds. He approached Professor X and volunteered to support the X-Men. The timing was fortuitous: Xavier needed to withdraw from active duty to fend off an impending alien invasion. The Changeling agreed to impersonate the Professor during his absence. However, his leadership of the X-Men was cut short when he was killed during a skirmish with the insane Prince Gor-Tok. AD

FACTFILE
REAL NAME
Unknown
OCCUPATION
Reformed criminal; one-time leader of the X-Men
BASE
Mobile

HEIGHT 5 ft 11 in
WEIGHT 180 lbs
EYES Brown
HAIR Black

FIRST APPEARANCE
X-Men #35 (August 1967

POWERS
A metamorph, the Changeling was able to adopt the appearance and voice of other humanoids; limited telekinetic ability.

Changeling turned over a new leaf by taking Professor X's place, at the latter's request.

Charcoal

FIRST APPEARANCE Thunderbolts #19 (October 1998)
REAL NAME Charles Burlingame
OCCUPATION Adventurer; student **BASE** Mt. Charteris.
HEIGHT 5 ft 7 in **WEIGHT** 135 lbs **EYES** Brown **HAIR** Black
SPECIAL POWERS/ABILITIES Transforms into a being composed of charcoal; manipulates heat and can reshape himself into any form of carbon, including flaming charcoal or rock-hard diamond.

When Charles Burlingame's father took him to a rally of the Imperial Forces of America, the scientist Arnim Zola ran a genetic test on the boy and discovered his potential for superhuman powers. Injecting Charles with chemicals, Zola transformed him into Charcoal, the Burning Man. At first, Charcoal joined a group called the Bruiser Brigade and battled the Thunderbolts. Later, as a member of the Thunderbolts, Charcoal witnessed the death of Jolt. He left the group to join the Redeemers, where he battled his father, who was still a member of the Imperial Forces. **MT**

Charlie-27

FIRST APPEARANCE Marvel Super Heroes #18 (January 1969)
REAL NAME Charlie-27
OCCUPATION Soldier; adventurer **BASE** The starship *Icarus*
HEIGHT 6 ft **WEIGHT** 555 lbs **EYES** Blue **HAIR** Red
SPECIAL POWERS/ABILITIES Superhuman strength and endurance; high resistance to injury and disease; withstands the gravity of Jupiter (11 times that of Earth); pilot and master strategist.

In one possible future, Charlie-27 is a space militia pilot and a member of a genetically bio-engineered race of humans that has been sent to live on and mine the planet Jupiter. After completing a solo tour of duty in space, Charlie-27 learned that an alien race called the Badoon had overrun the entire solar system and had slaughtered the inhabitants of his Jupiter, Pluto, Mercury and Earth. Joining with Martinex (Pluto), Nikki (Mercury), Yondo (Centauri V) and Vance Astro (Earth), Charlie-27 helped to expel the Badoon and later safeguarded the entire galaxy. **TD**

Luke Cage ended Chemistro's criminal career almost before it began.

Chemistro

Sad and slightly pathetic—that's how you might describe the story of the first man to bear the name Chemistro. Dissatisfied with his research position at Mainstream Motors, Curtis Carr embarked on a personal project–the development of an "Alchemy Gun" capable of changing one substance into another. When Carr was sacked for refusing to hand the weapon over to his boss, he disguised himself as a new supervillain, Chemistro, and began a series of revenge attacks against his employer. Carr's vengeful spree of destruction finally ended during a struggle with Power Man, when Carr accidentally shot his own foot and turned it to steel.

Crippled when his steel foot crumbled into dust, Carr was thrown into prison where he was forced to give the secrets of the Alchemy Gun to a fellow prisoner, Arch Morton. Although Morton's version of the gun exploded in his hand, the accident did endow his left hand with similar alchemical powers. On leaving prison, a reformed Carr developed a device called a Nullifier, and Luke Cage was able to use it to disable Morton.

The third Chemistro turned out to be Carr's brother, Calvin, who stole a new version of the Alchemy Gun but was again defeated, this time by both Power Man and Iron Fist. **AD**

FACTFILE
REAL NAME
Curtis Carr
OCCUPATION
Research scientist and reformed criminal
BASE
New York City

HEIGHT 5 ft 11 in
WEIGHT 185 lbs
EYES Brown
HAIR Black

FIRST APPEARANCE
Luke Cage, Hero for Hire #12 (August 1972)

POWERS
No superhuman powers; carried self-designed Alchemy Gun capable of transmuting one substance into another.

Although it made him look the part, Chemistro's spangly outfit did not prevent him from losing a foot when he accidentally shot himself.

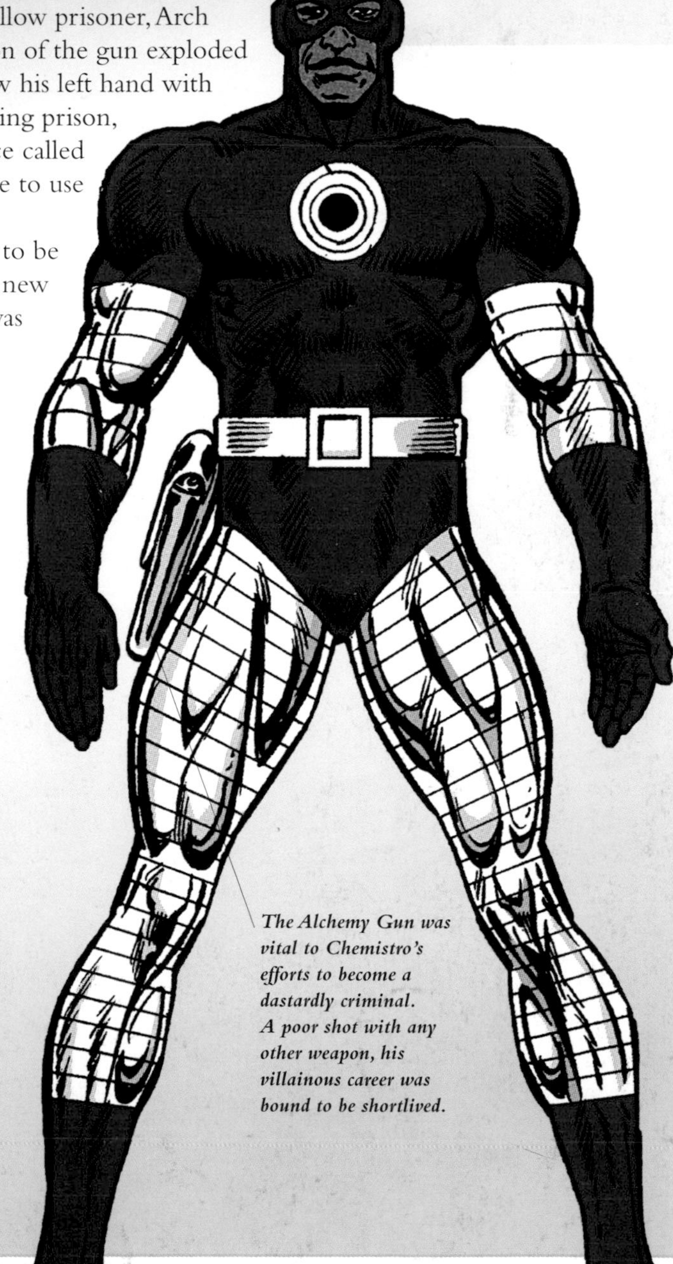

The Alchemy Gun was vital to Chemistro's efforts to become a dastardly criminal. A poor shot with any other weapon, his villainous career was bound to be shortlived.

Cheney, Lila

FIRST APPEARANCE New Mutants Annual #1 (1984)
REAL NAME Lila Cheney **OCCUPATION** Songstress; thief
BASE A Dyson sphere somewhere in the Milky Way Galaxy
HEIGHT 5 ft 8 in **WEIGHT** 120 lbs **EYES** Blue **HAIR** Black
SPECIAL POWERS/ABILITIES Lila Cheney possesses the mutant ability to teleport herself and other people and objects over intergalactic distances.

An acclaimed rock singer on Earth, Lila Cheney simultaneously pursued a very different career among the stars. Employing her mutant gift to teleport herself, Lila gained a reputation as one of the foremost thieves in the universe. She was an ally of the New Mutants, and a romance with Cannonball led her to curtail her criminal activities. Since their breakup, it remains to be seen whether she has abandoned her outlaw life for good. **TB**

Chthon

Chthon is one of the major Elder Gods who first appeared on Earth, shortly before humans appeared on the planet. Chthon and his sister god Gaea inhabited the portions of Earth which were covered by land (not the seas or the skies) and probably helped create Earth's land masses as they appear today.

Being a scholar, Chthon wrote upon a parchment all the mystical knowledge of the world he had acquired to that point. This document became known as the Darkhold. Chthon hoped to use the Darkhold as a way to manipulate Earthly pawns, as well as a magical talisman that could function as an Earthly portal, enabling Chthon to one day return to Earth. **MT**

FACTFILE
REAL NAME
Chthon
OCCUPATION
Elder God
BASE
An unknown extradimensional realm

HEIGHT Unknown
WEIGHT Unknown
EYES Red
HAIR None

FIRST APPEARANCE
Avengers #187 (September 1979)

POWERS
Chthon is a master of the forces of magic on a scale beyond human comprehension. In his own dimension, he has absolute control over every aspect of that dimension's reality.

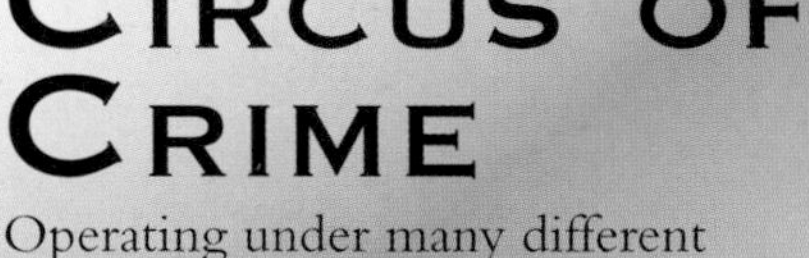

Circus of Crime

Operating under many different commercial names, the Circus of Crime is constantly traveling around the country. They usually enter a small town and give away a large quantity of free tickets in order to ensure a full house. Once the show has begun, the Ringmaster uses a hypnotic device in his top hat to place the audience in a deep trance. The audience is robbed and sometimes the entire town is looted. A post-hypnotic suggestion usually prevents the Ringmaster's victims from identifying any members of the Circus or from remembering any details of the crime. They only recall having had a great time at the circus!

Despite the Ringmaster's skills, and those of his accomplices, the Circus has not always got away with its mass robberies. When the Ringmaster tried to turn Hulk into a monstrous attraction, he was unable to hypnotize the enraged green giant—with inevitable results. **TB**

FACTFILE
MEMBERS
RINGMASTER (Maynard Tibolt), **STRONGMAN** (Bruno Olafsen), **CLOWN** (Eliot "Crafty" Franklin), **FIRE-EATER** (Tomas Ramirez), **THE GREAT GAMBONNOS** (Ernesto and Luigi), **HUMAN CANNONBALL** (Jack Pulver), **LIVE WIRE** (Rance Preston), **PRINCESS PYTHON** (Zelda DuBois), **RAJAH** (Kabir Mahadevu), **TEENA THE FAT LADY** (name unrevealed)

FIRST APPEARANCE
Incredible Hulk Vol. 1 #3 (July 1962)

POWERS
Most of the members of the Circus of Crime have skills and abilities that fit their job descriptions; these they then adapt for criminal purposes. Princess Python is a snake charmer; Rajah is an elephant trainer; and Live Wire possesses an electrified

Originally from Austria, the Ringmaster moved his circus to America where he believed he could strike it rich. However, he only turned to crime when his small band were unable to compete with the larger circus shows.

AND NOW, REPEAT AFTER ME...I MUST OBEY THE RINGMASTER!! HIS WILL IS MY WILL! HIS WILL IS MY WILL!!

The Ringmaster's mechanism has enough range to hypnotize a capacity crowd in a sports arena.

Dr. Strange meets Clea for the first time.

Clea

Until recently the ruler of the Dark Dimension, during her lifetime the Faltinian Princess Clea has experienced numerous trials and tribulations. The daughter of Prince Orini and Umar, influential figures in the Dark Dimension, Clea became involved in much of the political turmoil that afflicted that pocket universe. DOCTOR STRANGE first met Clea during one of his first forays to her homeland, and he was to have a significant influence on her life. Together they fought against the demon DORMAMMU and during these battles they fell in love. Inevitably, these struggles were not without their dangers and for a time Clea became trapped in a separate pocket universe with Dormammu. After her rescue by Strange, Clea spent several years in New York City, where she became his disciple and also his lover. When she returned to her home, she led a revolution against her mother, who had become ruler. Although she was to take her mother's place, it was only for a short time, for she was to be usurped as well: the upheavals of her early life seem set to continue throughout Clea's adulthood. **AD**

Even a burning head can't help Dormammu beat Dr. Strange.

FACTFILE

REAL NAME
Clea

OCCUPATION
Former ruler of the Dark Dimension

BASE
The Dark Dimension

HEIGHT 5 ft 8 in
WEIGHT 190 lbs
EYES Blue
HAIR White

FIRST APPEARANCE
Strange Tales #125 (November 1964)

POWERS
Formidable manipulator of mystical forces. Alien metabolism gives greater strength and endurance than a human being of similar height and weight.

Cloak and Dagger

Tyrone Johnson was an Afro-American teenager whose stutter tragically prevented him saving his friend Billy from being mistakenly shot as a thief by a policeman. A Caucasian teenager, Tandy Bowen, felt neglected and unloved by her wealthy mother. Johnson and Bowen each ran away from home, and met each other upon arriving in New York City at the Port Authority Bus Terminal.

They were offered a place to stay by men who worked for Simon Marshall, an unscrupulous chemist who was developing a new, highly addictive drug for the MAGGIA. Marshall was testing the drug on captured runaways. But whereas the drug killed the other runaways, it activated Johnson and Bowen's latent mutant abilities. Realizing he now resembled a living shadow, Johnson wrapped himself in fabric. He then entrapped some of Marshall's men in the blackness within this "cloak," while Bowen struck others down with "daggers" of "light." Johnson and Bowen decided to use their superhuman powers to save children and teenagers from drug dealers and other criminals and became the vigilante duo called Cloak and Dagger. **PS**

Despite differing backgrounds, runaways Tyrone Johnson and Tandy Bowen became the closest of friends.

FACTFILE

REAL NAMES
Tyrone Johnson, Tandy Bowen

OCCUPATION
Vigilantes

BASE The Holy Ghost Church, New York City

HEIGHT (Cloak) 6 ft (Dagger) 5 ft 5 in
WEIGHT (Cloak) 175 lbs, (Dagger) 115 lbs
EYES (Cloak) Brown, (Dagger) Blue
HAIR (Cloak) Black, (Dagger), Blonde

FIRST APPEARANCE
Spectacular Spider-Man #64 (March 1982)

POWERS
Cloak can open a portal into "Darkforce Dimension." Can project foes into this dimension, teleport himself and others. Dagger projects "daggers of light," psionic energy that deprives a victim of some life energy and can also cleanse people of drugs and poisons.

Dagger's "light-knives" are manifestations of the life energy that resides within all living beings. Dagger generates more of this life energy than normal humans do, and uses it to feed Cloak's hunger for such "light."

Cobra

FIRST APPEARANCE Journey into Mystery #98 (November 1963)
REAL NAME Klaus Voorhees
OCCUPATION Criminal **BASE** Manhattan, formerly the Serpent Citadels in New York State **HEIGHT** 5 ft 10 in
WEIGHT 160 lbs **EYES** Blue **HAIR** None
SPECIAL POWERS/ABILITIES Has flexible, virtually unbreakable bones: can perform superhuman contortionist feats.

Klaus Voorhees once worked in India as the assistant to a scientist who was conducting research into antidotes for snake venom. Voorhees fatally poisoned the scientist, but was himself bitten by an irradiated cobra. That cobra's venom and an experimental antidote radically mutated Voorhees. As the Cobra, Voorhees was first defeated by the thunder god THOR. As partners in crime the Cobra and MISTER HYDE have repeatedly battled Thor and DAREDEVIL. The Cobra has also joined other snake-themed criminals in the Serpent Squad and SERPENT SOCIETY. Shortly after assuming leadership of the Society, he changed his name to King Cobra. **PS**

Collector

FIRST APPEARANCE Avengers Vol. 1 #28 (June 1966)
REAL NAME Taneleer Tivan
OCCUPATION Curator **BASE** Mobile
HEIGHT 6ft 2in **WEIGHT** 450 lbs **EYES** White **HAIR** White
SPECIAL POWERS/ABILITIES Immortality, precognition and telepathy; can manipulate cosmic energy to change his size and shape; Temporal Assimilator permits time travel.

One of the immortal ELDERS OF THE UNIVERSE, the Collector foresaw the destruction of all life by THANOS, and began to collect specimens for future repopulation. He was slain by KORVAC, but returned to life when the GRANDMASTER, a fellow Elder, won a contest with Death. The Collector briefly held the Reality Gem, but lost it to Thanos who sought it for the Infinity Gauntlet. Recently, the Collector allowed the Brethren to invade Earth, hoping to collect survivors from the reduced population. **DW**

Colossus

FACTFILE

REAL NAME
Piotr Nikolaievitch Rasputin
OCCUPATION
Adventurer
BASE
Professor X's School for Gifted Youngsters, Salem Center, New York

HEIGHT 7 ft 5in (armored)
WEIGHT 500 lbs (armored)
EYES Blue
HAIR Blond

FIRST APPEARANCE
Giant Size X-Men #1 (1975)

POWERS
Mutant ability to change his body's tissue into an organic, steel-like material. This gives Colossus superhuman strength (he can lift at least 70 tons) and protects him from injury.

Piotr Rasputin was born and raised on a Soviet collective farm in Russia. His mutant powers first emerged during his adolescence, and at first he was content to use his great strength and invulnerability to help his fellow farmers on the collective. His armored form added 11 inches to his normal height and doubled his natural weight. When PROFESSOR X organized a new team of mutants to help him rescue his original team of X-MEN from the sentient island known as Krakoa, he contacted Rasputin and asked him to join. The young Russian agreed to leave his native land and accompany Xavier to the US. Training at the X-Men's mansion, Rasputin was given the code name Colossus. He then helped Professor X's other new recruits in their battle with Krakoa. When the battle was over, Rasputin decided to remain in the US as a member of the X-Men. **MT**

In armored form Colossus retains his normal degree of mobility, but his endurance and speed are greater.

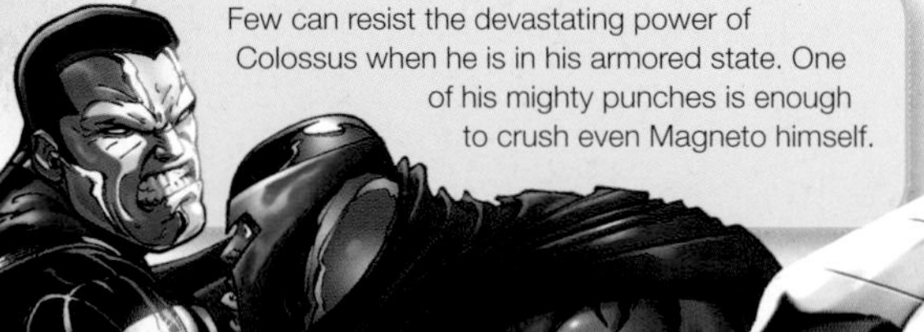

Few can resist the devastating power of Colossus when he is in his armored state. One of his mighty punches is enough to crush even Magneto himself.

His armor can withstand an explosion of 450 pounds of dynamite.

Collins, Rusty

FIRST APPEARANCE X-Factor #1 (February 1986)
REAL NAME Rusty Collins
OCCUPATION Adventurer **BASE** X-Factor HQ, New York City
HEIGHT 5 ft 11 in **WEIGHT** 160 lbs **EYES** Blue **HAIR** Red
SPECIAL POWERS/ABILITIES Rusty Collins was a pyrokinetic with the mutant ability to cause flames to spontaneously generate in his vicinity.

Leaving a troubled home life behind, Rusty Collins enlisted in the United States Navy while still underage. But his career as a sailor came to an end when his mutant ability to generate flames first manifested itself. Rusty was thereafter recruited by X-Factor, members of the original X-Men who had taken on the role of mutant hunters in order to conceal their activities in recruiting and training young mutants. Rusty eventually gained some control over his flaming abilities, and he adventured with X-Factor's junior team, the X-Terminators. However, he eventually perished due to injuries received during a battle with the villain Holocaust. **TB**

Comet

Comet aides Nova in the defence of the planet Xandar.

Harris Moore was one of the very first superpowered individuals to adopt a costume and take up the fight against crime. During an encounter with a gaseous, comet-like object in the 1950s, Moore was mutagenically affected by its radiation. Discovering that he could now fly and fire electrical energy from his hands, Moore decided to battle criminals on the streets of New York. His new vocation was not to end well. Moore was a wealthy individual with a wife and two children, but his good life was to come to an end when an enemy tracked him down to his suburban home and attacked him and his family. While he was hospitalised and appeared to have lost his powers, they were all thought to be dead. Moore retired his costume for many years until he was called upon to travel to the planet Xandar, along with other Earth superheroes, and help its people in the fight against the Skrulls. During this battle, Moore was reunited with his son, Frank, the high tech vigilante Crimebuster. Sadly, their renewed relationship was not to last long: Frank was killed during this battle while Moore later died during the Xandarians' battle against Nebula. **AD**

FACTFILE
REAL NAME
Harris Moore
OCCUPATION
Crimefighter
BASE
New York City/Xandar

HEIGHT 5 ft 11 in
WEIGHT 190 lbs
EYES Blue
HAIR Gray

FIRST APPEARANCE
Nova #21 (September 1978)

POWERS
Flies and projects energy blasts from his hands.

Comet Man

Comet Man *Max*

On a mission in space, Dr. Stephen Beckley lost control of his spacecraft, which entered a comet's tail. The comet's intense heat vaporized the ship and Beckley. However, within the comet was another spaceship piloted by Max, an alien from the Colony Fortisque. Max used Fortisquian technology to reconstruct Beckley's body and endow him with superhuman powers.

Returning to Earth, Beckley was quarantined by David Hilbert, a member of the Bridge, an intelligence agency headed by Beckley's brother John, the Superior. Hilbert captured Stephen's wife Ann and son Benny. Stephen escaped captivity, but in her own escape attempt Ann was killed. The Superior had scientist Dr. Fishler subject Benny to painful experiments in order to endow him with powers like Stephen's. Stephen found Benny, who used his new powers to kill Dr. Fishler before turning comatose.

Now known as Comet Man, Stephen accompanied Max to the Colony Fortisque, where Beckley mastered his powers. Comet Man then returned to Earth, where he used his powers to awaken Benny from his coma. **PS**

Max, a member of the Fortisquian race, is fascinated by Earth's popular culture. Revealing himself to be an alien, Max became a media celebrity.

About every 77 years, a Fortisquian spaceship, hidden within a comet, travels past Earth to observe the planet.

FACTFILE
REAL NAME
Dr. Stephen Beckley
OCCUPATION
Former astronaut, astronomer and astrophysicist
BASE
Mobile

HEIGHT 6ft 1in
WEIGHT 190lbs
EYES Blue
HAIR Brown

FIRST APPEARANCE
Comet Man #1 (February 1987)

POWERS
Possesses superhuman strength and self-healing ability. Can teleport himself and levitate himself and other objects. Projects concussive energy from his hands. By projecting part of his consciousness into people and higher animals, he can read and influence their minds.

THE CSA

FACTFILE

BASE
United States of America; various locations

FIRST APPEARANCE
Captain America #331 (July 1987)

The Commission on Superhuman Activities is tasked with maintaining national security in a world occupied by superhumans.

COMMISSION ON SUPERHUMAN ACTIVITIES

The Commission on Superhuman Activities is a special task force answerable only to the President of the United States. It is charged with the task of regulating security in an age when beings with superhuman abilities roam the world. The Commission, or the CSA as it is frequently known, has involved itself in numerous incidents since its inception: it recruited the BROTHERHOOD OF EVIL MUTANTS led by MYSTIQUE to form the nucleus of a government-sponsored team of operatives known as FREEDOM FORCE. It was responsible for choosing John Walker as the replacement for Steve Rogers when the latter gave up his identity as CAPTAIN AMERICA. Members of the CSA were also responsible for the creation of superhumans such as Nuke and the Julia Carpenter SPIDER-WOMAN. When a SENTINEL went rogue and attacked a school in Antigo, Wisconsin, the Commission sent agents to investigate. The CSA has also been responsible for pitting the THUNDERBOLTS against the NEW AVENGERS. While their resources have occasionally been used for nefarious purposes, in general the membership of the Commission remains dedicated to its mission statement of protecting the American people from any threat spawned by those possessing superhuman attributes. **TB**

CSA
1 Orville Sanderson **2** George Mathers
3 General Heyworth **4** Henry Peter Gyrich
5 Valerie Cooper **6** Raymond Sikorsky
7 Adrian Sammish

CONSTRICTOR

FACTFILE

REAL NAME
Frank Payne (alias Frank Schlichting)

OCCUPATION
Professional criminal and assassin

BASE
Mobile

HEIGHT 5 ft 11 in
WEIGHT 190 lbs
EYES Blue
HAIR Black

FIRST APPEARANCE
Incredible Hulk # 212 (June 1977)

POWERS
Battlesuit contains two cybernetically-controlled, electrically-powered adamantium cables, used as whips, as crushing coils, and to release electrical charges.

The cables in Constrictor's battlesuit are made of adamantium, the strongest metal ever forged by man.

CONSTRICTOR

SHIELD agent Frank Payne was sent undercover to infiltrate a criminal organization known as the Corporation, using the alias Frank Schlichting. When Payne was forced to kill several youths during a fight between the Corporation and a gang, he suffered a nervous breakdown. The Corporation then gave him the Constrictor battlesuit, and he became a criminal operative for them, battling the HULK and Nick FURY. When the Corporation was dissolved, Constrictor went freelance and fought CAPTAIN AMERICA, POWER MAN and IRON FIST, and SPIDER-MAN. For a while Constrictor teamed with SABRETOOTH, but preferring to work alone, he refused membership in the SERPENT SOCIETY. **MT**

CONTEMPLATOR

FIRST APPEARANCE Marvel Treasury Special #1 (1976)
REAL NAME Tath Ki
OCCUPATION Philosopher **BASE** Coal Sack Nebula
HEIGHT 5 ft **WEIGHT** 100 lbs **EYES** Blue **HAIR** None
SPECIAL POWERS/ABILITIES Control of his body's involuntary responses: heartbeat, perspiration, etc.; highly developed mental powers; acute awareness of this and alternate universes.

An ELDER OF THE UNIVERSE, the Contemplator is one of the most ancient beings in the cosmos. Born in the early days of the universe, he has spent most of his life in meditation, reflecting on and teasing out the universe's deepest secrets. On occasion, the Contemplator has intervened in human affairs—IRON FIST encountered him during a battle with HYDRA; he once gave CAPTAIN AMERICA a history tour, and he has had dealings with the SILVER SURFER. But, for the most part, this enigmatic, aged figure spends his days watching and learning. **AD**

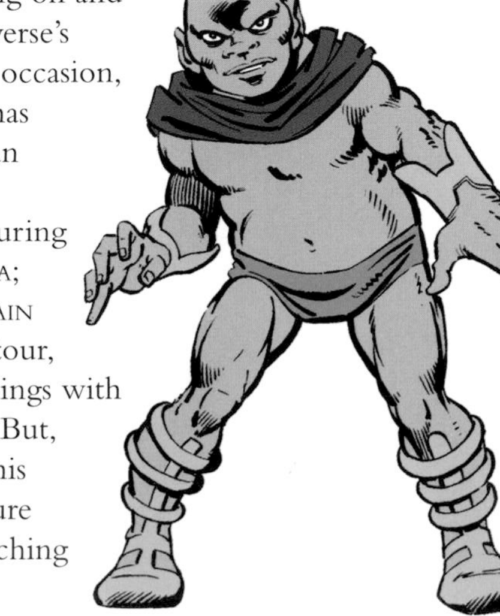

Controller

FIRST APPEARANCE Iron Man Vol. 1 #12 (April 1969)
REAL NAME Basil Sandhurst
OCCUPATION Criminal **BASE** Mobile
HEIGHT 6 ft 2 in **WEIGHT** 565 lbs **EYES** White **HAIR** Black
SPECIAL POWERS/ABILITIES Armored exoskeleton provides enhanced strength and damage resistance; can telepathically control victims wearing his slave discs.

Crippled in a lab accident while working for Cord Industries (one of Stark Industries' main rivals), scientist Basil Sandhurst built himself an exoskeleton powered by mental energy. By placing a slave disc on a victim's head or neck, Sandhurst could direct that person's actions and leech their brain power to charge up his suit. Calling himself the Controller, Sandhurst took command of an entire town with his slave discs until IRON MAN defeated him and freed all the people. Following the Controller's escape from the Vault prison, the RED SKULL forced him to act as a member of the Skeleton Crew. The Controller has also worked with the U-FOES. His current whereabouts and activities are unknown. **DW**

Cooper

FIRST APPEARANCE X-Men #176 (December 1983)
REAL NAME Valerie Cooper **OCCUPATION** Chair of the Commission on Superhuman Activities **BASE** Washington, D.C.
HEIGHT 5 ft 9 in **WEIGHT** 135 lbs **EYES** Green **HAIR** Blonde
SPECIAL POWERS/ABILITIES Highly intelligent, efficient, and loyal; superb organizer; trained in the use of weapons.

Special Assistant to the US National Security Advisor Dr. Valerie Cooper was concerned about the number of mutants in the world. She feared that if control of mutants fell into the wrong hands, they could be used as weapons against the US. When MYSTIQUE offered the help of the BROTHERHOOD OF EVIL MUTANTS, Cooper accepted, changing the group's name to FREEDOM FORCE. Later, as the head of the COMMISSION ON SUPERHUMAN ACTIVITIES, Cooper was the liaison with the mutant team X-FACTOR. When SHADOW KING mentally controlled Cooper and ordered her to kill Mystique, Cooper instead turned the gun on herself. For a while she was believed dead, but actually survived this incident. **MT**

Copycat

FIRST APPEARANCE New Mutants #98 (Feburary 1991, in the guise of Domino) **REAL NAME** Vanessa Geraldine Carlysle
OCCUPATION Professional criminal; mercenary **BASE** Mobile
HEIGHT Unrevealed **WEIGHT** Unrevealed
EYES Black with white pupils **HAIR** White
SPECIAL POWERS/ABILITIES Copycat can transform herself into a duplicate of any other person.

Vanessa Carlysle's mutant power to transform her appearance manifested itself in her early teens. She was kicked out by her family, and forced to make her way on the mean streets. She eventually came to the attention of the shadowy Mr. Tolliver, who used her to infiltrate X-FORCE in the guise of DOMINO. But Copycat came to like the members of X-Force, and she could not go through with the plan to blow them up along with their headquarters. Her deception discovered, Copycat was forced to return to being a mercenary, and She met her doom at the hands of SABRETOOTH after being recruited by the revived WEAPON X project. **MT**

Copycat's most successful impersonation was when she took the form of Domino and joined the New Mutants. Even the readers were unaware of the substitution for months.

Corruptor

FIRST APPEARANCE Nova #4 (December 1976))
REAL NAME Jackson Day
OCCUPATION Criminal mastermind
BASE Mobile
HEIGHT 6ft 1in **WEIGHT** 225 lbs **EYES** Red **HAIR** White
SPECIAL POWERS/ABILITIES His touch makes his victims susceptible to his commands. Left to themselves, they will behave in an unihibited, perhaps amoral fashion.

While employed by a drug company, factory worker Jackson Day was accidentally drenched with chemicals. They turned his skin blue-black, and removed his inhibitions against wrongdoing. He also gained the power to control the wills of others by touching them. As the Corruptor, Day turned the Asgardian thunder god THOR into a violent menace.

However, the Super Hero NOVA intervened, and together he and Thor captured the Corruptor. The villain subsequently escaped and formed a criminal organization called the Inner Circle. Nova remains his main enemy. **PS**

COUNT NEFARIA

FACTFILE

REAL NAME
Count Luchino Nefaria

OCCUPATION
Criminal; former head of Nefaria "family" of Maggia

BASE
Various, including castle originally located in Italy and reconstructed in the New Jersey Palisades.

HEIGHT 6 ft 2 in
WEIGHT 230 lbs
EYES Blue
HAIR Black

FIRST APPEARANCE
The Avengers #13 (Feb. 1965)

POWERS

Superhuman strength, speed, and resistance to injury; projects laser beams from eyes; regenerates after injury; drains energy from other beings powered by ionic energy.

COUNT NEFARIA

Italian nobleman Count Luchino Nefaria used his fortune both to finance technological research and to make himself a power in the MAGGIA crime syndicate. Nefaria's wife Renata died giving birth to their daughter Giulietta. Growing up in America as Whitney Frost, Giulietta would eventually become the Maggia leader called MADAME MASQUE. In retaliation for the AVENGERS' opposition to the Maggia, Nefaria framed them for treason. The Avengers were cleared, but Nefaria was publicly exposed as a criminal. Among his grandest schemes, Nefaria captured Washington DC and held it for ransom, and later took over the North American Defense Command base at Valhalla Mountain. On both occasions he was thwarted by the X-MEN.

Thunderbird, a Native American member of the X-Men, perished while trying to prevent Count Nefaria's escape from Valhalla Mountain.

Nefaria was the villain in the 1975 issue that relaunched the X-Men Super Heroes.

Later, Nefaria had Prof. Kenneth Sturdy endow him with the powers of the LIVING LASER, POWER MAN, and WHIRLWIND and again battled the Avengers. Soon afterwards, however, Nefaria aged into an ancient invalid, and seemingly died when his body was crushed. However, Nefaria revived as a superhuman powered by ionic energy, and continues to menace the entire world. PS

CRAZY GANG
1 Jack of Hearts *2* Jester
3 Tweedledope *4* Executioner
5 Red Queen

CRAZY GANG

FIRST APPEARANCE Marvel Super Heroes #377 (Sept. 1981)
BASE Mobile
MEMBERS AND POWERS
Executioner A hooded, scythe-wielding humanoid robot.
Jester Accomplished swordsman.
Knave Possesses superhuman strength.
Red Queen Her insanity twists all reality into negative situations.
Tweedledope Idiot-savant who devises advanced machinery.

The Crazy Gang is a team of professional criminals from another dimension (Earth-238, or the Crooked World) who look like characters from children's storybooks. They were assembled by that dimension's CAPTAIN BRITAIN (called Captain UK, real name: James Jaspers).

When the Crazy Gang was transported to the Earth of the Captain Britain, who was really Brian Braddock, they proved incompetent at committing crimes and so advertised for a new leader. They were taken over by Captain Britain's foe the Slaymaster, who masterminded a series of spectacular crimes which the Crazy Gang carried out for him. They were then recruited by master assassin ARCADE to abduct Courtney Ross, the former girlfriend of Captain Britain. Ross managed to escape from the bumbling group, but was taken prisoner by Arcade himself. The Crazy Gang later clashed with EXCALIBUR, who subsequently allowed them to remain in this dimension. MT

Creed, Graydon

FIRST APPEARANCE Uncanny X-Men #299 (April 1993)
STATUS Villain (deceased) **REAL NAME** Graydon Creed
OCCUPATION Politician; wheeler-dealer **BASE** New York City; New York State; mobile **HEIGHT** 6 ft **WEIGHT** 181 lbs
EYES Blue **HAIR** Brown
SPECIAL POWERS/ABILITIES Charismatic orator, skilled political operator and rabble-rouser.

Victor Creed was psychologically abused as a child and become the mutant menace Sabretooth; his son, Graydon Creed, was to grow up similarly disaffected. Born to the shapeshifting mutant Mystique, Graydon came to hate all mutants. He founded the Friends of Humanity, an organization that aimed to wipe out mutants. Standing for U. S. President on a Friends of Humanity platform, Graydon was cut down by an assassin's plasma beam. The murderer turned out to be his own mother, who had travelled back from the future especially to kill him. **AD**

Crimson Commando

FIRST APPEARANCE Uncanny X-Men # 215 (March 1987)
REAL NAME Frank Bohannan
OCCUPATION Federal agent **BASE** Washington, DC
HEIGHT 6 ft 1 in **WEIGHT** 235 lbs **EYES** White **HAIR** White
SPECIAL POWERS/ABILITIES The Crimson Commando is a mutant at the peak of physical perfection. He has been turned into a cyborg with even greater strength and power.

The Crimson Commando is a veteran Super Hero of World War II who, after the war, took to hunting down criminals and slaying them in a brutal vigilante style alongside his two partners, Super-Sabre and Stonewall. They were arrested when their activities were revealed after trying to execute the X-Man Storm. Recruited for the government-sponsored mutant team, Freedom Force, the Crimson Commando served with that unit until, on a mission to Kuwait, he was horribly wounded, losing both legs and part of an arm. Still alive, he was rebuilt into a cyborg by the government, and continues to operate as a covert agent. **TB**

Crimson Dynamo

FIRST APPEARANCE Tales of Suspense Vol. 1 #46 (October 1963)
STATUS Russian hero **REAL NAME** Valentin Shalatov
OCCUPATION Former KGB agent **BASE** Moscow, Russia
HEIGHT 6 ft 2 in **WEIGHT** 210 lbs **EYES** Brown **HAIR** Brown
SPECIAL POWERS/ABILITIES Armored suit provides flight, enhanced strength, and damage resistance; built-in weapons include missiles, guns, electrical generators, and a fusioncaster.

Six men have worn the Crimson Dynamo armor. The first, Russian inventor Anton Vanko, built the original battlesuit and battled Iron Man, but defected to work for Tony Stark. Vanko died killing the second Dynamo, Boris Turgenev, who had been sent to assassinate him. Vanko's protégé Alex Nevsky became the third Dynamo until his death at the hands of the KGB. The fourth, fifth, and sixth Crimson Dynamos (Yuri Petrovich, Dimitri Bukharin, and Colonel-General Valentin Shalatov), operated as Russian agents. Shalatov engineered the disgrace of Bukharin so that he could become the Crimson Dynamo. He wished to restore Russia to its former glory, but later changed his stance and helped Iron Man defeat the fanatical Titanium Man. **DW**

Crossbones

FIRST APPEARANCE Captain America #360 (October 1989)
STATUS Villain **REAL NAME** Brock Rumlow
OCCUPATION Brock Rumlow **BASE** Mobile
HEIGHT 6 ft 4 in **WEIGHT** 290 lbs **EYES** Brown **HAIR** Brown
SPECIAL POWERS/ABILITIES Brutal hand-to-hand combatant; highly adept with weapons and explosives, including pistols, throwing knives, which he keeps in his boots, and wrist blades, which are hidden in his wrist bands.

As a child, Brock Rumlow idolized the Red Skull. Therefore, it comes as no surprise that, as the mercenary Crossbones, he and his Skeleton Crew became regular employees of Adolf Hitler's old confidante. A brutal thug, Rumlow's work has repeatedly brought him face-to-face with Captain America. There is no love lost between these two, particularly given Rumlow's treatment of Rachel Leighton, aka Diamondback, Captain America's ex-girlfriend. When Rachel was 15 years old, Crossbones attacked her before killing her brother that same night. He has yet to pay for these horrendous crimes. **AD**

Crossfire

FIRST APPEARANCE Marvel Two-In-One #52 (June 1979)
REAL NAME William Cross
OCCUPATION Ex-CIA agent, criminal **BASE** Mobile
HEIGHT 6 ft **WEIGHT** 190 lbs **EYES** Blue **HAIR** Brown
SPECIAL POWERS/ABILITIES Marksman, spy, deadly hand-to-hand fighter; left eye replaced by infrared device allowing night vision; left ear replaced by audio sensor giving super-hearing.

William Cross learned all about espionage, and especially brainwashing techniques, as a CIA agent. Leaving the CIA, and taking the codename Crossfire, he organized an army of mercenaries with the goal of disrupting society and earning himself a hefty profit from the ensuing chaos. When his enemies set off an explosion in Crossfire's headquarters, he lost his left eye and left ear. Replacing these with an enhanced cybernetic eye and ear, Crossfire set about brainwashing costumed heroes. His attempts put him in conflict with the Thing, Moon Knight, and Hawkeye. **MT**

Crystal

FIRST APPEARANCE Fantastic Four #45 (December 1965)
REAL NAME Corystalia Amaquelin Maximoff
OCCUPATION Adventurer **BASE** City of Attilan, variously located in the Himalayas, on the Moon, and on Attilan Is., Atlantic Ocean
HEIGHT 5 ft 6 in **WEIGHT** 110 lbs **EYES** Green **HAIR** Red
SPECIAL POWERS/ABILITIES Elemental powers enable her to psionically control fire, air, earth, and water.

Crystal is an elemental and a member of the Royal Family of the INHUMANS, a genetically advanced offshoot of humanity. She is also the younger sister of MEDUSA. Forced into exile, the Royal Family wandered the world, eventually arriving in New York City, where Crystal met and fell in love with Johnny Storm, the HUMAN TORCH. Crystal subsequently became a substitute member of the FANTASTIC FOUR during INVISIBLE WOMAN Susan Richards' maternity leave. Crystal eventually married the temperamental QUICKSILVER of the AVENGERS. They had a daughter named Luna, but their marriage has been marred by repeated estrangements. Crystal has also served as a member of the Avengers, helping the team battle the GATHERERS. **PS**

Cybele

FIRST APPEARANCE Eternals #1 (July 1976)
REAL NAME Cybele **OCCUPATION** Goddess
BASE The forests of Colorado **HEIGHT** 5 ft 11 in
WEIGHT 125 lbs **EYES** Blue **HAIR** White-blonde
SPECIAL POWERS/ABILITIES Immortal projects cosmic energy from hands and eyes; levitates and flies; manipulates minds of others to render herself invisible.

The wife of Zuras, the ruler of the ETERNALS, Cybele has lived a life surprisingly remote from the affairs of her fellow immortals. Marrying Zuras in the days before the rise of the ancient Greek civilization, Cybele bore his child, Azura (later known as THENA) and tended to her upbringing. After Azura came of age, Cybele withdrew from the other Eternals. Despite her formidable powers, she chooses to live quietly in a forest in Colorado, where she uses her psionic abilities to remain invisible to humans, unless she wishes them to see or hear her. **AD**

Cyber's hatred of Wolverine spurred him to destroy this robotic doppelganger with particular enthusiasm.

Cyber

FIRST APPEARANCE Marvel Comics Presents #85 (August 1991)
REAL NAME Silas Burr **OCCUPATION** Mercenary
BASE Mobile **HEIGHT** 6 ft 4 in **WEIGHT** 365 lbs
EYES Hazel **HAIR** Unrevealed
SPECIAL POWERS/ABILITIES Superhuman strength; mutant healing; ability to track brain patterns; adamantium-laced skin; claws containing poisons or hallucinogens; cybernetic eye.

During World War I, Silas Burr served as the commanding officer of Logan (*see* WOLVERINE) in the "Devil's Brigade" of the Canadian army. He later killed Logan's girlfriend, beat Logan up and gouged out his eye, beginning a lifelong, bitter enmity between the two. During the subsequent decades, Burr turned himself into a formidable opponent: part-man, part-machine with skin laced with adamantium, to make it virtually impenetrable and indestructible. He enhanced his considerable fighting abilities by equipping each of his hands with an adamantium claw.

Taking the name Cyber, he crossed paths with Wolverine while working for a drug cartel based on the Southeast Asian island of Madripoor. In a fight with Wolverine, he lost an eye and fell victim to a new hallucinogenic drug that drove him insane. The drug's after-effects enabled him to track brain patterns over several miles.

Sporting a cybernetic left eye in place of the one he had lost, Cyber led a female crime organization known as Hell's Belles and clashed with X-FACTOR and EXCALIBUR. The mutant GENESIS ultimately lured Cyber into a trap, where he died, his flesh consumed by mutant death-watch beetles. **DW**

CYCLOPS *SEE OPPOSITE PAGE*

Cypher

FIRST APPEARANCE New Mutants #13 (March 1984)
REAL NAME Douglas Ramsey **OCCUPATION** Student
BASE Professor Xavier's School for Gifted Youngsters
HEIGHT 5 ft 9 in **WEIGHT** 150 lbs **EYES** Blue **HAIR** Blond
SPECIAL POWERS/ABILITIES Cypher possessed a mutant facility for translating any sort of language, whether human, extraterrestrial, or even computer code.

Doug Ramsey's interest in computer programming and games brought him into contact with Kitty PRYDE, and from there PROFESSOR X, who realized that Ramsey's ability to decipher languages was a mutant trait. Both the NEW MUTANTS and Emma FROST'S HELLIONS tried to recruit Ramsey; he eventually became a member of the New Mutants after they requested his aid in communicating with the newly-arrived alien child called WARLOCK. Cypher often complained that his gift was not of great value in a fight with Super Villains, but he proved his heroism when he sacrificed his life blocking a bullet meant for his teammate, WOLFSBANE. **TB**

CYCLOPS

Deputy Leader of the X-Men

Deadly solar energy continually crackles forth from the eyes of Cyclops, controlled only by his visor.

When PROFESSOR X set up his School for Gifted Youngsters, the first mutant he asked to join was Scott Summers. He joined the Professor's team, the X-MEN, adopting the codename Cyclops. Cyclops proved Professor X's most trusted X-Man, and quickly became the team's deputy leader and master strategist, displaying great tactical abilities.

Ruby quartz visor shields optic blasts, which he is unable to "turn off" due to his childhood brain injury.

FACTFILE

REAL NAME
Scott Summers

OCCUPATION
Adventurer, student, radio announcer

BASE
Xavier Institute, Westchester County, New York State; X-Factor Headquarters, New York City

HEIGHT 6 ft 3 in
WEIGHT 175 lbs
EYES Black (red when his optic power is active)
HAIR Brown

FIRST APPEARANCE
X-Men #1 (September 1963)

POWERS

Cyclops has the mutant ability to project ruby-colored beams of pure solar energy from his eyes. The power of these beams is drawn from the sun's rays. Cyclops' cells constantly absorb sunlight and transfer the solar energy to his eyes. Due to a brain injury as a child, Cyclops' optic beam is always "on." The only way to block it is by closing his eyes or wearing a visor or glasses. Cyclops' optic blasts are powerful enough to punch holes through a mountain.

A PERILOUS FLIGHT

Scott Summers was the elder of two sons of Air Force Major Christopher Summers and Katherine Anne Summers. Major Summers decided to fly his family home from a vacation aboard his private plane. But the plane was attacked by a space ship of the alien SHI'AR EMPIRE.

Scott's mother pushed him and his brother Alex out of the burning plane with the one available parachute. Having to share one parachute led the boys to plunge to Earth rapidly. When they hit the ground, both brothers were hurt and hospitalized. Scott struck his head and fell into a coma, which lasted for a year.

Scott suffered brain damage, which would eventually prevent him from controlling his mutant powers (optic blasts) once they emerged. Alex ended up in an orphanage and the boys lost contact for many years. They would be reunited once Alex's mutant powers emerged and he became known as HAVOK, and eventually joined the X-Men.

Target practice: Cyclops hones his skills by practicing pinpoint control using targets flying through the air.

ESSENTIAL STORYLINES

- ***X-Men #107*** First appearance of Corsair, Cyclops's father (Christopher Summers), whom Scott believed to be dead, but is now a member of the Starjammers, an alien group opposed to Shi'ar tyranny.
- ***X-Men #30*** Marriage X-men style: after years of romance, Scott Summers finally marries his beloved, Jean Grey.

Cyclop roars with anguish as he holds the dead body of his beloved, Jean Grey, in his arms.

THE X-MAN

In his mid-teens, Scott developed terrible headaches and eyestrain. Then his mutant powers emerged and he unintentionally released an optic blast that struck a crane at a construction site, endangering people on the street. He then fired another blast which destroyed the falling debris, saving the crowd, which was nonetheless enraged. Scott fled the scene and subsequently fell into an unwilling partnership with a powerful mutant criminal, the Living Diamond.

When Professor X learned about Scott and his ability, the professor rescued the young mutant from the Living Diamond and invited him to join his school. Scott became Cyclops, the first member of the X-Men. Scott later formed X-FACTOR, but always returned to the X-Men. Shy and reserved, he was in love with teammate JEAN GREY for years before they finally married. Their son is named Nathan. MT

DAREDEVIL

The Man Without Fear

FACTFILE

REAL NAME
Matthew Michael Murdock

OCCUPATION
Lawyer

BASE
Hell's Kitchen, New York City

HEIGHT 5 ft 11 in
WEIGHT 185 lbs
EYES Blue
HAIR Red/Brown

FIRST APPEARANCE
Daredevil #1 (April 1964)

POWERS

Despite his blindness, Daredevil's remaining four senses have been honed to superhuman levels. He also possesses a built-in Radar Sense that allows him to detect the contours of his environment. A trained athlete and acrobat, he carries a billy club that can be converted into a blind man's cane; it also contains a reeled throwing line that allows Daredevil to swing over the rooftops or entangle an enemy.

When he began his crime-fighting career, Daredevil wore a yellow and red costume similar to that of a wrestler.

Matt Murdock was the only son of professional boxer "Battling" Jack Murdock. But his father, forced to work as a mob leg-breaker in order to supplement his meager income as a prize-fighter, made Matt promise to get a good education, and not become a fighter like himself. As a dedicated student who would never compete in athletics with his fellows, Matt was nicknamed "Daredevil" by his taunting classmates. Not wanting to break his promise to his father, Matt took their insults—but he secretly kept up a rigorous training regimen all by himself.

RADIOACTIVE ACCIDENT

One fateful day, Matt saw a blind pedestrian about to be struck down by a truck. Matt rushed to the old man's aid, knocking him from the path of the vehicle. In the crash that followed, a canister of radioactive material fell from the truck and struck Matt in the face. Despite the best efforts of the doctors, Matt would thereafter be blind.

However Matt discovered that the accident had a second effect on him: all of his remaining senses had been enhanced to a superhuman degree. Additionally, he now possessed a kind of built-in radar Sense, which allowed him to detect the contours of his environment and compensated for his lack of sight.

Initially overwhelmed by his powers, young Matt sought out the former Ninja master known as Stick, who trained him to control his newfound abilities.

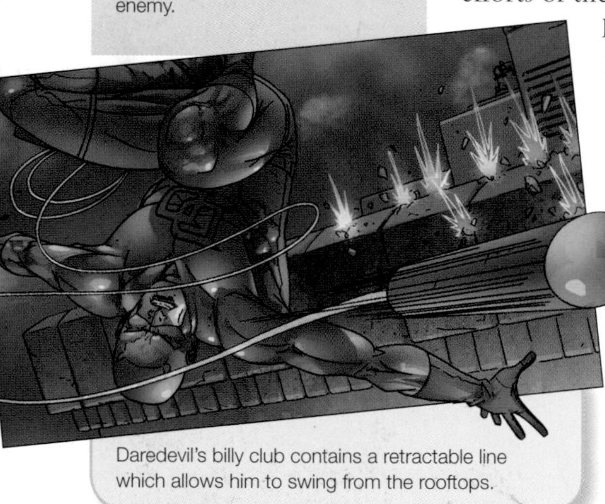

Daredevil's billy club contains a retractable line which allows him to swing from the rooftops.

REVENGE AND THE LAW

In the meantime, Jack Murdock's career had gone downhill, thanks to the Fixer, who paid Murdock's opponents to take dives. Now the Fixer demanded that Jack Murdock throw his next bout. With his son in the audience, Murdock couldn't do it—he defeated his much younger opponent, and was gunned down by the Fixer's men after the fight.

In order to track down the men who had murdered his father, Matt Murdock, now a successful lawyer, adopted the costumed identity of Daredevil, the Man Without Fear. After the Fixer had been brought to justice, Matt continued his crusade, fighting crime in the worst areas of New York City, hunting down by night some of the same perpetrators he would defend in court by day. TD

In college, Matt Murdock fell in love with exchange student Elektra Natchios. The two would one day become implacable foes.

ESSENTIAL STORYLINES

- ***Daredevil #168***
Daredevil has a reunion with his college sweetheart Elektra, now an assassin for hire.
- ***Daredevil #227–232***
The Kingpin methodically tears Matt Murdock's life apart, piece by piece.
- ***Daredevil Vol. 2 #32***
Daredevil's true identity as Matt Murdock is revealed to all the world.

Damage Control

FIRST APPEARANCE Marvel Comics Presents #19 (June 1989)
BASE Manhattan
MEMBERS
Anne Marie Hoag Director of Operations
Henry Ackerdson V.P. Marketing
Albert Cleary Comptroller
Eugene Strausser Head of R&D

Damage Control, Inc. is an engineering and construction company that specializes in cleaning up and repairing property damage caused by conflicts between Super Heroes and Super Villains. With its headquarters in Manhattan's Flatiron Building, and a warehouse in New Jersey, the company has about 300 employees. It was hired by the Avengers to clean up the damage done to their mansion by the Masters of Evil. After the Baxter Building was destroyed, Damage Control was hired to build the Fantastic Four's new HQ, Four Freedom's Plaza. **MT**

Dansen Macabre

FIRST APPEARANCE Marvel Team-Up #93 (May 1980)
REAL NAME Unknown **OCCUPATION** Criminal; exotic dancer; second-in-command of Night Shift **BASE** Los Angeles
HEIGHT 5 ft 10in **WEIGHT** 135 lbs **EYES** Blue **HAIR** Silver
SPECIAL POWERS/ABILITIES Her dancing can hypnotise or even kill; able to evade Spider-Man's telepathic "Spider-Sense."

Dansen Macabre was the high priestess of Kali, a religious cult. When Macabre believed the Shroud to be a member of a rival cult, she hypnotised Spider-Man into attacking him. Her plan failed and the pair defeated her. Realizing the impossibility of imprisoning Macabre, Spider-Man left her in the Shroud's care. She is now second-in-command of Night Shift, the Shroud's supposed criminal gang, unaware that it is a front for his crimefighting. **AD**

Daredevil *SEE OPPOSITE PAGE*

Dark Beast, The

FIRST APPEARANCE X-Men Alpha (1994)
REAL NAME Henry P. McCoy **OCCUPATION** Genetic engineer
BASE Formerly Sinister's slave pens in the "Age of Apocalypse"
HEIGHT 5 ft 11 in **WEIGHT** 355 lbs **EYES** Blue
HAIR Formerly brown, now blue-black
SPECIAL POWERS/ABILITIES Possesses superhuman strength, agility and durability. Expert in genetics and biochemistry.

In the alternate timeline called the "Age of Apocalypse," there was an evil counterpart to the X-Men's Beast. This "Dark Beast" was the head geneticist for that reality's Sinister, and experimented on the inmates in his slave pens. The Dark Beast transported himself to the "mainstream" reality of the X-Men, arriving 20 years in its past. The Dark Beast claims responsibility for genetically engineering the Morlocks. In recent times he captured the X-Men's Beast and impersonated him. (The Dark Beast resembles the other Beast's simian appearance, not his current feline form.) **PS**

Darkhawk

Darkhawk concentrates to use his android body.

While exploring an old amusement park, Christopher Powell discovered an amulet that was extraterrestrial in origin. It instantly exchanged Chris's body for the Darkhawk android, while simultaneous transferring the teenager's consciousness into the artificial construct. When not being used, the Darkhawk android or Chris's own body rested in a state of suspended animation within a living vessel in deep space. Whenever the Darkhawk body was damaged, the ship instantly surrounded it within a healing pod that immediately restored it to full health.

Chris eventually obtained a new android form with new powers, including the ability to become invisible. He managed to copy his mind so he could exist as both Chris and Darkhawk simultaneously, but later had to go back to one body at a time. Darkhawk joined the New Warriors and also helped out the West Coast Avengers. He was one of the Avengers who were captured by Morgan Le Fay and mind-controlled into becoming a member of her guard, but he later helped defeat her. Chris recently joined Excelsior, a group for former teenage heroes struggling with their current lot in life. Though he had vowed that he would never become Darkhawk again, he changed his mind and aided the group when they battled Ultron. **TD**

FACTFILE

REAL NAME
Christopher Powell

OCCUPATION
High-school student

BASE
Queens, New York City

HEIGHT 6 ft 1/2 in
WEIGHT 320 lbs
EYES Brown
HAIR Brown

FIRST APPEARANCE
Darkhawk #1
(Aug 1964)

POWERS
Bio-mechanical armored suit possesses enhanced strength, speed, agility and durability. Also possesses a pair of retractable glider wings and a claw-cable on his right hand that can act as a grappling hook. Can also generate defensive force-shields and concussive blasts of dark energy.

Darkstar

FIRST APPEARANCE Champions #7 (August 1976)
REAL NAME Laynia Petrovna
OCCUPATION Adventurer **BASE** Russia
HEIGHT 5 ft 6 in **WEIGHT** 125 lbs **EYES** Brown **HAIR** Blond
SPECIAL POWERS/ABILITIES Darkstar could tap into the extradimensional Darkforce to create solid objects, to teleport herself and others, and to fly.

Born a mutant, Laynia and her brother Nicolai were turned over to Professor Piotr Phobos, the Russian counterpart of Professor X, who was assembling a team of Russian mutants to serve the state. They became Darkstar and Vanguard. Darkstar was instrumental in defeating Phobos when it emerged that the real purpose of his academy was to increase his own power. Darkstar continued her activities as a Super Heroine in the Winter Guard (*see* Soviet Super-Soldiers), until she perished, with other members of X-Corps, fighting the villain Weapon X11. **TB**

Deadpool

FIRST APPEARANCE New Mutants #98 (February 1991)
REAL NAME Wade Wilson
OCCUPATION Mercenary **BASE** Mobile
HEIGHT 6ft 2in **WEIGHT** 210 lbs **EYES** Brown **HAIR** None
SPECIAL POWERS/ABILITIES Has advanced healing abilities, and is an expert marksman and hand-to-hand-combatant. Uses a teleportation device to travel instantly from one place to another.

When Wade Wilson was diagnosed with cancer, he allowed the scientists of Weapon X—the secret Canadian government project that had created Wolverine and Sabretooth—to try to cure him by attempting to recreate Wolverine's genetic healing ability. The cure was successful, but Wilson's skin was left a mangled mess, and Weapon X placed him in a prison lab as a failed experiment. After killing the guards and escaping, Deadpool began his career as one of the world's deadly mercenaries for hire, battling Cable and X-Force, among others. **MT**

Dazzler

Alison Blaire's father, Carter, was a lawyer and her mother was a jazz singer, who eventually deserted the family. Carter wanted his daughter to follow in his footsteps, but she dreamed of becoming a singer.

Alison's mutant power first manifested itself during a high-school talent show. After graduation she attempted to establish herself professionally and used her powers to create spectacular lighting effects while she sang. Her amazing powers soon helped to make her a star. Although originally Alison had no intention of using her mutant abilities to fight crime, she joined the X-Men after she was publicly exposed as mutant, and her popularity with the public plummeted. She later met and fell in love with Longshot. After he was reported dead, Alison returned to her singing career. **TD**

Rock singer Dazzler's mutant power creates a spectacular light show to match her dynamic vocals.

FACTFILE
REAL NAME
Alison Blaire
OCCUPATION
Singer, actress
BASE
Mobile

HEIGHT 5 ft 8 in
WEIGHT 115 lbs
EYES Blue
HAIR Blonde

FIRST APPEARANCE
X-Men #130 (February 1980)

POWERS
Mutant with the ability to convert sonic vibrations into various forms of light, including blinding, colorful, mind-numbing and hypnotic displays, high impact photon blasts, laser beams, holographic illusions and protective force fields.

The loss of her romantic love, Longshot, led Dazzler to return to her first love—music.

Dean, Laura

FIRST APPEARANCE Alpha Flight Vol. 1 #53 (December 1987)
REAL NAME Laura Dean
OCCUPATION Former adventurer
BASE Formerly Alpha Flight headquarters, Canada
HEIGHT 4 ft 8 in **WEIGHT** 90 lbs **EYES** Brown **HAIR** Black
SPECIAL POWERS/ABILITIES Possesses psionic ability to open portals into another dimension and also close them.

Darby Dean discovered to his horror that one of his wife's unborn twins was a mutant with an inhuman form, and attempted to kill the child. However, the other unborn twin, Laura, used her own mutant powers to save her sister by transporting her to another dimension, which she would later name "Liveworld." In her teens, Laura used her powers to change places with her twin, known as Goblyn. Hence, whenever Goblyn came to Earth, Laura went to Liveworld. Eventually both twins ended up on Earth simultaneously.

Laura and Goblyn then briefly served as members of Beta Flight, the training team for the Alpha Flight hero team, and Laura took the code name Pathway. **PS**

Laura and Goblyn's miserable early lives led to Laura calling Earth "Deadworld."

Death

FIRST APPEARANCE Captain Marvel Vol. 1 #27 (July 1973)
REAL NAME Not applicable
OCCUPATION Embodies principle of mortality **BASE** Mobile
HEIGHT Varies **WEIGHT** Varies **EYES** Varies **HAIR** Varies
SPECIAL POWERS/ABILITIES Often appears as a cowled skeleton, but has adopted various male and female guises; an arch-manipulator; extent of other powers remains unknown.

Just as the abstract being ETERNITY represents life, so Death is said to symbolise mortality, the pair serving to provide cosmic balance. Although they have been embarked on games of one-upmanship (Death once attempted to manipulate THANOS into destroying the universe) in large part Death works in partnership with Eternity to maintain universal equilibrium. When APOCALYPSE established his Four Horsemen, he recruited a number of people to be Death. Wolverine *(pictured right)* was the third individual to fill this role. **AD**

Deathbird

FIRST APPEARANCE Ms. Marvel #9 (September 1977)
REAL NAME Cal'syee Neramani **OCCUPATION** Adventurer
BASE Shi'ar Empire **HEIGHT** 5 ft 8 in **WEIGHT** 180 lbs **EYES** White **HAIR** None; black, purple and blue feathers
SPECIAL POWERS/ABILITIES Flight (18 ft wingspan); vast strength and stamina; razor-sharp talons; wrist-bands contain telescopic javelins; has javelins that emit gas or electric charges.

Deathbird was born a mutant into the ruling house of the SHI'AR; her full set of wings were a throwback to her people's avian ancestry. Her younger sister, Lilandra, aided by the X-MEN, assumed the Shi'ar throne before her, and Deathbird launched several coups in her efforts to become Majestrix. She eventually won the throne, but her rule was short-lived. During the Shi'ar war against the alien Phalanx, Deathbird struck up a short-lived romance with the X-Man BISHOP. Deathbird served as War, one of APOCALYPSE's Horsemen. **AD**

Deathcry

FIRST APPEARANCE Avengers #363 (June 1993)
REAL NAME Deathcry
OCCUPATION Warrior **BASE** The Shi'ar Empire
HEIGHT 6 ft 2 in **WEIGHT** 196 lbs **EYES** White **HAIR** Purple
SPECIAL POWERS/ABILITIES Deathcry possesses super-acute senses, superhuman reflexes, and natural claws which she can use as weapons.

The young warrior known only as Deathcry was dispatched to the AVENGERS' side by Lilandra, Empress of the SHI'AR, who feared reprisals by the KREE race against the Avengers for the role they had played in the Kree-Shi'ar War, in which the Shi'ar emerged victorious. Stripped of her true name due to this assignment, Deathcry journeyed to Earth, where she became an honorary member of the Avengers, aiding the group in fending off a Kree attack, and against other threats. Eventually, feeling that her mission had come to an end, Deathcry asked her teammate HERCULES to return her to the Shi'ar Empire. **TB**

Deathlok

Luther Manning is not the only man to bear the Deathlok mantle.

Luther Manning was born in an alternate timeline in which multinational corporations had used Operation: Purge to rid the Earth of all Super Heroes. A colonel in that world's US Army, Manning was wounded in battle and later transformed into the cyborg Deathlok by brothers Harlan and Simon Ryker. Although they intended to control him, Deathlok somehow managed to break free. With the help of Godwulf, Deathlok was transported to Earth-616, where Operation: Purge had yet to take place. Working with CAPTAIN AMERICA, Deathlok successfully prevented the program from being carried out.

In the years since, a number of other Deathloks have been created, with Michael Collins and Siege (John Kelly) both acting as brain donors. Although the original Deathlok has traveled to numerous realities, even fighting alongside DAREDEVIL for a time, his life continues to be a lonely one. **AD**

FACTFILE
REAL NAME
Luther Manning
OCCUPATION
Cyborg supersoldier
BASE Mobile

HEIGHT 6 ft 4 in
WEIGHT 395 lbs
EYES Red
HAIR Gray/brown

FIRST APPEARANCE:
Astonishing Tales #25 (Aug. 1974)

POWERS
Cybernetic brain and body parts enable superhuman strength, endurance and reactions; Deathlok's special armaments include a dagger and laser pistol.

Death's Head

FIRST APPEARANCE The Transformers #113 (May 1987)
REAL NAME Death's Head
OCCUPATION Bounty hunter **BASE** New York City
HEIGHT Varies **WEIGHT** Varies **EYES** Varies **HAIR** Varies
SPECIAL POWERS/ABILITIES Superhumanly strong; able to detach limbs and substitute for weapons; controls limbs even when separated from body; jets in feet enable short-range flight.

Death's Head is a cyborg originally built by techno-mage Lupex as a shell for his own mind. Lupex' plan was ruined by his wife, who activated the cyborg's consciousness and caused the automaton to flee. Ever since, Death's Head has hopped between realities and time periods. Following an encounter with the Time Lord known as the Doctor he was dumped in the year 8162. Since then he has visited contemporary Earth and Earth of the year 2020, meeting IRON MAN, SPIDER-MAN and the X-MEN. **AD**

De la Fontaine, Contessa

FIRST APPEARANCE Strange Tales #159 (August 1967)
REAL NAME Valentina Allegra de la Fontaine
OCCUPATION Former secret agent **BASE** Mobile
HEIGHT 5 ft 8 in **WEIGHT** 196 lbs
EYES Blue **HAIR** Black with white streak
SPECIAL POWERS/ABILITIES Superb strategist and hand-to-hand combatant; expert with most types of weapons.

Bored with life as a wealthy jet-setter, the Contessa began SHIELD training and caught the eye of Nick FURY by defeating him in a hand-to-hand combat exercise. The two became lovers and teammates, working to help SHIELD put down threats from HYDRA and AIM. The Contessa later led SHIELD's Femme Force, an elite group of female agents. Following SHIELD's takeover by artificial lifeforms called the Deltites, the Contessa helped Fury disband the agency and restructure it. **DW**

Demolition-Man

FIRST APPEARANCE The Thing Vol. 1 #28 (October, 1985)
REAL NAME Dennis Dunphy
OCCUPATION Adventurer **BASE** New York City
HEIGHT 6 ft 3 in **WEIGHT** 335 lbs **EYES** Blue **HAIR** None
SPECIAL POWERS/ABILITIES Enhanced strength and endurance, damage resistance; expert wrestler; trained in hand-to-hand combat by Captain America.

Given superhuman strength by the corrupt POWER BROKER, Dennis Dunphy became a member of the Unlimited Class Wrestling Federation. There, he befriended the THING, and later left the UCWF to become CAPTAIN AMERICA's unofficial partner as the costumed hero D-Man. On a mission to infiltrate the FLAG-SMASHER's Arctic stronghold, D-Man seemingly died in the explosion of an AVENGERS' Quinjet. However, D-Man survived among the Inuit for a time, before returning to New York City and becoming protector of the homeless in the subterranean Zerotown. **DW**

Defenders

The Defenders are a loose affiliation of heroes. In fact, the core four Defenders are often at odds with one another, and only band together when there is no other option available. Initially, the Defenders allied themselves to face the menace posed by an interdimensional scientist-sorcerer named Yandroth, and his Omegatron device which threatened to destroy the world.

Thereafter, when met by circumstances in which they required assistance, the individual Defenders would often seek each other out. Over the years, other heroes have become involved in the activities of this "non-team," notably NIGHTHAWK, the VALKYRIE, and HELLCAT, but despite efforts over the years to officialize the partnership, the individual Defenders remain too different in temperament and outlook to remain a unit for long. **TB**

Despite functioning as a "non-team", the Defenders have formed tight bonds.

THE DEFENDERS
1 Namor, the Sub-Mariner **2** The Hulk
3 The Silver Surfer **4** Doctor Strange

FACTFILE

KEY MEMBERS

DOCTOR STRANGE
Command of the mystic arts.

NAMOR, THE SUB-MARINER
Superhuman strength and durability; ability to fly; ability to breathe air and also survive beneath the ocean waves.

HULK
Rampaging monster of almost unlimited strength.

SILVER SURFER
Possesses the Power Cosmic, one of the fundamental forces of the universe.

BASE
The Defenders team usually operates out of Doctor Strange's sanctum in Greenwich Village, New York City.

FIRST APPEARANCE
Marvel Feature #1 (December 1971)

Destiny

FIRST APPEARANCE X-Men #141 (January 1981)
REAL NAME Irené Adler
OCCUPATION US government agent **BASE** Washington, D.C.
HEIGHT 5 ft 7 in **WEIGHT** 110 lbs **EYES** Unknown **HAIR** Silver
SPECIAL POWERS/ABILITIES Mutant power to see future allowed her to scan the probability spectrum of alternate futures, then focus on events before they happened.

Destiny was a longtime friend of the mutant Mystique. When Mystique formed the second Brotherhood of Evil Mutants, Destiny joined her. When the Brotherhood was renamed Freedom Force and went to work for the US government, Destiny accompanied Mystique on its first mission—the capture of Magneto. She was killed on a later mission by Legion (Professor X's son) who was possessed by the evil Shadow King at the time. **MT**

Devil Dinosaur

FIRST APPEARANCE Devil Dinosaur #1 (April 1978)
REAL NAME Inapplicable **OCCUPATION** Carnivore
BASE A jungle on the otherdimensional planet "Dinosaur World," later the Savage Land
HEIGHT 25 ft **WEIGHT** unknown **EYES** Yellow
SPECIAL POWERS/ABILITIES Has unusually high intelligence for a dinosaur. Possesses superhuman strength and stamina.

On an alien world similar to prehistoric Earth, dinosaurs coexisted with primitive, fur-covered human beings. A tribe called the Killer Folk tried to burn to death a creature that resembled one of Earth's tyrannosaurs. The reptile was rescued by a furry primitive known as Moonboy, but the fire had turned his hide bright red. Moonboy named him Devil Dinosaur, and they became loyal companions, battling various menaces. Later, they were transported to Earth, and joined the superhuman team called the Fallen Angels. Eventually they went to live in the primeval Savage Land. **PS**

Diablo

FIRST APPEARANCE Fantastic Four #30 (September 1964)
REAL NAME Esteban Corazon de Ablo
OCCUPATION Alchemist **BASE** Mobile
HEIGHT 6 ft 3in **WEIGHT** 190 lbs **EYES** Brown **HAIR** Black
SPECIAL POWERS/ABILITIES Alchemical elixir bestows extended life and vitality. Clothing lined with alchemical potions including a sleeping potion and nerve gas; a master of disguise.

Born into the aristocracy in 9th-century Spain, Diablo became fascinated with the alchemical arts. Realizing that time was against him, Diablo sold his soul to the demon Mephisto in exchange for knowledge. Developing an elixir of life and moving to Transylvania, Diablo spent the next millennia tyrannising the local villagers, until they rose up, trapping him in a crypt for over a century. Having tricked the Thing into freeing him, Diablo clashed with the Fantastic Four numerous times. Given his persistent vitality he is likely to remain a threat for years to come. **AD**

Diamondback

FIRST APPEARANCE Captain America #310 (October 1985)
REAL NAME Rachel Leighton
OCCUPATION Professional mercenary **BASE** Serpent Citadel
HEIGHT 5 ft 11 in **WEIGHT** 142 lbs **EYES** Green **HAIR** Magenta
SPECIAL POWERS/ABILITIES Expert gymnast; wields diamond-shaped throwing spikes filled with explosives, acid, poison, or drugs.

Diamondback was enlisted into the Serpent Society by Sidewinder. On her first mission, to track down and kill Modok, leader of AIM, Diamondback had the opportunity to kill Captain America but chose not to. After leaving the Serpent Society she became his partner and eventually his lover. Later, Diamondback joined Asp, Black Mamba, and Impala to form a mercenary group called "Bad Girls, Inc." An android version of Diamondback later teamed up with the Red Skull. **MT**

Digger

FIRST APPEARANCE Amazing Spider-Man Vol. 2 #51 (May 2003)
REAL NAME None (a combination of 13 mobsters)
OCCUPATION None **BASE** New York City sewers
HEIGHT 7 ft 1 in **WEIGHT** 275 lbs **EYES** Blue **HAIR** None
SPECIAL POWERS/ABILITIES Gamma-powered strength, but limited endurance; possesses the combined consciousnesses of the Vegas Thirteen, with their various 1950s predelictions.

In 1957, a meeting of 13 mobsters in Las Vegas turned nasty, resulting in the deaths of all of them. The bodies of the gangsters, who became known as the Vegas Thirteen, were secretly buried deep in the Nevada desert—a common resting place for Vegas' gangland casualties.

Many years later, scientists investigating the effects of gamma rays detonated a gamma bomb in the desert near the site of the grave. Somehow, the bomb's gamma radiation fused the 13 dead mobsters into a huge, powerful, green zombie who called himself Digger. Digger followed some old railroad tracks until he reached New York City. He then started on a mission of vengeance against the Forelli mob, who had bumped off the Vegas Thirteen in the first place. Spider-Man, hired by Forelli to investigate, went to Nevada and figured out that Digger was a gamma-mutated version of the Vegas Thirteen. Back in New York, during a long battle with Spider-Man, Digger eventually broke apart and died. **MT**

Dire Wraiths

FIRST APPEARANCE Rom #1 (December 1979)
BASE Formerly Wraithworld in the Dark Nebula
HEIGHT 5 ft 5 in (average) **WEIGHT** Unrevealed
EYES No pupils **HAIR** Inapplicable
SPECIAL POWERS/ABILITIES Shapeshifters who mimic other living beings. Female Wraiths kill their victims and gain their memories; they also have powers of sorcery.

The Dire Wraiths are offshoots of the SKRULLS who settled on a planet called Wraithworld. Male Wraiths are white-skinned, vaguely humanoid creatures. Female Wraiths have heavier, red bodies, tentacles and clawed feet. Centuries ago, the Wraiths attacked the planet Galador, but were defeated by Galadorian cyborgs called the Spaceknights, including ROM. Rom battled Wraiths on Earth and used his neutralizer to cast Wraithworld into the otherdimensional realm called Limbo. As a result, the Wraiths lost their powers, and Rom exiled them into Limbo as well. **PS**

Doctor Bong

FIRST APPEARANCE Howard the Duck #15 (August 1977)
REAL NAME Lester Verde **OCCUPATION** Genetic engineer
BASE An island in the Atlantic Ocean **HEIGHT** 8 ft 8 in
WEIGHT 225 lbs **EYES** Blue **HAIR** Reddish-brown
SPECIAL POWERS/ABILITIES When struck by the large metal ball he wears on his hand, Doctor Bong's helmet can produce sonic waves for a variety of effects.

Having adopted the aphorism "The pen is mightier than the sword" as his motto at an early age, bullied Lester Verde began to strike back at those who tormented him through his writing. Infatuated with Beverly SWITZLER, Lester reinvented himself as Doctor Bong, a melodramatic villain whose exploits were puffed by self-penned press releases. Intent on forcing Switzler to marry him, Bong was undone by Beverly's boyfriend, HOWARD THE DUCK. He has since gone on to be a thorn in the side of the SHE-HULK. **TB**

Doctor Demonicus

FIRST APPEARANCE Godzilla #4 (December 1977)
REAL NAME Douglas Birely
OCCUPATION Geneticist; criminal **BASE** Pacific Ocean
HEIGHT 5 ft 11 in **WEIGHT** 170 lbs **EYES** Gray **HAIR** Brown
SPECIAL POWERS/ABILITIES A brilliant geneticist who used a radioactive meteor to artificially mutate animals, turning them into monsters to do his bidding; no superpowers.

Geneticist Douglas Birely exposed himself to radiation hoping to acquire superpowers. Instead, he ended up with skin cancer. Embittered, he acquired a radioactive meteor he called the Lifestone, and perfected a process to mutate animals into monsters. As Doctor Demonicus, he recruited an army of criminals and battled SHIELD. He was captured by the West Coast AVENGERS. **MT**

Doc Samson

FACTFILE
REAL NAME
Dr. Leonard Samson
OCCUPATION
Psychiatrist
BASE
Mobile

HEIGHT 6 ft 6 in
WEIGHT 380 lbs
EYES Blue
HAIR Green

FIRST APPEARANCE:
Incredible Hulk #141 (July 1971)

POWERS
Gamma-radiation greatly increased Samson's body mass and musculature; he has the equivalent strength of a "relaxed" Hulk, plus great endurance and injury resistance. The gamma rays also turned his hair green. Unlike the Hulk, Samson's razor-sharp mind has been unaffected by the changes in his physiology.

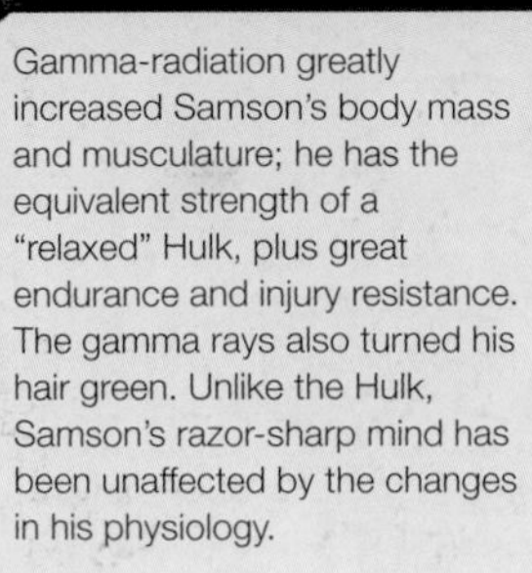

A dedicated psychiatrist, Doctor Leonard Samson was fascinated by gamma radiation's potential to help the mentally ill. When Betty ROSS was transformed into a crystalline creature, Samson used a specially developed machine to drain gamma radiation from the HULK and used it to cure Betty. Later he exposed himself to the remaining stored rays and gained Hulk-like powers.

In the years that followed, Samson has doggedly pursued Bruce Banner, hoping to rid Bruce of the Hulk. Samson's good intentions have not always been welcomed and he and the Hulk have fought repeatedly. At times the pair have been known to work together, fighting the LEADER after his capture of Gamma Base, for example. However, Samson has never lost sight of his primary goal. For the time being it looks like the fates of both Samson and the Hulk are to remain intertwined. **AD**

Doc Samson's good intentions are not welcomed by the Hulk, who likes a good fight.

Doctor Doom

The Lord of Latveria

Victor Von Doom was born in a gypsy camp in the tiny kingdom of Latveria in the Balkan Mountains of Eastern Europe. Victor's mother, Cynthia, was killed when he was an infant. When Victor was a boy, his father Werner, a gypsy healer, failed to save the wife of a Latverian baron from dying of cancer. With Victor, Werner fled the baron's retaliation, only to perish from exposure. Victor vowed vengeance on the world for his parents' deaths.

A mysterious order of Tibetan monks helped Doctor Doom forge the metal mask with which he conceals his hideously scarred features.

FACTFILE

REAL NAME
Victor Von Doom

OCCUPATION
Monarch of Latveria

BASE
Doomstadt, Latveria

HEIGHT 6 ft 2 in; (in armor) 6 ft 7 in
WEIGHT 225 lbs; (in armor) 415 lbs
EYES Brown
HAIR Brown

FIRST APPEARANCE
Fantastic Four #5 (July 1962)

POWERS
Scientific genius; knowledge of sorcery. Learned from alien Ovoids how to psychically transfer his consciousness into the body of another person. armor is actually a battlesuit that increases his strength to superhuman levels and contains highly advanced weaponry.

As king, Doom has brought peace and prosperity to his homeland, Latveria.

SCARRED

Victor discovered Cynthia's chest of magical artifacts and realized that she was a witch. He developed immense talents for sorcery and also science, eventually winning a scholarship for State University in the US. It was there he first encountered fellow student Reed Richards.

Determined to contact his mother in the hereafter, Von Doom invented an interdimensional communication device. Richards happened upon Von Doom's notes on the machine and pointed out an error in his calculations. Furious that Richards had invaded his privacy, Von Doom refused to heed his warning. When Von Doom activated his machine, it exploded, scarring his face. (According to one account the explosion left only one thin scar; however, Doom's ego could not tolerate even a single imperfection in his appearance.)

Doctor Doom led an army of Super Villains on the Beyonder's Battleworld in the first "Secret War."

The Metal Mask

Blaming Richards for the accident, Von Doom made his way to Tibet, where an order of monks helped him forge the metal mask and armor that he would wear in his new role as Doctor Doom. Donning the newly cast mask before it had fully cooled, Doom scarred his face for life. Returning to Latveria, Doom overthrew the monarch and made himself king.

Although Doom lives in a castle and Latveria appears unchanged since the 19th century, he has created technological wonders, including a robot army and a time machine. Doom has dedicated himself to world domination. As monarch of Latveria, he has diplomatic immunity that shields him from arrest. However, his plans have often been thwarted by his archnemesis Reed Richards and the Fantastic Four. Over the years Doom has clashed with many leading costumed crimefighters. **PS**

ESSENTIAL STORYLINES

- ***Fantastic Four #5***
  Doctor Doom first clashes with the world's greatest team.
- ***Fantastic Four Annual #2***
  The origin of Doctor Doom.
- ***Fantastic Four #39–40***
  Doctor Doom battles the Fantastic Four without their powers.
- ***Fantastic Four #57–60***
  Doom steals the power of the Silver Surfer.
- ***Fantastic Four #84–87***
  Doctor Doom traps the Fantastic Four in Latveria.

Doctor Druid

Dr. Druid

FACTFILE

REAL NAME
Dr. Anthony Ludgate Druid

OCCUPATION
Psychiatrist and master of the occult

BASE Mobile

HEIGHT 6 ft 5 in
WEIGHT 310 lbs
EYES Green
HAIR White

FIRST APPEARANCE
Amazing Adventures Vol. 1 #1 (June 1961)

POWERS
Master of the mystical arts; able to control his heartbeat, respiration, bleeding, etc.; can undertake telepathy, scan thoughts, control minds of others, and levitate objects.

For many years Harvard-educated Dr. Anthony Druid pursued a career as a psychiatrist, while harbouring an interest in all things mystical and occult. Growing older he began to devote more and more time to this area but it was only when called to the side of a dying Tibetan lama that he started to develop his abilities. After Druid survived a number of trials, the lama helped him to realise his latent potential while conferring upon the psychiatrist some of his own powers.

In the years that followed Druid was recruited by NSA agent Jake Curtiss to join his team of Monster Hunters, a team that also included Ulysses BLOODSTONE and the Eternal Makkari (*see* ETERNALS). Following the emergence of Super Heroes like the FANTASTIC FOUR, Druid aligned himself with the AVENGERS, becoming a member and helping to drive the MASTERS OF EVIL from Avengers Mansion.

The final years of Druid's life proved far less fulfilling. Twice he was manipulated into betraying his friends—he was held in the thrall of Terminatrix and later corrupted by his manipulative lover, NEKRA. She eventually killed him, his promising life finally ending in grief. **AD**

A powerful sorcerer, Dr. Druid could project images of himself.

Doctor Spectrum

Dr. Spectrum

FACTFILE

REAL NAME
Joseph Ledger

OCCUPATION
Squadron Supreme member

BASE
Squadron City

HEIGHT 6 ft
WEIGHT 190 lbs
EYES Brown
HAIR Blond

FIRST APPEARANCE
Avengers Vol. 1 #85 (March 1971)

POWERS
Internalized power prism permits flight, the discharge of energy blasts, and the ability to construct objects of solid energy.

On a parallel Earth in another dimension, astronaut Joe Ledger rescued an alien SKRULL who gave him a power prism. Using the prism's energies to become the heroic Doctor Spectrum, Ledger joined the SQUADRON SUPREME. After the defeat of the villainous OVERMIND, the Squadron Supreme repaired the damage to their world by becoming virtual dictators. A second group of heroes known as Nighthawk's Redeemers formed a resistance movement. One of their number, the Black Archer (formerly the GOLDEN ARCHER), shattered Doctor Spectrum's power prism with an arrow, only to watch as its energies became part of Ledger's own body. Doctor Spectrum no longer needs to rely on an outside source for his powers, and his body has been changed to a monochromatic white. **DW**

Seen here is Doctor Spectrum in an alternate incarnation.

Various versions of Doctor Spectrum, and other Squadron Supreme members, exist among the parallel Earths that compose the multiverse.

Doctor Octopus

Mastermind of mechanical menace

Otto was the son of Torbert and Mary Lavinia Octavius. He was a shy bookworm, but his father, a construction worker, believed that a man was measured by his brute strength. Mary Lavinia wanted Otto to rely on his brains, and when his father was killed in a construction accident, she convinced herself that an early grave was the destiny of all manual laborers.

ESSENTIAL STORYLINES

- *Amazing Spider-Man Annual #1* Octopus forms the Sinister Six to kill Spider-Man.
- *Spectacular Spider-Man #221* He appears to be killed by Peter Parker clone Kaine.
- *Amazing Spider-Man #426* Doc Ock is restored to life thanks to his protégée Carolyn Trainer.

Doc Ock can use his tentacles simultaneously, with each one performing a different action.

FACTFILE

REAL NAME
Otto Octavius

OCCUPATION
Criminal mastermind, former nuclear scientist

BASE
New York area

HEIGHT 5 ft 9 in
WEIGHT 245 lbs
EYES Brown
HAIR Brown

FIRST APPEARANCE
Amazing Spider-Man #3 (July 1963)

POWERS

Mental control over four electrically powered, 6-ft long, prehensile, titanium steel tentacles that can telescope to 24 ft in length and lift 3 tons; tentacles terminate in three single-jointed pincers that can rotate 360 degrees and grip with a force of 170 lbs per sq. in.

Tentacles can operate independently

Arm's Length

Otto became a scientist specializing in nuclear research and invented a mechanical harness that allowed him to perform dangerous experiments at a distance. He also began dating Mary Alice Anders, a fellow researcher, and even asked her to marry him. Believing that no woman was good enough for her son, Otto's mother forced him to break off the engagement. Shortly afterwards she died of a heart attack while arguing with her son over Mary Alice. Lost in a private world of grief and guilt, Otto caused a laboratory accident: he was bombarded with radiation and his mechanical arms somehow fused with his body.

Ock's tentacles can move at a speed of 90 feet per second and can strike with the force of a jackhammer.

Mind Control

After this accident, Doctor Octopus was misdiagnosed with brain damage. In reality his superior intellect was busily creating new neuro-pathways allowing him to mentally control his metal tentacles. He can now psionically control them even when they have been completely separated from him.

Doctor Octopus, also known as the Master Planner and Master Programmer, first fought and was defeated by Spider-Man shortly after he became a professional criminal. Sometimes as a member of the Sinister Six, sometimes on his own he has since battled heroes such as Daredevil, Captain America and the Fantastic Four; however Doc Ock's overriding obsession is to destroy the elusive web-swinger. **TD**

Doctor Strange

Sorcerer Supreme of Earth's dimension

FACTFILE

Doctor Strange

REAL NAME
Dr. Stephen Vincent Strange

OCCUPATION
Former surgeon, now Sorcerer Supreme of Earth's dimension

BASE
177A Bleecker St., Greenwich Village, Manhattan

HEIGHT 6 ft 2 in
WEIGHT 180 lbs
EYES Grey
HAIR Black; white at temples

FIRST APPEARANCE
Strange Tales #110 (July 1963)

POWERS
Greater mastery of the arts of magic than anyone else in Earth's dimension; astral projection and mental communication. Possesses various magical paraphernalia, including cloak of levitation which enables him to fly, and amulet the Eye of Agamotto.

According to the original account, Doctor Stephen Strange was a highly successful but arrogant surgeon whose brilliant career was abruptly cut short by an automobile accident. Strange suffered minor nerve damage, which prevented him from holding a scalpel steadily enough to perform surgery. Exhausting his fortune searching in vain for a cure, Strange ended up an alcoholic derelict.

The Ancient One not only instructed Stephen Strange in sorcery, but advised and guided him until his death.

ANCIENT WISDOM

Strange journeyed to Tibet to meet a healer known as the Ancient One. Initially, Strange, a man of science, refused to believe in the magic powers that the Ancient One claimed to have. However, Strange discovered the Ancient One's pupil Baron Mordo intended to murder his master. Mordo cast a spell on Strange that prevented him from uttering a warning to the Ancient One, but otherwise allowed him to speak. Not only did Strange now know that magic was real, but he also recognized the existence of evil and realized that it must be fought. Evading the restrictions of Mordo's spell, Strange asked the Ancient One if he could become his pupil. The Ancient One freed Strange from Mordo's spell, revealed that he was well aware of Mordo's treachery, and accepted Strange as his new apprentice.

Another version of Strange's origin claims he was injured in a skiing accident.

Sorcerer Supreme

Upon completing his training, Doctor Strange lived in New York City's Greenwich Village. The public does not believe in magic and considers Strange to be merely an eccentric authority on occult lore. Hence they are unaware that Strange has devoted his life to protecting humanity from supernatural menaces from our own world and mystic realms, such as his enemies Mordo, Nightmare and Dormammu. When the Ancient One died, Doctor Strange inherited his role as Sorcerer Supreme of Earth and the dimension in which it exists.

Doctor Strange has allied himself with Earth's leading costumed crimefighters, such as Spider-Man, the X-Men, and the Avengers. Doctor Strange also founded the Defenders, a team of superhuman champions that often included the Hulk and Namor. **PS**

Strange has long been associated with the Defenders, including Hellcat, the Hulk, Nighthawk, and the Sub-Mariner.

ESSENTIAL STORYLINES
- ***Strange Tales #130–146*** Doctor Strange battles Baron Mordo and Dormammu and first meets Eternity
- ***Strange Tales #150–168*** Doctor Strange first combats Umar and encounters the Living Tribunal.
- ***Doctor Strange (second series) #1–2, 4–5*** Doctor Strange battles Silver Dagger, dies and is resurrected.

Domino

FIRST APPEARANCE X-Force #8 (March 1992)
REAL NAME Neena Thurman (many aliases include "Beatrice")
OCCUPATION Covert operative **BASE** Mobile
HEIGHT 5 ft 8 in **WEIGHT** 196 lbs **EYES** Blue **HAIR** Black
SPECIAL POWERS/ABILITIES Able to influence the laws of probability to shift odds in her favor; weapons expert; her staff fires projectiles; a superb athlete, martial artist, and linguist.

A career mercenary during her early adult life, it was only after being employed as a bodyguard to the genius Milo Thurman that the mutant Domino became drawn into more official circles. She and Milo fell in love, only to be separated when an attack by AIM terrorists forced Milo into deeper cover. Believing that Milo was dead, Domino joined Six-Pack and became an ally of Cable. For a while she was impersonated by Copycat. Domino has since served with X-Factor, worked for the Hong Kong branch of X-Corporation and fought alongside the X-Men. **AD**

Doom 2099

FIRST APPEARANCE Doom 2099 #1 (January 1993)
REAL NAME Victor Von Doom
OCCUPATION Monarch **BASE** Latveria, in the year 2099
HEIGHT 6 ft 2 in **WEIGHT** 225 lbs **EYES** Brown **HAIR** Brown
SPECIAL POWERS/ABILITIES Superhuman strength; can put up a force field and fire concussion beams; also has some psionic and mystical power, and can exchange minds with another person.

In 2099, a man claiming to be the original Dr. Doom returned to the nation of Latveria. He had no memory of how he came to be transported into the future. Upon his arrival, Doom discovered that a man named Tiger Wylde, an elite corporate muscle man, had seized the throne of Latveria, declaring himself dictator. Wylde had caused the people to fall into violence and poverty, but Doom overthrew the pretender and once again made Latveria a great nation. **MT**

Dormammu

Although a member of the Faltine race, Dormammu has spent most of his life in the Dark Dimension, where his people had banished him. Following his arrival there, Dormammu allied himself to the Dark Dimension's ruler, Olnar, showing him how to expand his realm by absorbing other pocket universes into it. Inadvertently, this was to precipitate Dormammu's rise to power. One of these universes was occupied by the Mindless Ones, destructive beings that, once released in the Dark Dimension, began to wreak havoc. Before they were finally stopped, Olnar was killed and Dormammu had been named regent.

FACTFILE
REAL NAME
Dormammu
OCCUPATION
Sometime ruler of the Dark Dimension
BASE
Dark Dimension

HEIGHT 6 ft 1 in
WEIGHT Unknown
EYES Green
HAIR Black

FIRST APPEARANCE
Strange Tales Vol. 1 #126 (November 1964)

POWERS
One of the most powerful mystical beings in the universe; can teleport between dimensions, alter his size, travel in time, and perform telepathy.

Flames blazing from every limb, Dormammu is a fearsome being.

His appetite for power still not satisfied, Dormammu set his sights on conquering Earth but repeated attempts to invade were repelled by various mystical beings, including the Ancient One and, later, Dr Stephen Strange. Although less powerful than Dormammu, Strange has defeated him on several occasions, even trapping him in a separate pocket universe for a time. Hugely powerful, Dormammu is a difficult creature to destroy altogether. Although quelled at present, he is likely to re-emerge at some point in the future. **AD**

Dormammu is a little hotheaded.

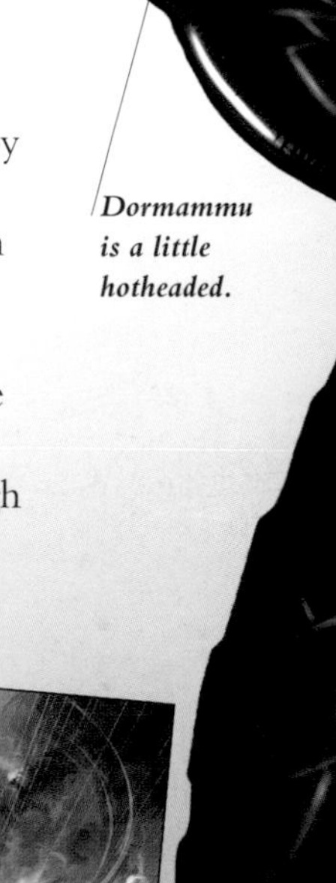
Only Dr. Strange stands in the way of Dormammu's domination of the Dark Dimension and a strike against the Earth itself.

Dracula

The most powerful vampire on Earth

Dracula

FACTFILE

REAL NAME
Vlad Tepes Dracula

OCCUPATION
Ruler of Earth's vampires

BASE
Castle Dracula, Transylvania; otherwise mobile

HEIGHT 6 ft 5 in
WEIGHT 220 lbs
EYES Red
HAIR Black

FIRST APPEARANCE
Tomb of Dracula #1 (April 1972)

POWERS
Drains blood from victims by biting, enabling him to control their wills. Those who die become vampires. Has superhuman strength, virtual immortality, and cannot be killed by conventional means. Transforms into a bat, wolf, or mist. Can mentally control other vampires and mesmerize human beings.

Vlad Tepes Dracula was born in 1430 in Schassberg, Transylvania. The following year his father, the Transylvanian nobleman Vlad Dracul, became prince of nearby Wallachia. Dracula's father was later assassinated by other Transylvanians. Dracula nevertheless went through with the marriage his father had arranged with Zofia, a Hungarian noblewoman. After the birth of their daughter, Dracula put an end to their marriage. Zofia committed suicide; her daughter would become the vampiress Lilith.

THE IMPALER

Dracula regained the throne of Wallachia in 1456, and had those responsible for his father's assassination impaled. He then fought a war with the Turks, during which he impaled huge numbers of them. Hence Dracula became known as "Vlad the Impaler." Dracula married his second wife, Maria, who bore him a son, Vlad Tepelus.

In 1459, Dracula was defeated in battle by the Turkish warlord Turac, who mortally wounded him. Turac took Dracula to the gypsy healer Lianda, who proved to be a vampiress and bit and killed Dracula, transforming him into a vampire. After Turac murdered Maria, Dracula slew him and turned his son Vlad Tepelus over to the care of gypsies. By defeating the vampire Nimrod, Dracula took his place as the ruler of Earth's vampires. The eldest vampire on Earth, Varnae, enhanced Dracula's blood with his own before killing himself. As a result Dracula became the most powerful vampire on the planet.

Dracula's most persistent modern adversaries were (from left to right) the team of Quincy Harker, Frank Drake, Rachel Van Helsing, and Blade.

THE VAMPIRE HUNTERS

In 1890 Dracula employed British solicitor Jonathan Harker to buy Carfax Abbey in England. Moving there, Dracula attacked Harker's fiancée Mina Murray. Vampire hunter Abraham Van Helsing intervened and led the pursuit of Dracula to Transylvania, where Van Helsing's allies impaled the vampire. However, Dracula has repeatedly returned from real or apparent death, and he has continued to menace humanity into the 21st century.

In recent years, Dracula's nemeses were a team led by Jonathan Harker's son, Quincy. Among his allies were Rachel Van Helsing, Abraham's descendant; Dracula's own descendant Frank Drake; and the vampire hunter Blade. Quincy Harker and Rachel Van Helsing have died, but Drake and Blade continue the hunt. Dracula has also battled such adversaries as Doctor Strange, the vampire detective Hannibal King, and the monster hunter Elsa Bloodstone. **PS**

ESSENTIAL STORYLINES
- ***Dracula Lives #2–3*** How Count Dracula first became a vampire
- ***Tomb of Dracula #45–59*** Dracula married Domini and fathers Janus, who rapidly becomes an adult who opposes him.
- ***Tomb of Dracula #64–70*** Dracula becomes human again. After regaining his powers, Dracula and Quincy Harker die in their final confrontation.

Drake, Frank

FIRST APPEARANCE Tomb of Dracula Vol. 1 #1 (April 1972)
REAL NAME Frank Drake
OCCUPATION Private Investigator; former vampire hunter
BASE Boston, Massachusetts
HEIGHT 6 ft **WEIGHT** 165 lbs **EYES** Blue **HAIR** Blond
SPECIAL POWERS/ABILITIES Adept at hand-to-hand fighting and a fair marksman.

A distant descendent of Dracula, Frank Drake's life was dogged by his vampiric ancestor. After frittering his considerable inheritance away, all Drake had left was his family's castle in Transylvania. Traveling there with an aim to selling up, Drake accidentally resurrected Dracula. The following years were marked by a series of battles against the undead fiend. Fighting alongside other vampire hunters, including Blade, Rachel Van Helsing and Quincy Harker, Frank met and lost many good friends and lovers. Exhausted by the fight, he eventually retired from vampire-hunting to become a private eye in Boston. AD

Dragon Man

FIRST APPEARANCE Fantastic Four #1 (February 1965)
REAL NAME Dragon Man
OCCUPATION None **BASE** Mobile
HEIGHT 15 ft 3 in **WEIGHT** 3.2 tons **EYES** Gray **HAIR** None
SPECIAL POWERS/ABILITIES Possesses colossal natural strength. He can exhale flame from his mouth, and his gigantic wings enable him to fly.

An artificial lifeform created by Professor Gregson Gilbert of State University and brought to life by Diablo the alchemist, Dragon Man has the intelligence of a dog. He has been used as a pawn by various Super Villains, including Diablo himself, the wealthy industrialist Gregory Gideon, and Machinesmith. But Dragon Man is not evil himself—he operates strictly by animal instinct. On occasion, the Fantastic Four have attempted to adopt Dragon Man as a pet, but he has proven to be too accidentally destructive to domesticate easily. TB

Dragon of the Moon

FIRST APPEARANCE The New Defenders #143 (May 1985)
REAL NAME Unrevealed **OCCUPATION** Demon
BASE Mobile **HEIGHT** Unknown **WEIGHT** Unknown
EYES Red **SCALES** Dark blue
SPECIAL POWERS/ABILITIES The Dragon is a virtually immortal, demonic entity with god-like powers; able to influence other beings to commit evil deeds.

The Dragon psychically bonded itself to Moondragon.

The sole survivor of an ancient race of demons, the Dragon of the Moon seeks to gain power by corrupting the human race. The Dragon once allied with Mordred, who was trying to overthrow King Arthur Pendragon of Britain, but it was defeated and imprisoned within Saturn's moon Titan by the Eternals. The Dragon later managed to corrupt Thanos, who murdered most of the population of Titan. It also began to corrupt Moondragon. With the aid of the Defenders, Moondragon was freed and the Dragon destroyed. However, it remains to be seen if the Dragon is really dead. TD

Drax the Destroyer

Mentor, the powerful Titanian, had been monitoring the reckless actions of his mad son Thanos on Earth.

When Thanos destroyed a car containing Arthur Douglas and his wife and daughter, fearing that they had seen his spaceship, Mentor took Douglas's daughter Heather, who was still alive, back to Titan to be raised. She would later return to Earth as Moondragon.

Then, with the aid of his father, Chronos, Mentor took the living consciousness of Arthur Douglas before it had completely left his body and placed it into a humanoid body he had created from the Earth's soil, granting it superhuman powers. This new being was known as Drax the Destroyer. Mentor blocked all of Douglas's human memories and instilled in him a single-minded desire to destroy Thanos. Once Thanos was killed, however, Drax wandered space searching for a new reason to exist. Drax was killed while trying to stop Moondragon from controlling the planet Ba-Banis, but later resurrected and roamed the galaxy once more. MT

Drax pauses after his latest session of carnage, plotting the next steps in his all-consuming quest to completely destroy Thanos.

FACTFILE

REAL NAME
Arthur Douglas

OCCUPATION
Former real estate agent; agent of Chronos

BASE
Titan

HEIGHT 6 ft 4 in
WEIGHT 680 lbs
EYES Red
HAIR None

FIRST APPEARANCE
Iron Man #55 (February 1973)

POWERS
Cosmic energy gives him superhuman strength, invulnerability, the ability to fly and make interplanetary voyages in a matter of weeks. He can survive for an indefinite time in outer space without air, food, or water. He fires concussive blasts from his hands.

Dreadknight

FIRST APPEARANCE Iron Man #101 (August 1977)
REAL NAME Bram Velsing
OCCUPATION Engineer; vengeful vigilante **BASE** Mobile
HEIGHT 5 ft 8 in **WEIGHT** 160 lbs **EYES** Red **HAIR** None
SPECIAL POWERS/ABILITIES High-tech suit of armor protects him from attack. Among his arsenal are a lance containing a number of offensive weapons, and a nerve-gas pistol.

Born in Latveria, Bram Velsing was a skilled engineer, carrying out the schemes of Doctor Doom. As punishment for an act of disobedience, Doom had an iron mask fused to Velsing's face, so that he would know what it meant to be Doom. Fleeing Latveria, Velsing took refuge in the castle of Victor Frankenstein. Calling himself Dreadknight, armed with his own inventions, and riding a winged horse that once belonged to the Black Knight, he vowed to take revenge on his former master—no matter how many innocent people got hurt along the way. **TB**

Dreadnought

FIRST APPEARANCE Strange Tales #154 (May 1940)
REAL NAME Dreadnought
OCCUPATION Weapons system **BASE** New York State
HEIGHT 8 ft **WIDTH** 40 in **WEIGHT** 2,200 lbs
SPECIAL POWERS/ABILITIES Portable fusion generator ensures 1.5 years of continuous use; travels at 35 mph; lifts up to 10 tons; armed with flamethrower, knuckle spikes, and electrical field.

A robotic juggernaut, the Dreadnought was built by the terror group HYDRA, but its first field trial proved unsuccessful: directed to kill Nick Fury, the SHIELD director's resourcefulness, combat training and arsenal of miniaturised weaponry combined to overwhelm the automaton. This wasn't the end of the machine, however; when the Maggia crime family stole the Dreadnought blueprints, eight more of these machines were built, the most sophisticated being a silver version of the robot. Numerous Super Heroes have contended with these new Dreadnoughts, including Iron Man, Spider-Man and the Fantastic Four, and each time the heroes have proved triumphant. **AD**

Dreamqueen

Eight hundred years ago, Nightmare, ruler of the dream dimension, captured a succubus called Zhilla Char, mated with her, and then confined her in a pocket dimension. Zhilla Char was consumed by flames giving birth to her daughter, the Dreamqueen. Three hundred and fifty years ago the Native American shaman Nanquato's astral self traveled into the Dreamqueen's realm in search of the sky gods that could save his tribe from drought. Believing the Dreamqueen to be a sky god, Nanquato accepted a totem from her. Through this totem, the Dreamqueen terrified Nanquato's tribe with hallucinations, as a means to escape to Earth. But her plan was thwarted when Nanquato's tribesmen slew the shaman and buried the totem.

In recent years, the mutant Laura Dean visited the Dreamqueen's dimension, which Dean named "Liveworld." The Canadian Super Hero team Alpha Flight inadvertently traveled to Liveworld, and when they returned to Earth, the Dreamqueen came with them. However, Alpha Flight's Puck and Laura Dean succeeded in forcing her back to Liveworld. By afflicting Alpha Flight with nightmares, the Dreamqueen escaped to Earth, where she took control of the minds of the people of the Canadian city of Edmonton. But Alpha Flight's sorceress Talisman defeated her and drove her from Earth. Still later, the Dreamqueen sided with Alpha Flight against their enemy, the Master. **PS**

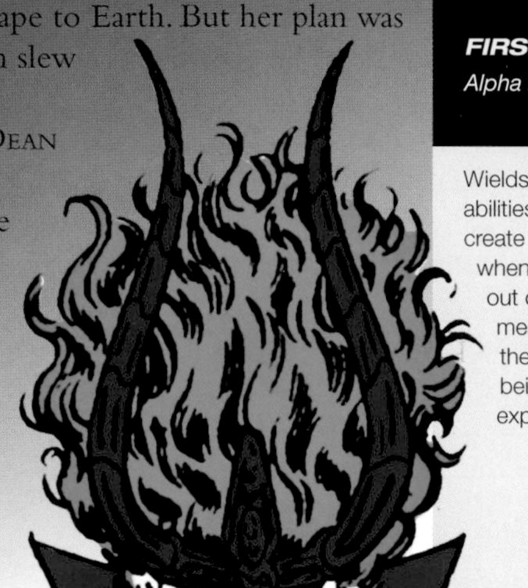

FACTFILE
REAL NAME
Unrevealed
OCCUPATION
Ruler of Liveworld
BASE
The dimension of Liveworld

HEIGHT Variable, normally 6 ft 3 in
WEIGHT Variable
EYES White
HAIR Green

FIRST APPEARANCE
Alpha Flight Vol. 1 #57 (April 1988)

DREAMQUEEN

POWERS

Wields virtually unlimited magical abilities, including the ability to create living beings, but only when she is in Liveworld. In or out of Liveworld, she can mentally control the minds and the perceptions of other beings, and cause them to experience hallucinations.

Drew, Jonathan

FIRST APPEARANCE Spider-Woman Vol 1, #1 (April 1978)
REAL NAME Jonathon Drew
OCCUPATION Scientist **BASE** Wundagore City
HEIGHT 6 ft 2 in **WEIGHT** 196 lbs **EYES** Blue **HAIR** Black
SPECIAL POWERS/ABILITIES Brilliant scientist who specializes in radiation and entomology—the study of spiders and insects.

A gifted scientist with a beautiful wife and child, the world was Jonathan Drew's oyster. Moving to the Balkans with Drew's colleague, Herbert Wyndham, his family was struck down by tragedy: Drew's daughter, Jessica, became critically ill with radiation poisoning and his wife died mysteriously. Unable to cope, Drew fled to England, leaving his daughter in Wyndham's hands. Years later, Drew also died in tragic circumstances. After developing a radiation antidote for Pyrotechnics, Inc, he was killed by his employers. It was left to Jessica Drew—now the first Spider Woman—to avenge his death. **AD**

Drew, Patience

FIRST APPEARANCE Marvel Fanfare Vol 1, #43 (April 1989)
REAL NAME Unknown
OCCUPATION Pirate Captain **BASE** Sargasso Sea
HEIGHT Unknown **WEIGHT** Unknown **EYES** Blue **HAIR** Black
SPECIAL POWERS/ABILITIES Skilled in the use of sabres, swords and pistols, and other weapons of her time. Possessed the same skills in death.

Patience Drew was a pirate captain who lived several hundred years ago. She and her crew were killed by a British ship which led them into a trap during battle. After they sunk into the Sargasso sea, they were doomed to experience their deaths forever. Namor rescued Drew and her ship on one of these occasions and the pair fell in love. Namor joined Drew as a pirate and she gave him an earring to remember her by. Later, Namor left her ship and never returned—despite still wearing her earring, he found her skeleton on the seabed and was uncertain whether he had ever known her. **ED**

D'spayre

FIRST APPEARANCE Marvel Team-Up Vol. 1 #68 (April 1978)
REAL NAME Unknown **OCCUPATION** Demonic being
BASE Extradimensional tower **HEIGHT** 6 ft 3 in
WEIGHT Unknown **EYES** Black **HAIR** None
SPECIAL POWERS/ABILITIES Enhanced strength; able to levitate; able to instill fear into other beings; various other unrevealed magical abilities.

D'spayre is an extradimensional demon created by another demon, the Dweller-in-Darkness. He feeds off the psychic energy of suffering. D'spayre has teamed with Nightmare, and is attended by a horde of small servant-beings, the D'sprites. One of D'spayre's first clashes with Super Heroes took place in the Florida Everglades, where he was defeated by Spider-Man and Man-Thing. He has since fought Cyclops, Doctor Strange, and served as a member of the Fear Lords, an alliance of demons. **DW**

Dugan, Dum Dum

FIRST APPEARANCE Sgt Fury and his Howling Commandos #1 (May 1963) **REAL NAME** Timothy Aloysius Cadwallader Dugan **OCCUPATION** Ex-SHIELD agent
BASE New York City **HEIGHT** 6 ft 2 in
WEIGHT 196 lbs **EYES** Blue **HAIR** Black
SPECIAL POWERS/ABILITIES Expert boxer, wrestler, marksman, and commando.

Touring 1941 Europe as a circus strongman, "Dum Dum" Dugan encountered Nick Fury, who was on a covert mission. Dugan struck up a strong, durable friendship with Fury. Throughout the war, the pair fought together in the military strike force, the Howling Commandos, and following Fury's appointment as director of the government agency SHIELD, Dugan served as one of his top operatives. When his health finally hobbled him, Dugan intended to live out his days with his family, but a contented retirement proved impossible—his wife was killed by a HYDRA splinter group and he rejoined SHIELD. **AD**

Dusk

FIRST APPEARANCE Slingers #0 (December 1998)
REAL NAME Cassie St. Commons
OCCUPATION Adventurer **BASE** New York City
HEIGHT 5 ft 6 in **WEIGHT** 125 lbs **EYES** Blue **HAIR** Black
SPECIAL POWERS/ABILITIES Receives power from the Negative Zone allowing her to melt into shadows or to teleport; possesses minor psychic abilities.

During a time when Spider-Man was accused of murder, he adopted four separate costumes and identities, including one called Dusk. Later, former World War II hero Black Marvel gave the costumes to four youths to create the Slingers. Cassie St. Commons, a moody Empire State University student from a rich family, became the new Dusk. After what seemed a fatal fall, she returned with the power of teleportation. The Slingers disbanded after saving Black Marvel's soul from Mephisto, and Dusk has since kept a low profile. **DW**

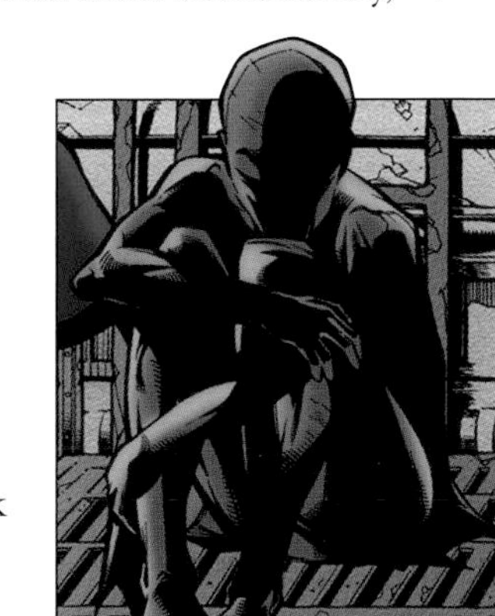

Earth Lord

FIRST APPEARANCE Thor #395 (September 1988)
REAL NAME Kyle Brock **OCCUPATION** Policeman
BASE New York City **HEIGHT** (as Brock) 6 ft 1 in; (as Earth Lord) 12 ft 2 in to unknown limit **WEIGHT** (as Brock) 194 lbs; (as Earth Lord) varies **EYES** Brown **HAIR** Brown
SPECIAL POWERS/ABILITIES Draws strength and mass from the Earth. Can increase his size and strength to superhuman levels.

Shot in the line of duty, Officer Brock was rushed to hospital, the same hospital where the god Hogun (*see* Gods of Asgard) was staying. He and two other dying patients attracted the attention of Seth, god of death (*see* Gods of Heliopolis), who claimed that Hogun was a threat to the Earth. Seth branded their left palms with the sign of Aton, the disc of the sun, and gave them superhuman powers. Brock and his teammates learned that Seth was the real menace and helped Thor defeat him. Brock returned to the police force, but becomes Earth Lord when necessary. **TD**

Eel

FIRST APPEARANCE Strange Tales #112 (October 1963)
REAL NAME Leopold Stryke **OCCUPATION** Criminal
BASE New York City **HEIGHT** 5 ft 10 in **WEIGHT** 192 lbs
EYES Brown **HAIR** Brown
SPECIAL POWERS/ABILITIES The Eel's costume contains devices that generate and shoot electrical charges; also contains layer of nearly frictionless synthetic fabric.

Leopold Stryke was the curator of an aquarium who turned to crime as the Eel. After being defeated by Johnny Storm, the Human Torch, the Eel worked as henchman for Mister Fear and for Count Nefaria. Later, Stryke joined his brother Jordan, the Viper, in the Serpent Squad. Finally, the Eel was murdered by another criminal, the Gladiator. Edward Lavell became a second Eel, gaining notoriety by battling the team of Power Man and Iron Fist. **PS**

Ecstasy

FIRST APPEARANCE Doctor Strange Vol. 1 #74 (December 1985)
REAL NAME Renée Deladier
OCCUPATION Drug kingpin **BASE** Marseilles, France
HEIGHT 5 ft 9 in **WEIGHT** 130 lbs **EYES** Green **HAIR** Blonde
SPECIAL POWERS/ABILITIES Formerly possessed the ability to project semi-solid tentacles of darkness, or to absorb beings into the Darkforce dimension.

Ecstasy, who can wield tendrils of Darkforce energy, proves more than a match for the light-generating heroine Dagger.

Renée Deladier, who headed up a French cartel distributing the drug ecstasy, adopted the drug's name as her alias. The vigilante Cloak tried to punish her by absorbing her into the Darkforce dimension, but instead the sentience inhabiting the Darkforce selected Ecstasy to be its new agent, and absorbed Cloak instead, transferring his powers to Ecstasy. Doctor Strange came to Cloak's assistance, and with the help of the Eye of Agamotto, Cloak was able to defeat Ecstasy and regain his powers. **DW**

Egghead

Egghead

FACTFILE

REAL NAME
Elihas Starr

OCCUPATION
Criminal; scientist

BASE
New York City

HEIGHT 5 ft 7 in
WEIGHT 210 lbs
EYES Blue
HAIR None

FIRST APPEARANCE
Tales to Astonish #38 (December 1962)

POWERS
Egghead created machines to enable communication with ants, powerful robots, and mind-controlling, prosthetic limbs; prone to delusions of grandeur and obsessed with destroying rival Henry Pym.

A brilliant scientist, Elihas Starr—or Egghead as he was known because of his unusually-shaped head—lacked a conscience and was prone to boredom. Seeking extra excitement, Egghead had been working for the US government when he was sacked for stealing and selling secrets.

Coming to the attention of the New York mobs, Egghead was contracted to rid them of the original Ant-Man, otherwise known as Henry Pym. In the years that followed, the pair were to become arch enemies. Egghead's strenuous efforts to destroy Ant-Man involved a range of intriguing devices: he built a machine to communicate with ants and persuaded them to turn against Pym, and on another occasion, he developed a bionic arm designed to control the thoughts of Pym's niece.

Although he often appeared fairly harmless, during his criminal career Egghead has been responsible for the destruction of an entire Mid-western town, an incident that brought him into direct conflict with the Avengers team of Super Heroes. As time went on, Egghead's schemes became ends in themselves: the more complex and convoluted they were, the happier he seemed to be. Had it not been for a gun exploding in his face, Egghead's schemings would probably have continued. Instead, the accident brought to an end both his life and his latest attempt to savage Henry Pym's reputation. **AD**

So much did he hate Harry Pym, nothing would stop Egghead from trying to get revenge—not even the prison bars.

Motivated by his hatred of Henry Pym, Egghead was inspired to create a device to communicate with ants.

Ego the Living Planet

FIRST APPEARANCE Thor #132 (September 1966)
REAL NAME Ego
OCCUPATION Not applicable **BASE** Mobile
DIAMETER 4,165 miles
SPECIAL POWERS/ABILITIES Vast intelligence and psionic powers, including telepathy and telekinesis; travels through space faster than light and can change its surface appearance.

Ego is a self-aware planet, which although formed from the same cosmic gases and dust resulting from the Big Bang as other planets, somehow also grew a huge brain. About the size of a small moon, Ego is from the Black Galaxy. Ego created armies of superhuman warriors from its own substance, which it sent to conquer other worlds. During a battle with Galactus, Thor sided with Ego, but later realized Ego's evil intentions and battled it with Galactus, Hercules, and Firelord. Eventually, Ego's size was condensed and contained within the body of the Super Hero Quasar. **MT**

Elders of the Universe

The Elders of the Universe are among the oldest sentient creatures in the universe. Although they do not belong to the same race, they have come to regard one another as brothers. This is because their lifespans date back to the formation of the first primordial galaxies, and because they have each chosen an area of speciality with which to fill their eons-long lives. In this way they manage to overcome the inevitable boredom that would otherwise accompany their virtual immortality.

The exact number of Elders in existence is not known, but several of their number have had dealings with the Super Heroes of Earth, including the Grandmaster, the Collector, the Gardener, the Contemplator, and the Champion. **TB**

Each Elder of the Universe has a specialty. The Grandmaster, for example, devotes his time to games of cosmic chance, while the Gardener is obsessed with the growing of beautiful plant life.

Electro

While working as a lineman for an electrical company during a thunderstorm, Max Dillon received a shock that endowed him with superhuman powers. He became the villain Electro. On his first outing, Electro robbed *Daily Bugle* publisher J. Jonah Jameson, who was sure that Electro was Spider-Man in disguise. To clear his name, Spider-Man defeated Electro by short-circuiting his powers with a water stream. Electro then allied himself with criminal teams, including the Sinister Six and the Frightful Four.

A chronic inferiority complex caused by an unhappy childhood led Electro to absorb all the power in downtown Manhattan, until calmed by Spider-Man. He then attempted to overload all of New York City's power stations until Spider-Man, wearing a specially insulated costume, bested him.

Electro recently broke Sauron and a number of other criminals out of the Raft prison, but wound up behind bars for his pains. **DW**

FACTFILE
REAL NAME
Maxwell Dillon
OCCUPATION
Professional criminal
BASE
New York City

HEIGHT 5 ft 11 in
WEIGHT 165 lbs
EYES Blue
HAIR Reddish-brown

FIRST APPEARANCE
Amazing Spider-Man Vol. 1 #9 (February 1964)

POWERS
Electro can store, release, and manipulate electricity to fire electric bolts, travel along power lines, and control machinery.

Electro can transmit so much electricity through the bodies of others that he can literally cook them from the inside out. The upper limit of his powers has never been established.

Mentally unbalanced Electro can shape electricity into whips, tendrils, and nets.

ELEKTRA

Assassin-for-hire

FACTFILE

REAL NAME
Elektra Natchios

OCCUPATION
Mercenary assassin

BASE
Mobile

HEIGHT 5 ft 9 in
WEIGHT 130 lbs
EYES Blue-Black
HAIR Black

FIRST APPEARANCE
Daredevil Vol 1 #168
January 1981

POWERS

Awesome martial arts skills, particularly proficient in Ninjutsu; skilled with martial art weaponry, especially the sai; Olympic-standard gymnast and athlete; limited telepathic abilities and partial control of nervous system.

From their first encounter, Elektra's fate was bound to Matt Murdock's.

The histories of so many superpowered individuals are marred by tragedy. While in some cases these tragedies drive them towards heroism others are compelled to pursue careers of villainy. For Electra Natchios this choice has never been clear-cut—while she continues to yearn for contentment, time and again her happiness has been spoiled by the intervention of others.

Elektra was not the first to be resurrected by the Hand. That fate fell to 16th-century warrior, Eliza Martinez.

ETCHED BY SADNESS

Even before she was born, misfortune was etched into Elektra's existence: her mother was shot while pregnant and died soon after giving birth. When Elektra's overprotective father became Greek ambassador to the US, she enrolled at Columbia University in New York City, but was followed everywhere by security guards.

Despite this restriction, a romance grew between Elektra and Matt Murdock, a fellow student. For a year, a clandestine relationship flourished, but when her father was killed during a hostage incident Elektra's whole world fell apart. Riven with grief she fled, leaving Matt and the US behind.

Armed with her trademark sai, few have stood against Elektra and survived.

Fatally injured, Elektra crawls to Matt's apartment to die.

KILLER FOR HIRE

In the years that followed Elektra trained as a Ninja, hoping to ease her tortured soul. For a year she belonged to the Chaste, a Ninja order led by Matt Murdock's own mentor, STICK. Ultimately, Elektra's "impure" heart disqualified her from membership, this rejection driving her to the Chaste's enemy—the HAND, an order of assassins. Elektra abandoned them and became an assassin for hire. This gruesome work ironically led her back to Matt Murdock, now established as the crime-fighter DAREDEVIL. Once lovers, they were now opponents but despite this, when Elektra was mortally wounded by BULLSEYE, it was to Matt's door that she crawled and in his arms that she died.

ELEKTRA REBORN

Matt refused to believe Elektra was dead and became involved in the Hand's attempt to resurrect her. Fighting alongside Stick, he tried to prevent the Hand from bringing Elektra back to life and claiming her soul. He failed to prevent her return, but his love purified her soul, making her useless to the Hand. Whether Elektra's path will ultimately end in heroism or villainy remains uncertain. **AD**

Following her resurrection, a purified Elektra fought evil, garbed in a white costume.

KEY STORYLINES

- ***Daredevil #168–9*** Elektra's first encounter with Matt Murdock; her origin is revealed.
- ***Daredevil #174–181*** Elektra fights the Hand with Matt, is recruited by the Kingpin, and dies at the hands of Bullseye.
- ***Daredevil #190*** Elektra is reborn and more about her past is revealed.
- ***Elektra Vol. 2 #11–15*** As her addiction to violence reaches new heights, relatives of Elektra's victims seek revenge.

Ellis, Ken

FIRST APPEARANCE Web of Spider-Man #118 (November 1994)
REAL NAME Kenneth Ellis
OCCUPATION Reporter **BASE** New York City
HEIGHT 5 ft 10 in **WEIGHT** 165 lbs **EYES** Brown **HAIR** Brown
SPECIAL POWERS/ABILITIES Professional journalistic skills; useful talent for coming up with a memorable moniker for a costumed hero or villain, or an eye-catching headline.

Ken Ellis was a reporter for the *Daily Bugle*, a major New York City newspaper published by the redoutable J. Jonah Jameson. He has reported on various stories involving the costumed crimefighter Spider-Man.

When Spider-Man's clone, Ben Reilly, adopted his first costumed identity, it was Ellis who named the new crimefighter "The Scarlet Spider" in one of his Daily Bugle" articles.

Since this high point in his journalistic career, however, Ellis has become less prominent in the New York newspaper business. **PS**

Emplate

FIRST APPEARANCE Generation X #1 (November 1994)
REAL NAME Marius St. Croix
OCCUPATION None **BASE** Mobile
HEIGHT 6 ft 3 in **WEIGHT** Variable **EYES** Red **HAIR** Gray
SPECIAL POWERS/ABILITIES Must consume the marrow of mutants to prevent being pulled into a pocket dimension of untold tortures; absorbs the abilities of each mutant he feeds on for a time.

The sister of Monet St. Croix of Generation X, Emplate's mutant power flung him into a pocket dimension, where his physical body was ravaged. Only by feeding on the marrow of the mutant Penance was he able to return to our world, albeit encased in a respirator unit he now needed to survive. In order to remain in our dimension, Emplate must constantly renew himself from the marrow of other mutants, and he specifically targeted Generation X after Penance was delivered into their care, allying himself with others who bore the team a similar grudge, such as the New Hellions. **TB**

Exiled to a horrific other dimension, Emplate could only remain in our reality by consuming the bone marrow of mutants like himself.

Empath

Empath is the son of a poor Castilian noble who can trace his ancestry back to ancient Rome. As a member of the mutant team the Hellions, Empath was trained in the use of his superhuman powers by Emma Frost, the White Queen of the Hellfire Club. But when Empath provided assistance to Thunderbird in his attack on the X-Men, Emma Frost temporarily removed Empath's powers. Seeking revenge for this, Empath helped arrange the kidnapping of Magma and Sunspot of the New Mutants by the Gladiator. **MT**

FACTFILE
REAL NAME
Manuel Alfonso Rodrigo de la Rocha
OCCUPATION
Student
BASE
Massachusetts Academy, Snow Valley, Massachusetts

HEIGHT 5 ft 11 in
WEIGHT 160 lbs
EYES Black
HAIR Light Brown

FIRST APPEARANCE
New Mutants #16 (June 1984)

EMPATH

POWERS
The Super-Soldier Serum brought him to the peak of physical perfection; able to lift twice his own body weight; expert military strategist; Olympic-level martial artist and gymnast; resistant to disease and fatigue.

New Mutants #16 (June 1984), featured "Away Game!" by Chris Claremont, Sal Buscema, Tom Mandrake, and Kim DeMulder.

Empath and his fellow Hellions were all students at the White Queen's Massachusetts Academy.

ENCHANTRESS

FACTFILE

REAL NAME
Amora

OCCUPATION
Goddess

BASE
Asgard, otherworldly home of the Norse gods

HEIGHT 6 ft 3 in
WEIGHT 450 lbs
EYES Green
HAIR Blonde

FIRST APPEARANCE
Journey Into Mystery #103 (April 1964)

POWERS

Possesses the enhanced lifespan, durability, and might of a goddess of Asgard. Adept at sorcery, specializing in spells that enhance her beauty and allow her to control the minds and emotions of men. Her kiss can enslave any man. Able to fire power bolts from her hands.

Enchantress

One of the immortals of the Norse realm of Asgard (see GODS OF ASGARD), the Enchantress studied under the master sorceress Karnilla. Vain and headstrong, she centered her magics on increasing her allure, so as to more easily ensnare the hearts and minds of those around her. When her desire for Odin's son THOR proved unrequited, she turned her mystic powers to evil, hoping to catch him one way or another. She especially resented Thor's love of humanity, and longed for him to rule Asgard with her as his queen. Her feelings for the Thunder God are genuine, and she has come close to realizing her dream; however Thor's love of humanity always gets in the way.

The Enchantress's Asgardian body is three times denser and heavier than that of a human being.

Not only can the Enchantress manipulate magical energy, but she uses various spells and potions to exert control over mortal men and other Asgardians.

The Femme Fatale

The Enchantress' love of manipulating others to do her will has resulted in her often teaming up with Skurge, the grim EXECUTIONER. He was hopelessly infatuated and would do anything to please her, and she contemptuously strung him along. The pair have even tried to conquer Asgard, and suffered banishment for their presumption.

The Enchantress has also plied her trade on Earth as a member of the MASTERS OF EVIL. She was also responsible for the creation of the heroic warrior-woman known as the VALKYRIE, in reality the Enchantress in disguise. **TB**

Enclave

FIRST APPEARANCE Fantastic Four #66 (September 1967)
BASE Various, including a North Atlantic island
MEMBERS AND POWERS
Maris Morlak Lithuanian Nuclear Physicist
Jerome Hamilton American Medical Biologist
Carlo Zota Spanish Electronics Technician
Wladyslav Shinski Polish Geneticist.

The group of scientists known as the Enclave believed they could establish a benevolent world dictatorship. Faking their deaths, the Enclave established a base on a remote North Atlantic island. They first endeavored to create a race of superbeings to control the human race. However, they failed to control the monsters, the first of which rampaged through their base, destroying it. Initially named "Him," this creature eventually came to be called Adam WARLOCK. The Enclave embarked on new schemes, such as attempting to dominate the race known as the INHUMANS and exploit the aliens' technology. Intervention by the AVENGERS resulted in two of the Enclave being imprisoned. Although they later broke out, nothing has been heard of the Enclave since. **AD**

Energizer

FIRST APPEARANCE Power Pack #1 (August 1984)
REAL NAME Katie Power **OCCUPATION** Student, adventurer
BASE New York City **HEIGHT** (age 5) 3 ft 7 in
WEIGHT (age 5) 41 lbs **EYES** Blue **HAIR** Strawberry blonde
SPECIAL POWERS/ABILITIES Can disintegrate objects in order to absorb energy, which she can release as "power balls" of destructive force—hence her codename.

Katie Power is the youngest child of Dr. James and Margaret POWER, and the sister of Alex, Jack and Julie Power. When Katie was five, she and her siblings met Aelfyre WHITEMANE of the alien Kymellians. Dying, "Whitey" endowed the children with superpowers, and they became the POWER PACK. At times the Pack has exchanged powers. Katie was Starstreak when she could fly, and Counterweight when she could alter her body density. **PS**

Enforcer

FIRST APPEARANCE Ghost Rider Vol. 1 #22 (February, 1977)
REAL NAME Charles L. Delazny, Jr. **OCCUPATION** Criminal
BASE Los Angeles, California **HEIGHT** 5 ft 11 in
WEIGHT 180 lbs **EYES** Brown **HAIR** Brown
SPECIAL POWERS/ABILITIES Wears bulletproof costume and carries automatic pistols; formerly possessed a disintegration amulet and ring

Son of a movie mogul, Charles Delazny left college to become the Enforcer. His primary weapon was a disintegration device, at times worn as an amulet or ring. The Enforcer, often going by the name of childhood acquaintance Carson Collier, built up a secret criminal empire from his father's Delazny Studios and clashed with GHOST RIDER and SPIDER-WOMAN. He was later shot and killed by THE SCOURGES OF THE UNDERWORLD. **DW**

Enforcers

FIRST APPEARANCE Amazing Spider-Man #10 (March 1964)
BASE New York City
MEMBERS AND POWERS
Fancy Dan Judo and karate expert—a nice line in suits, too.
Montana Proficient with the lariat. **Ox** Not superstrong but very strong. **Snake Marston** Entwines body around objects and people.
Hammer Harrison Expert boxer and unarmed combatant.
Big Man Would-be crime lord Frederick Foswell.

The Enforcers can give most Super Heroes a run for their money. Although they have been defeated by SPIDER-MAN a number of times, he has required the help of others to overcome them, calling on the NYPD, the HUMAN TORCH, or the reformed SANDMAN. Initially employed by the BIG MAN, during his bid to control New York's underworld, the Enforcers have also worked for the GREEN GOBLIN and the KINGPIN, until he was overthrown, forcing them back into the muscle-for-hire market. **AD**

ENFORCERS
1 Big Man
2 Ox
3 Montana
4 Fancy Dan

Eternals

The Eternal known as Thena is a powerful fighter with a brilliant mind. Like all Eternals she doesn't age or get sick.

About a million years ago the extraterrestrial CELESTIALS came to Earth to perform genetic experiments on the still-evolving human race. To test how adaptable the human gene was, the Celestials accelerated the evolution of a few early human test subjects, giving them the genetic potential to mentally control small amounts of cosmic energy.

The result of these experiments was a race known as the Eternals, who possess a number of superhuman powers and far longer lifespans than normal humans. With training an Eternal can further develop a specific superhuman ability. Subsequent genetic experimentation by the Celestials also led to the creation of the Deviants who, in time to come, would vie for power with the Eternals.

Eventually, the Eternals split into two factions, a peaceful, benevolent one, led by Chronos, and a warlike one, led by Uranos. Increasing tension led to a bitter civil war, which was won by Chronos and his followers. The group led by Uranos were exiled to outer space. In time, the survivors among Uranos's followers established a civilization of their own on Saturn's moon Titan.

The Eternals, led by Zuras, clashed with the fourth host of the Celestials, when the latter arrived to judge the Earth and its people. Although Zuras was killed, the Celestials spared the peoples of Earth and departed. **MT**

ETERNALS, THE

FACTFILE
KEY MEMBERS
CHRONOS, MENTOR (Alars), **ZURAS, IKARIS, URANOS, ARLOK, THENA, SERSI, MAKKARI, THE FORGOTTEN ONE, KINGO SUNEN, SPRITE, CYBELE, PHASTOS, KHORYPHOS, INTERLOPER, AJAK, DOMO, VALKIN, DRUIG, AGINAR, ZARIN, DELPHAN BROTHERS, SIGMAR, VIRAKO, VAMPIRO.**
BASE
Earth; Titan (moon of Saturn)

FIRST APPEARANCE
Eternals Vol. 1 #1 (July 1976)

POWERS
All Eternals have superhuman strength, can levitate themselves or other objects, can fly (up to 600 mph), create mental illusions, and project cosmic energy in beams from their eyes. Some Eternals can transform an object's shape.

Ancient Earth civilizations such as the Greeks, Romans, and Norse, worshipped the Eternals as gods, whom they called by names such as Zeus, Hera, and Athena. Those humans believed these gods resided in great temples in places such as Mount Olympus.

Eternity

FIRST APPEARANCE Strange Tales #138 (November 1965)
REAL NAME Inapplicable; (alias) Adam Quadmon
OCCUPATION None; abstract entity **BASE** Inapplicable
HEIGHT Inapplicable **WEIGHT** Inapplicable
EYES Inapplicable **HAIR** Inapplicable
SPECIAL POWERS/ABILITIES Unlimited ability to manipulate time, space, matter, energy or magic for any purpose.

Eternity is the collective consciousness of all life and is dependent on the many trillions of beings within it. It exits everywhere simultaneously. Eternity can take on humanoid form when it deigns to communicate with sorcerers and the like. Eternity once aided DOCTOR STRANGE against DORMAMMU, and Strange then helped Eternity escape NIGHTMARE's clutches. To have a greater understanding of humanity, Eternity has occasionally walked the Earth, using the name Adam Quadmon. **TD**

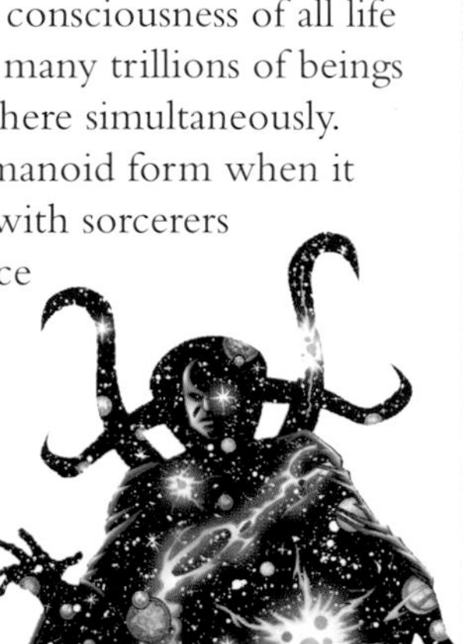

Executioner

Battling the Hulk, the Executioner finally met his match.

Born in the Asgardian province of Skornheim, Skurge was the child of a goddess and a Storm Giant. Although ostracized by the Storm Giants for his small height (he was only 7 ft tall), the Skurge became a great warrior. Turning against his father's people, Skurge killed many of them during a bloody war, earning himself the sobriquet "The Executioner." He fell under the ENCHANTRESS' spell, serving her in various bids to dominate Earth and Asgard. In time, Skurge realized she was just toying with him and rejected her. On a mission to the realm of Hela with THOR, Skurge restored his reputation by fighting to free mortal souls from this land of the dead. Skurge died a hero's death, guarding the escape of Thor's forces. **AD**

EXECUTIONER

FACTFILE
REAL NAME
Skurge
OCCUPATION
Giant-killer
BASE
Asgard

HEIGHT 7 ft 2 in
WEIGHT 1100 lbs
EYES Blue
HAIR Black

FIRST APPEARANCE
Journey into Mystery #103 (April 1964)

POWERS
A master of combat. Superhuman strength and stamina; wielded a magical double-bladed axe that can create dimensional rifts enabling time travel and also fired blasts of intense heat or cold; also possessed an unbreakable helmet.

EXCALIBUR

FACTFILE
ORIGINAL MEMBERS
CAPTAIN BRITAIN
Superpowered defender of Earth-616.
SHADOWCAT
Phases through solid objects.
NIGHTCRAWLER
Teleportation.
MEGGAN
Shapeshifter.
PHOENIX
(Rachel Summers-Grey)
Telepathy; telekinesis; projects force bolts.
LOCKHEED
Breathes fire and flies.

BASE
United Kingdom

FIRST APPEARANCE
Excalibur: The Sword is Drawn (1987)

Excalibur

Based at CAPTAIN BRITAIN's lighthouse, the Excalibur team of Super Heroes was formed following the X-MEN's apparent demise at the hands of the ADVERSARY. With a base located not just on the shores of the UK but also at the nexus of several realities, many of their battles have been fought across multiple alternate worlds. For instance, Excalibur has confronted the CRAZY GANG on Murderworld and its alternate universe counterparts, the Nazi Lightning Force.

Excalibur's unity has often been undermined by romantic tensions. When NIGHTCRAWLER developed feelings for Captain Britain's lover, MEGGAN, friction grew within the team, culminating in a brawl between the two men. Ultimately, it was the relationship between Captain Britain and Meggan that was to bring the team to an end—when the pair married the remaining team members decided to disband. Over time, Excalibur's lineup has evolved. **AD**

Excalibur missions are bywords for exotic travel to alien worlds and otherworldly dimensions.

EXCALIBUR
1 Nightcrawler ***2*** Pete Wisdom ***3*** Kitty Pryde ***4*** Meggan ***5*** Colossus ***6*** Wolfsbane

EXILES

FACTFILE

CURRENT MEMBERS

BLINK (leader)
Ability to teleport herself and others.

BEAK
Mutant power of flight.

MIMIC
Can duplicate the powers and abilities of others.

MORPH
Shapeshifting.

SABRETOOTH
Mutant healing factor, enhanced senses, retractable claws.

BASE
Mobile Panoptichron base

FIRST APPEARANCE
Exiles Vol. 1 #1 (August 2001)

Exiles

The Exiles are a group of heroes taken from alternate realities, tasked by the Timebroker with fixing snags in the multiverse of divergent timestreams. They receive guidance on repairing the timestream from a device called the Tallus. The founding Exiles team consisted of other-dimensional versions of BLINK, MIMIC, MAGNUS, THUNDERBIRD, NOCTURNE, and Morph. Later members included Sunfire, SASQUATCH, and MAGIK. During their dimension-hopping, the team faced off against HYPERION and the opposing team WEAPON X, and welcomed NAMORA and BEAK to their ranks. The Exiles later adventured within the Age of Apocalypse timeline, where they picked up that reality's version of SABRETOOTH as well as APOCALYPSE's former horseman HOLOCAUST. The current Exiles team has recently adventured within the alternate continuity of "House of M." **DW**

CHARACTER KEY
1 Morph
2 Sabretooth
3 Beak ***4*** Sasquatch
5 Mimic ***6*** Blink

Exodus

FIRST APPEARANCE X-Factor Vol. 1 #92 (July 1993)
REAL NAME Bennet du Paris
OCCUPATION Supervillain **BASE** Mobile
HEIGHT 5 ft 10 in **WEIGHT** 165 lbs **EYES** White **HAIR** Black
SPECIAL POWERS/ABILITIES Incalculable psionic powers including telepathy, telekinesis, and the ability to fire mental bolts; possesses enhanced strength, near-invulnerability, and flight.

Originally a crusader during the 12th century, the mutant Bennet du Paris crossed paths with APOCALYPSE, who placed him in suspended animation when he refused to kill the BLACK KNIGHT. Awakened by MAGNETO in the modern era, du Paris took the name of Exodus and became a devoted member of Magneto's Acolytes. Exodus led the Acolytes in struggles against the X-MEN, until Nate Grey (X-Man) sealed him in a mountain. Later, Exodus commanded the BROTHERHOOD OF EVIL MUTANTS in an assault on the X-Mansion, before being sucked into a black hole by Xorn. **DW**

Externals

The Externals, also known as the High Lords, were a small group of superhuman mutants whose lifespans were potentially unlimited. Their aging process was greatly retarded, and they could recover from injuries that would be fatal to normal humans.

Candra exacted payments of "tithes" from the Thieves and Assassins Guilds of New Orleans until GAMBIT stopped her. GIDEON was the owner of Ophrah Industries and a recurring foe of X-FORCE. Selene has lived for thousands of years and became Black Queen of the HELLFIRE CLUB. Most of the Externals proved not to be as immortal as they hoped. Burke and Nicodemus succumbed to the Legacy Virus. Candra perished in an encounter with the X-MEN. Having drained the life forces of Gideon and the others, Selene is the last living External. **PS**

Believing Sunspot was another External, Gideon arranged the murder of Sunspot's father. Later, Gideon fought Crule (left) and sent him to capture Cannonball.

Selene as the Black Queen of the Hellfire Club.

One of the oldest known mutants, Selene is also a powerful sorceress.

EXTERNALS

FACTFILE

KEY MEMBERS
(all have virtual immortality)

ABSALOM
Caused bone-like spikes to emerge from his skin.

BURKE Precognition.

CANDRA Telekinesis.

CRULE Superhuman strength.

GIDEON Duplicated powers of superhumans.

SELENE Drains life forces from others; telekinetic powers; superhuman strength and speed.

FIRST APPEARANCE
X-Force #10 (May 1992)

Falcon

FACTFILE
REAL NAME
Sam "Snap" Wilson
OCCUPATION
Hero and urban planner
BASE
Harlem, New York City

HEIGHT 6 ft 2 in
WEIGHT 240 lbs
EYES Brown
HAIR Black

FIRST APPEARANCE
Captain America #117 (September 1969)

POWERS
Falcon has a telepathic link allowing him to see through the eyes of his trained falcon, Redwing. Trained by Captain America, Falcon is skilled in numerous fighting styles, and possesses the agility of a skilled acrobat. Jet-powered glider wings enable him to fly.

When both his parents were murdered, his father trying to stop a street fight, and his mother in a mugging, community volunteer Sam Wilson became so disillusioned he turned to crime. While working for a smuggling gang he crash-landed on Exile Island in the Caribbean and encountered the Red Skull. In order to realize one of his diabolical schemes, the Skull used a Cosmic Cube to endow Sam with limited superpowers, moulding him to become Captain America's ideal sidekick.

After helping the Cap to defeat Red Skull, Sam branded himself the Falcon and entered into a long partnership with the famed supersoldier. A gift of jet-powered wings from Black Panther enabled him to become Captain America's airborne companion. Wilson accepted an invitation to join the Avengers, but soon came to believe that Earth's Mightiest team was just trying to fill its quota of black Super Heroes and left.

Although a Super Hero, Sam has never lost sight of his roots. He continues to work for and protect his community in Harlem—serving as its hero, role model, and protector. **AD**

Captain America's airborne ally, Falcon provides vital air support in the battle against evil.

Fenris

FIRST APPEARANCE Journey into Mystery #114 (March 1965)
REAL NAME Fenris Wolf
OCCUPATION Predator **BASE** Varinheim
HEIGHT 15 ft **WEIGHT** Unrevealed **EYES** Brown **HAIR** Gray
SPECIAL POWERS/ABILITIES Superhuman strength, speed and durability; razor-sharp claws and teeth; able to transform change into a humanoid god and wield weapons.

Said to be the offspring of Loki and the giantess Angrboda, Fenris is an immense wolf with human intelligence. Though kept chained by the Gods of Asgard, it is prophesied that the Fenris Wolf will devour Odin at Ragnarok.

Fenris was also the name taken by Andrea and Andreas von Strucker, the twin children of Baron von Strucker, for their terrorist organization. In his guise as Citizen V, Baron Zemo murdered Andrea, and Andreas later became the new costumed Swordsman. **PS**

Feral

FIRST APPEARANCE New Mutants #99 (March 1991)
REAL NAME Maria Callasantos **OCCUPATION** Terrorist
BASE New York City **HEIGHT** 5 ft 9 in **WEIGHT** 110 lbs
EYES Yellow **HAIR** Orange and white
SPECIAL POWERS/ABILITIES Enhanced strength, speed, and agility; superhumanly acute senses, especially her senses of sight and smell.

When Feral's mutant powers emerged at the age of 15, she killed her stepfather and her mother. Keeping this a secret, she joined X-Force. When X-Force tried to rescue Henry Gyrich from the terrorist group the Mutant Liberation Front, Feral switched sides, joining the terrorist group and trying to kill Gyrich. Cable subdued her, and Feral was arrested by the New York City Police for the murders of her parents. **MT**

Firebird

FIRST APPEARANCE Incredible Hulk #265 (November 1982) **REAL NAME** Bonita Juarez
OCCUPATION Social worker **BASE** New Mexico
HEIGHT 5 ft 5 in **WEIGHT** 125 lbs **EYES** Brown **HAIR** Black
SPECIAL POWERS/ABILITIES Firebird can generate a field of flame about herself, a fiery envelope that often manifests itself in the shape of a huge bird; this also enables her to fly.

Bonita Juarez gained her fiery powers when she was struck by a fireball from the heavens. Believing that her powers were from God, Bonita became Firebird, and used her abilities to help the people of her native New Mexico. She became a member of the Avengers, though she devoted much time to social work. She learned that the fireball was caused by an alien race, but still maintains that her abilities are god-given. **TB**

Firelord

FIRST APPEARANCE Thor Vol. 1 #225 (July 1974)
REAL NAME Pyreus Kril
OCCUPATION Former herald of Galactus **BASE** Mobile
HEIGHT 6 ft 4 in **WEIGHT** 220 lbs **EYES** White **HAIR** yellow
SPECIAL POWERS/ABILITIES Exposure to alien radiation granted Firelord the ability to fly and to understand the language of birds.

Pyreus Kril, an officer of the Xandarian Nova Corps, saw his commander abducted by GALACTUS, devourer of worlds, from aboard the ship *Way-Opener*. Kril's commander became AIR-WALKER, Galactus's herald, seeking out worlds for him to destroy. The loyal Kril followed his trail, eventually becoming Galactus's newest herald following Air-Walker's death. Remade as Firelord, Kril wielded the energies of a miniature sun. Firelord served with Galactus briefly, until THOR offered the Asgardian construct known as the Destroyer (*see* GODS OF ASGARD) to Galactus as a replacement herald. **DW**

Flag-Smasher

FIRST APPEARANCE Captain America #312 (December 1985)
REAL NAME Unknown
OCCUPATION Terrorist **BASE** Rumekistan
HEIGHT 6ft 2 in **WEIGHT** 235 lbs **EYES** Brown **HAIR** Brown
SPECIAL POWERS/ABILITIES Skilled at shotokan karate-do; multilingual, can speak Russian, German and Japanese; wields spiked mace, flame-throwing pistol, and tear-gas gun.

When his diplomat father died in a riot, Flag-Smasher committed himself to similar aims of peace; however, he opted to pursue them by violent means. Regarding nationalism as the enemy of concord, he initiated a terrorist campaign against symbols of national identity—embassies, national flags and the like. These activities brought Flag-Smasher face-to-face with that greatest living national symbol, CAPTAIN AMERICA, who repeatedly defeated him. Extending the scope of his campaign by forming the terrorist organization. ULTIMATUM, Flag-Smasher subsequently took over Rumekistan, a small, unstable country that became his new base of operations. **AD**

Firestar

Firestar has learned to focus her microwave energy so that prolonged exposure isn't dangerous to those nearby.

Angelica Jones's mutant powers began to emerge when she was 13 years old. She was soon recruited by the Massachusetts Academy, a school that trained young mutants how to use their powers, and she became a member of the HELLIONS. Emma FROST, who was both the school's headmistress and the White Queen of the Inner Circle of the HELLFIRE CLUB at the time, secretly trained Angelica to become an assassin who could kill without detection.

After the Hellions repeatedly clashed with the X-MEN and NEW MUTANTS, Angelica decided to leave the school. She joined the NEW WARRIORS and fell in love with Vance "Justice" Astrovik. They briefly became reserve members of the AVENGERS, a lifelong dream held by Justice. Angelica eventually learned that her powers were slowly causing her to become sterile and began to use them more sparingly. She later shared her medical problem with the team and Dr. Henry PYM cured her. Justice proposed to her and the couple decided to leave the Avengers to concentrate on their relationship and their education. **TD**

FACTFILE
REAL NAME
Angelica Jones
OCCUPATION
College student
BASE
Manhattan, New York

HEIGHT 5 ft 1 in
WEIGHT 101 lbs
EYES Green
HAIR Red

FIRST APPEARANCE
Uncanny X-Men #193 (May 1985)

FIRESTAR

POWERS

Firestar possesses mutant ability to project microwave energy and to generate intense heat. She can propel herself and others through the air by mentally pushing microwave energy behind or beneath herself.

When Firestar concentrates, she causes microwaves to swirl around her body. She can project toward a specific target by mentally pushing the waves toward it.

FANTASTIC FOUR

Superheroic planet protectors

FANTASTIC FOUR

FACTFILE

CURRENT MEMBERS

MR. FANTASTIC (Reed Richards) Scientific genius; elastic powers.

INVISIBLE WOMAN (Susan Richards) Can turn her body or any other object invisible; projects invisible force fields.

THE THING (Ben Grimm) Man monster with superhuman strength.

HUMAN TORCH (Johnny Storm) Generates fiery plasma over his entire body and can fly.

ADDITIONAL MEMBERS

CRYSTAL, MEDUSA, SHE-HULK, ANT-MAN (Scott Lang), **LUKE CAGE** (Carl Lucas), **SHARON VENTURE** (Ms. Marvel/She-Thing), **NAMORITA** (Namorita Prentiss)

BASE

Baxter Building, New York City

FIRST APPEARANCE

Fantastic Four #1 (November 1961)

ALLIES/FOES

ALLIES Spider-Man, Namor, The Sub-Mariner, Alicia Masters, Agatha Harkness, Wyatt Wingfoot, Silver Surfer, Lyja (Lyja Storm).

FOES Dr. Doom, Puppet Master, Red Ghost and his Super-Apes, Frightful Four, Galactus.

ISSUE #1

After being exposed to cosmic rays, the Fantastic Four kept a low profile and didn't reveal their powers to the public until giant monsters began attacking atomic research facilities.

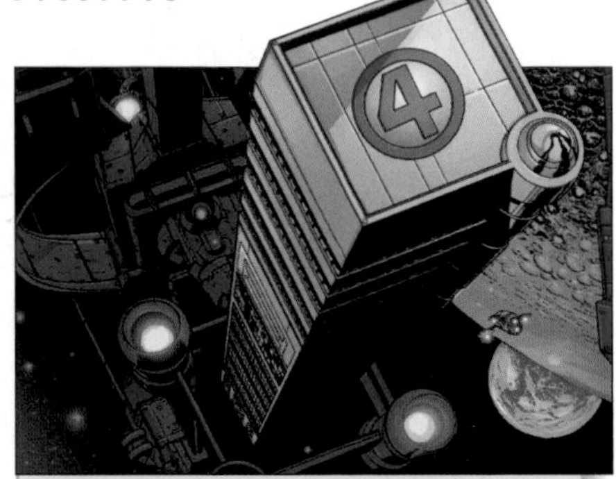

The Baxter Building was built by Noah Baxter, one of Reed's professors and mentor.

Reed Richards was a scientific genius who dreamed of exploring the stars. His roommate at New York's State University was football star Ben Grimm. Reed shared his dream of building a starship and Grimm, who wanted to become a pilot, promised to fly it. Grimm subsequently joined the US Air Force and became a test pilot and astronaut. Meanwhile, using his own family's fortune as well as money from the government, Richards built a starship.

COSMIC RAYS

When the government threatened to withdraw its funding, Richards decided to take his prototype ship on a test flight with Grimm at the helm. Richards' fiancée Susan Storm and her teenage brother Johnny came along for the ride. Soon after takeoff, a solar flare bombarded the ship with an unknown form of cosmic radiation that mutated their bodies and gave them fantastic powers. Richards became MR. FANTASTIC, Susan Storm became INVISIBLE WOMAN, Ben Grimm became the THING, and Johnny Storm became the HUMAN TORCH.

Fearing that Reed's ship didn't have sufficient shields, Ben tried to talk the others out of flying.

NO CHARGE

Pledging to use their new powers for the good of mankind, the four adventurers formed a legal corporation. The Fantastic Four safeguards the planet from human and extraterrestrial super-menaces, and also specializes in pure scientific research and explorations into the unknown. Funded by the patents on inventions and scientific discoveries made by Richards, the team offers its services without charge.

On their first public mission, the Fantastic Four prevented the MOLE MAN conquering the world. They later stopped the SKRULLS invading Earth and the MIRACLE MAN from blackmailing New York City. They were also responsible for the return of Prince NAMOR, the Sub-Mariner: the Human Torch found him living like a tramp in the Bowery slums and helped restore his lost memory. The FF also uncovered the menace of DOCTOR DOOM and made first contact with UATU THE WATCHER and the mysterious INHUMANS. They blocked GALACTUS from consuming the Earth and discovered the area of sub-space known as the Negative Zone. The team also battled the FRIGHTFUL FOUR, the OVERMIND, the SPHINX and aided the Planet Xandar against a Skrull invasion.

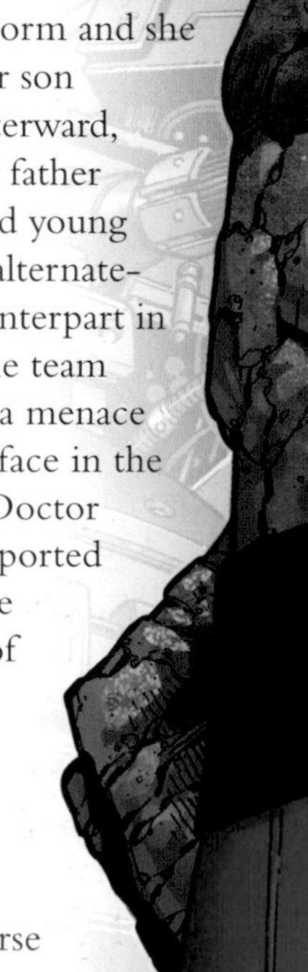

The Fantastic Four have vowed to safeguard Earth.

ALTERNATE WORLDS

After a prolonged engagement, Reed Richards married Susan Storm and she gave birth to their son Franklin. Soon afterward, Richards' scientist father Nathaniel switched young Franklin with his alternate-world teenage counterpart in an effort to help the team battle Hyperstorm, a menace they were destined to face in the future. Richards and Doctor Doom were later transported into a possible alternate future where the son of Franklin had conquered the universe.

A few months later, Franklin somehow created a pocket universe

1

THE FANTASTIC FOUR
1 The Thing *2* Mr. Fantastic
3 Invisible Girl *4* Human Torch

4

2

3

BASES AND EQUIPMENT

The team established its first headquarters on the top five floors of the Baxter Building in Manhattan, New York City. Although this building was later destroyed, Richards designed another base that was constructed in outer space by his former mentor Noah Baxter. The new Baxter Building is equipped with a state-of-the-art security system that is regularly upgraded. Roberta, the Fantastic Four's robot receptionist, is networked with the team's main computer and can undertake hundreds of tasks simultaneously.

Richards has also designed many different types of Fantasti-cars for easy travel around Manhattan (they're easy to park). Each team member is equipped with a wireless communications link, and an emergency flare gun. The FF also have a Pogo-Plane that is outfitted with vertical take off and landing capabilities, a captured Skrull starship that they use for galactic travel and a time platform and space/time sled that allow them to visit alternate time eras or dimensions. The team's costumes are composed of unstable molecules that are specifically designed to adjust to their individual powers.

Roberta is able to operate 24 hours a day and can answer various calls simultaneously.

ESSENTIAL STORYLINES

- ***Greatest Villains of the Fantastic Four* (tpb)** The FF battle Psycho-Man, Blastarr, Annihilus, Puppet Master, the Mad Thinker, and Doctor Doom.
- ***Fantastic Four: Monsters Unleashed* (tpb)** The Hulk, Ghost Rider, Wolverine and Spider-Man help the FF battle the Mole Man and the Skrulls.
- ***Fantastic Four: Nobody Gets Out Alive* (tpb)** The FF travel through time and various alternate dimensions on a hunt for the missing and presumed dead Reed Richards.
- ***Fantastic Four: Unthinkable* (tpb)** Dr. Doom attempts to use black magic as well as Reed and Sue's own children as weapons against the FF.
- ***Fantastic Four: Authoritative Action* (tpb)** To the world's horror and outrage, the FF seize control of Latveria after Doom is apparently destroyed.

called Counter Earth, where he transported his parents to protect them from a psychic monster called ONSLAUGHT. The FF later returned and soon faced another reality-altering cosmic entity called Abraxas. Shortly after they defeated him, the Invisible Woman gave birth to a daughter, named Valeria.

DOOMSDAY

Reed Richards eventually had a climactic battle with Doom, condemning him to a mystical dimension. Temporarily assuming control of Doom's beloved Latveria, Richards dismantled his regime and destroyed all his weapons of mass destruction.

The FF later journeyed into another alternate dimension to save the Thing from death and then faced bankruptcy and public disgrace at the hands of the PSYCHO MAN. They have since regained their fortune and are rebuilding their reputation as the world's greatest super-team. **TD**

The team have traveled into space and alternate dimensions.

Flux

FIRST APPEARANCE Incredible Hulk #17 (August 2000)
REAL NAME Benjamin Tibbetts
OCCUPATION US Army private **BASE** Washington, DC
HEIGHT Variable **WEIGHT** Variable **EYES** Green **HAIR** Green
SPECIAL POWERS/ABILITIES Exposure to gamma radiation and experimentation by the military gave Flux superhuman strength and durability; however his physiology is in a constant state of change.

Benny Tibbetts enlisted in the US army to fight in the Gulf War and was caught in the blast of gamma bombs dropped by a Black Ops team headed by General Ryker. Tibbetts survived, but like the Hulk before him, was forever changed by the gamma radiation. However his own self-doubts prevented his gamma-abilities from permanently catalyzing, with the result that, as Flux, his body was in a constant state of transformation. Flux was tricked by General Ryker into fighting the Hulk, but lost the battle. He eventually came to realize that he was being used as a pawn, and quit the battlefield. **TB**

General Ryker hoped that his creation Flux would defeat the Hulk, but Flux had too many mental insecurities.

Foolkiller

Paralyzed from the waist down, Ross Everbest's childhood was never going to be easy; then his parents were killed in the Korean War. However, when traveling revivalist preacher Reverend Mike Pike used faith-healing to restore his legs Everbest's life changed.. Joining Pike on the road, Everbest became increasingly angry with the "immoral fools" he encountered every day.

Foolkiller had a calling card warning victims that they had 24 hours to live and telling them to use the time wisely.

Vowing to rid the world of sinners and dissidents, he became Foolkiller, his murder spree beginning when he discovered Pike indulging in a drunken orgy. Everbest's psychotic reign of death ended when he was killed during a confrontation with the Man-Thing. However, his example was to inspire two more Foolkillers: Greg Salinger, who was eventually locked up in a mental institution; and Kurt Gerhardt, still at large in Albuquerque, New Mexico. **AD**

FOOLKILLER

FACTFILE
REAL NAME
Ross G. Everbest
OCCUPATION
Killer
BASE
Mobile

HEIGHT 6 ft
WEIGHT 185 lbs
EYES Blue
HAIR Blond

FIRST APPEARANCE
Man-Thing #3 (March 1974)

POWERS

Psychopathic energy gave him greater strength and endurance than an average man of his weight; possessed a raygun, he termed his "purification gun," capable of disintegrating victims.

FORCE WORKS

FACTFILE
MEMBERS AND POWERS
CENTURY
Composite being of 100 alien warriors.
IRON MAN
Powered armor; flight; energy blasts.
MOONRAKER
Emits electrical energy from hands.
SCARLET WITCH
Chaos magic.
SPIDER-WOMAN
Various spider powers; spins webs of psionic energy.
US AGENT
Enhanced strength, expert combatant.
WONDER MAN
Body composed of ionic energy.
BASE
The Works, Ventura, California

FIRST APPEARANCE
Force Works vol. 1 #1 (July 1994)

Force Works

After the disbanding of the Avengers West Coast, Tony Stark (Iron Man) founded Force Works to be a team with a more aggressive, proactive stance. By using the Scarlet Witch's hex powers, combined with data from a predictive supercomputer, the members of Force Works set out to squash budding threats before they could escalate to crisis levels.

On Force Works' first mission, Wonder Man seemingly died while battling a band of Kree warriors. The team bounced back from this loss by welcoming the alien Century into their ranks. Soon, the events known as the Crossing caused Iron Man to appear to turn traitor, behaving irrationally and murderously due to the mind-controlling Immortus. A new hero named Moonraker (claiming to be Libra) joining the group to distract them from Immortus's larger schemes. Force Works dissolved following the Crossing episode. **DW**

FORCE WORKS
1 Spider-Woman (Julia Carpenter) ***2*** Wonder Man
3 Iron Man ***4*** Scarlet Witch ***5*** US Agent

Forge

The Native American who became known as Forge was not only trained in mystic arts by Naze, a shaman in his Cheyenne tribe, but was also a mutant, with the ability to invent highly-sophisticated mechanical devices.

Forge lost a leg and a hand during the Vietnam War and designed mechanical limbs to replace them. When industrialist Anthony Stark (see Iron Man) stopped making advanced weaponry for the federal government, the US Defense Department began buying new weaponry designs from Forge. The genius inventor was soon at work, creating a scanning device that could detect the presence of mutants and extraterrestrials, and a neutralizing device capable of removing the powers of any superhuman being.

When government agent Henry Peter Gyrich shot the X-Men member codenamed Storm with Forge's device, depriving her of her mutant powers, Forge rescued her. Gyrich later hoped to use the neutralizing device to eliminate the superhuman powers of every being on Earth, but his typically devious plans were thwarted by Forge. **MT**

Forge shares a tender moment with Mystique, despite his deep feelings for Storm.

FACTFILE

REAL NAME
Unknown

OCCUPATION
Inventor, former soldier

BASE
Dallas, Texas

HEIGHT 6 ft
WEIGHT 180 lbs
EYES Brown
HAIR Black

FIRST APPEARANCE
X-Men #184 (August 1984)

POWERS

Mutant ability gives superhuman talent for inventing mechanical devices. While even the greatest inventors must work out the principals and designs of their inventions, the ideas for Forge's inventions spring fully formed from his mutant mind.

Forgotten One, The

FIRST APPEARANCE Eternals #13 (July 1977)
REAL NAME Unknown; has been known as Gilgamesh
OCCUPATION Adventurer; agent of the Celestials **BASE** Mobile
HEIGHT 6 ft 5 in **WEIGHT** 269 lbs **EYES** Brown **HAIR** Black
SPECIAL POWERS/ABILITIES Superhuman strength and stamina; immortality; full mental control over body; ability to manipulate matter on a subatomic scale.

A member of the god-like race of Eternals, the Forgotten One has lived for millennia. As punishment for his involvement in the affairs of humanity, for many centuries the Forgotten One was confined to the city of Olympia, only regaining his freedom after foiling an attack by the Deviants, grotesque, distant cousins of humanity. Adopting the name Gilgamesh, the Forgotten One went on to serve with the Avengers, but during a battle with Immortus is thought to have been killed. Given the power of the Eternals, talk of the Forgotten One's demise may be premature. **AD**

Frankenstein's Monster

FIRST APPEARANCE X-Men #40 (January 1968)
REAL NAME None
OCCUPATION Caretaker, wanderer **BASE** Baveria, Germany
HEIGHT 8 ft **WEIGHT** 325 lbs **EYES** Brown **HAIR** Brown
SPECIAL POWERS/ABILITIES The Monster possesses superhuman strength and stamina; able to go into suspended animation when exposed to intense cold.

In the late 18th century, Victor Frankenstein created a living humanoid creature from different corpses. Abandoned by his creator, the Monster learned to speak, and forced Frankenstein to create a mate for him. After Frankenstein killed her, the Monster slew Frankenstein's own bride. The Monster pursued his creator to the Arctic, where Frankenstein perished. The Monster was revived in 1898 and again in modern times. As "Adam," the Monster assisted monster hunter Elsa Bloodstone. **PS**

Freedom Force

FIRST APPEARANCE Uncanny X-Men Vol. 1 #199 (Nov. 1985)
BASE Washington DC **MEMBERS AND POWERS** **Mystique** (leader), shapeshifter [4]; **Avalanche**, groundquakes [7]; **Blob**, immovable; **Crimson Commando**, expert combatant [6]; **Destiny** (deceased), precognition [3]; **Pyro** (deceased), controls fire [5]; **Spider Woman**, spider powers; **Spiral**, spellcaster [2]; **Stonewall**, superstrength [1]; **Super Sabre** (deceased), superspeed
[Dazzler [8] is not a member]

Freedom Force was a government-sanctioned incarnation of the Brotherhood of Evil Mutants, formed to wipe out mutant threats to America. Group leader Mystique convinced US officials to issue pardons for her teammates' crimes in exchange for service. Freedom Force clashed with outlaw mutants such as the X-Men and X-Factor. The Force later teamed with the X-Men to help save Dallas, Texas from the Adversary, but the group disbanded after a disastrous mission to the Middle East. **DW**

Frightful Four

FACTFILE

MEMBERS AND POWERS

WIZARD
Brilliant scientist and inventor.

HYDRO-MAN
Can transform himself into semi-liquid form.

SALAMANDRA
Half-dragon, half-human; magical control of fire.

COLE
Controls and manipulates mass.

BASE
Subterranean Manhattan headquarters; mobile

FIRST APPEARANCE
Fantastic Four #36 (March 1965)

Frightful Four

The Wizard (Bentley Wittman) was a much-lauded scientist until the similarly brilliant Mr. Fantastic (Reed Richards) led the Fantastic Four into the limelight and forced him from the public eye. Insanely jealous, the Wizard committed himself to destroying Reed and his friends, by establishing the Frightful Four team of Super Villains. The original lineup was Wizard himself, Sandman, Trapster, and Medusa.

The Wizard has changed his team's roster many times, but it has continued to suffer defeats. Even when they took the Fantastic Four off guard—during Reed and Sue Storm's engagement party, for example—the Wizard's team was still beaten. The search for new members led the Wizard to look everywhere, even advertising in the *Daily Bugle*.

More recently, the Frightful Four's lineup has come to resemble a family—albeit a dysfunctional one—with the Wizard's ex-wife, Salamandra, and their daughter, Cole, signing up for duty.

Perhaps now the team will finally defeat its sworn enemies, the Fantastic Four. **AD**

FRIGHTFUL FOUR
1 Wizard
2 Hydro-Man
3 Trapster
4 Salamandra

Frog-Man

FIRST APPEARANCE Marvel Team-Up #121 (September 1982)
REAL NAME Eugene Paul Patilio
OCCUPATION High-school student **BASE** New York City
HEIGHT 5 ft 8 in **WEIGHT** 158 lbs **EYES** Brown **HAIR** Red
SPECIAL POWERS/ABILITIES Frog-man wears an electrically-powered suit with leaping coils built into his boots; can leap a maximum height of 60 ft and a maximum distance of 100 ft.

Eugene's inventor father designed a pair of electrically-powered leaping coils. Calling himself Leapfrog, he became a criminal to support his family, but soon ended up in jail. He returned to his wife and son a broken man. To redeem his father's name, Eugene donned one of his old costumes to become the crime fighter Frog-Man, helping Spider-Man and the Human Torch defeat the Speed Demon. Eugene tried to form his own team with the Toad and Spider-Kid (now called the Steel Spider). Though proud of his son's successes, his father has tried to discourage Eugene from risking his life and playing the hero. **TD**

Frost, Emma

FACTFILE

REAL NAME
Emma Frost

OCCUPATION
CEO of Frost International; Instructor, Massachusetts Academy

BASE
Massachusetts Academy

HEIGHT 5 ft 10 in
WEIGHT 125 lbs
EYES Blue
HAIR Ash blonde

FIRST APPEARANCE
X-MEN #132 (January 1980)

POWERS

Frost is a mutant with formidable telepathic powers. She can read minds, and project thoughts into others minds, controlling their actions, She can project pain and knock out victims by touching their brows; highly intelligent; expert designer of electronic devices that amplify psionic energy.

Frost, Emma

Emma was the chair of the Massachusetts Academy's board of trustees.

Emma Frost was born into a wealthy New England family. Gifted with a superb business brain, at a remarkably young age she was running a multi-billion-dollar corporation specializing in transportation and electronics, which she re-named Frost International. Her great wealth, intelligence, and charisma soon attracted the attention of the Hellfire Club, an elite social organization of powerful politicians and businessmen and women. She joined, becoming a close associate of Sebastian Shaw, who, like her, was also a mutant. When Frost and Shaw discovered a plot by Hellfire Club leader Edward Buckman to build massive Sentinel robots to hunt down and destroy mutants, they seized control of the organization, renaming it the Inner Circle, and taking the codenames Black King and White Queen.

In her role as the White Queen, Frost was at first an enemy of the X-Men. However, guilt over her inability to prevent the violent deaths of her former students, the Hellions, caused her to offer the Massachusetts Academy, the private school she had headed, to the X-men's leader Professor X, who turned it into his new School for Gifted Youngsters. Emma Frost now teaches there, instructing the young mutants of Generation X to develop and control their various mutant abilities. **MT**

Fury, Nick

Agent of SHIELD

Nick Fury grew up on the mean streets of Hell's Kitchen in New York during the Great Depression of the 1930s. Recruited by "Happy" Sam Sawyer, who would serve as his commanding officer for most of the war, Fury enlisted in the US Army at the outbreak of World War II, eventually becoming the Sergeant in command of the Howling Commandos, an elite unit of Able Company given the most dangerous missions.

As Director for the Strategic Hazard Intervention Espionage Logistics Directorate, Fury has access to the most state-of-the-art weapons and technologies on the planet.

INFINITY FORMULA

Fury and his Howlers raked up an impressive string of victories over the Axis forces, defeating such foes as Baron Von Strucker and his Blitzkrieg Squad, and even the legendary Red Skull himself. Wounded at the end of the war, Fury was injected with an experimental Infinity Formula by Professor Berthold Sternberg. The formula allowed Fury to survive what would have otherwise been fatal injuries (though he did eventually lose his left eye as a result of this injury), but the drawback was that Fury would need to ingest a yearly dosage to survive. On the plus side, the formula greatly extended Fury's natural lifespan—and for decades, Professor Sternberg blackmailed Fury for great sums in order to provide the necessary supply of the drug. After the War, Fury became an operative of the OSS, and then the CIA, earning the rank of Colonel.

Once a gung-ho Sergeant during World War II, Fury is now Director of SHIELD.

FACTFILE

REAL NAME
Nicholas Joseph Fury

OCCUPATION
Spymaster, director of SHIELD

BASE
SHIELD mobile Helicarrier

HEIGHT 6 ft 1 in
WEIGHT 225 lbs
EYES Brown
HAIR Brown, graying at temples

FIRST APPEARANCE
Sgt. Fury and His Howling Commandos #1 (May 1963)

POWERS

Nick Fury is a trained soldier with decades of experience. His youth and vigor have been maintained, despite his age, by the rejuvenating Infinity Formula. He is an expert martial artist and highly trained in the use of all kinds of weapons, both conventional and advanced.

THE PEACEKEEPER

When heroes such as the Fantastic Four began to appear, the CIA employed Fury as a liaison between them and the government. Thereafter, thanks to his sterling record, Fury was recruited to head up SHIELD, a worldwide peacekeeping force. SHIELD's first mission was to destroy the terrorist cartel HYDRA, which had been founded by Fury's old nemesis, Baron Von Strucker.

Fury's inner circle at SHIELD includes surviving members of the Howling Commandos.

As SHIELD's chief, Fury has battled threats to freedom all over the world, and proved a staunch ally to many of the Earth's Super Heroes, such as Captain America.

Answerable only to those world leaders in the highest positions of authority, Nick Fury stands as an important watchman on the walls of freedom. **MT**

ESSENTIAL STORYLINES

- ***Strange Tales #135*** Nick Fury is recruited by SHIELD to be its Director in its war against HYDRA.
- ***Nick Fury vs. SHIELD #1–6*** Having discovered corruption deep within his own spy organization, Fury must battle his own men.
- ***Secret War #1–5*** When Fury becomes aware of a clear and present danger to world security, he must organize a covert team of superhuman operatives to wage a secret war.

Resourceful, cool, courageous and committed to the cause, Fury is a superb field agent, as well as a brilliant leader of others.

GALACTUS

The Devourer of Worlds

GALACTUS

FACTFILE

REAL NAME
Galen

OCCUPATION
Consumer of planets

BASE
Mobile

HEIGHT 26 ft 9 in
WEIGHT 18.2 tons
EYES Unknown; to humanoids appear white
HAIR Unknown; appears black to humanoids

FIRST APPEARANCE
Fantastic Four #48 *(April 1966)*

POWERS
Manipulates vast cosmic power; can restructure matter and deliver a planet-shattering energy blast; able to teleport across the galaxy and create force fields; travels the galaxy in a worldship the size of the solar system; also pilots a smaller, circular "shuttle,"

In the last universe's final moments, Galactus awaited his death.

Older than the universe itself, the only survivor of the universe that came before our own, Galactus's fate is inextricably bound up with that of the entire cosmos. Although at times he has been a force for good, far more often he has brought doom, destroying whole peoples and consuming entire worlds, for his hunger for energy is insatiable; without it, he would cease to exist.

GALEN OF TAA

Born Galen, on the paradise world of Taa, Galactus was fated to live in the last days of his universe, just as it was entering the final stages of the Big Crunch. Realizing that his people were doomed, he persuaded them to pilot a vessel into the heart of the Crunch, to die in one last act of heroism. His people perished, but Galactus was somehow saved by the Phoenix Force of his universe.

For billions of years he slept, and when he awoke it was with an immense hunger that could only be sated by consuming the life-energies of a world. At first he searched for uninhabited worlds but his hunger gradually forced him to consume planets populated by sentient races. Galactus's conscience was only eased by a prophecy that he would ultimately make good on the devastation he wrought.

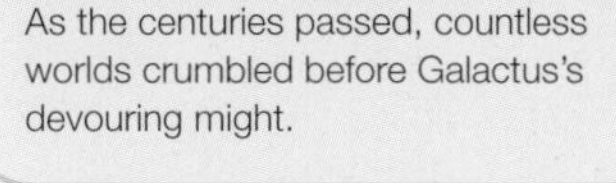

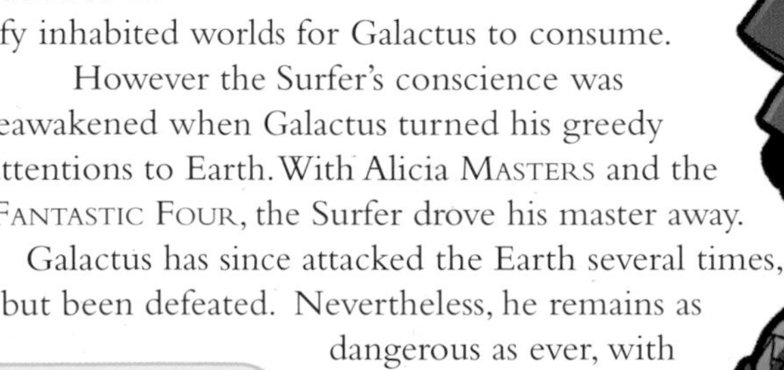

As the centuries passed, countless worlds crumbled before Galactus's devouring might.

GALACTUS'S HERALD

During a search for food, Galactus came upon the planet Zenn-La. To save his homeworld, a young man named Norrin Radd agreed to become Galactus's herald and to search out new planetary fodder. Transformed into the SILVER SURFER, Radd's emotions were subdued so he would be willing to identify inhabited worlds for Galactus to consume.

However the Surfer's conscience was reawakened when Galactus turned his greedy attentions to Earth. With Alicia MASTERS and the FANTASTIC FOUR, the Surfer drove his master away.

Galactus has since attacked the Earth several times, but been defeated. Nevertheless, he remains as dangerous as ever, with no sign of the earlier, hopeful prophecy coming to pass. **AD**

A being of immense power and size, only the very brave or foolish would stand against Galactus.

ESSENTIAL STORYLINES

- ***Fantastic Four #48–50***
Galactus discovers the Earth and, for the very first time in his immortal life, experiences defeat.
- ***Silver Surfer vol. 1 #1***
Galactus's first meeting with Norrin Radd, soon to become the Silver Surfer, is detailed.
- ***Galactus the Devourer #1–6***
Galactus is seemingly destroyed by the combined efforts of the Avengers, Fantastic Four, and the Shi'ar Empire.

Gaea

FIRST APPEARANCE Doctor Strange #6 (February 1975)
REAL NAME Gaea **OCCUPATION** Goddess **BASE** Earth
HEIGHT Variable **WEIGHT** Variable **EYES** Blue **HAIR** Black
SPECIAL POWERS/ABILITIES Possesses enormous mystical energies tied to the Earth; commands the forces of nature, such as storms and volcanic activity; power to heal and make things grow; telekinetic abilities; able to bestow magical powers.

Gaea is the embodiment of the spirit of life, growth, harvest and renewal on Earth. One of the foremost of the Elder Gods who ruled the world when mankind was not yet a glimmer, Gaea was the only one not to devolve into a demon, feeding on the spirits of others to survive. Instead, she became literally Mother Earth, and oversaw the growth of all living things. With Odin (see Gods of Asgard), Gaea conceived Thor, who is both of Asgard and of Earth, and the champion of both realms. **TB**

Galactus *see opposite page*

Gamora

FIRST APPEARANCE Strange Tales Vol. 1 #180 (June 1975)
REAL NAME Gamora
OCCUPATION Former assassin; member of the Infinity Watch
BASE Mobile
HEIGHT 6 ft **WEIGHT** 170 lbs **EYES** Green **HAIR** Black
SPECIAL POWERS/ABILITIES Expert gymnast and martial artist; proficient with all known weapons .

Gamora is the sole survivor of the Zen-Whoberi, an alien race wiped out by Magus and his Universal Church of Truth. The mad Titan Thanos rescued Gamora as an infant and trained her to become the deadliest assassin in the galaxy. Thanos killed her after a failed rebellion, and Adam Warlock absorbed her spirit into his soul-gem. She returned in a new form, and guarded the Time Gem as a member of the Infinity Watch. **DW**

Gardener

FIRST APPEARANCE Marvel Team-Up #55 (March 1977)
REAL NAME Ord Zyonyz
OCCUPATION Botanist **BASE** The known universe
HEIGHT 7 ft 1 in **WEIGHT** 390 lbs **EYES** Purple **HAIR** Gray
SPECIAL POWERS/ABILITIES Almost immortal, but not quite; Soul-Gem worn on forehead enables travel between worlds and to other dimensions; Soul-Gem also accelerates growth of plants.

One of the Elders of the Universe, the Gardener belonged to one of the first sentient species to roam the cosmos. Dedicating his life to horticulture, the Gardener spent his days collecting new seeds and cultivating barren worlds. The Gardener's fate was bound up with the two Soul-Gems that he used to travel between worlds and to accelerate plant growth. Abandoning the first Soul-Gem after using it in battle with the Stranger, the Gardener fought the Death-worshipping Eternal Thanos to retain his second gem, but the battle resulted in his death. **AD**

Gambit

The mutant Gambit was abducted soon after his birth by members of the Thieves Guild of New Orleans, and was later adopted by Jean-Luc LeBeau, the head of the Thieves' Guild.

Hoping to make peace between the Thieves' Guild and their rivals, the Assassins' Guild, Remy married the granddaughter of the Assassins Guild's leader. Her brother Julien was opposed to the union and challenged Remy to a duel, in which Remy killed him. Banished from New Orleans, Remy became the international master thief known as Gambit.

Gambit was employed by Mister Sinister to organize the mutant team of assassins called the Marauders, but he was shocked when Sinister sent the Marauders to massacre the Morlocks. Later, Gambit met and aided Storm, who sponsored his membership in the X-Men. He has had a longstanding romantic relationship with his X-Men teammate Rogue. Gambit served in the spinoff team, the X-Treme X-Men, before rejoining the main X-Men organization. **PS**

Gambit and Rogue's relationship had its explosive side: here, she nimbly avoids Gambit's "energy charge card."

More fiery fallings-out as Rogue gives Gambit a taste of his own medicine—an energy blast that knocks him off his feet.

GAMBIT

FACTFILE
REAL NAME
Remy LeBeau
OCCUPATION
Professional thief, adventurer
BASE
New Orleans, Louisiana; the Xavier Institute, Salem Center, New York State

HEIGHT 6 ft 1 in
WEIGHT 175 lbs
EYES Black (red pupils)
HAIR Brown

FIRST APPEARANCE
The Uncanny X-Men #266 (August 1990)

POWERS
Mutant ability to charge small objects with an unknown form of energy; when he throws the objects at a target, they explode on impact

Gargoyle

FACTFILE
REAL NAME
Isaac Christians
OCCUPATION
Caretaker
BASE
The estate of Daimon Hellstrom

HEIGHT 5 ft 10 in
WEIGHT 204 lbs
EYES Red
HAIR None

FIRST APPEARANCE
Defenders #94
(April 1981)

POWERS
Possesses the increased strength and mystic durability of one of the demon race. He can also levitate, fly and project bolts of eldritch force from his hands; leathery skin is bulletproof; impervious to disease and to aging.

In order to secure economic prosperity for his impoverished town, elderly Isaac Christians made a pact with a demonic group called the Six-Fingered Hand. He allowed his essence to be transplanted into the body of a demon, while the demon's mind would reside within his own human body. This demon had formerly been trapped in stone form as a gargoyle, as seen on ancient churches throughout Europe.

Isaac Christians made a deal with infernal forces that saw his soul cast into the body of a demon.

Despite his grotesque appearance, the Gargoyle was not truly evil, and after the destruction of his human body, he rebelled against the Six-Fingered Hand and came to be affiliated with the DEFENDERS. When that team disbanded, Christians tagged along with HELLCAT and her husband Daimon Hellstrom, eventually becoming the caretaker of Hellstrom's estate.

The Gargoyle should not be confused with a similarly-named Soviet agent (real name: Yuri Topolov) who attempted to capture the HULK on the eve of the latter's creation and was the father of the GREMLIN. **TB**

While inhabiting the body of a demon, the Gargoyle retains the essence of an elderly human. His mind and characteristics remain those of a human retiree.

Garokk

FIRST APPEARANCE Astonishing Tales #2 (October 1970)
REAL NAME Unrevealed **OCCUPATION** Sailor, wanderer, god
BASE The Savage Land **HEIGHT** 7 ft **WEIGHT** 355 lbs
EYES (as human) Brown; (as Garokk) Yellow
HAIR (as human) Brown; (as Garokk) Virtually none
SPECIAL POWERS/ABILITIES Can project heat, light, and concussive force from his eyes. Possesses virtual immortality.

Godlike wrath: Garokk the immortal Petrified Man lets fly with his powerful eye beams.

Some time in the 15th century, a British sailor from *HMS Drake* became stranded in the Savage Land. Immersion in a pool of mysterious liquid rendered the sailor virtually immortal. He wandered the world for centuries, and his body took on a gray, rock-like appearance, as if he were a "petrified man."

In recent times, the Petrified Man returned to the Savage Land, where he was worshipped by the Sun People as the incarnation of their god Garokk. As Garokk he regards himself as the guardian of the Savage Land, although his insanity and "offensive capability" makes him a thoroughly unpredictable menace. **PS**

Gateway

FIRST APPEARANCE Uncanny X-Men Vol. 1 #227 (March, 1988)
REAL NAME Unrevealed
OCCUPATION None known **BASE** Australia
HEIGHT 4 ft 6 in **WEIGHT** 80 lbs **EYES** Brown
HAIR Gray-black
SPECIAL POWERS/ABILITIES Ability to open teleportation doorways, transdimensional clairvoyant

The mysterious, silent Gateway is an Australian aborigine with the mutant ability to open teleportation doorways. The outlaw REAVERS forced Gateway to assist them in their crimes by threatening to destroy an aborigine sacred site. The X-MEN later evicted the Reavers, operating from their headquarters for a time, and Gateway became an unofficial member. Gateway has a special connection to the GENERATION X member M, and is an ancestor of the X-Man called Bishop. **DW**

Gatherers

FACTFILE

MAIN MEMBERS AND POWERS

PROCTOR
Teleportation; mind control.

CASSANDRA
Telepath; strategist.

MAGDALENE
Wields power lance.

SLOTH
Superstrong; razor-sharp claws.

SWORDSMAN
Sword fires energy beam.

FIRST APPEARANCE
Avengers #355 (October 1992)

The Gatherers serve PROCTOR, an extra-dimensional being. Each member of the Gatherers comes from an alternate Earth in another dimension. On each of their Earths, the Gatherers were AVENGERS. Also, on each of their Earths, Sersi, a member of the ETERNALS, went mad and killed everyone. The Gatherers were each the last survivors of their home worlds. They were recruited by Proctor to destroy SERSI and the Avengers of Earth-616. But in order for the Gatherers to exist on Earth-616, they had to each kill their own counterpart on Earth-616. This process was known as "gathering." The Gatherers infiltrated the Avengers' mansion on Earth-616 several times. In the final battle, Proctor tried to destroy all realities, but THUNDERSTRIKE hit Proctor with a bolt of lightning, and all the Gatherers collapsed. **MT**

THE GATHERERS
1 Cassandra
2 Magdalene
3 Swordsman
4 Sloth

Genesis

FIRST APPEARANCE Cable #18 (December 1994)
REAL NAME Tyler Dayspring
OCCUPATION Would-be conqueror, arms-dealer **BASE** Mobile
HEIGHT 6 ft 1 in **WEIGHT** 191 lbs **EYES** Blue **HAIR** Blond
SPECIAL POWERS/ABILITIES Mutant ability to create solid holograms from the memories of another person; trained in military tactics and combat techniques; wears armored suit.

The adopted son of CABLE in a future world ruled by APOCALYPSE, Tyler Dayspring was brainwashed by Cable's twisted clone STRYFE into becoming his father's enemy. Tyler traveled to the present, intent on ensuring that Apocalypse's rise to power would take place, and on avenging himself on Cable. He operated at first under the alias of a rogue arms dealer named Tolliver, but then abandoned that identity for direct action as Genesis. However, when Genesis attempted to restore WOLVERINE's lost adamantium to his skeleton, the pain-crazed mutant slew him. **TB**

Gemini

FIRST APPEARANCE Avengers Vol. 1 #72 (January, 1970)
REAL NAME Joshua Link
OCCUPATION Professional criminal **BASE** Mobile
HEIGHT 6 ft **WEIGHT** 185 lbs **EYES** Blue **HAIR** White
SPECIAL POWERS/ABILITIES Possessed psychic control over his twin brother's mind and body; could draw upon his twin to double his own strength.

Twin brothers Joshua and Damian Link followed opposite paths: Joshua became a street hoodlum, while Damian joined the police force. Exposure to experimental rays forged a psychic connection between the two. At first the connection worked both ways, but Joshua soon learned how to take complete control of Damian, both physically and mentally. Operating from his prison cell, he forced his brother to become the villainous Gemini, leaving Damian with no memory of the crimes he committed. Gemini worked as a criminal kingpin for the ZODIAC Cartel, aiding their plot to kill everyone in Manhattan born under the Gemini sign. Life model decoys, sent by the MAGGIA, later killed Gemini and most other Zodiac members. **DW**

Generation X

As one generation of X-MEN matures so another steps forward, in this case Generation X. Having experienced danger in the form of the alien collective intelligence, PHALANX, when the members of Generation X banded together they had a fair idea what fate had in store. Accepted by the Xavier Institute's new mutant high school at Massachusetts Academy, the team learned to hone its abilities and were introduced to PROFESSOR X's vision of the future. While at the Academy, the members of Generation X faced various foes, including EMPLATE, who preyed on the marrow of mutants. The team members were outed to the world as mutants and, with those in charge of the school—Emma FROST and Sean Cassidy (*see* BANSHEE)—becoming increasingly unstable, they decided to go their separate ways. **AD**

FACTFILE

MEMBERS/POWERS

HUSK
Sheds skin to reveal shape-shifted body beneath.

SKIN
Has 6 ft of extra skin, to manipulate as required.

M
Superstrength; invulnerability.

JUBILEE
Projects explosive energy bolts.

CHAMBER
Projects psionic energy blasts from chest.

SYNCH
Mimics powers of students.

PENANCE
Super-dense body.

BASE
Massachusetts Academy

FIRST APPEARANCE
Generation X #1 (November 1994)

CHARACTER KEY
1 Emma Frost ***2*** M ***3*** Banshee ***4*** Chamber ***5*** Synch ***6*** Jubilee ***7*** Penance ***8*** Skin ***9*** Husk

Genoshans

FIRST APPEARANCE Uncanny X-Men #235 (October 1988)
BASE The island of Genosha, Indian Ocean
SPECIAL POWERS/ABILITIES The inhabitants of Genosha were a mixture of ordinary humans and those with mutant abilities. The latter were called "Mutates" and were conditioned to fulfil specific, tasks tailored to their particular mutant ability. From time to time Mutates managed to rebel against their human masters.

Adolescent mutates were tatooed with a number on their foreheads, their identities were eliminated, and they faced a life of enslavement.

The Genoshans live on the island of Genosha located near the Seychelles in the Indian Ocean. Their economy was based on exploiting the labors of enslaved mutants. Genoshan adolescents were tested to see if they had mutant abilities. Those that did were genetically engineered to alter or enhance their abilities, had numbers tattooed on their foreheads, and lost their personal identities. A militia called the Magistrates enforced the enslavement laws and hunted down mutates who tried to escape.

The UN placed Magneto in charge of the Genoshan government, but a mutate called the Zealot leads a faction that opposes his rule. **MT**

Ghaur

FIRST APPEARANCE Eternals Vol. II, #2 (November 1985)
REAL NAME Ghaur **OCCUPATION** Priestlord
BASE "City of Toads", Deviant Lemuria
HEIGHT 6 ft 4 in **WEIGHT** 210 lbs **EYES** Yellow **HAIR** Blue-Black
SPECIAL POWERS/ABILITIES The extent of Ghaur's power is currently unknown.

The product of a centuries-long breeding programme run by Deviant Priests, Ghaur came to head this priestly order. His ambition did not end there, for Ghaur was determined to rule the Deviant race and to challenge the might of the alien Celestials themselves. These hubristic ambitions almost led to his death. For a time his disembodied consciousness floated through space, until a passing Silver Surfer inadvertently enabled him to regain corporeal form. Becoming a servant of the Elder God, Set, Ghaur sought to enable Set's return to Earth but his efforts came to naught. His whereabouts are currently unknown. **AD**

Ghost Rider

Centuries ago, Mephisto enslaved a demon, Zarathos. In the 18th century, Mephisto used a shard of the Medallion of Power to transform Noble Kale into a "spirit of vengeance," the Ghost Rider. Noble's descendant Naomi Kale and her husband, Barton Blaze, had three children, John, Daniel and Barbara. After Barton's death, John was raised by "Crash" Simpson, who taught John to become a stunt motorcyclist like himself.

The Ghost Riders are brilliant motorcyclists who can perform incredible stunts. Their mystical bikes enable them to ride up walls and even across water.

Posing as "Satan," Mephisto offered to cure Simpson of a fatal disease in exchange for Blaze's soul. Simpson died performing a stunt, and Mephisto bonded Zarathos to Blaze's body, causing him to transform into Ghost Rider. Blaze was freed of the curse when Zarathos became trapped in a "crystal of souls."

When criminals wounded Barbara Ketch, her brother Dan carried her to a junkyard. With Barbara's innocent blood on his hand, Dan touched a mysterious motorcycle and became Ghost Rider II.

Dan and John Blaze later learned they were brothers. John was again bonded to Zarathos and became a Ghost Rider once more. **PS**

FACTFILE
REAL NAME
John "Johnny" Blaze
OCCUPATION
Stunt motorcyclist
BASE
Mobile

HEIGHT (Ghost Rider) 6 ft 2 in
WEIGHT (Ghost Rider) 220 lbs
EYES (Ghost Rider) flaming red
HAIR (Ghost Rider) none

FIRST APPEARANCE
Marvel Spotlight Vol. 1 #5 (August 1972)

POWERS
Turns into a superhuman mystical being that projects "hellfire"; Ghost Rider I can create a mystical motorcycle from "hellfire." Ghost Rider II's "Penance Stare" causes wrongdoers to suffer the same emotional pain they inflicted.

Giant-Man

FIRST APPEARANCE Avengers Vol. 1 #32 (September 1966)
REAL NAME William Foster
OCCUPATION Adventurer **BASE** Los Angeles
HEIGHT 6 ft 10 in **WEIGHT** 200 lbs **EYES** Brown **HAIR** Black
SPECIAL POWERS/ABILITIES Could grow in size up to a maximum height of 25 ft; gained proportional strength as his size increased.

Dr. Hank Pym (the first Ant-Man) discovered how to use his "Pym particles" to increase his size and became the first Giant-Man. His lab assistant, Bill Foster, duplicated the growth serum and became a crimefighter with Dr. Pym's encouragement. Foster became Black Goliath, and fell victim to radiation fighting Atom-Smasher. He later became the second Giant-Man, and Spider-Woman (Jessica Drew) cured his radiation sickness with a blood transfusion. Foster lost his size-changing abilities in the process, though they have returned sporadically. **DW**

Gladiator

FIRST APPEARANCE Daredevil Vol. 1 #18 (July 1966)
REAL NAME Melvin Potter **OCCUPATION** Ex-criminal
BASE New York City
HEIGHT 6 ft 6 in **WEIGHT** 300 lbs
EYES Blue **HAIR** None
SPECIAL POWERS/ABILITIES Skilled athlete and combatant; wore armored suit with saw blades in gauntlets.

When Foggy Nelson rented a Daredevil outfit from Melvin Potter's costume shop, Potter agreed to dress up like a Super Villain to ambush Foggy. But Potter acquired a taste for crime, becoming the Gladiator and serving with Electro's Emissaries of Evil and the Maggia. After numerous defeats, usually at the hands of Daredevil, Gladiator reformed and married, and now has a young daughter. He still owns the Spotlight Costume Shop. Melvin Potter is not to be confused with the alien Gladiator who leads the Shi'ar Imperial Guard. **DW**

Glob

FIRST APPEARANCE Incredible Hulk #121
REAL NAME Joe Timms **OCCUPATION** Petty thief; swamp creature **BASE** Florida Everglades
HEIGHT 6 ft 6 in **WEIGHT** 900 lbs **EYES** Brown **HAIR** None
SPECIAL POWERS/ABILITIES Superhumanly strong, the Glob's mutated swampy body can withstand severe attacks; enhanced speed and stamina; not particularly intelligent.

Escaping prison to be with his dying wife, Joe Timms fled into the Florida Everglades only to drown in the marshes. Decades later the Hulk accidentally spilt radioactive waste there and Timms was resurrected as the swamp-like creature, the Glob. Mistaking Betty Ross (*see* Banner, Betty) for his wife, the Glob battled the Hulk for her. He was more than a match for the emerald ogre–every blow the Hulk struck merely sank into the Glob's muddy body. Realising the radioactive marsh might hurt Betty, the Glob gave her up, disappearing into the swamp, where some say he walks to this day. **AD**

Not a pretty sight, the Glob is, nevertheless, a well-meaning soul.

Gideon

FIRST APPEARANCE New Mutants #98 (February 1991)
REAL NAME Gideon **OCCUPATION** CEO of Ophrah Industries
BASE Denver, Colorado
HEIGHT 6 ft 8 in **WEIGHT** 265 lbs **EYES** Blue **HAIR** Green
SPECIAL POWERS/ABILITIES Mutant ability to duplicate the superhuman powers of others by aligning himself with their energy signatures. He also had a greatly extended lifespan.

A member of the long-lived mutants who call themselves the Externals, Gideon was a power broker who called the halls of big business his natural habitat. Utterly corrupt, Gideon attempted to take Roberto DaCosta, the New Mutant known as Sunspot, under his wing, and turn him into his protégé. However his attempts to turn Sunspot into an External like himself met with failure, and he soon turned his attentions to other pursuits. Gideon was subsequently slain by the External vampire Selene, who had embarked on a vendetta against her fellow Externals. **TB**

Glenn, Heather

FIRST APPEARANCE Daredevil Vol. 1 #126 (October 1975)
REAL NAME Heather Glenn
OCCUPATION Secretary; owner of Glenn Industries (after her father's death) **BASE** New York City
HEIGHT 5 ft 8 in **WEIGHT** 120 lbs **EYES** Blue **HAIR** Black
SPECIAL POWERS/ABILITIES Proficient secretarial skills; Heather had no superpowers.

The daughter of Maxwell Glenn, owner of Glenn Industries, Heather became romantically involved with lawyer Matthew Murdock. Zebediah Killgrave, the Purple Man, used his mind-controlling powers to force Maxwell Glenn to commit crimes. Murdock prosecuted Maxwell Glenn, who killed himself. Heather blamed Murdock for her father's death; she then discovered that he was the crimefighter Daredevil. Heather and Murdock were reconciled but, while drunk, Heather revealed Daredevil's identity to his enemy Tarkington Brown. When Murdock broke up with Heather, she committed suicide, as her father had. **PS**

Glorian

FIRST APPEARANCE Incredible Hulk #191 (September 1975)
REAL NAME Thomas Gideon
OCCUPATION Apprentice dream-shaper **BASE** Known universe
HEIGHT 5 ft 9 in **WEIGHT** 155 lbs **EYES** Pink **HAIR** Orange
SPECIAL POWERS/ABILITIES Glorian can control tachyons, small speed-of-light particles, forming them into rainbow-shaped bridges allowing him to travel across worlds or star systems at light speed. He can also mentally redefine small pockets of reality for short periods of time.

Thomas Gideon and his parents were flying in a private jet when it was caught in the explosion of a Russian nuclear test. Thomas alone survived radiation poisoning, thanks to the Shaper of Worlds, who taught Thomas, now called Glorian, to manipulate reality and dreams. On Earth, Glorian was saved by the Hulk from the demon Satannish. Glorian later aided Generation X when they were lost at sea. **MT**

Gods of Asgard

Immortals who rule the dimension of Asgard

FACTFILE

KEY ASGARDIANS

ODIN
(Monarch of Asgard) The most powerful god, possessing vast magical abilities. He can enchant objects or living beings, project energy bolts, and open gateways between dimensions. He also commands the life energies of all Asgardians, which he can absorb at will.

THOR
(God of Thunder) Asgard's finest warrior; exceptionally skilled in hand-to-hand combat, swordsmanship, and hammer-throwing.

BALDER
(God of Light) Thor's closest friend; almost invulnerable; skilled in hand-to-hand combat, swordsmanship, and horsemanship.

HELA
(Goddess of Death) Ruler of the underworlds of Hel and Niffleheim; holds the power of life and death over the gods; can levitate and travel in astral form; touch is fatal to mortals,

LOKI
(God of Evil) Great magical abilities; can shapeshift into any animal, god, or giant; can plant hypnotic suggestions into others' minds.

HERMOD
(God of Speed) Fastest of all Asgardians.

HODER
(God of Winter) has Psychic abilities that allow him to see into the future.

VALKYRIE
Brunnhilde the Valkyrie can see a "deathglow" around a person about to die. She can transport herself (and a dead or dying person) from one dimension to another.

HEIMDALL
Guardian of the Rainbow Bridge has extremely acute senses. He can focus on, or block out, any specific sensory information.

VOLLA
Prophetess who can see alternate futures.

BASE
The Otherdimensional Realm of Asgard

FIRST APPEARANCE
Journey into Mystery #85, (October 1962)

The otherdimensional planetary body known as Asgard.

The Gods of Asgard are a powerful race of beings who live in a dimension called Asgard, a small, otherdimensional planetary body whose laws of physics are different from the planets we know in the Earthly realm. Asgard is also home to five other races—Giants, Dwarves, Elves, Trolls, and Demons. The Gods of Asgard are the most human-looking and powerful of the six races of Asgard.

NINE WORLDS

All Asgardian refer to the known universe as the "Nine Worlds of Asgard." Four of those worlds—Asgard, home of the gods; Vanaheim, home of the Asgardians' sister race called the Vanir; Nidavellir, home of the Dwarves.; and Alfheim, home of the Light Elves—actually share the planetary body on which Asgard is located.

The other five worlds exist in separate dimensions connected by an unknown number of interdimensional nexuses. They are Midgard, the Asgardian name for Earth, home of humanity; Jotunheim, home of the giants; Svartalfheim, home of the dark elves; Hel, land of the dead and it's adjunct world Niffleheim, the frozen realm of the dishonored dead; and Muspelheim, land of the fire demons and home to Surtur, the Gods of Asgard's most deadly enemy.

Surtur rises from the flames of Muspelheim, land of the fire demons.

Rainbow Bridge

The origin of the Gods of Asgard is not clearly known, but it believed that unlike the other races of the realm, the gods are not native to Asgard. Legend has it that they were born on Earth, but moved to Asgard at some time in the far distant past. The Rainbow Bridge, also known as Bifrost—one of the interdimensional nexuses—connects Asgard to Earth. Although they look like humans, the Gods of Asgard possess superhuman physical abilities. They are extremely long-lived (although not immortal, unlike their Olympian counterparts) and age at an extremely slow pace once they reach adulthood.

Their skin and bones are three times as dense as that of a human and are invulnerable, to a degree, to physical attack. They possess great strength (able to lift 30 tons) and, due to their density, weigh far more than humans of comparable size. The Gods of Asgard are immune to all diseases found on Earth and their metabolism gives them superhuman endurance while performing physical activities.

All Asgardians are born with the potential to use and control mystical energies, although only a few (such as Loki) have developed this power to any significant degree.

The Fantastic Four cross Bifrost, the Rainbow Bridge to Asgard, which is guarded by Heimdall, Sentry of Asgard.

GODS OF ASGARD
1 Enchantress ***2*** Sif ***3*** Balder the Brave ***4*** Hela, Goddess of Death ***5*** Hermod, God of Speed ***6*** Loki ***7*** Thor ***8*** Heimdall, Guardian of the Rainbow Bridge ***9*** Thunderstrike ***10*** Odin ***11*** Karnilla, the Norn Queen ***12*** Kurse ***13*** Frigga ***14*** Fandral the Dashing ***15*** Volstagg the Enormous ***16*** Hogun the Grim ***17*** Thor Girl ***18*** Malekith ***19*** Surtur ***20*** Ulik, the Unstoppable Rock Troll

ESSENTIAL STORYLINES
- ***The Mighty Thor Vol. 2 #80–85*** The Ragnarok (Doom of the Gods) Saga. Loki and his followers unleash an attack on Asgard intended to destroy the home of the gods and all its inhabitants. Thor's hammer Mjolnir is shattered during the battle that follows.
- ***The Mighty Thor #418*** The fire demon Surtur possesses Odin and gains control of Asgard.

The Storm Giants, sworn enemies of the Gods, eat and drink their fill in Jotunheim, their Asgardian home. Odin challenged Thor and Loki (in foreground) to return the Golden apples of Iduna to the Storm Giants.

Odin, Thor, and Loki

ODIN, also called All-Father, is the leader of the Gods of Asgard. Odin is the grandson of Buri, the first of the Asgardians. He is the son of the God Bor and Bestia, of the race of frost giants.

For many ages, Odin has ruled Asgard wisely and effectively. Odin wields the enchanted, three-pronged spear Gungnir ("The Spear of Heaven"), which returns to his hand when thrown, and he travels through space in Skipbladnir, a Viking-style longboat with enchanted sails and oars.

Son of Odin

Although Odin made the Asgardian Goddess Frigga his queen, he desired a son that would combine the power of Asgard and Earth, and so he mated with GAEA, the patron Goddess of Earth, who bore him THOR, the God of Thunder, Odin's favorite son. However, from the time Thor was an infant, he was raised in Asgard by Frigga, whom he believed to be his mother.

When Thor was eight, Odin sent him to Nidavellir, land of the Dwarves, to ask them to create treasures for Asgard's rulers. Among the objects they created was the hammer Mjolnir, forged of the mystical metal uru. Odin enchanted the hammer so that only one worthy of wielding such a powerful weapon could lift it. He hoped that Thor would one day be that one.

Heroic Deeds

For the next eight years Thor strove to become powerful enough and worthy enough to possess Mjolnir, doing many heroic deeds to prove his valor. When Thor reached the age of sixteen, Odin finally presented him with the mighty hammer, and Thor became Asgard's greatest warrior.

Odin adopted Loki, who, although raised alongside Thor, quickly turned to sorcery and earned the nickname, "God of Mischief." Bitterly jealous of Thor, Loki vowed to destroy him and seize the throne of Asgard. Soon the God of Mischief became known as the God of Evil. **MT**

Ymir, King of the Ice Giants

In the early days of Asgard, the rampaging Ice Giants attempted to bring frost, desolation and eternal night to the land of the gods. They were defeated by Odin and his warriors.

GODS OF HELIOPOLIS

Deities of Ancient Egypt

GODS OF HELIOPOLIS

FACTFILE

NOTABLE GODS

OSIRIS (Ruler of the Gods) God of the Dead

BES God of Luck

GEB God of the Earth

HORUS God of the Sun

ISIS Goddess of Fertility

KHONSHU God of Light

NUT Goddess of the Sky

SETH God of Evil

THOTH God of the Moon

BASE

Celestial city of Heliopolis

FIRST APPEARANCE

Thor Vol. 1 #240 (October 1975)

The Path of the Gods enabled the Egyptian deities to visit Earth and meddle in human affairs.

In ancient times the pantheon of the Egyptian gods lived in Heliopolis, ruling Egypt until humans finally took their place as the dynastic kings known as the pharaohs. It was then that the Heliopolitan gods departed Earth, settling in a parallel dimension, where they established the celestial city of Heliopolis. However, like the Asgardian gods (*see* GODS OF ASGARD), the Heliopolitan deities retained strong links with Egypt, traveling to and from Earth on a golden bridge named the Path of the Gods.

Creeping up on the sleeping Osiris, Seth prepared to slice him into pieces.

CLASH OF THE GODS

Although essentially an extended family, the Heliopolitan gods were somewhat dysfunctional. When Osiris, God of the Dead, was appointed ruler of the Gods his younger brother Seth was overwhelmed with jealousy—the tensions between the pair were to reverberate far beyond their celestial home. Seth's first solution was drastic—he killed Osiris, slicing up his body and scattering the pieces. When Osiris' wife and son—Isis and Horus—managed to resurrect him, Seth employed a different tactic, imprisoning all three in a pyramid. Although trapped there for millennia, Osiris and Isis eventually made the pyramid appear in the 20th century. This attracted the attention of the Asgardian gods THOR and Odin but their efforts to free their fellow immortals did not prove straightforward. Odin was forced to join battle with Seth, their struggle finally culminating in the severing of Seth's left hand.

Releasing Osiris from his pyramid prison, Thor and Odin joined him in the battle to overthrow Seth. However, before they could reach him, they were forced to fight through Seth's skeletal legions.

CONTINUING MENACES

Seth has attempted time and again to destroy all life in the multiverse. An alliance of evil let loose the demonic Demogorge the God-Eater. Only when the entity attempted to consume Thor was its path of destruction brought to an end. On a separate occasion, Seth drained the energies of his fellow gods and invaded Asgard. He was only defeated by the combined forces of the AVENGERS and EARTH FORCE. Thanos also threatened the universe with his Infinity Gauntlet. Osiris attended a Council of the God Kings to discuss their response. Fortunately, Thanos was thwarted by other entities.

Although the time of the Heliopolitan Gods is now long over, they and their petty squabbles still spill over into human affairs. **AD**

For millennia, the god Seth has brooded and conspired to gain control of Heliopolis.

ESSENTIAL STORYLINES

- ***Thor Vol. 1 #240–241*** In the first story to feature the Heliopolitans, Seth traps Osiris and Isis in a pyramid and does battle with Odin and Thor.
- ***Thor Vol. 1 #386–400*** Seth conquers Heliopolis, battles Thor and the Avengers, and then tries to invade Asgard.

Gods of Olympus

Deities of Ancient Greece

Olympus was ruled by the stern and hirsute, Zeus.

Although for centuries they were worshipped by the Greeks it remains unclear where the Gods of Olympus first originated—was it on Earth or in the pocket dimension of Olympus where they currently reside? Wherever they came from, their influence on this planet has faded over the last two millennia, although a handful of their number still walk the Earth.

The court of Zeus was a byword for feasting and revelry. While most enjoyed the carefree hedonism of the place, some, including Venus and Hercules, yearned for a slightly more challenging existence.

THE GOLDEN AGE

Children of the Titans, the first generation of the Olympian Gods were imprisoned in the underworld realm of Tartarus as soon as they were born, their father Cronos fearing that they would eventually overthrow him. His anxiety proved to be well founded: the last of his children, Zeus, avoided being incarcerated and, when he was old enough, freed his siblings and led a ten-year-long war against Cronos.

Victorious, Zeus and his siblings became the Gods of Olympus, worshipped by peoples across Europe. It was only when Christianity began to dominate the Western world that the Gods chose to withdraw to the Olympus dimension and began to reduce their ties with the mortal realm. Although most of the Gods departed a handful either remained on the Earth or returned, time and again, in the years that followed. Of those that stayed on Earth, Neptune (or Poseidon, as the Greeks called him) remained to watch over and be worshipped by the Atlanteans, while Hercules and Venus (Aphrodite to the Greeks) spent time living with mortals.

This Mortal Life

In 1948 Venus arrived in the US, taking up a post as an editor at *Beauty Magazine*. In between writing features, she spent her days bringing couples together, warding off suitors, and foiling various sinister plots. She then became a college professor at UCLA.

Hercules became friends with the god Thor and they fought with the Avengers, against the Triumvirate of Terror and the Red Guardian.

However, Venus' and Hercules' presence on the Earth did not overly please Zeus, ruler of the Olympian Gods. He set tests for Venus forcing her to prove that being on the planet was worthwhile. Zeus' treatment of Hercules was much harsher: he stripped Hercules of his immortality and refused to let him return to Olympus. Fortunately for humanity, despite Zeus' isolationist tendencies it is likely that these ancient Gods will continue to walk amongst ordinary humans for a great many more years. **AD**

Zeus did not entirely approve of the life his son, Hercules, had chosen to lead.

FACTFILE

NOTABLE GODS

ZEUS (Ruler of the Gods) God of the Sky and Weather
APOLLO God of Light
ARES God of War
ARTEMIS Goddess of the Hunt
ATHENA Goddess of Wisdom
ATLAS Mountain God
BELLONA Goddess of Discord
CUPID God of Love
DEIMOS God of Terror
DEMETER Goddess of Fertility
DIONYSUS God of Wine
GAEA Mother-Earth
HEBE Goddess of Youth
HEPHAESTUS God of Fire
HERA Goddess of Marriage; Queen of the Gods
HERMES God of Commerce and Travel
NEPTUNE (POSEIDON) God of the Sea
NOX God of Night
PAN God of Shepherds, Flocks and Forests
PERSEPHONE Queen of the Underworld
PHOBOS God of Fear
PROMETHEUS Titan of forethought; benefactor of mankind
PSYCHE Goddess of Fidelity and Adoration
TYPHON God of Wind
VENUS (APHRODITE) Goddess of Love and Beauty

BASE

Mount Olympus, Greece; later in an otherdimensional world

FIRST APPEARANCE

Journey Into Mystery Annual #1 (1966)

ESSENTIAL STORYLINES

- ***Venus #1–5***
The goddess Venus becomes editor of Beauty Magazine and helps bring couples together.
- ***Thor #126–131***
Hercules fights Thor who then rescues him from the netherworld where he has been imprisoned. Their firm friendship is sealed.
- ***Avengers #281–285***
Angered by injuries suffered by Hercules, Zeus attacks the Avengers and forbids the Olympus Gods from travelling to Earth.

Goldbug

FIRST APPEARANCE Luke Cage, Power Man #41 (March 1977)
REAL NAME Unrevealed
OCCUPATION Criminal **BASE** New York City
HEIGHT 5 ft 9 in **WEIGHT** 170 lbs **EYES** Blue **HAIR** Blond
SPECIAL POWERS/ABILITIES Battlesuit contains electrically-powered exoskeleton that amplifies strength; "gold-gun" shoots gold-colored dust that hardens on contact; uses "bugship" hovercraft and submarine.

Goldbug is a thief obsessed with gold. Early in his career he clashed with Luke CAGE, POWER MAN, and Thunderbolt. Later, Goldbug captured the HULK as part of his plan to find and conquer the legendary city of El Dorado in South America. In El Dorado, Goldbug teamed up with the Hulk to defeat the subterranean conqueror TYRANNUS. He then sought an alliance with the criminal MAGGIA, but was thwarted by the intervention of SPIDER-MAN. Sometime afterwards, the Goldbug attempted to steal underwater gold but was foiled by NAMOR, the Sub-Mariner. **PS**

Golden Archer

FIRST APPEARANCE Avengers #141 (November 1975)
REAL NAME Wyatt McDonald **OCCUPATION** Government agent, former cab driver **BASE** Squadron City
HEIGHT 6 ft 3 in **WEIGHT** 150 lbs **EYES** Blue **HAIR** Black
SPECIAL POWERS/ABILITIES Expert archer who shot arrows with pin-point accuracy. Besides conventional arrows used a chemical mace arrow, a siren arrow, and a flash arrow.

Wyatt McDonald practiced until he became an expert archer. Deciding to use his skills as a costumed crimefighter he adopted the name Hawkeye. McDonald was the first recruit of the SQUADRON SUPREME, a team of Super Heroes who banded together to protect their world, known as "Earth-S." He later changed his name to Golden Archer. Eventually he was kicked out of the Squadron Supreme for using a Behavior Modification Machine on Lady Lark. He then joined NIGHTHAWK's Redeemers as Black Archer and was killed battling Blue Eagle. **MT**

Golddigger

FIRST APPEARANCE Captain America #389 (April 1990)
REAL NAME Angela Golden
OCCUPATION Enforcer **BASE** New Orleans, Louisiana
HEIGHT/WEIGHT Unknown **EYES** Blue **HAIR** Blonde
SPECIAL POWERS/ABILITIES Skilled hand-to-hand combatant.

Little is known about the woman known as Golddigger, save that she sells her skills to the highest bidder, and that she specializes in sneak attacks. She first crossed swords with CAPTAIN AMERICA in the service of Superia, who plotted to sterilize the world. Thereafter, she came to be employed by Damon Dran as an enforcer for his child slavery ring. But when Captain America and the brutal hero called Americop demolished Dran's operation, Golddigger attempted to flee in a helicopter, which was subsequently shot down. No one knows whether she truly perished in the crash. **TD**

GRANDMASTER

FACTFILE

REAL NAME
En Dwi Gast

OCCUPATION
Game player

BASE
Mobile throughout the universe

HEIGHT 7 ft 1 in
WEIGHT 240 lbs
EYES Red (no visible pupils)
HAIR White (pale blue skin)

FIRST APPEARANCE
Avengers Vol. 1 #69 (October 1969)

POWERS
The Grandmaster has an encyclopedic knowledge and comprehension of games and game theory played throughout the universe. Possesses a cosmic life force and is immune to aging, disease, or injury. Can levitate, project energy blasts, and travel through time, space, and alternate dimensions with the speed of thought. He can also rearrange matter on a planetary scale.

Like his kinsman, the COLLECTOR, the GRANDMASTER is one of the oldest living beings in the universe and a survivor of an intelligent extraterrestrial race that evolved shortly after the "Big Bang" that first created this universe. To combat the unending boredom of immortality, the Grandmaster has spent the eons amusing himself by engaging in various games, tournaments, and contests. He particularly relishes challenging other cosmic beings to games of skill and chance for incredibly high stakes.

Grandmaster discovered the alternate Earth inhabited by the SQUADRON SUPREME and created duplicates of these heroes which he pitted against the AVENGERS. He later decided to use Earth as a breeding ground for superhuman pawns for his games, but gave up this plan when he lost a bet to DAREDEVIL. He also challenged DEATH to a series of games, resulting in the banning of all the ELDERS OF THE UNIVERSE from her kingdom, making them all virtually immortal. He also once joined with the other Elders in a plot to kill GALACTUS, but that failed owing to intervention by the SILVER SURFER. **TD**

Daredevil challenges Grandmaster to a final game—with the Moon and the fate of the people of the entire Earth at stake.

Gorgon

FIRST APPEARANCE Fantastic Four Vol. 1 (November 1965)
REAL NAME Unrevealed
OCCUPATION Administrator **BASE** Attilan, blue Area, the Moon
HEIGHT 6 ft 5 in **WEIGHT** 450 lbs **EYES** Brown **HAIR** Black
SPECIAL POWERS/ABILITIES Immensely powerful legs and hooves give him the ability to create seismic tremors.

Gorgon is a member of the INHUMAN royal family and a cousin of their ruler, BLACK BOLT. Like all Inhumans, Gorgon underwent exposure to the mutating Terrigen mists as a youth and gained hooves in place of feet, complete with kinetic-release powers capable of creating seismic tremors measuring up to 7.5 on the Richter scale. Gorgon fled Attilan during the Inhumans' war against the Trikon, wandering Earth and encountering the FANTASTIC FOUR. Later, Gorgon and KARNAK teamed with DAREDEVIL in a search for Black Bolt's son. He is not to be confused with the Japanese villain called Gorgon who was recently killed by WOLVERINE. **DW**

Graviton

FIRST APPEARANCE Avengers Vol. 1 #158 (April 1977)
REAL NAME Franklin Hall
OCCUPATION Criminal **BASE** Mobile
HEIGHT 6 ft 1 in **WEIGHT** 200 lbs **EYES** Blue **HAIR** Black
SPECIAL POWERS/ABILITIES Control over gravity allows Graviton to levitate objects, generate force fields and shockwaves, and pin opponents to the ground.

Franklin Hall, a Canadian researcher, gained absolute control over gravity in an accident involving a particle accelerator. Dubbing himself Graviton, he raised the laboratory thousands of feet in the air in a demonstration of his power, until put in his place by the AVENGERS.

In subsequent adventures, Graviton fought the THUNDERBOLTS, SPIDER-MAN, and the West Coast Avengers (*see* Avengers, West Coast), and was the object of worship by the alien Ptah during a stay in an alternate dimension. Despite his abilities, Graviton has a deep-seated need for approval that makes him both insecure and megalomaniacal. **DW**

Grant, Gloria

Model Glory Grant befriended Peter Parker when they both lived in an apartment house on Manhattan's Lower West Side. Grant was looking for work, and Peter, a freelance photographer for the *Daily Bugle,* suggested she apply to be the paper's publisher J. Jonah JAMESON's secretary, a post recently vacated by Betty Brant LEEDS. The irascible Jameson liked Grant and she became Brant's replacement.

Mexican crimelord Eduardo Lobo seduced Grant to obtain the *Bugle*'s files on his enemy, the KINGPIN; in time, Grant and Lobo fell genuinely in love. During a battle between SPIDER-MAN and Lobo, Grant tried to shoot Spider-Man, but shot and killed Lobo instead. Later, Grant was possessed by the spirit of the voodoo sorceress CALYPSO as part of the latter's plan to return to life. Grant has enjoyed a more successful romantic relationship with Randy ROBERTSON, Joe's son. **PS**

FACTFILE
REAL NAME
Gloria "Glory" Grant
OCCUPATION
Administrative assistant, former model
BASE
New York City

HEIGHT 5 ft 8 in
WEIGHT 120 lbs
EYES Brown
HAIR Black

FIRST APPEARANCE
The Amazing Spider-Man #140 (February 1975)

GRANT, GLORIA

POWERS
Highly efficient secretarial skills, including typing and computer skills. Outgoing, romantic, and warm-hearted; prepared to do almost anything to help the man she loves.

Great Lakes Avengers

Formed by Craig Hollis (Mr. Immortal) the GLA was a self-proclaimed branch of the Avengers based in Wisconsin. Much mocked in the press and by other Super Heroes for their bizarre powers, lack of common sense, and high mortality rate, the GLA insisted on remaining together. Even when the team saved the entire Multiverse from destruction their success was totally overlooked on the evening news. The group's bills are met by Big Bertha, whose alter ego, supermodel Ashley Crawford, earns large sums modelling. Other misfit members have included: Squirrel Girl, Leather Boy, Monkey Joe, Tippy-Toe and Grasshopper. **AD**

THE GREAT LAKES AVENGERS
1 Mr. Immortal
2 Big Bertha
3 Dinah Soar
4 Flatman
5 Doorman

FACTFILE
FOUNDING MEMBERS AND POWERS
MR. IMMORTAL
Immortal; team leader
DINAH SOAR
Alien flying reptile, attacks with high-pitched shriek.
BIG BERTHA
Controls body mass; alternates between super-obesity and strength and supermodel skinniness.
DOORMAN
Can teleport self and others into the next room.
FLATMAN
Two-dimensional mutant with elasticated body.

FIRST APPEARANCE
The West Coast Avengers #46 (July 1989)

GREAT LAKES AVENGERS

GREEN GOBLIN

Spider-Man's greatest enemy

FACTFILE

REAL NAME
Norman Osborn

OCCUPATION
Criminal/Industrialist

BASE Mobile

HEIGHT 5 ft 11 in
WEIGHT 185 lbs
EYES Blue
HAIR Reddish-brown

FIRST APPEARANCE
Amazing Spider-Man #14 (July 1964)

POWERS
Superhuman strength, endurance, and reactions, endowed by Goblin Formula, have increased steadily over time; weaponry includes armoured costume, Goblin Glider and Pumpkin Bombs.

ALLIES/FOES
ALLIES The Enforcers, the Cable of Scrier, Crime-Master, Jackal, the Sinister Twelve

FOES Spider-Man

ISSUE #1
Teaming up with the Enforcers, the Green Goblin is determined to destroy Spider-Man.

Norman Osborn reveals himself to be the Green Goblin.

For almost as long as there has been a SPIDER-MAN, so too has the Green Goblin existed. Spider-Man's arch nemesis, the Green Goblin is the insane, malevolent alter ego of that once-respectable industrialist, Norman Osborn. Despite their mutual antagonism, the relationship between the pair is complex. Although the Green Goblin loathes and resents Spider-Man's very existence, for a long time Norman Osborn and Peter Parker shared a deep mutual respect and admiration. Osborn saw in the orphaned Peter the son he really wanted.

YOU MUST BE *NUTS* GOBLIN! I AIN'T LETTIN' *YOU* OR ANYONE ELSE TAKE OVER MY GANG! NOW HIT THE ROAD, MISTER, WHILE YOU STILL *CAN!*
DIG THAT CORNY COSTUME WILLYA?
BUT, UNDER *MY* LEADER-SHIP, WE COULD TAKE OVER EVERY RACKET IN THE CITY!

ESSENTIAL STORYLINES

- ***Amazing Spider-Man #39–40*** The Green Goblin discovers Peter Parker's secret identity, the Goblin is unmasked as Norman Osborn and we learn about his origins.
- ***Amazing Spider-Man #121–2*** A climactic battle between the Green Goblin and Spider-Man results in the death of Gwen Stacy and the Goblin's own, apparent, demise.
- ***Amazing Spider-Man #134–7*** Norman Osborn's son Harry discovers that Peter Parker is really Spider-Man and, looking for revenge, becomes the second Green Goblin.

GENESIS OF THE GOBLIN

Long before his transformation into the Green Goblin, Norman Osborn was an ambitious businessman, quite prepared to sacrifice others on the altar of his own success. The co-founder of chemical company Oscorp, Osborn gained total control by framing his business partner, Professor Mendel Stromm, for embezzlement. The Goblin Formula that was to prove Osborn's undoing was a concoction detailed in the professor's notes, but it was Osborn's attempt to manufacture it for himself that resulted in the solution exploding in his face. As a result of this explosion, Osborn's strength, stamina and reflexes were enhanced but his sanity began to erode.

As the Green Goblin, Osborn wished to lead New York's criminal underworld and he set out to gain the respect of the key gangs by destroying Spider-Man. He developed high-tech weaponry specifically designed to achieve this end. Despite discovering Spider-Man's true identity, the Green Goblin was ultimately defeated: an electric shock, sustained during a battle with the web-slinger, caused Osborn to regain his sanity and lose all memory of his malevolent alter ego. Peter Parker judged that it was better to allow Osborn to resume his old life.

STRIKING AT SPIDER-MAN

Osborn's regained sanity proved fragile. Time and again his inner demon—the Green Goblin—reasserted control, and

Tingling spider-sense, awesome strength, and superfast reflexes—Spider-Man needs all of these things to survive the Green Goblin's arsenal of weapons and enhanced body.

although Peter repeatedly brought Osborn back to reality, the businessman's grip on sanity became more and more tenuous. During this period, Peter's then-girlfriend, Gwen Stacy, met Osborn and, overwhelmed by his charisma, became pregnant by him. Nine months later, she gave birth to twins, Gabriel and Sarah, in France, keeping their existence a secret from Peter.

Following Gwen's return to New York, an angry altercation between her and a desperately unbalanced Osborn served to destabilize him further. Determined to punish both her and Spider-Man, when Osborn reverted to the Green Goblin he kidnapped Gwen and carried her to the top of Brooklyn Bridge.

OTHER GREEN GOBLINS

In becoming the Green Goblin, Norman Osborn inadvertently founded a Goblin dynasty. After witnessing his father's apparent death, a mentally unstable Harry Osborn adopted the Green Goblin mantle and attempted to destroy Spider-Man. Although Harry eventually put his father's legacy behind him, even settling down with a wife and child, life's pressures finally drove him back to the Goblin formula. Tragically, his body was killed by the deadly concoction. Twice, the Goblin name has been borne by non-Osborns, with Harry's psychiatrist, Bart Hamilton, and Phil Urich, the nephew of reporter Ben Urich, both being pretenders to the Goblin crown. More recently, Gabriel Stacy, the son of Norman Osborn and Gwen Stacy, injected himself with the Goblin formula to save his own life. Now the fifth Green Goblin, Gabriel remains at large, somewhere in Europe.

To protect his father, Harry Osborn says he is the Green Goblin.

The third Green Goblin is revealed.

All the Green Goblins have shared similar equipment.

The Goblin uses a variety of grenades which look like Halloween pumpkins.

A casualty of war, the Green Goblin throws Gwen Stacy to her death.

The ensuing confrontation with Spider-Man resulted in Gwen's death and in Osborn being impaled by his own Goblin Glider.

Peter Parker assumed that Osborn had been killed by this impact but he had not allowed for the extraordinary potency of the Goblin formula. While lying on a mortuary slab, Osborn's body suddenly revived. To keep his survival secret, Osborn substituted his own body with that of an anonymous drifter.

Osborn travelled to Europe, where he took control of a secret society known as the Scriers. At the same time he watched over Gwen's children, tending to their physical needs while warping their minds against Peter Parker by convincing them that Peter was their father and had abandoned them.

The War Becomes Personal

In the years that followed, Osborn's attacks on Peter were increasingly aimed at causing him emotional rather than physical harm. He created a clone of Peter but this failed to unsettle the Super Hero's self-belief. Osborn even tried to torture and drug Peter into becoming a new Green Goblin, but Peter's strength of personality proved to be unassailable.

At present, Osborn has gone to ground but Peter's recent discovery of Gabriel and Sarah's existence has shown that this unhinged criminal mastermind still has the ability to cause deep hurt. It may well be that their fates are forever intertwined. For as long as there is a Spider-Man perhaps there will always be an evil Green Goblin. **AD**

Harry Osborn prevents the Ultimate universe Green Goblin from destroying Spider-Man. Norman Osborn had injected himself with a spider-serum. Rather than endowing him with Spider-Man's powers, the serum transformed Osborn into a crazed demonic creature.

Gremlin

FIRST APPEARANCE Incredible Hulk vol. 2 #187 (May 1975)
REAL NAME Unrevealed
OCCUPATION Scientist **BASE** A secret base in Khystyro, somewhere in the Arctic and Bitterfrost, a secret base in Siberia
HEIGHT 4 ft 6 in **WEIGHT** 215 lbs **EYES** Blue **HAIR** None
SPECIAL POWERS/ABILITIES Mutant who inherited father's genius-level intelligence; battlesuit gave superhuman strength.

The Gremlin is the son of the dead Soviet scientist known as the GARGOYLE, who participated in atomic tests that vastly increased his intelligence but scarred his face and body. The Gargoyle died following an encounter with Bruce Banner, the HULK. The Gremlin's intelligence was so great that he achieved a position of authority while only a child. Unfairly blaming the Hulk for his father's death, the Gremlin frequently tried to destroy him. Wearing a battlesuit similar to TITANIUM MAN, he was eventually killed in a battle with IRON MAN. **TD**

Grey, Jean *see pages 122-3*

Grim Reaper

FIRST APPEARANCE Avengers #52 (May 1968)
REAL NAME Eric Williams
OCCUPATION Criminal **BASE** Mobile
HEIGHT/WEIGHT Unrevealed **EYES** Brown **HAIR** Black
SPECIAL POWERS/ABILITIES Wears a scythe in place of his right hand which can fire arcs of electrical energy, and make victims comatose; now a spirit with power to absorb life forces.

The criminal brother of the Avenger WONDER MAN, Eric Williams became the Grim Reaper to get revenge on the AVENGERS, whom he believed were responsible for Wonder Man's death. To that end, he allied with ULTRON, and then formed the LETHAL LEGION. Even after Wonder Man revived, the insane Reaper refused to believe it, and died pursuing his vendetta. He was revived by a vampiric ally, NEKRA, and is now a malevolent spirit. **TD**

Guardian

FIRST APPEARANCE X-Men #109 (February 1978)
REAL NAME James MacDonald Hudson
OCCUPATION Scientist, adventurer **BASE** Canada (Dept. H)
HEIGHT 6 ft 2 in **WEIGHT** 196 lbs **EYES** Blue **HAIR** Black
SPECIAL POWERS/ABILITIES Electromagnetic battlesuit has built-in force-field, allows him to fly, and discharge force bolts; also uses gravity to slingshot him in a westward direction at 1000 mph.

James MacDonald Hudson stole the prototype battlesuit he was developing when he discovered that his employers, Am-Can Petro-Chemical, intended to turn it over to the US military. Hudson took the suit to the Canadian government, and proposed they create a superhuman team like the FANTASTIC FOUR. This team became ALPHA FLIGHT, led by Hudson (codenamed Vindicator). Eventually, Alpha Flight was suspended by the Canadian government, but its members remained together. Hudson took the name Guardian to symbolize his new role. Despite many travails, including his seeming death and resurrection, Hudson continues to lead Alpha Flight to this day. **TD**

Grey Gargoyle

French chemist Pierre Paul Duval inadvertently spilled a potion that had been contaminated by an unknown organic substance onto his right hand. To his astonishment, his right hand permanently transformed into stone; however, he could still move it as if it were ordinary flesh. When Duval discovered that he could transform his *entire body* into mobile, living stone, he decided to become a costumed criminal named the Grey Gargoyle.

Hoping to learn the secret of immortality, the Grey Gargoyle battled THOR, who remains his principal enemy. Over the years, the Gargoyle has also contended against IRON MAN, CAPTAIN AMERICA, SPIDER-MAN, the HULK, the AVENGERS and the FANTASTIC FOUR. The Grey Gargoyle also briefly served as a member of BARON ZEMO'S MASTERS OF EVIL.

For a time the Grey Gargoyle used a secret identity as "sculptor" Paul St. Pierre, transforming real people into supposed stone sculptures. **PS**

Grey Gargoyle

FACTFILE
REAL NAME
Paul Pierre Duval
OCCUPATION
Chemist, criminal
BASE
Mobile
HEIGHT 5 ft 11 in
WEIGHT 175 lbs (human form); 750 lbs (stone form)
EYES Blue (human form); white (stone form)
HAIR Black (human form); gray (stone form)

FIRST APPEARANCE
Journey into Mystery #107 (August 1964)

POWERS
Can transform himself into living stone without losing mobility, thereby gaining superhuman strength and durability. By touching people or objects with his right hand, he can transform them into an immobile, stone-like substance for about an hour.

The Grey Gargoyle retains his normal agility when in stone form, despite his increased weight. With his superhuman strength, he can leap nearly twenty feet into the air.

Guardians of the Galaxy

FACTFILE

NOTABLE MEMBERS AND POWERS

MAJOR VICTORY
(Vance Astrovik) Psychokinesis, mental force blasts.

ALETA
Can create objects of solid light.

CHARLIE-27
Enhanced strength and stamina.

MARTINEX
Enhanced strength, projection of heat and cold.

NIKKI
Resistant to heat and bright light, sharpshooter.

STARHAWK
Flight, enhanced strength, energy projection.

YONDU
Skilled archer, mystical sensory abilities.

BASE
Mobile

FIRST APPEARANCE
Marvel Super Heroes Vol. 1 #18 (January 1969)

In an alternate timeline of the 31st century, the Guardians of the Galaxy act as protectors of the Milky Way. The group formed in response to the Badoon invasion of 3007, which decimated Pluto, Mercury, Jupiter, and Earth. The Guardians defeated the Badoon by 3015, then became adventurers. They have traveled to Earth's current reality several times, becoming honorary members of the AVENGERS. The Guardians' adventures in their own time included a quest for Captain America's shield. At this time, Vance Astrovik convinced his younger self to follow a different path, leading to his mainstream version becoming MARVEL BOY (later Justice). Other teammates have included Hollywood (a future WONDER MAN); the feline Talon, the shapeshifting SKRULL Replica, a time-traveling Yellowjacket II, and the former herald of GALACTUS, FIRELORD. **DW**

CHARACTER KEY
1 Spirit of Vengeance (Ghost Rider)
2 Martinex ***3*** Replica ***4*** Phoenix IX
5 Firelord ***6*** Hollywood (Wonder Man)

Guardsman

FACTFILE

REAL NAME
Kevin O'Brien

OCCUPATION
Research scientist

BASE
Long Island, New York

HEIGHT 5 ft 10 in
WEIGHT 195 lbs
EYES Blue
HAIR Red

FIRST APPEARANCE
Iron Man #43 (November 1971)

POWERS
Armor augments strength and enables flight; it is also equipped with radiation shielding and pulsed laser.

Kevin O'Brien headed up Stark Industries' research department and aided IRON MAN against the SPYMASTER and the Espionage Elite. After revealing that he was Iron Man, Stark asked O'Brien to substitute for him if the need arose. That day came before O'Brien's Guardsman armor had been fully tested. Stark was kidnapped; O'Brien put on his armor, but its circuitry malfunctioned, stimulating areas of O'Brien's brain responsible for rage and jealousy. Guardsman and Iron Man clashed and Kevin was accidentally killed. Furious, Kevin's brother Michael obtained the Guardsman armor, and fought Stark. They have since become reconciled, and Michael led a Guardsman force guarding the high-tech Vault prison. **AD**

Kevin O'Brien tries on the Guardsman armor for the first time.

Ultimately, Tony Stark's victory over the Guardsman depended on his greater experience.

Gyrich

FIRST APPEARANCE Avengers #168 (February 1978)
REAL NAME Henry Peter Gyrich
OCCUPATION Adventurer **BASE** Washington, DC
HEIGHT 6 ft 8 in **WEIGHT** 225 lbs **EYES** Green **HAIR** Red
SPECIAL POWERS/ABILITIES Gyrich is a normal human being with no superhuman powers; a cunning, ruthless strategist and highly efficient administrator.

Henry Peter Gyrich was appointed by the US National Security Council to be a government liaison to the AVENGERS. He threatened to cut off the Super Hero team's unlimited airspace access and use of top secret government equipment unless the team followed his rules. After overseeing Avengers activities for many months, Gyrich was made special consultant to Project Wideawake, a plan to oversee mutant activity in America and combat the threat of foreign mutants and alien invaders. To this end, he took the BROTHERHOOD OF EVIL MUTANTS and changed their name to FREEDOM FORCE. **MT**

Jean Grey

Telepath of virtually unlimited psychic power

ESSENTIAL STORYLINES
- ***Uncanny X-Men #129 –137***
The Dark Phoenix Saga.
- ***Fantastic Four #286, X-Factor #1***
Jean Grey returns from apparent death and reunites with Scott Summers (Cyclops).
- ***X-Men Vol. 2 #30***
At long last the wedding of Jean Grey and her beloved Scott Summers takes place.

JEAN GREY

FACTFILE

REAL NAME
Jean Grey-Summers

OCCUPATION
Adventurer, former fashion model

BASE
Formerly the Xavier Institute, Salem Center, New York State; now the "White Hot Room"

HEIGHT 5 ft 6 in
WEIGHT 110 lbs
EYES Green
HAIR Red

FIRST APPEARANCE
X-Men #1 (September 1963)

POWERS

As Marvel Girl, possessed mutant abilities of telepathy and telekinesis. The Phoenix Force amplified these powers to a virtually unlimited extent. The Phoenix Force can manifest itself as a fiery corona in the shape of a bird that surrounds Jean Grey's body.

ALLIES/FOES

ALLIES Professor Charles Xavier, Cyclops, Archangel, Beast, Iceman, Storm, Wolverine, Marvel Girl (Rachel Summers), Cable

FOES Magneto, Mastermind, Hellfire Club, Apocalypse, Sentinels, Xorn I

ISSUE #1

In the first *X-Men* comic, Jean Grey arrived at Professor Xavier's school, met her future husband Scott Summers, became Marvel Girl, and first battled Magneto.

Jean's telekinetic power enables her to levitate objects.

When Jean Grey was ten years old, her best friend, Annie Richardson, was hit by an automobile. Jean's anguish as she held her friend activated her mutant telepathic powers, and Jean thus shared Annie's emotions as she died. Traumatized, Jean suffered from deep depression and was unable to control her new telepathic powers.

MARVEL GIRL

Jean Grey was only a small child when she first met Charles Xavier. She joined the X-Men in her mid-teens.

When Jean was eleven, her parents turned to Professor Charles Xavier (*see* PROFESSOR X) for help. Xavier created psychic shields in Jean's mind to prevent her from utilizing her telepathic powers until she was mature enough to control them. He also began training her telekinetic ability to mentally manipulate objects. As a teenager, Jean enrolled in Xavier's School for Gifted Youngsters, becoming the fifth member of the original X-MEN, the team of young mutants whom Xavier was training to combat mutant menaces to humanity. Grey was given the codename "Marvel Girl."

Grey and her fellow student Scott Summers (CYCLOPS) quickly fell in love, although they did not reveal their feelings to each other for a long time. After she had trained for years at his school, Xavier finally enabled Grey to use her telepathic powers.

Following Xavier's recruitment of a new class of X-Men, Grey left the team. However, soon afterwards she and other X-Men were abducted by SENTINELS to a space station orbiting the Earth. The X-Men had to escape back to Earth in a space shuttle during a solar radiation storm. Grey volunteered to pilot the shuttle, although she had to sit in a section without sufficient radiation shielding. Grey's powers proved insufficient to hold back the intense radiation, and it began killing her.

Phoenix Force: This primal power of creation and destruction manifests itself as a gigantic bird of prey composed of cosmic flame.

PHOENIX FORCE

A sentient cosmic entity of limitless power, the Phoenix Force, made contact with the dying Grey. The Phoenix Force created a human host body for itself that was a duplicate of Grey's, and infused it with a portion of her consciousness. The Phoenix Force placed Grey's original body into suspended animation within a large cocoon, in which it would slowly heal. When the shuttle crash-landed in Jamaica Bay, the Phoenix Force's new host body rose from the water, declaring herself to be Phoenix. The X-Men believed that Phoenix was the real Jean Grey, and Phoenix/Grey joined the team.

The X-Men's old foe the criminal Mastermind began manipulating Phoenix/Grey's mind to prove his worthiness to join the Inner Circle of the

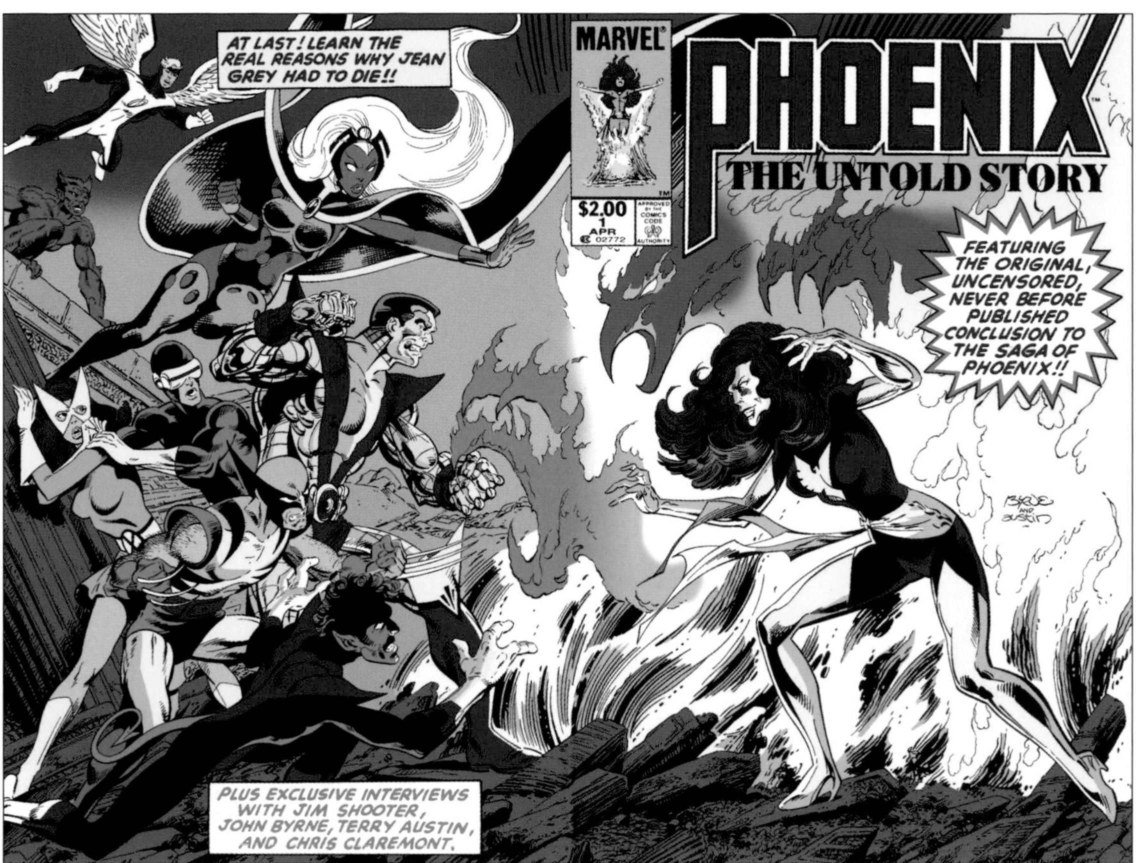

In this cover, Jean Grey appears as Marvel Girl (on the left, with the X-Men) confronting herself as Dark Phoenix (on the right). in the classic "Dark Phoenix Saga."

BLACK QUEEN

The mutant Mastermind projected illusions directly into Phoenix's mind, in which she led a dissolute life in the 18th century. Thus he brainwashed her into becoming the sinister new Black Queen of the Inner Circle of the Hellfire Club. Phoenix regained her free will and sent Mastermind into a coma. However his malevolent tampering with her mind triggered her metamorphosis into the evil Dark Phoenix.

Hellfire Club, thereby awakening the dark side of her personality. Finally, Mastermind mesmerized her into becoming the new Black Queen of the Hellfire Club. However Mastermind could not control her for long: Phoenix/Jean Grey not only turned against him, she transformed into the insane Dark Phoenix.

Dark Phoenix battled the X-Men, and inadvertently destroyed an inhabited planet. Finally, Jean's original personality reasserted itself. To prevent herself from reverting to Dark Phoenix, she committed suicide as the horrified Cyclops looked on.

Back from the Dead

Upon the death of Phoenix's body, the portion of Jean's consciousness within it returned to her original body within the cocoon at the bottom of Jamaica Bay. Scott Summers eventually married Madelyne Pryor, who later proved to be a Jean Grey clone created by Mister Sinister. Scott and Madelyne had a child, Nathan, who became the warrior Cable.

Eventually the cocoon was found by the Avengers, and a revived Jean Grey emerged from it. Soon she, Cyclops, and the other three original X-Men rejoined to found the original X-Factor team. Pryor went mad, developed superhuman powers as the Goblin Queen, and died in combat with Grey.

The series *X-Men: The End* depicts an alternate future timeline in which Jean Grey returns once more as Phoenix in time for the team's last adventure.

Inevitably, Grey and the other X-Factor founders rejoined the X-Men.

Finally, Jean Grey and Scott Summers were married, with the other X-Men in attendance. During their honeymoon, Jean and Scott's souls were transported into an alternate future by Mother Askani (Rachel Summers) and infused into new bodies. As "Redd" and "Slym," Jean and Scott raised Nathan Summers for ten years. Jean and Scott's souls were then sent back to their original bodies in their native time period.

Drifting Apart

Jean assumed the name "Phoenix" and linked herself with the Phoenix Force. Jean and Scott began drifting apart from one another, and Jean discovered that Scott was having an affair with Emma Frost, the former White Queen.

Later, the first Xorn, posing as Magneto, slew Grey. But the Phoenix Force resurrected Grey and bonded with her once again. Jean Grey is now "the White Phoenix of the Crown" and inhabits a higher level of reality, known as the "White Hot Room." PS

MARVEL IN THE

1970s

Marvel Comics began to experiment with its line of comics during the 1970s. *The Fantastic Four* celebrated its 100th issue in 1970, and new titles such as *Claws of the Cat*, *Marvel Team-Up*, *Red Wolf*, *Shanna the She-Devil*, *The Tomb of Dracula*, *Warlock*, *Werewolf By Night* and *Luke Cage, Hero for Hire* were launched in 1972. *The Monster of Frankenstein*, *Ghost Rider* and *Tales of the Zombie* followed in 1973. Marvel also published black and white magazines and Treasury-sized editions. *The Man-Thing* and *Marvel Two-In-One* both debuted in 1974.

The Champions, The Invaders, Iron Fist and Skull the Slayer were all awarded titles in 1975. The first issues of *Black Goliath*, *The Eternals*, *Howard the Duck*, *Nova*, *Omega the Unknown* and *Peter Parker, the Spectacular Spider-Man* appeared in 1976. The Black Panther finally starred in his own title in 1977, accompanied by *Ms. Marvel* and *What If*. *The Defenders*, *Devil Dinosaur*, *Machine Man*, and *Spider-Woman* all had first issues in 1978. As the decade drew to a close, the Avengers challenged Korvac, reality went wild when the X-Men first met Proteus and the Fantastic Four were artificially aged as Galactus battled the Sphinx.

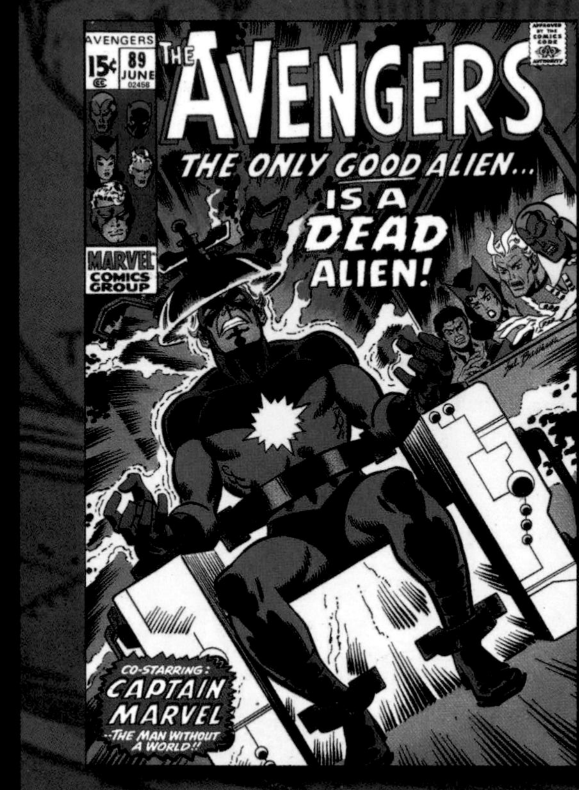

AVENGERS #89 (1971)

The Avengers suddenly find themselves in the middle of a war between the space-born Kree and the alien Skrulls.

TOMB OF DRACULA #1 (1972)

The first appearance of Dracula in the Marvel Universe and the start a new slew of comics based on classical monster.

AMAZING SPIDER-MAN #121 (1973)

Peter Parker's girlfriend Gwen Stacy is captured and murdered by his greatest enemy—Norman Osborn, the original Green Goblin.

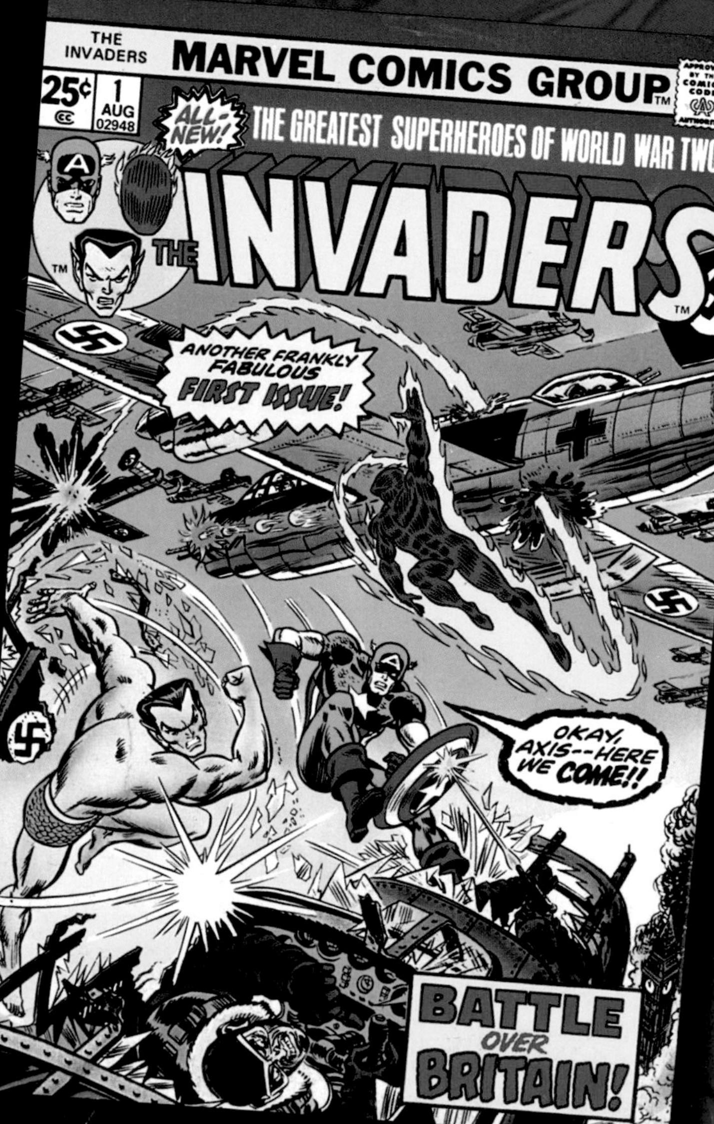

INVADERS #1 (1975)

Captain America, Bucky Barnes, the Human Torch, Toro, and Namor the Sub-Mariner unite to battle the Nazi menace during World War II.

AVENGERS #152 (1976)

After apparently dying in Avengers # 9, Wonder Man is resurrected and rejoins the team.

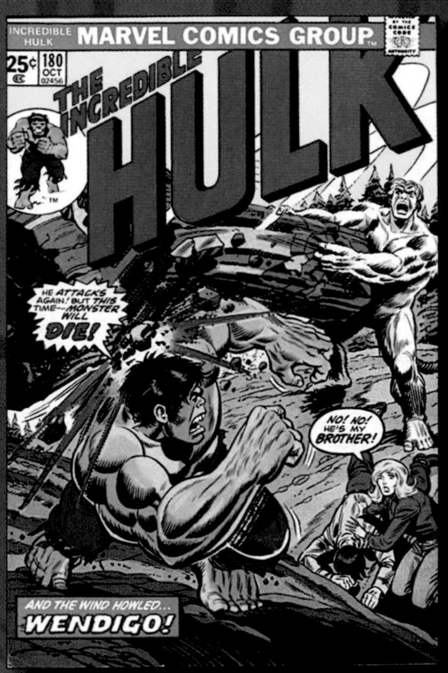

The Incredible Hulk #180 (1974)

Aside from fighting the mysterious Wendigo, the Hulk must also play host to the very first appearance of Wolverine.

Giant-Sized X-Men #1 (1975)

After a brief hiatus, the X-Men return with new members and a new concept as Nightcrawler, Storm and Thunderbird are introduced.

Spider-Woman #2 (1978)

Jessica Drew, the original Spider-Woman, teams up with the legendary Merlin the Magician to battle a menace from the golden age of Camelot.

Devil Dinosaur #2 (1978)

Moon Boy and his faithful companion battle strange monsters at the dawn of time.

Iron Man #128 (1979)

Tony Stark faces his greatest enemy—himself—as he finally admits that he has become an alcoholic.

Haller, Gabrielle

FIRST APPEARANCE The Uncanny X-Men #161 (September 1982)
REAL NAME Gabrielle Haller
OCCUPATION Israel's ambassador to the United Kingdom
BASE Tel Aviv, Israel; London, England
HEIGHT/WEIGHT Unrevealed **EYES** Brown **HAIR** Black
SPECIAL POWERS/ABILITIES Gabrielle Haller has no superpowers, but is a highly accomplished diplomat.

Gabrielle Haller is a survivor of the concentration camp in Dachau, Germany. There Nazis implanted in her mind the location of a hidden cache of gold. After the war, Haller was afflicted with catatonic schizophrenia and hospitalized in Israel. Charles Xavier (*see* Professor X) used his telepathic powers to cure her and they fell in love. When Baron Von Strucker and his HYDRA agents kidnapped Haller to find the gold, Xavier and "Magnus" (the future Magneto) rescued her.

Many years later Xavier learned that Gabrielle had given birth to a son, David (*see* Legion). Haller is now Israel's ambassador to UK. **PS**

Hammer, Justin

FIRST APPEARANCE Iron Man #120 (March 1979)
REAL NAME Justin Hammer
OCCUPATION Criminal financier **BASE** Mobile
HEIGHT 6 ft 2 in **WEIGHT** 170 lbs **EYES** Blue **HAIR** Gray
SPECIAL POWERS/ABILITIES A financial and business genius, Hammer has cunningly preserved his wealth despite being worldwide *persona non grata*.

Whatever Justin Hammer lacked in guile he made up for with low cunning. Infuriated by Stark International's success, Hammer resolved to undermine Tony Stark's business by compromising its corporate emblem, the Iron Man. Using a hypersonic device to take control of the armored suit, Hammer used it to kill a foreign ambassador. After Stark cleared his name, Hammer went into hiding and took to funding various criminals, including Blizzard, Boomerang, and Water Wizard. Another showdown with Stark left Hammer frozen in a block of ice and floating through space. **AD**

Hammerhead

Hammerhead's style recalls the Prohibition gangsters of the 1920s.

Once a small-time criminal, so obscure his real name is not known, Hammerhead was found, severely injured, by the criminal scientist Dr. Jonas Harrow after an apparent gang showdown. Harrow saw this as an opportunity to use some of his untested medical techniques on his nameless guinea pig. The doctor's experiments reconstructed the criminal's shattered skull, reinforcing it and making it as strong as steel—hence his new name.

Hammerhead was restored to health, but retained no knowledge of his past life, save that he had been a criminal. Taking his inspiration from the poster of a gangster movie, *The Al Capone Mob,* which was the last thing he saw before he was shot down, Hammerhead returned to the New York underworld. But this time he was determined to become the boss of bosses and prepared to violently dispatch anyone who stood in his way, including crimelords such as Doctor Octopus, the Kingpin and Maggia boss Don Fortunato. One of his few Super Villain allies is the Chameleon. **TB**

HAMMERHEAD

FACTFILE
REAL NAME
Unknown
OCCUPATION
Criminal; gang boss of Hammerhead "family"
BASE
Manhattan, New York City

HEIGHT 5 ft 10 in
WEIGHT 195 lbs
EYES Blue
HAIR Black

FIRST APPEARANCE:
Amazing Spider-Man #113 (October 1972)

POWERS

Hammerhead's reinforced skull allows him to head-butt with devastating effect, and even smash through walls. He can also use his head as a shield against blows. He has strong criminal organizational skills, and his favorite weapon is a Tommy gun.

A full-powered Spider-punch means nothing to the criminal with the hardest head in the business.

Hammerhead's skull is reinforced with an unbreakable steel alloy.

THE HAND

FACTFILE
NOTABLE MEMBERS
THE BEAST
Demon with mystical powers
KIRGI
Martial arts and occult magic
SHADOW
Martial arts and occult magic
THOUGHT
Martial arts and occult magic
PAIN
Martial arts and occult magic
KWANNON
Martial arts and occult magic
MANDARIN
Martial arts and occult magic

FIRST APPEARANCE
Daredevil #168 (Jan. 1981)

POWERS

In addition to possessing various mystical powers, Hand operatives are trained in the way of the ninja: expert spies and assassins skilled at unarmed combat, and with all kinds of weapons.

Hand, The

The Hand is a cult of mystical ninjas involved with organized crime and often hired to carry out assassinations. The Hand dates back to 16th-century Japan, where the cult adapted classical ninjitsu techniques to its own evil purposes. The Hand's activities have now spread throughout the world. Hand operatives are servants of a demon known only as the Beast. Skilled in the use of powerful occult magic, they can kill a person, then bring that person back to life as a member of the Hand. Only Elektra and Wolverine have ever been able to reverse this process. If one of the Hand is killed, his body magically turns to dust in order to prevent identification.

The Hand has most often clashed with Daredevil, Elektra, and other members of the clan of warriors once led by Stick, the late martial arts master. They have also battled Wolverine, Spider-Man, the Avengers, and the X-Men. **MT**

Implacable, faceless killers, the Hand cult remains one of the most feared groups of assassins at large in the modern world.

Harkness, Agatha

FIRST APPEARANCE Fantastic Four #94 (March 1969)
REAL NAME Agatha Harkness
OCCUPATION Witch **BASE** New York City
HEIGHT 5 ft 11 in **WEIGHT** 130 lbs **EYES** Blue **HAIR** White
SPECIAL POWERS/ABILITIES Could manipulate magical forces through the recitation of spells; possessed magical familiar named Ebony, a pet cat that could transform into a vicious panther.

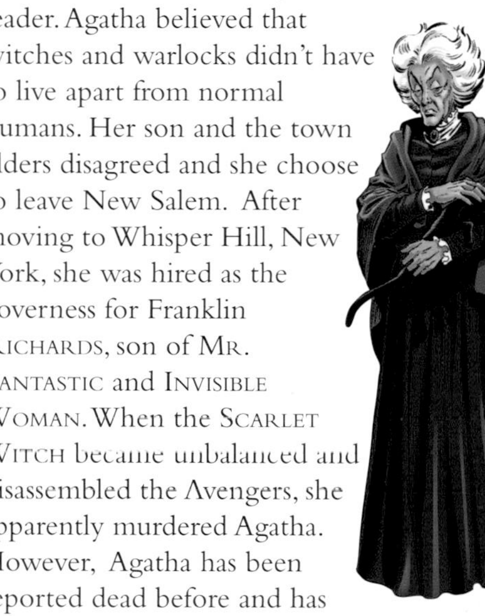

Agatha Harkness was raised in the town of New Salem, Colorado, whose inhabitants practiced magic. She excelled in her craft and eventually became the town's most powerful sorceress and leader. Agatha believed that witches and warlocks didn't have to live apart from normal humans. Her son and the town elders disagreed and she choose to leave New Salem. After moving to Whisper Hill, New York, she was hired as the governess for Franklin Richards, son of Mr. Fantastic and Invisible Woman. When the Scarlet Witch became unbalanced and disassembled the Avengers, she apparently murdered Agatha. However, Agatha has been reported dead before and has returned. **TD**

Havok

Holidaying in Mexico, Havok and Wolverine battle Dr. Neutron.

The brother of the X-Man Cyclops, Alex Summers was separated from his sibling following the deaths of their parents. Although Alex's mutant abilities developed during puberty, it was his mutant college professor, Ahmet Abdol, who was the first to recognize them. After absorbing the cosmic energy stored in Alex's body, Abdol became the Living Monolith but was defeated by the X-Men. Reunited with his brother, Alex was taken under the X-Men's wing, taught to control his abilities, and became a sometime member of Professor X's team.

Alex has fought alongside Wolverine, led X-Factor, and fought to save a dark and twisted alternate-reality Earth. Throughout these adventures, he has often felt stifled by his brother's reputation, and harboured a love for fellow mutant Lorna Dane (Polaris). Although their relationship has been repeatedly undermined, Alex is looking to rebuild bridges with Lorna and renew their romance. **AD**

HAVOK

FACTFILE
REAL NAME
Alexander "Alex" Summers
OCCUPATION
Adventurer; X-Man
BASE
New York State

HEIGHT 6 ft
WEIGHT 180 lbs
EYES Brown
HAIR Blond

FIRST APPEARANCE
X-Men #54 (March 1969)

POWERS

Havok can absorb solar energy and project it either in an omni-directional wave or iin the form of plasma bolts of intense heat, which causes objects to shatter or burn up.

Hawkeye

The Marksman

FACTFILE

REAL NAME
Clinton "Clint" Barton

OCCUPATION
Super Hero; Avengers member

BASE
Manhattan, New York City

HEIGHT 6 ft 3 in
WEIGHT 20 lbs
EYES Blue
HAIR Blond

FIRST APPEARANCE
Tales of Suspense #57 (September 1964)

POWERS
Expert archer with perfect accuracy. Employs an arsenal of custom-made bows and a variety of trick arrows. Extensive training as an aerialist and acrobat. Skilled in hand-to-hand combat.

An orphan who ran away to join a traveling carnival, Barton was only fourteen years old when he attracted the attention of the show's star attraction Jacques Duquesne, the SWORDSMAN. Duquesne began to train Barton in the art of throwing knives, but quickly realized the boy was a natural at archery and turned him over to Trickshot, the carnival's archer. After mastering the bow and arrow, Barton took on the stage name of Hawkeye the Marksman.

Wickedly sarcastic, Hawkeye has developed some of his trick arrows to both defeat and humiliate his foes.

Hawkeye and Black Widow on a mission.

GOING WRONG

After learning that Duquesne robbed the carnival's payroll to pay gambling debts, Barton was severely injured when his former mentor cut a tightrope out from under him. Rejoining the carnival after recovering from his injuries, Barton later witnessed IRON MAN in action and became inspired to use his archery skills to fight crime. However, when Hawkeye tried to prevent a robbery, he was mistaken for a thief and soon found himself battling Iron Man. He met Natalia "Natasha" Romanova, the BLACK WIDOW, who was a professional spy at the time. He quickly fell in love with her and was soon committing crimes to impress her.

REFORMED CHARACTER

Hawkeye later decided to reform and begged to be admitted into the AVENGERS. Impressed by his sincerity, his old enemy Iron Man sponsored him for membership. Hawkeye remained a member of the Avengers for many years, though he occasionally took brief breaks and even joined the Defender during one of them. To help the team, Hawkeye sometimes borrowed Hank Pym's growth formula and became a new version of Goliath.

Hawkeye and Mockingbird were partners in every sense of the word.

While on leave, Hawkeye married Bobbi Morse (MOCKINGBIRD). They moved to California when Hawkeye was assigned to set up the West Coast branch of the Avengers. After Mockingbird was killed in action and the West Coast branch was disbanded, Hawkeye rejoined the Avengers. He died in one of the many battles that recently caused the Avengers to disassemble. **TD**

ESSENTIAL STORYLINES

- ***Hawkeye (tpb)*** While working as head of security for Cross Industries, Hawkeye meets and marries Mockingbird.
- ***Solo Adventures #1-6*** Hawkeye's former mentor Trickshot returns and we learn Clint's true origin.
- ***West Coast Avengers Limited Series #1-4*** Hawkeye opens a branch office for the Avengers.
- ***Avengers #502*** Hawkeye courageously sacrifices his life to protect his Avengers teammates.

Headmen, The

The Headmen comprised four brilliant individuals, each so confident of their abilities they were convinced that they should rule the Earth. United by Dr Arthur Nagan they agreed to combine their talents to gain control of the planet. Despite obvious ability, their tactics were at best questionable.

Looking to obtain superhuman powers for themselves, the Headmen targeted the Defenders and succeeded in implanting Chondu's brain into the head of Kyle Richard, alias Nighthawk. When his consciousness was subsequently transferred into the body of a vile monster, Chondu went mad. Although his sanity had returned by the time his brain was transferred into a She-Hulk clone, this proved to be one step too far. Furious at having been given a woman's body, Chondu attacked the Headmen with the help of Spider-Man. The group reunited and attempted to take over the world, starting with Manhattan, by manipulating a hugely powerful, extra-dimensional entity named Orago the Unconquerable. **AD**

The Headmen
1 Gorilla-Man ***2*** Ruby Thursday ***3*** Orago the Unconquerable (not a member) ***4*** Chondu the Mystic ***5*** Shrunken Bones

FACTFILE

MEMBERS AND POWERS

GORILLA-MAN
(Dr. Arthur Nagan)
A brilliant scientist, whose head has been mysteriously transplanted onto a gorilla's body.

SHRUNKEN BONES
A biologist and biochemist, experiments on own body led to skeleton shrinking but not skin.

CHONDU THE MYSTIC
A minor adept in the mystic arts; powers determined by body occupied by brain.

RUBY THURSDAY
Artificial head serves as "organic computer", capable of superhuman storage and processing.

BASE Mobile

FIRST APPEARANCE
Defenders #21 (March 1975)

Hellcat

Patsy Walker had a teenage crush on Reed Richards of the Fantastic Four.

As a teenager, Patsy Walker was the subject of popular comic written by her mother. As an adult, Walker wed Air Force officer Buzz Baxter (later Mad Dog), though the marriage ended unhappily. She had always idolized Super Heroes, so Walker decided to become one, donning a costume once worn by Greer Nelson (Tigra). Calling herself Hellcat, she aided the Avengers and served with the Defenders for years. Eventually she married master of the occult Daimon Hellstrom, the Son of Satan. The couple moved to San Francisco, becoming paranormal investigators. Hellcat later took her own life, but her spirit lived on in Hell. There she encountered Hawkeye and the Thunderbolts, who had journeyed to the underworld to rescue Mockingbird. The team returned to Earth with Hellcat, who rededicated herself to the heroic life. She has since thwarted Dormammu's scheme to conquer Hell. **DW**

Hellcat with the Defenders
1 Doctor Strange ***2*** Hellcat ***3*** Nighthawk ***4*** Valkyrie ***5*** Damion Hellstrom

FACTFILE

REAL NAME
Patricia "Patsy" Walker Hellstrom

OCCUPATION
Adventurer

BASE
San Francisco, California

HEIGHT 5 ft 8 in
WEIGHT 135 lbs
EYES Blue
HAIR Red

FIRST APPEARANCE
Fantastic Four Vol. 1 #3 (March 1962)

POWERS
Minor psionic abilities, skilled acrobat and combatant (received combat training from Moondragon on Saturn's moon Titan). Costume enhances strength and agility; steel-tipped claws in gloves and boots; a wrist device fires a 30-ft cable with grappling hook for scaling tall buildings.

FACTFILE

HELLFIRE CLUB

MEMBERS
***1* SHINOBI SHAW**
(White King)
***2* SELENE**
(Black Queen)
***3* SEBASTIAN SHAW**
(Black King)
***4* EMMA FROST**
(White Queen)
***5* HARRY LELAND**
(Black Bishop)
***6* EMMANUEL DA COSTA**
(White Rook)
***7* JASON WYNGARDE**
(Mastermind)
***8* TESSA**
(Sage)
***9* DONALD PIERCE**
(White Bishop)
***10* FRIEDRICH VON ROEHM**
(Black Rook)
***11* MADELYNE PRYOR**
(Black Rook)
***12* TREVOR FITZROY**
(White Rook)

BASE
London, Manhattan, Paris, and Hong Kong

FIRST APPEARANCE
(as Council of the Chosen) X-Men (first series) #100 (August 1976); (as Hellfire Club) The Uncanny X-Men #129 (January 1980)

Hellfire Club

Founded in England in the mid-18th century, the Hellfire Club was an exclusive social organization for Britain's upper classes. According to legend, the Club provided a place where members could secretly pursue illicit pleasures. In the 1770s, Sir Patrick Clemens and Lady Diana Knight established the Hellfire Club's American branch in New York City. Today, the Hellfire Club is a worldwide organization with branches in London, Manhattan, Paris, and Hong Kong. Its members include socialites, celebrities, wealthy businessmen, and politicians. Despite the Club's outward respectability, its Inner Circle secretly seeks world domination through accruing political and economic influence. Inner Circle members hold positions named after chess pieces. The men dress in 18th-century costume and the women in risqué clothes.

Inner Circle

Industrialist Sebastian Shaw ruled as Black King over an Inner Circle that included his fellow mutant Emma Frost, the White Queen, and cyborg Donald Pierce. To win admission to the Inner Circle, Mastermind mesmerized Phoenix into becoming the Club's Black Queen. Other members of American Inner Circles in recent years have included Magneto, Selene, Daimon Hellstorm, Blackheart, the Viper, Sunspot, and Cassandra Nova. **PS**

Hellions

FIRST APPEARANCE New Mutants #16 (June 1984)
BASE Snow Valley, MA
CURRENT MEMBERS AND POWERS
Rockslide (Santo Vaccarro) Made of granite, can fire hands as projectiles [1]; **Emma Frost** Telepath [2]; **Wither** (Kevin Ford) Touch disintegrates organic matter [3]; **Dust** (Sooraya Qadir) Turns into a sandlike substance [4]; **Mercury** (Cessily Kincaid) Shapeshifter made of non-toxic mercury [5]; **Hellion** (Julian Keller) Telekinesis [6]; **Tag** (Brian Cruz) Tags others, causing them to emit a psionic signal [7]

Three groups of young mutants have called themselves the Hellions. The original Hellions were students at Emma Frost's Massachusetts Academy who served the Hellfire Club. They were wiped out by a psychotic criminal. The second band were formed by the brother of X-Force member Bedlam, and were out solely for their own interests. The third group of Hellions, students at the Xavier Institute for Higher Learning, had a reputation as bad boy rebels. They ceased to exist in the aftermath of M-Day. **TB**

Hellstorm

FIRST APPEARANCE Marvel Spotlight #12 (October 1973)
REAL NAME Daimon Hellstrom
OCCUPATION Demonologist, occult investigator, exorcist, former priest **BASE** San Francisco, CA.
HEIGHT 6 ft 1 in **WEIGHT** 180 lbs **EYES** Blue **HAIR** Red
SPECIAL POWERS/ABILITIES Trident projects "soulfire;" can cast spells to transport himself and others into mystical dimensions.

Daimon Hellstrom is the son a demon father named Satan and a human mother. Sent to an orphanage after his mother's breakdown, Daimon returned home to discover her diary and thus learned the truth about his father. Satan brought him to the demon's netherworld domain, where Daimon vowed to battle his father. As Son of Satan he joined the Defenders and eventually defeated his father. Daimon married Patsy Walker (Hellcat of the Defenders) and the two lived in San Francisco working as supernatural investigators. Daimon uses the costume identity of Hellstorm to secretly battle supernatural menaces. **MT**

Hercules *SEE OPPOSITE PAGE*

High Evolutionary

FIRST APPEARANCE Thor #134 (November 1966)
REAL NAME Herbert Edgar Wyndham
OCCUPATION Founder of the Knights of Wundagore **BASE** ?
HEIGHT 6 ft 2 in **WEIGHT** 200 lbs **EYES** Brown **HAIR** Brown
SPECIAL POWERS/ABILITIES Highly evolved intelligence; immense psionic powers; armor reconstructs body when injured enabling virtual immortality; able to grow to 300 ft.

At Oxford in the 1930s, Herbert Wyndham built a genetic accelerator that evolved any entity placed inside it. Ostracised by his peers, he joined up with scientist Jonathan Drew to establish a research center at Wundagore Mountain in the Balkans. Wyndham used his accelerator to evolve his own mind, becoming the High Evolutionary. He created a series of humanoid animals, and, calling them the Knights of Wundagore, charged them with defending Wundagore Mountain. The High Evolutionary later founded a new planetary home for his knights, established Counter-Earth, and tried to evolve humanity to a new state of being. The Avengers stopped this last effort, but the High Evolutionary is likely to meddle in human affairs again at some time. **AD**

Hercules

Super-strong demigod son of Zeus

During his 12 labors, Hercules killed a flock of man-eating birds belonging to his half-brother Ares, the god of war, who has hated him ever since.

Hercules is the son of Zeus, king of the Gods of Olympus, and a mortal woman. He is best known for his Twelve Labors, which he carried out to prove that he was worthy of immortality. He also made three enemies during the course of these labors: Ares, the god of war, Pluto (Hades), the lord of the underworld and Typhon, the giant son of Titan.

PRINCE OF POWER

Hercules is known throughout Olympus as the Prince of Power and he lives for the thrill of battle. He also believes that it is a great honor to fight him and often bestows this so-called "gift" on both friends and foes alike. Instead of a handshake, Hercules likes to greet his fellow Avengers with a friendly punch in the face!

In modern times, Hercules met and battled Thor when the thunder god accidentally journeyed to Olympus. Hercules later traveled to Earth to renew his acquaintance with the Asgardian and unwittingly signed a contract that made him Pluto's slave. After being rescued by Thor, Hercules returned to Olympus until the Enchantress cast a spell on him and sent him to battle the Avengers. He later joined the team when Zeus temporarily exiled him to Earth. He was taken prisoner by Ares and his minions, but rescued by the Avengers. Hercules joined Thor on a journey to the far end of the galaxy, where they battled the Destroyer, Firelord and Ego, the Living Planet. He also joined the Los Angeles super-team known as the Champions and spent time as one of the Defenders.

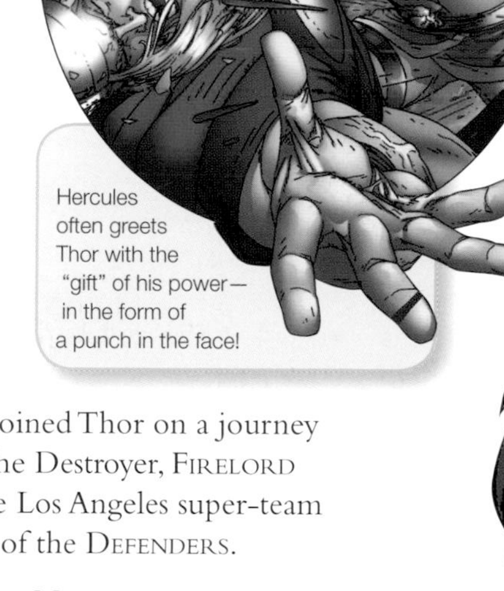

Hercules often greets Thor with the "gift" of his power— in the form of a punch in the face!

THE TRIALS OF HERCULES

Hercules was nearly beaten to death and left in a coma when the Masters of Evil seized control of Avengers Mansion. He eventually recovered, but fought the Avengers during a brief bout of insanity. While fighting the High Evolutionary during the so-called "Evolutionary Wars,",, Hercules was mutated beyond godhood, but later regained his normal appearance. His stepmother Hera, who had always resented him, conjured an illusion of a mortal woman and cast a spell on Hercules so that he fell in love with it. He was heartbroken when he learned the truth. **TD**

Hercules has been unlucky in love. He falls for mortal women who grow old and die while he remains young.

Though outnumbered, Hercules tried to defeat the Masters of Evil and almost paid the price.

FACTFILE

REAL NAME
Hercules; aliases Heracles, Harry Cleese

OCCUPATION
Adventurer

BASE
Olympus

HEIGHT 6 ft 5 in
WEIGHT 325 lbs
EYES Blue
HAIR Dark brown

FIRST APPEARANCE:
Journey Into Mystery Annual #1 (1965)

POWERS
Virtually immortal. Trained in hand-to-hand combat and ancient Greek wrestling skills. Excellent archer. Wields a practically indestructible golden mace.

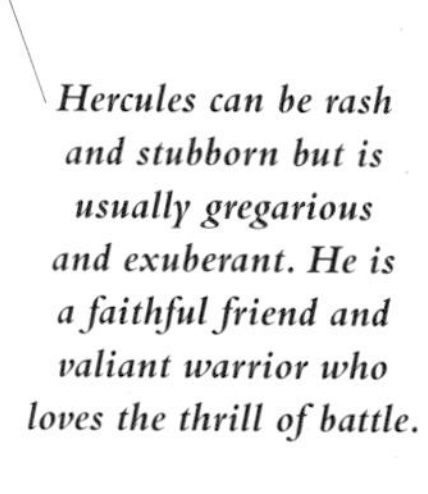

Hercules can be rash and stubborn but is usually gregarious and exuberant. He is a faithful friend and valiant warrior who loves the thrill of battle.

ESSENTIAL STORYLINES
- ***Thor #124 –130*** Hercules' first journey to Earth in modern times: enslaved by Pluto, rescued by Thor.
- ***The Avengers: Under Siege tpb*** Zemo's new Masters of Evil invade Avengers Mansion and almost beat Hercules to death.
- ***Hercules: Prince of Power tpb*** Hercules confronts Galactus in the far future.

HOBGOBLIN

FACTFILE

REAL NAME
Roderick Kingsley

OCCUPATION
Super Villain

BASE
Mobile

HEIGHT 5 ft 11 in
WEIGHT 185 lbs
EYES Blue
HAIR Gray

FIRST APPEARANCE
Spectacular Spider-Man #43 (June 1980)

POWERS
Hobgoblin's strength and agility are enhanced by improved Goblin formula; flies upon a vertical-thrust Goblin glider; wears electro-shock gloves; carries Jack O'Lantern-shaped grenades in a pouch. Possessed an armor-plated battle-van with an arsenal of weaponry.

Hobgoblin

When one of the victims of his unscrupulous dealings—Belladonna—attempted to kill him, Roderick Kingsley looked for ways to defend himself. He uncovered a cache of the Green Goblin's costumes and weaponry, hidden in the New York sewers. Thus equipped, he sought to dominate New York's criminal underworld as Hobgoblin; however, his efforts were undermined by Spider-Man.

To defeat the Wallcrawler, Kingsley has manipulated two other men into taking the Hobgoblin role. Petty crook Lefty Donovan served as a human guinea pig when Kingsley wanted to test his own version of the Goblin formula; and, after being brainwashed by Kingsley, Ned Leeds also acted as Kingsley's substitute until his death. Since Betty Leeds outed Kingsley as the Hobgoblin, he has been in hiding, plotting revenge from the sanctuary of the Caribbean. AD

The various Hobgoblins have all tested Spider-Man's mettle, but the doughty wall-crawler is always victorious.

Hodge, Cameron

FIRST APPEARANCE X-Factor #1 (February 1986)
REAL NAME Cameron Hodge
OCCUPATION Businessman **BASE** Mobile
HEIGHT 6 ft 2 in **WEIGHT** 196 lbs **EYES** Blue **HAIR** Black
SPECIAL POWERS/ABILITIES Cunning manipulator; due to a pact with the demon N'astrih, Cameron Hodge cannot die; since becoming a cyborg, he has vast strength and weaponry.

Cameron Hodge grew up secretly hating mutants, becoming the leader of the anti-mutant radical group the Right. Hodge suggested that the X-Men go undercover as mutant hunters called X-Factor, so as to conceal their activities in recruiting and training mutants. However, his real objective was to stir up anti-mutant sentiment. Hodge later made a pact with the demon N'astrih that gave him immortality. Even after his head was cut off and he was consumed by the techno-organic race known as the Phalanx, Hodge remained a thorn in the X-Men's side. TB

Hogan, Harold

FIRST APPEARANCE X-Men Alpha #1 (February 1995)
REAL NAME Harold "Happy" Hogan
OCCUPATION Tony Stark's right-hand man; chauffeur
BASE New York City **HEIGHT** 5 ft 11 in **WEIGHT** 221 lbs
EYES Brown **HAIR** (as human) Brown; (as Freak) None
SPECIAL POWERS/ABILITIES As the Freak, Hogan possesses superhuman strength and durability.

When former boxer "Happy" Hogan saved Tony Stark from a car crash, Stark hired him as his chauffeur. Hogan eventually realized that Stark was secretly the famous Super Hero Iron Man. When the need arose, Hogan would occasionally don an Iron Man battlesuit and stand in for Stark. Doctors used Stark's invention, the Enervator, to save Hogan's life, but its cobalt radiation had the unfortunate side-effect of transforming Hogan into a virtually mindless monster known as the Freak. Iron Man subsequently employed the Enervator to change Happy Hogan back to his normal human form, although Hogan has sometimes reverted to the Freak. PS

Holocaust

FIRST APPEARANCE X-Men Alpha #1 (February 1995)
REAL NAME Unknown
OCCUPATION Horseman of the Apocalypse **BASE** Mobile
HEIGHT 6 ft 2 in **WEIGHT** 240 lbs **EYES** Red **HAIR** Blond
SPECIAL POWERS/ABILITIES Holocaust is a flaming skeleton held inside a containment suit; able to absorb energy and release it as concussive power blasts.

Sired in the Age of Apocalypse timeline, Holocaust claimed to be the son of Apocalypse and served as the leader of Apocalypse's Four Horsemen. Escaping from that timeline just moments before it was obliterated, Holocaust was transported to Earth-616, where he destroyed the Avalon space station and battled another timeline refugee, X-Man. Press-ganged into joining reality-hopping heroes the Exiles, an encounter with a tyrannical Hyperion led to Holocaust's demise. After cracking his containment suit, Hyperion literally absorbed his entire being. AD

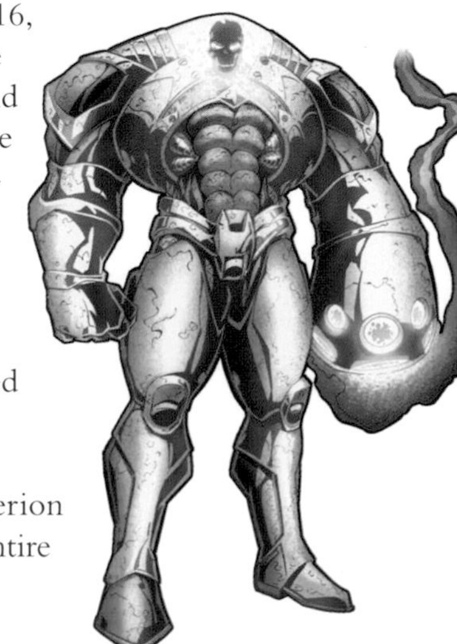

Hornet

FIRST APPEARANCE Slingers #0 (December 1998)
REAL NAME Eddie McDonough
OCCUPATION Adventurer **BASE** New York City
HEIGHT 5 ft 11 in **WEIGHT** 175 lbs **EYES** Blue **HAIR** Black
SPECIAL POWERS/ABILITIES Cybernetic suit has built-in electrical stingers and provides flight, enhanced strength, and damage resistance.

SPIDER-MAN created the identity of the Hornet during a time when he adopted four separate personas in response to a bogus murder charge. The discarded costumes later found their way into the hands of the Black Marvel, who gave them to four youths to create the Slingers. Empire State University student Eddie McDonough became the new Hornet, and found that the armored exoskeleton permitted him to use his normally palsied right arm. The Slingers soon disbanded when the members discovered that the Black Marvel had received the costumes from the demon MEPHISTO, and the Hornet later died at the hands of a brainwashed WOLVERINE. DW

Howard the Duck

Howard feels the strain of life in a world not his own.

Howard the Duck was born on Duckworld, a planet in another dimension, where the most intelligent life evolved from waterfowl. When the demon Thog the Nether-Spawn caused the Interdimensional Cosmic Axis to Shift, Howard was dropped into the Florida Everglades on Earth, the site of the Nexus of All Realities, where many dimensions meet.

Hoping to correct the Cosmic Axis and get home, Howard joined up with Korrek the Barbarian, the Earth sorceress Jennifer KALE, Dakimh the Enchanter, and the MAN-THING. As this group battled Thog in an inter-dimensional mêlée, Howard fell off the Stepping-Stones of Oblivion and tumbled back to Earth, landing in the city of Cleveland, Ohio. There he met Beverly SWITZLER, when the two were attacked by the costumed criminal accountant Pro-Rata. Howard and Beverly escaped, and began living together, attempting to have as normal a life as possible in a human-duck relationship. MT

FACTFILE
REAL NAME
Howard (last name unknown)
OCCUPATION
Many, including former candidate for President of the United States; most often unemployed.
BASE
Cleveland, Ohio

HEIGHT 2 ft 7 in
WEIGHT 40 lbs
EYES Brown
FEATHERS Yellow

FIRST APPEARANCE
Fear #19
(December 1973)

POWERS
Howard is skilled in the little-known martial art of Quack Fu, and a formidable opponent in hand-to-hand combat.

Howling Commandos

The Howling Commandos was the first attack squad of Able Company during World War II, a unit specifically designed and peopled so as to take on the most dangerous missions of the war. Under orders from Captain "Happy" Sam SAWYER, Sgt. Nick FURY led his ragtag group of soldiers against the worst the Axis powers could throw at them, including the legendary Blitzkrieg Squad of BARON VON STRUCKER, and the malevolent RED SKULL himself. The Howlers racked up an impressive record during the war, and many members of the unit survived to become the nucleus of the UN peace-keeping force known as SHIELD. Recently, the Howling Commandos name has been reactivated within SHIELD, and used to refer to a top-secret squad comprised of monsters and dedicated to battling supernatural forces against which normal SHIELD operatives would prove ineffective. TB

The Howling Commandos were heroes of World War II.

HOWLING COMMANDOS
1 Sgt. Nick Fury
2 Jonathan "Junior" Juniper
3 Reb Ralston
4 Cpl. Dum Dum Dugan
5 Gabe Jones
6 Dino Manelli
7 Izzy Cohen

FACTFILE
MEMBERS
Sgt. Nick Fury; Corporal Thaddeus "Dum Dum" Dugan; Privates Dino Manelli, Izzy Cohen, Gabe Jones, Percival Pinkerton, Reb "Rebel" Ralston, Jonathan "Junior" Juniper (killed in action), Eric Koenig

BASE
Pacific Theater of Operations, World War II

FIRST APPEARANCE
Sgt. Fury and His Howling Commandos #1
(May 1963)

POWERS
Apparently ill-assorted group welded into crack unit by Sgt. Fury's unmatched leadership qualities. Each member was a highly trained commando, with skills in hand-to-hand combat, the use of explosives, and proficiency with a variety of firearms.

THE HULK

The strongest man-like creature on Earth!

THE HULK

FACTFILE

REAL NAME
Robert Bruce Banner

OCCUPATION
Scientist; wanderer

BASE
Mobile

HEIGHT 7 ft
WEIGHT 1,040 lbs
EYES Green
HAIR Green

FIRST APPEARANCE:
Incredible Hulk #1 (May 1962)

POWERS

Fueled by gamma radiation, the Hulk possesses almost unlimited physical strength. The madder he gets, the stronger he gets. He can leap several miles in a single bound. His body heals almost instantly, He possesses a strong homing instinct for the desert where he was "born."

ALLIES/FOES

ALLIES Rick Jones, Betty Ross-Banner, Doc Samson, Jennifer Walters (She-Hulk), Jarella, the Avengers.

FOES The Leader, The Abomination, Rhino, Sandman, Juggernaut, Absorbing man, General Thaddeus "Thunderbolt" Ross, Bi-Beast, Zzzax.

ISSUE #1

In his first appearance in The incredible Hulk #1 (May 1962), the Hulk was colored grey, rather than the more familiar green.

Bruce had a troubled childhood; his father called him a monster, and eventually killed his mother.

A child prodigy, Bruce Banner grew up in an abusive household, one that would have a profound long-term effect on his psyche. An introverted child, Bruce was ill-equipped to deal with the outbursts of his father, who called young Bruce a monster and terrorized both him and his mother. Bruce developed a multiple personality disorder, shunting aside and repressing all of his negative emotions when the trauma became too much to take. This cycle of abuse continued until the day Brian Banner slew his wife in a fit of rage. Thereafter, Bruce was shuttled from relative to relative, and grew ever more socially awkward, even as his remarkable intellect became more apparent.

FIRST LOVE

The US Army recruited Banner to develop new weapons systems while he was still in high school. Bruce was placed under the authority of General Thaddeus "Thunderbolt" Ross, a blustering no-nonsense veteran. It was in the person of Ross's daughter Betty that Bruce found a kindred spirit. Both he and Betty had lost mothers, and were subjected to the outbursts of raging fathers; an attraction soon developed between them.

Recruited by the military, Bruce Banner worked on developing new weapons systems on the military base commanded by hard-nosed general "Thunderbolt" Ross.

The Hulk can withstand cannon fire.

THE GAMMA BOMB

Prodded by his military handlers, Banner developed the G-Bomb, a weapon harnessing the power of gamma radiation. On the day the bomb was to be tested, a reckless teenager, Rick Jones, drove out onto the test range on a dare, little realizing that he was standing on ground zero of the most potent explosive device ever developed. In an uncharacteristic moment of heroism, Bruce Banner rushed out onto the test site, and dragged Jones to the safety of a nearby trench before the G-Bomb detonated. However Banner was exposed to the full force of the weapon, his every atom bombarded by gamma radiation.

Banner is bathed in gamma rays trying to save the life of Rick Jones.

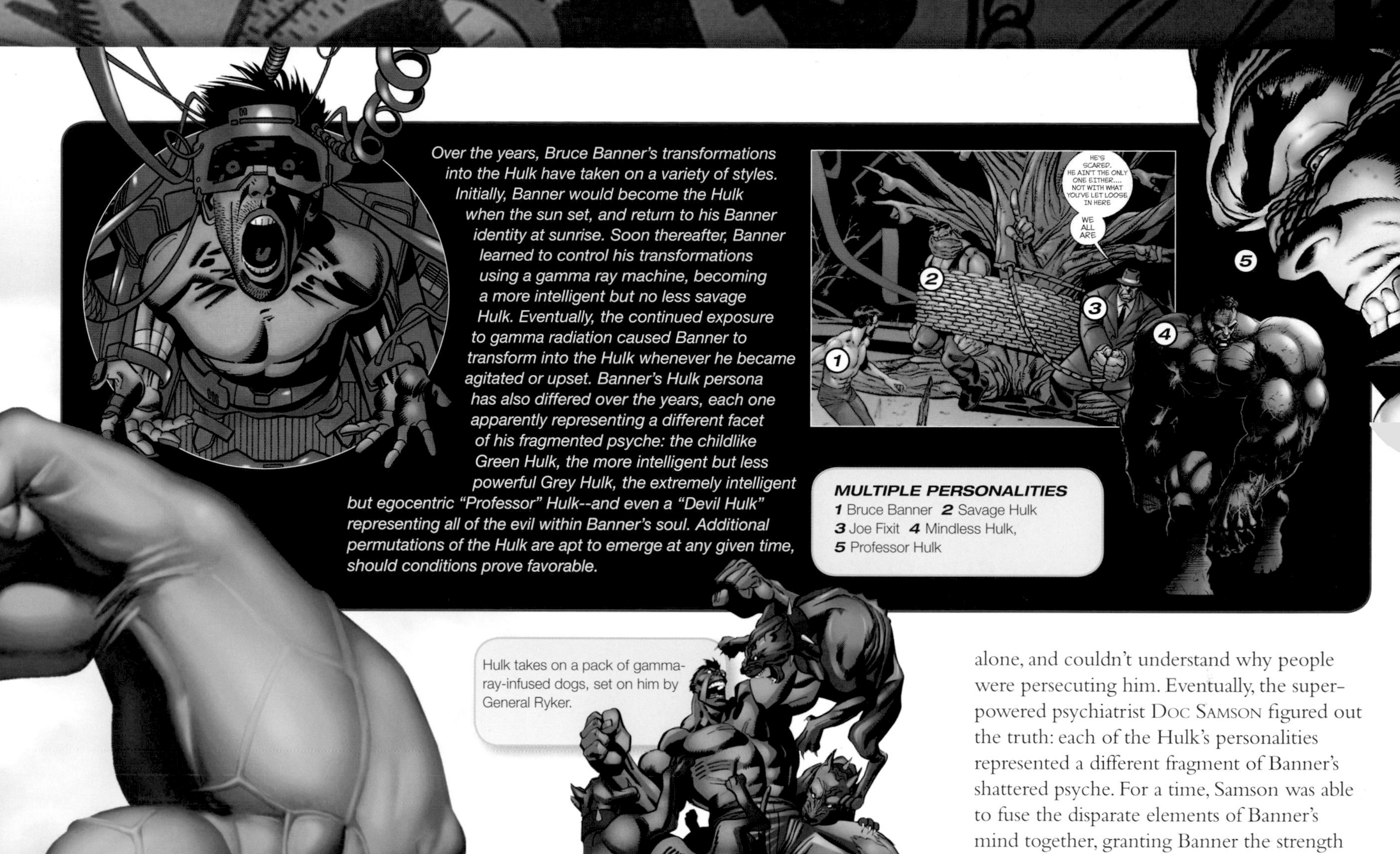

Over the years, Bruce Banner's transformations into the Hulk have taken on a variety of styles. Initially, Banner would become the Hulk when the sun set, and return to his Banner identity at sunrise. Soon thereafter, Banner learned to control his transformations using a gamma ray machine, becoming a more intelligent but no less savage Hulk. Eventually, the continued exposure to gamma radiation caused Banner to transform into the Hulk whenever he became agitated or upset. Banner's Hulk persona has also differed over the years, each one apparently representing a different facet of his fragmented psyche: the childlike Green Hulk, the more intelligent but less powerful Grey Hulk, the extremely intelligent but egocentric "Professor" Hulk--and even a "Devil Hulk" representing all of the evil within Banner's soul. Additional permutations of the Hulk are apt to emerge at any given time, should conditions prove favorable.

MULTIPLE PERSONALITIES
1 Bruce Banner **2** Savage Hulk
3 Joe Fixit **4** Mindless Hulk,
5 Professor Hulk

Hulk takes on a pack of gamma-ray-infused dogs, set on him by General Ryker.

A day later, Banner was still silently screaming. But the military doctors could find nothing wrong—he had miraculously escaped the blast unscathed. Or so it seemed. For the gamma radiation Banner had been exposed to had unlocked long-repressed feelings of hate and rage. When conditions were right, Banner found himself transforming into an unstoppable juggernaut of destruction, the personification of his long-denied dark side: the incredible Hulk!

At first, the Hulk only manifested at nightfall. When the sun went down, Banner would inexorably change into a green-skinned powerhouse and remain out of control until daybreak. Eventually, due in part to Banner's attempts to cure himself of these unwanted transformations, the appearance of the Hulk would be brought on by stress and anxiety. Whenever Bruce became outraged or fearful, the change in his emotional state would trigger the gamma radiation within his system, and the Hulk would live again. For a time, with the aid of Rick Jones, Bruce kept his dual identity secret, even while the Hulk was hunted by the same military forces for whom Banner toiled. But eventually the truth was revealed to the world, forcing Banner to become a fugitive, both to escape those who desired the Hulk's destruction, and to protect those who might be harmed during his uncontrollable episodes.

MIND OF A CHILD

The character of the Hulk changed over time. Initially, he had a strong dislike for humanity. However he mellowed as the years went by, resulting in a more childlike Hulk. He simply wanted to be left alone, and couldn't understand why people were persecuting him. Eventually, the super-powered psychiatrist Doc Samson figured out the truth: each of the Hulk's personalities represented a different fragment of Banner's shattered psyche. For a time, Samson was able to fuse the disparate elements of Banner's mind together, granting Banner the strength of the Hulk while allowing him to maintain his own intellect. But this construct proved unstable, and eventually splintered once again.

Over the years, the Hulk has proved a force for good almost as often as he has been an engine of destruction. He was instrumental in the formation of the Avengers, Earth's Mightiest Heroes, though friction between himself and his teammates quickly led to him leaving the group. He has stood side-by-side with the Defenders, Doctor Strange, the Sub-Mariner, and the Silver Surfer in defense of our planet. But for the most part, the Hulk calls no man friend. Bruce Banner and his superhuman alter ego remain ever at odds, as they strive to stay one step ahead of forces who would see the Hulk destroyed, or exploit his power for their own ends. **TB**

ESSENTIAL STORYLINES

- ***Incredible Hulk #312*** The truth about Bruce Banner's multiple personality disorder and traumatic childhood is revealed.
- ***Incredible Hulk #377*** Doc Samson unites Banner's splintered psyche into an intelligent Hulk.
- ***Incredible Hulk #24-25*** General "Thunderbolt" Ross unleashes the Hulk against the Abomination, who had secretly poisoned Ross's daughter and Hulk's beloved, Betty Banner!

HUMAN TORCH

The Super Hero who is literally "hot stuff!"

HUMAN TORCH

FACTFILE

REAL NAME
Jonathon Lowell Spencer Storm

OCCUPATION
Adventurer

BASE
New York City

HEIGHT 5 ft 10 in
WEIGHT 170 lbs
EYES Brown
HAIR Brown

FIRST APPEARANCE
Fantastic Four #1
(November 1961)

POWERS

Able to control heat energy and cover his body with fiery plasma for over 16 hours before needing to rest, for about 12 hours. He can release a single "Nova-burst" which strikes with the force of a nuclear warhead. The Torch can create shapes from flame, including letters which burn in the sky for 3 minutes. He can also control the temperature of objects with his mind. Clothing is made of special fire-resistant fabric.

ALLIES/FOES

ALLIES Invisible Woman, the Thing, Mr. Fantastic, Lyja the Laserfist, Alicia Masters, Spider-Man.

FOES Doctor Doom, Onslaught, Gormuu, Frightful Four, Galactus.

ISSUE #1

When Johnny Storm's sister, Sue, accompanied her fiancé, Reed Richards, into space, Johnny insisted on tagging along. Transformed into the Human Torch, he battled the Mole Man.

The Human Torch can generate and control fire from any part of his body.

Johnny Storm and his older sister Susan grew up on Long Island, New York, the children of a doctor and his wife. In spite of the fact that Johnny's mother was killed in a car crash when he was nine years old, the boy developed a passion and skill for building, fixing, and driving cars. He overhauled his first transmission at the age of 15. The following year his father bought him his first hot rod.

FATEFUL FLIGHT

While a teenager, Johnny went to California to visit his sister Susan who had moved out west to become an actress. Susan Storm (see INVISIBLE WOMAN) was engaged to marry a brilliant physicist and engineer named Reed Richards (*see* MISTER FANTASTIC). Richards was developing a starship that would be capable of exploring other galaxies.

While Johnny was in California, the government threatened to cut off Richards' funding and so he decided to prove his ship's worth by taking it on a test flight to the stars. Reed's best friend Ben Grimm (see THE THING) piloted the craft. Susan and Johnny insisted on coming along.

In space, inadequate shielding on the starship allowed a huge dose of cosmic radiation to bombard the crew. They managed to return to earth using the autopilot, but all four were changed forever.

The cosmic rays altered Johnny's genetic structure allowing him to create fiery plasma that covered his entire body in flames without causing him harm.

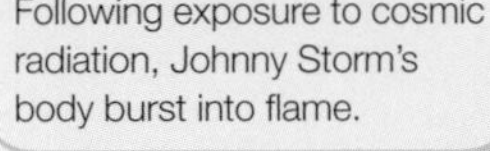

Following exposure to cosmic radiation, Johnny Storm's body burst into flame.

The Human Torch creates multiple flaming images of himself in an attempt to escape from fireproof natives with poison-tipped spears.

THE FIRST HUMAN TORCH

The original Human Torch was an android, created by Professor Phineas T. Horton. But the professor's dream of creating a perfect human being failed when the android's body, which was covered in photoelectric solar cells, burst into flames upon contact with oxygen. Astonishingly, the android itself was not harmed by the fire.

At first the public, fueled by the news media, labeled this Human Torch a menace. The Torch then rejected his creator's "ownership," claiming he didn't want to be a "slave" to someone more concerned about his own fame than about his creation's well-being.

Once he learned to control his flames, the Human Torch vowed never to use his power for evil or harm, and he became a crimefighter. When World War II broke out, the Human Torch teamed with other super heroes, using his abilities to fight the Axis Powers.

Over the years, the Human Torch found himself involved with Heroes for Hire, the West Coast Avengers, and even the Fantastic Four, the group containing the second hero to be known as the Human Torch.

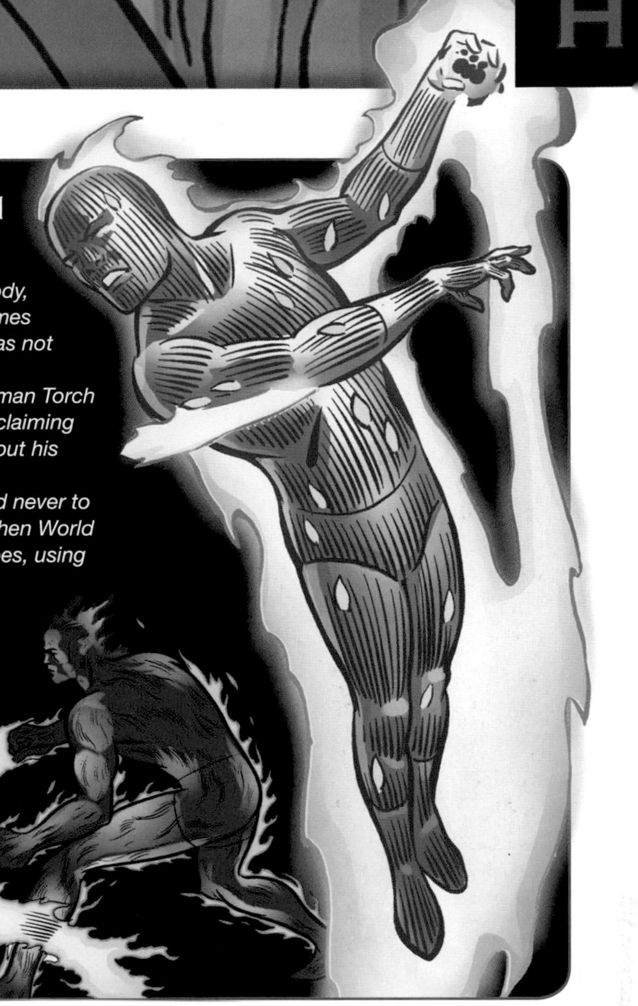

Exposure to oxygen caused the photoelectric cells in the original Human Torch's skin to burst into flame, to the surprise of the android and its creator.

The original Human Torch faces off against Johnny Storm, the Human Torch of Fantastic Four fame!

ESSENTIAL STORYLINES

- ***Fantastic Four #4*** The Human Torch quits the Fantastic Four. He meets the Sub-Mariner (for the first time since the revival of both characters), who threatens the human race.
- ***Essential Fantastic Four Vols. 1–3 (tpb)*** The Human Torch's classic adventures with the Fantastic Four.
- ***The Essential Human Torch Vol. 1 (tpb)*** A collection of some of the Human Torch's key adventures.
- ***Human Torch Vol. 1: Burn (tpb)*** A fiery tale, in which Johnny's high-school rival reappears in his life years later.
- ***Spider-Man/Human Torch #1–5*** The Human Torch teams up with Spider-Man in these new adventures.

He also discovered that he was able to fly, shoot flames, and absorb heat.

Calling themselves the FANTASTIC FOUR, the transformed astronauts decided to team up and use their new powers to help humankind. Johnny chose to call himself the Human Torch, the same name used by an android hero of the 1940s.

For a while, Johnny tried living with his sister on Long Island, attempting to complete high school while at the same time trying to keep that fact he was the Human Torch a secret. This proved far more difficult than he had anticipated. After he finished high school, Johnny moved into the Baxter Building, the Fantastic Four's original headquarters in New York City.

The Human Torch can release concussive blasts of heat energy, each packing a powerful punch.

LOVE RIVALS

Johnny always loved to tease the unfortunate THING, Ben Grimm, who was easily angered and jealous of Johnny's good looks and charm. Still, they felt a great affection for each other. This however was greatly strained when Johnny fell in love with and eventually married the blind sculptress Alicia MASTERS, the only woman that had ever returned Ben's affection.

Later, Alicia Masters was revealed to be a spy named LYJA from the alien race of shape-changers known as the SKRULLS. The deception devastated Johnny. Usually hotheaded, wisecracking, and outgoing, he changed, becoming sullen and brooding for long periods.

Johnny's ability as a mechanic has come in handy, as he has souped-up and redesigned the Fantastic Four's Fantasti-Car. MT

Flaming on (except for his left arm), Johnny rescues a woman from an attacking Sentinel.

Huntara

FIRST APPEARANCE Fantastic Four #377 (June 1993)
REAL NAME Huntara Richards
OCCUPATION Guardian of the Sacred Timelines **BASE** Elsewhen
HEIGHT 6 ft 2 in **WEIGHT** 185 lbs **EYES** Brown **HAIR** Black
SPECIAL POWERS/ABILITIES Psionic scythe cuts through almost any material, fires concussive bolts and teleports her between dimensions and across space; superior athlete and combatant.

Huntara was born on an alternate Earth. The daughter of Nathaniel Richards and the half-sister of MISTER FANTASTIC, she was taken to Elsewhen, a barbaric alien dimension. Huntara was trained in the arts of war and combat alongside her nephew Franklin and they both became Guardians of the Sacred Timelines, who prevent and repair time paradoxes.

When her father created a time paradox by exchanging the teenager Franklin RICHARDS with his younger self, Huntara was forced to journey to this timeline where she eventually met the FANTASTIC FOUR. She later returned to Elsewhen and resumed her duties as a Guardian. **TD**

Hunter, Stevie

FIRST APPEARANCE The Uncanny X-Men #139 (November 1980)
REAL NAME Stephanie "Stevie" Hunter
OCCUPATION Dance instructor **BASE** Salem Center, New York State **HEIGHT** 5 ft 9 in **WEIGHT** 121 lbs
EYES Brown **HAIR** Dark brown
SPECIAL POWERS/ABILITIES A talented dancer and athlete and an excellent dance teacher.

Stevie Hunter was a ballet dancer, until a broken leg forced her to retire. She became a dance instructor and opened a school in Salem Center, New York State. Professor Charles Xavier's School for Gifted Youngsters, the headquarters of the X-MEN, was located nearby. One of Xavier's students, Kitty PRYDE, began taking lessons at Hunter's school. Eventually, Hunter discovered that Xavier's students were mutants. Xavier hired Hunter to be a physical trainer and therapist at his school.

Hunter has since returned to operating her own dance academy. **PS**

Husk

Husk, Archangel and Iceman are surrounded by a pack of slavering wolf men.

Condemned to a humdrum life on a struggling family farm in West Virginia, Paige Guthrie envied her elder brother who, as CANNONBALL, had forged a career among the NEW MUTANTS team. Although she underwent a mutation of her own, Paige kept this hidden until she was forced into a battle of wits with the Gamesmaster. This mutant with psionic powers had formed the UPSTARTS, who specialized in assassinating mutants. Paige's intervention freed her brother and several of his friends from the Grandmaster's clutches.

Shortly afterward, she was captured by PHALANX, an alien collective intelligence, along with several other young mutants. Its effort to assimilate them into its consciousness was foiled and Paige was invited to join the Xavier Institute's new school, Massachusetts Academy, and become a member of GENERATION X. Paige subsequently joined X-CORPS, helping to police mutants in Europe, and then went traveling with ARCHANGEL. Her dream of a life of adventure had been realized. **AD**

FACTFILE
REAL NAME
Paige Elisabeth Guthrie
OCCUPATION
X-Man
BASE
New York State

HEIGHT 5 ft 7 in
WEIGHT 127 lbs
EYES Blue
HAIR Black

FIRST APPEARANCE
X-Force #32 (March 1994)

HUSK

POWERS

A mutant metamorph, Husk can shed skin and transform her body into any form with similar or less mass. She frequently turns her body into a different substance, such as steel or stone, taking on the properties of that substance, for example increased strength.

Husk tears off her skin to reveal a woman of steel.

HYDRA

FACTFILE

KEY MEMBERS

BARON VON STRUCKER
Master criminal strategist; founder of HYDRA.

ARNOLD BROWN
Brilliant bureaucrat who transformed HYDRA.

RED SKULL
Instructed Strucker to found HYDRA.

MADAME HYDRA
Leader of New York City HYDRA

LAURA BROWN
Daughter of Arnold Brown; one of the first women to serve in HYDRA.

BASE Mobile

FIRST APPEARANCE
Strange Tales #135 (August 1965)

HYDRA

"Cut off one limb and two more shall take its place!" This is the motto of HYDRA, the global terrorist organization that has threatened the world since the end of World War II. Created by Baron von Strucker, HYDRA was a conventional organization with a base on a Pacific island. When US Marines destroyed this, HYDRA began to decentralise, becoming less easy to attack. Under Strucker's guidance HYDRA twice attempted to blackmail the world, first with a Betatron bomb and later with a biological weapon, the Death Spore. After his death, HYDRA focused on criminal activities. In recent years HYDRA has been reinvigorated, allying with the Hand to destroy all Super Heroes and preparing for a confrontation with "Earth's mightiest," the Avengers. **AD**

The personalities of HYDRA personnel are subordinate to the organization they serve.

Hydro-Man

FIRST APPEARANCE Amazing Spider-Man #212 (January 1981)
REAL NAME Morris Bench
OCCUPATION Criminal **BASE** New York City
HEIGHT 6 ft 2 in **WEIGHT** 265 lbs **EYES** Brown **HAIR** Brown
SPECIAL POWERS/ABILITIES Changes body into watery liquid; can merge with larger bodies of water; propels liquid body as if it were shooting through a fire hose; can turn body into ice or steam.

While working as a crewman on a cargo ship lowering an experimental generator into the ocean, Morris Bench was accidentally knocked overboard by Spider-Man. Exposed to the energy-conversion process of the generator, which mixed with volatile volcanic gases, Bench gained the ability to change his body into water. As Hydro-Man he sought revenge against Spider-Man. Later, in a battle with Sandman, Hydro-Man fused with the Super Villain and the two became a mud creature. Eventually they were separated. Hydro-Man joined the Sinister Syndicate and later, Green Goblin's Sinister Twelve, and continues to battle Spider-Man, Black Cat, and the Avengers. **MT**

Hyperion

A member of the race of Eternals on a parallel earth, Hyperion, unaware of his lineage, was raised by human beings, and taught to use his tremendous powers for the benefit of all men. Adopting the costumed identity of Hyperion, he became the foremost champion of his world, and a founding member of the heroic Squadron Supreme.

After the Squadron was manipulated by the Overmind into participating in a plan that left their world decimated, Hyperion and his fellow Squadron members embarked on a bold plan. They resolved to take control of their world for one year, and to turn it into a utopian state within that time.

Despite initial success, their program met with resistance from one of the Squadron's former members, Nighthawk, and before too long, Hyperion and the others realized the error of their ways; unfortunately by the time the team were ready to dismantle the government they had set up, it had turned into a corrupt, totalitarian regime. Ever since, Hyperion and the remaining Squadron members have functioned as freedom fighters, trying to liberate their homeland. **TB**

In one world visited by the reality-hopping Exiles, Hyperion had murdered most of humanity.

HYPERION

FACTFILE

REAL NAME
Unrevealed; adopted the human identity of Mark Milton for a time.

OCCUPATION
Adventurer, world leader

BASE
Squadron City on the Squadron Supreme's parallel Earth.

HEIGHT 6 ft 4 in
WEIGHT 460 lbs
EYES Blue
HAIR Red

FIRST APPEARANCE
Avengers #85 (February 1971)

POWERS

Hyperion possesses almost limitless strength, speed, and endurance. He is impervious to virtually any injury, can fly through the air, and project radioactive beams of energy from his eyes as "Flash-Vision."

ICEMAN

FACTFILE

REAL NAME
Robert Drake

OCCUPATION
Adventurer

BASE
The Xavier Institute for Higher Learning

HEIGHT 5 ft 8 in
WEIGHT 145 lbs
EYES Brown
HAIR Brown

FIRST APPEARANCE
Uncanny X-Men #1 (September 1963)

POWERS
Iceman can manipulate temperatures around him to freeze the water vapor in the air, forming a variety of icy weapons, protective ice shields, and ice slides.

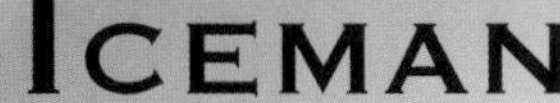

ICEMAN

Born a mutant, young Bobby Drake was almost lynched when his ability to freeze moisture in the air was discovered. Bobby was saved by CYCLOPS of the X-MEN, and became the second recruit to Professor Charles Xavier's School for Gifted Youngsters (*see* PROFESSOR X), where he would learn to control his mutant gifts. Adopting the codename Iceman, Drake fought as one of the X-Men, battling such menaces as MAGNETO's BROTHERHOOD OF EVIL MUTANTS, the JUGGERNAUT, and the robotic SENTINELS. Upon graduation, Iceman attempted to forge a super-heroic career on his own, founding the Champions of Los Angeles. However, his path eventually led him back to Xavier's School, where he remains as a member of the X-Men today. His command of his icy abilities has also increased, to the point where, rather than simply sheathing his body in an icy coating, Drake's entire form now transmutes into living, sentient ice. **TB**

Iceman creates weapons of all kinds from ice, from single missiles to hailstones. Here he lets fly with an ice beam.

Iceman can transform back into an ordinary-looking human being at will.

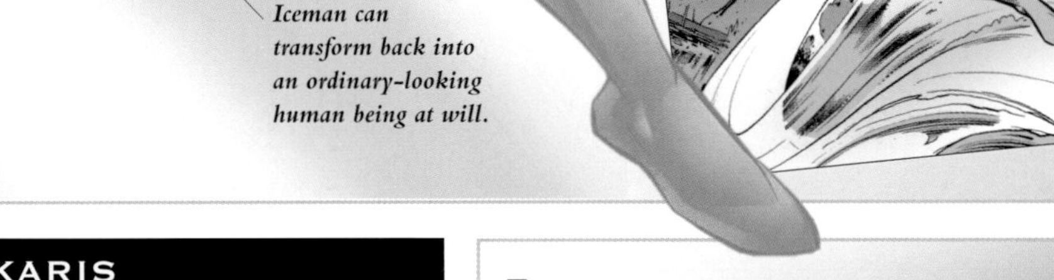

Iceman slides along at superhuman speeds thanks to a path of ice that he creates himself.

IKARIS

FIRST APPEARANCE The Eternals Vol. 1 #1 (July 1976)
REAL NAME Unrevealed
OCCUPATION Prime Eternal **BASE** Olympia, Greece
HEIGHT 6 ft 2 in **WEIGHT** 230 lbs **EYES** Blue **HAIR** Blond
SPECIAL POWERS/ABILITIES Superhuman strength; virtual immortality and indestructibility; psionic abilties, including flight through levitation; projects cosmic energy from eyes or hands.

Born over 20,000 years ago, Ikaris is one of the Polar ETERNALS, who lived in the city of Polaria in Siberia. Over the millennia, Ikaris has battled the Eternals' enemies, the Deviants. He calls himself Ikaris in memory of his deceased son. Under the name "Ike Harris," Ikaris accompanied archeologist Dr. Daniel Damian and his daughter Margo to the Andes, where they witnessed the arrival of the Fourth Host of the CELESTIALS. Since then Ikaris has succeeded THENA as Prime Eternal, ruler of the Eternals of Earth. **PS**

IMMORTUS

Immortus was born in the 31st Century of one of Earth's alternate futures. It was a time of peace and prosperity, but Immortus craved adventure. Using parts found in the ruins of his ancestors' property, he built a time machine and set off traveling through time.

In each time era he arrived at, Immortus adopted a new guise, among them Rama-Tut and KANG THE CONQUEROR. He left behind countless temporal counterparts capable of existing on their own and of further time travel. The being who became Rama-Tut journeyed to Limbo, a realm existing outside the timestream itself. There he was visited by the TIME-KEEPERS, who helped him unlock the secrets of time. Immortus then set about untangling the many timelines he and his counterparts had created by their time travel. **MT**

IMMORTUS

FACTFILE

REAL NAME
Unknown

OCCUPATION
Ruler of Limbo

BASE
Limbo, outside the timestream

HEIGHT 6 ft 3 in
WEIGHT 230 lbs
EYES Green
HAIR Gray

FIRST APPEARANCE
Avengers #10 (November 1964)

POWERS
Immortus has no superhuman powers. His abilities come from his use of the vast knowledge and advanced technology he has accumulated on his travels through time.

Impossible Man

IMPOSSIBLE MAN

FACTFILE

REAL NAME
Unknown

OCCUPATION
Trickster and student of Earth's popular culture

BASE
Mobile

HEIGHT 6 ft 4 in
WEIGHT 165 lbs
EYES White
HAIR None

FIRST APPEARANCE
Fantastic Four Vol. I #11 (February 1963)

POWERS
Limitless shape-shifting abilities; can mirror properties of objects he imitates (if he's a hose he can spray water, as a light bulb he can light up); asexual reproduction.

The planet Poppup was an inhospitable world, its people surviving through asexual reproduction and their shape-changing abilities and group mind. Then a Poppupian was born who had a degree of individuality. Bored by life, this creature transformed himself into a spacecraft and traveled to Earth where he encountered the FANTASTIC FOUR. Finding him unbearably annoying, the THING told the creature that he was "impossible", and so "Impossible Man" was born.

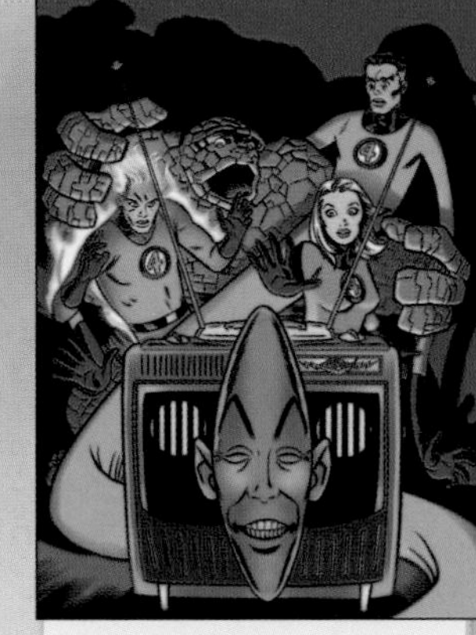

Impossible Man can change himself into just about anything.

To the Fantastic Four's annoyance, the team has encountered Impossible Man several times. When GALACTUS was threatening to consume Counter-Earth, Impossible Man tricked him into eating Poppup instead, giving him a bad case of cosmic indigestion. With his peoples' consciousness living on through him, Mr Impossible set about rebuilding the Poppup race, first creating a wife—Impossible Woman—and later scores of children. Despite his newfound responsibilities, Impossible Man has continued to visit Earth, oblivious of humanity's ambivalence toward him. **AD**

Transformed into a rocket, Impossible Man left his homeworld far behind him.

In-Betweener

FIRST APPEARANCE Warlock Vol. 1 #10 (December 1975)
REAL NAME Inapplicable
OCCUPATION Cosmic entity **BASE** Mobile
HEIGHT 15 ft **WEIGHT** Unrevealed
EYES White **HAIR** None
SPECIAL POWERS/ABILITIES Near-infinite cosmic power, often held in check by its own need for balance.

The In-Betweener, the creation of LORD CHAOS and MASTER ORDER, is the living synthesis of balance, representing both life and death, good and evil, logic and emotion, reality and illusion, existence and nothingness, and god and man. When the Titan THANOS tried to plunge the universe into death, the In-Betweener tried to restore balance by abducting Adam WARLOCK and turning him into a champion of life. The In-Betweener later clashed with the sorcerer DOCTOR STRANGE and GALACTUS, and briefly had possession of the reality-warping Soul Gem until Thanos stole the item in his quest to build the Infinity Gauntlet. **DW**

Infectia

FIRST APPEARANCE X-Factor #28 (May 1988)
REAL NAME Not known
OCCUPATION Genetic manipulator **BASE** New York City
HEIGHT 5 ft 6 in **WEIGHT** 120 lbs **EYES** Brown **HAIR** Black
SPECIAL POWERS/ABILITIES Perceives molecular structure of organic lifeforms, and is able to mutate the lifeforms genetically by kissing them.

The daughter of a geneticist, Infectia gained an enormous amount of knowledge from her father, which enabled her to understand her mutant ability to mutate organic life. Following her father's death while she was still at high school, Infectia inherited a small fortune and withdrew from society. Re-emerging as a dangerous and manipulative mutant, she set her sights on obtaining the X-Factor's skycraft headquarters. Her plan was to transform ICEMAN into a form she could manipulate, but because he was a mutant her effort caused an explosion. It was the last time she was to pose a threat—shortly thereafter, Infectia was stricken by the fatal Legacy virus and died in BEAST's care. **AD**

Inferno

FIRST APPEARANCE (as Inferno) Avengers #192 (August 1977)
REAL NAME Joseph Conroy
OCCUPATION Steelworker **BASE** Pittsburgh, Pennsylvania
HEIGHT/WEIGHT Unrevealed **EYES** Red **HAIR** None
SPECIAL POWERS/ABILITIES Possessed superhuman strength and durability; could radiate intense heat; could absorb and redirect electrical energy.

Thor once repaired his enchanted uru hammer at the Paretta Steel Mill in Pittsburgh. Steel worker Joseph Conroy kept a flake from the hammer for luck. Later Conroy threatened to expose the criminal activities of his boss, Vince Paretta, and was knocked into a vat of electrified molten steel. The magic of the uru flake transformed Conroy into Inferno, a being made of "living slag." Inferno's revenge mission led to a clash with the Avengers. When Captain America promised that Paretta would be jailed, Inferno committed suicide by walking into a river. **PS**

Interloper

FIRST APPEARANCE Defenders Vol. 1 #147 (September 1985)
REAL NAME Unknown
OCCUPATION Hermit **BASE** Washington, D.C.
HEIGHT 6 ft 2 in **WEIGHT** 196 lbs **EYES** Blue **HAIR** Black
SPECIAL POWERS/ABILITIES Virtually immortal through total mental control of his body; levitation; projects cosmic energy in form of beams from hands or eyes.

Although one of the Eternals of Earth, for most of his life, the Interloper lived as a hermit, emerging for periodic battles against his nemesis, the malevolent Dragon of the Moon. Only three of these battles have been chronicled, the first taking place on the Saturn moon of Titan and the second during the final days of King Arthur Pendragon. Believing that he had finally bested the Dragon, Interloper withdrew to the Siberian wastelands, but his destiny was still bound up with the creature. Returning to fight one more time, the Interloper sacrificed his life to destroy the dragon altogether. **AD**

Inhumans

The Inhumans are a race who diverged from mainstream human beings on Earth about 25,000 years ago. The aliens known as the Kree created this separate race using genetic experimentation on early humans, in order to create a race of superhuman warriors to serve the Kree.

The Inhumans are an incredibly technologically advanced race descended from early humans.

Following these experiments, however, the Kree abandoned this plan, leaving a small tribe of these genetically enhanced humans to fend for themselves on Earth. This group became known as the Inhumans. The Inhumans settled on an island in the North Atlantic that they named Attilan. There, they developed technology and culture at an astounding rate.

An Inhuman geneticist named Randac developed a substance called Terrigen which he believed would accelerate genetic advances. Subjecting himself to immersion in the Terrigen Mist, Randac developed advanced mental powers. But the Terrigen had a genetic side-effect on others, causing nonhuman mutations in about half of those exposed to the Mist. **MT**

FACTFILE

KEY MEMBERS AND POWERS

SUPER-RANDAC
Mental manipulation ability.

BLACK BOLT
Amazing mental powers, the most powerful Inhuman who ever lived.

TRITON
Super-fast swimmer; resists crushing water pressure.

FALCONA
Mental control over birds of prey.

CRYSTAL
Mentally manipulates the four basic elements of nature.

STALLIOR
Speed and endurance; powerful hooves for fighting.

BASE
Attilan Island, North Atlantic

FIRST APPEARANCE
Fantastic Four #45 (December 1965)

THE INHUMANS
1 Medusa ***2*** Gorgon
3 Triton ***4*** Karnac
5 Black Bolt

Invaders

The greatest Super Heroes of World War II

The Invaders were brought together in 1941 by Winston Churchill.

During the opening days of World War II, before the United States had formally entered the conflict, an elite fighting unit was banded together by British Prime Minister Winston Churchill to halt Nazi aggression. The first great gathering of superhuman champions ever recorded—Captain America and Bucky Barnes, Namor the Sub-Mariner, the Human Torch and Toro, Union Jack, Spitfire, Miss America and the Whizzer—this alliance, known formally as the Invaders, cut a swath through enemy forces until the Axis powers were defeated.

As a team, the Invaders battled both conventional forces, and Nazi superhuman operatives such as the Atlantean U-Man.

FACTFILE

CURRENT MEMBERS AND POWERS

USAGENT
Super-strong soldier.

BLAZING SKULL
Immortal; impervious to flame.

THIN MAN
Can distend body and teleport by twisting dimensions.

UNION JACK
Trained fighter who specializes in battling monsters.

TARA
Android life form that bursts into flame and can fly.

BASE
The Infiltrator, a battleship capable of interdimensional travel

FIRST APPEARANCE
Giant-Size Invaders #1 (June 1975)

The All-Winners

Although they disbanded after the war, for a time combating crime on the homefront as the All-Winners Squad, the Invaders established a legend and a tradition that would inspire others to follow in their footsteps over the years. Some of those heroes associated with the Invaders joined forces with Parisian resistance fighters to form the covert V-Battalion, maintaining world order secretly through the decades.

ESSENTIAL STORYLINES

- ***Invaders #5–6 and Marvel Premiere #29–30*** The Invaders are joined by the homefront heroes of the Liberty Legion to thwart a scheme by the Red Skull
- ***Avengers #83–85, New Invaders #0*** When the Avengers become a global organization, a modern day team of Invaders is assembled by the US government to do the jobs that they will not.

The New Invaders

In the early years of this century, the demonic Red Skull infiltrated the highest levels of government in the guise of US Secretary of Defense Dell Rusk. He proceeded to organize a new incarnation of the Invaders, malevolently intending it to forcibly protect US interests worldwide, and thus foment greater distrust among nations.

This new incarnation of the Invaders, recruited by the right-wing US Agent (whose title as Captain America had been restored by Rusk), and led by the Nazi-hunting Thin Man, soon realized the truth. Instead of following Rusk's agenda the new Invaders turned their efforts towards the destruction of Axis Mundi, a secret cabal of sinister superhumans organized in the waning days of World War II.

TB

The Machiavellian Thin Man, once imprisoned for his murder of a former Nazi agent, was the brains behind the modern-day Invaders' operation.

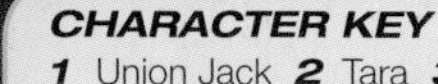

CHARACTER KEY
1 Union Jack ***2*** Tara ***3*** The USAgent (as Captain America) ***4*** The Blazing Skull

INVISIBLE WOMAN

The Fantastic Four's female presence

FACTFILE

REAL NAME
Susan Storm Richards

OCCUPATION
Adventurer

BASE
New York City

HEIGHT 5 ft 6 ins
WEIGHT 120 lbs
EYES Blue
HAIR Blonde

FIRST APPEARANCE
Fantastic Four Vol. 1 #1 (November 1961)

POWERS
Can turn herself invisible, and is able to project energy around other people or objects that makes them invisible too; can generate protective force fields, or shape invisible objects of psionic force. By projecting force fields beneath her, she can travel through the air.

Actress Susan Storm had already struck up a romance with the scientist Reed Richards when she volunteered to join him on an experimental mission into space. Along with her brother Johnny Storm and the starship's pilot Ben Grimm, Sue received a mutagenic dose of cosmic rays that gave her the power to turn invisible at will. The others had also received superhuman powers, and Sue became a member of their new team, the FANTASTIC FOUR, under the identity of the Invisible Girl. Sue's powers evolved over time, giving her the ability to project impenetrable force fields and to turn objects invisible through mental control.

Sue's ability to generate force fields is more versatile than her power of invisibility, making her one of the team's strongest members.

MOTHERHOOD AND MALICE

Sue soon married Reed, and battled threats to the Earth including the planet-devouring GALACTUS. Complications with her first pregnancy forced Reed to stabilize her labor with the exotic energies of ANNIHILUS' Cosmic Control Rod, and Sue safely gave birth to a boy, FRANKLIN RICHARDS. Later, she briefly separated from Reed and left the Fantastic Four, allowing MEDUSA to fill her spot. Sue's second pregnancy ended in a stillbirth. During this vulnerable period, PSYCHO-MAN controlled Sue's mind and caused her to assume the villainous identity of Malice. After shaking off Psycho-Man's influence, Sue rechristened herself the Invisible Woman.

LEADING LADY

Sue and Reed briefly joined the AVENGERS, but returned to their original team. After Reed's apparent death at the hands of DOCTOR DOOM, Sue served as the Fantastic Four's leader, rejecting romantic overtures from NAMOR the Sub-Mariner. It transpired that the child from Sue's earlier stillbirth had been preserved in another dimension by Franklin. After a battle with Abraxas, the unborn girl returned to Sue's womb.

Doctor Doom assisted with Sue's second delivery, naming the baby girl Valeria and trying to take control of her. Sue fought to save Franklin from Hell during one of Doom's cruelest revenge schemes. Later, her relationship with her husband suffered a new strain when the Fantastic Four usurped control of Latveria. Ben Grimm's death (*see* THING) prompted her to separate from Reed again; however the two have reconciled since Ben's return from the afterlife. **DW**

Sue can shape her force fields into tentacles that grasp and stab. Here, she unleashes her rage on Doctor Doom.

ESSENTIAL STORYLINES

- ***Secret Wars II #2***
  Sue assumes the villainous identity of Malice while under the influence of the Psycho-Man.
- ***Fantastic Four Vol. 1 #284***
  It's goodbye to the venerable codename Invisible Girl, as Sue reinvents herself as the Invisible Woman.
- ***Fantastic Four Vol. 3 #54***
  Sue gives birth to her second child, Valeria Richards, assisted in the delivery by the Fantastic Four's archenemy, Doctor Doom.

Iron Fist

Wendell Rand was the son of the ruler of K'un-L'un, a city in another dimension. He came to the US, married, and had a son, Danny. When Danny was nine, he accompanied Wendell, his wife Heather, and his business partner Harold Meachum on an expedition to K'un-L'un. Meachum caused Wendell's death, and Heather was killed by wolves. Only Danny reached K'un-L'un. Aged 19, Danny slew the dragon Shao-Lao the Undying and gained the power of the "Iron Fist." As Iron Fist, he confronted Meachum, but spared him; a ninja slew Meachum instead. Rand became wealthy as co-owner of Rand-Meachum, Inc. and, as Iron Fist, partnered Luke Cage, (alias Power Man), in Heroes for Hire, Inc. **PS**

Iron Fist's hand glows with superhuman energies.

Iron Fist's supreme mastery of the K'un-L'un martial arts and his "iron fist" make him a match for even superhuman opponents.

FACTFILE

REAL NAME
Daniel Thomas Rand-K'ai (Daniel Thomas Rand in US)

OCCUPATION
Adventurer; co-owner of Rand-Meachum, Inc.

BASE
New York City

HEIGHT 5 ft 11 in
WEIGHT 175 lbs
EYES Blue
HAIR Blond

FIRST APPEARANCE
Marvel Premiere #15 (May 1974)

POWERS
Master of the martial arts of K'un-L'un. Can focus his chi (natural energy) and superhuman energy in his hand, endowing his fist with superhuman strength, durability, or healing power.

Iron Man *see pages 146–7*

Ironclad

FIRST APPEARANCE Incredible Hulk #254 (December 1980)
REAL NAME Michael Steel
OCCUPATION Superpowered villain **BASE** Mobile
HEIGHT 6 ft 2 in **WEIGHT** 450 lbs **EYES** White **HAIR** None
SPECIAL POWERS/ABILITIES Metallic armored hide protects him from most forms of attack, and increases strength and endurance to superhuman levels; can also increase his body's density.

Ironclad was one of the U-Foes, organized by industrialist Simon Utrecht, who hoped to recreate the accident that had empowered the Fantastic Four. Bruce Banner (*see* Hulk), believed the spaceship carrying the U-Foes was in trouble and recalled it, limiting Ironclad's exposure to radiation and his power. **MT**

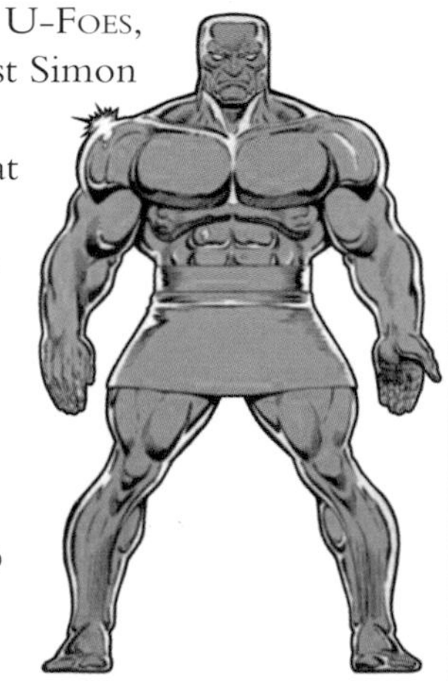

It

It, the Living Colossus was a statue supposed to celebrate the might of the Soviet Union. The night before its unveiling, the statue was animated by a stranded alien Kigor. It rampaged through Moscow until other Kigor fetched their companion. It was transferred to Los Angeles and once again animated by the Kigor, however special-effects expert Robert O'Bryan tricked the aliens with a booby-trapped prop and uploaded his own mind into It. Thus began a tug of war with the scheming Dr. Vault. Since then, O'Bryan has twice rebuilt It, once for a movie, and once while under the thrall of crime boss Lotus Newmark. Fortunately, O'Bryan was freed from Newmark before any harm could be done. **AD**

FACTFILE

REAL NAME
None

OCCUPATION
Instrument of destruction

BASE
Los Angeles

HEIGHT 100 ft (later reduced to 30 ft)
WEIGHT approximately 1,000 tons (later 100 tons)
EYES White
HAIR None

FIRST APPEARANCE
Tales of Suspense #14 (September 1961)

POWERS
Outside consciousness needed to animate—or reassemble– statue. Vast strength. Granite construction impervious to bullets, shells, and electric shocks; limited flying ability. Vulnerable to gas attack.

IRON MAN

The billion-dollar man

IRON MAN

FACTFILE

REAL NAME
Anthony Stark

OCCUPATION
Businessman and philanthropist, hero and leader of the Avengers

BASE
Stark Tower ("Avengers Tower"), Manhattan, New York

HEIGHT 6 ft 1 in
WEIGHT 225 lbs
EYES Blue
HAIR Black

FIRST APPEARANCE
Tales of Suspense #39 (March 1963)

POWERS

Prodigious inventiveness and business acumen. Standard Iron Man armor provides superhuman strength and durability, jet-boot powered flight, repulsor beams in gauntlets, and chest-mounted uni-beam. Armor's underlayer is now incorporated into Stark's body, letting him control Iron Man remotely.

ALLIES/FOES

ALLIES The Avengers, James Rhodes (War Machine), SHIELD, Virginia Potts, Bethany Cabe, Edwin Jarvis.

FOES Obadiah Stane, Justin Hammer, Madame Masque, Titanium Man, Spymaster, Mandarin.

ISSUE #1

Injured in Vietnam, Stark's first Iron Man armor saves his life and helps him escape capture. From that day on, he could not survive without it.

Billionaire industrialist and philanthropist Tony Stark is perhaps the most influential superpowered individual on the planet. While PROFESSOR X has the respect of the Earth's mutant community, Stark's work as Iron Man, his long-term membership of the AVENGERS, and position as head of Stark International arguably gives him even wider authority.

FORGING THE IRON MAN

The son of a wealthy industrialist, Tony Stark's parents died in a car crash when he was young, leaving him their business conglomerate, Stark Industries. Taking over the company when he was 21, in retrospect some of Tony's early business decisions were ethically circumspect. An engineering prodigy, many of Tony's early inventions were designed for use by the US military and it was his dealings with the army that ultimately led him to create his Iron Man armor.

In the nick of time, the first Iron Man armor saved Tony Stark's life.

Developing mini-transistors for use on the battlefield, Tony travelled to Vietnam to see them in use on the ground. The trial ended badly when an exploding bomb left a piece of shrapnel dangerously close to his heart and Tony was captured by the North Vietnamese warlord, Wong-Chu.

Told that the shrapnel would only be removed if he developed a weapon for the North Vietnamese, Tony responded with typical tenacity. Teaming with a fellow prisoner, Nobel prize-winning physicist Ho Yinsen, Tony developed an iron suit that would protect his heart as well as allow him to fight the warlord and his men and escape.

Iron Man—corporate mascot, bodyguard, or armored Super Hero?

SOCIAL CONSCIENCE

In the following years, Tony donned this armor many times. Claiming the Iron Man was his bodyguard and corporate emblem, at first he simply used it to fight communists and threats to his business empire. With the advent of new technologies and ideas the armor evolved, becoming increasingly, at times dangerously, sophisticated.

Initially a defender of Stark Industries, gradually Iron Man began to serve the general public.

Over the years Tony's own world view also began to evolve: he halted sales to the military, recognizing that they caused more harm than good, and established a number of charitable foundations. He became a founder member of the AVENGERS, allowing the team to use his mansion as their base and providing financial backing via the Maria Stark foundation—a non-profit-making organization named for his mother.

ESSENTIAL STORYLINES

- ***Iron Man Vol. 1 #120–129 #153–156*** Tony Stark's first encounter with Justin Hammer and his battle with alcohol.
- ***Iron Man Vol. 2 #162–200*** Stark's long dark fall to the gutter at the hands of Obadiah Stane, and his gradual resurrection.
- ***Iron Man Vol. 3 #27–30*** The Iron Man armor becomes sentient and attacks Stark.

OLD FLAMES

Wealthy, charming, handsome—over the years, countless women have been drawn to Tony Stark, and many hearts have been broken, including his own. Time and again, his dual identity and multiple responsibilities have sabotaged any hope at a settled, long-term romance.

JANICE CORD *Daughter of Stark rival Drexel Cord.*

BETHANY CABE *Tony's lover until her husband returned.*

SUNSET BAIN *Seduced Tony and stole his secrets.*

VIRGINIA POTTS *One of Tony's most loyal confidantes.*

NATASHA ROMANOVA *Sometime adversary and former fiancée.*

Although immensely strong-willed, at times the pressures upon Tony Stark have proved overwhelming—twice he has succumbed to the lure of alcohol. Tony's first fall from grace was precipitated by a series of attacks from supervillains hired by business rival Justin Hammer. While fending these off, Iron Man was framed for the murder of a diplomat, and at the same time national security agency SHIELD were attempting to buy his company and so gain his military secrets. Gradually, with the support of his friends, Tony overcame these threats and defeated his addiction.

This episode was nothing compared to Tony's second dance with drink. As a result of the emotional manipulations of his competitor Obadiah Stane, Tony entered a deep depression and for a time became a homeless vagrant. His epiphany came when he was forced to deliver the child of a homeless woman, who died soon after.

Like his father before him, Tony Stark was cursed by the demon drink. With Iron Man labeled a murderer and his company under siege, Tony was driven to the bottle.

After waking up in hospital, he began to rebuild his life, creating a new business empire from scratch—Stark Enterprises—and defeating Stane in combat.

Battling armored humans is now commonplace for Iron Man.

In the House of M universe, Tony Stark is a competitor in Sapien Death Match, a televised gladiatorial contest. There he competes against other armored humans.

An Enemy of America

Although a long-term member of the Avengers, at times Tony's decisions have brought him into direct conflict with his Super Hero friends, as well as with the US government. When Justin Hammer stole Stark technology and distributed it to criminals across the world, Tony began a quest to find each item of missing technology. It was his effort to track down the US military's Stark-derived Guardsmen suits that resulted in the Iron Man being branded an outlaw by the US government. This action also antagonized Captain America.

A Heavy Burden

Tony's life has gone through many dramatic changes. When he publicly admitted to being the Iron Man, his initial relief at no longer having to lead a double life was short-lived. Successfully campaigning to become US Secretary of Defense, he tried to use his government position to control the use of his various inventions. At the same time he continued to serve as Iron Man. Eventually, the mounting conflicts of interest led him to resign from the government and announce that the role of Iron Man was now being borne by someone else.

Despite his life's many ups and downs Tony Stark remains the same man he always was, adhering to his principles with an iron will. **AD**

Although sometimes at odds with his fellow Avengers, Tony Stark remains one of the team's most constant members. While his money keeps the team afloat, it is as Iron Man that he really leaves his mark.

J2

FIRST APPEARANCE What If? Vol. 2 #105 (February 1998)
REAL NAME Zane Yama
OCCUPATION High-school student **BASE** New York City
HEIGHT 5 ft 5 in (Zane); 6 ft 6 in (J2) **WEIGHT** 137 lbs (as Zane) 725 lbs (as J2) **EYES** Blue **HAIR** Brown
SPECIAL POWERS/ABILITIES Superhuman strength and durability; virtually unstoppable and indestructible.

In one possible future, Zane's parents are Cain Marko, the original JUGGERNAUT, and Sachi Yama, an Assistant District Attorney. They fell in love shortly after Marko renounced his criminal ways, joined the X-MEN, and was pardoned for his past crimes. They married, but Sachi kept her last name for professional reasons. While on an X-Men mission, Marko was lost in an alien dimension. Years later, Zane discovered that he could temporarily gain the mass and power of the Juggernaut. Calling himself J2, Zane joined the AVENGERS of his timeline and eventually freed his father from an alien sorcerer who had been holding him prisoner. TD

JACK OF HEARTS

Jack Hart's mother was an extraterrestrial Contraxian, and his father a human scientist. He was born with volatile energy powers that would have killed him, and his father created Zero Fluid in an attempt to give his son control. After an accidental drenching in the fluid when agents of the criminal Corporation killed his father, Jack became the costumed hero Jack of Hearts, but he required regular periods of isolation in a SHIELD facility to keep from exploding. After learning of his origins, Jack traveled to Contraxia to rekindle the planet's waning star. He became romantically involved with Ganymede of the Spinsterhood during the fight against GALACTUS's offspring TYRANT, and joined the AVENGERS upon his return to Earth. Frustrated by the segregation required by his condition, Jack detonated himself in space after saving the life of ANT-MAN II's daughter, Cassie Lang (Stature). A doppelganger of Jack of Hearts, created by the SCARLET WITCH, later killed Ant-Man II in an explosion. DW

JACK OF HEARTS

FACTFILE
REAL NAME
Jonathan "Jack" Hart
OCCUPATION
Adventurer
BASE
Mobile

HEIGHT 5 ft 11 in
WEIGHT 175 lbs
EYES Blue (right), white (left)
HAIR Brown

FIRST APPEARANCE
Deadly Hands of Kung Fu #22 (March, 1976)

POWERS

Enhanced strength, resistance to injury and accelerated healing rate, ability to release massive quantities of explosive energy as shock waves. Power of flight is achieved by controlling blasts of energy. Computerized intelligence enables him to think at phenomenal speeds.

An undead version of Jack of Hearts appeared at the Avengers Mansion, moments before the events known as "Avengers Disassembled."

JACKAL

FIRST APPEARANCE Amazing Spider-Man #31 (December 1965)
REAL NAME Dr Miles Warren
OCCUPATION Criminal, former university lecturer
BASE New York City **HEIGHT** 5 ft 10 in **WEIGHT** 175 lbs
EYES Green **HAIR** Gray; (as Jackal) none
SPECIAL POWERS/ABILITIES Expert in cloning; superhuman strength and poison-tipped, razor-sharp claws; used gas bombs.

Peter Parker's biochemistry teacher was obsessed with Peter's girlfriend, Gwen STACY. Grief-stricken by her death he became unhinged, creating clones of Gwen and Peter and killing his lab assistant when he was discovered. Unable to face what he had done, he developed an alternate personality, the Jackal, who gradually became dominant. The Jackal blamed SPIDER-MAN for what had happened to Gwen, and forced Peter to face up to his own guilt for her death. Their last confrontation was in the *Daily Bugle* offices, where the Jackal met his maker. TB

JACK FROST

FIRST APPEARANCE USA Comics #1 (August 1941)
REAL NAME Unrevealed **OCCUPATION** Adventurer
BASE North Pole; mobile in US in World War II
HEIGHT 5 ft 11 in **WEIGHT** 172 lbs
EYES Blue-white **HAIR** Blue
SPECIAL POWERS/ABILITIES Possesses innate superhuman ability to generate sub-freezing temperatures.

Jack Frost may have been the human-sized offspring of Frost Giants (*see* GODS OF ASGARD). In the 1940s, he joined the Liberty Legion, a hero team that battled Axis agents on the American home front. Jack Frost was later swallowed by a gigantic Ice Worm in the Arctic yet remained alive. Dr. Gregor Shapanka, whose costume generated intense cold, adopted the name "Jack Frost" as his original criminal identity. A foe of IRON MAN, Shapanka later called himself the BLIZZARD. He was killed by Arno Stark, the time-traveling Iron Man of an alternate future. PS

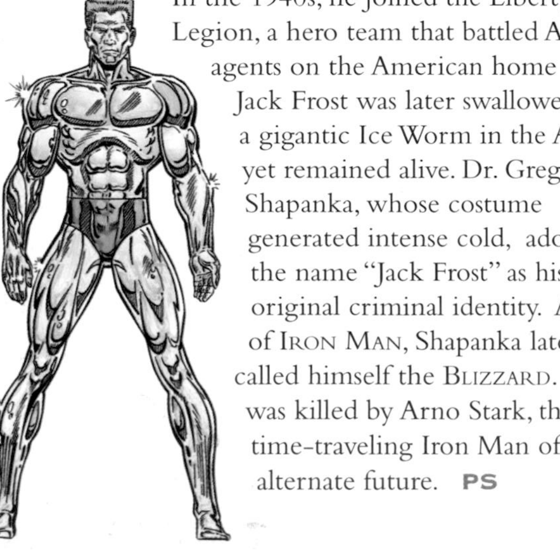

JAMESON, JOHN

FIRST APPEARANCE Amazing Spider-Man #1 (March 1963)
REAL NAME John Jameson
OCCUPATION Former astronaut **BASE** Manhattan
HEIGHT 6 ft 2 in **WEIGHT** 200 lbs **EYES** Brown
HAIR Red-brown
SPECIAL POWERS/ABILITIES Possesses the physical fitness of a top-notch astronaut.

The only son of Daily Bugle publisher J. JONAH JAMESON, John was rescued by SPIDER-MAN when his space capsule went out of control. Spider-Man also helped John when exposure to space-spores gave him superhuman strength and caused him to run wild, and when a lunar gemstone caused him to transform into the MAN-WOLF. Jameson joined the AVENGERS support staff as CAPTAIN AMERICA's pilot, before serving as the head of security for Ravenscroft Asylum, wherein the superhumanly insane were incarcerated. Presently, he is dating Jennifer Walters, the SHE-HULK. TB

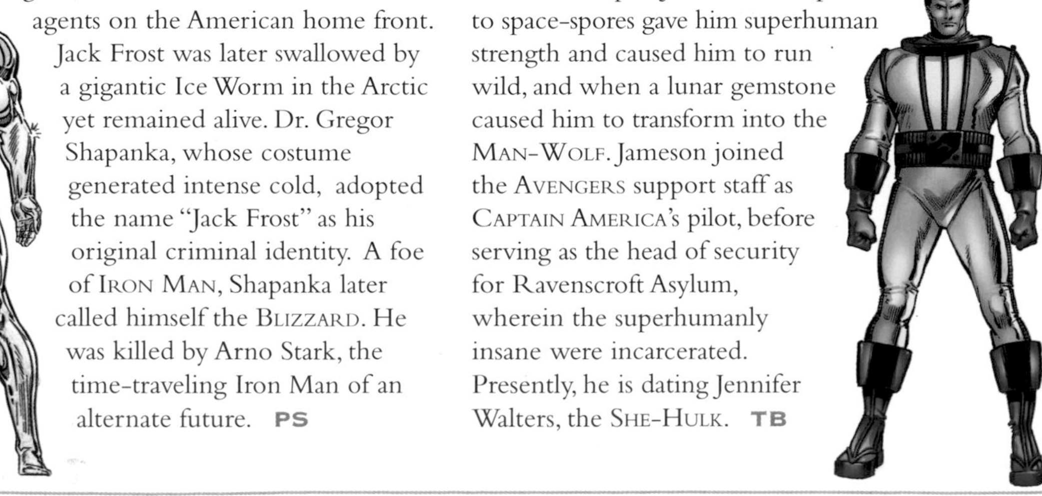

JAMESON, J. JONAH

Crusading publisher of the Daily Bugle

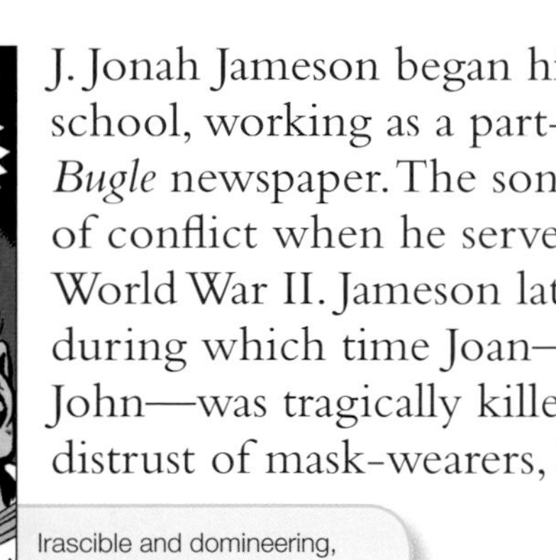

Irascible and domineering, Jameson had no time for costumed Super Heroes.

J. Jonah Jameson began his career in journalism while he was still in high school, working as a part-time copy boy for New York's prestigious *Daily Bugle* newspaper. The son of a war hero, he obtained firsthand experience of conflict when he served as a war correspondent in Europe during World War II. Jameson later spent three years covering the Korean War, during which time Joan—his first wife and the mother of his son, John—was tragically killed by a masked mugger, sparking a lifelong distrust of mask-wearers, be they villain or hero!

CRIME FIGHTER

Jameson reacted to the grief by throwing himself even more fully into his professional life, rising to become editor-in-chief of the *Bugle*. He eventually became the paper's publisher, relinquishing the editor-in-chief position to Joe "Robbie" ROBERTSON. In time, Jameson bought the paper. For many years Jameson used his newspaper to fight for civil rights and to battle organized crime. The KINGPIN of Crime tried to have him killed, but this attempt on his life did nothing to change Jameson's uncompromising attitude. The stubborn, belligerent, but courageous publisher continued to print exposés of big-time criminals—even when his old friend, Norman Osborn, turned out to be one of them.

The *Bugle*'s staff soon learned to cope with Jameson's outbursts!

Jameson began writing editorials against costumed Super Heroes, criticizing them as vigilantes who took the law into their own hands. When the Amazing SPIDER-MAN appeared in New York and began fighting crime as a costumed hero, J. Jonah Jameson focused his most pointed attacks on the Wall Crawler. He called Spider-Man a menace, claiming that the Web Swinger was a danger to the citizens of New York.

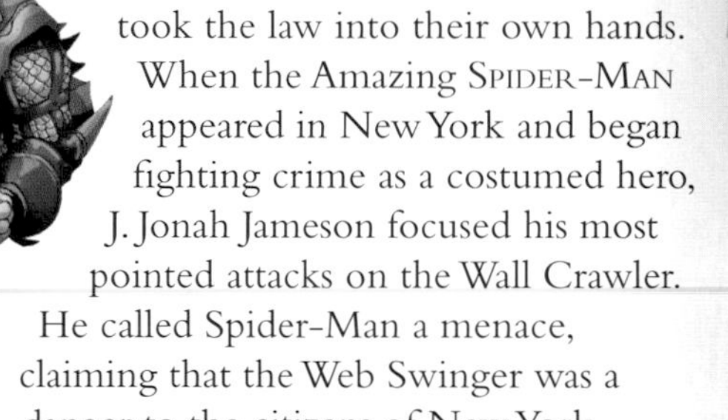

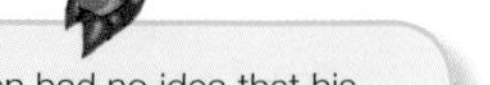

Jameson had no idea that his fellow club member Norman Osborn was the Green Goblin.

SPIDER SEEKER

Ironically, Jameson has bought many photos of Spider-Man in action from freelance photographer Peter Parker. Unknown to the *Bugle*'s publisher, Peter Parker is Spider-Man's secret identity. Jameson has tried unsuccessfully for years to uncover Spider-Man's true identity, even hiring private detectives and offering rewards for information. He has never suspected that the Webbed Wonder is in fact one of his most prized freelancers.

Over the years, Jameson has made a number of attempts to capture Spider-Man, including hiring Dr. Marla Madison to build him a Spider-Slayer robot. He later fell in love with Marla and the two were married.

Despite his hatred for Spider-Man, Jameson is not a murderer and only hopes to capture and unmask Spider-Man, not to kill him. TB

FACTFILE

REAL NAME
J. Jonah Jameson

OCCUPATION
Owner and publisher, Daily Bugle newspaper

BASE
New York City

HEIGHT 5 ft 11 in
WEIGHT 210 lbs
EYES Blue
HAIR: Black, white at the temples

FIRST APPEARANCE
Amazing Spider-Man #1 (March 1963)

POWERS

J. Jonah Jameson has no superhuman powers, but his stubborn, uncompromising attitude makes him a formidable opponent. Outspoken and tenacious, he refuses to back down when he believes he is right.

Jarella

FACTFILE

REAL NAME
Jarella

OCCUPATION
Empress of K'ai

BASE
The city-state of K'ai

HEIGHT (on Earth) 5 ft 6 in
WEIGHT (on Earth) 126 lbs
EYES Green
HAIR Blonde

FIRST APPEARANCE
The Incredible Hulk Vol. 2 #140 (May 1971)

POWERS
Jarella was an excellent swordswoman and formidable hand-to-hand combatant; a brilliant military leader and a wise and compassionate ruler of her people.

A creature called Psyklop subjected the Hulk to a ray that caused him to shrink, until he was shunted into an alternate dimension called a "microverse." The Hulk found himself outside the city of K'ai on an unnamed planet, whose humanoid inhabitants had green skin like his own. After defeating huge beasts called warthos, the Hulk was hailed as a hero by the people of K'ai. Its warrior queen, Jarella, chose the Hulk to become her husband and king of the city-state. K'ai's Pantheon of Sorcerers cast a spell that enabled the personality and intellect of Dr. Bruce Banner to dominate the superhuman form of his alter ego, the Hulk. Believing he would never return to Earth, Banner came to love Jarella. However, the day before their wedding, Psyklop returned the Hulk to Earth, where the spell no longer had effect.

Jarella visited Banner on Earth, and the Hulk twice returned to K'ai, before returning to Earth with Jarella. The Hulk later battled a robot, the Crypto-Man, causing a wall to collapse. Saving a child from the toppling wall, Jarella was crushed to death by it instead. PS

Hulk was so in love with Jarella that he was willing to spend the rest of his life on K'ai and never see Earth again.

Jarvis, Edwin

FACTFILE

REAL NAME
Edwin Jarvis

OCCUPATION
Butler

BASE
Stark Tower, New York City

HEIGHT 5 ft 11 in
WEIGHT 160 lbs
EYES Blue
HAIR Black

FIRST APPEARANCE
Tales of Suspense #59 (November 1964)

POWERS
Former boxing champion of the Royal Air Force. Resourceful under pressure, courageous, and loyal; an excellent, manager, administrator and organizer. World's leading authority on cleaning otherworldly stains from clothing, rugs and fabrics.

Jarvis keeps track of all the Avengers' expenditures.

Edwin Jarvis is a war hero and a former pilot in Britain's Royal Air Force. After retiring to the US, he become the butler of Howard and Maria Stark and continued to work for their son Tony (*see* Iron Man) after their deaths. When Stark transferred ownership of his mansion to the Avengers, he asked Jarvis to stay on as the team's principal domestic servant. Jarvis agreed and served the team loyally until he was captured, hypnotized and transformed into the Crimson Cowl by Ultron. Under Ultron's control, Jarvis allowed the second version of the Masters of Evil to enter Avengers Mansion and capture the team. Ultron also hypnotized Jarvis into believing that he had betrayed the Avengers to secure funds for his ailing mother's medical care. After regaining his true memory, Jarvis convinced the Avengers of his innocence and returned to his duties. Although he supervised an enormous staff, Jarvis was the only servant who actually lived in the mansion. The Scarlet Witch, in a temporary fit of madness, used her reality-altering powers to "disassemble" the Avengers team and destroy the mansion. Jarvis fortunately survived this disaster, and subsequently moved to the new team's headquarters, Stark Tower, resuming his role as the Avengers' major domo. TD

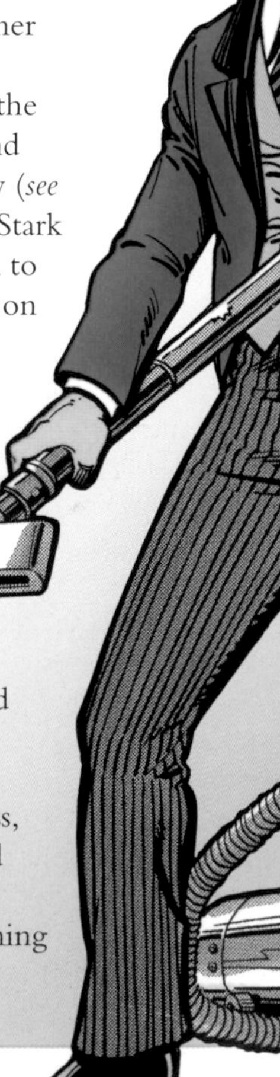

FACTFILE
REAL NAME
Jonathan Powers
OCCUPATION
Former actor; criminal
BASE
New York City

HEIGHT 6 FT 2 IN
WEIGHT 190 lbs
EYES Blue
HAIR Brown

FIRST APPEARANCE
Daredevil Vol. 1 #42 (July 1968)

POWERS
While the Jester has no superhuman powers, he is an above-average athlete, skilled in gymnastics, swordsmanship, and unarmed combat. He also uses a variety of toys which have been turned into deadly weapons or special tools.

JESTER

Struggling actor Jonathan Powers thought he had got his big break in an off-Broadway play. Unfortunately his performance was panned by the critics and booed by the audience. He began studying fencing, gymnastics, and bodybuilding, hoping to win additional roles, but all he landed was a job as a comic foil on a children's TV show.

Deciding to turn to crime, Powers contacted the TINKERER, who specialized in creating unusual weapons from toys. Donning a harlequin-style jester's costume, Powers began calling himself the Jester, and set out on a crime spree in New York, using his deadly toys and gimmicks.

Jester soon came into conflict with the costumed hero DAREDEVIL, who halted Jester's criminal activity and helped to put him in jail. **MT**

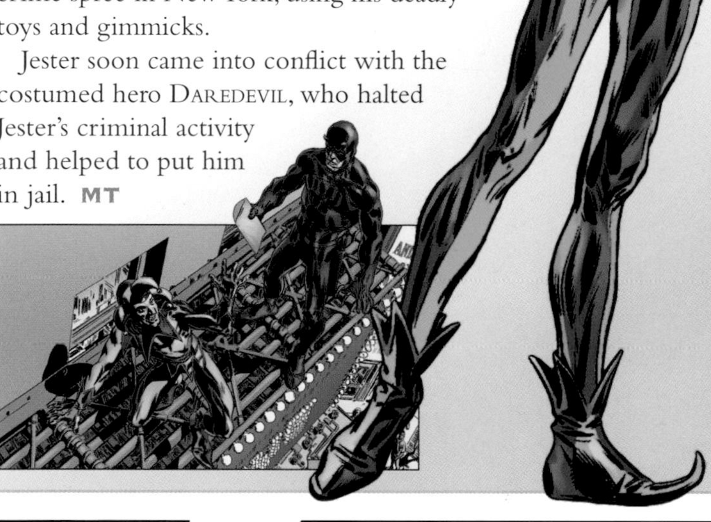

The Jester finally runs out japes when cornered by Daredevil on a fire escape high above the streets of New York City.

JETSTREAM

FIRST APPEARANCE New Mutants #16 (June 1984)
REAL NAME Haroun ibn Sallah al-Rashid
OCCUPATION Hellion team-member
BASE Massachusetts Academy
HEIGHT 5 ft 7 in **WEIGHT** 145 lbs **EYES** Black **HAIR** Black
SPECIAL POWERS/ABILITIES Body generates thermo-chemical energy; able to fly.

Mutants often have difficulty learning to use their powers, but Haroun al-Rashid struggled more than most. Codenamed Jetstream, Haroun had difficulty controlling and releasing the thermo-chemical energy his body was constantly generating. When these energies caused his flesh to catch fire, it was only the intervention of the HELLIONS that saved his life. The Hellions provided him with a bionic system that enabled him to control his powers.

After all they had done for him, Haroun felt obliged to remain with the team; however his membership was not destined to last long. During an attack on the HELLFIRE CLUB by White Rook (Trevor Fitzroy), Haroun was killed when his life energy was drained away. **AD**

JOCASTA

FIRST APPEARANCE Avengers #162 (August 1977)
REAL NAME Jocasta
OCCUPATION Former adventurer; computer **BASE** Mobile
HEIGHT 5 ft 9 in **WEIGHT** 750 lbs **EYES** Red **HAIR** None
SPECIAL POWERS/ABILITIES Superhuman ability to process information; superhuman strength, durability and senses of sight and hearing; projects energy blasts from eyes and hands.

The robot Jocasta was created by another robot, the hate-filled ULTRON, to be his mate. Jocasta's personality is based on that of the WASP, who was the wife of Ultron's creator, Henry PYM. Although Ultron programmed Jocasta to serve him, she turned against him. She repeatedly aided the AVENGERS and became a member of their team. Later Jocasta's artificial intelligence entered the main computer in the Seattle mansion of Tony Stark (IRON MAN), and she became his personal ally. Subsequently, Jocasta appeared in a robot body that resembles her original form. **PS**

JOLT

FIRST APPEARANCE Thunderbolts #1 (April 1997)
REAL NAME Helen "Hallie" Takahama
OCCUPATION Adventurer **BASE** Counter-Earth
HEIGHT 5 ft 5 in **WEIGHT** 110 lbs **EYES** Brown **HAIR** Black
SPECIAL POWERS/ABILITIES Jolt is suffused with biokinetic energy which gives her enhanced strength, speed and agility and the ability to throw hyperkinetic punches.

After her parents were killed during the rampage of ONSLAUGHT, Hallie Takahama had to fend for herself on the streets of New York. Abducted by mad geneticist Arnim ZOLA, Hallie was rescued by the THUNDERBOLTS—Super Villains posing as heroes. Not realizing their motives, Hallie joined the team as Jolt, to the consternation of its leader, BARON ZEMO. She inspired some members to turn against Zemo, before leaving the team and opting to live on the ravaged Counter-Earth on the other side of the sun. **TB**

JONES, GABE

FIRST APPEARANCE Sgt. Fury and his Howling Commandos #1 (May 1963) **REAL NAME** Gabriel Jones
OCCUPATION SHIELD agent **BASE** New York City
HEIGHT 6 ft 2 in **WEIGHT** 225 lbs **EYES** Brown **HAIR** White
SPECIAL POWERS/ABILITIES Formidable hand-to-hand combatant when younger; excellent marksman and combat tactician; expert jazz trumpeter.

Like so many other members of World War II heroes the HOWLING COMMANDOS, Gabe Jones was to continue fighting alongside its commander, Nick FURY, for most of his life. Reuniting with the rest of the military strike squad during the Korean and Vietnam wars, Gabe became a key aide to Fury when he was made director of SHIELD. Responsible for infiltrating and bringing down the insidious organization known as the Secret Empire, Gabe remained loyal to Fury even after the android Deltites infiltrated SHIELD. He went on to play a key role when the organization was re-established as a leaner, more focused operation. **AD**

Jones, Jessica

FIRST APPEARANCE Alias #1 (November 2001)
REAL NAME Jessica Jones
OCCUPATION Private investigator **BASE** New York City
HEIGHT 5 ft 4 in **WEIGHT** 120 lbs **EYES** Brown **HAIR** Brown
SPECIAL POWERS/ABILITIES As the Super Hero Jewel, Jessica Jones possessed the powers of flight, superhuman strength, and a high resistance to injury.

When the car she and her family were in collided with a truck full of radioactive chemicals, young Jessica Jones acquired superpowers. The rest of her family was killed. Taking the identity Jewel, she used her powers to battle criminals until the evil Zebediah Killgrave, known as the PURPLE MAN, took control of her mind and enslaved her. After losing a battle with the AVENGERS, Jessica fell into a coma and underwent psychic therapy with Jean GREY. She gave up being a hero and opened a detective agency specializing in cases involving superpowered beings. MT

Jones, Marlo

FIRST APPEARANCE Incredible Hulk #347 (September 1998)
REAL NAME Marlo Chandler-Jones
OCCUPATION Talk show host, comic shop owner
BASE Las Vegas, Los Angeles
HEIGHT 5 ft 8 in **WEIGHT** 135 lbs **EYES** Green **HAIR** Red
SPECIAL POWERS/ABILITIES In excellent physical shape. At one point she acquired the ability to see the spirits of dead people.

Marlo Chandler met and dated the HULK when he was in his grey Joe Fixit personality and working as a bodyguard for Las Vegas casino-owner, Michael BERENGETTI.

She broke off the relationship after witnessing the Hulk savagely kill an enemy. Marlo later met the Hulk's friend Rick JONES, when he was on a book tour promoting his memoirs. Rick and Marlo married and hosted a television talk show called *Keeping Up With the Joneses*. Rick and Marlo separated, made up, then broke up again. Despite their many ups and downs, Rick and Marlo are still together. MT

Jones, Rick

A shiftless teenager, Rick Jones had no idea how his life and the world would change the day he snuck onto a military testing facility on a dare. For the test of a new Gamma Bomb was being carried out, and it was only through the sacrifice of Bruce Banner that Jones survived the blast—the same blast that cursed Banner with becoming the HULK whenever he became enraged.

Feeling enormous guilt over his catalytic role in this chain of events, Rick remained by Banner's side, helping him to conceal his secret from the military. Thereafter, when the AVENGERS were formed in response to the threat of the Hulk, Rick became an honorary member. Trained by CAPTAIN AMERICA, Rick served as his partner for a time, and subsequently worked in concert with both CAPTAIN MAR-VELL and his son, Genis-Vell (*see* CAPTAIN MARVEL), and with the space knight known as Rom. Most recently, Rick secretly bankrolled the young superhuman help group known as Excelsior. TB

FACTFILE
REAL NAME
Richard Jones
OCCUPATION
Adventurer
BASE
Various

HEIGHT 5 ft 9 in
WEIGHT 165 lbs
EYES Brown
HAIR Brown

FIRST APPEARANCE
Incredible Hulk #1
(May 1962)

POWERS
Rick Jones possesses a courageous spirit and the expert fighting skills of one trained by Captain America.

For a time, Rick's molecules were merged with those of the Kree hero Captain Marvel.

Joseph

FIRST APPEARANCE Uncanny X-Men #327 (December 1995)
REAL NAME Unknown **OCCUPATION** Adventurer
BASE Xavier Institute, New York State
HEIGHT 6 ft 2 in **WEIGHT** 190 lbs
EYES Blue-gray **HAIR** White
SPECIAL POWERS/ABILITIES As Magneto's clone Joseph has the same power as Magneto—the ability to control magnetism and magnetic forces—frequently to devastating effect.

Astra of the BROTHERHOOD OF EVIL MUTANTS created a clone of her enemy MAGNETO hoping that it would kill the original. The clone physically resembled the 20-year-old Magneto. The clone and Magneto clashed in Guatemala. Magneto knocked the clone unconscious and escaped. When the clone came to, he had lost his memory. Sister Maria de la Joya nursed him back to health and a child at the orphanage where she worked named him Joseph. Sister Maria sent Joseph to the US to seek help from the X-MEN, but they believed that he was really Magneto, only younger and with amnesia. Nevertheless, they allowed him to join the team.

In a final confrontation with the real Magneto, Joseph bravely sacrificed his life in order to save the world from Magneto's attack on the Earth's magnetic fields. Magneto's dreams of world conquest would have to wait a little longer. MT

Jubilee

Born to a wealthy Asian-American family, Jubilee was raised in Beverly Hills and became a top-class gymnast. After her parents lost their fortune and then their lives, Jubilee was left orphaned and embittered. Jubilee ran away, living at the Hollywood Mall, where her mutant powers became manifest. Having evaded mall security with the help of various X-Men, Jubilee followed them through a teleportal to their Australian base, remaining hidden there until it was abandoned. She left the base with Wolverine and they travelled through Asia: he found her directness, sarcasm and honesty refreshing; she came to regard Wolverine as a surrogate father. Since returning to the US, Jubilee has been a member of the X-Men and Generation-X. While she still has some sharp edges, much of Jubilee's faith in humanity has been restored. AD

JUBILEE

FACTFILE

REAL NAME
Jubilation Lee

OCCUPATION
X-Corporation employee

BASE
Mobile

HEIGHT 5 ft 5 in
WEIGHT 105 lbs
EYES Blue
HAIR Black

FIRST APPEARANCE
Uncanny X-Men #244
(May 1989)

POWERS

Generates and projects energy globules—"fireworks"—from her fingers; Jubilee is also able to control, direct and reabsorb these.

Juggernaut

After the death of her husband, Sharon Xavier married his colleague, atomic scientist Dr. Kurt Marko. Dr. Marko often beat his son Cain, who in turn bullied his new stepbrother, Charles Xavier (*see* Professor X), whom he came to hate. Marko joined the army, but deserted while in Korea. In a cave he came upon a temple to the god Cyttorak. Marko seized a large ruby, which magically transformed him into a "human juggernaut," an unstoppable super-being. Enemy bombs then caused the cave to collapse, burying him alive.

Years later, Marko resurfaced as the Juggernaut, invading Xavier's mansion and trying to kill him. The Juggernaut had several battles with the X-Men often teaming up with Black Tom Cassidy, whom he had met in prison.

In time, the Juggernaut lost much of his power, made peace with Xavier, and fell out with Cassidy. Marko even joined the X-Men, and later became a member of the third incarnation of Excalibur. PS

JUGGERNAUT

FACTFILE

REAL NAME
Cain Marko

OCCUPATION
Former soldier, later mercenary, professional criminal, adventurer

BASE
Mobile

HEIGHT 6 ft 10 in
WEIGHT 900 lbs
EYES Blue
HAIR Red

FIRST APPEARANCE
X-Men #12
(July 1965)

POWERS

At full power, possessed virtual invulnerability, extraordinary superhuman strength, and could generate an impenetrable force field around himself. Wore a helmet that protected him from psychic attack.

Juggernaut uses his colossal might against one of Callisto's soldiers.

KAINE

FACTFILE
REAL NAME
None; clone of Peter Parker
OCCUPATION
Assassin, criminal
BASE
Various

HEIGHT 6 ft 4 ins
WEIGHT 250 lbs
EYES Brown
HAIR Brown

FIRST APPEARANCE
Web Of Spider-Man #118, November 1994

POWERS
Kaine possesses the strength, speed and agility of Spider-Man himself, as well as the ability to burn the "mark of Kaine" onto the skin of his victims. Kaine also receives prophetic visions of the future from his imperfect spider-sense.

Kaine

The first, flawed clone of Peter Parker created by the JACKAL, Kaine developed cellular degeneration and was able to survive only by wearing a special life-support suit. His condition left him badly scarred, and caused his spider-powers to become twisted and magnified. Abandoned by his creator, and knowing himself to be nothing more than a mockery of true life, Kaine wandered the world taking on work as an assassin to survive. Kaine would duplicate his own facial scarring on his victim's faces, leaving it as a calling card—the "mark of Kaine."

Kaine believed that the Ben Reilly clone of Peter Parker was the true SPIDER-MAN, and made it his mission in life to torture and torment Reilly for having the life that he never would, even framing him for a series of murders.

Eventually, Kaine was drawn back into Spider-Man's orbit as part of a far-reaching plot of the JACKAL's, and he was a participant in the Maximum Clonage affair which resulted in him finally learning the truth about Reilly and Parker. In the end, Kaine gave himself up to the authorities to pay for his crimes; however, he later escaped from prison, and his current whereabouts are unknown. **TB**

The assassin Kaine always left his vicious mark—a network of scars on the face of each victim.

KALA

FIRST APPEARANCE Tales Of Suspense #43 (July 1963)
REAL NAME Kala
OCCUPATION Queen **BASE** The Netherworld and Subterranea
HEIGHT 5 ft 8 in **WEIGHT** 135 lbs **EYES** Blue **HAIR** Black
SPECIAL POWERS/ABILITIES Kala possess no superhuman powers, although she can see clearly in very low light due to her years of living underground.

Kala is the queen of an underground realm known as the Netherworld. She had threatened to attack the surface world, but IRON MAN captured her and brought her up to the surface. The sudden change in atmospheric conditions caused the young and beautiful Kala to age rapidly. She renounced her plans of conquest and was returned to the Netherworld, where she reverted to her youthful self. Kala allied with MOLE MAN of Subterranea, but the two later went to war. **MT**

KALE, JENNIFER

FIRST APPEARANCE Adventures Into Fear #11 (December 1972)
REAL NAME Jennifer Kale
OCCUPATION Sorceress **BASE** Citrusville, Florida
HEIGHT 5 ft 6 in **WEIGHT** 122 lbs **EYES** Blue **HAIR** Blonde
SPECIAL POWERS/ABILITIES Jennifer Kale is a highly knowledgeable sorcereress with developing skill in manipulating various magical forces.

Jennifer is the granddaughter of Joshua Kale, a leader of the Cult of Zhered-Na, named after a sorceress who lived in Atlantis before it sank. Jennifer and MAN-THING were magically transported to another dimension, where they met the wizard Dakimh, last surviving pupil of Zhered-Na. As Dakimh's apprentice, Jennifer became a sorceress. An ally of MAN-THING and HOWARD THE DUCK, she is a founder of the Legion of Night and teamed with TOPAZ and Satana as the Three Witches. **PS**

KALUU

FIRST APPEARANCE Strange Tales Vol. I #147 (August 1966)
REAL NAME Kaluu
OCCUPATION Sorcerer **BASE** Not known
HEIGHT 6 ft 5 in **WEIGHT** 190 lbs **EYES** Yellow **HAIR** Black
SPECIAL POWERS/ABILITIES Arguably most powerful living black magician; has knowledge of vast number of spells including all those contained in Book of the Vishanti.

Born five hundred years ago in Tibet, Kaluu trained alongside the being that came to be known as the ANCIENT ONE. Whereas the Ancient One became a force for good, Kaluu was corrupted by the vampire VARNAE. Over the centuries he threatened Earth numerous times but redeemed himself in more recent years, helping DR. STRANGE to destroy a hoard of demons the Doctor had inadvertently released. Unable to complete the journey to eradicate the greatest of these demons, Shuma-Gorath, Kaluu was left behind by Strange. His whereabouts are currently unknown. **AD**

Kang

Time-traveling conqueror

Born in an alternate timeline in 3000 AD, Nathaniel Richards (a descendant of Mr. Fantastic's father, who bore the same name) discovered time-travel technology that enabled him to journey virtually anywhere he liked in the timestream.

TIME TRAVELER

Richards' first stop was ancient Egypt, where he seized power and ruled for a decade as Pharaoh Rama-Tut until forced to flee after a fight with the Fantastic Four. Arriving in the 40th century, he briefly became the Scarlet Centurion before settling on the name Kang the Conqueror. Kang found the century in turmoil and easy to subjugate.

Looking for new challenges, Kang traveled to 1901 and established the city of Timely, Wisconsin in his guise as Victor Timely. He assembled an elite warrior class, the Anachronauts, from all eras of history before returning to the 40th century. There he fell in love with Princess Ravonna. After her death during a revolt by Kang's troops, he tried and failed to become the consort of the Celestial Madonna (Mantis), killing the original Swordsman in the process. A future version of Kang, calling himself Immortus, tried to thwart his younger self's aggressive schemes, but Kang would not be contained, and assembled the original Legion of the Unliving.

Despite having the entirety of time and space at his disposal, the only thing for which Kang truly cared was the beautiful princess Ravonna. His obsession for her inspired several of his early schemes.

FACTFILE

REAL NAME
Nathaniel Richards

OCCUPATION
Conqueror

BASE
Mobile

HEIGHT 6 ft 3 in
WEIGHT 230 lbs
EYES Brown
HAIR Brown

FIRST APPEARANCE
Avengers Vol. 1 #8 (September 1964)

POWERS
Master of time travel; suit provides enhanced strength, force field projection, and energy projection; Kang is typically armed with futuristic weaponry.

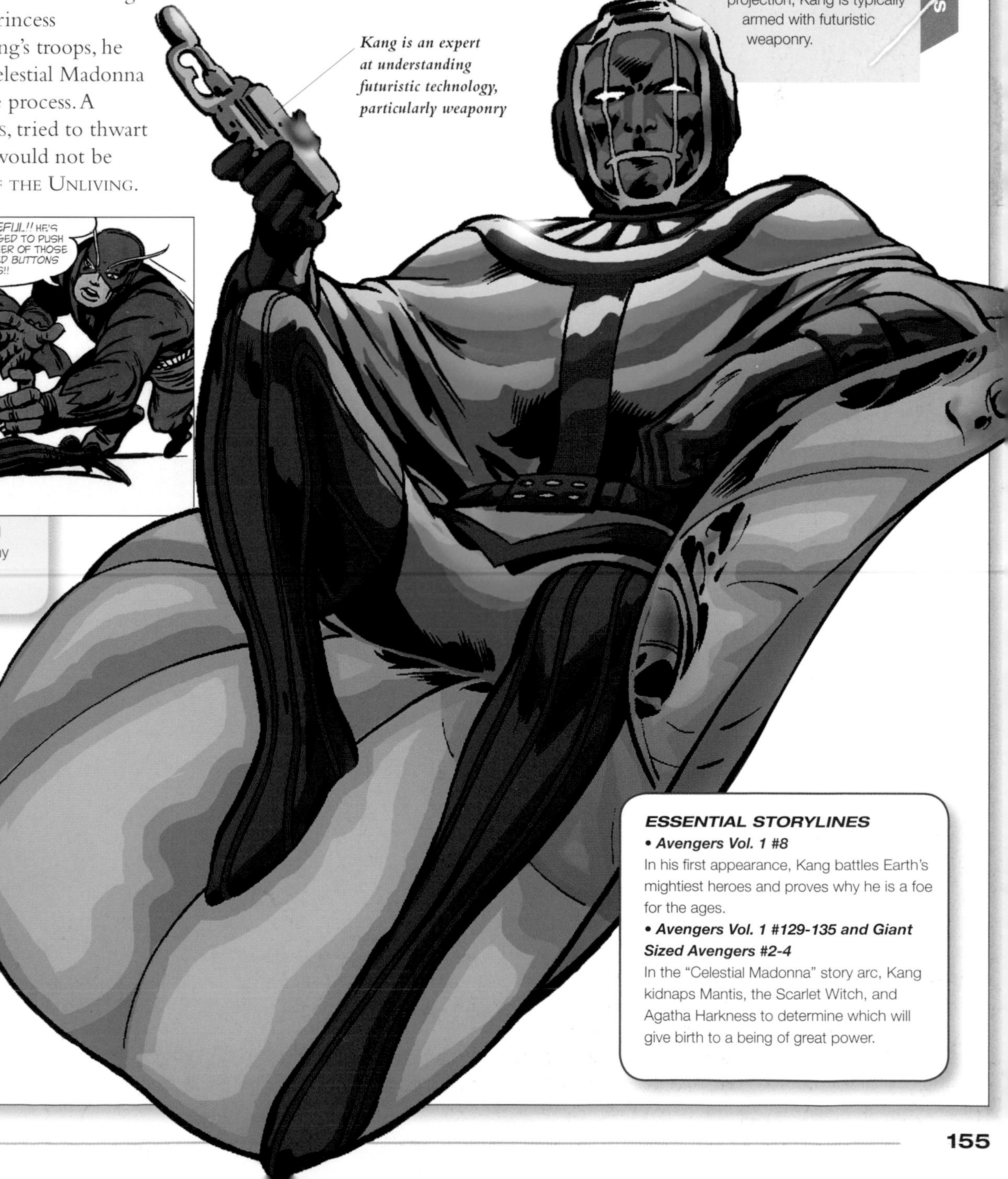

Kang is an expert at understanding futuristic technology, particularly weaponry

The Avengers faced Kang shortly after the team's founding, and have clashed with him countless times since. During the "Destiny War," Kang handpicked a group of Avengers from across the timestream to aid in his fight against Immortus.

Kang's Gang

After a stint in 1873 Arizona and many other time hops, Kang gathered alternate versions of himself from branching timestreams and formed the Council of Kangs. The Kangs killed any duplicates deemed unworthy until only the prime Kang remained.

Kang joined with Libra, the Kree Supreme Intelligence, and the Avengers to prevent Immortus and the Time Keepers from wiping out a multitude of alternate realities. During the battle, Kang and Immortus's histories diverged. Kang then conquered modern-era Earth with his son Marcus (the new Scarlet Centurion), but met defeat at the hands of the Avengers. DW

ESSENTIAL STORYLINES

- ***Avengers Vol. 1 #8***
In his first appearance, Kang battles Earth's mightiest heroes and proves why he is a foe for the ages.
- ***Avengers Vol. 1 #129-135 and Giant Sized Avengers #2-4***
In the "Celestial Madonna" story arc, Kang kidnaps Mantis, the Scarlet Witch, and Agatha Harkness to determine which will give birth to a being of great power.

Karkas

FIRST APPEARANCE The Eternals Vol. 1 #8 (January 1977)
REAL NAME Karkas
OCCUPATION Scholar **BASE** Olympia
HEIGHT 8 ft 3in **WEIGHT** 1,260 lbs **EYES** Black **HAIR** None
SPECIAL POWERS/ABILITIES Possesses superhuman strength. His thick hide, resembling an elephant's, gives him superhuman resistance to injury.

The Deviants are an evolutionary offshoot of humanity with an unstable genetic code. Those whose genetic makeup varies beyond standards set by the Deviant priesthood are labeled mutates. The Deviant mutate Karkas was raised to be a gladiator, but at heart he was a philosopher. He was defeated in the arena by another mutate, Ransak the Reject. Then Karkas asked THENA, a visiting ETERNAL, to grant sanctuary to himself and the Reject. She transported them to Olympia, home of the Eternals. Ever since then Karkas has been a staunch ally of the Eternals. **PS**

Karma

FIRST APPEARANCE Marvel Team-up #100 (December 1980)
REAL NAME Xi'an Coy Manh
OCCUPATION Adventurer **BASE** Mobile
HEIGHT 5 ft 4 in **WEIGHT** 90 lbs **EYES** Brown **HAIR** Black
SPECIAL POWERS/ABILITIES Has the ability to psionically possess other people, controlling their actions and turning them into virtual puppets.

Xi'an and her twin brother Tran had the ability to possess the minds of others. Tran worked for the criminal organization of their uncle, General Coy, and Coy tried to force Xi'an to do the same by abducting their younger siblings Leong and Nga. With the aid of SPIDER-MAN and the FANTASTIC FOUR, Xi'an rescued the children, but had to absorb Tran's psyche into her own. She attended Professor Xavier's School for Gifted Youngsters, and became the first member of the NEW MUTANTS, but has since left. **TB**

Karnak

FIRST APPEARANCE Fantastic Four #45 (December 1965)
REAL NAME Unrevealed **OCCUPATION** Priest/philosopher
BASE Attilan, Blue Area, the Moon
HEIGHT 5 ft 7 in **WEIGHT** 150 lbs **EYES** Blue **HAIR** Black
SPECIAL POWERS/ABILITIES Superhuman strength and ability to control his heartbeat and other autonomic body functions. Has the extrasensory ability to perceive weakness in objects and people.

A member of the royal family of the INHUMANS, Karnak is the second son of the Inhuman priest Mander. Mander and his wife Azur had sent their first son, TRITON, into the Terrigen Mist which produced genetic mutations. They decided not to expose Karnak to the mist, instead sending him to his father's religious seminary in the Tower of Wisdom. There, he trained in physical and mental disciplines, martial arts, and religious study until the age of eighteen. Karnak was involved in the Kree-Skrull Wars, and aided DAREDEVIL in his attempt to find Karnak's cousin BLACK BOLT's son. **MT**

Karnilla

FIRST APPEARANCE Journey into Mystery #107 (August 1964)
REAL NAME Karnilla
OCCUPATION Sorceress and Queen of Nornheim
BASE Nornheim, Asgardian dimension
HEIGHT 6 ft 6 in **WEIGHT** 475 lbs **EYES** Purple **HAIR** Black
SPECIAL POWERS/ABILITIES Long-lived; superhuman strength; can project magical power bolts and create a magical shield.

For centuries, Karnilla, Queen of Nornheim and the most powerful sorceress in the Asgardian dimension, vied with the GODS OF ASGARD, often allying herself with the mischievous god LOKI. Karnilla fell in love with the heroic warrior god BALDER THE BRAVE, but he repeatedly spurned her advances. After fighting alongside her in the war against the demon Surtur however, Balder relented and the pair became lovers, to the consternation of others in Asgard. The pair have forged a deep love and mutual respect, with Balder committing himself to a life in Nornheim. **AD**

Ka-Zar

FIRST APPEARANCE Uncanny X-Men vol. 1 #10 (March, 1965)
REAL NAME Lord Kevin Plunder
OCCUPATION Hunter, trapper, lord of the Savage Land
BASE The Savage Land
HEIGHT 6 ft 2 in **WEIGHT** 215 lbs **EYES** Blue **HAIR** Blond
SPECIAL POWERS/ABILITIES Expert physical combatant, hunter and forager.

Son of British nobleman Lord Robert Plunder (the discoverer of Antarctic vibranium), Ka-Zar grew up in the Antarctic "Savage Land" following the murder of his father at the hands of MAN-APES. Raised by the intelligent sabertoothed tiger ZABU, Ka-Zar learned to survive against dinosaurs and Man-Apes. His enemies have included his brother Parnival, also known as the Plunderer, and the Savage Land Mutates. Ka-Zar eventually married SHANNA THE SHE-DEVIL, and the two are currently raising a son, Matthew. **DW**

Kelly, Senator

FIRST APPEARANCE X-Men #135 (September 1980)
REAL NAME Senator Robert Kelly
OCCUPATION Politician **BASE** Washington D.C.
HEIGHT 5 ft 10 in **WEIGHT** 175 lbs **EYES** Brown
HAIR Brown (graying temples)
SPECIAL POWERS/ABILITIES Charismatic individual with rabble-rousing public speaking skills.

In one alternate future, the successful assassination of Senator Kelly led to the death or imprisonment of all mutants.

As senator for Massachusetts, Robert Kelly proposed strong anti-mutant legislation. Repeated assassination attempts and his wife's death hardened his stance until, while standing for president on an anti-mutant platform, he was saved from another attempt on his life by the sacrifice of PYRO. Kelly then changed his stance dramatically, only to be killed by a non-mutant who accused him of betraying humanity. **AD**

Killraven

FIRST APPEARANCE Amazing Adventures Vol. 1 #18 (May 1973)
REAL NAME Jonathan Raven
OCCUPATION Freedom fighter **BASE** Mobile
HEIGHT 6 ft 1 in **WEIGHT** 185 lbs **EYES** Blue **HAIR** Red
SPECIAL POWERS/ABILITIES An expert combatant and swordsman who can take mental control of a Martian's body. A natural leader who has keen survival instincts suited for a post-apocalyptic world.

In an alternate timeline, Martian invaders conquered Earth in the year 2001. The Martians forced many of the survivors to battle in gladiatorial pits, where Jonathan Raven first won fame as "Killraven." Keeper Whitman, a scientist employed by the Martians but secretly working against them, was given the task of rehabilitating Killraven following an unsuccessful escape attempt. Whitman genetically modified Killraven giving him the ability to seize mental control of his Martian masters. Killraven led a team of Freemen in a cross-country trek, striking out against the Martian overlords while searching for his lost brother. **DW**

Armed only with his trademark swords, Killraven faces off against a horde of alien warriors, exhibiting the cocky courage that won him fame in the gladiator pits.

Like his adversary Iron Man, Killer Shrike wears armor: his costume is a head-to-toe battlesuit composed of steel alloy mesh that can resist small-arms fire.

Killer Shrike

FIRST APPEARANCE The Rampaging Hulk #1 (January 1977)
REAL NAME Simon Maddicks
OCCUPATION Criminal **BASE** Mobile
HEIGHT 6 ft 5 in **WEIGHT** 250 lbs **EYES** Brown **HAIR** Brown
SPECIAL POWERS/ABILITIES Posesses enhanced strength and ability to fly. Wears bracelets with titanium talons and power-blasters that fire electrical bolts of concussive force.

Former soldier Simon Maddicks worked as a mercenary before becoming a covert operative for the Roxxon Oil company. The mutagenics laboratory of the Brand Corporation, Roxxon's subsidiary, boosted Maddicks' strength to superhuman levels and implanted an anti-gravity generator at the base of his spine, which enabled him to fly.

Roxxon assigned Maddicks, in his new costumed identity of Killer Shrike, to infiltrate the cabal called the Conspiracy. This mission led to his defeat by the monster hunter Ulysses Bloodstone.

Eventually Killer Shrike became a free agent, hiring out his services or committing crimes on his own. In the course of his criminal career, he has battled the Super Heroes Spider-Man, Moon Knight, and the She-Hulk. **PS**

Kincaid, Dr.

FIRST APPEARANCE Thor #136 (January 1967)
REAL NAME Dr. Keith Kinkaid
OCCUPATION Medical doctor **BASE** California
HEIGHT 5 ft 7 in **WEIGHT** 155 lbs **EYES** Blue **HAIR** Blond
SPECIAL POWERS/ABILITIES Dr. Keith Kincaid is a normal human with no superhuman powers. He possesses the normal degree of physical fitness of a man of his age and weight.

Following the temporary transformation of Thor's mortal love Jane Foster into a goddess by Odin (*see* Gods of Asgard) and her defeat at the hands of the Unknown (a formless creature composed of living fear), Odin returned her to Earth. Jane had no memory of either Thor or his alter ego Dr. Donald Blake. Foster went to work for Dr. Keith Kincaid. She fell in love with Kincaid, whose personality and appearance were virtually identical to Blake's. They married and had a son named Kevin. As it turned out, Odin had originally used Kincaid as the model for the Don Blake persona he created as a punishment for Thor. **TB**

King, Hannibal

FIRST APPEARANCE Tomb of Dracula #25 (October 1974)
REAL NAME Hannibal King
OCCUPATION Private Investigator **BASE** Boston, Massachusetts
HEIGHT 6 ft 2 in **WEIGHT** 196 lbs **EYES** Blue **HAIR** Black
SPECIAL POWERS/ABILITIES Has all of the abilities typical to a vampire, but prefers not to use them due to his self-loathing about his condition.

A low-rent private investigator, Hannibal King was slain by the vampire Deacon Frost and three days later rose from the dead himself a vampire. Repulsed by his new condition, King's force of will was so strong that he refrained from feasting on human blood. Resuming his career as a private eye, albeit one who only operated at night, King clashed with the vampire lord Dracula, which brought him into the sphere of the man called Blade, who had his own grievances against Deacon Frost. Together, the two men tracked Frost to his lair, and ended his menace forever. Thereafter, King and Blade formalized their professional relationship, becoming the Nightstalkers, dedicated to hunting down and eradicating supernatural evil. **TB**

KINGPIN

Bulky criminal mastermind

KINGPIN

FACTFILE

REAL NAME
Wilson Grant Fisk

OCCUPATION
Criminal mastermind

BASE
New York City

HEIGHT 6 ft 7 in
WEIGHT 450 lbs
EYES Blue
HAIR None

FIRST APPEARANCE
Amazing Spider-Man Vol 1 #50 (July 1967)

POWERS

Brilliant criminal mind and superb fighting skills; his body, though huge and heavy, is composed of almost solid muscle.

Fisk was so in love with the beautiful Vanessa that he agreed to renounce his criminal ways—until fate took a hand.

Wilson Fisk, the Kingpin, is the most formidable figure in organized crime, and a perennial enemy of the Super Heroes SPIDER-MAN, the PUNISHER, and, most frequently, DAREDEVIL. The Kingpin's operations are global and the assassins that have done his dirty work are legion, including such names as BULLSEYE, ELEKTRA, and TYPHOID MARY.

ESSENTIAL STORYLINES

- ***Daredevil Vol. 1 #227–233***
In the acclaimed "Born Again" storyarc, the Kingpin's malicious schemes bring Daredevil to the edge of a mental breakdown.

- ***Daredevil Vol. 2 #46–50***
In a shocking turn of events, Daredevil defeats the Kingpin and takes over as boss of New York City's notorious Hell's Kitchen.

UNDERWORLD KING

As a youth, Fisk bulked up his body to strike back against the bullies who tormented him, committing his first murder at the age of 12. At 15, he led a gang of street toughs, and came to be called the "Kingpin of Crime." Employed by crimelord Don Rigoletto, he ended up killing Rigoletto and assuming control of his operation. He married Vanessa, a beautiful socialite, and they had a son, Richard. The Kingpin also became the guardian of Maya Lopez (Echo), the daughter of one of his murdered business partners. After decades in power, the Kingpin organized the various New York gangs and challenged the MAGGIA, triggering a war that Spider-Man helped to end.

POWER STRUGGLES

The Kingpin believed that his son Richard had died in a skiing accident. In truth, Richard had become a rival crimelord, the SCHEMER, who lured his father into an alliance with a HYDRA faction. The Kingpin left his empire behind to pursue a new life with Vanessa in Japan, but returned with a vengeance after Vanessa's apparent death. Richard Fisk then became a new criminal rival, the ROSE.

After the Kingpin learned Daredevil's secret identity, he destroyed the hero's life and nearly killed him. The Kingpin also participated in a gang war between New York crime families, and defeated the RED SKULL. The Kingpin's empire crumbled when HYDRA agents cleaned out his bank accounts and assaulted his headquarters, Fisk Towers. The Kingpin rebuilt his empire by controlling multinationals such as Fujikawa Industries. His foster daughter Echo blinded him by shooting him in the face, and the Kingpin's inner circle—including his son Richard—stabbed him many times and left him for dead. Vanessa nursed her husband, killed Richard for betraying his father, and the Kingpin returned stronger than ever. Recently, however, Daredevil beat his longtime nemesis senseless and declared *himself* the new Kingpin. **DW**

Sabotage by various costumed crimefighters have hobbled the Kingpin's illicit empire.

The Kingpin's son, Richard Fisk, became a rival to his father as the masked Rose.

Sheer muscle mass makes the Kingpin surprisingly strong and tough, allowing him to withstand Spider-Man's powerful blows

Klaw

FIRST APPEARANCE Fantastic Four #53 (August 1966)
REAL NAME Ulysses Klaw
OCCUPATION Scientist, professional criminal **BASE** Mobile
HEIGHT 5 ft 11 in **WEIGHT** 175 lbs **EYES** Red **HAIR** None
SPECIAL POWERS/ABILITIES Can turn sound waves into matter and reshape his body, which is made of sound waves. Able to project deafening sounds and fire concussive blasts of sound waves.

Physicist Ulysses Klaw was working on a device to turn sound into physical objects and needed Vibranium, an element found only in the African nation of Wakanda. He traveled to the country and tried to seize the element from the Cult of the BLACK PANTHER, but in the battle, Klaw's right hand was destroyed by his own sonic blaster. Eventually buying vibranium on the black market, Klaw made a prosthetic device that could turn sound into matter, to replace his hand. He has frequently battled the FANTASTIC FOUR. **MT**

Knight, Misty

FIRST APPEARANCE Marvel Team-Up #1 (March 1972, as bystander); Marvel Premiere #20 (January 1975, identified)
REAL NAME Misty Knight **OCCUPATION** Private investigator
BASE Nightwing Restorations, New York City
HEIGHT 5 ft 9 in **WEIGHT** 136 lbs **EYES** Brown **HAIR** Black
SPECIAL POWERS/ABILITIES Misty Knight is a trained fighter whose right arm has been replaced with a bionic substitute.

Once a highly-decorated police officer, Misty Knight's days on the Force came to an end when she lost her right arm to a terrorist's bomb. In recognition of her bravery, Stark International arranged for Misty to receive a bionic prosthetic to replace her lost limb. Unwilling to accept a desk job with the police department, Misty instead went into business as a private investigator with her friend, samurai Colleen WING. As the Daughters of the Dragon, the two women have shared innumerable adventures, often in the company of Power Man (*see* CAGE, LUKE) and Misty's longtime lover, IRON FIST. **TB**

Kofi

FIRST APPEARANCE Power Pack #16 (November 1985)
REAL NAME Lord Kofi Whitemane
OCCUPATION Student **BASE** Kymellian homeworld
HEIGHT 5 ft **WEIGHT** Not known **EYES** Pink **HAIR** Black
SPECIAL POWERS/ABILITIES Able to teleport himself short distances; like other Kymellian's, Kofi has the potential to control mass, energy, and gravity but these skills are as yet undeveloped.

A young member of the Kymellian race of aliens, Kofi was the son of Lord Yrik Whitemane, the interstellar ambassador to the Z'nrx (*see* SNARKS). As he became older, Kofi grew to resent the time and energy his father committed to his work. Things came to a head when Kofi discovered a Z'nrx plot to kidnap the junior team of Earth Super Heroes known as POWER PACK, and to use them in a game of political brinksmanship. Traveling to Earth, Kofi defeated the schemers, his efforts earning the admiration of his father and forging a reconciliation between them. **AD**

Korvac

FIRST APPEARANCE Giant-Size Defenders #3 (January 1975)
REAL NAME Michael Korvac **OCCUPATION** Computer technician; would-be master of the universe **BASE** Mobile
HEIGHT 6 ft 3 in **WEIGHT** 230 lbs **EYES** Blue **HAIR** Blond
SPECIAL POWERS/ABILITIES Cosmic power on an unimaginable scale. Capable of time travel, astral projection, projecting lethal energy blasts and of power absorption from any source.

Korvac comes from the same possible 31st-century future as the GUARDIANS OF THE GALAXY. When the Badoon invaded Earth, he quickly offered to help the alien conquerors. They rewarded his loyalty by amputating the lower half of his body and replacing it with a mobile computer module. Realizing the potential of his new form, Korvac began to plot against the Badoon. He also managed to siphon energy from the GRANDMASTER and absorbed the power cosmic from the world-sized starship that belonged to GALACTUS. Now seemingly omnipotent, Korvac traveled to the 20th century with the intention of restructuring the universe in his image, but he later faked his own death during a battle with the AVENGERS. **TD**

Michael Korvac possessed a level of cosmic power that easily made him the equal of gods like Odin and Zeus and alien entities such as the Collector and Grandmaster.

Krang

FIRST APPEARANCE Fantastic Four Annual #1 (1963)
REAL NAME Krang **OCCUPATION** Warlord ***Base*** Formerly Atlantis, now mobile in the Atlantic Ocean.
HEIGHT 6 ft **WEIGHT** 290 lbs **EYES** Blue **HAIR** Black
Special powers/abilities Like all Atlanteans, Krang has superhuman strength, gills for breathing water, and other physical adaptations forundersea living.

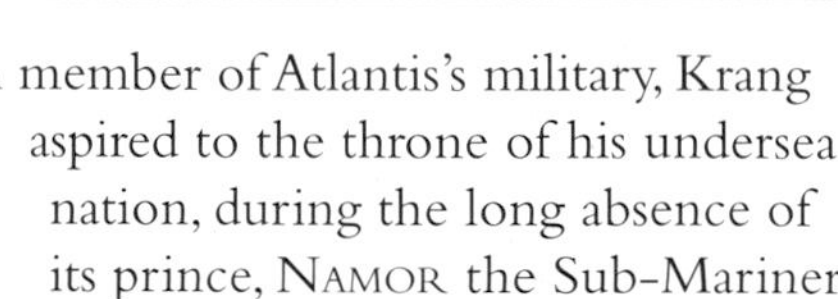

A member of Atlantis's military, Krang aspired to the throne of his undersea nation, during the long absence of its prince, NAMOR the Sub-Mariner. When Namor finally returned, he appointed Krang as his warlord. But Krang staged a coup d'etat, seized the throne and plotted to conquer the surface world. Namor bested Krang in single combat and exiled him from Atlantis. Since then Krang has continued to scheme against Namor and Atlantis, and has allied himself with Namor's enemies ATTUMA and Byrrah. Krang also once fell under the sway of the Serpent Crown and joined forces with the second VIPER's Serpent Squad. **PS**

Kraven

KRAVEN

FACTFILE

REAL NAME
Sergei Kravinoff

OCCUPATION
Professional game hunter and mercenary

BASE
Mobile

HEIGHT 6 ft
WEIGHT 235 lbs
EYES Brown
HAIR Black

FIRST APPEARANCE:
Amazing Spider-Man Vol. 1 #15 (August 1964)

His parents were Russian aristocrats, who died while he was a child. Sergei Kravinoff found employment with an African safari, learning to track and kill big game. A mystical serum augmented his strength and speed, and Kravinoff became the world's greatest hunter. After anglicizing his name to Kraven, he took up a challenge from his criminal half-brother, the CHAMELEON, to hunt the most dangerous game of all—the American Super Hero SPIDER-MAN.

After suffering numerous defeats, both on his own and as one of the SINISTER SIX, Kraven tranquilized Spider-Man and buried him alive. Kraven then assumed the hero's identity in a bid to prove himself the better crime fighter. In the end, confident that life held no further challenge, Kraven shot and killed himself. Spider-Man later helped Kraven's spirit find its final rest. Kraven's son Vladimir briefly served as the Grim Hunter, while his son Alyosha has since become the second Kraven the Hunter. **DW**

POWERS

Enhanced strength, speed, and agility; expert tracker and skilled hand-to-hand fighter

Despite his modest superpowered abilities, Kraven's combat skill allowed him to hold his own against multiple metahuman opponents.

Kraven was skilled with whips, crossbows, and all bladed weapons, as well as an expert in every form of unarmed combat.

KREE, THE ***SEE OPPOSITE PAGE***

Kro

FIRST APPEARANCE The Eternals Vol. 1 #1 (July 1976)
REAL NAME Kro **OCCUPATION** Monarch of Earth's Deviants
BASE Deviant Lemuria **HEIGHT** 6 ft 5 in **WEIGHT** 320 lbs
EYES Red **HAIR** Bald with black facial hair
SPECIAL POWERS/ABILITIES Superhuman strength; mental control over his body, giving him virtual immortality; the power to heal from severe injuries, and limited shapeshifting abilities.

Unlike other members of the Deviants, an offshoot of humanity, Kro is virtually immortal, and has lived more than 20,000 years. Kro has concealed his longevity by pretending to be his own descendants. Kro fell in love with THENA of the ETERNALS, the Deviants' foes. They have mostly remained apart, but decades ago they had twins known as Donald and Deborah Ritter. Formerly a warlord, Kro has become ruler of the Deviants on Earth. **PS**

Kulan Gath

FIRST APPEARANCE Conan the Barbarian #15 (May 1972)
REAL NAME Kulan Gath
OCCUPATION Sorcerer **BASE** Mobile
HEIGHT n/a **WEIGHT** n/a **EYES** Red **HAIR** Black
SPECIAL POWERS/ABILITIES Manipulates magic to a very high level. Can summon demonic entities, mentally control individuals, project beams of mystical force, and restructure flesh and bone.

Kulan Gath once held a high position among the sorcerers of Stygia during the Hyborian era. He married his bitter rival, the sorceress Vammatar, to gain access to the Iron-Bound Books of Shuma-Gorath and together they opened the books, unleashing a Nether Demon. Kulan Gath also studied under the master sorcerer Thoth-Amon, a longtime enemy of Conan the Barbarian. The wizard's physical body has been killed more than once but his spirit always survives, often in a necklace, to enslave others. He has clashed with DR STRANGE, SPIDER-MAN, THE AVENGERS and the X-MEN, among others. **MT**

Kurse

FIRST APPEARANCE Thor #347 (September 1984, as Algrim), Secret Wars II #4 (October 1985, as Kurse)
REAL NAME Valgoth, formerly Algrim the Strong
OCCUPATION Vengeance-seeker ***Base*** Asgard
HEIGHT 7 ft **WEIGHT** 840 lbs **EYES** Yellow **HAIR** None
SPECIAL POWERS/ABILITIES Almost limitless strength, and is invulnerable to almost all harm. Can sense the presence of those he hunts from a world away.

Kurse began life as Algrim the Strong, mightiest of the Dark Elves who served their ruler Malekith. Chosen to battle THOR on behalf of his master, Algrim fell into a pit of lava. His desire for vengeance was so strong he survived, but he no longer knew who he was. The BEYONDER decided to use Algrim to study vengeance. He transformed Algrim into the vastly more powerful Kurse, who pursued Thor across the Nine Worlds. Kurse eventually learned that his true enemy was his one-time ruler Malekith. After he slew the Dark Elf Lord, his craving for revenge was sated, and he became a sword protector of Asgard and its children, taking the name Valgoth. **TB**

Kree, The

Extraterrestrial empire-builders

The Kree are aliens, similar in appearance to humans but possessing twice the strength and endurance. They originated on the planet Hala in the Pama system, located in the Greater Magellanic Cloud, a planet they shared with another intelligent species, the plant-like Cotati. Kree consist of two primary races: the original blue-skinned race and a pink-skinned race which emerged millennia later.

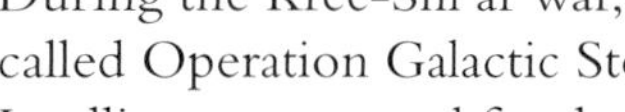

Armored mobile infantry platforms decimate the Kree enemy and protect Kree operators from counterattack.

War Years

Nearly a million years ago, the Skrulls landed on Hala and set up a contest between the Kree and the Cotati. When the Cotati were named as victors, the enraged Kree killed the contact team, stole their starship technology, and launched the Kree-Skrull war that raged for eons. They took a special interest in Earth, creating the offshoot of humanity known as the Inhumans. Kree society was ruled by the Supreme Intelligence, a computer consciousness formed by the collective minds of the greatest Kree thinkers. In the modern era, the Kree officer Mar-Vell scouted Earth for a possible invasion, but defected to Earth's side as the superheroic Captain Marvel.

Kree Evolution

During the Kree-Shi'ar war, a later conflict sometimes called Operation Galactic Storm, the Supreme Intelligence arranged for the detonation of a nega-bomb in Kree space in the hope of jumpstarting the species' evolution. Over ninety percent of the Kree died, and the survivors became vassals of the Shi'ar. The Avengers executed the Supreme Intelligence, but it survived, and using the Forever Crystal, accelerated the evolution of some Kree into a new breed, the Ruul, which could spontaneously produce adaptations such as the ability to fly or to breathe underwater. During Avengers Disassembled, Hawkeye seemingly died while fighting a Kree invasion force, but these Kree were probably manifestations of the Scarlet Witch's formidable reality-warping powers. **DW**

The Kree have created many technological wonders, including Kree Sentries and the Psyche-Magnetron, which can conjure up any weapon from Kree history.

ESSENTIAL STORYLINES

- ***"Operation: Galactic Storm" (19-part crossover in Avengers, Avengers West Coast, Captain America, Iron Man, Quasar, Thor, and Wonder Man)*** The Kree-Shi'ar war comes to an explosive conclusion when a nega-bomb nearly exterminates Kree society.
- ***Maximum Security #1-3*** A new galactic species, the Ruul, are revealed to be Kree agents, hatching a scheme to restore their decimated empire.

Warships, bristling with weaponry form the Kree defense fleet and its expeditionary strike teams.

FACTFILE

BASE
Kree-Lar, Turunal system, Greater Magellanic Cloud

FIRST APPEARANCE
Fantastic Four vol. 1 #65 (August, 1967)

POWERS
Strength and endurance that are twice the human average

Warriors dominate Kree society. Other respectable professions include politician and scientist, since both can use their unique talents to advance the glory of the Kree empire.

Lady Deathstrike

FACTFILE

REAL NAME
Yuriko Oyama

OCCUPATION
Assassin; CEO of Oyama Heavy Industries

BASE
Japan, later mobile

HEIGHT 5 ft 9 in
WEIGHT 128 lbs
EYES Brown
HAIR Black

FIRST APPEARANCE
Daredevil Vol. 1 #197 (August 1983)

POWERS
Cyborg whose bones have been laced with adamantium molecules, rendering them unbreakable. Her fingers were replaced with adamantium talons. Can interface with computers.

Yuriko Oyama is the daughter of Lord Dark Wind, a Japanese scientist who created a process for binding the indestructible metal adamantium to human bone. Seeking vengeance on her father for the death of her brothers and the scarring of her face, Oyama joined forces with the costumed champion Daredevil against him. She killed Lord Dark Wind just as he was about to murder Daredevil. However the man she loved, Kira, a member of Lord Dark Wind's private army, then committed suicide.

Oyama believed that the secret of her father's process had been stolen and used to lace Wolverine's skeleton with adamantium.

Lady Deathstrike is not only a mistress of Japanese martial arts, but, as a cyborg, has increased strength, speed and agility.

Cyborg Assassin

As the samurai warrior Lady Deathstrike, Oyama attempted to kill Wolverine and take his skeleton. However, she was defeated by Wolverine's friend Heather Hudson in her costumed identity of Vindicator.

Subsequently, Lady Deathstrike was converted into a cyborg by the extradimensional being Spiral. In this new form, Lady Deathstrike's own skeleton has been reinforced with adamantium.

Although Lady Deathstrike heads Oyama Heavy Industries, she also works as a professional assassin. For a time she was a member of the Reavers, Donald Pierce's team of cyborgs. She severed the legs of the Japanese hero Sunfire. Wolverine remains her principal adversary. PS

Like her archfoe Wolverine, Lady Deathstrike also has an adamantium-laced skeleton and adamantium claws. Normally a foot long, her claws can extend to about twice that length.

Lava Men

FIRST APPEARANCE Journey Into Mystery #97 (October 1963)
BASE Various; deep underground **HEIGHT** Up to 20 ft
WEIGHT Unknown **EYES** Black **HAIR** None
SPECIAL POWERS/ABILITIES Able to stand in molten lava; constantly release heat into surrounding area; possess double the strength of normal humans; possess ability to transform themselves into sentient giants.

Moulded into their current form by an unknown demon, the Lava Men were originally descended from the Gortokians, a genetically engineered offshoot of humanity. There are two known tribes of Lava Men. For a time, the first was led by a witch doctor known as Jinku, but his reign ended when Thor thwarted efforts to ignite every volcano on the planet. The second tribe lives in caverns beneath the Project: PEGASSUS research facility. Researchers became aware of these Lava Men when the creatures were disturbed by a drilling project. The Avengers resolved the situation and the Lava Men haven't been seen since. AD

Leap-Frog

FIRST APPEARANCE Daredevil Vol. 1 #25 (February 1967)
REAL NAME Vincent Patilio
OCCUPATION Inventor, professional criminal
BASE New York City
HEIGHT 5ft 9in **WEIGHT** 170 lbs **EYES** Brown **HAIR** Gray
SPECIAL POWERS/ABILITIES Electrical coils in boots enable leaps up to 60 feet high; exoskeleton provides enhanced strength.

Vincent Patilio started out as a toy inventor before seeing a chance to make some money when he created a set of electrically-powered jumping coils. He devised a frog costume and embarked on a criminal career as Leap-Frog. He met with a string of pathetic setbacks, including a disastrous stint with Electro's Emissaries of Evil and numerous humiliations at the hands of Daredevil and Spider-Man. Vincent's son Eugene later donned his father's costume and became Frog-Man, an identity that Vincent has sometimes assumed as he continues in his modest calling. DW

Leader

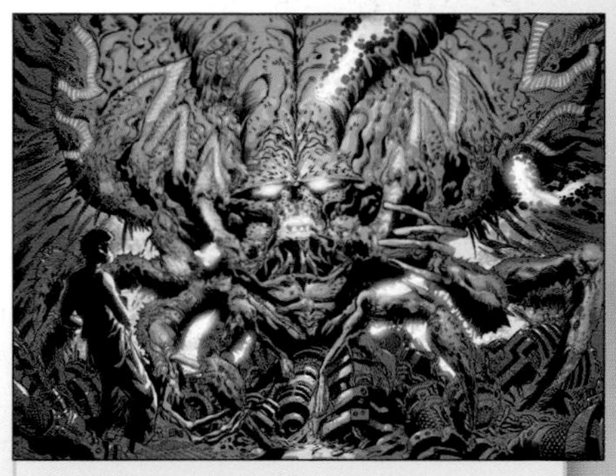
Bruce Banner shares the Leader's final moments in the physical world and witnesses his ascension to a new plane of existence.

After dropping out of school, Samuel Sterns took a menial job in a US government research facility, where an accident led to his body being bombarded by intense gamma radiation. In the days that followed, Sterns developed an insatiable thirst for knowledge, and as his intelligence expanded at exponential rates, so too did his cranium.

Unfortunately, Sterns' increased intellectual capacity was not matched by emotional maturity. Disgusted by government corruption, he decided that he should command the human race, and restyled himself as the Leader.

Over the years, the Leader's efforts to dominate the world have been repeatedly foiled by the Hulk and undermined by his own impatience. The Leader has battled that green behemoth with robotic humanoids and even pitted Super Villains like the Rhino and the Glob against him, but global domination has remained elusive. However, he has had some successes, in particular the construction of Freehold, a utopian city hidden in Canada's icy north.

An increasingly lonely individual, the Leader came to believe that only the Hulk truly understood him. Believing that his brain was about to ascend to a higher plane, he asked Banner to come to him. Did the Leader find the enlightenment that he anticipated? It may be too soon to say. **AD**

FACTFILE
REAL NAME
Samuel Sterns
OCCUPATION
Would-be world conqueror
BASE
Another dimension

HEIGHT 5 ft 10 in
WEIGHT 140 lbs
EYES Green
HAIR Black

FIRST APPEARANCE
Tales to Astonish #62 (December 1964)

POWERS
Superhuman intelligence, several times that of a genius, with an incredible memory for facts and information. Specializes in creating robots, computer systems, high-tech weapons. Has devized methods of telepathic control.

Leech

FIRST APPEARANCE Uncanny X-Men #179 (March 1984)
REAL NAME Unrevealed
OCCUPATION Adventurer **BASE** Various
HEIGHT 4 ft 2 in **WEIGHT** 67 lbs **EYES** Yellow **HAIR** None
SPECIAL POWERS/ABILITIES Leech can dampen the superhuman powers of any Super Heroes or Villains, mutant or not, within his proximity, up to a range of 30 feet.

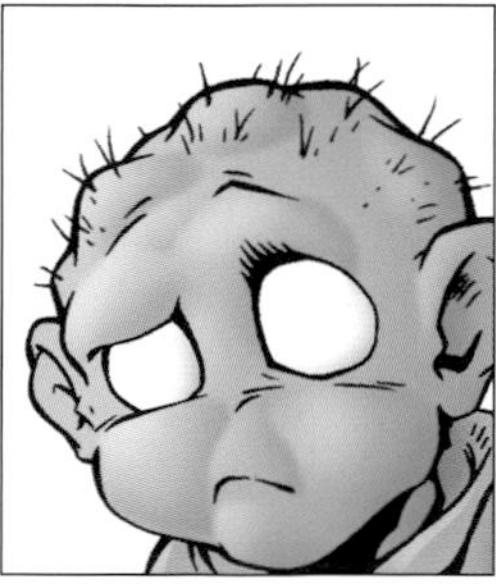

Abandoned by his parents when they discovered he was a mutant, Leech was found by Caliban, who brought him into a mutant community known as the Morlocks, who lived in the sewers beneath Manhattan. Leech was happy there—until Mister Sinister sent the Marauders to wipe the Morlocks out. Leech was saved by Power Pack and X-Factor. The green-skinned boy lived with X-Factor as one of their junior team, the X-Terminators, then associated with Generation X and a group of adventurous children known as the Daydreamers. **TB**

Leeds, Betty Brant

Although unfazed by the rantings of her bullish boss, J. Jonah Jameson, Betty Brant's positive outlook was gradually worn down as events drove her from one calamity to another.

Betty was Spider-Man Peter Parker's very first girlfriend, and when their relationship ended, she married *Daily Bugle* reporter Ned Leeds. Ned's obsession with his work caused constant tension, which he blamed on Spider-Man. She was dismayed to discover that Ned had become the evil Hobgoblin, and suffered a mental breakdown following his death. Since then, Betty has rebuilt her life, becoming an investigative reporter. It was she who discovered that Roderick Kingsley was the original Hobgoblin. Having experienced the worst that life can deal, Betty can now look to the future with confidence. **AD**

FACTFILE
REAL NAME
Betty Brant Leeds
OCCUPATION
Investigative journalist
BASE
New York City

HEIGHT 5 ft 7 in
WEIGHT 125 lbs
EYES Brown
HAIR Brown

FIRST APPEARANCE:
Amazing Spider-Man #4 (September 1963)

POWERS
Expert investigative reporter with a strong personality and a hugely generous soul.

Left-Winger

FIRST APPEARANCE Captain America #323 (November 1986)
REAL NAME Hector Lennox
OCCUPATION Former wrestler **BASE** Mobile
HEIGHT 6 ft 5 in **WEIGHT** 265 lbs **EYES** Blue **HAIR** Black
SPECIAL POWERS/ABILITIES Left-Winger possessed superhuman strength and stamina thanks to the Power Broker's strength-augmentation program.

When his ex-army buddy John Walker (*see* US Agent) became the Super-Patriot, Lennox became one of his Bold Urban Commandos ("Buckies"). Walker was then selected to replace Steve Rogers as Captain America. Angered, Lennox and his partner took on guises as Left-Winger and Right-Winger, and set out to destroy Walker's tenure as Captain America. They revealed Walker's true identity to the media, Walker's parents were killed as a result, and he vowed vengeance. Left-Winger was so badly burned in an ensuing explosion that he took his own life. **TB**

Legion

FIRST APPEARANCE New Mutants #25 (March 1985)
REAL NAME David Charles Haller **OCCUPATION** Student
BASE Muir Island, off the coast of Scotland
HEIGHT 5 ft 9 in **WEIGHT** 130 lbs **EYES** (left) Green; (right) Blue **HAIR** Black **SPECIAL POWERS/ABILITIES** Telepathic ability; telekinesis enables him to lift objects and protect self with force field; also able to start fires with his mind.

Some time ago, a relationship between Charles Xavier (Professor X) and Gabrielle Haller led to the birth of a boy, David, though years passed before Xavier learned of this. When David was ten, his mutant abilities began to emerge. He developed multiple personalities, each of which controlled different powers. His psychological condition gradually deteriorated but David would be in his late teens before Xavier was asked to help and finally discovered that David was his son. With his father's aid, David's core persona reasserted itself, allowing him to live a happier, more contented life. **AD**

Legion of the Unliving
SEE OPPOSITE PAGE

Lethal Legion

When Simon Williams (*see* Wonder Man) sacrificed his life to save the Avengers, his altruism had untold consequences. His grieving brother, Eric, blamed the Avengers for Simon's death and determined to destroy them, adopting the guise of the Grim Reaper and forming the Lethal Legion of Super Villains. The Legion's efforts ended in failure, while Eric's own enmity to the Avengers was compromised following his brother's resurrection. Nevertheless the Lethal Legion lived on under the leadership of Count Nefaria. Not much of a team player, Nefaria stole the powers of his fellow legionnaries but was still defeated, despite his augmented abilities.

Following Grim Reaper's death, the Legion's name was adopted by the demon lord Satannish, who resurrected various historical figures—including Josef Stalin and Heinrich Himmler—to capture the souls of the Avengers. Although this plot was also foiled, the Lethal Legion's name continues to inspire fear. **AD**

CHARACTER KEY
1 Living Laser
2 Power Man
3 Swordsman
4 Grim Reaper
5 Man-Ape

FACTFILE

MEMBERS AND POWERS

GRIM REAPER
A mechanical scythe replaces right hand.

LIVING LASER
A collection of light particles possessing human consciousness.

MAN-APE
Superhuman strength, endurance, and agility.

POWER MAN
Can grow from 6 ft to 60 ft, with tenfold increase in strength.

SWORDSMAN
Superb athlete and master swordsman.

COUNT NEFARIA
Superhuman strength, speed and the power of flight.

WHIRLWIND
Achieves superhuman speed by spinning body.

ULTRON
A robot with vast strength, speed and deadly weapons.

BLACK TALON
Can create and control zombies.

BASE
Mobile

FIRST APPEARANCE
Avengers #78 (July 1970)

Libra

FIRST APPEARANCE Avengers Vol. 1 #72 (January 1970)
REAL NAME Gustav Brandt **OCCUPATION** Professional criminal
BASE Mobile **HEIGHT** 6 ft **WEIGHT** 195 lbs
EYES None (formerly blue) **HAIR** Blond
SPECIAL POWERS/ABILITIES Skilled martial artist, psychic sight, can access the "Place Between Places" in order to teleport.

Gustav Brandt served as a mercenary in Asia, where he fathered a daughter, later known as Mantis, before losing his sight in the fire that killed his wife. A pacifist group called the Priests of Pama taught him to see via psychic means, but because Brandt was a soldier they took his daughter away and raised her themselves. The Zodiac Cartel later recruited Brandt as a criminal kingpin, and he took the name of Libra. His ability to access the "Place Between Places" made it possible for him to disappear and appear at will, and several times he vanished suddenly and mysteriously while serving prison sentences. Libra was eventually briefly reunited with his daughter. He considered himself the balance point between good and evil and acted accordingly, switching sides to aid the Avengers and Kang against the forces of Immortus and the Time Keepers. **DW**

Legion of the Unliving

The undead are on the march!

THE ORIGINAL LEGION
1 Wonder Man **2** Midnight
3 Baron Zemo
4 Human Torch
5 Flying Dutchman
6 Frankenstein's Monster

The Legion of the Unliving are foes of the AVENGERS, their ranks made up of deceased heroes and villains brought together by outside entities. Legion members have variously appeared as duplicates or animated zombies and, most disturbingly, have included former Avengers. KANG the Conqueror, allied with IMMORTUS, assembled the original Legion. Scouring the timestream, Kang brought together FRANKENSTEIN'S MONSTER, Midnight, Flying Dutchman, villain-turned-hero WONDER MAN, BARON ZEMO and the heroic HUMAN TORCH.

DEFEATED

Despite their combined powers, Kang's Legion failed to defeat the Avengers, and Immortus—after defeating the turncoat Kang—restored the Legion members to their proper places in the timestream.

The second Legion of the Unliving came about through the efforts of the GRANDMASTER, who raised such figures as Bucky BARNES, the SWORDSMAN, CAPTAIN MAR-VELL, KORVAC, DRACULA, and the RED GUARDIAN to guard "life bombs" that threatened to wipe out the universe. As the Avengers struggled to thwart the Grandmaster's scheme, their slain members joined the ranks of the Legion of the Unliving. Fortunately, all the Avengers returned to life after the resolution of the crisis.

THE SECOND LEGION
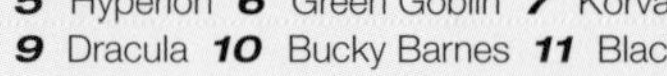
1 Swordsman **2** Nighthawk **3** Executioner **4** Terrax
5 Hyperion **6** Green Goblin **7** Korvac **8** Death Adder
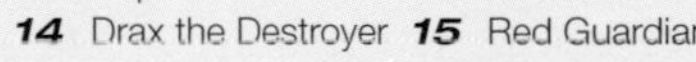
9 Dracula **10** Bucky Barnes **11** Black Knight
12 Captain Mar-Vell **13** Baron Blood
14 Drax the Destroyer **15** Red Guardian

THE THIRD LEGION
1 Iron Man (Arno Stark)
2 Grim Reaper
3 Swordsman
4 Left-Winger
5 Right-Winger
6 Oort the Living Comet

Never Say Die

A third Legion included such notable figures as the GRIM REAPER, the BLACK KNIGHT (Nathan Garrett), and Toro. They were gathered by Immortus in order to help him capture the SCARLET WITCH.

Following Immortus's failure, the undead Grim Reaper gained additional power from the demon Lloigoroth and gathered a fourth version of the Legion of the Unliving. Grim Reaper's Legion included copies of villains such as COUNT NEFARIA and INFERNO, but the team once again met defeat in battle against the Avengers.

The fifth Legion of the Unliving were once more pawns of the Grim Reaper against the Avengers. It consisted of the deceased heroes Captain Mar-Vell, DOCTOR DRUID, HELLCAT, MOCKINGBIRD, Swordsman, Wonder Man, and THUNDERSTRIKE (Eric Masterson). The Scarlet Witch used her powers to send the spirits of this Legion into the afterlife, and her love for Wonder Man restored him to life. Likewise, Wonder Man restored his brother the Grim Reaper to full physical health, thus ending his threat. DW

THE FOURTH LEGION
1 Wonder Man
2 Captain Mar-Vell
3 Swordsman
4 Doctor Druid
5 Thunderstrike
6 Mockingbird

FACTFILE

ORIGINAL MEMBERS AND POWERS

KANG THE CONQUEROR
Master of time travel

FRANKENSTEIN'S MONSTER
Enhanced strength, damage resistance.

BARON ZEMO
(Heinrich Zemo)
Extended longevity, brilliant criminal mind.

WONDER MAN
Flight, enhanced strength, body suffused with ionic energy.

HUMAN TORCH
(Jim Hammond)
Flight, flame projection.

FLYING DUTCHMAN
Projection of energy blasts.

MIDNIGHT
Master martial artist.

BASE
Mobile

FIRST APPEARANCE
Avengers Vol. 1 #131 (January 1975)

Lifeguard

FIRST APPEARANCE X-Treme X-Men #6 (December 2001)
REAL NAME Heather Cameron
OCCUPATION Member of X-Corp **BASE** Mumbai, India
HEIGHT 5 ft 10 in **WEIGHT** 156 lbs **EYES** Blue **HAIR** Blonde
SPECIAL POWERS/ABILITIES Possesses bio-morphic ability—powers adapt to circumstances. In past Lifeguard has grown wings, extra arms, and developed ability to breath underwater.

Targeted by the Chinese Triad, only the X-Men's intervention saved the lives of Heather Cameron and her brother, Davis. Forced to reveal her mutant abilities during this encounter, Heather was invited to join the X-Men and forsake her career as an Australian lifeguard. As her powers developed, Heather's appearance changed, becoming increasingly alien, and it became apparent that her mother was a member of the Shi'ar race. Unable to cope with this revelation, Davis disappeared and Heather left the team to find him.

Now working for the X-Corporation in Mumbai, it is not yet known whether Heather has ever found her brother. AD

Lightmaster

FIRST APPEARANCE Peter Parker, the Spectacular Spider-Man #1 (December 1976) **REAL NAME** Dr. Edward Lansky
OCCUPATION Physics professor **BASE** New York City
HEIGHT 5 ft 11 in **WEIGHT** 175 lbs **EYES** Brown **HAIR** Brown
SPECIAL POWERS/ABILITIES Lightmaster possesses the ability to generate light, including lasers, to create simple solid objects out of light, and to fly.

In a bid to prevent budget cuts that might affect his position at Empire State University, Dr. Edward Lansky donned a high-tech suit designed to harness the power of light and became the criminal Lightmaster. His intent was to hold various key government officials hostage, but his scheme was foiled by Spider-Man. During the conflict, Lansky's suit was damaged, transforming him into an energy being. Since that time, Lightmaster has resurfaced, attempting to cash in on his light-based powers. But each time heroes such as Dazzler, Quasar, Cable, and the aforementioned Spider-Man have succeeded in putting his lights out. TD

Lilith

FIRST APPEARANCE Ghost Rider #98 (August 1992)
REAL NAME Kiskillilla **OCCUPATION** Sumerian Goddess
BASE The Shadowside Dimension, Atlantis
HEIGHT 6 ft **WEIGHT** 140 lbs **EYES** Yellow **HAIR** Black
SPECIAL POWERS/ABILITIES Superhuman strength and stamina; manipulates the dark forces of the universe. She can summon her children from other dimensions, giving them new bodies on Earth.

Lilith is believed to be the daughter of Aehr, the ancient god of darkness. She lived on the island of Atlantis and survived its destruction, escaping in the form of a storm demon to the desert beyond the Euphrates River. Later, Atlantean sorcerers imprisoned her within the belly of a Leviathan believed to be Tiamat. On emerging, Lilith saw a vision of the future in which her children, the Lilin, were defeated by Ghost Rider and Blaze. She then traveled through a portal to gather her children to her side. Lilith and the Lilin later came into conflict with Doctor Strange. AD

Lilith

FIRST APPEARANCE Giant-Size Chillers Vol. 1 #1 (June 1974)
REAL NAME Unrevealed
OCCUPATION Adventureress **BASE** South of France
HEIGHT 6 ft **WEIGHT** 125 lbs **EYES** Red **HAIR** Black
SPECIAL POWERS/ABILITIES Unique among vampires, Lilith could walk in sunlight and was unaffected by religious talismen; superhuman strength; hypnotic abilities; could transform into a bat.

The daughter of Dracula and his first wife, Zofia, Lilith hated her father for throwing them out of their castle home and driving her mother to suicide. Lilith was raised by a gypsy woman called Gretchin. When Dracula killed her son, Gretchin used magic to transform Lilith into a vampire, condemning her to hunt Dracula for the rest of her life.

For centuries, Lilith stalked and battled her father until, in a final, climactic confrontation he tore open his shirt and goaded her to kill him. To her dismay, Lilith discovered that she was unable to slay her own father. She resigned herself to failure and withdrew to the south of France. AD

Lipscombe, Dr. Angela

FIRST APPEARANCE The Incredible Hulk Vol. 3 #12 (March 2000)
REAL NAME Angela Lipscombe
OCCUPATION Neuropsychologist **BASE** Mobile
HEIGHT 5 ft 9 in **WEIGHT** 125 lbs **EYES** Blue **HAIR** Blonde
SPECIAL POWERS/ABILITIES Genius-level knowledge of the science of neuropsychiatry; kind-hearted and a loyal and courageous friend to Bruce Banner in his hour of need.

Angela Lipscombe and Bruce Banner (*see* Hulk) dated in medical school, but Banner broke off the relationship, jealous when Lipscombe received a coveted grant for graduate study and he did not. Doctor Lipscombe became one of the world's foremost experts in the field of neuropsychiatry. Many years later, Bruce Banner looked her up in terrible distress, believing he had contracted an incurable disease. Lipscombe used the opportunity to study the bizarre and disturbing multiple personalities that Banner exhibited as the Hulk. She is the partner of Doc Samson. DW

Living Laser

FIRST APPEARANCE Avengers Vol. 1 #34 (November, 1966)
REAL NAME Arthur Parks
OCCUPATION Criminal **BASE** Mobile
HEIGHT 5 ft 11 in **WEIGHT** (formerly) 125 lbs
EYES (formerly) Blue **HAIR** (formerly) Brown
SPECIAL POWERS/ABILITIES Composed entirely of light, he can travel at light speed or transform himself into an offensive laser.

Technician Arthur Parks strapped laser projectors to his wrists to become the costumed criminal Living Laser. Obsessed with the beautiful Wasp, he kidnapped her until the Avengers broke her out. The Living Laser escaped from prison and worked as a criminal henchman for the Mandarin, Batroc's Brigade, and the Lethal Legion. He later attempted to implant laser diodes beneath his skin, but the process drew too much energy into his body and he exploded. He continues to exist as a sentient being made entirely of light. **DW**

Living Mummy

FIRST APPEARANCE Supernatural Thrillers #5 (August 1973)
REAL NAME N'Kantu
OCCUPATION Wanderer **BASE** Egypt
HEIGHT 7 ft 6 in **WEIGHT** 650 lbs **EYES** Brown **HAIR** None
SPECIAL POWERS/ABILITIES Blood replaced by life-preserving fluid removing human need for food, water, or sleep; enhanced strength, rock-hard body, near-immortality; limited mobility.

Chief N'Kantu of the Swarili of North Africa became a prisoner of the pharaoh Aram-Set, and organized a slave rebellion. Although Aram-Set was killed, the rebellion was crushed and N'Kantu's punishment was to be embalmed and entombed while still alive. Preserved in a sarcophagus for 3,000 years by mystical means, N'Kantu reawakened in the modern era and went on a rampage before being shocked back to relative sanity when he seized a power line. As the Living Mummy, N'Kantu lumbers through Africa searching for meaning in what passes for his life. He aided Captain America during the Bloodstone Hunt. **DW**

Living Tribunal

FIRST APPEARANCE Strange Tales #157 (June 1967)
REAL NAMES Equity, Necessity, and Vengeance
OCCUPATION Guardian of the continuum of alternate universes
BASE The Multiverse
HEIGHT n/a **WEIGHT** n/a **EYES** n/a **HAIR** n/a
SPECIAL POWERS/ABILITIES Immensely powerful; can cause a sun to go supernova by firing a single bolt of its cosmic energy.

The Living Tribunal has existed as long as the universe itself. Its purpose is to safeguard the multiverse (the totality of all alternate universes) from an imbalance of mystical forces. Thus the Living Tribunal will pass judgment on any crisis that threatens to affect the cosmic balance. It will prevent one universe from acquiring more mystical power than any other. The Living Tribunal will also intervene to prevent an imbalance between the mystical forces of good and evil within a single universe.

The Living Tribunal is capable of destroying entire planets in order to maintain the cosmic balance. In its humanoid form, the Living Tribunal has three faces—its fully visible face represents equity, its partially hooded face represents vengeance, and its fully hooded face represents necessity. It will only pass judgment when all the three sides are in agreement. **MT**

Living Lightning

FIRST APPEARANCE Avengers West Coast #63 (October 1990)
REAL NAME Miguel Santos
OCCUPATION Student **BASE** California
HEIGHT 5 ft 9 in **WEIGHT** 170 lbs **EYES** Brown **HAIR** Black
SPECIAL POWERS/ABILITIES Living Lightning can transform his body into sentient electrical energy, which he uses for various effects, including to fly.

The eldest son of the Lightning Lord, head of a radical organization called the Legion of the Living Lightning, who had designs on overthrowing the US government. The Legion's plans were destroyed by the rampaging Hulk, and the Lightning Lord was killed in the collapse of his hidden base.

Miguel intended to follow in his footsteps, and excavated the Legion's base. An accident with one of his father's devices transformed him into a being of pure electrical energy, who needed a containment suit to remain stable. Though driven temporarily insane, Living Lightning eventually became a member of the Avengers. **TB**

Living Pharaoh

FIRST APPEARANCE Marvel Graphic Novel #17
REAL NAME Ahmet Abdol
OCCUPATION Would-be world conqueror, now living planet
BASE Formerly Egypt, now distant solar system
HEIGHT 5 ft 8 in **WEIGHT** 196 lbs **EYES** Blue **HAIR** Black
SPECIAL POWERS/ABILITIES Absorbs cosmic energy and wields it as destructive force; at times able to increase body size.

Egyptian academic Ahmet Abdol was obsessed with the Egyptian Pharaohs, so when a traumatic incident caused his own mutant powers to become evident he renamed himself the Living Pharaoh. The discovery that his abilities were muted by those of Alex Summers (*see* Havok) led to many encounters with the X-Men, during which he occasionally transformed himself into the 30-ft-high Living Monolith. Terrible destruction always ensued, including his daughter's own death, and eventually Ahmet faced up to this. Asking Thor to hurl him into deep space, cosmic energy gradually transformed him into a rich and verdant Living Planet. **AD**

LIZARD

FIRST APPEARANCE The Amazing Spider-Man #6 (November 1963)
REAL NAME Dr. Curtis Connors
OCCUPATION Research biologist **BASE** New York City
HEIGHT 5 ft 11 in **WEIGHT** 175 lbs **EYES** (as human) Blue, (as Lizard) Red **HAIR** (as human) Brown, (as Lizard) None
SPECIAL POWERS/ABILITIES Superhuman strength and speed. Can cling to walls like a gecko, and can telepathically control reptiles.

When Dr. Curt Connors was an Army surgeon, his wounded right arm had to be amputated. Back in civilian life, he researched the ability of some reptiles to regenerate missing limbs and created a serum to grow his arm back. It worked, but transformed him into a savage humanoid lizard. SPIDER-MAN restored him to human form, but he has repeatedly reverted into the Lizard. Though the Lizard is one of Spider-Man's main enemies, Dr. Connors has acted as a friend to both Spider-Man and his true identity, Peter Parker. PS

LLYRA

FIRST APPEARANCE Sub-Mariner #32 (December 1970)
REAL NAME Llyra Morris
OCCUPATION Subversive **BASE** Mobile
HEIGHT 5 ft 11 in **WEIGHT** 220 lbs **EYES** Green **HAIR** Green
SPECIAL POWERS/ABILITIES Amphibious—can live under water or on land—and able to change skin colour to pass as human or homo mermanus; can manipulate brains of primitive marine life.

Daughter of a *Homo mermani* (*see* ATLANTEANS) and a human woman, Llyra was raised on land by her mother following her father's death. Confused by her hybrid status, Llyra became increasingly unstable, and caused great angst to those she encountered. On her first visit to the underwater kingdom of Lemuria, Llyra seized the throne, only to be overthrown by NAMOR the Sub-Mariner. Llyra made Namor the focus of her rage. Before Namor finally captured her, Llyra was responsible for murdering his fiancée. Prison is definitely the best place for her. AD

LOBO BROTHERS

FIRST APPEARANCE Spectacular Spider-Man #143 (Oct. 1988)
REAL NAMES Edwardo and Carlos Lobo
OCCUPATION Drug traffickers **BASE** Dallas, Texas
HEIGHT (Edwardo) 6 ft 1 in, (wolf) 6 ft 4 in; (Carlos) 6 ft, (wolf) 6 ft 4 in **WEIGHT** (Edwardo) 225 lbs, (wolf) 275 lbs; (Carlos) 210 lbs, (wolf) 260 lbs **EYES** (both) Brown **HAIR** (both) Black
SPECIAL POWERS/ABILITIES Mutant shape changers.

Twin boys, the Lobo Brothers grew up alone on the streets of Puebla de Zaragoza, Texas, never having known their parents. Their mutant powers began to emerge when they were teenagers and they used them to unite all the independent criminal mobs in South Texas. They eventually bought an oil refinery and began shipping drugs in their oil tankers. Believing that they were cutting into his profits, the KINGPIN of Crime took out a contract on them. They escaped and came to New York for revenge, where Edwardo met and fell in love with Glory GRANT, J. Jonah JAMESON's secretary. Edwardo was later accidentally shot and killed by her during a battle with Spider-Man. Carlos was captured and is currently in prison. TD

LOCKHEED

FIRST APPEARANCE Uncanny X-Men Vol. 1 #166 (February 1983) **REAL NAME** Unknown
OCCUPATION None
BASE Westchester County, New York
HEIGHT 2ft **WEIGHT** 20 lbs
EYES White **HAIR** None
SPECIAL POWERS/ABILITIES Can fly and breathe fire; empathic ability.

Lockheed is a small dragon belonging to the alien species known as the Flock. He encountered the X-MEN during their fight with the BROOD, and took a liking to Kitty PRYDE (Shadowcat). He returned with the team to Earth, where Kitty gave him the name Lockheed (after the Lockheed SR-71 Blackbird aircraft used by the X-Men). Lockheed is Kitty's constant companion, serving with her as a member of EXCALIBUR as well as on the current team of X-Men. DW

LOCKJAW

FIRST APPEARANCE Fantastic Four #45 (December 1965)
REAL NAME Not known
OCCUPATION Dog **BASE** Attilan, Blue Area, the Moon
LENGTH 6 ft 8 in **WEIGHT** 1, 240 lbs **EYES** Brown **HAIR** Brown
SPECIAL POWERS/ABILITIES Immense physical strength; can teleport self and up to a dozen others the distance from the Earth to the Moon; can also teleport to other dimensions.

When they come of age, INHUMANS are exposed to the Terrigen Mists, from which they gain their unique powers. For the Inhuman known as MEDUSA, exposure gave her living hair, while another Inhuman, CRYSTAL, gained the ability to manipulate elements.

The Mists transformed another child into a teleporting dog, now known as Lockjaw, who serves as a companion to the Inhuman Royal Family. Lockjaw is able to teleport not only himself, but a number of others up to a maximum combined weight of one ton. Although he has the intelligence of a human, Lockjaw still has canine tendencies: he likes to chase other animals, fetch sticks, and enjoy other doggy pleasures. He has also been known to speak, but that's another story. AD

Loki

God of Mischief with a will to rule Asgard

Loki was a megalomaniac, who aimed to overthrow his father and rule over Asgard.

Loki was born the son of Laufey, king of the Frost Giants of Jotunheim. Ashamed of Loki's small size, Laufey hid him away, but the child's existence came to light after the Frost Giants were defeated in a battle with the Asgardians. Odin (see Gods of Asgard), the ruler of Asgard, discovered Loki in the Frost Giants' fortress. Realizing that Loki was the son of Laufrey, a king whom he had slain, Odin took the boy back to Asgard and raised him as his own son.

FACTFILE

REAL NAME
Loki Laufeyson

OCCUPATION
God of Mischief; later God of Evil

BASE
Asgard

HEIGHT 6 ft 4 in
WEIGHT 525 lbs
EYES Green
HAIR Black-gray

FIRST APPEARANCE
Journey Into Mystery Vol. 1 #85 (October 1962)

POWERS
Enhanced strength, stamina, longevity, and limited invulnerability; uses his vast skills in sorcery to fly, generate force fields, teleport between dimensions, animate objects, and change his own shape.

ASGARD'S MISFIT

Unfortunately, Loki never fitted in among the inhabitants of Asgard. He nursed a virulent grudge against his stepbrother Thor, the God of Thunder, who possessed in abundance the heroic qualities prized by the Asgardians that Loki himself lacked. Jealous of the praise Odin showered on Thor, Loki took up the dark arts of sorcery and plotted for a way to become ruler of Asgard. His love of trickery earned him a reputation first as the God of Mischief, and then, as he grew more and more cruel, the God of Evil. After many attempts by Loki to usurp the throne of Asgard, Odin lost patience with him and imprisoned him within a mystical tree. He eventually freed himself and went in search of Thor, now living on Earth in the mortal guise of Donald Blake.

Loki's vast magical talents allowed him to overpower Earth's most powerful heroes. Only Thor's efforts—and Loki's own insecurities—stopped the Trickster God from achieving his ultimate triumph.

EARTH-SHAKER

Thor and his adopted home, Earth, became the focus of Loki's attentions. He accidentally precipitated the formation of the Avengers by inciting the Hulk to violence, and transformed Crusher Creel into Thor's foe, the Absorbing Man. He occasionally allied with the Enchantress, an Asgardian villainess, and turned all of Earth's major Super Villains into his pawns during the Acts of Vengeance conspiracy. Loki never ceased vexing Thor, yet he never intended to destroy Asgard, and willingly defended the kingdom against threats such as the fire demon Surtur.

By leading armies against Asgard, Loki helped achieve the end-cycle of Ragnarok.

THE END OF ASGARD

During the last days of Asgard just prior to Ragnarok, Loki finally conquered Asgard and remade it in his own image. But Thor succeeded in decapitating Loki, carrying his mystically-preserved head to observe the final act of Ragnarok. When Thor severed the tapestry that wove the reality of his dimension, Asgard and all its inhabitants vanished from existence. DW

ESSENTIAL STORYLINES

- ***Avengers #1*** Loki hatches a plot to destroy his brother Thor, accidentally inspiring the world's greatest heroes to form the Avengers.
- ***Loki #1—4*** In this limited series, told from Loki's point of view, the Trickster God temporarily succeeds in winning power over all of Asgard.
- ***The Mighty Thor #582—588*** As Ragnarok unfolds around them, Loki and Thor face off for their final battle, then tour the end of the world.

FACTFILE
REAL NAME
Unknown
OCCUPATION
Former slave; former movie stuntman; rebel leader
BASE
Mobile

HEIGHT 6 ft 2 in
WEIGHT 80 lbs
EYES Blue
HAIR Blond

FIRST APPEARANCE
Longshot #1 (September 1985)

POWERS
His genetically engineered powers include the ability to affect probability to bring him what is commonly called "good luck." He can telepathically read a person's memories by touching the person and can read psychic imprints left on objects touched by someone.

LONGSHOT

Longshot and his team of rebels prepare to do battle with the manipulative Mojo, the Spineless One.

Longshot is from a world in another dimension, whose inhabitants have no spines. A scientist named Arize created an artificial exoskeleton which allowed members of his race to stand upright. Under Arize's guidance their civilization thrived.

A group called the Spineless Ones refused to use the exoskeletons yet became the planet's rulers. They forced Arize to create a race of slaves for them using genetic engineering. Longshot was one of these slaves. From the moment he achieved consciousness, however, Longshot refused to be anyone's slave. He helped organize a slave revolt. Captured by the Spineless Ones, Longshot escaped through an interdimensional portal, arriving on Earth. MOJO, the Spineless One who claimed to own Longshot, followed him to Earth, hoping to stop him returning home and telling the slaves about this world where they could live freely. Longshot with his ally Quark, and help from DOCTOR STRANGE, defeated Mojo. **MT**

When Longshot lets fly with his deadly throwing knives, the probability is that he won't miss!

LORD CHAOS

FIRST APPEARANCE Marvel Two-in-One Annual #2 (1977)
REAL NAME None
OCCUPATION Abstract entity **BASE** Everywhere
HEIGHT/WEIGHT Unknown **EYES** None **HAIR** None
SPECIAL POWERS/ABILITIES Can teleport self and a dozen others the distance from the Earth to the Moon; can also teleport to other dimensions.

An abstract entity (depicted as a disembodied purple head) Lord Chaos embodies the concept of Chaos, just as other entities represent DEATH, Order (depicted as a bald head with black eyebrows), and even ETERNITY. Alongside Order, Chaos strives to maintain a cosmic balance, only intervening in mortal affairs on rare occasions. When THANOS was attempting to destroy the universe, SPIDER-MAN released Adam WARLOCK from a Soul Gem, allowing him to save the day. After these events, Order and Chaos implied that Peter Parker's destiny had been manipulated since birth, in order for him to perform this very act. No one knows if this is true. **AD**

LORD TEMPLAR

FIRST APPEARANCE The Avengers Vol. 3 #13 (Feb. 1999)
REAL NAME Unrevealed (last name presumably Tremont)
OCCUPATION Operative of Jonathan Tremont **BASE** Mobile
HEIGHT/WEIGHT Unrevealed **EYES** Red **HAIR** Gray
SPECIAL POWERS/ABILITIES Various powers include the ability to fire energy blasts; can summon counterparts of himself called the Avatars of Templar, each of whom has a different super-power.

Jonathan Tremont's two older brothers died from a disease. Years later Tremont acquired a cosmic artifact in the form of a triangle and used it to resurrect his brothers as the superhumans Lord Templar and Pagan.

Jonathan Tremont founded the Triune Understanding, a cult allegedly devoted to world peace. In actuality, Tremont sought to amass power for himself. He used Lord Templar to combat the AVENGERS. Ultimately, Tremont absorbed the life forces of Lord Templar and Pagan into himself, only to be defeated by the Avenger TRIATHLON. **PS**

Lorelei

FIRST APPEARANCE Thor #339 (January 1984)
REAL NAME Lorelei
OCCUPATION Seductress **BASE** Asgard
HEIGHT 5 ft 5 in **WEIGHT** 320 lbs
EYES Blue-green **HAIR** Reddish-blonde
SPECIAL POWERS/ABILITIES Superstrength, enhanced stamina, longevity, and resistance to injury.

Lorelei, a member of the godlike Asgardians, is the younger sister of the ENCHANTRESS – one of THOR's direst enemies. She doesn't share her sister's malevolent streak, but she does enjoy using her beauty and certain magical enchantments to ensnare men with passions of the heart. On several occasions, Lorelei has assisted LOKI by attempting to place THOR into lovesick spells. Lorelei has loved LOKI due to enchantments, and has even died and returned to life. She was not with the other Asgardians when the apocalyptic Ragnarok event destroyed their kingdom, and therefore may have escaped their grim fate. DW

Lubensky, Nathan

FIRST APPEARANCE Spectacular Spider-Man #47 (October 1980)
REAL NAME Nathan Lubensky
OCCUPATION Retired **BASE** New York City
HEIGHT 5 ft 8 in **WEIGHT** 125 lbs **EYES** Brown **HAIR** White
SPECIAL POWERS/ABILITIES Wheelchair-bound and elderly, he had no special physical powers but was a charming and likeable personality and a skilled entertainer.

Nathan Lubensky met Peter Parker's Aunt May at the Restwell Nursing Home, and the two struck up a romance that culminated in a brief engagement. An ex-Vaudeville entertainer, Lubensky had considerable personal charm, but his struggles with gambling threatened to ruin him. He ultimately wagered everything he had on the outcome of a criminal assassination by the VULTURE and CHANCE to eliminate billionaire Richard Trask. During the attempted hit, the Vulture grabbed Aunt May as a hostage. Lubensky intervened, saving her life but suffering a fatal heart attack in the process. DW

Lumpkin, Willie

FIRST APPEARANCE Fantastic Four #11 (Februaryt 1963)
REAL NAME William "Lumpy" Lumpkin
OCCUPATION United States Postal Courier **BASE** New York City
HEIGHT 5 ft 8 in **WEIGHT** 165 lbs **EYES** Blue **HAIR** White
SPECIAL POWERS/ABILITIES None, although he believes that he possesses a special talent when it comes to wiggling his ears; good at his job, courageous, and loyal.

After working as a postman for a small town, Lumpkin moved to New York City, where he was assigned a mail route that included the Baxter Building. Soon after the FANTASTIC FOUR moved into the top five floors of the Baxter, Lumpkin half-jokingly petitioned for membership on the grounds that he had the ability to wiggle his ears. Although he never joined the team, he has been involved with them on many occasions. He once rang a bell that allowed the team to escape the MAD THINKER and a SKRULL once impersonated him to gain access to the FF headquarters. Lumpkin is currently semi-retired and his curvaceous niece Billie has replaced him as the FF's mail carrier. TD

Lotus

FIRST APPEARANCE Avengers Spotlight #30 (March 1990)
REAL NAME Lotus Newmark
OCCUPATION Mob leader **BASE** California
HEIGHT/WEIGHT Unrevealed **EYES** Brown **HAIR** Black
SPECIAL POWERS/ABILITIES Lotus is a trained martial artist and an experienced criminal leader. She possesses some skill at hypnotizing others to do her will.

As a child, Lotus was traded to Hong Kong underworld leader Li Fong to cover her father's gambling debts. She became Fong's protégée, trained in martial arts, and eventually ascending to a high position within his organization. Lotus emigrated to California to set up her own criminal operation. As she increased her power, she began to run afoul of various heroes, including HAWKEYE, WONDER MAN, and NIGHT THRASHER.

As a cover for her illegal activities, Lotus took over a film studio and became a movie producer. However, proof of her misdeeds was uncovered by Wonder Man and the BEAST, and she was taken into police custody. TB

Lucifer

FIRST APPEARANCE X-Men #9 (January 1965)
REAL NAME Unknown
OCCUPATION Agent for the Arcane **BASE** Mobile
HEIGHT 6 ft 2 in **WEIGHT** 325 lbs **EYES** Blue **HAIR** Black
SPECIAL POWERS/ABILITIES Initially merely possessed limited telepathic powers; later able to manipulate ionic energy to increase strength, generate protective shield and fuse self with other beings.

Belonging to the planet-conquering Arcane race, the alien Lucifer served as one of their leading agents and was responsible for the capture of numerous worlds. Ordered to obtain Earth for the Arcane, Lucifer was thwarted by a young Charles Xavier (*see* PROFESSOR X). Furious at his defeat, before fleeing, Lucifer used a stone slab to cripple Xavier's legs. This encounter motivated Xavier to create the X-MEN. That mutant organization claimed victory over Lucifer several more times. Angry at their agent's failures, the Arcane leaders had him terminated. AD

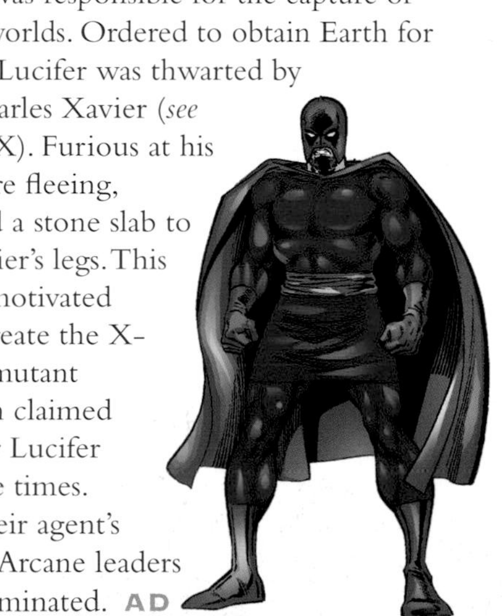

Lyja the Laserfist

FIRST APPEARANCE (as Alicia) Fantastic Four Vol. 1 #265 (April 1984); (as Lyja) Fantastic Four Vol. 1 #357 (October 1991)
REAL NAME Lyja
OCCUPATION Skrull agent **BASE** Mobile
HEIGHT 5 ft 5 in **WEIGHT** 120 lbs **EYES** Green **HAIR** Green
SPECIAL POWERS/ABILITIES A shapeshifter, like all Skrulls; able to fly and project energy bursts.

The SKRULL called Lyja used her natural shapeshifting abilities to masquerade as Alicia MASTERS, in an attempt to further a scheme by her commander, Paibok, to destroy the FANTASTIC FOUR. In her guise as Alicia she married the HUMAN TORCH, though he discovered the ruse and broke off their relationship. Lyja became "the Laserfist" after Paibok bestowed her with energy powers, and from then on she alternated between fighting the FANTASTIC FOUR and seeking to reconcile with the Human Torch. After losing her energy powers during a false pregnancy, Lyja assumed the identity of a human named Laura Greene. DW

M

FIRST APPEARANCE Uncanny X-Men #316 (September 1994)
REAL NAME Monet St. Croix
OCCUPATION Investigator **BASE** Mutant Town area of New York
HEIGHT 5 ft 7 in **WEIGHT** 125 lbs **EYES** Brown **HAIR** Black
SPECIAL POWERS/ABILITIES M possesses superhuman strength and durability, flight and telepathy.

Having lived much of her young life mystically trapped in the speechless form of PENANCE by her brother EMPLATE, Monet St. Croix's existence was usurped by her two younger sisters Claudette and Nicole. They used their mutant abilities to combine into a single entity that resembled Monet. Both Penance and the amalgam-Monet became members of GENERATION X, the satellite team of young X-MEN at the Massachusetts Academy. Later, the truth of M's situation became apparent, and she and her sisters were restored to their rightful forms. M joined Jamie Madrox's detective agency, X-Factor Investigations. **TB**

MacTaggart, Dr.

FIRST APPEARANCE Uncanny X-Men vol.1 #96 (December 1975)
REAL NAME Moira Kinross MacTaggart
OCCUPATION Geneticist **BASE** Muir Island, Scotland
HEIGHT 5 ft 7 in **WEIGHT** 135 lbs **EYES** Blue **HAIR** Brown
SPECIAL POWERS/ABILITIES Brilliant geneticist with expertise in the mutant genome.

Moira MacTaggart met CHARLES XAVIER (PROFESSOR X) at Oxford University. They agreed to wed but she later broke off their engagement, as she was already locked into an abusive marriage. She bore a child (PROTEUS) to her husband but kept his existence a secret, and also adopted the mutant child Rahne Sinclair (WOLFSBANE). Later, she struck up a romance with Sean Cassidy (BANSHEE). MacTaggart established a Mutant Research Center on Muir Island off the coast of Scotland, where she found a cure for the Legacy virus. She later died in an explosion caused by MYSTIQUE. **DW**

Mach-4

FIRST APPEARANCE Strange Tales vol. 1 #123 (August 1964)
REAL NAME Abner Jenkins
OCCUPATION Superhero, former criminal **BASE** New York City
HEIGHT 5 ft 11 in **WEIGHT** 175 lbs **EYES** Brown **HAIR** Brown
SPECIAL POWERS/ABILITIES Armored flight suit provides enhanced strength and supersonic flight; has a built-in tactical computer and a generator that can fire electrostatic blasts.

Abner Jenkins' career began as the BEETLE, a criminal whose armored suit allowed him to fly. He later joined the MASTERS OF EVIL and agreed to BARON ZEMO's scheme that the team pose as Super Heroes, the THUNDERBOLTS. As the supersonic MACH-1, Jenkins learned that being a hero had its rewards, and most of the team decided to go straight. Jenkins became MACH-2 and MACH-3 while serving prison sentences for past crimes. He currently leads the Thunderbolts as MACH-IV, serving alongside his longtime love interest Songbird. **DW**

Machine Man

FACTFILE
REAL NAME
X-51
OCCUPATION
Insurance investigator
BASE
Manhattan, New York

HEIGHT 6 ft
WEIGHT 850 lbs
EYES Red Imaging Sensors
HAIR Black (artificial)

FIRST APPEARANCE
2001: A Space Odyssey #8 (July 1977)

POWERS
Robot composed of titanium alloy. Motorized endoskeleton which houses a vast array of weapons systems.

A self-motivated mobile weapons system, X-51 was designed to be a killer. He was part of a government project to build robot soldiers that could make independent decisions. His limbs could extend 100 feet and his endoskeleton housed solar power augmented batteries, multi-optical imaging devices with zoom and magnifying sensors, and anti-gravity devices allowing flight. His fingers were equipped with miniature lasers, concussive blasters and a .357 Magnum pistol. Believing that a robot could only act like a man if he was treated like one, Dr. Aaron Stack took X-51 into his home and even designed a human face for him. The project was later terminated and only X-51 escaped destruction. Assuming the identity of Aaron Stack, he attempted to assimilate into human society and later met Gears Garvin, a mechanic who repaired any damage to his robot body. X-51 befriended the robot called JOCASTA. He felt so guilty when ULTRON destroyed her that he agreed to fight the AVENGERS in return for the SUPER-ADAPTOID's promise to rebuild her. To make amends for these actions, X-51 later aided the West Coast Avengers against Terminus and the original HUMAN TORCH's old enemy the HYENA. **TD**

As long as Machine Man's programming or "conscious mind" is secure, his body can be destroyed and rebuilt. This means he's virtually immortal.

Machinesmith

FIRST APPEARANCE Marvel Two-In-One #47 (January 1979)
REAL NAME Samuel "Starr" Saxon
OCCUPATION Robot maker, professional criminal **BASE** Mobile
HEIGHT 6 ft 1 in **WEIGHT** 295 lbs **EYES** Green **HAIR** Bald
SPECIAL POWERS/ABILITIES A living computer program, his consciousness can be placed into multiple robot bodies which approximate human beings.

Master robot builder Starr Saxon built robots for criminals. When Daredevil defeated one of his robots, Saxon sought revenge, but died during the battle. One of his robots, following its programming, took Saxon's body back to his workshop and transferred his brain patterns into a robotic body. On recovery, Saxon replaced this body with a human-looking one. Calling himself Machinesmith, he resumed his career of building robots for the underworld. He has come into conflict with SHIELD and Captain America. He now exists as a computer program which can be placed into robot bodies. **MT**

Mad Dog

FIRST APPEARANCE (as Baxter) Amazing Adventures vol. 2 #13 (July 1972); (as Mad-Dog) Defenders #125 (November 1983)
REAL NAME Robert "Buzz" Baxter
OCCUPATION Criminal, retired US Air Force Colonel **BASE** Mobile
HEIGHT 6 ft 2 in **WEIGHT** 270 lbs **EYES** Blue **HAIR** Blue
SPECIAL POWERS/ABILITIES Possesses superhuman strength, smell and hearing. Enhanced speed and agility. Has hollow fangs which secrete poison to which he is immune.

In the comics she wrote, Dorothy Walker based her characters on her daughter Patsy and Patsy's friend "Buzz" Baxter. After the real Patsy and Baxter graduated from high school, they married and Baxter joined the Air Force. As a security consultant for the Brand Corporation, Baxter hunted the mutant Beast. Patsy divorced Baxter and became the Hellcat. When Brand captured the Avengers, Hellcat forced Baxter to free them. Baxter underwent treatment by Roxxon Oil's Mutagenics Department that gave him superhuman powers. Thus Baxter became Mad-Dog, who has battled not only Hellcat, but also other costumed adventurers. **PS**

Mad Thinker

For many years the police did not know of the Mad Thinker's existence, despite the various criminal activities he had masterminded over that period. He only leapt into the public eye when he went head-to-head with the Fantastic Four. A brilliant strategist, he tempted each of them away from New York with various impossible-to-refuse jobs. He subsequently used their absence to enter the Baxter Building and steal Reed Richards' inventions. Manufacturing superhuman androids based on Richards' designs he used them to battle the Fantastic Four. However, the Mad Thinker failed to account for a circuit breaker Richards had built into the designs for just this eventuality. Once the circuit was activated all the robots became disabled. Since then, the Mad Thinker has spent much of his time in prison but he has somehow managed to continue his activities from inside. His motives remain unclear—perhaps no one is brilliant enough to understand them or could the Mad Thinker just be enjoying the game? **AD**

With low cunning the Fantastic Four are almost duped into defeat.

FACTFILE

REAL NAME
Unknown

OCCUPATION
Criminal mastermind

BASE
Mobile

HEIGHT 5 ft 11 in
WEIGHT 195 lbs
EYES Blue
HAIR Brown

FIRST APPEARANCE
Fantastic Four Vol. 1 #15 (June 1963)

POWERS
Brilliant criminal mind. Created a way to project his mind into an android body to continue criminal activities in his absence.

The Mad Thinker's first robotic creation, the Awesome Android, could emulate certain Super Heroes, even mimicking the rocky epidermis of the Thing.

Madame Hydra

FIRST APPEARANCE (Viper as MH) Captain America #110 (February 1969); (MH VI) Nick Fury vs. SHIELD #3 (August 1988)
REAL NAME (both) Unrevealed **OCCUPATION** (both) Subversive
BASE (Both) Mobile **HEIGHT** (Viper) 5 ft 9 in ; (MH VI) 5 ft 11 in
WEIGHT (Viper) 141 lbs; (MH VI) 135 lbs **EYES** (both) Green
HAIR (Viper) Black, green highlights; (MH VI) Brown, dyed green
SPECIAL POWERS/ABILITIES (both) Formidable combatant.

Originally the subversive organization HYDRA restricted its membership to men. The first female HYDRA agent was Laura Brown. Another female operative seized command of HYDRA's New York operations, took the name Madame Hydra, and battled CAPTAIN AMERICA. Eventually she took a new alias, the VIPER, and became one of the world's most dangerous terrorists. Another female Hydra agent, Madame Hydra VI, clashed with SHIELD and allied with the YELLOW CLAW. (Five other Madame Hydras outranked her.) She committed suicide to avoid capture. Viper has now reassumed the name of Madame Hydra. **PS**

Madame Masque

Raised by wealthy financier Byron Frost, Whitney Frost grew up anticipating the easy life of a New York socialite, but when her adoptive father died, her world collapsed. Learning that her biological father was the Italian COUNT NEFARIA, head of the MAGGIA criminal organization, she was manipulated into becoming his heir.

Following Nefaria's imprisonment she became head of the Maggia, now based in New York, but her appointment led to yet more tragedy. A raid on Stark Industries' headquarters resulted in cruel facial disfigurements. At the suggestion of Mordecai Midas, her new employer, Whitney hid these with a golden mask, and took the name Madame Masque.

It was Mordecai Midas who first suggested the golden mask.

Falling in love with Tony Stark (IRON MAN), she impersonated his assistant to spend time with him. The relationship ended when Whitney betrayed her lover.

Back to Her Roots

IRON MAN's intervention in an attempt to rescue Whitney's father from Avenger's Mansion accidentally resulted in the the Count's death. Griefstricken, Whitney returned to her criminal roots, once again taking the reins of the Maggia.

Now fiercely opposed to Tony Stark, she has even made efforts to kill him. She remains at large, a lingering chink in the armor of the Iron Man. **AD**

FACTFILE

REAL NAME
Countess Giulietta Nefaria (adopted name Whitney Frost)

OCCUPATION
Head of Maggia criminal organisation

BASE
Unknown

HEIGHT 5 ft 9 in
WEIGHT 130 lbs
EYES Gray
HAIR Black

FIRST APPEARANCE
Tales of Suspense #97 (January 1968)

MADAME MASQUE

POWERS
Gymnast and athlete trained to Olympic standards; superb markswoman and exceptional mistress of strategy.

FACTFILE
REAL NAME
Cassandra Webb
OCCUPATION
Professional medium
BASE
New York City

HEIGHT 5 ft 7 in
WEIGHT 115 lbs
EYES Pale gray
HAIR Black and silver

FIRST APPEARANCE
Amazing Spider-Man #210 (November 1980)

POWERS
Through clairvoyancy Madame Web can predict the future, read minds and perform psychic surgery.

"Reading" tarot cards was central to Madame Web's clairvoyant abilities.

Madame Web

A one-time ally of Spider-Man, Cassandra Webb was born blind but developed skills as a clairvoyant that compensated for her sightlessness. Cassandra's first encounter with Spider-Man came when businessman Rupert Dockery was scheming to take over the Daily Globe. At first sceptical of the help she offered, Spider-Man later acknowledged her usefulness and they worked together to prevent the assassination of a local congressman.

At times Cassandra could be hugely manipulative. When Norman Osborn invited her to become part of his mystical "Gathering of Five", she tricked Spider-Man into obtaining a mystical object for her, so that she could gain the youthful immortality she so wanted. Since then, she has used her powers for good, even agreeing to mentor the third Spider-Woman, Mattie. AD

Madcap

FIRST APPEARANCE Captain America #307 (July 1985)
REAL NAME Not known
OCCUPATION Prankster **BASE** New York City
HEIGHT 5 ft 9 in **WEIGHT** 145 lbs **EYES** Blue **HAIR** Brown
SPECIAL POWERS/ABILITIES Remarkable self-healing ability, able to survive almost any injury; causes others to lose inhibitions with embarrassing and sometimes lethal consequences.

A devoted member of a Christian church, Madcap began his descent into insanity following a terrible accident. He was traveling on a bus with his family and forty church members when it collided with a truck carrying an experimental nerve agent. Madcap was the only survivor, and in the days that followed he developed the ability to heal himself and cause temporary insanity in others. He has used these talents to cause repeated havoc on the streets of New York. In between short spells in Bellevue Hospital, Madcap has encountered a number of superpowered individuals, including Ghost Rider, Nomad, and Wolverine. AD

FACTFILE
REAL NAME
Phillip Sterns
OCCUPATION
Scientist
BASE
Mobile

HEIGHT Variable
WEIGHT Variable
EYES Pupils uncolored
HAIR None

FIRST APPEARANCE
(as Phillip Sterns) Incredible Hulk #363 (January 1990). (as Madman) Incredible Hulk #364 (February 1990)

POWERS
Super-human strength, ability to increase and decrease his mass, and to change his shape and form.

Madman

Phillip Sterns, brother of Samuel Sterns who became the Hulk's enemy, the Leader, was a classmate of Bruce Banner (the Hulk) in graduate school. Banner was always at the top of his class, Phillip Sterns at the bottom. After graduation, both Banner and Sterns began researching the use of gamma radiation as a potential weapon. But the government funded Banner's research, not Sterns', increasing Sterns' envy of Banner. When Sterns learned that Bruce Banner had become the Hulk through exposure to gamma radiation, Sterns grew even more jealous, believing that the enormous power of the Hulk should have been his. Sterns began intentionally exposing himself to gamma radiation over a period of years, trying to duplicate the accident that created the Hulk. As a result of this exposure Stern's gained the powers of the Madman. Sterns and Madman are two separate personalities both existing in the same body. Over the years Madman has battled the Hulk many times. MT

MAELSTROM

FACTFILE

REAL NAME
Unrevealed

OCCUPATION
Nihilist

BASE
Mobile

HEIGHT 8 ft 2 in
WEIGHT 425 lbs
EYES Purple
HAIR White

FIRST APPEARANCE
Marvel Two-In-One #71 (January 1981)

POWERS

Increases his own powers through control of kinetic energy and draining the energy of others; projects force blasts.

He might own some nice spandex, but Maelstrom sometimes seemed out of his depth.

Maelstrom

The seeds of a Super Villain's behavior can often be found in their childhood. The hybrid child of a Deviant and an Inhuman, Maelstrom's birth caused consternation. His mother was killed for giving birth to him, and as a child he was forced to work in Deviant slave pits until rescued by his father, the brilliant geneticist Phaeder.

Following in his father's footsteps, Maelstrom traded information on genetics with various dubious individuals including Red Skull, Magneto, and the High Evolutionary. Their use of this knowledge caused untold suffering: the Nazi genetic atrocities and various clones of Spider-Man were direct results of Maelstrom's collaborations.

A desperately lonely individual, Maelstrom looked for an antidote to his unhappiness in plans to end the Multiverse. Destroyed by Quasar when he first attempted this, he was resurrected and tried again. This time, Mr. Immortal of the Great Lakes Avengers tricked Maelstrom into committing suicide—a humiliating way to die. **AD**

Maggia

THE MAGGIA
1 Silvermane
2 Count Nefaria
3 Hammerhead

The Maggia is the world's most powerful crime syndicate. The organization's operations are worldwide, though its roots began in southern Europe during the 13th century and it spread to the United States in the 1890s. The Maggia has its fingers in gambling, narcotics, loan-sharking, organized labor, and crooked politics. Those who betray the Maggia are executed, often with a death-grip to the chin nicknamed the "Maggia touch."

The three largest Maggia families active in New York City include the Silvermane family, the Hammerhead family, and the Nefaria family. The Silvermanes are a traditionally-structured crime network controlling the narcotics trade. The Hammerheads are styled in the fashion of 1920s gangsters, and are led by the flat-topped Hammerhead. The Nefarias, organized by Count Nefaria, are the most colorful of the three families, frequently employing costumed criminals to further their schemes. Early in his career, the gang boss Kingpin was one of the Maggia's most successful rivals. **AD**

MAGGIA

FACTFILE

NOTABLE MEMBERS

TOP MAN (Hammerheads, deceased) Cunning mind.

HAMMERHEAD (Hammerheads) Enhanced strength through metal exoskeleton.

COUNT NEFARIA (Nefarias) Vast powers of ionic energy.

MADAME MASQUE (Nefarias) Skilled martial artist.

SILVIO "SILVERMANE" MANFREDI (Silvermanes) Cybernetic body.

JOSEPH MANFREDI (Silvermanes) Formerly had control over bats.

BASE Worldwide

FIRST APPEARANCE
Avengers Vol. 1 #13 (February 1965)

Maggott

FIRST APPEARANCE Uncanny X-Men #345 (June 1997)
REAL NAME Japheth
OCCUPATION Former X-Man **BASE** Mobile
HEIGHT 6 ft 8 in **WEIGHT** 350 lbs **EYES** Brown **HAIR** Black
SPECIAL POWERS/ABILITIES Two semi-sentient slugs can leave and re-enter Maggott's body. They feed on anything and use it to nourish him. He can replay in mind's eye past events in local area.

A sickly child, unable to eat solid food, young Japheth felt that he was nothing but a burden to his poor South African family. Heading into the desert to die, Japheth encountered MAGNETO who activated his mutation, allowing two slugs to leave his body and feed on his behalf. Now calling himself Maggott, Japheth went searching for Magneto. In Antarctica, he first encountered the X-MEN, and briefly joined the mutant team. Unfortunately, Maggott's life was not to end happily: captured by the WEAPON X facility, he became an inmate at the Neverland concentration camp and was eventually executed by the authorities there. AD

Thanks to her seismic mutant talents, Magma is impervious to heat and, by encasing herself in fiery molten rock, is as comfortable inside the crater of an erupting volcano as she is in the open air.

Magma

FIRST APPEARANCE New Mutants #8 (October 1983)
REAL NAME Amara Aquilla
OCCUPATION Adventurer **BASE** Mobile
HEIGHT 5 ft 6 in **WEIGHT** 124 lbs **EYES** Brown **HAIR** Blonde
SPECIAL POWERS/ABILITIES Projects bursts of heat and molten rock, and causes shifts in the tectonic plates beneath the surface of the Earth to produce volcanic eruptions.

Raised in the hidden city of Nova Roma in the Amazon jungles of Brazil, Amara was selected for sacrifice by Selene, a nigh-immortal mutant who drains the life essences of others. Hurled into an active volcano, Amara's mutant ability to control molten rock surfaced, and she was reborn as Magma. Magma was rescued from Selene by the NEW MUTANTS, students of PROFESSOR X, and she became a longtime member of the group. Questions about her past—for a time, she believed herself to be Allison Crestmere, daughter of an English Ambassador—caused her to part ways with the New Mutants, but she still reappears in the circles frequented by the X-MEN. TB

Magik

Illyana Rasputin is the younger sister of Piotr Rasputin, the X-Man known as COLOSSUS. A few years after Piotr left their home in Russia and joined the X-MEN, Illyana was kidnapped by Miss Locke, assistant to the assassin ARCADE. Rescued by the X-Men, Illyana decided to stay with her brother at PROFESSOR X's school for mutants in New York State.

Later, the sorcerer Belasco brought Illyana and the X-Men to his extradimensional realm, Limbo. The X-Men escaped from Limbo, but Belasco managed to keep Illyana there as his captive. He turned a portion of her soul evil, which she called her darksoul. This change gave her powers of sorcery. Belasco hoped eventually to turn Illyana completely evil. Illyana eventually mastered the magic in Belasco's books and did battle with him using her soulsword, a construct of her magic power. With Belasco defeated, she returned to Earth, and joined the NEW MUTANTS under the code name, Magik. MT

Mutant Illyana Rasputin (code name Magik) joined her brother Piotr (code name Colossus) at the Professor Xavier's school for mutants, where they became X-Men.

FACTFILE
REAL NAME
Illyana Nikolievna Rasputin
OCCUPATION
Student
BASE
Professor Xavier's School for Gifted Youngsters, New York; the extradimensional realm, Limbo

HEIGHT 5 ft 5 in
WEIGHT 120 lb
EYES Blue
HAIR Blond

FIRST APPEARANCE
(as a child) Giant-Size X-Men #1 (1975)

MAGIK

POWERS
Magik is both a mutant with superhuman powers and an expert sorceress. She can teleport herself and others through time, perform astral projection, and sense the presence of magic.

Magik is not only a powerful mutant, she is also a skilled sorceress, which helps to make her a formidable warrior.

MAGNETO

Master of magnetism

MAGNETO

FACTFILE

REAL NAME
Unrevealed, uses the name Erik Magnus Lehnsherr

OCCUPATION
Conqueror

BASE
Mobile

HEIGHT 6ft 2 in
WEIGHT 190 lbs
EYES Blue-grey
HAIR White

FIRST APPEARANCE
X-Men #1, (September 1963)

POWERS
Mutant ability to manipulate magnetism and all forms of electromagnetic energy

ALLIES/FOES
ALLIES Brotherhood of Evil Mutants, (sometimes) Professor Charles Xavier, (formerly) the X-Men, the New Mutants

FOES Professor Charles Xavier, the X-Men, the Avengers, the Fantastic Four

Magneto's sufferings in his youth inspired his hatred of humankind.

One of the most powerful and dangerous of all mutants, Magneto has been both the foremost enemy of the X-MEN and, sometimes, their ally. As a boy, he was imprisoned in the Nazi death camp in Auschwitz, Poland. Sickness and malnourishment prevented Magneto's mutant powers from emerging there. In Auschwitz, Magneto's family perished, and he witnessed the inhumanity that people can show to those who are considered different.

MUTANT RAGE

Magneto magnetically shielded Magda and Anya in a burning inn, but could not save Anya's life.

Following World War II Magneto married Magda, and they had a daughter, Anya. When Anya was trapped in a burning building, an insensitive crowd prevented Magneto from rescuing her. Infuriated, Magneto lashed out with his powers, killing them.

Frightened by what her husband had done, Magda fled from him. She had not told Magneto that she was pregnant. Eventually Magda arrived at Wundagore Mountain, where she gave birth to twins, Wanda and Pietro. She then ran away into the wilderness, where she presumably died.

While searching for Magda, Magneto employed a forger named George Odekirk to create a false identity, "Erik Magnus Lehnsherr," for him. Eventually Magneto settled in Israel, where he became friends with the young Charles Xavier (*see* Professor X) They continually debated their different views on whether mutants could peacefully coexist with the rest of humanity.

SUPERIORITY COMPLEX

When their friend Gabrielle HALLER was abducted by BARON VON STRUCKER and his HYDRA agents, Magneto and Xavier rescued her. Magneto used his powers to make off with a cache of Nazi gold that Strucker had sought. Magneto decided that the only way to prevent humanity from oppressing the emerging race of mutants was for mutants to conquer the rest of the human race. Indeed, Magneto believed that mutants were superior to ordinary humans and deserved to rule them.

Magneto's first step in his war against the human race was to seize a missile base at Cape Citadel, Florida. By now Xavier had founded the X-MEN, who foiled Magneto's takeover of the base.

ISSUE #1
In the first *X-Men* comic, Magneto captured the Cape Citadel missile base, only to be defeated by the original X-Men in their initial battle.

ESSENTIAL STORYLINES

- ***X-Men Vol. 1 #4-7, 11***
Magneto's original Brotherhood of Evil Mutants battles the original team of X-Men.
- ***X-Men Vol. 1 #62-63***
Magneto's unmasked face is revealed when he combats the X-Men in the Savage Land.
- ***Uncanny X-Men #161***
The story of how Magneto first met Charles Xavier in Israel.
- ***Classic X-Men #12***
Magneto's captivity at Auschwitz and the death of his daughter.

A resistance movement including Cyclops, Spider-Man, and Wolverine attacked Magneto's House of M before the Scarlet Witch finally restored reality to its previous normalcy.

When Magneto next battled the X-Men, it was as leader of the original BROTHERHOOD OF EVIL MUTANTS. The other members were Mastermind, the Toad, and Pietro and Wanda (QUICKSILVER and the SCARLET WITCH), who felt obligated to Magneto for saving them from a mob. Neither Magneto nor Wanda and Pietro realized that Magneto was their father.

After numerous clashes with the X-Men, Magneto tried to force a superhuman being known as the STRANGER to serve him. He little knew that the Stranger was actually an alien with seemingly limitless powers who captured Magneto and the Toad.

Weary of Magneto's crusade against humanity, Quicksilver and the Scarlet Witch quit the Brotherhood and soon joined the Avengers.

Magneto eventually escaped back to Earth from the Stranger's planet and resumed his war on humanity, battling the X-Men, Avengers, Fantastic Four, and Defenders. He also formed several new versions of the Brotherhood.

Using his advanced knowledge of genetic engineering, Magneto created a being called Alpha the Ultimate Mutant. But Alpha turned against Magneto and devolved him into a powerless infant. Xavier turned the infant Magneto over to his colleague Dr. Moira MacTaggart, who began experiments to alter the baby's mind. Davan Shakari, an alien Shi'ar agent, later restored Magneto to his adult physical prime. Hence Magneto is

THE HOUSE OF M
1 Quicksilver **2** Scarlet Witch
3 Scarlet Witch's sons Thomas and William
4 Magneto **5** Polaris

THE HOUSE OF MAGNUS

Urged by her brother Quicksilver, the Scarlet Witch utilized her mutant power over probability to alter history. As a result, Magneto had led mutants in a successful war against the rest of humanity. Magneto was now monarch of Earth. His royal family was known as the "House of Magnus" or "House of M" and was comprised of his son Quicksilver, his daughters the Scarlet Witch and Polaris, and his grandsons Thomas and William.

physically considerably younger today than his contemporaries from the World War II period.

Magneto resumed his battles against the X-Men, but eventually MacTaggart's tampering with his mind took effect, and he became the X-Men's ally. During an extended absence from Earth by Xavier, Magneto even took over as headmaster of Xavier's school, mentoring the New Mutants. Around this time, Magneto, Quicksilver and the Scarlet Witch learned their true relationship

The Truce Is Over

In time Magneto's previous personality reemerged, and his war against humanity began anew. After he created an electromagnetic pulse that deactivated technology all over the world, the United Nations gave him control of the island nation of Genosha, which was mainly populated by mutants. Magneto hoped to turn Genosha into base from which to conquer the world. However, the island was devastated by Sentinels sent by Xavier's evil twin, Cassandra Nova.

During a fit of madness, the Scarlet Witch used her powers to alter reality so that Magneto ruled the world. She later restored the status quo, and also deprived most superhuman mutants of their super-powers, including Magneto. How long Magneto will remain powerless, however, remains to be seen.

TB

An alternate reality Magneto and his Brotherhood attempted to destroy Earth.
1 Wolverine **2** Rogue **3** Ice-Man **4** Mystique **5** Magneto

Once merely an arms merchant, Moses Magnum was transformed by Apocalypse into a world-shaking villain with command of the Earth itself.

Magnum, Moses

FIRST APPEARANCE Giant-size Spider-Man #4 (April 1975)
REAL NAME Moses Magnum
OCCUPATION Terrorist, arms merchant **BASE** Various
HEIGHT/WEIGHT Not known **EYES** Brown **HAIR** Black
SPECIAL POWERS/ABILITIES Moses Magnum can generate vibrational force, which he can use to bolster his own strength and durability or release outwards to cause earthquakes.

Once a noted arms merchant, Moses Magnum's operation was dismantled by Spider-Man and the Punisher. Narrowly escaping death, Magnum was found by Apocalypse, who offered the arms dealer power in exchange for help in fomenting chaos. Reconstructed by Apocalypse with the power to cause shifts within the Earth's crust, Magnum attempted to blackmail Japan but was foiled by the X-Men. Displeased, Apocalypse destabilized Magnum's abilities so that he would cause earthquakes simply by coming into contact with the Earth. Magnum tried to regain Apocalypse's favor through a show of power but was undone by the Avengers. He was last seen plummeting toward the center of the Earth. **TB**

Magnus

FIRST APPEARANCE Exiles #1 (August 2001)
REAL NAME Magnus Lensherr
OCCUPATION Adventurer **BASE** Mobile
HEIGHT 6 ft **WEIGHT** 177 lbs **EYES** Brown **HAIR** Brown
SPECIAL POWERS/ABILITIES Ability to manipulate magnetic fields, heat, radiation and radio waves; when makes skin-to-skin contact with other lifeforms, he transforms them into steel.

Born in an alternate reality, Magnus was the product of a union between Magneto and Rogue. Inheriting his father's powers of magnetism, Magnus was also born with a corrupted version of his mother's abilities—everything he touched turned to steel. Concerned about the harm he might cause, Magnus became something of a hermit, only to be coerced into joining the Exiles. In an attempt to free yet another version of Magneto from incarceration, Magnus sacrificed himself whilst containing the force of a nuclear explosion. **AD**

Magus

FIRST APPEARANCE New Mutants Vol. 1 #18 (August 1984)
REAL NAME Magus **OCCUPATION** Monarch **BASE** Mobile
HEIGHT Variable **WEIGHT** Variable **EYES** Black
HAIR In true form he has no hair, but parts of his head resemble it.
SPECIAL POWERS/ABILITIES Able to grow to the size of a star and destroy it. Can exist in outer-space and change his shape to that of any being or machine. Can replenish his life energies.

The Magus is the leader of an unknown world in outer space populated by sentient "techno-organic" beings, a species with an organic structure resembling metal. Each child of the Magus must face him in a battle to the death, before they reach adulthood. One of his sons, Warlock, fled to avoid combat and joined the New Mutants on Earth. The Magus came to Earth to search for Warlock, arriving in New York, where he fought three X-Men: Colossus, Nightcrawler, and Rogue. The X-Men managed to hurt the Magus. He warned them that unless Warlock was returned to him he would cause great destruction on earth. The Magus departed and has not been met since. **MT**

Major Domo

FIRST APPEARANCE Longshot #4 (December 1985)
REAL NAME Major Domo
OCCUPATION Principal aide to Mojo
BASE Mojoworld
HEIGHT/WEIGHT Not known **EYES** Blue **HAIR** Gray
SPECIAL POWERS/ABILITIES Constantly monitors Mojoworld's markets, enabling ongoing evaluation of his master's businesses.

The sycophantic yet contemptuous aide to Mojo, the ruler of Mojoworld, Major Domo's job is to ensure the smooth running of his master's household. An android, Major Domo provides information on and analysis of Mojo's businesses, while at the same time soothing his paranoid ego. These abilities make him Mojo's most prized servant. Although treated as nothing more than a glorified toaster, Major Domo remains at Mojo's side, playing a key role in curbing the worst excesses of his master's personality. Despite finding Mojo repulsive, Major Domo's position gives him almost unparalleled influence over Mojoworld. Not bad for a mere android. **AD**

Malus

FIRST APPEARANCE Spider-Woman #30 (September 1980)
REAL NAME Dr. Karl Malus
OCCUPATION Former surgeon, now criminal scientist
BASE Los Angeles, California
HEIGHT 5 ft 9 in **WEIGHT** 155 lbs **EYES** Brown **HAIR** Black
SPECIAL POWERS/ABILITIES Advanced knowledge of genetic engineering, expertise in biochemistry, radiology, and surgery.

Fascinated with superhuman beings, scientist Karl Malus became involved with the criminal underworld to obtain funding for his research. Malus attempted to capture the original Spider-Woman. He restored the superhuman strength of Eric Josten (now known as Atlas) and enabled him to grow to gigantic size. Working for the Power Broker, Malus gave many clients superhuman strength. Later, he became the head of the criminal organization called the Corporation. **PS**

Man-Ape

FIRST APPEARANCE Avengers #62 (March 1969)
REAL NAME M'Baku
OCCUPATION Mercenary, renegade **BASE** Mobile
HEIGHT 7 ft **WEIGHT** 355 lbs **EYES** Brown **HAIR** Brown
SPECIAL POWERS/ABILITIES Possesses superhuman strength, agility, and resistance to injury. He is a powerful fighter whose combat ability is based on that of gorillas.

Clad in the pelt of the rare Wakandan white gorilla, M'Baku the Man-Ape takes up a battle position at the head of a band of his followers in the White Gorilla cult.

While T'Challa, the Black Panther, and king of the warriors of the African nation of Wakanda was away helping the Avengers in the US, M'Baku schemed to seize his throne. Reviving the outlawed White Gorilla cult, M'Baku killed a rare white gorilla, then bathed in its blood and ate its flesh, which gave him the power of the ape. Calling himself Man-Ape, he battled Black Panther and his Avenger teammates both in Wakanda and in the US. Eventually defeated by Captain America, Man-Ape did not try to return to Wakanda, where he would have faced the death penalty. Instead, he teamed with the Grim Reaper and the Lethal Legion to exact his revenge on the Avengers. But the Reaper's racist attitudes caused the group to split up. **MT**

Man-Beast

Man-Beast

Created by scientific accident, the Man-Beast was born when a wolf was placed inside the High Evolutionary's genetic accelerator. Despite creating an entire evil army using the same device, the Man-Beast was eventually defeated by Thor, placed in a shuttle, and exiled into space.

The Man-Beast sought revenge on the High Evolutionary when he landed on Counter-Earth—a world created by that being. There, he introduced the people of Counter-Earth to the concept of evil and even attempted to destroy the planet altogether. In the years since, the Man-Beast has gone into battle several more times, fighting both Adam Warlock and the Hulk. When he attempted to raise a second army, using the Legion of Light religious cult as a front, the Man-Beast went head-to-head with Spider-Man.

Repeated defeats have demoralized the Man-Beast, and he seems to have disappeared from view. **AD**

FACTFILE
REAL NAME
Man-Beast
OCCUPATION
Would-be world conqueror
BASE
Somewhere below New York City

HEIGHT 6 ft 10 in
WEIGHT 320 lbs
EYES Red
HAIR Brown

FIRST APPEARANCE
Thor #134 (November 1966)

POWERS
Superhuman strength, speed, endurance, and senses; remarkable scientific ability, particularly in genetics and engineering.

During confrontations, the Man-Beast could employ his mental powers as a weapon.

Despite his great strength and mental agility, the Man-Beast was no match for the mighty Thor.

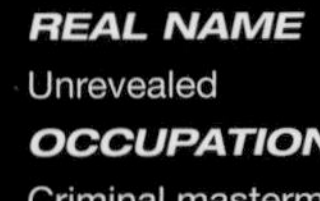

MANDARIN

FACTFILE
REAL NAME
Unrevealed
OCCUPATION
Criminal mastermind
BASE
The "Palace of the Star Dragon" in the "Valley of Spirits" within China

HEIGHT 6 ft 2 in
WEIGHT 215 lbs
EYES Blue-black
HAIR Black

FIRST APPEARANCE
Tales of Suspense #50 (1941)

POWERS
One of the world's greatest scientific mind and a superb athlete. Possesses ten rings of extraterrestrial origin that have amazing powers.

Not only is the Mandarin a great scientific genius, he is also a superb athlete with extensive training in martial arts.

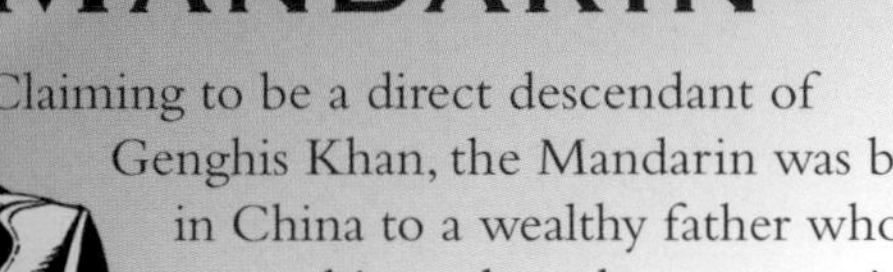

MANDARIN

Claiming to be a direct descendant of Genghis Khan, the Mandarin was born in China to a wealthy father who lost everything when the communists took over the country. A brilliant scientist, he embarked on a quest to gain personal power and explored the forbidden "Valley of Spirits". There, he found a starship that had crashed centuries ago containing ten alien rings with amazing powers. Some rings could be used to seize control of another's mind, rearrange matter, fire a disintegration beam, or create a vortex. Others could produce deadly gases and ice blasts, or discharge electricity, flames, bursts of blinding light and clouds of darkness. After mastering the extraterrestrial technology, the Mandarin conquered the villages that bordered the valley and began making plans to seize control of the entire world, often clashing with IRON MAN and the AVENGERS. He once hired the SWORDSMAN to place a bomb in Avengers Mansion. He also built a device capable of spreading hatred around the world and assembled a team of Super Villains to battle the Avengers. The Mandarin is currently residing in his castle, devising new plans for world conquest. **TD**

Mandarin is trained martial artist and his rings pack a punch, but Spider-Man is just too quick for him!

Since the Mandarin believes he can use technology to achieve world domination, he often crosses paths with Iron Man who always spoils his plans.

MANDRILL

FACTFILE
REAL NAME
Jerome Beechman
OCCUPATION
Professional criminal
BASE
Mobile

HEIGHT 6 ft
WEIGHT 270 lbs
EYES Black
HAIR Brown

FIRST APPEARANCE
Shanna the She-Devil #4 (June 1972)

POWERS
Mandrill has the ability to emit powerful pheromones which give him the power to attract and enslave adult women causing them to submit to his will.

MANDRILL

Jerome Beechman's parents worked at the atomic testing grounds in New Mexico, where exposure to radiation caused mutations in their son. Jerome was born with animal-like fur on his body and an ape-like appearance. He grew up hated by his peers and his parents because of his freakish appearance.

When Jerome was ten, his parents abandoned him in the desert. There he met NEKRA Sinclair, a mutant whose mother had also worked at the atomic testing grounds. Nekra too had been mistreated and abandoned. Jerome took the name Mandrill, and the two teamed up and traveled the American Southwest together, avoiding all human contact. Mandrill and Nekra formed Black Spectre, an organization of black women who hoped to overthrow the American government. This group was defeated by DAREDEVIL. After Nekra was taken into custody by SHIELD, Mandrill formed Fem-Force, an army of radical women under his control. Fem-Force teamed up with MAGNETO's Mutant Force, but was eventually stopped by the DEFENDERS. **MT**

MANSLAUGHTER

FIRST APPEARANCE Defenders #133 (July 1984)
REAL NAME Not known
OCCUPATION Former hired assassin **BASE** Mobile
HEIGHT 5 ft 7 in **WEIGHT** 115 lbs **EYES** Blue **HAIR** Red
SPECIAL POWERS/ABILITIES Low-level telepath: influences peripheral vision and subliminal hearing of others in order to render himself invisible; uses abilities to enhance skills as a huntsman.

Manslaughter was born with mutant powers ideal for tracking and hunting. He impressed the Eternal known as the INTERLOPER by successfully tracking him down in the Siberian wastelands. The Interloper agreed to help Manslaughter hone his powers but, concerned about the young man's unstable personality, he did not train him fully. This was just as well, for Manslaughter later became a ruthless assassin for hire. Eventually he redeemed himself, sacrificing his life in the effort to destroy the DRAGON OF THE MOON. **AD**

Man-Thing

All who fear burn at the Man-Thing's touch!

Unflappable insurance claims adjustor Nathan Mehr comes face to face with the shambling, monstrous Man-Thing.

Ted Sallis was a research scientist on a project aiming to replicate the Super-Soldier formula that empowered Captain America in the 1940s. But he was betrayed to the sinister criminal think-tank known as AIM, who wanted his research. Fearing that his work would fall into evil hands, Sallis destroyed his notes and injected himself with the only sample of his serum. But while fleeing for his life, he crashed his car in the swampland surrounding his laboratory, and was seemingly killed.

TRANSFORMATION

Unknown to Sallis, the area in which he'd located his lab was close to the Nexus of All Realities, a mystical gateway that linked all of the myriad dimensions of existence. In some mysterious fashion, Sallis's serum combined with the ambient mystical energies of the Nexus, and caused the vegetation of the swamp that surrounded his almost lifeless body to reconstitute him as a mindless, shambling mass—the Man-Thing.

Feeling the Burn

Possessing scant intellect of its own, the Man-Thing is instead empathetically attuned to his surroundings. While Ted Sallis's soul still resides within the great beast, in general the Man-Thing is mindless, reacting only to the emotions of those around him. Fear causes the Man-Thing great pain, and he will journey forth from his swampy home to put an end to any source of fear that causes him distress. Because of a quirk of chemistry in his make-up, any creature who feels fear in the Man-Thing's presence burns at his touch.

The Man-Thing seldom leaves the confines of his swamp, but he can occasionally be drawn forth by strong emotions, which affect him painfully through his animalistic empathy.

ESSENTIAL STORYLINES

- ***Adventures Into Fear #17–19 & Man-Thing #1*** The Man-Thing and a ragtag band of allies including Dakimh the Sorcerer, Jennifer Kale, Korrek the Barbarian and Howard the Duck defend the Nexus of All Realities from Thog the Netherspawn.
- ***Giant-Size Man-Thing #4*** The Man-Thing is drawn to the pain experienced by an angst-ridden high school student.

MAN-THING

FACTFILE

REAL NAME
Ted Sallis

OCCUPATION
Guardian of the Nexus of All Realities

BASE
Swamp in the Florida everglades that conceals the Nexus of All Realities

HEIGHT Around 7 ft
WEIGHT Around 500 lbs
EYES Red, bulbous
HAIR None

FIRST APPEARANCE
Savage Tales #1, May 1971

POWERS

Virtually indestructible, he has superhuman strength. Fear causes him pain, and changes his chemical makeup so that the touch of his body burns those who feel fear in his presence.

Man-Thing guards the Nexus of All Realities, an interdimensional gateway at the center of his swamp.

Swamp Protector

Empowered by the Nexus to serve as its silent, unsleeping guardian, the Man-Thing rarely strays from the vicinity of the swamp, and if circumstances force him to do so, he always returns. But anything that might threaten the sanctity of the Nexus, or that of the swamp itself, soon comes to know the mindless rage of its unspeaking protector! **TB**

MANTIS

FACTFILE
REAL NAME
Unknown
OCCUPATION
Adventuress
BASE
Temple of the Priests, Pama, Vietnam; Ho Chi Minh City, Vietnam; Avengers Mansion, New York City

HEIGHT 5 ft 6 in
WEIGHT 115 lbs
EYES Green
HAIR Black

FIRST APPEARANCE
Avengers #112 (June 1973)

POWERS
Mantis has superior agility, extraordinary martial arts skill, and the ability to sense the emotions of others. She can also will herself to heal.

Giant-Size Avengers #4 features Vision and Scarlet Witch's wedding, and Mantis's transformation and departure from Earth.

Mantis

Born in Vietnam, Mantis was raised by the Priests of Pama, a pacifist sect of the humanoid alien KREE. The priests educated Mantis in the ways of peace and also in their defensive martial arts. She took the name Mantis after defeating many male opponents in martial arts competition.

When Mantis had completed her training at the age of 18, the priests sent Mantis to live among humans, removing her childhood memories of growing up at the temple, and implanting false memories of life as an orphan, struggling for survival on the streets of Ho Chi Minh City.

She eventually teamed up with the SWORDSMAN, a costumed criminal, whom Mantis helped rehabilitate. When the Swordsman joined the AVENGERS, Mantis went with him to take up residence at the Avengers Mansion. She was also made a member of the team.

After her marriage to the eldest Cotati, an alien race of telepathic plant-beings, Mantis transformed into pure energy and left Earth. **MT**

Mantis is caught in the clutches of Thanos, an Eternal who augmented his superhuman abilities to become the most powerful of the Eternals.

Man-Wolf

FIRST APPEARANCE (as Man-Wolf) The Amazing Spider-Man #124 (September 1973) **REAL NAME** John Jameson
OCCUPATION Former astronaut, pilot, security chief
BASE New York City
HEIGHT 6 ft 6 in **WEIGHT** 350 lbs **EYES** Red **HAIR** White
SPECIAL POWERS/ABILITIES As Man-Wolf: superhuman strength, speed, agility, durability, and heightened senses.

The son of *Daily Bugle* publisher J. Jonah JAMESON, John Jameson discovered a gem on the Moon. On Earth, this gem caused him to transform into a wolflike creature under a full moon. The Moongem contained the essence of Stargod, ruler of "Other-Realm" in another dimension. Man-Wolf journeyed to "Other-Realm" where he helped its people defeat their enemy Arisen Tyrk.

John later underwent radiation treatment, which destroyed the Moongem, curing him of being Man-Wolf. Since then he has worked as a pilot for the AVENGERS and as security chief for the Ravencroft asylum. **PS**

Marauders

The personal army of mutant eugeneticist, MR. SINISTER, the Marauders are one of the most effective forces the X-MEN have ever faced. Mutants that fell short of the mark disgusted Mr. Sinister. He particularly loathed the MORLOCKS, mutants hiding from society in the tunnels beneath New York, and so the Marauders first mission was to obliterate them. In large part they were successful: despite being opposed by both the X-MEN and X-FACTOR, the Marauders killed most of the Morlocks while almost fatally injuring both Shadowcat (see PRYDE, KITTY) and NIGHTCRAWLER. The Marauders have gone head-to-head with the X-Men since then, even destroying the Xavier Institute. They are particularly feared because Sinister has created clones of each of the Marauders: if one falls a duplicate will replace them. The threat they pose looks set to continue for years to come. **AD**

THE MARAUDERS
1 Scrambler ***2*** Sabretooth ***3*** Malice
4 Scalphunter ***5*** Vertigo ***6*** Harpoon ***7*** Riptide

MARAUDERS

FACTFILE
MEMBERS
MR. SINISTER Telepathy.
MALICE Telepathy.
VERTIGO Affects equilibrium.
ARCLIGHT Seismic shocks from hands.
HARPOON Bio-energetic projectiles.
RIPTIDE A mutant whirlwind.
BLOCKBUSTER Super-strong.
PRISM Captures powers then projects back at source.
SABRETOOTH Adamantium skeleton; supersenses.
SCALPHUNTER Manipulates mechanical components.
SCRAMBLER Disrupts living and mechanical systems.

FIRST APPEARANCE
Uncanny X-Men #210 (October 1986)

Marrow

MARROW

FACTFILE

REAL NAME
Sarah; last name may be Rushman

OCCUPATION
Genetic terrorist, adventurer

BASE
Various

HEIGHT 6 ft
WEIGHT Unknown
EYES Green
HAIR Magenta

FIRST APPEARANCE
Uncanny X-Men #325 (October 1995)

She is a young mutant who left her normal life behind to journey into the sewers controlled by the mysterious MORLOCKS. Marrow was one of the few survivors of the Mutant Massacre which decimated the Morlocks' ranks. Escaping to the dimension ruled by Mikhail RASPUTIN, Marrow became a member of Gene Nation, a radical mutant group dedicated to striking back at their human oppressors.

After a number of encounters with the X-MEN, Marrow came to join with them in common cause. However, her fiery personality and natural savageness meant that she never fitted in at Xavier's School and she left under mysterious circumstances. More recently, she was recruited by the newly-reformed WEAPON X program, who have boosted her powers so as to allow her to control her appearance. **PS**

POWERS

Marrow's mutant physiognomy allows her to rapidly regrow the protruding bone spurs which protrude from her body, and which she uses as weapons. She also possesses two hearts and enhanced durability, making her difficult to kill.

Bony projections from her body can be broken off and used as vicious weapons.

Marrow's bone-spikes would grow wildly throughout her body, causing her discomfort and disfiguring her appearance.

Marrina

FIRST APPEARANCE Alpha Flight Vol. 1 #1 (August 1983)
REAL NAME Marinna Smallwood
OCCUPATION Adventuror **BASE** Mobile
HEIGHT 6 ft **WEIGHT** 200 lbs **EYES** Black **HAIR** Green
SPECIAL POWERS/ABILITIES Enhanced strength and stamina; able to breathe both air and water; can swim at high speed and generate waterspouts.

The Plodex alien life form who became known as Marinna hatched from an egg that had soaked in the Atlantic Ocean, giving her aquatic adaptations that surfaced when she assumed the humanoid forms of her adoptive guardians, the Smallwoods.

Her superhuman abilities allowed her to join ALPHA FLIGHT, and she later married NAMOR the Sub-Mariner. Tragedy struck when, during her pregnancy, she turned into a monstrous leviathan. Namor was forced to kill her, but her alien biology may have preserved her in a coma-like state. **DW**

Marvel Boy

FIRST APPEARANCE Marvel Boy #1 (September 2000)
REAL NAME Noh-Varr
OCCUPATION Would-be conqueror **BASE** New York City
HEIGHT 5 ft 10 in **WEIGHT** 165 lbs **EYES** Black **HAIR** White
SPECIAL POWERS/ABILITIES Enhanced strength, speed, and stamina; can mentally control his body's growth; nanobots reroute pain sensations.

The name Marvel Boy has been adopted by five individuals. Martin Burns wielded the power of Hercules in the 1940s, Robert Grayson received cosmic bracelets from the ETERNALS of Uranus in the 1950s, Wendell Vaughn used the name (and the bracelets) before becoming QUASAR, and Vance Astrovik took the identity before becoming Justice. The most recent is Noh-Varr of the KREE. When his ship crashed on Earth, he became the prisoner of Doctor Midas. He escaped thanks to Midas's daughter Oubliette and declared war on Earth. He has since been imprisoned by SHIELD. **DW**

Master Khan

FIRST APPEARANCE Strange Tales #77 (October 1960)
REAL NAME Khan **OCCUPATION** God to the people of K'un-Lun
BASE K'un-Lun, New York City
HEIGHT Unknown **WEIGHT** Unknown **EYES** Red **HAIR** Black
SPECIAL POWERS/ABILITIES Magical powers allow him to distort reality, levitate and shrink objects, alter his appearance, form energy shields, fire energy blasts, and cast mystic spells.

Master Khan is worshiped as a god on the alien planet of K'un-Lun. The dominant life form on the planet is a sentient plant called the H'ylthri, although humanoid life forms live there as well. Master Khan is a human, but has the magical powers of a sorcerer. He is the protector of the inhabitants of K'un-Lun, and his power comes from their worship. On Earth Khan was a scholar but also a student of the occult. Once on K'un-Lun, Master Khan became a mortal enemy of IRON FIST. Later Khan appeared in the midst of a battle among WOLVERINE, NAMOR, NAMORITA, and the H'ylthri, which resulted in the banishment of Wolverine. **MT**

Master Order

FIRST APPEARANCE Marvel Two-in-One Annual #2 (December 1977)
REAL NAME None **OCCUPATION** Cosmic entity
BASE Everywhere
HEIGHT/WEIGHT/EYES/HAIR Unknown
SPECIAL POWERS/ABILITIES Scope of powers is unknown although can change destinies of specific individuals.

DEATH, LORD CHAOS, ETERNITY, and Master Order—enigmatic beings all, each embodying a distinct abstract concept. Their origins are unknown and so are their powers, although many surmise that these are without limit. The "brother" of Lord Chaos, Master Order strives to maintain a cosmic balance with his sibling, intervening in mortal affairs on the rarest of occasions. Following the defeat of the would-be universe-destroyer, THANOS, Chaos and Order implied that they were responsible for manipulating SPIDER-MAN's destiny to ensure his intervention in the crisis at a critical moment. No one knows if this is truly the case. **AD**

Master Pandemonium

FIRST APPEARANCE West Coast Avengers #4 (January 1986)
REAL NAME Martin Preston **OCCUPATION** Demon commander
BASE Los Angeles, California
HEIGHT 6 ft 1 in **WEIGHT** 205 lbs **EYES** Blue **HAIR** Black
SPECIAL POWERS/ABILITIES Amulet of Azmodeus permits inter-dimensional teleportation. Can detach his own arms as living demons, fire energy beams from his hands, levitate, and breathe fire.

A Hollywood actor given a second chance at life by demon MEPHISTO, Master Pandemonium appeared as a monstrous being with demons in place of arms and a star-shaped hole in his chest that represented the five fragments of his missing soul. Pandemonium identified the SCARLET WITCH's twin sons as repositories of two of the soul fragments and absorbed them, apparently wiping the two children from existence. **DW**

Masters, Alicia

FACTFILE
REAL NAME
Alicia Reiss Masters
OCCUPATION
Sculptress
BASE
Manhattan

HEIGHT Not known
WEIGHT Not known
EYES Blue
HAIR Blond

FIRST APPEARANCE
Fantastic Four #8 (November 1962)

POWERS
A talented sculptress despite her blindness; able to see the good in people despite their appearance.

As a child, Alicia Masters was blinded in the same accident that took the life of her father, Jacob Reiss. The man responsible for the accident, Philip Masters, married her mother and adopted Alicia. She discovered that despite her handicap she had a talent for sculpting. When her step-father, as the notorious PUPPET MASTER, fell into conflict with the FANTASTIC FOUR, Alicia, a pawn in his scheme, was rescued by Ben Grimm, the THING. A strong relationship developed between them, and she found herself embroiled in many of the Fantastic Four's most dangerous adventures.

Perhaps her most shining moment was when she appealed to the humanity buried deep within the sky-spanning SILVER SURFER and convinced him to rebel against his master, the world-devouring GALACTUS, in defense of Earth. In recent times, the romance between Alicia and the Thing has cooled, and she has dated other men. But it is only a matter of time before fate casts Alicia together with Ben Grimm once again. **TB**

Alicia had a powerful effect on the deep-buried emotions of the Silver Surfer. She convinced him to rebel against his master, the world-devouring Galactus, and fight for Earth by appealing to his inner goodness.

Despite her blindness, Alicia Masters is a world-renowned sculptress who practices her art through touch.

Masters of Evil

A villainous alliance against the Avengers

Believing that there's strength in numbers, the original Baron Zemo forms a sinister super-team equal in power to the mighty Avengers.

The Masters of Evil are perennial foes of the AVENGERS, assembling multiple times over the years, often with no link between the various groupings other than their name. The first Masters of Evil came about through the efforts of Nazi mastermind BARON ZEMO.

DECADES OF VILLAINY

Zemo schemed to defeat his wartime nemesis CAPTAIN AMERICA by enlisting the most notorious enemies of Captain America's comrades in the Avengers. He gathered the Melter to fight IRON MAN, the RADIOACTIVE MAN to fight THOR, and the BLACK KNIGHT to battle both the WASP and GIANT MAN (Henry Pym). Later, Zemo welcomed the ENCHANTRESS and the EXECUTIONER into the Masters of Evil. The team disbanded after Zemo's death.

A second Masters of Evil took its place, founded by the robot ULTRON, in his cover identity as the Crimson Cowl. The team obtained blueprints of Avengers' Mansion from butler Edwin JARVIS and struck at the Avengers in their own home. The new Black Knight, DANE WHITMAN, turned on his teammates in the Masters of Evil and helped the Avengers scatter the villains.

ESSENTIAL STORYLINES

- ***Avengers Vol. 1 #6*** Baron Zemo assembles the first Masters of Evil, featuring a villainous counterpart for each member of the Avengers.
- ***Avengers Vol. 1 #270-277*** The Masters of Evil raid their enemies' headquarters in the classic storyline "The Siege of Avengers Mansion."
- ***Thunderbolts #24-25*** The most recent grouping of the Masters of Evil unites 25 Super Villains, providing a formidable foe for the Thunderbolts.
- ***Guardians of the Galaxy #28–29*** Doctor Octopus' Masters of Evil team clash with the Guardians of the Galaxy.

FACTFILE

ORIGINAL MEMBERS AND POWERS

BARON ZEMO Extended longevity, brilliant criminal mind.

MELTER Could melt any metal with a molecular beam.

RADIOACTIVE MAN Can release blasts of lethal radioactive energy.

BLACK KNIGHT (Nathan Garrett) Skilled combatant; carried power lance.

EXECUTIONER Enhanced strength, carried enchanted axe.

ENCHANTRESS Sorceress

FIRST APPEARANCE

Avengers Vol. 1 #6 (July 1964)

CHARACTER KEY
1 Flying Tiger
2 Cyclone
3 Klaw
4 Man-Killer
5 Tiger Shark

The criminal mastermind EGGHEAD organized a third Masters of Evil, hoping to take vengeance on Henry Pym but met defeat (and death) soon after. Helmut Zemo, son of the original Baron Zemo, brought together the fourth incarnation of the Masters.

The Darkest Hour

Baron Zemo II gathered more than a dozen criminals to crush the Avengers through force of numbers. Their most infamous achievement was the siege of Avengers' Mansion.

DOCTOR OCTOPUS assembled a fifth Masters of Evil and fought the GUARDIANS OF THE GALAXY. Baron Zemo II returned to organize a sixth team, the THUNDERBOLTS, who masqueraded as heroes. Before long, most of the Thunderbolts had become heroes for real!.

Justine HAMMER, the new Crimson Cowl, assembled a seventh version of the team that included a staggering 25 members. These Masters of Evil failed in an attempt to blackmail the United Nations for one trillion dollars. **DW**

CHARACTER KEY
1 Black Knight
2 Melter
3 Radioactive Man

MAXIMUS

FACTFILE
REAL NAME
Maximus
OCCUPATION
Would-be conqueror
BASE
City of Attilan in the Blue Area of the Moon

HEIGHT 5 ft 11 in
WEIGHT 180 lbs
EYES Blue
HAIR Black

FIRST APPEARANCE
Fantastic Four #47, February 1966

POWERS
Maximus possesses a genius-level intellect unhampered by sanity, and possesses the ability to overwhelm the thought-processes of those in close proximity, taking over their conscious minds.

MAXIMUS

Son of Agon and brother to BLACK BOLT, the young Maximus exhibited no outward sign of change after his first exposure to the gene-altering Terrigen Mists that make the INHUMANS who they are. But secretly, Maximus exhibited a strong desire to rule, a desire he knew could never be fulfilled while his brother, Black Bolt, lived.

Black Bolt caught Maximus forging an alliance with the Kree, the alien race who were responsible for the creation of the Inhumans. Black Bolt's sonic scream destroyed the Kree warship, and also shattered Maximus' grip on sanity. Thereafter he became known as Maximus the Mad.

However, his desire for power only increased with his madness, and Maximus has devoted his every resource to wresting control of the Hidden Land of the Inhumans from his noble brother in a *coup d'état*. **AD**

Black Bolt is Maximus' older brother. Since just a whisper from his voice can trigger sonic shockwaves, Black Bolt remains silent most of the time.

Despite his boast, Maximus' attempt to destroy humanity failed utterly.

MAYHEM

FIRST APPEARANCE Cloak and Dagger Vol 1 #1 (October 1983)
REAL NAME Brigid O'Reilly
OCCUPATION Former policewoman, vigilante **BASE** New York City
HEIGHT 5 ft 4 in **WEIGHT** 120 lbs **EYES** Green **HAIR** Green
SPECIAL POWERS/ABILITIES Skin constantly secretes a poisonous gas; this can cause paralysis if it gets in bloodstream and can serve as truth drug; Mayhem is also able to fly.

As a New York police detective, Brigid O'Reilly confronted the vigilante partnership CLOAK AND DAGGER. Feeling that their approach endangered innocent lives, Brigid was initially hostile to them, but became more tolerant when she learned of their origins. Following a confrontation with several corrupt police officers while she was investigating a drug-smuggling operation, Brigid was killed by poisonous gas. However, the intervention of Cloak and Dagger led to her resurrection as a superpowered individual, enabling her to exact revenge. Since then, Brigid has adopted the alias Mayhem and become a vigilante, targeting New York drug pushers. **AD**

The poisonous gas produced by Mayhem's body is used in her fight against crime.

Medusa

FACTFILE

REAL NAME
Medusalith Amaquelin

OCCUPATION
Royal Interpreter

BASE
Attilan, Blue Area, Earth's Moon

HEIGHT 5 ft 11 in
WEIGHT 130 lbs
EYES Green
HAIR Red

FIRST APPEARANCE
Fantastic Four #36 (March 1965)

POWERS
Can use her 6-ft-long hair to attack, lift weights, pick locks, or as a whip or a rope.

MEDUSA

A member of the INHUMANS Royal Family on Attilan, Medusa was exposed to the mutagenic Terrigen Mist as a baby. She gained the ability to use her hair like extra limbs, controlling it with her mind.

Following the first coming of Trikon, Medusa left Attilan and suffered amnesia in a plane crash. As she wandered through Europe, her powers caught the attention of the criminal called the WIZARD. He brought her to America and made her part of the FRIGHTFUL FOUR. When her second cousin BLACK BOLT, to whom she was betrothed, took the throne of Attilan, Medusa returned home to act as his interpreter. She also replaced INVISIBLE GIRL in the FANTASTIC FOUR during the time Sue Storm was estranged from her husband. **MT**

Medusa uses her long hair to tangle up the amazing Spider-Man in a different kind of web.

MEGGAN

FIRST APPEARANCE Mighty World of Marvel #7 (December 1983)
REAL NAME Meggan
OCCUPATION Adventurer **BASE** England
HEIGHT Variable **WEIGHT** Variable
EYES Variable **HAIR** Variable
SPECIAL POWERS/ABILITIES Meggan is a shapeshifter whose forms are influenced by the emotions of others; she can fly and project energy blasts drawn from the Earth.

Born to gypsies, Meggan grew up in a fur-covered form and considered herself a freak. Only later, after being taken in by Brian Braddock (CAPTAIN BRITAIN), did she discover that she could consciously alter her appearance. She transformed herself from her furry form into a strikingly beautiful woman with long, golden hair. Not long after this, Meggan and Braddock started a relationship and founded the supergroup EXCALIBUR, and the two eventually married. As Captain Britain's wife, Meggan is the queen of Otherworld, assisting in the management of the dimensional realities that make up the Omniverse. **DW**

MELTDOWN

When he learned of his daughter's burgeoning mutant abilities, Tabitha Smith's father beat her, driving her to leave home and flee to Xavier's School for Gifted Youngsters. It would be some time before she got there. Encountering the BEYONDER on the way, she went on a series of cosmic adventures before falling in with the VANISHER's gang of thieves, the Fallen Angels.

Perhaps Tabitha's childhood explains her subsequent fickleness. She oscillated between X-FACTOR and the Fallen Angels before becoming a member of the NEW MUTANTS where her attraction to CANNONBALL helped steady her. In recent years Tabitha has become a protégé to Nathan Summers, joining him in an attack on the WEAPON X facility and the Neverland mutant concentration camp. Now more settled and having greater control over her powers, Tabitha is maturing into a happy, stable and formidable young woman. **AD**

A founding member of X-Force, in the early days Meltdown was known as Boom-Boom.

MELTDOWN

FACTFILE

REAL NAME
Tabitha Smith

OCCUPATION
Adventurer

BASE
New York State

HEIGHT 5 ft 5 in
WEIGHT 120 lbs
EYES Blue
HAIR: Blonde

FIRST APPEARANCE
Secret Wars II, #5 (November 1985)

POWERS
Generates and throws "time bombs"—energy balls of concussive force. She is able to vary the size and power of her time bombs at will.

Mentallo

FIRST APPEARANCE Strange Tales #141 (February 1966)
REAL NAME Marvin Flumm
OCCUPATION Professional criminal **BASE** Mobile
HEIGHT 5 ft 10 in **WEIGHT** 175 lbs **EYES** Brown **HAIR** Brown
SPECIAL POWERS/ABILITIES Possesses telepathic powers. Can read the thoughts of anyone within five miles, locate a particular brain pattern and project his own thoughts into the minds of others.

Marvin Flumm was born with telepathic powers. He went to work for SHIELD where his powers became more fully developed. Hoping to take control of SHIELD, Flumm stole a battle suit and telepathic-enhancing equipment and took the name Mentallo. Teaming with the Fixer (later known as Techno), Mentallo tried to take over SHIELD headquarters but the two were captured. They escaped and joined HYDRA.

While battling the Micronauts, Mentallo's mind was overloaded. Later, when Professor X tried to help him, the two battled on a psychic plane and Mentallo was overpowered by the Professor. **MT**

Mercado, Joy

FIRST APPEARANCE Moon Knight Vol. 1 #33 (September 1983)
REAL NAME Joy Mercado
OCCUPATION Reporter **BASE** New York City
HEIGHT 5 ft 10 in **WEIGHT** 135 lbs **EYES** Blue **HAIR** Blonde
SPECIAL POWERS/ABILITIES Normal human strength for a woman of her build who exercises regularly; has some skill at unarmed combat; accomplished writer and interviewer.

Joy Mercado, formerly a top writer for *NOW* magazine, is among the elite investigative reporting staff of the *Daily Bugle*. She was partnered with staff photographer Peter Parker on a number of stories, including an assignment to England and Northern Ireland, where Spider-Man prevented the assassination of the British prime minister. Joy seemed suspicious of Peter's relationship with Spider-Man and, at one time, accused Peter of using Spider-Man to further his career.

Joy is an incorrigible flirt, but her relationship with Peter never progressed to anything more than friendship. **DW**

Mephisto

Mephisto is an extradimensional demon of immense power. He is not the Biblical Satan, and his realm is not the Hell of Scripture. However, Mephisto appears to Earthmen in the traditional form of the Devil, and often poses as Satan. By one account, Mephisto, like other rulers of hell dimensions, originated ages ago as a portion of a mass of dark mystical energy. Mephisto continually schemes to make bargains with mortals and gods to gain possession of their souls, which he confines to his netherworld. Mephisto especially covets the souls of heroes for their purity and has repeatedly sought to corrupt and enslave the soul of the noble Silver Surfer. Mephisto has also contended with Thor, Doctor Strange, Daredevil, the Fantastic Four, and many others. It was Mephisto, posing as Satan, who bonded the demon Zarathos to Johnny Blaze, turning him into the Ghost Rider. Mephisto has a son, Blackheart, and a daughter, Mephista. **PS**

FACTFILE
REAL NAME
Unrevealed
OCCUPATION
Ruler of an extradimensional realm of the dead
BASE
A hell dimension

HEIGHT 6 ft 6 in
WEIGHT 310 lbs
EYES Variable, usually white with no visible pupils or irises
HAIR Variable, usually black

FIRST APPEARANCE
The Silver Surfer Vol. 1 #3 (December 1968)

POWERS
Possesses virtually unlimited ability to manipulate magical energies; potentially incalculable strength; godlike durability; immortality; and shapeshifting ability. He can possess the souls of those who hand them over willingly.

Mephisto can magically augment his strength to an immeasurable extent, rivalling even the possibly limitless power of the Hulk.

In his fiery netherworld Mephisto rules over lesser demons and the souls of deceased humans, which have been imprisoned in demonic bodies.

Merlin

FIRST APPEARANCE Journey into Mystery #96 (September 1963)
REAL NAME Merlin
OCCUPATION Wizard **BASE** British Isles
HEIGHT 6 ft **WEIGHT** 210 lbs **EYES** Gray **HAIR** Gray-white
SPECIAL POWERS/ABILITIES Able to predict the future; wields vast magical powers; has incredible powers in his astral form, the extent of which are unknown.

For a time, the wizard Merlin guided the destiny of the British Isles. He could foretell what Fate had in store, help it along, or even stave it off, for a time. Merlin enabled the birth of King Arthur PENDRAGON, led him to the throne and advised him. He also brought the BLACK KNIGHT to Camelot to foil the plots of MORDRED and MORGAN-LE-FAY and prolong Arthur's reign. Sadly, destiny cannot be put off forever and eventually Arthur's reign ended. What happened to Merlin is unknown. **AD**

Merlyn

FIRST APPEARANCE Black Knight #1 (May 1955)
REAL NAME Merlyn
OCCUPATION Sorcerer, guardian of the multiverse
BASE Otherworld **HEIGHT/WEIGHT/EYES/HAIR** Variable
SPECIAL POWERS/ABILITIES Almost unlimited command of sorcerous energies allow him to perform innumerous feats, including extending his natural lifespan.

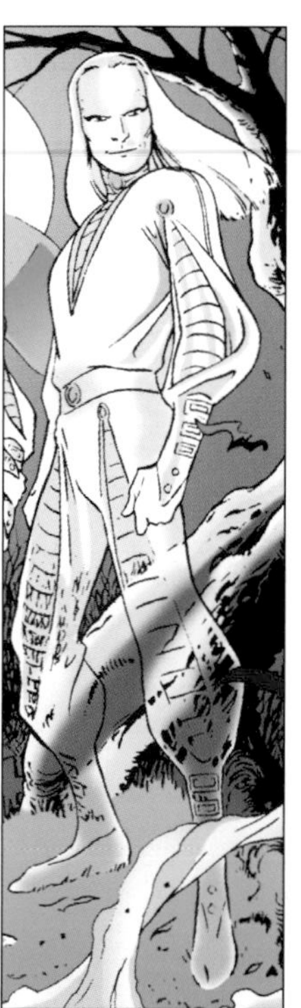

The son of a demon who seduced a mortal woman, Merlyn may or may not be the sorcerer who aided King Arthur PENDRAGON during the rise of Camelot. Eventually, Merlyn returned to his "star-home" in the interdimensional realm called Otherworld. With his daughter ROMA, he created the CAPTAIN BRITAIN CORPS to safeguard all the parallel Earths of the multiverse. Though he has appeared to perish many times, ceding authority of Otherworld first to Roma and later to Brian Braddock, Merlyn is a master manipulator, and it is uncertain whether his last demise was genuine. **TB**

Mesmero

Mesmero started out as a party hypnotist, using his mutant powers to convince guests to surrender their valuables. He branched out into supervillainy when the MACHINESMITH recruited him to lead the robotic "Demi-Men" alongside a robot duplicate of MAGNETO. Mesmero, who didn't realize that his comrades were robots, hypnotized POLARIS into becoming his partner until the X-MEN crushed the Machinesmith's plot.

Mesmero later found work as a stage hypnotist and clashed with SPIDER-MAN. He recently served as a field agent for the WEAPON X program in exchange for treatments that augmented his hypnotic abilities. His powers let him entrance crowds into doing anything he wished, putting Mesmero's mind-control abilities in the same class as PROFESSOR X. Mesmero helped hide the locations of Weapon X installations, but his superiors abandoned him when his power levels dipped after the death of his mother.

Mesmero was one of the mutants who saw their abilities stripped by the SCARLET WITCH during the Decimation event. Without his hypnotism, Mesmero finally forged a relationship with a woman that didn't rely on trickery. He has rededicated himself to starting a new life as an ordinary human. **DW**

Mesmero, who knew that he was a supremely powerful mutant, was also an insufferable egotist.

FACTFILE

REAL NAME
Vincent (full name unrevealed)

OCCUPATION
Professional criminal

BASE
Mobile

HEIGHT 5 ft 10 in
WEIGHT 180 lbs
EYES Red
HAIR Green

FIRST APPEARANCE
X-Men Vol. 1 #49 (October 1968)

MESMERO

POWERS

Mutant powers of hypnotism allow him to take control of others. Mesmero does this by making eye contact. His powers can induce amnesia, put memories into a victim's head or even change their personality.

Microchip

FIRST APPEARANCE Punisher Vol. 2 #4 (November 1987)
REAL NAME Linus Lieberman
OCCUPATION Mechanic, computer hacker, inventor
BASE New Jersey **HEIGHT** 5 ft 8 in **WEIGHT** 220 lbs
EYES Green **HAIR** Brown
SPECIAL POWERS/ABILITIES No superhuman abilities; highly skilled computer hacker; weapons engineer.

A former weapons engineer, Linus Lieberman became the PUNISHER's sidekick, putting his skills to work building the Punisher's arsenal. Calling himself Microchip, he became a close friend and confidante of the Punisher. Because he was the Punisher's assistant on many missions and the brains behind a number of the Punisher's operations, Microchip became a target of the Punisher's enemies. The most powerful of these enemies was the KINGPIN, who had Microchip kidnapped and held prisoner, then cut off his finger and sent it to the Punisher in the mail. Microchip was finally killed by Sudden Death, a rogue SHIELD agent. **MT**

Skilled in strategy, Microchip often planned the Punisher's missions.

Millie the Model

FIRST APPEARANCE Millie the Model #1 (1945)
REAL NAME Millicent "Millie" Collins
OCCUPATION Fashion model, actress, business executive
BASE Hanover Modeling Agency, New York
HEIGHT 5 ft 7 in **WEIGHT** 137 lbs **EYES** Blue **HAIR** Blonde
SPECIAL POWERS/ABILITIES None but has the poise and grace of a top fashion model; some fighting ability.

Having grown up in a rural farming town, Millie Collins left home for the big city, where she found employment as a model for the Hanover Modeling Agency. Over the years, Millie became involved in all sorts of outlandish adventures, often accompanied by her photographer boyfriend Clicker Holbrook and her rival, Chili Storm. Millie retired from active modeling to run an agency of her own. In recent years, Millie's niece Misty has become embroiled in comedic adventures herself. **TB**

Mindless Ones

FIRST APPEARANCE Strange Tales #127 (December 1964)
REAL NAME None
OCCUPATION None **BASE** Dormammu's Dark Dimension
HEIGHT/WEIGHT/EYES/HAIR Variable
SPECIAL POWERS/ABILITIES All possess incalculable strength, near-invulnerability, and the ability to fire energy blasts from their cyclopean eyes.

Dormammu and his sister Umar, master sorcerers, sought refuge in the Dark Dimension following their exile from the dimension of the Faltine. There, they taught the wizard-king Olnar how to absorb other dimensions into his own, a trick that backfired when the Mindless Ones appeared in the Dark Dimension. These soulless creatures, many thousand strong, exist just to destroy anything that lies in their path.

The rampaging monsters killed Olnar and ran riot over the Dark Dimension until Dormammu and Umar imprisoned them behind a mystical barrier, where they remain to this day. **DW**

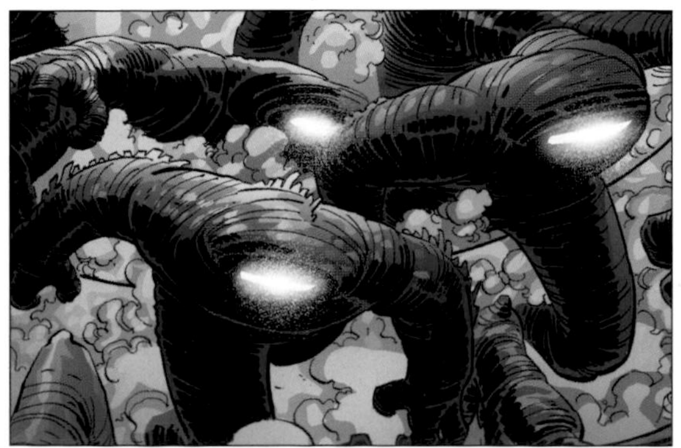

Mimic

The son of a research scientist, Calvin Rankin spilt a chemical over himself while exploring his father's laboratory. He became able to emulate the abilities of others, whether they be athletes, scientists, or even mutants. Naming himself Mimic, he sought to imitate the X-Men, but when he was eventually found out, Professor X invited Mimic to join the team.

Mimic's membership of the X-Men was short-lived—his arrogance made him difficult to work with—and, following his expulsion, he was thought to have died battling the Hulk. **AD**

By absorbing Wolverine's healing factor, Mimic actually survived his encounter with the Hulk. His present whereabouts are unknown.

FACTFILE
REAL NAME
Calvin Rankin
OCCUPATION
Adventurer
BASE
Mobile

HEIGHT 6 ft 2 in
WEIGHT 225 lbs
EYES Brown
HAIR Brown

FIRST APPEARANCE
X-Men #19 (April 1966)

POWERS
Can ape the powers and abilities of up to five individuals at a time; can only wield powers at half strength.

Mindworm

FIRST APPEARANCE Amazing Spider-Man Vol. 1 #138 (November 1974)
REAL NAME William Turner
OCCUPATION None **BASE** New York City
HEIGHT 6 ft 1 in **WEIGHT** 210 lbs **EYES** Brown **HAIR** Brown
SPECIAL POWERS/ABILITIES Feeds on emotions of others; can cause death; can control others; extraordinarily brilliant.

A mutant born with an oversized cranium and brilliant mind, William Turner was cursed with the need to absorb the emotions of others. Unable to understand or control his psychic hunger, he fed off his parents, causing their deaths. William's hunger continued into adulthood, when he took to feeding off the residents of his apartment block, until Spider-Man intervened. Before he could exact revenge, William had an epiphany, realizing his actions were motivated by guilt at his parents' death. After developing mental illness, William became homeless and was killed by a street gang. **AD**

Miracle Man

FIRST APPEARANCE Fantastic Four #3 (March 1962)
REAL NAME Unrevealed
OCCUPATION Stage magician **BASE** New York, Cheemuzwa
HEIGHT 6 ft 4 in **WEIGHT** 220 lbs **EYES** Brown **HAIR** Black
SPECIAL POWERS/ABILITIES Master hypnotist, able to mesmerize people with a glance and make them see what he wants; occasionaly telekinesis, animating objects, and restructuring matter.

A brilliant illusionist and stage magician, Miracle Man most likely had some mutant abilities. During a performance, he spotted the FANTASTIC FOUR in the audience and began taunting them about how much greater his powers were than theirs. Enraged, the THING challenged him but was outdone by Miracle Man's abilities. After escaping from prison following a crime spree, Miracle Man studied the mystical powers of the Cheemuzwa or the Silent Ones. Using his newfound powers, Miracle Man remained a constant and powerful foe of the Fantastic Four until he was shot dead by SCOURGE. **MT**

Missing Link

FIRST APPEARANCE Incredible Hulk #105 (July 1968)
REAL NAME Lincoln Brickford
OCCUPATION Miner **BASE** Lucifer Falls, West Virginia
HEIGHT/WEIGHT Not known **EYES** Yellow **HAIR** None
SPECIAL POWERS/ABILITIES Possesses superhuman strength and durability. His core is radioactive, and he can project heat from his epidermis.

A Neanderthal man born millennia ago, the Missing Link was accidentally sealed in a cave, where a mysterious mist kept him in suspended animation. He was awakened from his sleep by an atomic test that changed his molecular structure. Not understanding the modern world in which he found himself, the Missing Link went on a rampage and battled the HULK. Seemingly destroyed, the Link reconstructed himself, and was found and adopted by the kindly Brickford family. They called him Lincoln and got him a job in the local mines. After further battles with the Hulk, he was turned over to the authorities. **TB**

Miss America

Madeline was the ward of radio tycoon James Bennet. A scientist sponsored by Bennet claimed to have invented a device that gave him superpowers. Madeline tampered with the device during an electrical storm and gained the ability to fly.

Madeline chose to use her gifts in the service of her country. She became the costumed adventurer Miss America, fighting foreign spies and saboteurs alongside super-speedster the WHIZZER. Miss America and the Whizzer joined the Liberty Legion at the invitation of CAPTAIN AMERICA's sidekick Bucky, then became members of the INVADERS when the United States entered the Second World War. After the war, the Invaders changed their name to the ALL-WINNERS SQUAD.

Miss America and the Whizzer married. In 1949, the two took jobs at a government nuclear facility. Sabotage exposed them to dangerous levels of radiation, and Miss America's son, Nuklo, was born a mutant who was kept for decades in suspended animation.

Years later, Miss America gave birth to a stillborn child at the HIGH EVOLUTIONARY's Wundagore Mountain. Madeline did not survive the stress of giving birth and was buried at the mountain's base.

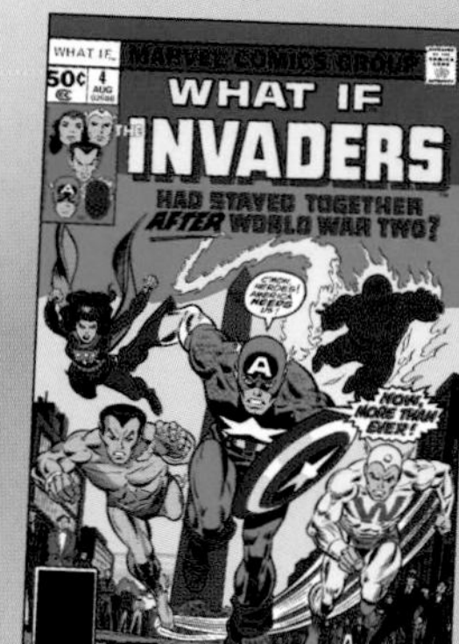

On an alternate Earth, Miss America and the Invaders continued in their roles long past WWII.

FACTFILE
REAL NAME
Madeline Joyce Frank
OCCUPATION
Adventurer
BASE
Mobile

HEIGHT 5 ft 8 in
WEIGHT 130 lbs
EYES Blue
HAIR Auburn

FIRST APPEARANCE
Marvel Mystery Comics Vol. 1 #49 (November 1943)

POWERS
Enhanced endurance; could levitate herself and fly at a limited speed.

THE INVADERS
Miss America, seen here with fellow Invaders the Sub-Mariner and the Human Torch, was one of the first female costumed adventurers. She was announced in the press as the female equivalent of Captain America, and she served as a public icon while aiding the Invaders in combat against Hitler's armies during World War II. **DW**

Mr. Fantastic

Leader of the Fantastic Four

Mr. Fantastic

FACTFILE

REAL NAME
Reed Richards

OCCUPATION
Scientist, adventurer

BASE
New York City

HEIGHT 6ft 1in
WEIGHT 180lbs
EYES Brown
HAIR Brown

FIRST APPEARANCE
Fantastic Four #1 (November 1961)

POWERS
A scientific genius, specializing in physics, aeronautics; Mr. Fantastic can stretch, reshape, compress, or expand his entire body or parts of his body into any shape. He can stretch his neck, limbs or torso up to 1,500 feet without pain. He can create a canopy, sheath, umbrella, or parachute with his body.

ALLIES/FOES
ALLIES Susan Storm (Invisible Woman), Ben Grimm (the Thing), Johnny Storm (Human Torch), Lyja the Skrull, Alicia Masters

FOES Gormuu, Doctor Doom, Frightful Four, Galactus, Puppet Master, the Skrulls, Annihilus, Blastaar, Diablo

ISSUE #1
In November 1961, issue number one of Fantastic Four ushered in the Marvel Age of Comics and introduced millions to what would become the Marvel Universe. Comic books would never be the same!

He's the leader of one of the world's most important Super Hero teams. He's also a brilliant scientist. Reed Richards is Mr. Fantastic. As leader of the super hero group, the Fantastic Four, Mr. Fantastic uses both his ability to stretch his body and his sharp scientific mind in his quest to help mankind.

ESSENTIAL STORYLINES

- ***Fantastic Four #5***
Victor Von Doom blames Reed for the facial scar he receives when a machine explodes. He dons a mask and becomes Doctor Doom, Mr. Fantastic's worst enemy.
- ***Fantastic Four Annual #6***
The cosmic radiation that gave Sue her invisibility power affects her red bloods cells, putting her life and the life of her unborn child in danger.

A BRILLIANT STUDENT

The son of highly intelligent parents, Reed Richards was a child prodigy and a brilliant student. His father Nathaniel Richards was a wealthy physicist. Reed's mother, Evelyn, died when the boy was seven years old.

Young Reed showed a genius for math, physics, and mechanics, which his father encouraged. Nathaniel guided his son's scientific studies. By the time Reed was fourteen, he was already taking and excelling in college-level courses. When he reached college age, Reed attended several universities, including Empire State University in New York.

Reed Richards' attempt to make friends with fellow student Victor Von Doom were rudely brushed aside.

It was there that Reed Richards met several people who would play a major role in his later life as Mr. Fantastic. Victor Von Doom was a foreign student from the nation of Latveria. This scientific genius was assigned to be Reed's first college roommate, but Von Doom disliked Reed from the moment he met him and asked for a new roommate. Later, as Doctor Doom, he would become Mr. Fantastic's and the Fantastic Four's greatest enemy.

Replacing Von Doom as Reed's roommate was Benjamin J. Grimm, a former high school football star who, though very different in temperament, intellect, and personality, quickly became Reed's best friend.

In college, Reed began working on plans to build a starship that would enable him to travel to other solar systems. When he told his new roommate about this plan, Ben joked that if Reed could build the ship, Ben would pilot it. This would not only turn out to be true, but would also be the pivotal event in both their lives.

After transferring to Columbia University in Manhattan, Reed rented a room from a woman whose daughter, Susan Storm, immediately fell for Reed. One day she would be his wife, as well as his partner in the Fantastic Four.

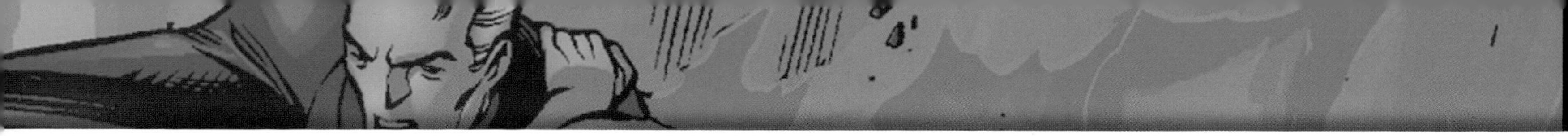

A Fateful Journey

Using money left to him by his father, Nathaniel, who arranged for the fortune to be given to Reed while Nathaniel was on an alternate Earth, Reed began developing his starship shortly after college. When his own funds began to run out, Reed got funding from the US Federal Government to complete the project.

However, shortly before Reed could complete the ship, the government threatened to cut off funding to the project. Desperate to prove that his starship would fly, Reed decided to take the ship up on a test flight himself. Ben argued against the idea, telling Reed that he thought the ship's shielding would be inadequate against the powerful cosmic radiation found in space.

Reed finally convinced Ben to pilot the ship on its test voyage. By this time, Reed and Sue Storm were engaged. Sue insisted in coming along on the flight, as did her younger brother Johnny Storm. The quartet snuck onto the launch pad, slipped onto the ship, and blasted off into space.

Before they could achieve hyperspace and a journey to another solar system, an unexpected solar flare shot intense levels of cosmic radiation at the ship. Ben had been right. The ship's shields were not enough to withstand this ultra-burst of cosmic radiation, which flooded the passenger compartment, irradiating the four astronauts and disrupting the ship's controls. Ben was forced to cut short the flight and land back on Earth.

Big Changes

Upon their return to Earth each member of the foursome soon discovered that the cosmic radiation had changed the very structure of their bodies. Reed discovered that he could bend and stretch his body at will. Sue could turn herself invisible. Johnny could cover his body with flames and also fly. Ben's skin was transformed into a orange, rock-like substance, and he gained tremendous strength.

Reed became the team's leader, calling himself Mr. Fantastic. Sue called herself Invisible Girl (and later Invisible Woman). Johnny called himself the Human Torch, and Ben called himself the Thing. All four agreed to use their newfound powers to help humanity.

Guided by the brilliant Reed Richards, the Fantastic Four has become the most respected Super Hero team on Earth. They have saved the planet from conquest and destruction at the hands of Super Villains and alien forces many times.

Reed and Sue eventually got married and had a son named Franklin Benjamin Richards, named for Sue's father, Franklin Storm, and for Ben Grimm, Reed's best friend. **MT**

Able to shape his body into a highly malleable state, Mr. Fantastic can stretch his neck to peek around corners, or even look over entire buildings!

AT THE CROSSROADS

Mr. Fantastic floats at the Crossroads of Infinity, where all dimensions and universes intersect. A traveler can journey from one dimension to another by carefully navigating through the Crossroads. Doctor Doom proved this, using the Fantastic Four as his test subjects.

Mr. Fantastic battles Crucible, a member of the Enclave. Crucible stole Mr. Fantastic's creative genius to launch a genetics program designed to create life itself, but went insane, unable to handle the flood of amazing ideas.

Mr. Fantastic can stretch his body well over 1,000 feet

Mister Hyde

FIRST APPEARANCE Journey Into Mystery #99 (December 1963)
REAL NAME Calvin Zabo **OCCUPATION** Professional criminal
BASE New York City **HEIGHT** 5 ft 11 in; (as Hyde) 6 ft 5 in
WEIGHT 185 lbs; (as Hyde) 420 lbs **EYES** Brown
HAIR Gray; (as Hyde) Brown
SPECIAL POWERS/ABILITIES Superhumanly strong; astonishing recuperative ability and resistance to pain.

Inspired by the story *Dr. Jekyll and Mr. Hyde* by R. L. Stevenson, medical research scientist Calvin Zabo concocted a formula with similar transformational effects. Zabo became a formidable superpowered adversary, taking on THOR then SPIDER-MAN and DAREDEVIL. Teaming up with COBRA, Hyde executed a number of bank heists until his venomous ally betrayed him. As with the fictional Dr. Jekyll, repeated use of the formula gradually eroded Zabo's sanity, making him a less formidable opponent. He is currently residing in prison. **AD**

Mockingbird

FIRST APPEARANCE Astonishing Tales Vol. 1 #6 (June 1971)
REAL NAME Barbara "Bobbi" Morse-Barton
OCCUPATION Adventurer **BASE** Mobile
HEIGHT 5 ft 9 in **WEIGHT** 135 lbs **EYES** Blue **HAIR** Blonde
SPECIAL POWERS/ABILITIES Expert hand-to-hand combatant and gymnast; her battle-stave can be used as a quarterstaff or broken into two smaller segments.

Bobbi Morse began her career as a SHIELD agent, by striking up a romance with the Super Hero HAWKEYE. The two eventually married and became founding members of the West Coast AVENGERS.

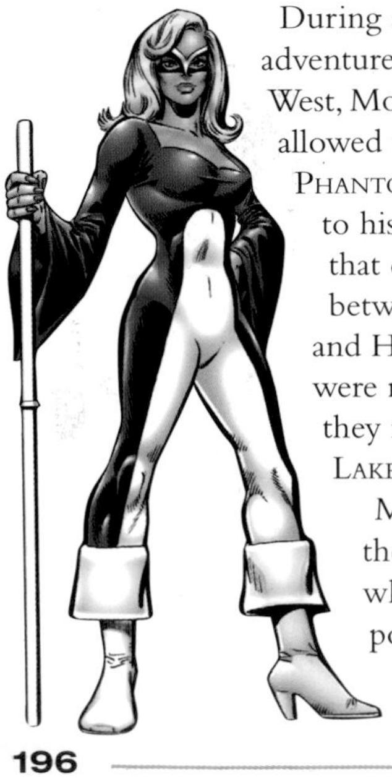

During a time-travel adventure to the Old West, Mockingbird allowed the abusive PHANTOM RIDER to fall to his death, an action that drove a wedge between Mockingbird and Hawkeye. The two were reconciled when they mentored the GREAT LAKES AVENGERS.

Mockingbird later died at the hands of MEPHISTO, when she intercepted a power blast meant for Hawkeye. **DW**

Mister Sinister

A visionary doctor living in 19th-century London, Dr. Nathaniel Essex was recruited by the Eternal mutant warlord APOCALYPSE, his genetic structure enhanced so as to provide him with virtual immortality and superhuman physical attributes. Taking the name Mister Sinister, Essex dispensed with any pretense of human morality as he continued his forbidden experiments into the secrets of mutation over the course of the next century.

Sinister will do anything to further his knowledge of genetics, and he has played a hidden role in the upbringing of the Summers brothers, CYCLOPS and HAVOK. He is also the guiding hand behind the MARAUDERS, a band of killers comprised of mutants and augmented humans whom Sinister once sent into the MORLOCK tunnels to carry out the Mutant Massacre. **TB**

FACTFILE
REAL NAME
Nathaniel Essex
OCCUPATION
Geneticist
BASE
Various

HEIGHT 6 ft 5 in
WEIGHT 285 lbs
EYES Red
HAIR Black

FIRST APPEARANCE
Uncanny X-Men #221 (September 1987)

MISTER SINISTER

POWERS
Enhanced strength and durability, and some command over his own genetic structure. Essex's advanced knowledge of cloning allows him to transfer his intellect into a pristine new body whenever his current one starts to wears out.

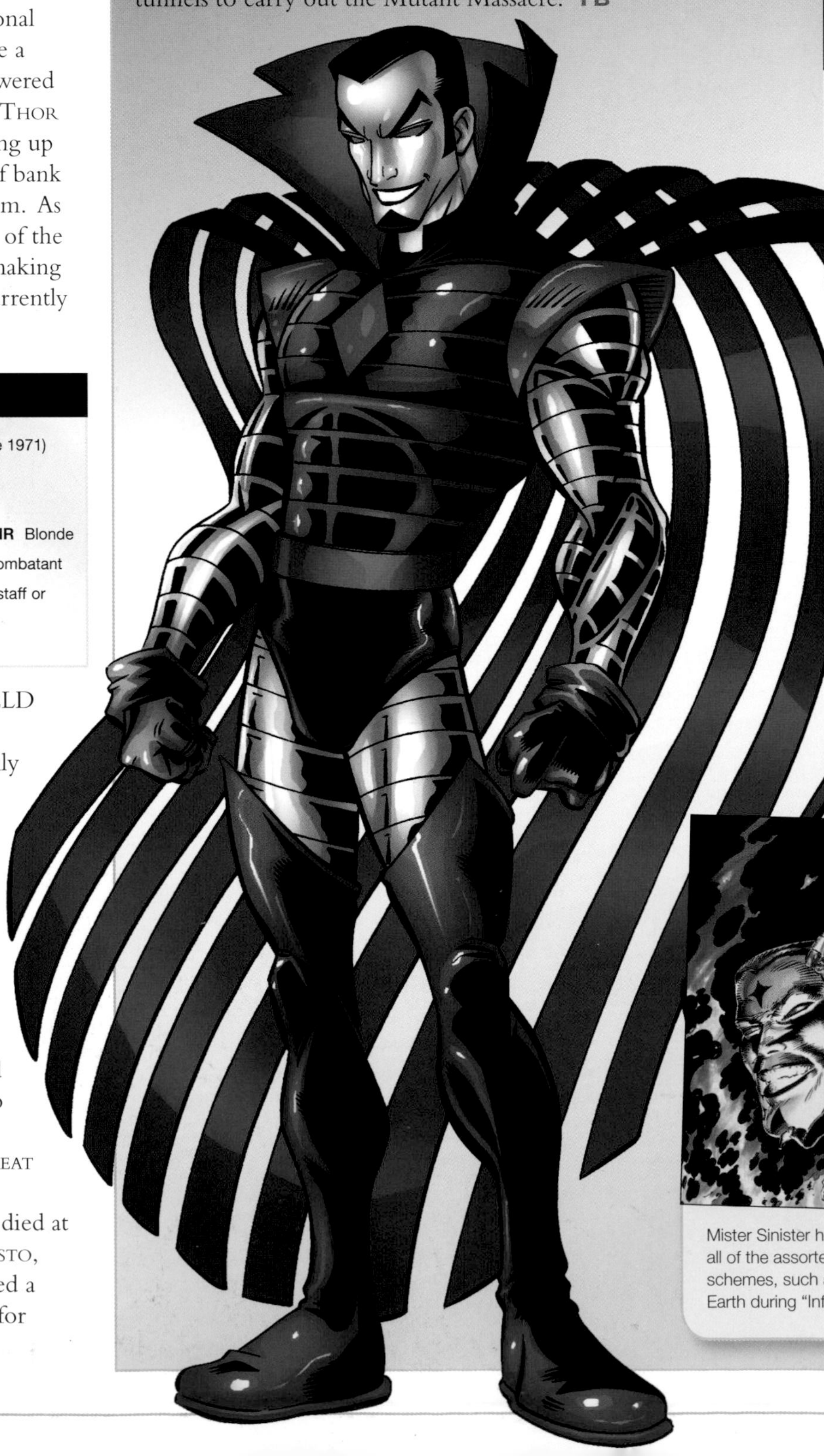

Mister Sinister has embroiled members of all of the assorted X-related teams in his evil schemes, such as the creation of a hell-on-Earth during "Inferno."

MODOK

FIRST APPEARANCE Tales of Suspense #93 (October 1967) **REAL NAME** George Tarleton **OCCUPATION** Leader of AIM **BASE** Various **HEIGHT** 12 ft **WEIGHT** 750 lbs **EYES** Red **HAIR** Brown **SPECIAL POWERS/ABILITIES** Superhuman mental and psionic powers; computer-like brain; headband enabled him to teleport from one AIM base to another; possessed a hover-chair that could fly and was equipped with weaponry.

An agent for the subversive organization AIM (Advanced Idea Mechanics), Tarleton was mutated by AIM's bio-engineers into a living computer named MODOK, which stands for "Mental Organism Designed Only for Killing." MODOK soon turned on his creators and later used his superior mental powers to seize control of AIM. He began making plans for world conquest, but was often thwarted by SHIELD, Captain America, the Hulk and Iron Man. Disgusted by his many failures, rebels within AIM finally managed to oust MODOK and later hired the Serpent Society to assassinate him. **TD**

Mojo

A literally spineless mass of yellow flesh, Mojo is ruler of Mojoworld, a bizarre, media-orientated planet. A manipulative tyrant, Mojo produces movies and TV shows to keep the masses amused. The need to maintain these entertainments' popularity has drawn him to Earth.

Mojo's first visit occurred when his slave, Longshot, tried to persuade the X-Men to help overthrow his master. Although they triumphed, Mojo's successor—"Mojo II, the Sequel"—proved to be even more tyrannical, and Mojo quickly reclaimed the reins of power. Since the X-Men are such crowd pleasers, Mojo has repeatedly involved them in his entertainment programmes, but they are rarely willing participants. Frustrated by this, he created younger versions of the X-Men, the so-called X-Babies, but they proved no easier to work with. **AD**

He may be spineless but Mojo simply refuses to accept defeat.

Equipped with a sophisticated exoskeleton that enabled humanoid movement, Mojo II was less grotesque than his predecessor. A corrupt tyrant, he was not popular and eventually Mojo overthrew him.

FACTFILE

REAL NAME
Mojo

OCCUPATION
Ruler of Mojoworld

BASE
The airborne Body Shoppe, Mojoworld

HEIGHT Unknown
WEIGHT Unknown
EYES Yellow
HAIR None

FIRST APPEARANCE
Longshot #3 (November 1985)

POWERS
Travels on robotic platform that moves on metal spiderlike legs; projects energy bolts from hands; his very presence can kill life nearby.

Mole Man

Shunned and ridiculed for his bizarre appearance, Mole Man turned his back on the surface world and sought a legendary underground kingdom. He eventually found an entrance to it on Monster Island, in the Bermuda Triangle—an underground world filled with advanced technical devices (left by a race known as the Deviants).

Mole Man also found a race of semi-human creatures, whom he enslaved. Sometimes in partnership with Red Ghost, Kala or the Outcasts, his deadly plots against the surface world have been thwarted by the Fantastic Four, the Avengers, Iron Man, and the Hulk.

Mole Man declared himself the sole ruler of the underground kingdom, which he named Subterranea. But Tyrannus, another man from the surface world, who also possessed Deviant technology, challenged Mole Man for control of Subterranea, leading to many epic battles between the two. **MT**

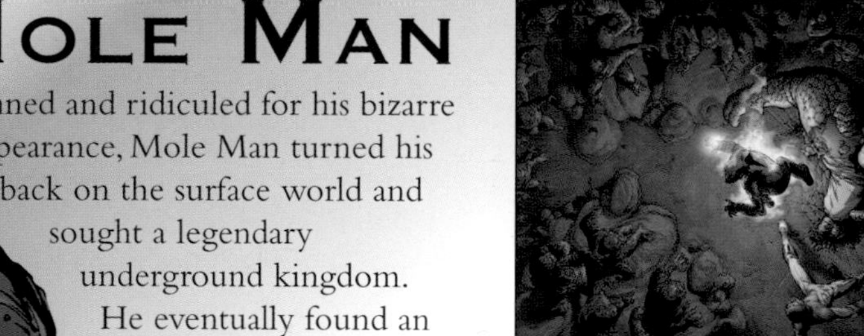

Hideous and lonely, Mole Man found solace in the depths of Subterranea.

Mole Man as he appears in the Ultimates series.

FACTFILE

REAL NAME
Unknown

OCCUPATION
Former nuclear engineer; ruler of the Subterraneans

BASE
Subterranea

HEIGHT 4 ft 10 in
WEIGHT 165 lbs
EYES Brown
HAIR Gray

FIRST APPEARANCE
Fantastic Four #1 (November 1961)

POWERS
Ingenious inventor of weapons capable of seismic disturbance; dominating personality; heightened senses, including a radar sense that enables him to navigate in pitch darkness, or to sense the presence of objects, or people behind him.

Molecule Man

FIRST APPEARANCE Fantastic Four #20 (November 1963)
REAL NAME Owen Reece
OCCUPATION Atomic plant worker turned criminal
BASE Brooklyn, New York; later a suburb of Denver, Colorado
HEIGHT 5 ft 7 in **WEIGHT** 140 lbs **EYES** Brown **HAIR** Brown
SPECIAL POWERS/ABILITIES Possesses psionic ability to manipulate all forms.

Lab assistant Owen Reece inadvertently activated a machine that opened a "pinhole" into another dimension, exposing him to radiation that scarred his face and endowed him with the power to control matter. An embittered misfit, Reece used his powers to evil ends, but was defeated by the Fantastic Four. Uatu the Watcher imprisoned Reece in another dimension, but he eventually returned to Earth. During the first "Secret War," Reece fell in love with another superhuman, Volcana. The two retired to live peacefully together in a Denver suburb, but Volcana has since left him. **PS**

Moon Boy

FIRST APPEARANCE Devil Dinosaur #1 (April 1978)
REAL NAME Moon Boy
OCCUPATION Adventurer **BASE** The Valley of Flame, located on an extra-dimensional planet
HEIGHT 6 ft 2 in **WEIGHT** 196 lbs
EYES Blue **HAIR** Black
SPECIAL POWERS/ABILITIES Able to communicate with Devil Dinosaur and possibly other unrevealed powers.

Moon Boy grew up in the Valley of Flame on an unnamed extra-dimensional world, where tribes of ape-like humanoids coexisted with dinosaurs. His people called themselves the Small-Folk, and struggled for survival against the Hill-Folk and Killer-Folk. When Moon Boy saved a tyrannosaurus rex from the Killer-Folk, the red-skinned dinosaur became his constant companion. Devil Dinosaur and Moon Boy defended the Small-Folk and briefly served with the Fallen Angels team on Earth, before returning to their own world through a space warp. **DW**

Molten Man

FIRST APPEARANCE Amazing Spider-Man #28 (September 1965)
REAL NAME Mark Raxton
OCCUPATION Security guard for Osborn Industries
BASE New York City
HEIGHT 6 ft 5 in **WEIGHT** 225 lbs **EYES** Brown **HAIR** Gold
SPECIAL POWERS/ABILITIES Superhuman strength and durability. Metallic epidermis is capable of producing flames and heat.

The stepbrother of Liz Allen, Mark Raxton worked as a laboratory assistant to Professor Spencer Smythe, creator of the Spider-Slayer robots. Envious of his employer's fame, Raxton stole his latest creation, a synthetic metallic liquid. The liquid spilled over him and was absorbed into his system. He became the super-strong criminal Molten Man, and clashed with Spider-Man. When Raxton's molten skin threatened to destroy him, Spider-Man saved his life. Molten Man then became an ally of the Wall-Crawler, and took a job as a security guard at the company owned by his stepsister's husband, Harry Osborn. **TB**

Montesi, Victoria

FIRST APPEARANCE Darkhold #1 (October 1992)
REAL NAME Victoria Montesi
OCCUPATION Occult investigator **BASE** Rome, Italy
HEIGHT 5 ft 11 in **WEIGHT** 130 lbs **EYES** Brown **HAIR** Black
SPECIAL POWERS/ABILITIES She possesses the ability to sense when someone has accessed a page from the Darkhold tome.

For generations, the Montesi line has guarded the Darkhold book of black magic to prevent the rise of the Elder god Chthon. Victoria Montesi, daughter of Monsignor Vittorio Montesi, grew up believing that her family's involvement with the Darkhold was just superstition, but her skepticism vanished when pages from the Darkhold became scattered around the world. To retrieve them, Victoria founded the Darkhold Redeemers with Louise Hastings and Interpol agent Sam Buchanan. She later learned that Monsignor Montesi was not her real father; unable to have children, he had used magic to ensure an heir. In reality, Victoria was Chthon's daughter, and was carrying Chthon himself in a demonic pregnancy. Fortunately, Doctor Strange prevented Chthon's birth into this world. **AD**

Moon Knight

SEE OPPOSITE PAGE

Moondragon

FIRST APPEARANCE Iron Man Vol. 1 #54 (January 1973)
REAL NAME Heather Douglas
OCCUPATION Adventurer **BASE** Mobile
HEIGHT 6 ft 3 in **WEIGHT** 150 lbs **EYES** Blue **HAIR** None
SPECIAL POWERS/ABILITIES Telepathy; telekinetic levitation of objects; ability to fire mental blasts; trained martial artist.

Moondragon grew up on Titan after Thanos killed her parents (though her father was later resurrected as Drax the Destroyer). An evil entity, the Dragon of the Moon, tried to corrupt her, but she believed she had resisted him. As Moondragon, she traveled to Earth, where her haughty attitude won few friends. Moondragon joined the Defenders, but the influence of the Dragon of the Moon sometimes turned her into a villain. She became a reservist of the Avengers, and later safeguarded the Mind Gem as a member of the Infinity Watch. **AD**

MOON KNIGHT

FACTFILE

REAL NAME
Marc Spector

OCCUPATION
Millionaire playboy and taxi driver

BASE
New York City

HEIGHT 6 ft 2 ins
WEIGHT 225 lbs
EYES Dark brown
HAIR Brown

FIRST APPEARANCE
Werewolf by Night Vol I, #32 (August 1975)

POWERS

His strength waxes and wanes with the moon. He bears weapons given to him by the Egyptian god Khonshu: scarab throwing darts, a golden ankh that glows when danger is near, and an ivory boomerang.

MOON KNIGHT

A mercenary left for dead in the Egyptian desert, Marc Spector was found by followers of the Egyptian god Khonshu. They carried Spector to their temple and presented him to their god, who saved his life, at the same time bestowing upon him superhuman powers. Returning to the US with a statue of Khonshu, Marc adopted the role of crimefighter, calling himself the Moon Knight and assuming two more alter egos: those of millionaire Steven Grant and taxi driver Jake Lockley. Aided by his pilot friend, Frenchie, and his lover, Marlene Alraune, Marc fought crime for many years, battling against Midnight Man and Black Spectre, and alongside SPIDER-MAN and the PUNISHER. But the strain of keeping up his various identities caught up with Marc. Eventually, exhaustion set in and he was persuaded to retire his alter egos and sell the Khonshu statue.

In his struggle against the more nefarious denizens of New York, Moon Knight is partnered by his lover, Marlene Alraune, and his good friend Frenchie.

NEW MOON

Before long, Marc began to have strange dreams and felt compelled to travel to Egypt. There he was met by members of the cult of Khonshu who explained to him that being the Moon Knight was his destiny, and not one he could shirk. Reinvigorated, and equipped by Khonshu with a new costume and a selection of special weapons, Marc's life as the Moon Knight has begun anew. **AD**

MOONSTAR

FIRST APPEARANCE Marvel Graphic Novel #4: The New Mutants (June 1982) **REAL NAME** Danielle "Dani" Moonstar
OCCUPATION Former SHIELD agent, later adventurer and teacher
BASE The Xavier Institute, Salem Center, New York State
HEIGHT 5 ft 6 in **WEIGHT** 105 lbs **EYES** Brown **HAIR** Black
SPECIAL POWERS/ABILITIES Created three-dimensional images of thoughts in others' minds. Had rapport with higher animals.

Danielle "Dani" Moonstar is the granddaughter of Black Eagle, a Cheyenne chief. When Black Eagle was murdered by agents of HELLFIRE CLUB member Donald Pierce, Dani joined forces with Professor Charles Xavier (see PROFESSOR X) to defeat Pierce. She then joined Xavier's NEW MUTANTS, at first being known as Psyche and later as Mirage and Moonstar. For a time Dani served as a Valkyrie in Asgard before becoming a SHIELD agent and then a member of X-FORCE. Recently, she worked as a teacher at the Xavier Institute, but lost her mutant powers. **PS**

MOONSTONE

FIRST APPEARANCE Captain America vol. 1, #192 (December 1975)
REAL NAME Dr Karla Sofen
OCCUPATION Psychologist, criminal adventurer **BASE** Mobile
HEIGHT 5 ft 11 in **WEIGHT** 130 lbs **EYES** Blue **HAIR** Blonde
SPECIAL POWERS/ABILITIES Able to fly and become intangible; creates blinding flashes and emits laser beams from hands.

An arch manipulator, during her childhood Karla Sofen learnt how to use others to get what she wanted. Karla became a psychologist in adulthood, and tricked the original Moonstone, Lloyd Bloch, into giving up the gem that endowed him with superpowers. Using the gem for herself she became a superpowered villain, driving GENERAL ROSS to a nervous breakdown and serving with the MASTERS OF EVIL for a time. Although she attempted to reform, Karla relapsed into her old ways and eventually lost her Moonstone to BARON ZEMO. The manipulator had herself been played. **AD**

Morbius

FIRST APPEARANCE Amazing Spider-Man #101 (October 1971)
REAL NAME Dr. Michael Morbius
OCCUPATION Biochemist **BASE** Mobile
HEIGHT 5 ft 10in **WEIGHT** 170 lbs **EYES** Blue **HAIR** Black
SPECIAL POWERS/ABILITIES A pseudo-vampire who can glide on air currents, Morbius has superhuman strength and healing ability. He can hypnotize people and force them to do his bidding.

Nobel Prize-winning biochemist, Dr. Michael Morbius discovered that he was dying from a rare blood disease which dissolved his blood cells. Morbius tried an experimental treatment in an attempt to cure himself which involved fluids made from the bodies of vampire bats combined with electric shock treatment.

This potent combination transformed Morbius, giving him the superhuman powers and the overwhelming bloodlust of a vampire. He was not a true "undead" vampire, however, as he was still a mortal man. Morbius grew fangs and killed to satisfy his craving for blood. However, after drinking his victim's blood, his mind would return to normal and he became filled with guilt, remorse, and self-loathing. He often battled SPIDER-MAN. **MT**

Mordred the Evil

FIRST APPEARANCE Black Knight #1 (May 1955)
REAL NAME Sir Mordred
OCCUPATION Conqueror **BASE** Various
HEIGHT 5 ft 10 in **WEIGHT** 185 lbs **EYES** Blue **HAIR** Black
SPECIAL POWERS/ABILITIES An expert swordsman, Mordred's mystic power is enhanced when he functions as the male familiar to the sorceress Morgan Le Fay.

The illegitimate son of King Arthur PENDRAGON, Mordred was eventually made a knight of the realm, though evil grew in his heart. Mordred repeatedly tried to usurp the throne of England, but was frequently foiled by Sir Percy, the mysterious BLACK KNIGHT. Eventually, the two men slew each other, but Mordred's ally, the sorceress MORGAN LE FAY drew his essence to her side where she lay, imprisoned in the Netherworld.

Revived and sent into the modern world by the Nether Gods for their own purposes, Mordred frequently battled Dane Whitman, the descendant of Sir Percy, and his allies, the AVENGERS. **TB**

Morgan Le Fay

FIRST APPEARANCE Spider-Woman Vol. 1 #2 (May 1978)
REAL NAME Morgan (or Morgana) Le Fey
OCCUPATION Sorceress **BASE** The astral plane
HEIGHT 6 ft 2 in **WEIGHT** 140 lbs **EYES** Green **HAIR** Magenta
SPECIAL POWERS/ABILITIES One of the most powerful sorceresses of all time; able to manipulate the natural environment of Earth and the astral plane. She can also fly and shapeshift.

The half-sister of King Arthur PENDRAGON of Camelot, Morgan's father was a member of an ancient magical race that once inhabited Britain. After learning the arts of sorcery, Morgan plotted against King Arthur until MERLIN the Magician magically imprisoned her within Castle Le Fey. Although her body couldn't leave the castle, her astral form was free to travel to various time periods. She once tried to use Jessica Drew, the first SPIDER-WOMAN, to break Merlin's spell and later stole the Twilight sword, a weapon of monumental power, which she used to recreate a distorted version of Camelot where the AVENGERS briefly served as her knights. **TB**

The mutant Morlocks' bizarre physical deformities made it impossible for them to pass as normal humans. They hid away in tunnels below the streets of Manhattan.

Morlocks

FIRST APPEARANCE Uncanny X-Men Vol. 1 #169 (May 1983)
BASE New York City; Kenya
KEY MEMBERS/POWERS **Callisto** (former leader) Strength, agility, senses **Ape** Shapeshifter **Caliban** Strength and speed, projects fear **D'Gard** Empathic ability **Leech** Projects force field **Marrow** Bone growth, recuperation **Masque** Alters features of other beings **Plague** Creates and projects deadly diseases.

The Morlocks were failed experiments by the DARK BEAST who established their own outcast society in the tunnels beneath New York City. The MARAUDERS, organized by the ruthless geneticist MISTER SINISTER, slaughtered many Morlocks in what became known as the Mutant Massacre. Mikhail RASPUTIN, the brother of COLOSSUS, transported most of the survivors to the alternate dimension of "The Hill," where a second generation grew to adulthood. One of their number, named MARROW, founded the terrorist group Gene Nation. Other Morlocks resettled in Africa, where D'Gard led them until Marrow killed him. **DW**

Mother Night

FIRST APPEARANCE Captain America #356 (August 1989)
REAL NAME Susan Scarbo
OCCUPATION Agent of the Red Skull **BASE** Red Skull's chalet
HEIGHT 5 ft 7 in **WEIGHT** 133 lbs **EYES** Green **HAIR** Black
SPECIAL POWERS/ABILITIES Expert hypnotist; could generate illusions, make herself appear to be invisible, and force others to obey her will.

Susan Scarbo and her brother Melvin were stage hypnotists whose ambitions grew beyond show business. They turned to crime, Susan took the name "Suprema," and was enlisted by the RED SKULL. Changing her identity to Mother Night, she took command of the SISTERS OF SIN, formerly led by the Red Skull's daughter Synthia (also known as Sin). In this role, Mother Night battled CAPTAIN AMERICA. When the Red Skull was captured by MAGNETO, Mother Night joined with the Skeleton Crew (Red Skull's main operatives) to try and free him. Mother Night was killed by the Winter Soldier. **MT**

Moy, Dr. Alyssa

FIRST APPEARANCE Fantastic Four #5 (May 1998)
REAL NAME Dr. Alyssa Moy
OCCUPATION Scientist and explorer **BASE** Mobile
HEIGHT 5 ft 9 in **WEIGHT** 129 lbs **EYES** Brown **HAIR** Black
SPECIAL POWERS/ABILITIES A scientific genius on a par with Reed Richards himself, she carries a universal skeleton key and drives a flying car.

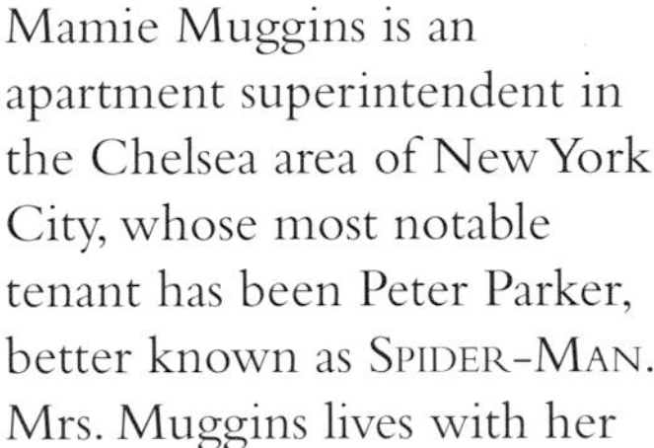

Alyssa Moy knew Reed Richards before he founded the FANTASTIC FOUR. The pair became romantically involved and Reed once even proposed to her. They remained in contact after Reed's cosmic mutation and, in recent years, Alyssa has lent occasional support to the Fantastic Four who returned the favor by curing her of a mystical virus. Things did become a little strained when Sue Richards (INVISIBLE WOMAN) learned of Reed's proposal all those years ago, but Alyssa is likely to remain a Fantastic Four ally for some time. **AD**

Muggins, Mamie

FIRST APPEARANCE Amazing Spider-Man Vol. 1 #139 (December 1974) **REAL NAME** Mamie Muggins
OCCUPATION Landlady **BASE** New York City
HEIGHT 5 ft 7 in **WEIGHT** 140 lbs
EYES Blue **HAIR** White
SPECIAL POWERS/ABILITIES An uncanny ability to sense when the rent is due.

Mamie Muggins is an apartment superintendent in the Chelsea area of New York City, whose most notable tenant has been Peter Parker, better known as SPIDER-MAN. Mrs. Muggins lives with her husband Barney, and was known for nagging Peter over his rent payments, and interrogating him about the crashing sounds she heard coming from his residence. Her niece Candi lived across the hall from Peter, along with Candi's roommates Bambi and Randi. The trio often sunbathed on the building's roof, hampering Peter's ability to sneak in unnoticed through the building's skylight. **DW**

Multiple Man

After his parents died, Jamie Madrox mutant power to duplicate himself ran riot. The Fantastic Four subdued Madrox, and turned him over to PROFESSOR X so he could learn how to control his mutant talent. But Madrox wasn't comfortable around other people, and chose instead to work with Dr. Moira MACTAGGART at her Muir Island complex.

Madrox became a member of X-FACTOR, making the first true friends of his life. After X-Factor was disbanded, Madrox sent his duplicates out into the world to experience all the possibilities life had to offer. Recently, however, he has opened a detective agency, X-Factor Investigations, in the heart of Manhattan's Mutant Town district. **TB**

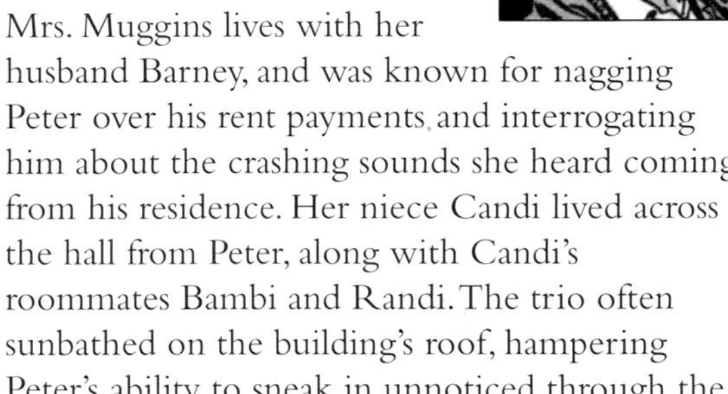

FACTFILE
REAL NAME
Jamie Madrox
OCCUPATION
Detective
BASE
"Mutant Town," New York City

HEIGHT 5 ft 11 in
WEIGHT 155 lbs
EYES Blue
HAIR Brown

FIRST APPEARANCE
Giant-Size Fantastic Four #4 (October 1974)

MULTIPLE MAN

POWERS

Madrox has just one superhuman ability: when struck, he can create duplicates of himself. Each duplicate lasts as long as he wishes and embodies an aspect of his personality. He also has a special suit, which prevents duplication taking place.

Because each of his duplicates is a facet of his personality, Madrox can have problems when he has to make a quick decision.

Uncanny X-Men #125 featured Madrox the Multiple Man and Moira MacTaggart in "The Mystery of Muir Island."

Mutant Liberation Front

FACTFILE

NOTABLE MEMBERS

STRYFE
REIGNFIRE
REAPER
FOREARM
TEMPO
STROBE
THUMBELINA
WILDSIDE
ZERO
SKIDS
RUSTY COLLINS
SUMO
KAMIKAZE
CORPUS DERELICTI
DRAGONESS
MOONSTAR
LOCUS
FERAL
SELBY
BLASTFURNACE
BLINDSPOT
BURNOUT
DEADEYE
THERMAL

FIRST APPEARANCE
New Mutants #86 (February 1990)

In an altered reality in which Egypt was the sole world power, a Mutant Liberation Front led by Magneto joined forces against that world's ruler, the Sphinx.

Mutant Liberation Front

Ostensibly an extremist terrorist cell working forcibly to promote mutant rights, the Mutant Liberation Front most often functioned as the shock troops fighting for the corrupt goals of their various leaders. Initially formed by Stryfe, a clone of Cable from the future, the MLF staged assorted terrorist events which initially brought them into conflict with the New Mutants, and subsequently with Cable's X-Force unit.

When they were of no further use to Stryfe, this incarnation of the MLF was left to its own devices. Reformed by Reignfire, who had been infused with the DNA of the New Mutant Sunspot, and who seemed to be Sunspot himself. Again, the MLF clashed repeatedly with X-Force, and eventually they were defeated and the truth of Reignfire's identity was exposed.

The third incarnation of the MLF wasn't composed of mutants, but of humans in armored costumes who posed as mutants so as to increase tensions between humans and mutants. Based at the Last Stand compound of the right wing group Friends of Humanity in Oklahoma, the MLF were later destroyed by the Punisher and SHIELD. **TB**

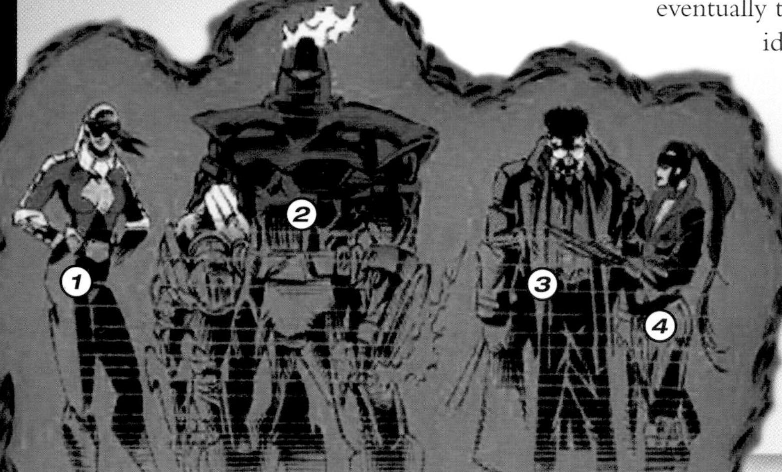

THE MLF (3RD VERSION)
1 Blindspot
2 Blastfurnace
3 Corpus Derelicti
4 Burnout

Mutant X

FACTFILE

MEMBERS AND POWERS

HAVOK (Alex Summers)
Projects concussive force and heat.
BLOODSTORM (Ororo Munroe)
Vampiric powers, controls the weather.
BRUTE (Hank McCoy)
Superhuman strength and agility.
FALLEN (Warren Worthington III)
Has wings enabling flight.
ICE-MAN (Bob Drake)
Generates intense cold.
MARVEL WOMAN (Madelyne Pryor)
Telekinetic powers.

FIRST APPEARANCE
Mutant X #1 (October 1998)

Mutant X

Alex Summers, alias the Super Hero Havok, a former X-Man on "mainstream" Earth (Earth-616), was seemingly killed in an explosion. At the same time on the Earth of an alternate reality (Earth-1298), its own Havok was brutally killed by a Sentinel robot. The spirit of the Havok of Earth-616 took possession of the body of the Havok of Earth-1298 and thus returned to physical life.

In this "Mutant X" universe Havok became the leader of a mutant team called the Six, who were counterparts of various members of the X-Men.

Eventually, the Havok of Earth-616 returned to physical existence on his native Earth. **PS**

Mutant X #1: The Six battle the Sentinels.

Madelyne Pryor, founder of the Six, along with Havok, in her Goblyn Queen persona.

THE SIX OF MUTANT X UNIVERSE
1 Bloodstorm ***2*** Ice-Man ***3*** Nick Fury of Earth-1298 ***4*** Brute ***5*** Havok, alias Mutant X ***6*** SHIELD agent of Earth-1298

MYS-TECH BOARD

FACTFILE

CURRENT MEMBERS AND POWERS
(All board members possess immortality)
ALGERNON CROWE
BRONWEN GRYFFN
RANULPH HALDANE (deceased)
PORLOCK
RATHCOOLE
GUDRUN TYBURN
ORMOND WYCHWOOD

BASE
London, England

FIRST APPEARANCE
Warheads #1 (June 1992)

Mys-Tech Board

In the year 987, seven members of a Druid cult made a bargain with the demon Mephisto: in exchange for immortality, they agreed to funnel souls into Mephisto's realm. Over the subsequent millennium, the mages acquired great wealth and became the board members of a London-based corporation named Mys-Tech. To pay their debt to Mephisto, the Mys-Tech board plotted to take over the world and kill vast numbers of innocents. Their assets included the Un-Earth, a model of the planet that operated like a voodoo doll, and the Warheads, mercenaries who could travel through wormholes to other dimensions or times. The board members eventually transformed themselves into beings of even greater power known as the Techno-Wizards. **AD**

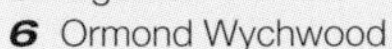

MYS-TECH BOARD
1 Porlock
2 Rathcoole
3 Bronwen Gryffn
4 Godrun Tyburn
5 Algernon Crowe
6 Ormond Wychwood

Mysterio

FIRST APPEARANCE Amazing Spider-Man #13 (June 1964)
REAL NAME Quentin Beck
OCCUPATION Criminal **BASE** New York City
HEIGHT 5 ft 11 in **WEIGHT** 175 lbs **EYES** Blue **HAIR** Black
SPECIAL POWERS/ABILITIES Extraordinary skill in devising special effects and stage illusions, master hypnotist, uses holograms, robots, and hallucinogens.

Quentin Beck began his Hollywood career as a stuntman, but rapidly became a leading special effects designer. Ambitious for fame, Beck created the costumed identity of Mysterio. Using illusions to confound Spider-Man, Mysterio became one of his greatest foes, operating both on his own and as a member of the Sinister Six. Mysterio devised an elaborate scheme to drive Daredevil insane. When it failed, Beck apparently killed himself. He was seemingly succeeded by Daniel Berkhart, then Francis Klum acquired Mysterio's costume and equipment. **PS**

Mystique

Mystique learned to use her mutant shape-shifting powers at a very early age. She quickly established her human Raven Darkhölme identity. She hid her powers and evil intentions so well that, as Darkhölme, she rose to a position of great power within the US Defense Department, giving her access to military secrets and advanced weaponry which she used for her own criminal purposes.

As Mystique, she organized the second Brotherhood of Evil Mutants, teaming with Avalanche, the Blob, Destiny, and Pyro. The Brotherhood attempted to assassinate Senator Robert Kelly, a vocal enemy of all mutants. The X-Men stopped the assassination attempt, in the first of many clashes between the Brotherhood and the X-Men. The Brotherhood later changed its name to Freedom Force, giving up its criminal activity, and began working for the US government. **MT**

Moving with lightning-quick reflexes, Mystique narrowly avoids the path of a guided missile!

MYSTIQUE

FACTFILE

REAL NAME
Raven Darkhölme

OCCUPATION
Deputy Director, Defense Advanced Research Planning Agency, US Defense Department.

BASE
The Pentagon, Washington DC

HEIGHT 5 ft 10 in
WEIGHT 120 lbs
EYES Yellow
HAIR Red-orange

FIRST APPEARANCE
Ms. Marvel #16 (April 1978)

POWERS
A mutant shape-shifter who can make herself look like any human, humanoid, or semi-humanoid being, male or female, copying every detail including retina, fingerprints, and voice pattern.

MARVEL IN THE 1980s

Extended storylines and limited series were in vogue in the 1980s. The decade began with "The Dark Phoenix Saga" in *X-Men* and the first titles to star Moon Knight and She-Hulk. *Ka-Zar the Savage*, *Dazzler* and "The Court Martial of Yellowjacket" in *Avengers* took center stage in 1981. In 1982, Hercules, Vision and Scarlet Witch and Wolverine were all had limited series and "The Mystery of the Hobgoblin" began in *Amazing Spider-Man*. "The Trial of Reed Richards" in *Fantastic Four* and new series featuring Alpha Flight, Falcon, Hawkeye, the Thing and the New Mutants began in 1983. *Jack of Hearts*, *Iceman*, *Prince Namor*, *Power Pack* and *West Coast Avengers* appeared in 1984, as did *Secret Wars*, a 12-issue series that crossed over many other Marvel titles. *Balder the Brave*, *Gargoyle*, *Longshot*, *Nightcrawler* and *Squadron Supreme* were highlights of 1985. Along with *X-Factor*, *Firestar* and *Elektra: Assassin*, the New Universe was launched in 1986 with six titles including *Justice*, *Kickers, Inc.*, and *Spitfire and the Troubleshooters*. Spider-Man was married in 1987, and 1988 saw the first appearances of Excalibur, Speedball and Wolfpack. Damage Control, Nth Man: the Ultimate Ninja and Quasar were all introduced in 1989.

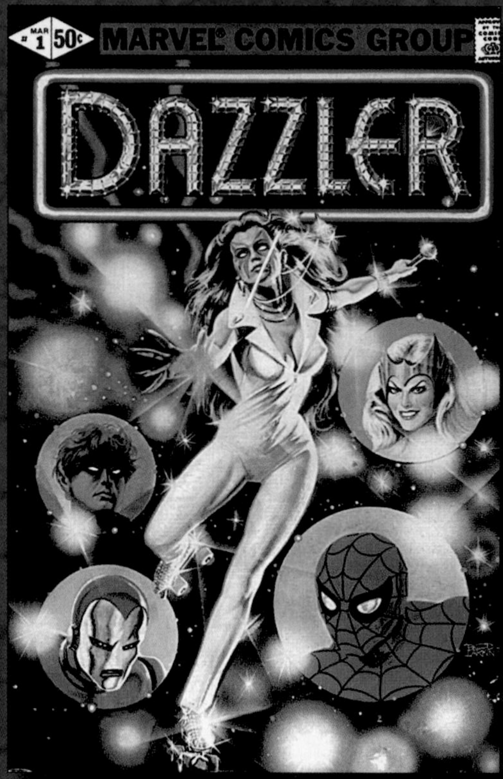

DAZZLER #1 (1981)
Dazzler's first issue is the first monthly Marvel title that is sold exclusively through comic book specialty stores.

CAPTAIN AMERICA #255 (1981),
Marvel celebrates the 40th Anniversary of Cap's first appearance by revealing never-before-seen facts about his origin.

DAREDEVIL #181 (1982)
Daredevil's first true love challenges his greatest enemy to a battle that ends in her death. (But don't worry—*she eventually gets better!*)

THE AVENGERS #236 (1983)
The Amazing Spider-Man temporarily joins Earth's Mightiest Heroes.

THOR #337 (1983)
The Thunder God learns that he isn't the only one worthy enough to lift his magic hammer in the first chapter of "The Saga of Beta Ray Bill."

Contest of Champions #1 (1981)

Marvel's first crossover series featured its most popular Super Heroes battling for their lives.

The Death of Captain Marvel (1982)

Marvel launches its first all-original graphic novel with a story that shows a hero and his final battle with cancer.

Amazing Spider-Man #252 (1984)

Spider-Man returns from the Secret Wars with a new costume, which is later revealed to be an alien symbiote.

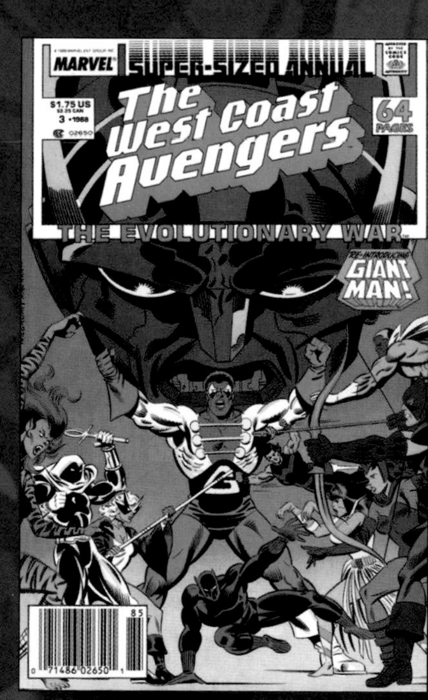

The West Coast Avengers Annual #3 (1988)

Giant-Man guest-stars when the High Evolutionary decides to genetically jumpstart the human race in a storyline that crosses into other Avengers-related annuals.

Wolverine Vol. 2 #1 (1988)

After a very successful limited series, Marvel's most popular mutant is finally awarded his own

Nth Command

FACTFILE

KEY MEMBERS

HENRY AKAI
As Timestream, he can travel forward or backward in time.

ALBERT DEVOOR
Director of the Nth Project.

ABNER DOOLITTLE
Scientist who designed the dimensional transporter.

DR. T.W. ERWIN
Mathematician famous for his theories of parallel time.

GODWULF
Cybernetic technology allows him to link with computers.

DR. THOMAS LIGHTNER
Magical abilities, on par with Dr. Strange.

BENNETT PITTMAN
Was in charge of Roxxon's extra-dimensional oil drilling facilities.

ANGLER
Passes through solid material, teleports, travels through hyper-space.

DEATHLOK THE DEMOLISHER
Superhuman strength, agility.

FIRST APPEARANCE
Marvel Two-In-One March #53 (July 1979)

Nth Command was formed by the Roxxon Corporation to gain total control of the world's energy supply. This was done by operatives, known as Nth Commandoes, using devices called Nth projectors, that could transport material from one dimension to another. The sorcerer, Thomas Lightner, was hired to destroy Project Pegasus, so that the Nth Command could gain a monopoly on energy research. Lightner took control of the time-traveling cyborg, DEATHLOK, removed his organic parts, then reprogrammed him to serve Nth Command. Breaking into Project Pegasus with Deathlok, Lightner hoped to use an Nth projector to transport the entire facility to another dimension. He was stopped by the THING, QUASAR, GIANT-MAN, THUNDRA, and the AQUARIAN. **MT**

THE WORLD AWAITS.

Albert DeVoor, Director of the Nth Project, addresses the Nth Commandoes.

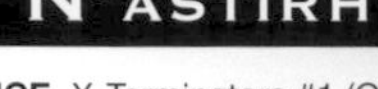

N'astirh

FIRST APPEARANCE X-Terminators #1 (October 1988)
REAL NAME N'astirh
OCCUPATION Conqueror, sorcerer **BASE** Washington, D.C.
HEIGHT/WEIGHT Variable **EYES** Red **HAIR** Greenish
SPECIAL POWERS/ABILITIES Able to turn humans into demons, fly and change size; considerable mystical abilities; knowledge of a vast number of magical spells.

N'astirh by name, nasty by nature—that's what they said about this demon from the Limbo dimension. Angered when Limbo's ruler made the human mutant, MAGIK, his apprentice, N'astirh felt compelled to rebel, and when a plan was hatched to take over the Earth, N'astirh usurped the scheme so that he could rule the Earth.

His efforts were foiled by Magik, however N'astirh made a second attempt to become a world conqueror by transforming Madelyne PRYOR into the Goblin Queen. Eventually, the X-MEN destroyed him, and Madelyne Pryor died not long after, proving that no bad deed goes unpunished. **AD**

NAMOR *SEE OPPOSITE PAGE*

Namora

FACTFILE

REAL NAME
Namora

OCCUPATION
Queen of Atlantis, ruler of Earth

BASE
An alternate Earth

HEIGHT 5 ft 7 in
WEIGHT 145 lbs
EYES Blue
HAIR Black

FIRST APPEARANCE:
Exiles #46 (July 2004)

POWERS
Namora had superhuman strength and durability and could breathe in air or underwater.

The Namora of "mainstream" Marvel Earth (Earth-616) was the cousin of Prince NAMOR the Sub-Mariner. Her mother was a surface human and her father an ATLANTEAN.

Like Namor she had pink skin and possessed similar powers. She is considered the "mother" of NAMORITA, who is her genetically altered clone. Namora was murdered by LLYRA of Lemuria.

Another Namora is a parallel Earth's female counterpart of Namor, but had blue skin. As queen of Atlantis, she conquered this alternate Earth before joining the EXILES, a team of interdimensional adventurers. She was finally slain by the Exiles' version of Hyperion. **PS**

Wings on Namora's heels enabled her to fly.

The original Namora married an Atlantean named Talan. After Talan was accidentally killed, Namora moved to Lemuria and married Prince Merro.

Unlike Namor, the Exiles' Namora had two water-breathing Atlantean parents. In conquering the surface world, Namora killed her alternate Earth's Avengers and Fantastic Four.

NAMOR

Ruler of the undersea realm of Atlantis

Occasionally Namor helps protect the surface world but his priority is the welfare of the people of Atlantis.

Prince Namor is the mutant son of a blue-skinned Atlantean princess and an American sea captain. He was raised in the underwater kingdom of Atlantis and grew up hating all surface dwellers. During World War II, Namor briefly sided with the Allies against the Axis Powers and joined the super-teams known as the INVADERS and the Liberty Legion.

After repeatedly battling the Fantastic Four, Namor eventually made peace with them and is now their greatest ally.

FACTFILE

REAL NAME
Prince Namor, aka Namor McKenzie, aka the Sub-Mariner

OCCUPATION
Lord of Atlantis, CEO of Oracle, Inc.

BASE Atlantis

HEIGHT 6 ft 2 in
WEIGHT 278 lbs
EYES Blue-gray
HAIR Black

FIRST APPEARANCE
Motion Picture Funnies Weekly #1 (1939)

NAMOR

POWERS

Super-strength, stamina and durability (these traits decline the more time he spends out of water). Amphibious; can swim underwater at 60 mph; can see clearly in the ocean depths. Telepathic rapport with marine life and can duplicate many of their abilities; wings on ankles enable flight; long-lived.

THE ALL-WINNER

After the war, Namor became a member of the ALL-WINNERS SQUAD, but returned to Atlantis when the Squad disbanded in 1949. He returned to the surface world in the late 1950s where he encountered a man called DESTINY who removed his memory and sent him to New York where he lived as a derelict. His memory was restored by Johnny Storm, the HUMAN TORCH, but Namor turned against the human race when he learned that the city of Atlantis had been destroyed in his absence. During his first battle with the FANTASTIC FOUR, Namor fell in love with the INVISIBLE WOMAN (who was called the Invisible Girl at the time) and offered to spare mankind if she became his bride. He later attempted to win her by buying a movie studio and offering the Fantastic Four a million dollars to star in a major motion picture when they briefly ran short of funds.

While traveling in the arctic, Namor once stumbled upon a tribe of Eskimos who were worshiping a figure frozen in ice. In a fury, Namor hurled the figure into the sea. The ice melted to reveal CAPTAIN AMERICA, who was later picked up and revived by the AVENGERS.

Namor became smitten with Sue Storm, but gallantly stepped aside once she decided to marry Reed Richards.

TRAGIC LOVES

Namor eventually fell in love and married the Lady Dorma, but she was later murdered by one of his enemies on their wedding day. His second wife MARRINA, a member of another undersea race, died after being transformed into a monstrous creature.

After occasionally battling the Avengers, Namor made peace with them and even became a member of the team. He used the vast riches of the sea to form Oracle, Inc., a company that he uses to fight the pollution caused by major corporations around the world. TD

ESSENTIAL STORYLINES
- ***Fantastic Four #4*** Namor regains his memory and declares war on the surface world.
- ***Fantastic Four Annual #1*** Namor is reunited with the kingdom of Atlantis and invades New York City.
- ***Tales To Astonish #70-76*** Namor seeks the sacred trident of Neptune and proves that he is worthy to rule Atlantis.
- ***Marvel Feature #1*** Helps form the Defenders.
- ***Avengers #262*** Namor joins the Avengers.

Namorita

FACTFILE
REAL NAME
Namorita Neptunia
(a.k.a. Namorita Prentiss)
OCCUPATION
College student
BASE
New York City

HEIGHT 5 ft 6 in
WEIGHT 225 lbs
EYES Blue
HAIR Blonde

FIRST APPEARANCE
Sub-Mariner vol. 1 #50 (June 1972)

POWERS

Namorita is amphibious: able to survive on land and in the sea; power of flight; her hands exude a paralyzing toxin; chameleon-like ability to camouflage herself.

Half-human, half-Atlantean, Namorita was a clone of her mother, Namora, although she was an adult before she discovered this fact. Orphaned when she was still a child, Namorita was watched over by NAMOR the Sub-Mariner and his friend Betty Prentiss. It was their love and support that carried Namorita through the tragic and traumatic loss of her mother. When she became an adult, they also helped and encouraged her to attend a US college.

An Atlantean in a human world, the New Warriors helped Namorita stave off isolation.

Not long after starting college, Namorita became a founder member of the NEW WARRIORS, a team of young Super Heroes, with whom she fought against the HELLIONS, PROTEUS and TERRAX. The group provided Namorita with a certain amount of security and stability, but not all her time with them was happy: her first attempt to lead the team resulted in the kidnap of many team members' families. They were eventually rescued and Namorita has continued as an active team member. **AD**

Nebula

FIRST APPEARANCE Avengers #257 (July 1985)
REAL NAME Nebula
OCCUPATION Space pirate **BASE** Various throughout galaxy
HEIGHT/WEIGHT Unrevealed **EYES** Blue **HAIR** Black
SPECIAL POWERS/ABILITIES Nebula's cybernetic components provide her with enhanced strength and durability, and a number of built-in weapons.

Claiming to be the grand-daughter of the mad Titan THANOS, Nebula embarked on a career as a space pirate, hijacking Thanos' old flagship *Sanctuary II* and attempting to conquer the fragmented SKRULL Empire. Her ambitions were thwarted by the AVENGERS, but not before she inflicted catastrophic damage upon the planet Xandar. When Thanos was reborn, he denied any relationship to Nebula, who nevertheless almost succeeded in wresting the omnipotent Infinity Gauntlet away from him. She then attacked NOVA, claiming that her father had been Zorr, a menace destroyed by the hero's predecessor, Nova Prime. Nebula's identity was also adopted for a time by RAVONNA the Terminatrix. **TB**

Nekra

FIRST APPEARANCE Shanna the She-Devil #5 (August 1973)
REAL NAME Nekra Sinclair
OCCUPATION Subversive, cult priestess **BASE** Mobile
HEIGHT 5 ft 11 in **WEIGHT** 140 lbs **EYES** Black **HAIR** Black
SPECIAL POWERS/ABILITIES Mutant whose feelings of hatred for the world and humanity in general endow her with superhuman strength, agility, and durability.

Gemma Sinclair and Frederick Beechman were accidentally exposed to radiation at the Los Alamos Atomic Proving Grounds. As a result, Gemma's daughter Nekra was born a mutant with chalk-white skin. An outcast, she teamed up with Beechman's mutant son Jerome, who had apelike features. As they grew older, they discovered their superhuman powers. As Nekra and the MANDRILL, they attempted to conquer three African nations and later the United States.

Nekra became leader of a fanatical religious cult. Afterwards, she became the ally of the Avengers' foe, the GRIM REAPER. He killed her, but she was resurrected by HELLSTORM. **PS**

Nelson, Foggy

Legal student Foggy Nelson roomed with Matt Murdock at Columbia University and Harvard Law School, never suspecting that Murdock possessed the superhuman powers of Daredevil. After graduation, the two friends opened Nelson & Murdock, and hired a secretary, Karen Page. Although Nelson pursued Page romantically, he also maintained a relationship with his old girlfriend Deborah Harris. Nelson won the election for New York City District Attorney, failed in his bid for reelection, and briefly opened Storefront Legal Services before reestablishing Nelson & Murdock.

Nelson and Deborah Harris married but soon divorced, and the Nelson & Murdock partnership came to an end when the Kingpin learned that Murdock was secretly Daredevil. Nelson took a position with Kelco Industrials, resigning when it became clear that Kelco was in the Kingpin's pocket. Nelson later believed Murdock dead as part of a faked scheme, and subsequently learned Murdock's secret identity. The two have since reconciled and reopened their law firm, specializing in superhuman clients. DW

THREE PEOPLE! A BLIND MAN--A GIRL--BUT, THE THIRD--!

THAT HAS TO BE-- HIM!

Foggy's law practice has put him on first-name terms with many Super Heroes.

FACTFILE

REAL NAME
Franklin P. Nelson

OCCUPATION
Lawyer, former District Attorney

BASE
New York City

HEIGHT 5 ft 10 in
WEIGHT 220 lbs
EYES Blue
HAIR Brown

FIRST APPEARANCE
Daredevil Vol. 1 #1 (April 1964)

NELSON, FOGGY

POWERS

Foggy has a brilliant legal mind and is a skilled debater. He is honest and loyal to his friends, particularly Matt Murdock, and usually good at keeping secrets.

New Mutants

Believing that his X-Men were dead, Charles Xavier (see Professor X) felt he had no choice but to begin again from scratch, and so his New Mutants were formed. A group of adolescents, they were charged with mastering their own powers at the same time as learning about themselves and fighting for Professor X's cause of mutant-hero harmony. Life as a New Mutant was not always easy—some members died in action—but for the most part it was rewarding. Following their graduation from Xavier's school, the New Mutants remained together to form X-Force, with some of them also becoming teachers at the Institute.

Noriko Ashida—Surge—belonged to the second New Mutants team.

More New Mutants

With his school expanding, Professor X decided to divide his students into squads. The New Mutants was one of these teams and was placed under the tutelage of Danielle Moonstar. The lineup was Prodigy (absorbs skills and knowledge from those nearby); Wind Dancer (creates winds upon which she is able to fly); Wallflower (pheromone release causes others to match her mood); Elixir (heals herself and others); Surge (projects electricity in power blasts or uses it to accelerate to superspeeds); and Icarus (flies on angel-like wings, healing ability, mimics sounds). Competition between these squads became as significant as their battles against more malevolent forces. AD

FACTFILE

ORIGINAL MEMBERS

CANNONBALL
Invulnerable in flight.

WOLFSBANE
Transforms into a wolf.

PSYCHE
Creates illusions representing the fears and desires of others.

KARMA
Possesses the minds of others.

SUNSPOT
Sunlight lends her superhuman strength.

BASE
Xavier School for Gifted Youngsters, New York State

FIRST APPEARANCE
Marvel Graphic Novel #4 (1982)

NEW MUTANTS

NEW MUTANTS II
1 Psyche
2 Wolfsbane
3 Magma
4 Cannonball
5 Karma
6 Sunspot

FACTFILE

ORIGINAL MEMBERS

NIGHT THRASHER
Master of martial arts; creator of various technological devices.

NOVA
Strength; resistance to injury; flight.

MARVEL BOY
Flight; the projection of blinding light; telepathy; superstrength.

FIRESTAR
Generates and manipulates microwaves.

NAMORITA
An amphibious flying girl.

SPEEDBALL
Surrounds himself with "bouncy" forcefield; travels within it.

BASE
New York City

FIRST APPEARANCE:
Thor #411
(December 1989)

New Warriors

After battling Galactus' herald, Terrax, the New Warriors officially came into being.

When his first vigilante partnership ended with the apparent death of the Super Hero Silhouette, Night Thrasher refused to hang up his costume. Envious of the Fantastic Four, Night Thrasher sought to establish his own quartet of heroes, bullying and cajoling Nova, Marvel Boy and Firestar to join. When the Super Heroes Namorita and Speedball leant their support during a battle against Galactus' former herald, Terrax, this foursome became a sextet and the New Warriors was established.

From their base at Night Thrasher's New York penthouse suite, the New Warriors were to fight against and alongside Psionex, and to battle the White Queen (*see* Frost, Emma) and her Hellions, as well as the mutant Proteus. Over the years the team lineup has undergone regular changes and as its members became adults it has become a part-time outfit. Despite this, when the team is together it continues to be a force to be reckoned with. The current lineup consists of Namorita, Night Thrasher, Nova, and Speedball. **AD**

CHARACTER KEY
1 Speedball ***2*** Night Thrasher ***3*** Namorita ***4*** Microbe ***5*** Nova

N'Garai

FIRST APPEARANCE Uncanny X-Men #96 (December 1975)
BASE The extra-dimensional "Realm of the N'Garai"
SPECIAL POWERS/ABILITES Super-strong, bloodthirsty demon race; immune to aging, disease; deadly poisonous fangs and claws; leathery skin; some have wings; leaders have greater intelligence.

In the timeless past, the Elder God Chthon created the race of demons called the N'Garai, and their ruler, Kierrok. Ages ago, the N'Garai returned to our dimension and for a period ruled the Earth, before being driven back and trapped within their extra-dimensional realm. Since then, they have been released onto the Earth again when one of the mystic cairns that seal the passageway to their native dimension is disturbed. These cairns are located ouside Salem Center in New York and on Magneto's island in the Bermuda Triangle. They have frequently been combated by the X-Men, as well as Doctor Strange and the Hulk. Several demonic sorcerers have called upon the N'Garai, including Belasco and Kulan Gath. **TB**

Nightcrawler
SEE OPPOSITE PAGE

Nighthawk

Kyle Richmond was a wealthy playboy who discovered he had a weak heart and took an experimental potion that dramatically increased his strength and reflexes, but only worked at night. Recruited into the Squadron Sinister by the Grandmaster, he later gave up crime and joined the Defenders until an explosion left him in a coma. He recovered and rejoined the Defenders.

On one alternate world, his adopted son Neil eventually took over his identity and became the new Nighthawk. On another alternate world, Kyle Richmond is an African-American entrepreneur who lost his parents to a hate crime and uses high-tech weaponry, stealth and fighting prowess to get revenge on criminals. **TD/MT**

ULTIMATE SERIES NIGHTHAWK
1 Valkyrie ***2*** Power Man
3 Nighthawk ***4*** Giant-Man
5 Son of Satan ***6*** Hellcat

FACTFILE

REAL NAME
Kyle Richmond

OCCUPATION
Former president of Richmond Enterprises, adventurer

BASE
New York City, Richmond Riding Academy, Long Island

HEIGHT 5 ft 11 in
WEIGHT 180 lbs
EYES Brown
HAIR Red-brown

FIRST APPEARANCE
AVENGERS #71
(December 1971)

POWERS
Nighthawk's powers of superhuman strength, increased endurance, and speedy reaction time only emerge at night.

NIGHTCRAWLER

Demonic face of the X-Men

Although Nightcrawler looks like a demon, he is actually a deeply religious Catholic who studied for the priesthood.

Kurt Wagner is the son of AZAZEL, a mutant who resembles a demon, and the shapeshifting mutant MYSTIQUE. When Kurt was born in Bavaria, Mystique posed as an ordinary human and married a German baron, Eric Wagner. The local populace was horrified by newborn Kurt's demonic appearance: he had pointed ears, three fingers on each hand, two toes on each foot, and a tail. Pursued by a mob, Mystique threw the infant down a waterfall.

CIRCUS FREAK

Azazel saved the baby, who was raised by gypsy sorceress Margali Szardos. Kurt grew up in a Bavarian circus where Szardos was a fortuneteller. The circus performers accepted Kurt as part of their family. His best friend was Szardos's son Stefan, and Kurt fell in love with her daughter Jimaine. With his great agility, Wagner became the circus's star acrobat and trapeze performer. Audiences assumed that his inhuman appearance was merely a costume.

However, when Texas millionaire Amos Jardine bought the circus, he insisted that Wagner be exhibited as a freak. Outraged, Wagner quit the circus. Two nights later he battled Szardos's son Stefan, who had become a serial killer, and accidentally killed him.

Charles Xavier of the X-Men arrives just in time to save Nightcrawler from a lynch mob.

Nightcrawler briefly used an image inducer to make himself look like a normal person.

Believing Wagner was a demon and responsible for the murders, a mob would have killed Wagner, but Charles Xavier (*see* PROFESSOR X) arrived and immobilized the crowd with his telepathic powers. Xavier recruited Wagner into his second team of X-MEN, based in the US, Wagner taking the name "Nightcrawler." In America he was reunited with Jimaine, now calling herself Amanda Sefton, and was reconciled with Margali Szardos, who had blamed him for Stefan's death.

After serving in the X-Men for years, Nightcrawler became a founding member of the British-based team EXCALIBUR. He returned to the X-Men briefly, then left again to study to become a priest. However, he was never ordained and returned to the X-Men.

Nightcrawler has since learned the identities of his parents, and discovered that Mystique's foster daughter ROGUE is his foster sister. He has also met his half-brothers Nils Styger, alias Abyss, and Kiwi Black. With them, Nightcrawler defeated Azazel, who had tried to use him as a pawn in conquering Earth. **PS**

Nightcrawler appears out of nowhere in a puff of smoke

FACTFILE

REAL NAME
Kurt Wagner

OCCUPATION
Adventurer

BASE
The Xavier Institute, Salem Center, New York State

HEIGHT 5 ft 9 in
WEIGHT 195 lbs
EYES Yellow, no visible pupils
HAIR Indigo

FIRST APPEARANCE
Giant-Size X-Men #1 (May 1975)

POWERS

Mutant power to teleport himself, his clothing, and a limited amount of additional mass, by traveling through another dimension. When he teleports, part of the atmosphere of that dimension escapes onto Earth, accompanied by a "bamf" sound and the smell of brimstone.

ESSENTIAL STORYLINES
- ***X-Men Vol. 1 Annual #4***
Margali Szardos seeks vengeance on Nightcrawler for killing her son.
- ***Nightcrawler #1-4***
Nightcrawler journeys through various dimensions in a quest to return to earth.
- ***X-Men Unlimited Vol. 1 #4***
Nightcrawler learns that Mystique is his mother.
- ***X-Men: Days of Future Past, tpb***
Turns the spotlight on Nightcrawler's interesting origins.

Nightmare

FIRST APPEARANCE Strange Tales #110 (July 1963)
REAL NAME Unknown **OCCUPATION** Ruler of the Nightmare World **BASE** The Nightmare world within the Dream Dimension
HEIGHT/WEIGHT Variable **EYES** Black **HAIR** Black
SPECIAL POWERS/ABILITIES A demon who draws power from the psychic energies of the subconscious minds of dreaming sentient beings; can draw the life energy from sleeping people, leaving then in comas; manipulates the substance of the Dream Dimension.

Nightmare, who has battled Doctor Strange, is the ruler of the Nightmare World within the Dimension of Dreams, where the life essence of humans is brought while they sleep. Nightmare monitors the collective unconscious of humans, and can manipulate the dreams of an individual, giving them nightmares, to gain control of that person. Nightmare is a creation of the human need to dream; if humans did not have this need, or if all humans vanished, Nightmare would cease to exist. His ultimate goal is to incorporate the waking world into his own domain. **MT**

Night Thrasher

FIRST APPEARANCE Thor #411 (December 1989)
REAL NAME Dwayne Michael Taylor **OCCUPATION** Crime-fighter
BASE Ambrose Building and a former factory in New York City.
HEIGHT 6 ft 3 in **WEIGHT** 220 lbs **EYES** Brown **HAIR** Black
SPECIAL POWERS/ABILITIES Weapons in battle-suit include truncheons, aerosols, a pneumatically-fired piton-line and an Uzi submachine gun. Fiberglass skateboard doubles as a shield.

After his wealthy parents were murdered, Dwayne Taylor grew up determined to fight crime. Encouraged by his guardians Chord and Tai, he gathered and funded a group of heroes whom he named the New Warriors. But it emerged that Tai was really a sorceress from Kampuchea, who planned to sacrifice the New Warriors to gain control of a breach into a mystical dimension called the Well of All Things, and thus rule the world. Night Thrasher traveled to Kampuchea and helped destroy the Well. On his return, he continued to serve with the New Warriors as well as running the Taylor Foundation. **TD**

Nocturne

FIRST APPEARANCE Exiles #1 (August 2001)
REAL NAME Talia Josephine Wagner
OCCUPATION Adventurer **BASE** England
HEIGHT 5 ft 7 in **WEIGHT** 125 lbs **EYES** Yellow **HAIR** Indigo
SPECIAL POWERS/ABILITIES Nocturne can inhabit the body of another person and remain in control of it for one lunar cycle. She can also fire blasts of energy, and possesses a prehensile tail.

The daughter of Nightcrawler and the Scarlet Witch in a parallel reality, Nocturne became "unstuck in time" and was the first recruit to the interdimensional team of reality-fixers, the Exiles. She was close to her fellow Exile Thunderbird, and was devastated when he was slain. After a mission to the prime reality in which she met our world's version of her father, Nocturne opted to remain here. She infiltrated the Brotherhood of Evil Mutants as a double agent for the X-Men, but was captured by Mojo. Freed by the X-Men, Nocturne accompanied her father to the UK, where she joined Captain Britain's Excalibur team. **TB**

Nightshade

FIRST APPEARANCE Captain America #164 (August 1973)
REAL NAME Tilda Johnson
OCCUPATION Criminal mastermind **BASE** New York City
HEIGHT 5 ft 4 in **WEIGHT** 115 lbs **EYES** Brown **HAIR** Black
SPECIAL POWERS/ABILITIES A fair athlete and accomplished street fighter; brilliant scientist and inventor; in the past has created mind-controlling chemicals and lifelike robots.

A child prodigy growing up in an poor Harlem neighbourhood, Tilda Johnson developed a sophisticated understanding of physics, genetics and cybernetics. However she hid her brilliance behind a veneer of childish behaviour. Determined never to experience poverty again, Tilda saw crime as a way to get rich quick and assumed the name Nightshade. Using various chemicals to control others, she rose to a prominent position in New York's underworld but drew the attention of Power Man and Iron Fist. Their repeated interventions eventually led to an extended prison sentence. **AD**

Nitro

FIRST APPEARANCE Captain Marvel Vol. 1 #34 (September 1974)
REAL NAME Robert Hunter
OCCUPATION Professional criminal **BASE** Mobile
HEIGHT 6 ft 3 in **WEIGHT** 235 lbs **EYES** Blue **HAIR** White
SPECIAL POWERS/ABILITIES Can explode his body, or any part of his body, and reconstitute himself at will. Cannot reintegrate if any of his molecules become separated from the rest.

Nitro is the result of experiments by the renegade Kree scientists of the Lunatic Legion, who took electrical engineer Robert Hunter and transformed him into a near-indestructible being able to explode and reassemble his molecules. He can explode either his whole body or any part of it. On an early criminal mission, Nitro exposed Captain Mar-Vell to nerve gas, giving the hero the cancer that later killed him. Nitro is only able to reconstitute himself if all his molecules are present. He can be stopped by trapping a portion of his molecules in an airtight container while he is in an exploded state, thereby preventing his body from reintegrating. **DW**

Nomad

FIRST APPEARANCE Captain America Vol. 1 #282 (June 1983)
REAL NAME Jack Monroe
OCCUPATION Adventurer **BASE** Mobile
HEIGHT 5 ft 11 in **WEIGHT** 200 lbs
EYES Brown **HAIR** Brown
SPECIAL POWERS/ABILITIES Physical perfection through the super-soldier formula; skilled at throwing stun discs.

During the 1950s, young Jack Monroe became the "Bucky" sidekick of the replacement Captain America active during that period. The two battled Communists until the super soldier formula affected their sanity; the US government then placed Monroe in suspended animation. SHIELD helped cure Monroe's madness upon his reawakening decades later, and he worked with the real Captain America as Nomad. Later, government agent Henry Gyrich placed Nomad under nanobot control and forced him to become the newest Scourge of the Underworld. The mysterious Winter Soldier recently assassinated Nomad. **DW**

North, Dakota

FIRST APPEARANCE Dakota North #1 (June 1986)
REAL NAME Dakota North
OCCUPATION Private investigator; former fashion model
BASE Mobile **HEIGHT** 5 ft 7 in **WEIGHT** 130 lbs
EYES Blue-gray **HAIR** Auburn
SPECIAL POWERS/ABILITIES Adept hand-to-hand combatant and skilled gymnast; accomplished with various firearms.

The daughter of a US intelligence agent, Dakota North pursued a career as a model before establishing a highly successful private investigation firm named North Security. Boasting branch offices across the globe, North Security rapidly gained a formidable reputation, taking on a multitude of cases that ranged from the mundane to the outright dangerous.

During one particularly difficult case, an international arms dealer who was attempting to gain possession of an experimental nerve gas pursued Dakota across Europe. However Dakota survived this encounter and her organization is still thought to be going strong. AD

Northstar

FIRST APPEARANCE Uncanny X-Men Vol. 1 #120 (April 1979)
REAL NAME Jean-Paul Baubier
OCCUPATION Member of Alpha Flight
BASE Tamarind Island, British Columbia, Canada
HEIGHT 5 ft 11 in **WEIGHT** 185 lbs **EYES** Blue **HAIR** Black
SPECIAL POWERS/ABILITIES Can redirect the kinetic motion of his body's molecules, giving him flight and superspeed.

Jean-Paul and his twin sister Jeanne-Marie (Aurora) were adopted separately. Jean-Paul joined a terrorist group and became a champion skier, then joined Alpha Flight as Northstar. One of the first Super Heroes to come out as gay, he later joined the X-Men. He was killed by a HYDRA-brainwashed Wolverine and resurrected as a HYDRA drone. Northstar then attacked the SHIELD helicarrier but was taken into custody. Recent manipulations of the timestream have created duplicates of Northstar and the other original Alpha Flight members. DW

Nova

High school student Rider became cosmic adventurer Nova.

Rhomann Dey was a Centurion of the Nova Corps, the space militia of the alien Xandarians. Mortally wounded, Dey transferred his powers to a student, Richard Rider. As Nova, Rider became a crimefighter on Earth. Nova later traveled into space and became one of the Champions of Xandar. Returning to Earth, Nova joined a team of young adventurers, the New Warriors.

Frankie Raye, who was to become the second Nova (*see also* Silver Surfer), was the stepdaughter of Phineas T. Horton, creator of the first Human Torch. Raye was exposed to Horton's chemicals, which gave her powers similar to the Torch's. Horton hypnotized her into forgetting him and her powers. Raye later became the girlfriend of Johnny Storm, the second Human Torch. She regained her memories and her powers and became the new herald of Galactus. She was killed by the alien Morg, but in an alternate timeline she is Galactus' herald at the death of the universe. PS

FACTFILE

REAL NAME
Richard Rider

OCCUPATION
Adventurer

BASE
New York City

HEIGHT 5 ft 9 in
WEIGHT 145 lbs
EYES Brown
HAIR Brown

FIRST APPEARANCE
Nova Vol. 1 #1 (September 1976); (as Frankie Raye) Fantastic Four #164 (November 1975)

NOVA

POWERS

The first Nova has superhuman strength and durability and the power to fly at supersonic speed. The second Nova could manipulate cosmic energy as stellar fire. She could project stellar energy, had nearly total invulnerability, and could survive unprotected in space.

Nova initially operated solo, but he has also worked with heroes like Doctor Strange, the Hulk and Wolverine. Nova has been a member of the New Warriors, the Champions of Xandar and the Nova Corps.

Occulus

FIRST APPEARANCE Fantastic Four #363 (April 1992)
REAL NAME Unrevealed **OCCUPATION** Absolute Monarch of an unnamed world in the Inniverse **BASE** Castle Occulus
HEIGHT 6 ft 4 in **WEIGHT** 290 lbs **EYES** Black **HAIR** Black
SPECIAL POWERS/ABILITIES Gem in place of his right eye draws energy from power crystals. Fires beams of concussive force, heat, and light from his gem-eye and hands. Can fly and form force-fields.

Occulus and his brother Wildblood were children of the Inniverse, a dimensional plane that exists between the subatomic particles of matter. Like all their kind, they were tested by the Gem Guild to see if they possessed the ability to manipulate the power gems that supplied their world with energy. Occulus had the gift and joined the Guild. He grew in power until he ruled his entire world. When Wildblood escaped to Earth, soldiers sent by Occulus to capture him also kidnapped Sue and Franklin RICHARDS. Occulus intended to use Franklin's psionic abilities for his own ends, but MR. FANTASTIC arrived with the rest of the FANTASTIC FOUR to rescue his wife and son. **TB**

Ogun

FIRST APPEARANCE Kitty Pryde and Wolverine #2 (December 1984)
REAL NAME Ogun
OCCUPATION Assassin **BASE** Japan
HEIGHT 5 ft 9 in **WEIGHT** 146 lbs **EYES** Blue **HAIR** Black
SPECIAL POWERS/ABILITIES A master martial artist and expert swordsan. As a spirit, Ogun can possess the bodies of others, and is immune to physical harm.

A legendary sorcerer and warrior who may have been born as early as the 17th century, Ogun trained WOLVERINE in the martial arts. Originally a man of integrity, Ogun was eventually corrupted by the dark sorceries that kept him alive and invulnerable to harm, and he turned to the path of evil. As revenge against his former pupil, Ogun mentally enslaved Kitty PRYDE, training her and sending her to kill Wolverine. But Wolverine ultimately freed Kitty, and together they slew Ogun's physical form. However, Ogun survived as a spirit, bound to the demon mask he once wore, and now can possess other beings of weaker will and employ them as puppets in the material world. **TB**

Omega Red

FIRST APPEARANCE X-Men Vol. 2 #4 (January 1992)
REAL NAME Arkady Rossovich
OCCUPATION Crime lord **BASE** Crime lord
HEIGHT 6 ft 11 in **WEIGHT** 425 lbs **EYES** Red **HAIR** Blonde
SPECIAL POWERS/ABILITIES Possesses enhanced strength and mutant healing factor; body secretes deadly pheromones; has carbonadium coils implanted in arms.

Omega Red is the product of the Russian KGB's attempt to create a Soviet super-soldier. The test subject, former serial killer Arkady Rossovich, gained mutant powers after receiving carbonadium implants and genetic treatments, though complications required him to drain the life-energy of victims to survive. Placed in suspended animation by the Soviets, Omega Red reemerged after the fall of Communism and sought a carbonadium synthesizer to stabilize his condition. He currently leads New York's Red Mafia. **DW**

Onslaught

During a ferocious battle between the X-MEN and MAGNETO'S Acolytes, PROFESSOR X succeeded in temporarily shutting down Magneto's brain. In the place where their minds touched, Xavier's own dark fears, doubts and frustrations combined with Magneto's anger and lust for revenge, to form a new being—Onslaught.

This creature lay dormant in Xavier's mind for some time, only manifesting itself when the Professor's own frustrations came to the fore. When Onslaught finally took over the Professor's body, the X-Men quickly realised what had happened. However, they were unable to prevent Onslaught's capture of Franklin RICHARDS, the son of Reed and Sue Richards, and a mutant with reality-altering powers. Inevitably, Onslaught's activities came to the attention of the FANTASTIC FOUR and the AVENGERS. Although Xavier was eventually freed and Onslaught was destroyed, the cost was significant—many Super Heroes were catapulted to a pocket universe, only returning to the Earth several months later. **AD**

By trapping Franklin Richards inside his body, Onslaught could tap into the boy's power to restructure reality.

FACTFILE
REAL NAME
Not applicable
OCCUPATION
Would be world-conqueror
BASE
New York City

HEIGHT 10 ft
WEIGHT 900 lbs
EYES Red
HAIR None

FIRST APPEARANCE
X-Men #15 (May 1996)

POWERS
Onslaught possessed Xavier's mental abilities combined with Magneto's powers of magnetism. He was able to induce illusions, amnesia, or paralysis, and manipulate magnetic fields. He also had powers of telekinesis and astral projection.

Orphan

FIRST APPEARANCE X-Force #117 (June 2001)
REAL NAME Guy Smith
OCCUPATION Adventurer **BASE** X-Force/X-Statix Tower in Santa Monica, California.
HEIGHT 5 ft 10 in **WEIGHT** 190 lbs **EYES** Green **HAIR** White
SPECIAL POWERS/ABILITIES Superhuman senses, superhuman speed, and the ability to levitate himself.

Guy Smith believed his parents died in a house fire (which was later proven to not be true) and was raised as an orphan. His mutant powers began to emerge in his early teens and he became extremely sensitive to his surroundings. After trying drugs and later martial arts to deal with this extreme sensitivity, he came to the attention of PROFESSOR X. The professor designed a special costume for him that allowed him to control his senses, and he began calling himself Mister Sensitive. When he joined the mutant team X-FORCE (later called X-STATIX), he changed his code name to Orphan. **MT**

Orphan-Maker

FIRST APPEARANCE X-Factor Vol. 1 #30 (July 1988)
REAL NAME Peter (last name unrevealed)
OCCUPATION Warrior **BASE** Mobile
HEIGHT 7 ft 1 in **WEIGHT** Unrevealed
EYES Unrevealed **HAIR** Unrevealed
SPECIAL POWERS/ABILITIES Carries an arsenal of guns; armored battlesuit protects against most damage.

Never seen out of his armored battlesuit, the Orphan-Maker was once a mutant child named Peter. Peter was subject to the cruel experimentations of Mister Sinister, who planned to kill the boy when he had no further use for him. The cyborg known as Nanny saved Peter and indoctrinated him in her philosophy of rescuing mutant children from threats both real and imaginary. As the first of Nanny's "Lost Boys and Girls," Orphan-Maker abducted young mutants and killed their parents, clashing with X-FACTOR and GENERATION X. **DW**

Osborn, Liz

Liz Allan, a high school classmate of Peter Parker's, married Harry Osborn (GREEN GOBLIN II) and had a son with him, whom they named Norman Osborn II. Liz had a keen business brain, and after Harry's tragic death she became the major shareholder of the multinational corporation Osborn Industries. However she lost control of the company after the original Norman Osborn's shocking return from the grave. Liz had a brief relationship with Foggy Nelson, but is now busy raising her son. **DW**

FACTFILE
REAL NAME
Elizabeth Allan-Osborn
OCCUPATION
Former businesswoman
BASE
Mobile

HEIGHT 5 ft 9 in
WEIGHT 135 lbs
EYES Blue
HAIR Blonde

FIRST APPEARANCE
Amazing Fantasy Vol. 1 #15 (August 1962)

In high school, Liz sometimes joined in when Flash Thompson mocked Peter Parker. She soon matured and befriended Peter.

Overmind

FIRST APPEARANCE Fantastic Four #113 (August 1971)
REAL NAME Grom
OCCUPATION Conqueror **BASE** Various
HEIGHT 10 ft **WEIGHT** 750 lbs **EYES** Black **HAIR** Red
SPECIAL POWERS/ABILITIES Possesses vast psionic powers. He can lift up to 70 tons, read the minds of others and manipulate matter through the power of his mind.

Grom led the interplanetary conquerors known as the ETERNALS to victory as they enslaved a thousand worlds. But they finally faced defeat when they attacked the enormous world Gigantus. Selecting Grom to be the sole survivor of their race, the Eternals transferred their mental energies to him, transforming him into the Overmind. After gestating for centuries, the Overmind tried to carry out the dread prophesy of the Eternals: "From Beyond the Stars Shall Come the Overmind—And He Shall Crush the Universe!" But his designs on conquest were foiled by the FANTASTIC FOUR. Since then, the many minds that make up the Overmind have begun to fragment, leaving him mentally unstable. **TB**

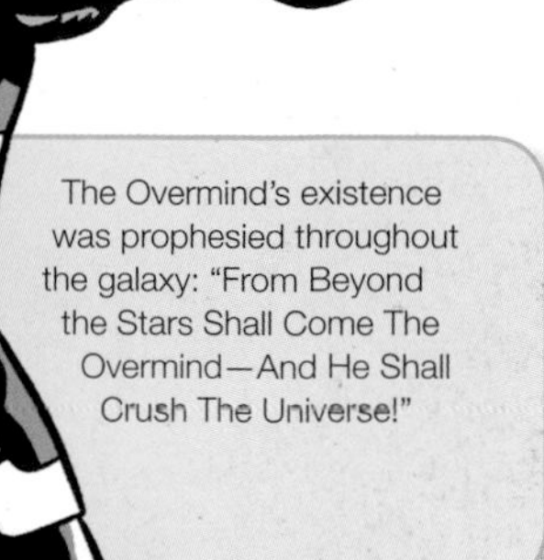

The Overmind's existence was prophesied throughout the galaxy: "From Beyond the Stars Shall Come The Overmind—And He Shall Crush The Universe!"

Page, Karen

FACTFILE

REAL NAME
Karen Page

OCCUPATION
Sometime secretary, actress and radio personality

BASE
New York City

HEIGHT 5 ft 7 in
WEIGHT 125 lbs
EYES Blue
HAIR Blonde

FIRST APPEARANCE:
Daredevil #1 (April 1964)

POWERS
Efficient secretarial skills and fair ability as an actor and presenter; some aptitude for street fighting, having battled alongside both Daredevil and Black Widow.

Karen's love for Matt was always troubled.

Karen Page's relationship with Matt Murdock spawned happiness but also much mutual heartache. Matt hired her as his secretary, but their relationship only blossomed when he told her about his secret identity. This happiness was not to last: in the middle of wedding preparations, Karen asked Matt to give up his Daredevil alter ego. When he refused she ended the engagement and entered a long vicious cycle of self-destruction. Embarking on a career as an actress, things went badly. As film and TV work dried up she became involved in the porn industry and fell prey to heroin addiction. At her very lowest ebb, Karen told a dealer Matt's secret identity in exchange for drugs. Fortunately, Matt is a man with a forgiving heart. After helping her kick the habit, their relationship continued intermittently until she was killed—just the latest of Matt's lovers to fall at Bullseye's hand. **AD**

Paladin

FIRST APPEARANCE Daredevil Vol. 1 #150 (January 1978)
REAL NAME Paul Denning
OCCUPATION Mercenary **BASE** Mobile
HEIGHT 6 ft 2 in **WEIGHT** 225 lbs **EYES** Brown **HAIR** Brown
SPECIAL POWERS/ABILITIES Enhanced strength, stamina, and reflexes; carries a nerve-scrambling stun gun; costume deflects most small-arms fire and goggles permit vision in darkness.

Paladin has teamed with Spider-Man to advance his mercenary career.

The for-hire adventurer Paladin is infamous for his arrogance and his "anything for money" attitude, yet his considerable charm has gotten him far in life. Little is known about Paladin's origins. On an early mission, he teamed up with Daredevil to pursue the Purple Man. He later became romantically involved with the Wasp. Paladin has allied with Captain America and Spider-Man to hunt foes, but he won't hesitate to abandon his partners if he's not getting paid. Other heroes dislike his methods, but many have grown to respect him. Paladin has frequently accepted employment with Silver Sable's Wild Pack. **DW**

Pantheon, The

Making a secret stand for human rights

The Pantheon is a family of long-lived superhumans who style themselves after the Greek gods of old. Centuries ago, Vali, their patriarch, bartered with the alien race known as the Troyjans for the secret of eternal youth. Afterwards, now known as Agamemnon, he fathered several children and adopted others, creating an organization of superhuman operatives bolstered by non-enhanced doctors, scientists and technicians.

THE PANTHEON
1 Paris **2** Ajax **3** Hector
4 Ulysses **5** Atalanta

The Pantheon operated as a covert strike team, pledged to maintaining the stability of the world.

ENTER THE HULK

Agamemnon feared that mankind would destroy or despoil the Earth, so he and his clan moved in secret to prevent potential disasters before they could reach fruition. The Pantheon's existence first became known to the world at large when it moved to recruit Bruce Banner, the incredible Hulk, to its ranks. At that time, the Hulk's fragmented psyche had been somewhat restored, giving him the intellect of Banner with the massive strength and power of the Hulk. Wanting to make amends for the destruction he'd caused to the world while he was no more than a rampaging brute, the Hulk agreed to joining Agamemnon's cause, and eventually came to function as the Pantheon's field leader.

The Pantheon at War

For a time, the Hulk led the Pantheon, as in this battle against the Endless Knights.

But things went wrong when the Troyjans returned to Earth, and the truth about Vali's deal with them came out: in exchange for the secret of bestowing his godly attributes and extended lifespan on his offspring, Vali had promised to give the best of them up to the Troyjans to use as they saw fit. A vast battle ensued, in which the Troyjans were repelled and Agamemnon was taken into custody by the Pantheon. He responded by summoning the Endless Knights, massive zombie warriors whose ranks included undead former members of the Pantheon itself, and commanding them to destroy the Pantheon's base, the Mount. Though the Pantheon survived this attack, its ranks were decimated, and the Hulk left, having gone through another psychological shift that changed the nature of his transformations. Since then, the Pantheon has gone back underground. It is presumed to have returned to covertly interfering in the affairs of man whenever the future of mankind is imperiled. TB

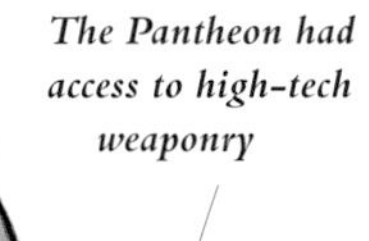

The Pantheon had access to high-tech weaponry

FACTFILE

NOTABLE MEMBERS

ACHILLES Virtually invulnerable; his invulnerability is weakened by the presence of gamma radiation.

AGAMEMNON Immortality; ability to project a holographic representation of himself.

AJAX Massive superhuman strength and a childlike intellect.

ATALANTA Fires energy arrows.

CASSIOPEIA Fires energy blasts fueled by starlight.

DELPHI Able to see glimpses of the future.

HECTOR Trained fighter; can walk on air; carries a plasma mace.

PARIS Possesses an empathetic sense of those around him.

PROMETHEUS Drives a high-tech armored vehicle.

ULYSSES Expert fighter; carries an energy sword and shield.

OTHER MEMBERS

ANDROMEDA, JASON, PERSEUS

BASE

The Mount, Arizona

FIRST APPEARANCE

Incredible Hulk vol. 2 #377 (January 1991)

ESSENTIAL STORYLINES

- ***Hulk #372–379***
The Pantheon recruits the newly-intelligent Hulk into their organization.

- ***Hulk #422–425***
During his trial, Agamemnon summons the Endless Knights to destroy the Pantheon and the Hulk.

PARKER, AUNT MAY

FACTFILE

REAL NAME
May Reilly Parker

OCCUPATION
Homemaker

BASE
New York City

HEIGHT 5 ft 5 in
WEIGHT 110 lbs
EYES Blue
HAIR White

FIRST APPEARANCE:
Amazing Fantasy #15 (August 1962)

POWERS
Amazing cook, (particularly her corn beef hash) and formidable personality—even Wolverine is afraid of her.

It may not have always been easy, but May Parker's life has certainly been eventful. Following a difficult childhood, May found love with Ben Parker, their marriage being further enriched when they became guardians to Ben's nephew, Peter. Sadly, their life together ended prematurely when Ben was shot dead by a burglar. The years that followed would be testing.

Happening upon Peter's ragged Spider-Man costume, May finally realised the startling truth about her nephew.

Concerned for his aunt's health, Peter kept the knowledge of his super-powered alter ego from her. However, his secrecy left May feeling lonely and did not protect her from danger. She was repeatedly kidnapped—the GREEN GOBLIN, DOCTOR OCTOPUS and the Beetle (*see* MACH-4) all held her hostage. It was only when May discovered the truth that the pair rediscovered their old closeness. Although physically frail, May's spirit is indomitable—she remains a bastion of strength, continuing to support Peter through his darkest days. **AD**

Spider-Man intervened just in time to prevent Dr. Octopus from marrying May.

PARKER, UNCLE BEN

FACTFILE

REAL NAME
Benjamin Parker

OCCUPATION
Retired

BASE
New York City

HEIGHT 5 ft 9 in
WEIGHT 175 lbs
EYES Blue
HAIR White

FIRST APPEARANCE
Amazing Fantasy #15 (August 1962)

POWERS
Wisdom, charisma, integrity, strength of personality and high moral standards.

Although never rich, his wisdom and fair-mindedness earned Ben Parker the respect of everyone he met. A carnival barker in his youth, Ben grew up in the same neighbourhood as May Reilly, for whom he harbored deep feelings. Love did not come easily to the pair, though—Ben was forced to compete for May's affections with the glamorous Johnny Jerome. It was only when May learnt that Johnny was a petty crook that she finally accepted Ben into her life.

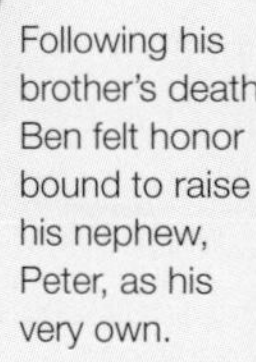

Following his brother's death, Ben felt honor bound to raise his nephew, Peter, as his very own.

Throughout their time together, Ben and May were to struggle financially, and these monetary straits only worsened when they adopted Ben's nephew, Peter, as their own. In spite of these pressures, however, Peter brought considerable joy into their lives. Tragically that joy would be cut short, when Ben was killed by a burglar's bullet. The memory of his kindly uncle inspired Peter to use his newfound spider powers to do good in the world, and so Ben Parker's spirit lives on. **AD**

Ben's tragic murder continues to inspire Peter Parker, even to this day.

PARKER, MARY JANE

The Webslinger's wife and one true love

Mary Jane was the daughter of Philip and Madeline Watson. Her mother was a drama student who dreamed of being an actress, while her father was an aspiring novelist. They met and fell in love at college, and married as soon as they graduated, with Philip taking a teaching job to support his family while he worked on his first novel. The couple had two daughters, Gayle and Mary Jane, and Madeline put her acting career on hold to stay at home and care for the girls.

After always missing each other, Peter finally met Mary Jane.

FACTFILE

REAL NAME
Mary Jane Watson-Parker

OCCUPATION
Fashion model, "B" movie actress, former star of daytime TV drama.

BASE
New York City

HEIGHT 5 ft 8 in
WEIGHT 120 lbs
EYES Green
HAIR Red

FIRST APPEARANCE
Amazing Spider-Man #25, (June 1965)

POWERS
Mary Jane has no special powers, but she is a talented dancer, model and actress; retains her fun-loving and optimistic outlook despite the numerous dangers and trials of being married to Spider-Man.

ESSENTIAL STORYLINES
- ***Amazing Spider-Man #42*** After months of missing each other, Peter Parker finally meets Mary Jane Watson for the first time.
- ***Amazing Spider-Man: Parallel Lives, tpb*** The early lives of Mary Jane and Peter are shown to have a lot in common.
- ***Amazing Spider-Man Annual #21*** Mary Jane finally marries Peter Parker.

UNSETTLED YOUTH

Frustrated with his inability to complete his novel, Philip began switching jobs, hoping each new location would spark his creativity. As a result, Mary Jane was constantly changing schools and having to make new friends. To cope with this, she developed an extrovert personality and became a bit of a class clown. The marriage of Mary Jane's parents was never happy, and they eventually called it quits. But Madeline and the girls had a good relationship with Philip's elderly sister, Anna Watson, who lived next door to the Parker family, and kept in touch with her after the split.

After repeatedly refusing to marry Peter, Mary Jane finally accepted his proposal. They were married at City Hall.

FIRST MEETING

Gazing out of her Aunt Anna's window, Mary Jane first saw Peter Parker when she was 13 years old. She later discovered that he was secretly SPIDER-MAN when she spotted him sneaking out of his Aunt May's house. Aunt Anna kept trying to get them together, but the outgoing Mary Jane didn't want anything to do with the bookish, sensitive boy who hid behind a mask. When they eventually met, however, she discovered that she was attracted to Peter after all. Feigning indifference, she flirted with his rival Flash THOMPSON and dated Harry Osborn (*see* GREEN GOBLIN), his best friend and roommate.

Though she has no superpowers of her own (unless you count her amazing patience), Mary Jane has aided her husband against various super-foes.

SPIDEY'S BRIDE

Mary Jane became a close friend of Gwen STACY, who was dating Peter at the time. When Gwen tragically died, Mary Jane comforted Peter. Peter eventually proposed to her, but she declined and left town. However, she returned a few years later and they resumed their relationship. Peter proposed again, and this time Mary Jane accepted.

Mary Jane tried to get used to Peter's double life, but being married to Spider-Man put a lot of strain on the marriage. The couple separated for a while after Peter rescued Mary Jane from a stalker, who had taken her hostage and faked her death. Although Mary Jane has always wanted to be an actor, she has worked mainly as a professional dancer and as a fashion model. However she did land a small role on a soap opera called *Secret Hospital.* TD

Patriot

FACTFILE

REAL NAME
Elijah Bradley

OCCUPATION
Student

BASE
New York City

HEIGHT 6 ft 2 ins
WEIGHT 205 lbs
EYES Brown
HAIR Black

FIRST APPEARANCE
Young Avengers #1 (April 2005)

POWERS
For a time, the Patriot used the drug MGH (Mutant Growth Hormone) to give himself enhanced strength, speed and durability.

Elijah Bradley is the grandson of Isaiah Bradley, the long-rumored "black Captain America" of World War II, whose mind had been reduced to that of a child by the super-soldier serum that empowered him. Eli possessed no inherent superhuman abilities of his own, but when Iron Lad sought out his aid to battle his future self, Kang the Conqueror, Eli resorted to using the designer drug MGH to give himself superhuman powers.

Alongside Iron Lad, Patriot became a founding member of the Young Avengers, determined to carry on in the tradition of the original Avengers Super Hero team, who had by that time been disassembled.

When his fellow Young Avengers teammates learned that Eli was using dangerous drugs to empower himself, they managed to convince him to give them up.

At the present time, Patriot still leads the Young Avengers, relying on his own intelligence and natural athletic skills rather than artificially induced superpowers. **TB**

YOUNG AVENGERS
1 Wiccan
2 Stature
3 Hulkling
4 The Patriot
5 Kate Bishop

Payback

FIRST APPEARANCE Punisher War Journal #48 (November 1992)
REAL NAME Edward "Eddie" Dyson
OCCUPATION Unknown, former vigilante
BASE Possibly Madison, Wisconsin. Formerly New York.
HEIGHT 5 ft 10 in **WEIGHT** 170 lbs **EYES** Brown **HAIR** Brown
SPECIAL POWERS/ABILITIES Skilled in both unarmed and armed combat and uses a wide range of firearms.

Eddie Dyson was a rookie police officer in the NYPD when he discovered his squad were taking payment to the local mob. He sought the Punisher's advice who persuaded him to expose their corruption to Internal Affairs. The mafia took revenge and killed Dyson's family. Dyson became Payback to avenge his family's death. At first, he blamed the Punisher for their murders, but the two made peace when the Punisher helped Payback kill Steve Venture—the mobster responsible for the family's death. Dyson retired for a short time, but he was attacked by Vigil, and became Payback again. He fought Vigil, Heathen and the Trust with Lynn Michaels then fled for the Midwest with her and her father.

Pendragon, King Arthur

Arthur reigned supreme as King of England.

FACTFILE

REAL NAME
Arthur Pendragon

OCCUPATION
King of the Britons

BASE
Avalon, Otherworld

HEIGHT 6 ft 2 in
WEIGHT 230 lbs
EYES Blue
HAIR Brown

FIRST APPEARANCE
Black Knight Comics vol. 1 #1 (May 1955)

POWERS
Inspirational and courageous leader and strategist; a highly skilled horseman and swordsman; he wielded the indestructible, magical sword Excalibur, which protected whoever wielded it against injury in battle.

King Arthur, who ruled England in the 6th century, is one of history's most celebrated figures. The son of Uther Pendragon, Arthur grew up in the care of Sir Ector, with the wizard Merlin as his tutor. When Arthur pulled an enchanted sword from a stone and anvil, he became the king of all Britons, with his rule centered on his court at Camelot. After breaking the sword in battle, Arthur received the mystical Excalibur from the Lady of the Lake.

Arthur had a son, Mordred, by his half-sister, and married Guinevere. When an affair between Guinevere and Lancelot became known, Arthur sentenced both to execution, though Lancelot rescued Guinevere. Morgan Le Fay allied with Mordred and raised armies against Camelot, and Arthur died while striking a mortal blow against Mordred. In the Otherworld realm of Avalon, Arthur awaited his return, and reappeared in modern times to battle the Necromon. The mystical Pendragon spirit has been used to empower the warriors known as the Knights of Pendragon. **DW**

King Arthur, legendary ruler of Britain, lived in a time of courtly chivalry, armored knights, and strange magical forces.

Persuasion

FIRST APPEARANCE Alpha Flight #41 (December 1986)
REAL NAME Kara Killgrave
OCCUPATION Adventurer **BASE** Mobile
HEIGHT 5 ft 3 in **WEIGHT** 120 lbs **EYES** Brown **HAIR** Black
SPECIAL POWERS/ABILITIES Has the mutant power to secrete psychoactive will-sapping pheromones from her pores that allow her to link with the minds of others and make them do her bidding.

After her mutant powers emerged, Kara Killgrave joined Beta Flight, Alpha Flight's training group. The group later split up, and Kara, whose code name was Persuasion, went home to her mother, taking teammates Laura Dean and Goblyn with her. When Beta Flight reformed, Persuasion was left out of several key missions, and left the team in anger. But she rejoined to battle Llan, the Sorcerer, and has served well, sometimes taking a leadership role. She hopes to graduate to become a full Alpha Flight member. **AD**

Petrovich, Ivan

FIRST APPEARANCE Amazing Adventures Vol. 2 #1 (August 1970)
REAL NAME Ivan Petrovich
OCCUPATION Chauffeur **BASE** Mobile
HEIGHT 6 ft 5 in **WEIGHT** 300 lbs **EYES** Brown **HAIR** Brown
SPECIAL POWERS/ABILITIES Does not posses superpowers, but is a skilled hand-to-hand combatant; a reliable chauffeur and steadfast ally of the Black Widow.

After the devastating siege of Stalingrad during World War II, Russian soldier Ivan Petrovich had been searching the city without success for his lost sister. As he was walking through the city's ruins he heard a woman's cries from a burning building. As the woman died in the fire, she let her baby fall into his arms. Petrovich decided to raise the girl as his own. She was Natasha Romanova who eventually became the Black Widow, Russia's top spy. Petrovich, feeling responsible for Natasha, accompanied her to America as her chauffeur. He lived with the Black Widow and Daredevil while the two heroes struck up a romance in San Francisco. His son Yuri Petrovich briefly served as the fourth Crimson Dynamo. He remains in good health, despite his age. **DW**

Phalanx

Every race feeds in its own way but the Technarchy's method is particularly convoluted. A techno-organic race, the release of their transmode virus converts organic matter into Phalanx, a collective intelligence lifeform. Members of the Technarchy then feed on the Phalanx, draining away their life energy.

While experimenting on Adam Warlock, a member of the Technarchy, human scientists obtained a strain of the transmode virus and injected it into humans, hoping to create a new generation of sentinel robots. Their experiment quickly got out of control. Transformed into Phalanx, their subjects began assimilating other humans.

Fortunately, the Phalanx found mutants to be somewhat indigestible. After capturing a number of younger mutants the Phalanx drew the ire of the X-Men and were almost destroyed. The survivors fled into space where they went on to threaten the Shi'ar Empire. **AD**

FACTFILE
REAL NAME
Inapplicable; alien being with collective intelligence
BASE
Outer space

HEIGHT Variable
WEIGHT Variable
EYES Unknown
HAIR None

FIRST APPEARANCE
Uncanny X-Men #305 (October 1993)

POWERS
Transforms sentient beings into techno-organic lifeforms and assimilates them into its collective. Superhumanly strong, also possess ability to teleport and shapeshift—molding their limbs into weapons or mimicking the appearance of others.

Sentient biological weapons, the Phalanx are formidable adversaries.

Phantom Eagle

FIRST APPEARANCE Marvel Super Heroes #16 (September 1968)
REAL NAME Karl Kaufman
OCCUPATION Pilot **BASE** Mobile
HEIGHT 5 ft 11 in **WEIGHT** 175 lbs **EYES** Blue **HAIR** Brown
SPECIAL POWERS/ABILITIES Although he had no superhuman powers, Phantom Eagle was an extraordinary pilot, exceptionally skilled in aerial combat.

When World War I broke out, ace flyer Karl Kaufman wanted to use his skills against the Germans, but he feared reprisals against his German parents. So he donned a costume and mask and took the name Phantom Eagle. He became one of the greatest aerial warriors of the war, wining many dogfights, and then joined the Freedom's Five, a team of costumed heroes who assisted the Allies. Kaufman's identity was discovered by a German pilot, who killed him and his parents. The ghost of the Phantom Eagle hunted the pilot down and killed him. MT

Phastos

FIRST APPEARANCE Eternals vol. 2 #1 (October 1985)
REAL NAME Phastos **OCCUPATION** Technologist, weaponsmith
BASE Ruhr Valley, Germany **HEIGHT** 6 ft 3 in
WEIGHT 410 lbs **EYES** Brown **HAIR** Bald (black beard)
SPECIAL POWERS/ABILITIES Able to fly and levitate objects; virtually invulnerable, super-strong, and projects cosmic energy from eyes or hands; ingenious inventor; hammer fires energy bolts.

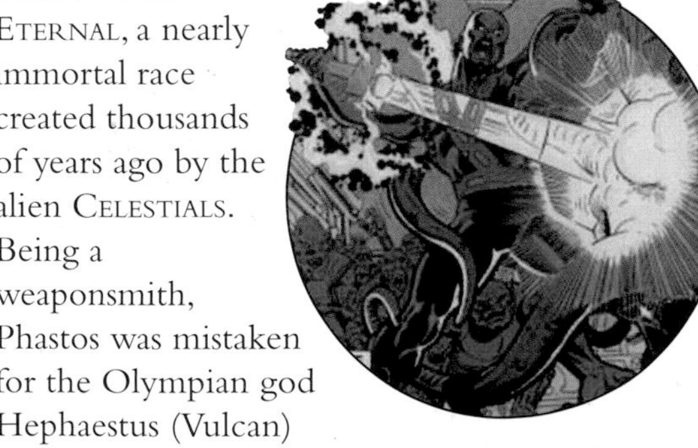

Phastos is an Eternal, a nearly immortal race created thousands of years ago by the alien Celestials. Being a weaponsmith, Phastos was mistaken for the Olympian god Hephaestus (Vulcan) during the days of ancient Greece (*see* Gods of Olympus). Phastos is more reticent than his fellows, having a melancholy spirit and an ambivalence toward fighting. When Apocalypse tried to incite a new war with the Deviants, the Eternals decided to go public as Super Heroes. In his new identity, Phastos adopted the codename Ceasefire. DW

Phantom Rider

With his luminescent cloak and magician's skills, the Phantom Rider appeared to be flying.

The greatest vigilante in the Wild West, that's what people said about Carter Slade, the Phantom Rider. Originally a schoolteacher, Carter was shot and seriously wounded by a ruthless local land baron. His life was saved by a Comanche Indian called Flaming Star, who recognized that the young man was destined for great things. When Carter had made a full recovery, Flaming Star provided him with a white horse and a cloak covered with a phosphorescent dust. Styling himself the Phantom Rider, Carter began a one-man battle against injustice.

Not knowing that the Phantom Rider was his brother, Marshall Lincoln Slade teamed up with him to battle the Reverend Reaper. A vicious gunfighter, the reverend was set on taking control of Bison Bend, the town Carter was dedicated to protect. Their final confrontation resulted in the death of both the reverend and Carter Slade. Finally discovering the truth about his brother, Lincoln decided to follow in his footsteps. In more recent times, Lincoln's descendent, Hamilton Slade, has become a modern day Phantom Rider. AD

FACTFILE
REAL NAME
Carter Slade
OCCUPATION
Schoolteacher, vigilante
BASE
Bison Bend in the Old West

HEIGHT 6 ft 1 in
WEIGHT 200 lbs
EYES Blue
HAIR Reddish-blond

FIRST APPEARANCE
Ghost Rider #1 (September 1973)

POWERS
A fast draw and a brilliant marksman; formidable hand-to-hand combatant; notable horseman.

With guile and some magnificent devices, the Phantom Rider stayed one step ahead of local miscreants.

Phobius

FIRST APPEARANCE Marvel Two-In-One #71 (January 1974)
REAL NAME Unknown
OCCUPATION Interrogator; servant **BASE** Unknown
HEIGHT 5 ft 9 in **WEIGHT** 122 lbs **EYES** Green **HAIR** Black
SPECIAL POWERS/ABILITIES Possesses the ability to psionically stimulate the fear centers of a person's brain in order to implant terrifying phobias; also wielded an energy whip.

Phobius was the chief interrogator of a gang known as Maelstrom's Minions. His role was to instill terror in victims to further his master Maelstrom's lust for scientific knowledge, particularly in the field of genetics. He also used his powers to protect Maelstrom's base. Maelstrom thought highly enough of his servant to create clone bodies for him to take over when Phobius was slain during clashes with the Fantastic Four, the Avengers, and Quasar. Phobius was also defeated by Sersi who turned him into a rat. Phobius' whereabouts are unknown since he helped revive Maelstrom after the scientist had been killed by Quasar. ED

Phobos, Professor

FIRST APPEARANCE The Incredible Hulk #258 (April 1981)
REAL NAME Professor Pieter Phobos
OCCUPATION Teacher **BASE** Russia
HEIGHT/WEIGHT/EYES Unrevealed **HAIR** Gray
SPECIAL POWERS/ABILITIES Possessed telepathic abilities artificially derived from draining the energies of superhuman mutants. Wore battle armor.

Professor Phobos was appointed by the Russian government to head the secret Super Soldier School, training the Russian mutant siblings Darkstar, Ursa Major, and Vanguard. Phobos secretly drained their power to give himself psionic abilities and turned against his government. Phobos teamed with Bruce Banner to imprison two Russian superhumans, Sergei the Presence and the Red Guardian. Sergei was the father of Darkstar, Ursa Major and Vanguard, who all intervened, calling Phobos a traitor. In the ensuing battle, the Hulk and Ursa Major apparently crushed Phobos to death. PS

Photon

Firing electrical energy, Photon disrupts the circuits of some complex equipment.

Monica Rambeau was working as a lieutenant in the New Orleans Harbor Patrol when she was struck by extradimensional energy from an "energy disruptor" weapon being developed by a South American terrorist. This exposure gave Rambeau her superpowers.

Dubbed "Captain Marvel" by the media she tried to put her new abilities to good use. Early in her career she met Spider-Man who introduced her to the Avengers. They agreed to help train her to use her powers more skilfully. In time she became a valuable member of the Avengers, and was even their leader for several stints.

When Genis-Vell (*see* Captain Marvel) the son of Captain Mar-Vell wanted to use his father's name, Rambeau gladly gave up the name and became Photon. Later, Genis-Vell changed *his* name to Photon, forcing Rambeau to change her super hero name yet again, this time to Pulsar. MT

FACTFILE
REAL NAME
Monica Rambeau
OCCUPATION
Adventurer
BASE
New Orleans; New York City

HEIGHT 5 ft 8 in
WEIGHT 145 lbs
EYES Black
HAIR Black

FIRST APPEARANCE
Amazing Spider-Man Annual #16 (1982)

POWERS
Photon can turn into any type of energy, including light, electricity, microwaves, radio waves, ultra-violet waves, gamma rays, or lasers. She can travel at the speed of light and fire blasts of whatever type of energy she becomes.

Becoming or controlling any form of energy gives Photon almost limitless power

Piecemeal

FIRST APPEARANCE Incredible Hulk #403 (March 1993)
REAL NAME Unrevealed
OCCUPATION Criminal **BASE** Loch Ness, Scotland
HEIGHT 7 ft 6 in **WEIGHT** 1,400 lbs **EYES** Red **HAIR** Gray
SPECIAL POWERS/ABILITIES Possesses all of the abilities of the criminal New World Order, including superhuman strength, the ability to fire energy blasts, and razor-sharp claws.

The man who would become Piecemeal was an operative from the Commission on Superhuman Activities sent to spy on the Red Skull. The Skull captured him, intending to make him into a living symbol of his criminal organization, the New World Order. Imbued with the properties of

members of the Order, and with memories of his previous life erased, Piecemeal became enthralled with being alive. He began using his powers to absorb the life-experiences of others, until the Hulk seemingly ended his menace. TB

Pip the Troll

FIRST APPEARANCE Strange Tales #179 (April 1975)
REAL NAME Pip Gofern
OCCUPATION Former bearer of the Space Gem, prince of Laxidazia and painter **BASE** Mobile with the Milky Way Galaxy
HEIGHT 4 ft 4 in **WEIGHT** 144 lbs **EYES** Pink **HAIR** Red
SPECIAL POWERS/ABILITIES Claims to be irresistible to women; could teleport anywhere in the universe when he possessed the Space Gem.

Born a prince on the alien world of Laxidazia, Pip was exiled from the court for befriending a tribe of trolls. Missionaries from the Universal Church of Truth came to Laxidazia to convert the natives. When the trolls resisted, the Church began exterminating them. Pip was captured and placed on a Death-Ship where he met Adam Warlock. They became friends and later overthrew the Church. Warlock called upon Pip to help stop Thanos from using the Infinity Gems to control reality and later gave him the Space Gem as a reward, making him a member of the Infinity Watch. The Watch disbanded after losing control of the gems and Pip was last seen in New York City with Warlock and Gamora. TD

Strange Tales #113 was Plantman's first appearance.

Plantman

While working in London as a botanist's assistant, Samuel Smithers became involved with experiments to explore the mental activity of plants. After ten years the botanist died, and Smithers moved to the United States where he planned to continue his work in trying to increase the intelligence of plants so that humans could communicate with them. However, due to his lack of formal education he had difficulty in finding support for his ideas and was forced to take a job as a gardener. Smithers tried to combine the job with his research, but was eventually fired for spending too much time on his experiments.

FACTFILE
REAL NAME
Samuel Smithers
OCCUPATION
Professional criminal, formerly a gardener
BASE
A submarine in the Atlantic Ocean

HEIGHT 6 ft
WEIGHT 190 lbs
EYES Green
HAIR Dark gray

FIRST APPEARANCE
Strange Tales #113 (October 1963)

POWERS
Plantman's projector weapons allow him to control plants, animating their limbs to attack a victim; and manipulate plants so they look like duplicates of humans.

Revenge

Not long after Smithers lost his job, a bolt of lightning struck his experimental plant ray-gun, charging the device with the power to control and animate plant life. Smithers put on a costume and, taking the name Plantman, sought revenge on the man who had fired him, but was stopped by the Human Torch, who destroyed the plant-gun. Undeterred, Plantman built a second, more powerful weapon, and tried to kill the Human Torch, but his plan failed. Later he joined the international crime syndicate, the Maggia. Creating plant duplicates of himself, Plantman battled the X-Men, the Avengers, Sub-Mariner, Triton, and SHIELD, among others.

The Plantman simuloid possessed all the powers of the original Plantman.

CHARACTER KEY
1 Plantman
2 Porcupine
3 The Eel
4 The Scarecrow

Crimewave

Plantman created a copy of himself, a simuloid, over which he had total control, in order to take part in the Crimewave. This criminal society included the Cowled Commander (Brian Muldoon, a police commander) Eel, Porcupine, Scarecrow, Viper and various unnamed others. They aimed at creating chaos in New York City to bring about the introduction of a tougher police force and were repeatedly fought by Captain America, Falcon and Redwing. Plantman captured Falcon and Captain America and brought them to the Cowled Commander to be killed. The heroes managed to escape and defeat the Crimewave, Plantman losing his fight against Falcon and Redwing. After their demise, the Crimewave were sent to prison. MT

Polaris

While her green hair marked her as a mutant, Lorna Dane had no idea growing up that she had been adopted—and that her true father was MAGNETO, the mutant master of magnetism! But when her mutant powers manifested, she found herself at the center of an all-out war between the X-MEN and the demoniac MESMERO for control of her abilities. Falling in love with the X-Man HAVOK, Lorna desired nothing more than to retreat into seclusion and live a normal life. But fate would not let her be, and time and again she was pulled to the center of mutant strife as Polaris, mistress of magnetism. Over the years, her magnetic powers have taken a toll upon the electromagnetic energies in her brain, driving Lorna half out of her mind. Nevertheless, she reluctantly continues to fight for PROFESSOR XAVIER'S dream of co-habitation for mutants, first alongside X-FACTOR and today as a member of the X-Men. TB

As the years have gone by, Polaris' mutant magnetic powers have had a detrimental effect on her mental stability, interfering with the electrical impulses in her brain.

FACTFILE

REAL NAME
Lorna Dane

OCCUPATION
Adventurer

BASE
The Xavier Institute for Higher Learning

HEIGHT 5 ft 7 in
WEIGHT 115 lbs
EYES Green
HAIR Green

FIRST APPEARANCE
Uncanny X-Men #49 (October 1968)

POWERS

Polaris possesses control of the Earth's electromagnetic field, and can employ it to fly, create force-fields, and manipulate anything composed of magnetic materials

Porcupine

FIRST APPEARANCE Tales to Astonish #48 (October 1963)
REAL NAME Alexander Gentry
OCCUPATION Weapons designer/criminal **BASE** New York City
HEIGHT (With battlesuit) 6 ft 7 in **WEIGHT** (With battlesuit) 305 lbs
EYES Blue-gray **HAIR** Brown
SPECIAL POWERS/ABILITIES Battlesuit fired quills, laser beams, bombs, gases, and other weapons. Belt jets enabled him to fly.

A weapons designer for the US government, Alexander Gentry invented a battlesuit inspired by a porcupine. It was covered in razor-sharp quills that he could fire at opponents, and quill-like tubes through which other weapons could be fired. Believing the government would not pay him enough for the suit, Gentry used it to become a criminal, the Porcupine, but his criminal career was a failure. CAPTAIN AMERICA agreed to buy the battlesuit from Gentry if he would help the AVENGERS to defeat the SERPENT SOCIETY. Gentry agreed, but was fatally impaled on his own quill during the battle. Though Gentry died believing his life had been a failure, Captain America honored the deceased Porcupine as a hero. PS

Potts, Virginia "Pepper"

FIRST APPEARANCE Tales of Suspense Vol. 1 #45 (September 1963)
REAL NAME Virginia Potts
OCCUPATION Former executive aide to Tony Stark **BASE** Mobile
HEIGHT 5 ft 4 in **WEIGHT** 110 lbs **EYES** Green **HAIR** Red
SPECIAL POWERS/ABILITIES No special powers, but is intelligent and extremely quick-witted.

"Pepper" Potts became Tony Stark's secretary early in the industrial magnate's career. She was promoted to that position after she impressed Stark by noticing an accounting error that would have cost the company a lot of money. Stark valued Potts as a confidante, entrusting her with the secret of his identity as IRON MAN, but didn't realize that she harbored a secret infatuation with him. Potts eventually married Stark's chauffeur, Harold "Happy" HOGAN, though they later divorced. Potts' feelings for Stark had never quite died, and since her divorce there have been brief attempts between the two to kindle a romance. DW

Powderkeg

FIRST APPEARANCE Captain Marvel Vol. 2 #1 (December 1995)
REAL NAME Frank Skorina
OCCUPATION Prisoner **BASE** The Big House
HEIGHT/WEIGHT/EYES Unrevealed **HAIR** Red
SPECIAL POWERS/ABILITIES Secretes nitro-glycerine through skin; when body strikes object with sufficient force the chemical ignites, causing an explosion.

Powderkeg was a member of the MASTERS OF EVIL during DOCTOR OCTOPUS' ill conceived turn as leader. Following the failure of the group's attempt to invade Avengers Mansion and their subsequent demise, Powderkeg began running a protection racket in the neighbourhood where Ben Grimm (*see* THING) grew up. The villain's treatment of a pawnbroker soon drew the attention of Grimm, who made short shrift of Powderkeg's operation. Currently an inmate in the experimental penitentiary The Big House, in which all the prisoners have been shrunk to reduce costs, Powderkeg was recently involved in an unsuccessful attempt at a mass breakout. AD

Power, Dr. James

FIRST APPEARANCE Power Pack #1 (August 1984)
REAL NAME Dr. James Power **OCCUPATION** Physicist
BASE New York City; later Bainbridge Island, Washington State
HEIGHT 6 ft **WEIGHT** 155 lbs **EYES** Blue **HAIR** Brown
SPECIAL POWERS/ABILITIES A brilliant and innovative physicist, Dr. Power has the normal human strength of a man of his age who engages in minimal regular exercise.

Dr. James Power is the inventor of the matter/antimatter converter, a comparatively inexpensive means of producing energy. Learning of Power's invention, an alien Kymellian named Aelfyre Whitemane ("Whitey") grew concerned, since a similar device had destroyed the Kymellian homeworld. Another alien race, the Z'nrx, or "Snarks," intending to utilize the converter as a weapon, abducted Dr. Power and his wife Margaret. The dying Whitemane bestowed superhuman powers upon the Powers' young children, Alex, Jack, Julie and Katie, who rescued their parents. The children continued to operate under the name Power Pack. **PS**

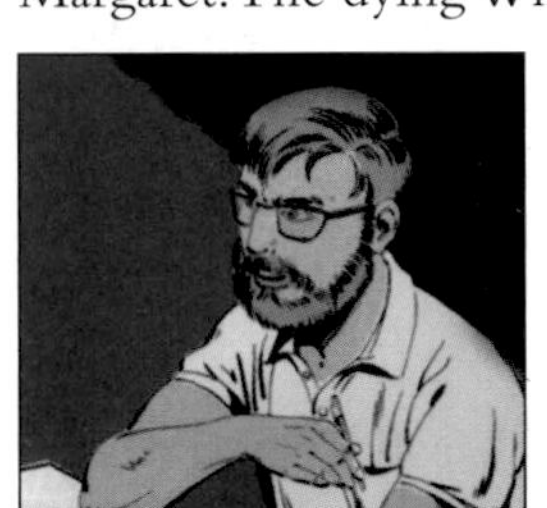

Power Broker

FIRST APPEARANCE Machine Man #6 (September 1978)
REAL NAME Curtiss Jackson
OCCUPATION Criminal **BASE** Los Angeles
HEIGHT 7 ft 6 in **WEIGHT** 600 lbs **EYES** Brown **HAIR** Black
SPECIAL POWERS/ABILITIES Once a normal man, Jackson possesses superhuman strength. However, his body is so overdeveloped that he cannot move without a steel exo-skeleton.

Curtiss Jackson was once an agent of the Corporation, a criminal organization run along the lines of a business firm. After he encountered Dr. Karl Malus, Jackson formed his own company, Power Broker, Inc., which claimed that it could give any client superhuman strength. He was responsible for empowering numerous heroes and villains, including US Agent, Demolition Man, and most of the wrestlers on the UCWF circuit. Hunted by the criminal-killing Scourge, Jackson tried to use the process upon himself, but wound up so musclebound that he cannot move without outside aid. **TB**

Power Pack
SEE OPPOSITE PAGE

Power Princess

FIRST APPEARANCE Defenders #112 (October 1982)
REAL NAME Zarda
OCCUPATION Princess **BASE** Capital City
HEIGHT 5 ft 9 in **WEIGHT** 145 lbs **EYES** Brown **HAIR** Black
SPECIAL POWERS/ABILITIES Incredible healing ability, and an incredibly long lifespan. She can also shoot a flash from her eyes which can heal others, or if she chooses, destroy them.

Princess Zarda lived on Utopia Island, where her people, the Utopians developed a culture of peace, fellowship, and learning. It is believed that the Utopians are the result of genetic experimentations performed by the Inhumans. Thus, while the rest of humanity was still in its early stages of development, the Utopians had developed an advanced civilization. When humans developed the atomic bomb, the Utopians felt threatened, built a spaceship and left Earth. Princess Zarda remained behind as their emissary on Earth. She took the role of Power Princess and moved to Capital City. **MT**

Powerhouse

POWERHOUSE

FACTFILE
REAL NAME
Rieg Davan
OCCUPATION
Syfon warrior
BASE
The planet Xandar

HEIGHT 6 ft 3 in
WEIGHT 265 lbs
EYES Brown
HAIR Brown

FIRST APPEARANCE
Nova #2
(October 1976)

POWERS
Powerhouse could siphon energy from external sources, including living beings to amplify his strength or discharge energy blasts.

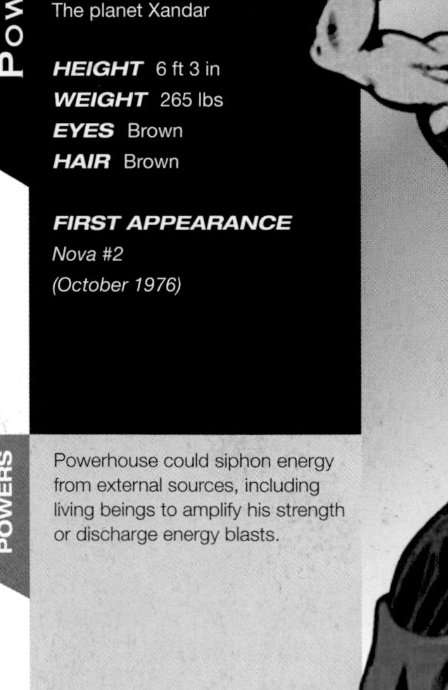

A member of the alien Xandarians, Rieg Davan was a Syfon warrior in the elite Nova Corps. He was sent to Earth to locate Centurion Nova-Prime Rhomann Dey. Davan's starship crash landed on Earth. He was found and brainwashed by the Condor, a costumed criminal.

As the Condor's accomplice Powerhouse, Davan battled Nova, the young Earthman who had inherited the deceased Dey's powers. Eventually Davan recovered his memory and with Nova and other heroes journeyed to Xandar. As the Champions of Xandar, they helped the Xandarians defeat the invading Skrulls.

Davan later perished in combat defending Xandar against a successful invasion by the forces of the space pirate Nebula.

The name Powerhouse has since been used by a criminal mutant Earthwoman who also has the power to drain energy from other living beings through touch to amplify her own. She has battled Spider-Man and Wolverine, among others.

Alex Power of Power Pack also used the name Powerhouse when he temporarily possessed the superhuman powers of his siblings. **PS**

The female Powerhouse is super-strong, can fly, and discharge energy blasts.

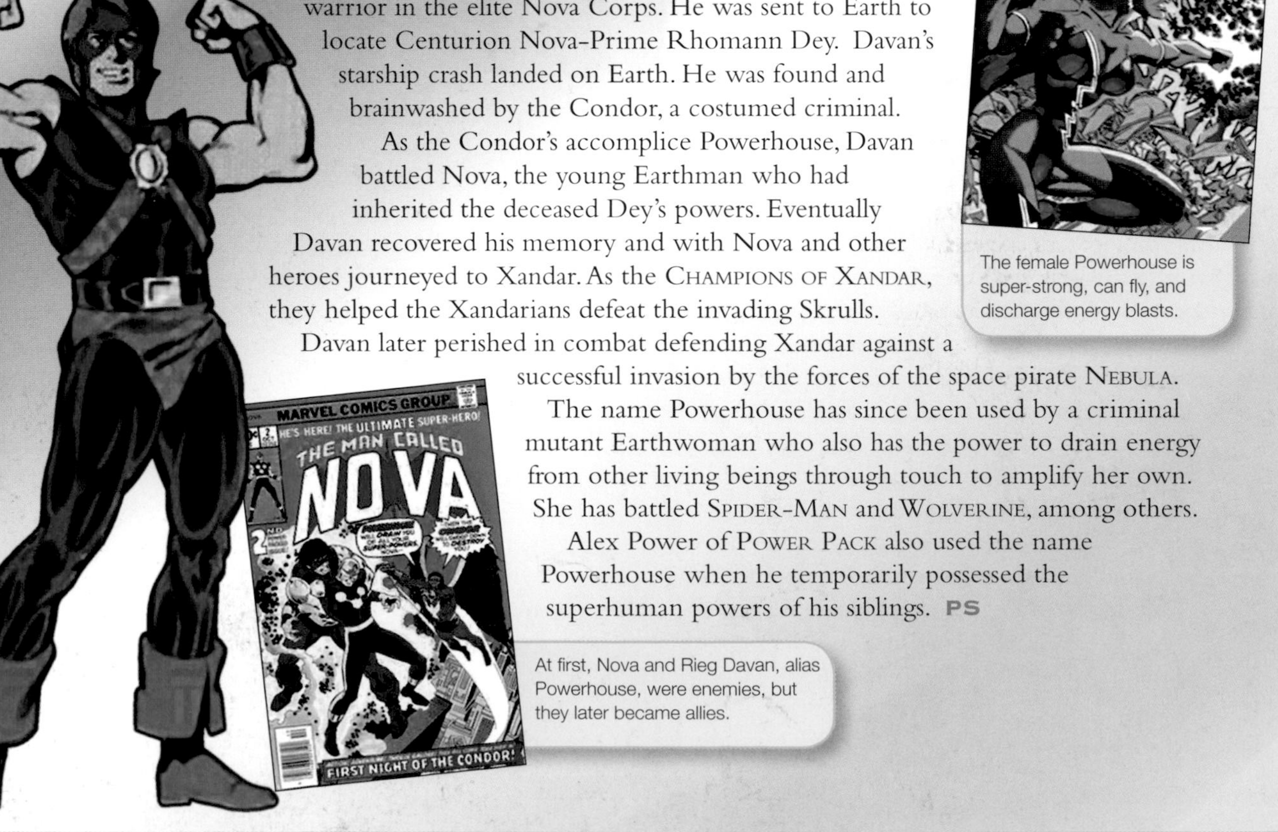

At first, Nova and Rieg Davan, alias Powerhouse, were enemies, but they later became allies.

Power Pack

Young hero team with power to burn

Dr. James Power inadvertently caused his children to join the ranks of Earth's Super Heroes.

Professor James Power, father of Alex, Julie, Jack, and Katie, invented an antimatter generator that siphoned energy from an alternate dimension. Aelfyre "Whitey" Whitemane, a member of the alien Kymellian race, arrived on Earth to prevent the machine being used, knowing it had the potential to wipe out entire planets. A rival species, the Snarks, attempted to steal the device.

Secret Super Heroes

Whitemane suffered fatal injuries in the ensuing struggle, but before dying he bestowed one of his abilities on each of the four Power children. They became the superheroic Power Pack, and adopted the identities of Gee (Alex), Lightspeed (Julie), Mass Master (Jack), and Energizer (Katie). Hiding their dual identities from their parents, the Pack dealt with extraterrestrial threats and employed Whitey's intelligent spacecraft, the Smartship Friday. Power Pack aided the Morlocks during the Mutant Massacre, and fought Apocalypse's horsemen during the Fall of the Mutants. Franklin Richards, using the name Tattletale due to his ability to perceive possible futures, became an unofficial member of the team, as did Kofi, a Kymellian relative of the late Whitemane.

Frequent contact with the Kymellians and the Snarks have turned the members of Power Pack into veteran interstellar adventurers.

Energy Swapping

Power Pack's powers often switched from one member to another. After one such incident, the children adopted the names of Destroyer (Alex), Molecula (Julie), Counterweight (Jack), and Starstreak (Katie). The team and helped the Kymellians relocate to a new world. Alex even appeared to transform into a Kymellian, though this was revealed to be a pseudoplasm duplicate planted by Technocrat a domineering Kymellian.

Alex joined the New Warriors, stealing the energies of his brother and sisters to become Powerpax and then Powerhouse. He restored his siblings' powers when he left the New Warriors.

Power Pack is again active, with Alex going by the name of Zero-G. The team recently fought off a squad of Snark invaders. DW

Despite their youth, the Power Pack members combine their abilities to defeat some of the strongest villains.

Essential Storylines

- ***Power Pack Vol. 1 #1***
  Power Pack debuts, launching a popular 62-issue series.
- ***Power Pack Vol. 2 #1-4***
  The heroes return—now a few years older—in a limited series that pits them against their perennial enemies, the Snarks.
- ***X-Men and Power Pack #1-4***
  Power Pack returns to its roots in a limited series that guest-stars such famous mutants as Cyclops, Beast, and Wolverine.

Factfile

Current Members

Zero-G
(Alex Power, leader) Ability to control the gravity of himself or other objects.

Lightspeed
(Julie Power) Flight, super-speed.

Mass Master
(Jack Power) Can compress or disperse his body's mass.

Energizer
(Katie Power) Can absorb and release energy.

Base
Bainbridge Island, Washington

First Appearance
Power Pack vol. 1 #1 (August 1984)

Power Pack
1 Mass Master
2 Energizer
3 Lightspeed
4 Zero-G

Pratt, Agent

FIRST APPEARANCE Incredible Hulk Vol. 3, #40 (July 2002)
REAL NAME Agent Pratt
OCCUPATION Agent for clandestine organisation **BASE** Mobile
HEIGHT/WEIGHT/EYES Unrevealed **HAIR** None
SPECIAL POWERS/ABILITIES Body able to regenerate itself as a result of H Section Programming; injection of Hulk blood endowed him with Hulk-like powers.

When he first met Bruce Banner, this ruthless operative was posing as an FBI agent. In truth he belonged to the sinister, clandestine organisation Home Base. After forcing Banner to change into the HULK, Pratt obtained a sample of his blood, but a police officer snatched it and, plunging it into Pratt's own bloodstream, caused him to explode. Pratt's H Section Programming enabled his body to regenerate itself, and he soon returned to taunt Banner again. This time the Hulk emerged to tear Pratt's body apart. AD

Prester, John

FIRST APPEARANCE Fantastic Four Vol. 1 #54 (September 1966)
REAL NAME Prester John
OCCUPATION Traveler **BASE** Traveler
HEIGHT 6 ft 1 in **WEIGHT** 210 lbs **EYES** Blue **HAIR** Red
SPECIAL POWERS/ABILITIES Skilled swordsman; a weapon called the Evil Eye allowed him to fire energy blasts, generate force fields, and rearrange matter.

Prester John, monarch of a 12th-century Christian kingdom in Asia, came to the aid of Richard the Lion-Heart during the Crusades. He then traveled around the world before discovering the fabled isle of Avalon. While he was there, a plague struck Avalon and left him the sole survivor. Prester John entered a period of suspended animation seated in the Chair of Survival. After reawakening in the modern era, Prester John has crossed paths with Super Heroes including the FANTASTIC FOUR and CABLE. He carries the powerful Stellar Rod, a weapon refashioned from the Evil Eye. DW

Princess Python

FIRST APPEARANCE Amazing Spider-Man Vol. 1 #22 (March 1965)
REAL NAME Zelda DuBois
OCCUPATION Snake charmer, professional criminal **BASE** Mobile
HEIGHT 5 ft 8 in **WEIGHT** 140 lbs **EYES** Green **HAIR** Red-brown
SPECIAL POWERS/ABILITIES Can control her trained rock python; sometimes carries an electric prod.

Princess Python is a snake charmer who possesses an uncanny rapport with her pet rock python. She has trained the snake to attack on her command. Princess Python served with the CIRCUS OF CRIME as well as its second incarnation, the Masters of Menace, before going on to pursue a solo career. She was distraught when her original python died in a pool of acid during a scheme to extort money from IRON MAN, but has since acquired several replacements.

Princess Python briefly joined the mercenaries of the SERPENT SOCIETY. However, she deserted her teammates during a mission to assassinate MODOK, and as a result the Serpent Society expelled her after brainwashing her to remove Society secrets from her memory. DW

Presence

FIRST APPEARANCE Defenders Vol. 1 #52 (October 1977)
REAL NAME Sergei Krylov
OCCUPATION Supervillain **BASE** Mobile
HEIGHT 6 ft 0 in **WEIGHT** 200 lbs **EYES** Yellow **HAIR** None
SPECIAL POWERS/ABILITIES Body produces lethal radiation which can be harnessed as flight, energy blasts, force fields, enhanced strength, or telepathy.

Sergei Krylov, a nuclear physicist who became an important player in Russian politics, sought to further increase his power by subjecting himself to experimental radiation. He succeeded in bestowing himself with radioactive energy deadly to unprotected persons in his presence, and which could also be used to control the minds of others. The Presence used his powers to brainwash Dr. Tania Belinskya (the RED GUARDIAN) into becoming his partner. Driven by his megalomania, he became a foe of the DEFENDERS and QUASAR. His children are DARKSTAR and VANGUARD. DW

Pretty Persuasions

FIRST APPEARANCE New Warriors Vol. 1 #4 (October 1990)
REAL NAME Heidi P. Franklin
OCCUPATION Professional criminal **BASE** Sayville, Long Island
HEIGHT 5 ft 6 in **WEIGHT** 120 lbs **EYES** Brown **HAIR** Black
SPECIAL POWERS/ABILITIES Can manipulate the pleasure centers of the brain, particularly in men, and create whips and other weapons from solidified psionic energy.

A former exotic dancer, Heidi Franklin gained the ability to influence the sexual drives of others through her association with GeneTech, a sinister genetic research facility in Long Island, New York. She also became capable of transforming psionic energy into a selection of different weapons. Under the name Pretty Persuasions, Franklin joined with other psionically-gifted individuals to form Psionex, GeneTech's villainous enforcement squad. The group frequently battled the NEW WARRIORS, and later became a squad of crime-fighting New York vigilantes. DW

Proctor

The man who came to be called Proctor was actually the BLACK KNIGHT of an alternate Earth. While serving as a member of the AVENGERS, he met and fell in love with the SERSI of his world. He became her "gann josin," a mate that was forever bound to her by a mental link that allowed them to share their powers, thoughts and souls. His Sersi eventually became mentally unstable, destroying their world and rejecting Proctor.

Desperate for revenge, Proctor and his companions used a gateway into alternate dimensions and journeyed across the multiverse. They were on a quest to kill every alternate world version of Sersi, along with every world and Avenger that had ever befriended her. They gathered and rescued all the alternate-Avengers that they deemed worthy of life.

After defeating the Black Knight of the real Earth, Proctor was slain by this world's Sersi. TD

Proctor possessed the battle prowess of the real Black Knight, and the mental and physical powers of an Eternal because he had become one with the Sersi of his world.

PROCTOR

FACTFILE

REAL NAME
Dane Whitman (of an alternate dimension)

OCCUPATION
Former Super Hero turned destroyer of worlds

BASE
A secret citadel hidden on the edge of reality

HEIGHT 6 ft
WEIGHT 190 lbs
EYES Brown
HAIR Black

FIRST APPEARANCE
Avengers #344 (March 1941)

POWERS

Expert combatant; immune to aging; can psionically manipulate matter, and project cosmic blasts from eyes and hands. Possesses ten rings that produce, among other things, ice blasts, flames, bursts of light and deadly gases.

Prodigy

High above the US Capitol, Prodigy tangles with fellow X-Men member Wind Dancer

Prodigy is a mutant and a member of the second team to go under the name of NEW MUTANTS. He has the ability to instantly absorb skills and knowledge of those close to him, but a mental block prevents him from retaining any of this knowledge once the subject is out of range.

Prodigy asked Emma FROST to help remove this block, so that he could remember everything he learned from his knowledge absorbing, and thus become the smartest man on Earth. Although MOONSTAR objected to this plan, Emma agreed to help him, and Prodigy gained all the knowledge of his professors, plus knowledge that allowed him to cure all known diseases, end poverty, and work for world peace.

However, his great power, originally a force for good, eventually led to death and destruction. It was only then that the whole thing was revealed to be just an illusion created by Moonstar and Emma Frost to show Prodigy why he was better off leaving his mental block in place. Eventually, Prodigy lost his mutant powers. MT

PRODIGY

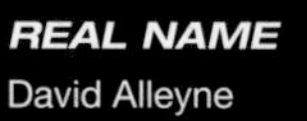

FACTFILE

REAL NAME
David Alleyne

OCCUPATION
Adventurer

BASE
Professor X's School for Gifted Youngsters, Salem Center, New York

HEIGHT 6 ft 3 in
WEIGHT 230 lbs
EYES Brown
HAIR Black

FIRST APPEARANCE
Captain America Comics #1, (March 1941)

POWERS

Prodigy has the mutant ability to absorb (although not permanently) the skills and knowledge of those near him. He cannot, however, absorb their mutant powers.

Professor X

Mastermind of the X-Men

Professor X

FACTFILE

REAL NAME
Charles Francis Xavier

OCCUPATION
Mutant rights activist, teacher

BASE
Mobile

HEIGHT 6 ft
WEIGHT 190 lbs
EYES Blue
HAIR None

FIRST APPEARANCE
Uncanny X-Men vol. 1 #1 (September 1963)

POWERS
Vast psionic abilities including mind-reading, mind-erasing, astral projection, the projection of illusions, the ability to take mental control of others, and the ability to fire mental blasts.

ALLIES/FOES
ALLIES The X-Men, the Starjammers

FOES Magneto, Juggernaut, Cassandra Nova, the Sentinels, the Hellfire Club

ISSUE #1
In *X-Men #1*, Professor X's team unites to fight off the menace of Magneto, marking the first appearance of both the heroic X-Men and their arch-foe.

Growing up in a time before widespread superpowers, Charles Xavier hid his telepathic abilities to shield himself from unwanted attention.

Widely considered the most powerful mutant on Earth, Charles Xavier has dedicated his life to the ideal that humans and mutants can coexist peacefully. His father Brian died when Charles was a child. Kurt Marko, his father's research partner, married Charles's mother Sharon, but only valued her for her fortune. Charles became a rival of his stepbrother Cain (who one day gained the powers of the JUGGERNAUT), and saw both his mother and stepfather die in separate incidents.

FIRST LOVE

Xavier attended graduate school at Oxford University, England, where he fell in love with Moira MACTAGGART; however their relationship ended when Charles joined the US Army. Following his tour of duty, Xavier traveled the world. At a clinic for Holocaust survivors in Israel, he befriended the man who would become MAGNETO. Magneto and Xavier teamed up to fight BARON VON STRUCKER, but Magneto's ruthless methods made it clear that the two had incompatible philosophies concerning the use of violence. Xavier left Israel, leaving behind Gabrielle HALLER, not realizing that Haller was pregnant with his child (the boy, David, would grow up to become the mutant LEGION). A rockslide caused by the villainous alien Lucifer, left Xavier a paraplegic.

IF THINGS HAD BEEN DIFFERENT, WE MIGHT HAVE BEEN FRIENDS...WE MIGHT HAVE TRULY BEEN BROTHERS! BUT YOU WOULD HAVE IT NO OTHER WAY! THIS FINAL CHAPTER WAS WRITTEN WHEN WE FIRST MET! THIS IS THE ONLY WAY IT COULD HAVE ENDED!

UHHHHHHHH....!

Professor X can disable opponents, such as the Juggernaut, with mental blasts.

THE X-MEN

As Professor X, Charles Xavier founded Xavier's School for Gifted Youngsters in Westchester County, New York to train mutant children in the use of their powers. Xavier identified potential students with the machine Cerebro, which amplified his telepathic powers and allowed him to pinpoint mutants from afar. His initial Super Hero team, the X-MEN, consisted of CYCLOPS, Angel (*see* ARCHANGEL), Marvel Girl (*see* Jean GREY), ICEMAN and BEAST, who sought to improve the image of mutants by selfless deeds.

The X-Men repeatedly faced off against Magneto, who had dedicated himself to subjugating humanity through his powers as the master of magnetism.

Professor X founded a second team of X-Men, whose members included NIGHTCRAWLER, COLOSSUS, STORM, BANSHEE, and WOLVERINE. The new X-Men helped Xavier battle SHI'AR emperor D'ken and the Imperial Guard. Xavier then fell in love with the new Shi'ar empress, Lilandra. He entered into the Shi'ar equivalent of marriage with Lilandra, and adventured with the STARJAMMERS.

Although his love for Shi'ar empress Lilandra took him across the galaxy, Professor X eventually returned to the X-Men.

Back on Earth, Xavier organized a third grouping of students, the NEW MUTANTS, but fell under the influence of the alien BROOD. To prevent his transformation into a Brood Queen, Xavier shifted his consciousness into a clone body with fully-functional legs. After suffering injuries as a result of a hate crime, Xavier reunited with Lilandra to recuperate among the Shi'ar, leaving Magneto to run the academy in his absence. Xavier again lost the use of his legs battling the SHADOW KING, and brought together a fourth team of young mutants, GENERATION X.

The relationship between Magneto and Xavier took a turn for the worse, culminating in a terrible moment when Magneto ripped the adamantium from Wolverine's skeleton. Enraged by Magneto's brutality, Xavier mind-wiped his former friend, unwittingly creating a powerful psionic being known as ONSLAUGHT. All of Earth's heroes united to destroy Onslaught, leading to the apparent deaths of the AVENGERS and the FANTASTIC FOUR. In the aftermath, Xavier briefly lost his telepathic powers and became a prisoner of the US government. He later uncovered a SKRULL plot to infiltrate the X-Men, and trained a promising group of Skrull mutants calling themselves Cadre K.

BATTLING MAGNETO

The philosophies held by Professor X and Magneto are diametrically opposed, but share some similarities. Both men profess the goal of protecting mutantkind, but Magneto wants to subjugate or eliminate human opposition, while Professor X dreams of a world where humans and mutants can co-exist. After Professor X founded the X-Men, Magneto created the Brotherhood of Evil Mutants. Over the years, the two men have been friends and foes. Recently, the pair united to help rebuild the island nation of Genosha. The Scarlet Witch's manipulations of reality during the House of M event seem to have temporarily de-powered both men.

TRANSITIONS

Xavier's genetic twin, the sinister Cassandra Nova, had died in Sharon Xavier's womb yet somehow maintained her life-essence. Nova re-entered Xavier's life with spectacular malevolence, orchestrating the devastation of the mutant nation of Genosha, and taking mental control of Xavier. In Xavier's guise, she outed him as a mutant to the world, and incited the Shi'ar Imperial Guard to attack the X-Mansion. Xavier's students helped free him from Nova's influence, and Xavier regained the use of his legs through the actions of academy student Xorn (actually a Magneto impostor in disguise.) Xavier later founded the X-Corporation, stepping down as head of the academy. He lost the use of his legs when the Magneto impostor revealed himself, and left for Genosha to help the real Magneto rebuild that island's shattered society.

Professor X designed the Danger Room, not realizing it would develop a mind of its own.

An artificial lifeform calling itself Danger tracked down Xavier on Genosha, intent on killing him. During the battle, it became clear that Danger was the self-aware consciousness of the X-Mansion's Danger Room training center, a fact that Xavier had known but suppressed in order to continue exploiting Danger in order to hone his students' combat skills.

Xavier later helped Magneto's daughter, the SCARLET WITCH to recover from a mental breakdown, although he was unable to prevent her altering reality to "cure" more than 98 per cent of the world's mutants. PS

ESSENTIAL STORYLINES
- ***Giant-Size X-Men #1*** Professor X recruits a new batch of X-Men to replace the originals, welcoming such future favorites as Nightcrawler and Storm.
- ***New X-Men #118–126*** The "Imperial" storyarc sees Professor X's genetic twin, Cassandra Nova, impersonating Xavier to imperil the Shi'ar empire.
- ***Astonishing X-Men #7–12*** A failure from his past returns to haunt Professor X, as he confronts the self-aware consciousness of the X-Men's Danger Room.
- ***X-Men: Mutant Genesis, tpb*** The X-Men stand in the way of Magneto's world-conquering schemes.

X-Men
(from top) Nightcrawler, Colossus, Storm, Cyclops, Wolverine, Professor X, Kitty Pryde (Shadowcat)

Proteus

FIRST APPEARANCE Uncanny X-Men #125 (September 1979)
REAL NAME Kevin MacTaggert
OCCUPATION None **BASE** Muir Island, Scotland
HEIGHT Inapplicable **WEIGHT** Inapplicable
EYES Inapplicable **HAIR** Inapplicable
SPECIAL POWERS/ABILITIES Able to warp reality. Made of psionic energies, he must inhabit a host body, which burns up over time.

The son of Moira MacTaggert, Proteus grew up a prisoner in his mother's Mutant Research Facility on Muir Island, where a special energy field prevented his mutant power to alter reality from consuming his body. When his cell was breached during an attack by Magneto, Proteus escaped into the world, shifting from host-body to host-body as each wore out. Only the intervention of the X-Men and Proteus' vulnerability to metal stopped him. Proteus was later reconstituted by the terrorist group AIM and resumed his deadly travels. **TB**

Proteus escaped incarceration on Muir Island and took over the body of his mother Moira's estranged husband Joe.

Proudstar

FIRST APPEARANCE New Mutants #16 (June 1984)
REAL NAME James Proudstar
OCCUPATION X-Force Team member **BASE** San Francisco
HEIGHT 7 ft 2 in **WEIGHT** 350 lbs
EYES Brown **HAIR** Black
SPECIAL POWERS/ABILITIES Superhuman strength, speed, endurance, agility and reflexes; also able to fly.

Like his Native American brother (the original Thunderbird) James Proudstar was born a mutant. When his brother died on an X-Men mission, James blamed Professor Xavier, and joined the Hellions. He left, disenchanted, to discover that his tribal community had been destroyed. Reconciling with Xavier, James joined the New Mutants, taking the name Warpath when they reformed as X-Force.

He has since learned that the man who caused his tribe's destruction is dead. **AD**

Prowler

Hobie Brown's gift for inventions is rivaled only by that of Peter Parker (Spider-Man).

While working as a window washer, mechanical genius Hobie Brown invented gadgets to make his job easier, including wrist-mounted, high-pressure sprayers. When his boss dismissed his ideas, Brown quit in frustration. He turned to crime, refashioning his contraptions into climbing gear and miniaturized weapons, and adopting the costumed identity of the Prowler. Seeking recognition rather than profit, Brown intended to return what he stole as the Prowler under his real identity. Almost immediately, he came into conflict with Spider-Man, though the two later put aside their differences and became allies.

A second Prowler appeared when the villainous Cat Burglar stole Brown's costume and worked with Belladonna to commit a string of crimes. Brown resumed his role as the original Prowler, joining the team of reformed criminals called the Outlaws, but suffered a severe spinal injury at the hands of El Toro Negro. A third Prowler, medical student Rick Lawson, briefly adventured while Brown recuperated in the hospital, but Brown has since retaken the role he created. **DW**

FACTFILE

REAL NAME
Hobie Brown

OCCUPATION
Adventurer

BASE
New York City

HEIGHT 5 ft 11 in
WEIGHT 170 lbs
EYES Brown
HAIR Dark brown

FIRST APPEARANCE
Amazing Spider-Man Vol. 1 #78 (November 1969)

POWERS

The cape of Prowler's costume allows him to glide; wrist cartridges fire compressed air; steel-tipped claws allow him to scale buildings.

Pryde, Kitty

By slipping her atoms past those of solid objects, Kitty can walk through walls.

As a schoolgirl in Deerfield, Illinois, Kitty Pryde began suffering intense headaches. They were a sign that her mutant power to "phase" through solid matter was about to emerge.

Emma Frost, the White Queen of the Hellfire Club visited Kitty's parents to recruit her as a student. Professor X and three of his X-Men soon followed, to try to convince Kitty's parents to let her attend his "School for Gifted Youngsters."

After the White Queen kidnapped the visiting X-Men, Kitty helped Cyclops and Phoenix (see Grey, Jean) rescue them. Kitty entered Xavier's school and joined the X-Men. She and fellow student Colossus fell in love, and Kitty briefly adopted the codenames Sprite and Ariel. During an adventure in Japan, where Wolverine taught her martial arts, she chose the name Shadowcat, which she uses today.

Pryde later became a founding member of the original Excalibur, a British-based team of adventurers. She also worked for the law enforcement agency SHIELD for a short time.

After Excalibur disbanded, Pryde rejoined the X-Men. She left to pursue college studies in Chicago but soon returned to the X-Men once more. **PS**

Kitty's loyal companion is the alien dragon Lockheed.

FACTFILE

REAL NAME
Katherine "Kitty" Pryde

OCCUPATION
Adventurer, student, former SHIELD employee

BASE
The Xavier Institute, Salem Center, New York State

HEIGHT 5 ft 6 in
WEIGHT 110 lbs
EYES Brown
HAIR Brown

FIRST APPEARANCE
The Uncanny X-Men #129 (October 1994)

POWERS
Mutant ability to pass ("phase") through solid matter by altering the vibratory rate of the atoms of her body, her clothing, and a limited amount of other matter. Highly adept with computers.

Pryor, Madelyne

FACTFILE

REAL NAME
Madelyne Jennifer Pryor-Summers

OCCUPATION
Vengeance-seeker

BASE
Mobile

HEIGHT 5 ft 6 in
WEIGHT 110 lbs
EYES Green
HAIR Red

FIRST APPEARANCE
Uncanny X-Men #168 (April 1983)

POWERS
Most of Madelyne's abilities stem from her status as a clone of Jean Grey. She possesses vast psionic powers including telepathy and telekinesis, Madelyne is able to generate energy and manipulate it so that she can fly, project powerful force blasts, and create force fields that act as shields.

Mr. Sinister was obsessed with obtaining the spawn of a union between Jean Grey and Scott Summers (*see* Cyclops), but it was only after Jean's death that he achieved his goal. Using stored genetic material, he successfully cloned Jean. He named his creation Madelyne Pryor, provided her with false memories, and manipulated Scott Summers into marrying her. Their relationship resulted in a son—Nathan Summers (*see* Cable)—but when the real Jean Grey was resurrected, Scott left Madelyne. Insanely jealous, Madelyne began to lose her grip on reality, and her journey towards madness accelerated when Sinister kidnapped Nathan. As Madelyne's mutant powers began to emerge, so did her thirst for vengeance, and she transformed herself into the Goblin Queen.

She was killed in a showdown with the X-Men, during which she tried to sacrifice her son. The machinations of the vile Mr. Sinister had once more resulted in desperate unhappiness. **AD**

Psycho-Man

FIRST APPEARANCE Fantastic Four Special #5 (November 1967)
REAL NAME Unrevealed
OCCUPATION Scientist; conqueror **BASE** Traan; his World-Ship
HEIGHT Indeterminate **WEIGHT** Indeterminate
EYES Unrevealed **HAIR** Unrevealed
SPECIAL POWERS/ABILITIES Superhuman intelligence; his main weapon projects a "psycho-ray" that stimulates fear, doubt, and hate.

The Psycho-Man was chief scientist of Traan, a planet in an alternate reality known as the "microverse." He traveled to Earth to conquer the planet by means of his "psycho-ray," but was thwarted by the Fantastic Four's Human Torch and Thing, the Black Panther, and the Inhumans' Royal Family. The Psycho-Man's true size and appearance are mysteries: on Earth he remained tiny while encased in a human-sized suit of body armor. He continues to clash with the Fantastic Four, both on Earth and within the microverse. **PS**

The Psycho-Man can operate suits of armor far larger than himself—or his foes.

Psyklop

FIRST APPEARANCE Avengers #88 (May 1971)
REAL NAME Psyklop
OCCUPATION Servant of the Dark Gods **BASE** Mobile
HEIGHT 8 ft **WEIGHT** 450 lbs **EYES** Red **HAIR** None
SPECIAL POWERS/ABILITIES Possessed of superhuman strength and durability, Psyklop can also fire beams of energy from his eye that can hypnotize an opponent, or make him experience illusions.

The devoted servant of the Dark Gods who ruled the Earth at the dawn of time, Psyklop hibernated for millennia until called upon to serve his masters once more. He tried to offer up the HULK as a sacrifice to his sinister lords, but was prevented from doing so by the AVENGERS. The Hulk ended up miniaturized, and fell into the Microverse, alighting on the planet K'ai. Pursuing the Hulk, Psyklop engaged him in battle and was defeated. For his failure, the Dark Gods exiled Psyklop to K'ai, where he seemingly met his end, consumed by the spirits of all the people he had slain. **TB**

Puck

FIRST APPEARANCE Alpha Flight Vol. 1 #1 (August 1983)
REAL NAME Eugene Milton Judd
OCCUPATION Alpha Flight member **BASE** Tamarind Island
HEIGHT 3 ft 6 in **WEIGHT** 225 lbs **EYES** Brown **HAIR** Black
SPECIAL POWERS/ABILITIES Superb athlete and gymnast; formidable hand-to-hand combatant with unique fighting style; trained bullfighter; limited knowledge of sorcery.

In 1939, Eugene Judd discovered the Black Blade of Baghdad and released the evil sorcerer imprisoned inside. Although he managed to entrap the sorcerer in his own body, extending his life considerably, Judd found that he had been reduced to the height of a dwarf. Decades later, Judd was invited to join Beta and then ALPHA FLIGHT, the Canadian team of Super Heroes. Given the codename Puck, in recognition of his diminutive size, Judd became a key team member. **AD**

Puma

FIRST APPEARANCE Amazing Spider-Man Vol. 1 #256 (Sept. 1984)
REAL NAME Thomas Fireheart
OCCUPATION CEO of Fireheart Enterprises; mercenary
BASE Mobile **HEIGHT** 6 ft 2in **WEIGHT** 240 lbs
EYES Green **HAIR** Red; (as Fireheart) black
SPECIAL POWERS/ABILITIES As Puma Fireheart has superhuman strength, agility, heightened senses, and slashing claws

Puma is the heir to a long tradition of mystical champions, created by a Native American tribe through a program of selective breeding and shamanistic magic. Raised to oppose the omnipotent BEYONDER, Thomas Fireheart donned the mantle of the Puma and kept his fighting skills sharp by becoming a mercenary, where he often fought (or aided) SPIDER-MAN.

Fireheart enjoys vast wealth as the head of Fireheart Enterprises (a multinational that supplies Puma with high-tech weaponry and vehicles), but struggles for control over his animalistic Puma persona. **DW**

Psylocke

FACTFILE
REAL NAME
Elisabeth "Betsy" Braddock
OCCUPATION
Adventurer
BASE
The Xavier Institute, Salem Center, New York State

HEIGHT 5 ft 11 in
WEIGHT 155 lbs
EYES (current body) blue
HAIR (current body) black, dyed purple

FIRST APPEARANCE
Captain Britain Vol. 1 #8 (December 1976)

POWERS
Possesses telekinetic powers. Can focus her psionic powers into a "psychic knife" to stun or kill an adversary. Former telepath. Highly skilled in martial arts.

Psylocke's psychic knife appears from her right hand

James Braddock, Sr. was an inhabitant of Otherworld who came to Britain and fathered three children, James, Jr., Brian and Elisabeth. Brian became the hero Captain Britain, a role Betsy later briefly took over at the behest of the British government agency RCX. Blinded and nearly killed by the villain Slaymaster, Betsy was abducted by MOJO, who gave her new artificial eyes. She was rescued by the NEW MUTANTS and joined the X-MEN as Psylocke. SPIRAL switched the minds of Psylocke and the Japanese assassin KWANNON into each other's bodies. Discovering that her new body was dying, Kwannon had the crimelord Matsu'o Tsurayaba kill her. Elisabeth survives in Kwannon's original body. Psylocke sacrificed her telepathy to defeat the X-Men's enemy, the Shadow King. Subsequently, she gained telekinetic abilities. While with the X-Treme X-Men, Psylocke was seemingly slain by their enemy Vargas. Psylocke returned, however, and after a spell with the X-Men, joined the EXILES. **PS**

Psylocke forfeited her telepathic powers in order to imprison the Shadow King, one of the X-Men's deadliest foes, in the Astral Plane.

PUNISHER

War hero turned vengeful vigilante

Marine Captain Frank Castle was a decorated hero during the Vietnam War. Winner of the Bronze and Silver Star, and recipient of four Purple Hearts, Castle was an exceptionally skilled combat veteran. Then came the event that changed his life. While on leave in New York, Castle took his family for a picnic in Central Park. There they witnessed a mob murder. The mobsters then killed Castle's wife and two young children.

Frank Castle, family man, in happier days.

The big white skull on Punisher's costume draws criminal fire to his heavily armored body rather than to his unprotected head

ONE-MAN ARMY

With his whole world destroyed, Castle deserted from the Marines and dropped out of sight for a few months. When he resurfaced, it was as a vigilante named the Punisher, who conducted a one-man, anti-crime campaign throughout New York City.

Equipped with an arsenal of weapons, the Punisher took his vengeance on the mob gang who had killed his family, but he didn't stop there. He vowed to kill all criminals of every kind.

The Punisher has devoted his life to destroying organized crime, drug dealers, street gangs, muggers, killers, or any other criminal element. His actions have brought him into conflict with several costumed heroes, such as SPIDER-MAN (with whom he has also cooperated), and DAREDEVIL, who strictly opposes Punisher's lethal methods.

FACTFILE

REAL NAME
Frank Castle (born Castiglione)

OCCUPATION
Vigilante

BASE
Mobile

HEIGHT 6 ft 1 in
WEIGHT 200 lbs
EYES Blue
HAIR Black

FIRST APPEARANCE
Amazing Spider-Man #129 (February 1974)

PUNISHER

POWERS

The Punisher is seasoned combat veteran of exceptional skill. He has undergone SEAL (Sea, Air, Land), UDT (Underwater Demolition Team), and LRPA (Long Range Patrol) military training. He is an expert using all types of small arms and large caliber guns, he has extensive training using explosives and tactical weapons, and he is a superior martial artist and hand-to-hand combatant.

Punisher battles Daredevil, who objects to the deadly force Punisher uses as a self-proclaimed vigilante.

WEAPONS AND ENEMIES

To carry out his one-man war on crime, the Punisher uses machine guns, rifles, handguns, shotguns, knives, grenade launchers, armor-piercing bullets, and explosives. His weapons are customized with tactical scopes, night-vision scopes, silencers, and tripods. Among those he has battled are the Italian and Russian Mafia, the Japanese Yakuza, Chinese Triads, drug cartels, biker gangs, and corrupt cops. MT

Evil beware! On the streets of Manhattan, no one escapes the Punisher's vigilante vengeance!

ESSENTIAL STORYLINES

• Marvel Preview #2
Marine captain Frank Castle takes his wife and two children for a picnic in New York's Central Park. There, they witness a mob killing, after which the mobsters kill Castle's wife and children. Traumatized, Castle take vengeance against the killers and continues his one-man vigilante campaign against all criminals as The Punisher.

• The Punisher Vol. 1 Welcome Back, Frank (tpb)
After a long absence, the Punisher returns to the streets of Manhattan to take on Ma Gnucchi and her crime family.

FACTFILE
REAL NAME
Phillip Masters
OCCUPATION
Professional criminal
BASE
Sunshine City, Florida

HEIGHT 5 ft 6 in
WEIGHT 150 lbs
EYES Blue
HAIR None

FIRST APPEARANCE:
Fantastic Four vol. 1 #8 (November 1962)

POWERS
A brilliant biologist and technician; Able to control the actions and thoughts of others by making models of them out of special radioactive clay. He then turns the models into marionettes, attaching strings to their limbs.

Puppet Master

Born in the Balkan country of Transia, Phillip Masters moved to the US at a young age. A talented biologist, he became the research partner of Jacob Reiss. Resentful of Reiss's success, Masters killed his partner during Masters's botched robbery of their lab, triggering an explosion that blinded Reiss's daughter, Alicia. Masters later married Reiss's widow and became Alicia's stepfather (*see* Masters, Alicia). Learning he could control others with his clay sculptures, Masters became the Puppet Master, one of the earliest enemies of the Fantastic Four. He also teamed up with the villains Egghead, Mad Thinker, and Doctor Doom. To his horror, his daughter Alicia fell in love with the Thing, though in time the Puppet Master was reconciled to their relationship. The US government recruited the Puppet Master to run their Sunshine City project, where mind-controlled criminals safely served out their prison sentences. DW

The Fantastic Four look on helplessly as the Puppet Master tinkers with a robot clutching a model of an atomic bomb. What can the villain be up to?

Pym, Hank *see opposite page*

Pyro

FIRST APPEARANCE Uncanny X-Men Vol. 1 #141 (January 1981)
REAL NAME St. John Allerdyce
OCCUPATION Professional criminal **BASE** Mobile
HEIGHT 5 ft 10 in **WEIGHT** 150 lbs **EYES** Blue **HAIR** Blond
SPECIAL POWERS/ABILITIES Could control and manipulate flames within his immediate vicinity, though he could not produce flames himself. His insulated costume had built-in flamethrowers.

Born in Sydney, Australia, St. John Allerdyce won fame as a novelist until Mystique convinced him to join her Brotherhood of Evil Mutants. As the flame-shaping Pyro, Allerdyce battled the X-Men and remained with his teammates when they transitioned into the US government-sanctioned Freedom Force. Pyro eventually contracted the fatal Legacy virus, and succumbed to its effects after saving Senator Robert Kelly from a team of assassins that belonged to a new Brotherhood of Evil Mutants. DW

FACTFILE
REAL NAME
Zebediah Killgrave
OCCUPATION
Former spy, professional criminal, conqueror
BASE
Mobile

HEIGHT 5 ft 11 in
WEIGHT 165 lbs
EYES Purple
HAIR Purple

FIRST APPEARANCE:
Daredevil vol. 1 #4 (October 1964)

POWERS
Killgrave's body secretes psychoactive chemicals that deaden the will of people in his vicinity, rendering them susceptible to his commands. Individuals with unusually strong will power can resist him.

Purple Man

Born in Yugoslavia, Zebediah Killgrave was a spy who attempted to steal an experimental nerve gas. Firing his gun at Killgrave, a guard hit a canister of the gas, stored in liquid form. The chemical spilled over Killgrave, permanently dying his hair and skin purple. It also gave him the power to compel others to obey his commands.

Killgrave turned to crime and became known as the Purple Man. He was repeatedly defeated by Daredevil, one of the few people able to resist his power—he forced the crimefighter Jewel to become his servant for months.

Inasmuch as the Purple Man could have anything he wanted just by asking for it, he decided to give up crime. However, the Kingpin and Doctor Doom exploited the Purple Man's abilities for their own ends. The Purple Man attempted to compel the mutant Nate Grey, alias X-Man, to help him conquer the world, but Grey defeated him.

The Purple Man has a daughter, Kara Killgrave, who has purple skin and similar powers. She became the adventurer known as the Purple Girl and Persuasion. PS

Pym, Hank

Scientific genius behind Ant-Man, Giant-Man, and Goliath

As Ant-Man, Henry Pym could shrink himself so small that he could ride atop an ant.

Dr. Henry Pym, a brilliant scientist, discovered a rare group of subatomic particles which became known as "Pym Particles." When ingested through a serum (and later through a gas and a capsule) the particles could either shrink a person down to the size of an ant, or increase a person's size to 10, 25, even 100 feet in height.

FACTFILE

REAL NAME
Dr. Henry "Hank" Pym

OCCUPATION
Adventurer, biochemist, roboticist, manager of Avengers Compound

BASE
Cresskill, New York; Avengers Compound, LA, California

HEIGHT 6 ft
WEIGHT 185 lbs
EYES Blue
HAIR Blond

FIRST APPEARANCE
Tales To Astonish #27 (January 1962)

POWERS
By ingesting Pym Particles, either as a serum, gas, or capsule, Henry Pym can shrink to the size of an ant, or grow up to 100 ft tall. He can also change the size of objects. Using his cybernetic helmet, Pym can communicate with ants and command them to do his bidding.

Ant-Man's cybernetic helmet contains technology that allows him to communicate with and command ants to do his bidding.

ANT AND WASP

Undertaking a study of ants, Pym also developed a cybernetic helmet which allowed him to communicate with and control ants. Developing a costume to go along with his size changing ability and helmet, Pym reduced himself to the size of an ant and fought evil as Ant-Man. Pym and his future wife Janet Van Dyne were founding members of the Avengers as Ant-Man and the Wasp. Later, Pym decided to use his size-changing power to grow rather than shrink, and he began fighting crime as the costumed hero Giant-Man. Eventually, Pym realized that changing his size was putting too great a strain on his body and he stopped.

The Pym Particles in the serum that Henry Pym uses to alter his size can prove difficult to control. Here, the effort it took to return to normal size caused Pym to lose consciousness.

With each change of Henry Pym's Super Hero identity came a costume change as well.

A Troubled Mind

When Janet was kidnapped by Attuma and then the Collector, Pym decided to help the Avengers rescue her by using his growing power once again. He donned a new costume and became Goliath. While experimenting with unknown gases, an accident changed Pym's personality and gave him amnesia. He claimed that he had murdered Henry Pym and assumed the identity of Yellow Jacket. During this time, Pym married Janet, later regaining his memory, but the two were eventually divorced due to his tendency toward domestic violence. MT

ESSENTIAL STORYLINES
- ***Tales to Astonish #49*** Hank Pym first uses his size-changing Pym Particles to grow in size, transforming himself from Ant-Man into Giant-Man.
- ***Avengers #54*** Hank Pym creates Ultron, an incredibly powerful robot, which he implants with his own brain patterns. However Ultron rebels against his inventor.
- ***Avengers Forever, tpb*** Pym (as Giant-Man) and the Avengers battle Kang with humanity's future at stake.

FACES OF PYM
1 Ant-Man
2 Goliath
3 Yellowjacket

MARVEL IN THE

1990s

As the popularity of extended storylines and multi-title crossovers grew, Marvel produced more new titles and added gimmicks like holograms, foil-stamping and die-cut designs to covers. New versions of *Deathlok* and *Ghost Rider* joined titles like *New Warriors* and *Guardians of the Galaxy* in 1990. "The Infinity Gauntlet," the first of three major crossovers, arrived in 1991. "Operation: Galactic Storm" sprawled across the Avengers-related titles and a series set in the year 2099 began with Ravage 2099 and Spider-Man 2099 in 1992. "Maximum Carnage" threatened all the Spider-Man titles and Daredevil experienced a "Fall from Grace" as *Cable*, *Night Thrasher* and *Thunderstrike* graced 1993. New team books like *Fantastic Force*, *Force Works* and *Generation X-Men* marked 1994, and 1995 was highlighted by the "Age of Apocalypse", an event that briefly re-named all the X-Men titles and launched *X-Man*. The crossovers "Onslaught" and "Heroes Reborn," dominated 1996 and the spotlight fell on *Heroes For Hire* and *Thunderbolts* in 1997. "Heroes Return" was the big news in 1998, and *Earth X*, set in an alternate reality, debuted in 1999.

SPIDER-MAN #1 (1990)

With multiple covers and sales topping a million-and-a-half copies, a new Spider-Man is launched and begins a six-part extended storyline.

SILVER SURFER #50 (1991)

The Silver Surfer battles Thanos and celebrates 50 issues by being the first Marvel comic to possess a foil-stamped cover.

X-MEN #1 (1991)

Selling over 12 million copies with multiple covers, a second X-Men title establishes a new high that has yet to be equaled.

THUNDERSTRIKE #1 (1993)

After briefly replacing Thor, Eric Masterson is given his own enchanted mace, a new name and a new monthly title to face the menace called Bloodaxe.

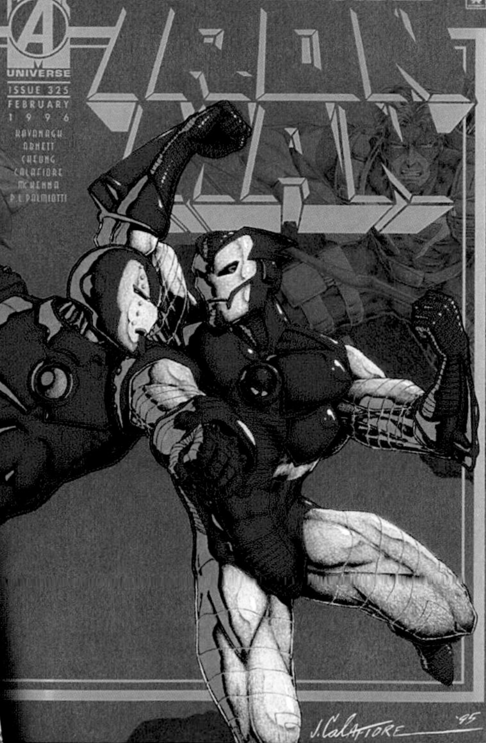

IRON MAN #325 (1996)

After learning that Tony Stark is being controlled by Kang, the Avengers enter a "Timeslide" to recruit a teenage Tony from an alternate timeline to assist them and battle his older self.

INCREDIBLE HULK #388 (1991)

The Hulk learns that one of his former partners is slowly dying from a deadly disease when he confronts the assassin called Speedfreak.

SPIDER-MAN 2099 #1 (1992)

A new universe set in a possible alternate future begins when a genetic experiment turns a corporate scientist into a reluctant Super Hero.

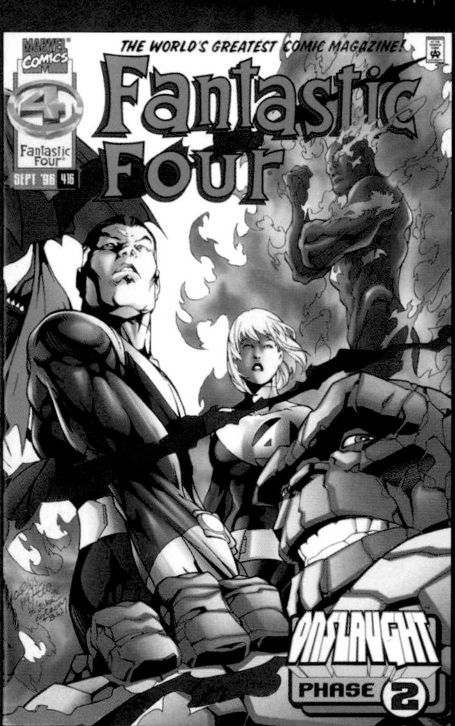

FANTASTIC FOUR #416 (1996)

As "Onslaught" draws to a climax, the title that spawned the Marvel Universe ends its first run, only to be relaunch in "Heroes Reborn."

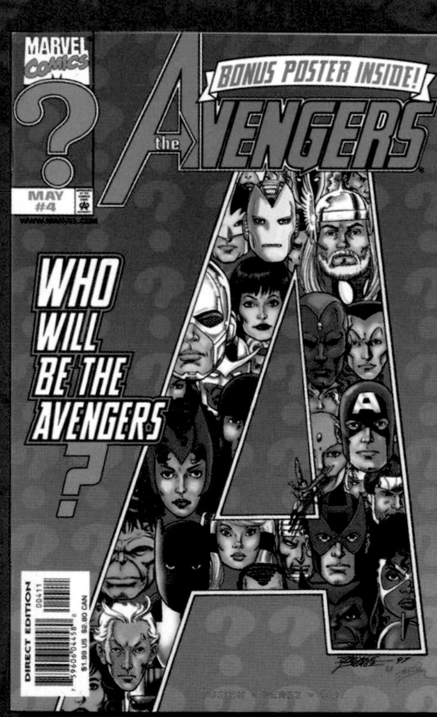

AVENGERS VOL. 3 #4 (1998)

Though the volume has changed, some traditions live on as the Avengers change their lineup once more.

AVENGERS FOREVER #1 (1998)

When Immortus decides that Rick Jones is a threat to all existence, Avengers from the past, present and future are forced to team up with Kang the Conqueror to save him.

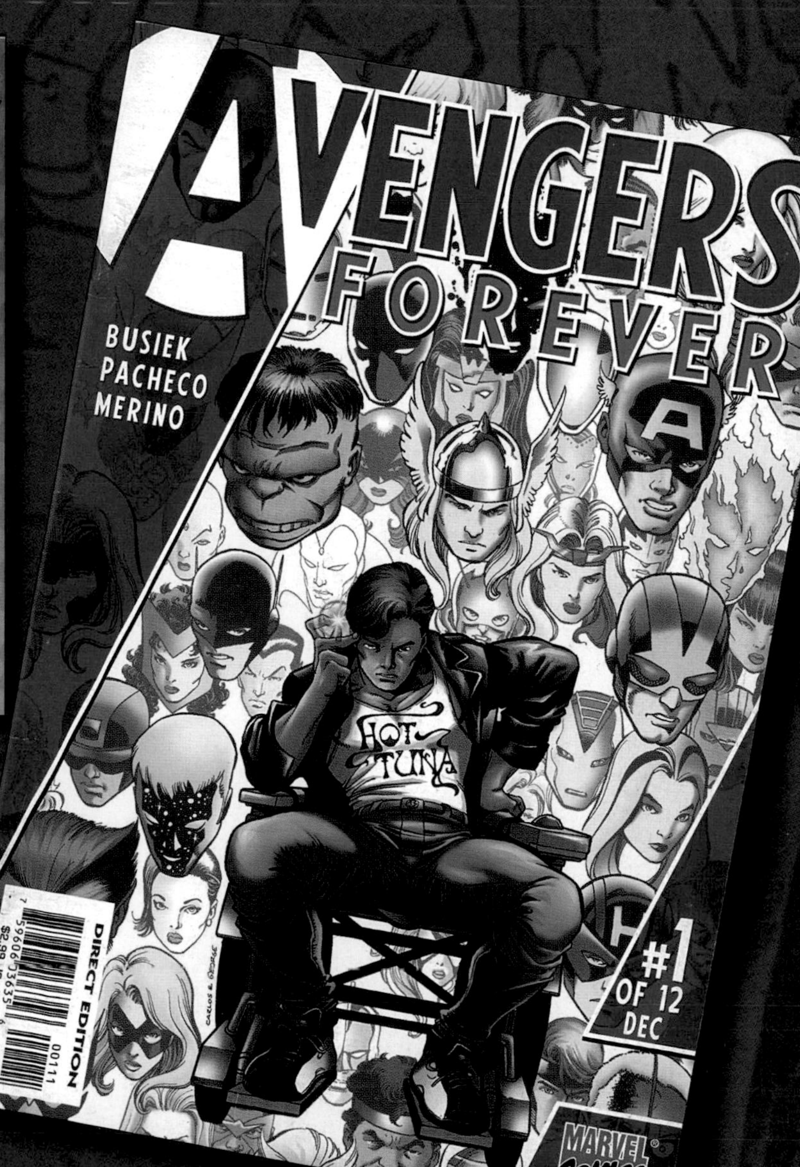

Quasar

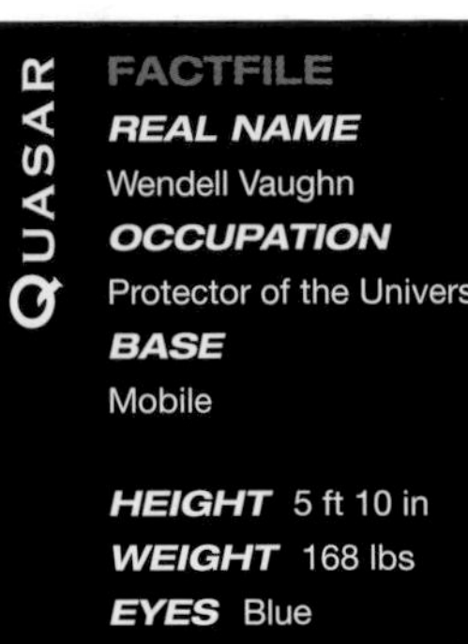

QUASAR

FACTFILE

REAL NAME
Wendell Vaughn

OCCUPATION
Protector of the Universe

BASE
Mobile

HEIGHT 5 ft 10 in
WEIGHT 168 lbs
EYES Blue
HAIR Blond

FIRST APPEARANCE
Captain America vol. 1 #217 (January 1978)

POWERS
Quantum-bands permit flight, teleportation, and the ability to form quantum energy constructs, including weapons and armor.

Wendell Vaughn attended SHIELD academy with Kenjiro TANAKA, and upon graduation found himself in the middle of a raid by AIM terrorists. Vaughn drove off the AIM agents by donning quantum-band bracelets worn by the 1950s Marvel Boy. As the new Marvel Boy, Vaughn became a member of SHIELD's Super-Agent program, later calling himself Marvel Man before settling on Quasar.

Vaughn later learned that he had been chosen by the cosmic entity Eon to become the new Protector of the Universe, replacing the late CAPTAIN MAR-VELL. Quasar also became a member of the AVENGERS, but could not prevent the villainous Maelstrom from killing Eon. When EGO THE LIVING PLANET threatened to devour Earth, Quasar proved his worth by absorbing the entity into his quantum-bands. Quasar exiled himself into space to prevent Ego's release, but he has returned to aid the Avengers and the FANTASTIC FOUR. **DW**

Using his quantum-bands, Quasar can project bubbles of energy that act as force shields. They can also transport things through space.

Initially hesitant about becoming Protector of the Universe, Quasar has become a selfless representative of Earth, and his understanding of his near-limitless powers has deepened.

Quasar is Earth's foremost cosmic hero, regularly dealing with representatives from interstellar empires such as the Kree, the Skrulls, and the Shi'ar. He has even held his own against Galactus-level threats.

Quasimodo

FIRST APPEARANCE Fantastic Four Special #4 (November 1966)
REAL NAME Quasi-Motivational Destruct Organism
OCCUPATION Former computer **BASE** Mobile
HEIGHT 6 ft **WEIGHT** 1,350 lbs **EYES** White **HAIR** None
SPECIAL POWERS/ABILITIES Computer brain; superhuman strength (when in physical form); left eye projects force blasts; can exist as pure consciousness without a physical body.

Quasimodo originated as a sentient computer created by the MAD THINKER. Endowed with a grotesque face that appeared on a screen, Quasimodo longed for a more human form. However, despite promising to fulfill his wish, the Thinker abandoned him. The SILVER SURFER took pity on Quasimodo and transformed him into a mobile, humanoid creature, but the ungrateful Quasimodo fought the Surfer, who rendered him immobile. Eventually Quasimodo regained his mobility, and has since battled such champions as SPIDER-MAN, the BEAST, the VISION, and the original CAPTAIN MAR-VELL. **PS**

QUICKSILVER
SEE OPPOSITE PAGE

Qnax

FIRST APPEARANCE Tales to Astonish #74 (December 1965)
REAL NAME Qnax (also known as Amphibian)
OCCUPATION Gladiator **BASE** The planet Xantares
HEIGHT 7 ft 9 in **WEIGHT** 915 lbs **EYES** Green **HAIR** None
SPECIAL POWERS/ABILITIES A product of centuries of scientific breeding to create the ultimate fighting machine; can travel fast and breathe underwater.

Xantares' Council of Elders sent Qnax on a mission to obtain the Sphere of Ultimate Knowledge, telling him the Sphere was needed to save the planet. Arriving on the homeworld of the WATCHERS, Qnax encountered the HULK, who was also searching for the Sphere. They fought and Qnax was hurled into space. Exiled from Xantares for this failure, Qnax travelled the cosmos as a gladiator for hire. He eventually discovered that the Council of Elders wanted the Sphere in order to dominate Xantares. Dismayed by this, Qnax returned home, hoping to bring justice to his people. **AD**

Quicksilver

The super-fast Super Hero

The son of Magneto, Pietro and his twin sister Wanda, the Scarlet Witch grew up never knowing their father's identity. Their mother, Magda, had fled from Magneto after witnessing his mutant powers in action, and gave birth to her twin offspring in the hills of Wundagore Mountain. The children were raised by the gypsy family of Django Maximoff. But at maturity, when their mutant powers first showed, Pietro and Wanda were persecuted as demonspawn.

THE BROTHERHOOD

In one attack, Wanda was surrounded by villagers who intended to burn her at the stake. Rescue came in the form of Magneto himself, who had been scouring the globe for mutants to recruit into his Brotherhood of Evil Mutants. Using his magnetic powers to scatter the frightened villagers, Magneto convinced Wanda and Pietro to join him and his Brotherhood.

Quicksilver eventually turned against Magneto (in reality, his long-lost father), and became a valued member of the Avengers along with his sister.

Quicksilver and Scarlet Witch engaged in a series of battles with the X-Men. However they only remained with the Brotherhood because of the debt they felt they owed Magneto. When the first incarnation of the Brotherhood was dissolved, Pietro and his sister went into seclusion, vowing never again to use their powers for evil.

Hearing that the Avengers were looking for new members, Pietro and Wanda resumed their costumed identities, and were accepted as members. But all did not remain well for long. Quicksilver, overprotective of his sister, did not approve of her marriage to the android Vision, causing a rift between them.

Quicksilver was later injured during a mission and nursed back to health by Crystal of the Inhumans. The two were married and had a daughter, Luna. Since then, Quicksilver has worked with the Avengers, served with the mutant team X-Factor, as well as leading the Knights of Wundagore for a time. **TB**

While in the Brotherhood of Evil Mutants, Quicksilver experienced superhuman combat against the X-Men, including Cyclops.

Since childhood, Quicksilver has been overly protective of his unstable sister, the Scarlet Witch.

QUICKSILVER

FACTFILE

REAL NAME
Pietro Maximoff

OCCUPATION
Adventurer

BASE
Various

HEIGHT 6 ft
WEIGHT 175 lbs
EYES Blue
HAIR Silver

FIRST APPEARANCE
X-Men #4 (March 1964)

POWERS

Quicksilver possesses the mutant ability to run at superhuman speeds over great distances. His top speed is alleged to be 175 mph. He can create a whirlwind by running in a circle; his temper can be a quick as his feet.

ESSENTIAL STORYLINES

- ***Avengers #16*** Quicksilver and his sister the Scarlet Witch join the Avengers.
- ***Avengers #127/Fantastic Four #150*** Quicksilver marries Crystal of the isolationist Inhumans.
- ***Avengers #185-187*** Quicksilver and the Scarlet Witch return to Wundagore Mountain in Eastern Europe to discover the strange secrets of their birth and their parentage.

Quicksilver is a member of the Ultimates team of Avengers who hail from a parallel Earth in another dimension of the mulitverse.

Radioactive Man

FIRST APPEARANCE Journey Into Mystery #93 (June 1963)
REAL NAME Dr. Chen Lu
OCCUPATION Former scientist; criminal **BASE** Mobile
HEIGHT 6 ft 6 in **WEIGHT** 310 lbs **EYES** Brown **HAIR** None
SPECIAL POWERS/ABILITIES Manipulates radioactivity given off by body; emits radiation as heat or blinding light and can incinerate a city block; hypnotic abilities; superhuman strength.

Dr. Chen Lu was a nuclear physicist in the People's Republic of China. After Thor stopped China invading India, the Chinese government asked its top scientists to find a way to defeat the thunder god. Lu exposed himself to massive doses of nuclear radiation, which transformed his body. As Radioactive Man, he traveled to New York and battled Thor, but was defeated. Baron Zemo then enlisted him in his Masters of Evil. Eventually he changed his ways and joined the Thunderbolts, a team of reformed villains. MT

Rage

FIRST APPEARANCE Avengers #326 (November 1990)
REAL NAME Elvin Daryl Haliday
OCCUPATION Student **BASE** Oatridge School for Boys
HEIGHT 6 ft 6 in **WEIGHT** 450 lbs **EYES** Brown **HAIR** None
SPECIAL POWERS/ABILITIES Exposure to alien radiation granted him the ability to fly and to understand the language of birds.

Twelve-year-old Elvin Haliday plunged into Newtown Creek to escape a vicious gang of racist thugs. The chemicals in the water caused the boy's body to grow, almost overnight, into that of an adult with superhuman strength.

Although Elvin could have used his new powers for all kinds of nefarious activities, his only relation, the devout Granny Staples, convinced him to follow a more heroic path. Elvin slipped from this road just once—when Granny Staples herself was murdered. A member of various Super Hero teams, including the Avengers and the Warriors, Elvin has since hung up his cloak and returned to school. AD

Rasputin, Mikhail

FIRST APPEARANCE Uncanny X-Men #284 (January 1992)
REAL NAME Mikhail Rasputin **OCCUPATION** Cosmonaut
BASE The Hill, in an unspecified dimension
HEIGHT 6 ft 5 in **WEIGHT** 255 lbs **EYES** Blue **HAIR** Black
SPECIAL POWERS/ABILITIES Manipulates matter on a sub-atomic level. He uses this power to fire destructive blasts, warp reality, and teleport through space and between dimensions.

During a spaceflight, Soviet cosmonaut Mikhail Rasputin was pulled into another dimension. There he fell in love with and married a princess. Her father, however, was a tyrant and Rasputin got involved in a civil war. During a battle another dimensional rift was opened and Rasputin used his powers to close it, but a backlash effect from closing the rift killed hundreds of people, including his beloved wife. Overcome with grief, he exiled himself to the desert where he was found by Sunfire and Iceman who helped bring Rasputin back to Earth. MT

Ravonna

In the 41st century of an alternate future, Kang had conquered all of Earth except the small kingdom of Princess Ravonna, who refused his offer of marriage. Kang's army ultimately overwhelmed Ravonna's kingdom.

But when Kang refused to execute Ravonna, his commander Baltag rebelled against him. Kang then joined forces with Ravonna and the Avengers to defeat Baltag. The grateful Ravonna fell in love with Kang. When the vengeful Baltag fired a blaster at Kang, Ravonna pushed Kang out of the way, and the blast struck her instead. Kang placed Ravonna in suspended animation. To restore her to life, Kang played a game with the alien Grandmaster, who gave him temporary power over life and death when Kang won. However, Kang wasted this short-lived power in an unsuccessful attempt to kill the Avengers.

After this point different timelines diverge, in which Ravonna leads different lives. In one timeline Kang saves Ravonna from Baltag's attack, but she becomes the ally and consort of Kang's own future counterpart, Immortus.

In another timeline the Grandmaster revives Ravonna, who seeks vengeance on Kang. She assumes a number of identities, including Nebula, the Temptress, and the Terminatrix. A future counterpart will take the name Revelation. PS

Ravonna was willing to sacrifice her life to save her lover Kang the Conqueror.

FACTFILE

REAL NAME
Ravonna Lexus Renslayer

OCCUPATION
Princess

BASE
Originally an unnamed kingdom on 41st century Earth in an alternate future.

HEIGHT 5 ft 8 in
WEIGHT 142 lbs
EYES (as Ravonna) Brown; (as Nebula/Terminatrix) Blue
HAIR (as Ravonna) Red-brown; (as Nebula/Terminatrix) Blonde

FIRST APPEARANCE
Avengers #23 (December 1965)

POWERS
As Terminatrix or Revelation: has enhanced durability, speed and agility, is a formidable hand-to-hand combatant, and uses highly advanced technology.

Rawhide Kid, The

FIRST APPEARANCE Rawhide Kid Vol. 1 #1 (March 1955)
REAL NAME Johnny Bart
OCCUPATION Gunslinger **BASE** The American Old West
HEIGHT 5 ft 10 in **WEIGHT** 185 lbs **EYES** Blue **HAIR** Red
SPECIAL POWERS/ABILITIES Skilled brawler and horseman; among the quickest draws in the Old West.

The Rawhide Kid learned to handle a six-shooter thanks to his adoptive father, a Texas Ranger, after his real parents were killed by Cheyenne warriors. When his adoptive father died in a rigged duel, the Rawhide Kid took revenge on the killers and then wandered the West astride his horse Nightwind, keeping one step ahead of the sheriff who suspected the Kid of murder. By means of time travel, the Rawhide Kid occasionally crossed paths with modern-era Super Heroes. AD

Reaper

FIRST APPEARANCE New Mutants Vol. 1 #87 (March 1990)
REAL NAME Pantu Hurageb
OCCUPATION None **BASE** Unknown
HEIGHT/ WEIGHT/ EYES/HAIR Unrevealed
SPECIAL POWERS/ABILITIES Neurosynaptic energy generated by Reaper slows reflexes and movements of those nearby; scythes focus energy and can be used to paralyse others.

Not to be mistaken for the demon raised to battle Blade, nor for an adversary of the Phantom Rider, the Reaper otherwise known as Pantu Hurageb was a mutant in the Mutant Liberation Front. The work was hazardous and during his time there, Reaper lost a hand and a lower leg, both of which were replaced by artificial limbs. Following Reaper's incarceration in the mutant concentration camp Neverland, Nathan Summers (Cable) tried to prise the camp's location from his mind, causing him severe brain damage and robbing him of the power of speech. AD

Reavers

The cyborg mercenaries known as the Reavers originally operated from an underground complex in Cooteman's Creek, located in Australia's Northern Territory. They exploited the teleportation mutant Gateway in order to commit robberies around the world until the X-Men forced them from their base. Ex-Hellfire Club member Donald Pierce reorganized the team, bringing in Cole, Macon, Reese, and Lady Deathstrike. The new Reavers nearly killed Wolverine, and launched a failed attack on Moira MacTaggart's Muir Island laboratory. A squad of Sentinels nearly destroyed the Reavers, though most members survived due to their half-machine physiologies.

The Reavers later won a contract from the psionic entity the Shadow King to kidnap Rogue of the X-Men, but failed to capture their quarry. Pierce chose to remake the Reavers into a grassroots anti-mutant movement, and swayed many citizens with his hateful propaganda. Recently, Pierce's group clashed with the latest incarnation of the New Mutants. During the battle, Reaver member Josh Foley discovered that he had mutant healing powers, and later joined the New Mutants under the code name Elixir. DW

FACTFILE

KEY MEMBERS

DONALD PIERCE (LEADER)
Adamantium-enhanced body, enhanced strength; morphing cyborg limbs emit energy blasts.

BONEBREAKER
Cyborg strength, tank treads, built-in weaponry.

PRETTY BOY
Extendible cyborg limbs and capture coils; reprograms the personalities of others.

SKULLBUSTER
Cyborg strength, robot legs; uses machine guns, grenade launchers.

SKULLBUSTER/CYLLA
Cyborg strength, reflexes; wrist claws, thermite launchers.

LADY DEATHSTRIKE
Augmented strength, reflexes; talons extend from fingertips.

COLE, MACON, AND REESE
Cyborg strength, reflexes; bionic scanners and tracking devices.

BASE Mobile

FIRST APPEARANCE
Uncanny X-Men Vol. 1 #229 (May 1988)

KEY
(from left to right)
Skullbuster, Bonebreaker, Pretty Boy

Red Ghost

FIRST APPEARANCE Fantastic Four Vol. 1 #13 (April 1963)
REAL NAME Ivan Kragoff **OCCUPATION** Villain
BASE Mobile **HEIGHT** 5 ft 11 in **WEIGHT** 215 lbs
EYES Brown **HAIR** White, balding
SPECIAL POWERS/ABILITIES Renders himself and nearby objects intangible and transparent; ingenious scientist and brilliant engineer.

Russian scientist Ivan Kragoff was consumed with envy by the achievements and powers of the Fantastic Four. Determined to beat them to the Moon, he designed his spacecraft to maximize exposure to cosmic rays, hoping to duplicate the freakish accident that had created his rivals.

Kragoff's experiment succeeded: while he gained the ability to become intangible, his three ape companions became more intelligent and obtained powers of strength, magnetism, and shapeshifting. Now known as the Red Ghost, Kragoff and his super-ape companions became formidable adversaries to the Fantastic Four, clashing with them repeatedly and even creating problems for the Avengers and Spider-Man. AD

Red Guardian

FACTFILE

REAL NAME
Alexi Shostakov

OCCUPATION
Espionage agent for Soviet Union; later for People's Republic of China

BASE
Various secret KGB bases in USSR; later a military base in the People's Republic of China

HEIGHT 6 ft 2 in
WEIGHT 220 lbs
EYES Blue
HAIR Red

FIRST APPEARANCE
Avengers #43 (August 1967)

POWERS
Brilliant athlete and test pilot, trained in espionage techniques and hand-to-hand combat by the KGB. Disc on Red Guardian's belt could be detached and used as a throwing weapon; magnetic force returned the disc after throwing.

Alexi Shostakov's life was destined to be radically different from that of his wife, Natasha Romanoff. A talented athlete and test pilot, Alexi came to the attention of the KGB, the Soviet secret service, which was eager to recruit new agents. The KGB faked Alexi's death and trained him to become a top operative codenamed Red Guardian. At the same time they coached his wife Natasha, keeping Alexi's survival a secret from her, and turning her into a secret agent codenamed Black Widow.

It was at this time that Alexi and Natasha's paths began to diverge. While she became disillusioned with her KGB masters and defected to the USA, Alexi remained loyal and increasingly ruthless and vindictive. The pair were to meet one more time, in China, but their reunion was short-lived: just minutes after revealing his identity to Natasha, Alexi was shot and killed. **AD**

After encountering the Avengers, the Red Guardian battles Hawkeye, Black Widow's lover.

The Red Guardian's identity is revealed.

Red Raven

FIRST APPEARANCE Red Raven Comics #1 (August 1940)
REAL NAME Unknown
OCCUPATION Adventurer **BASE** Mobile
HEIGHT 6 ft **WEIGHT** 180 lbs **EYES** Black **HAIR** Red
SPECIAL POWERS/ABILITIES Can fly using anti-gravity metallic wings, which can also deflect bullets and fire energy beams

Raised by a lost tribe of Inhumans known as the Bird-People, on a hovering island in the Atlantic, Red Raven was a heroic member of the World War II-era Liberty Legion. After the war, he placed himself and his people into suspended animation to prevent aggression between them and humanity. Later, the Angel (see Archangel) discovered Red Raven, who made it appear that his island had been destroyed to ensure the privacy of the Bird-People. His daughter Dania has also assumed the identity of Red Raven. **DW**

Red Skull ***SEE OPPOSITE PAGE***

Red Wolf

FIRST APPEARANCE Avengers #80 (September 1970)
REAL NAME William Talltrees
OCCUPATION adventurer **BASE** American Southwest
HEIGHT 6 ft 4 in **WEIGHT** 240 lbs **EYES** Brown **HAIR** Black
SPECIAL POWERS/ABILITIES Superhuman senses. Skilled hand-to-hand combatant. Expert tracker and archer. Employs a coup stick (a 6ft wooden staff used as a bo or javelin), tomahawk and knife.

The first Red Wolf is believed to have tamed the first horse and conquered the American plains for the Cheyenne. The second was Johnny Wakeley, a Cheyenne orphan who forged peace between his people and the US Cavalry. The current Red Wolf is Will Talltrees who grew up on the Cheyenne Reservation, in Wolf Point, Montana. After his family was murdered by businessmen, he begged the gods for the power to avenge them. The Wolf Spirit Owayodata heard his prayers. Following the legend of previous Red Wolves, Talltrees later trained a wolf until they almost thought as one. **TD**

Redeemer

FIRST APPEARANCE Incredible Hulk Vol. 2 #343 (May 1988)
REAL NAME Craig Saunders
OCCUPATION Former demolitions expert **BASE** New York
HEIGHT 6 ft 1 in **WEIGHT** 205 lbs **EYES** Brown **HAIR** White
SPECIAL POWERS/ABILITIES Bonded with combat suit armed with twin plasma canons on each hand, a rocket and grenade launcher, and rocket boots enabling 30 minutes of flight.

After joining the military as a demolitions expert, Craig Saunders' world came crashing down when he failed to defuse a bomb in an airport terminal, causing the death of two civilians. Desperate, he joined a new paramilitary team called the Hulkbusters, but their effort to defeat the Hulk also ended in disappointment. Taking advantage of Saunders' despair, the Leader persuaded him to become the Redeemer and integrated Saunders' body into a formidable yellow combat suit. Sadly, redemption was not to be his—Saunders died during his very first confrontation with old greenskin. **AD**

RED SKULL

The most dangerous of all Nazi agents

The Red Skull's Cosmic Cube, could alter reality.

Johann Shmidt was born in a German village. His mother died giving birth to him and, after failing to drown the newborn child, Johann's father committed suicide. The orphaned Shmidt became a beggar and thief, though he sometimes took menial jobs. Shmidt was working as a bellboy in a hotel when Adolf Hitler, the dictator of Nazi Germany, paid a visit there.

A PERFECT NAZI

Recognizing in Shmidt's eyes a hatred of all humanity that mirrored his own, Hitler decided to turn him into "the perfect Nazi." Hitler oversaw Shmidt's training, presented him with a skull-like head mask, and named him "The Red Skull." Answerable only to Hitler himself, the Red Skull undertook a wide range of missions for the Third Reich, especially acts of terrorism.

During World War II the Red Skull repeatedly battled Captain America and his partner Bucky.

It was in order to have an American counterpart to the Red Skull that the US government gave "super-soldier" Steve Rogers the identity of CAPTAIN AMERICA. Shortly before America entered World War II, the Red Skull first battled his greatest enemy, Captain America. During the war the Red Skull commanded numerous military missions. He rose to become the second most powerful man in the Third Reich, feared even by Hitler.

During the fall of Berlin, Captain America fought the Skull in Hitler's bunker. A bomb caused a cave-in that seemingly killed the Skull. However, an experimental gas kept the villain in suspended animation for decades.

BACK FROM THE DEAD

In the 1950s, the Skull was impersonated by Communist agent Albert Malik—the real Skull later had him killed. Eventually the original Red Skull was found and revived. With Hitler dead, the Skull was determined to become master of the world. However, his bids for global domination have repeatedly been thwarted by Captain America.

At one point the effects of the experimental gas wore off, and the Skull aged and died. The Nazi genetic engineer Arnim ZOLA transferred the Skull's consciousness into a body cloned from Captain America's. By accident, his own "dust of death" caused the Skull's new head to resemble a living red skull.

Although the Red Skull has seemingly died on numerous occasions, he always returns to continue his decades-long war against Captain America and the free world. **PS**

FACTFILE

REAL NAME
Johann Shmidt

OCCUPATION
Terrorist; conqueror

BASE
Nazi Germany, later various secret bases around the world.

HEIGHT (original body) 6 ft 1 in; (cloned body) 6 ft 2 in

WEIGHT (original body) 195 lbs; (cloned body) 240 lbs

EYES (both bodies) Blue

HAIR (original body) Brown; (cloned body) Formerly blond, later none

FIRST APPEARANCE
Captain America Comics #7 (October 1941)

POWERS

Totally ruthless, brilliant subversive strategist; excellent hand-to-hand combatant and marksman. Uses lethal "dust of death," which causes a victim's head to resemble a ghoulish red skull.

The Red Skull and Captain America are symbolic of tyranny and freedom.

The Red Skull so hates Captain America that he will even murder people who impersonate the real Captain and Bucky.

ESSENTIAL STORYLINES

- ***Tales of Suspense #66***
  The first time that the fascinating origin of the Red Skull was revealed.
- ***Tales of Suspense #79–81***
  The Red Skull is revived in modern times and steals the Cosmic Cube.
- ***Captain America #101–104***
  The Red Skull unleashes the Fourth Sleeper robot and leads his Nazi army of Exiles.

Revanche

FIRST APPEARANCE X-Men #17 (February 1992)
REAL NAME Kwannon **OCCUPATION** Assassin **BASE** Japan
HEIGHT (both bodies) 5 ft 11 in **WEIGHT** (both bodies) 155 lbs.
EYES (original body) Blue, (Braddock's body) Violet
HAIR (original body) Black, (Braddock's body) Brown, dyed purple
SPECIAL POWERS/ABILITIES Martial arts; (as Revanche) telepath; manifested psychic energy in form of Samurai sword.

Kwannon was a Japanese assassin and the lover of crimelord Matsu'o Tsurayaba. When Kwannon was mortally injured, Tsurayaba made a deal with Spiral, who transferred Kwannon's mind into the body of Elisabeth Braddock, Psylocke of the X-Men. Spiral also transferred Braddock's mind into Kwannon's body. Gaining Braddock's memories and powers, Kwannon claimed to be the real Psylocke and called herself Revanche (French for "revenge".) Discovering that she was infected with the Legacy Virus, she begged Matsu'o to kill her with a ceremonial dagger. **PS**

Ricochet

SEE OPPOSITE PAGE

Rictor

FIRST APPEARANCE X-Factor #17 (June 1987)
REAL NAME Julio Esteban Richter
OCCUPATION Private Investigator **BASE** New York City
HEIGHT 5 ft 9 in **WEIGHT** 162 lbs **EYES** Brown **HAIR** Brown
SPECIAL POWERS/ABILITIES By touching objects can cause them to vibrate and crumble; applied to buildings his powers have earthquake-like effect.

Before joining X-Factor Investigations, Julio Richter led an unsettled life. As a boy he saw his father, a black market arms dealer, murdered by the mutant clone, Stryfe. Julio developed mutant powers himself, and was captured and used by the Right to cause mayhem in San Francisco. Freed by X-Factor, he was caught up in the ideological turf war between Nathan Summers and Professor X, but now looks forward to a straightforward life as a private investigator. **AD**

Ringer

FIRST APPEARANCE Defenders Vol. 1 #51 (September 1977)
REAL NAME Anthony Davis
OCCUPATION Professional criminal **BASE** Mobile
HEIGHT 5 ft 8 in **WEIGHT** 145 lbs **EYES** Brown
HAIR Black, later dyed blonde
SPECIAL POWERS/ABILITIES Weapons included constricting rings, freeze rings, and explosive rings; could condense solid rings from air.

The Ringer was a second-tier villain throughout his short career. Although he developed a gimmick centered around ring weapons, he suffered humiliating defeats at the hands of crimefighters including Nighthawk II and Spider-Man. After his release from prison, the Ringer joined other criminals at the Ohio-based "bar with no name" to discuss the threat of the villain-killer known as the Scourge of the Underworld. Unknown to the criminals, the Scourge was also in the bar at the time. The Scourge shot everyone in the bar and left Ringer for dead. **DW**

Rhino

FIRST APPEARANCE Amazing Spider-Man #41 (October 1966)
REAL NAME Alex O'Hirn (possibly an alias)
OCCUPATION Criminal **BASE** Mobile
HEIGHT 6 ft 5 in **WEIGHT** 710 lbs **EYES** Brown **HAIR** Brown
SPECIAL POWERS/ABILITIES The Rhino possesses the strength and enhanced durability of his namesake due to his protective suit, which is bonded to his body.

A career criminal, the man who would become the Rhino was selected for experimentation by a group of spies because of his low intelligence. After months of chemical and radiation treatments, he was given his protective suit, which resembled a rhinoceros' hide. He was sent to abduct astronaut John Jameson, but was foiled by Spider-Man. The Rhino has subsequently used his strength in a number of criminal endeavors. Believing himself to be trapped permanently within his costume, the Rhino is subject to periodic bouts of insanity. **TB**

Richards, Franklin

SEE OPPOSITE PAGE

Right, The

FIRST APPEARANCE X-Factor #17 (June 1987)
MEMBERS AND POWERS
Cameron Hodge (commander) Brilliant planner; made immortal through a mystical pact
Ani-Mator Genius-level geneticist
Other unnamed operatives and soldiers.
BASE Mobile

The Right is a secret organization dedicated to preserving human freedoms by the eradication of mutantkind. Cameron Hodge, a former public relations director for X-Factor, founded the Right using X-Factor's own profits. Hodge's double-dealing soon became all too obvious and he engaged his former colleagues in combat, clashing with both X-Factor and the New Mutants. Agents of the Right wear armored battlesuits equipped with built-in machine guns and flight jets. Their battlesuits have facemasks that bearing a distinctive "smiley face" design. **DW**

Riordan, Dallas

FIRST APPEARANCE Thunderbolts #1 (April 1997)
REAL NAME Dallas Riordan
OCCUPATION Adventurer **BASE** New York City
HEIGHT 5 ft 1 in **WEIGHT** 150 lbs **EYES** Blue **HAIR** Red
SPECIAL POWERS/ABILITIES Expert swordswoman and adept hand-to-hand combatant.

The granddaughter of Paulette Brazee and one-time lover of the original Citizen V, for a time Dallas Riordan was to bear the Citizen V mantle herself. Working as the assistant to the New York mayor, Dallas served as his liaison to the Thunderbolts until Baron Zemo discredited the team and caused Dallas' own reputation to be called into question. Invited to become the new Citizen V, Dallas' career as this costumed crusader was cut short when she was crippled in battle. Now wheelchair-bound, Dallas can only walk when she merges her consciousness with that of her lover, Erik Josten, the Super Hero, Atlas. **AD**

Richards, Franklin

Son of Reed and Sue Richards of the Fantastic Four, Franklin Richards was once one of the most powerful mutants on Earth. Before his birth, strange energies flowing through Sue's body nearly killed both mother and baby until Annihilus' Cosmic Control Rod suppressed them. Agatha Harkness acted as Franklin's nanny in his earliest years. The boy soon began to exhibit immense psionic powers. Using his ability to see possible futures, he became a member of Power Pack under the name Tattletale. Nathaniel Richards, his grandfather, later raised him in a realm outside of time, where he became the adult adventurer Psi-Lord, and founded the Fantastic Force before Hyperstorm erased his adult form from existence. When the Avengers and the Fantastic Four seemingly perished fighting Onslaught, Franklin temporarily sent them to a "Counter-Earth" of his own creation. He used his powers to restore Galactus to life and return his sister Valeria to his mother's womb, but lost his powers in the process. Recently, Doctor Doom banished Franklin to Hell, causing psychological trauma that persisted long after his rescue. DW

The enemies of the Fantastic Four have frequently made Franklin the target of their aggression.

FACTFILE

REAL NAME
Franklin Benjamin Richards

OCCUPATION
Occasional adventurer

BASE
New York City

HEIGHT 4 ft 8 in
WEIGHT 100 lbs
EYES Blue
HAIR Blond

FIRST APPEARANCE
Fantastic Four Annual #6 (1968)

POWERS

Formerly possessed vast powers of telepathy and telekinesis, as well as the ability to fire psionic blasts, reshape reality, appear in astral form, and perceive future events.

Ricochet

Peter Parker as Ricochet, wearing a costume designed by his partner, the fashion-conscious Mary Jane.

When Spider-Man was falsely accused of murder, a $5 million reward was placed on his head and he was forced to adopt a new identity in order to find the real killer. Instead of temporarily assuming one new persona, he created four: Ricochet, Dusk, Hornet, and Prodigy. After clearing his name, Spider-Man discarded these identities and their costumes. The costumes came into the possession of a former Super Hero called the Black Marvel, who gave them to four teenagers and formed a new super-team called the Slingers. One of the members was Johnny Gallo, a troubled youth who had grown apart from his father after his mother was killed in a car accident. Johnny literally leaped at the chance to use his mutant powers in the Slingers, but like the other members of the team he was disillusioned when it emerged that the Black Marvel had obtained the costumes from Mephisto. Nevertheless, the Slingers battled to save the Black Marvel's soul from Mephisto and won, although the battle claimed the life of the Black Marvel. The Slingers then disbanded and Gallo moved to Los Angeles. He joined a group of former teenage heroes who were adjusting to civilian life and trying to dissuade other teenagers from becoming costumed heroes. TD

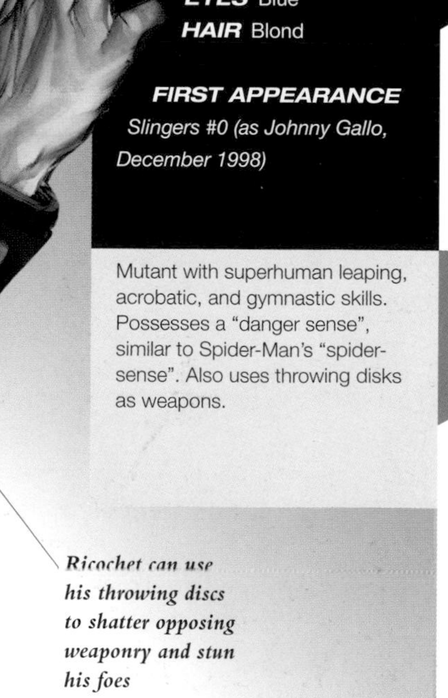

Ricochet can use his throwing discs to shatter opposing weaponry and stun his foes

FACTFILE

REAL NAME
Jonathon "Johnny" Gallo

OCCUPATION
College student

BASE
Los Angeles, California; formerly Brooklyn, New York

HEIGHT 5 ft 10 in
WEIGHT 155 lbs
EYES Blue
HAIR Blond

FIRST APPEARANCE
Slingers #0 (as Johnny Gallo, December 1998)

POWERS

Mutant with superhuman leaping, acrobatic, and gymnastic skills. Possesses a "danger sense", similar to Spider-Man's "spider-sense". Also uses throwing disks as weapons.

Riot Squad

FACTFILE

CURRENT MEMBERS AND POWERS

JAILBAIT
Can project psionic force fields.

HOTSHOT
Can project psionic force fields.

OGRESS
Enhanced strength and damage resistance.

OMNIBUS
Super-genius intellect.

SOUL MAN (deceased)
Possessed ability to resurrect the dead.

FIRST APPEARANCE
(As normal humans) Incredible Hulk Vol. 2 #345 (July 1988); (as Riot Squad) Incredible Hulk vol. 2 #366 (February 1990)

CHARACTER KEY
1 Rock **2** Soul Man
3 Ogress **4** Hotshot
5 Jailbait **6** Redeemer

Riot Squad

The Riot Squad came into being when the villainous Leader detonated a gamma bomb on the town of Middletown, Arizona. Amazingly, a few residents survived, mutated by gamma radiation in the same manner as the Hulk. These five took the cover names Jailbait, Hotshot, Ogress, Omnibus, and Soul Man, and became the Leader's elite guards. Charged with protecting the Freehold base, where the Leader gave sanctuary to those suffering from radiation sickness, the team fought the Hulk on several occasions.

During an attack on the Freehold base by HYDRA, Soul Man was killed, and with the Leader also presumed dead, Omnibus took control of the Riot Squad. His teammates later put him on trial after he orchestrated terrorist bombings in an effort to gain more power. Despite his protestations that he had been under the control of the Leader when he committed the crimes, they found him guilty and banished him to the Arctic. The Troyjans later decimated Freehold despite the efforts of Riot Squad. The team is likely to continue as a mercenary outfit. DW

Risque

FIRST APPEARANCE X-Force vol 1, #51 (August 1991)
REAL NAME Gloria Dolores Munoz
OCCUPATION X-Corporation Employee (deceased)
BASE Hong Kong
HEIGHT 5 ft 9 in **WEIGHT** 120 lbs **EYES** Brown **HAIR** Black
SPECIAL POWERS/ABILITIES Compresses matter, inorganic and organic; can destroy smaller objects, like a mobile phone, altogether.

Gloria Munoz had a lonely childhood. Her parents divorced when she was 12 and she left home at 16. Forced to fend for herself, Gloria developed a cold, distant personality and her first encounters with the mutant group, X-Force did not endear her to them. However, she became romantically involved with Warpath, even falling in love with him, before betraying him to the Deviant known as Sledge. After making recompense for her misdeeds, Gloria was invited to join X-Corporation's Hong Kong office, but she wasn't there long. While investigating the trade in mutant body parts, Gloria was killed by the U-Men, a group of humans seeking mutant body parts to graft onto themselves. AD

Robertson, Joe

Robertson defeated his nemesis Tombstone after years of trying.

Joseph "Robbie" Robertson, editor in chief of the *Daily Bugle*, grew up in Harlem alongside the brutal Lonnie Thompson Lincoln (Tombstone). While working as a newspaper reporter in Philadelphia, Robertson saw Tombstone kill a man, but, intimidated, kept silent about the murder for nearly two decades. After years with New York's *Daily Bugle*, he finally gathered evidence of the murder and Tombstone's other crimes, only for Tombstone to break his back in retaliation. Robertson recovered and testified against Tombstone in court, receiving a jail sentence of his own for withholding evidence. He resigned from the *Daily Bugle* when Norman Osborn (the Green Goblin) purchased the newspaper, but later returned to the job. His son Randy attended college with Peter Parker, and Robertson is believed to have guessed that Peter Parker is Spider-Man. He remains one of the few people who can keep *Daily Bugle* publisher J. Jonah Jameson under control. DW

FACTFILE

REAL NAME
Joseph Robertson

OCCUPATION
Editor-in-chief of the *Daily Bugle*

BASE
New York City

HEIGHT 6 ft 1 in
WEIGHT 210 lb
EYES Brown
HAIR White

FIRST APPEARANCE
Amazing Spider-Man Vol. 1 #51 (August 1967)

Robertson, Joe

POWERS

Highly skilled writer and dogged investigative reporter.

Rock

FIRST APPEARANCE The Incredible Hulk vol. 1 #343 (May 1988)
REAL NAME Samuel J. Laroquette
OCCUPATION Warrior **BASE** Mobile
HEIGHT 6 ft **WEIGHT** Unrevealed
EYES Brown **HAIR** Black
SPECIAL POWERS/ABILITIES Able to shape his rock-like exoskeleton into any form he imagines.

A former explorer, Sam Laroquette became a member of the Hulkbusters at a time when the HULK had been separated from Bruce Banner. Later recruited by would-be world conqueror the LEADER, Laroquette received treatments that encased him in a rocklike substance responsive to his mental commands. As Rock, he went into action against the Hulk alongside his fellow operative REDEEMER. The stone projections Rock created by reshaping his exoskeleton proved to be one of the few things capable of puncturing the Hulk's tough skin. The Rock has since worked alongside the U-FOES and the RIOT SQUAD. DW

Rocket Racer

FIRST APPEARANCE Amazing Spider-Man #172 (September 1977)
REAL NAME Robert Farrell
OCCUPATION Student **BASE** New York City
HEIGHT 5 ft 10 in **WEIGHT** 160 lbs **EYES** Brown **HAIR** Black
SPECIAL POWERS/ABILITIES Rides jet-powered, skateboard to which boots are magnetically attached; mini-rockets on gloves can tear holes in three-inch thick steel.

The eldest of seven children, Robert Farrell became responsible for his younger siblings when his mother died. Robert was a scientific prodigy, and when he realised he couldn't earn enough to support his family, he turned to a life of crime. He developed a superpowered skateboard which was cybernetically controlled by crude walkman device, and, wearing a weapon-equipped costume, became the Rocket Racer. Repeated defeats at the hands of SPIDER-MAN and several brushes with the law, including a short jail sentence, convinced Robert to reform. He has since gained a scholarship to Empire State University and even assists Spider-Man from time to time. AD

Rogue

Rogue stole and retained the powers of Ms. Marvell.

As a girl, the mutant called Rogue lived in Mississippi. Orphaned, Rogue ran away and was adopted by MYSTIQUE and DESTINY. Rogue's mutant power manifested itself when she kissed her friend Cody Robbins, involuntarily absorbing his memories. In her teens, Rogue joined Mystique's terrorist group, BROTHERHOOD OF EVIL MUTANTS.

After fighting the original Ms. Marvel, Rogue had superhuman strength, durability, and the power of flight. Distraught over her inability to control her absorption power, Rogue turned to her enemies, the mutant X-MEN, for help. Invited by Professor Xavier (*see* PROFESSOR X) to join them, she fell in love with GAMBIT. Rogue later joined the spin-off team, the X-Treme X-Men. She lost her superhuman powers but regained her absorption power and has rejoined the X-Men. Rogue recently (and apparently permanently) absorbed the power of SUNFIRE to absorb and discharge solar energy. PS

ROGUE

FACTFILE
REAL NAME
Unrevealed
OCCUPATION
Former terrorist, now adventurer
BASE
The Xavier Institute, Salem Center, New York State

HEIGHT 5 ft 8 in
WEIGHT 120 lbs
EYES Green
HAIR Brown

FIRST APPEARANCE
Avengers Annual #10 (1981)

POWERS
Mutant ability to absorb the memories, knowledge, talents, personality, and physical abilities of another person through physical contact with them.

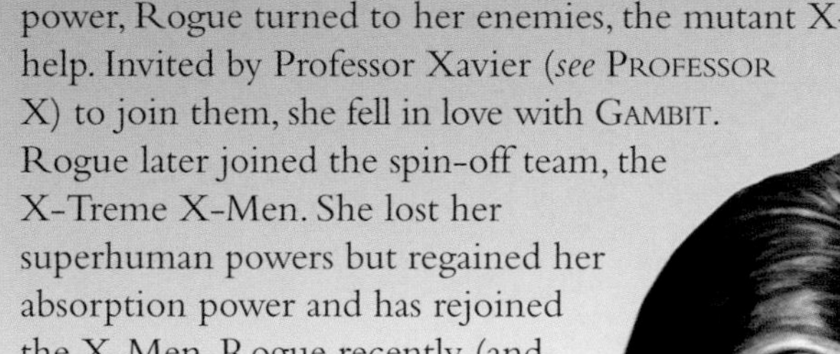

Rogue has striking white streaks in her long hair

Roma

FIRST APPEARANCE Captain Britain #1 (January 1985)
REAL NAME Roma
OCCUPATION Sorceress **BASE** Otherworld
HEIGHT 5 ft 10 in **WEIGHT** 135 lbs **EYES** Green **HAIR** Black
SPECIAL POWERS/ABILITIES Sorceress with mystical abilities; casts spells that restore life to the dead or block her own presence or others' presence from detection by organic or technological means.

The daughter of the sorcerer MERLIN, Roma appeared to a man named Brian Braddock as the Goddess of the Northern Skies and gave him the Amulet of Right. The amulet's mystical energy turned him into CAPTAIN BRITAIN and Roma became one of his advisors. Roma was imprisoned by the ADVERSARY but was freed by COLOSSUS, Madelyne Pryor (*see* PRYOR, MADELYNE), and FORGE, who all died but were brought back to life by Roma. Roma was then seized by the sentient computer, Mastermind, but was freed by Captain Britain. **MT**

Ronan the Accuser

FIRST APPEARANCE Fantastic Four #65 (August 1967)
REAL NAME Ronan
OCCUPATION Supreme Public Accuser
BASE Citadel of Judgement, on planet Kree-Lar
HEIGHT 7 ft 5 in **WEIGHT** 480 lbs **EYES** Blue **HAIR** Unknown
SPECIAL POWERS/ABILITIES Wields Universal Weapon—fires concussive energy bolts, disintegrates matter, creates force fields.

Born to an aristocratic Kree family (*see* KREES), Ronan was automatically accepted into the Accuser Corps when he came of age, and was in charge of bestowing justice across the Kree Empire. Rising to the position of Supreme Public Accuser, mighty Ronan became the third most powerful person in the Empire and was responsible for punishing the FANTASTIC FOUR when they defeated an Earth-based Kree Sentry. The foursome humiliated Ronan, so, when the Kree leader decided to let matters lie, Ronan tried, and failed, to wrest control of the Empire. Ronan has since resigned himself to working with his superiors for the betterment of his people. **AD**

Ross, General T.E

FIRST APPEARANCE Incredible Hulk Vol. 1 #1 (May 1962)
REAL NAME Thaddeus E. Ross
NICKNAME Thunderbolt
OCCUPATION Lieutenant General, US Air Force **BASE** Mobile
HEIGHT 6 ft 1 in **WEIGHT** 245 lbs **EYES** Blue **HAIR** White
SPECIAL POWERS/ABILITIES Is a capable combatant and has an advanced military mind.

General Ross comes from a long line of military officers. During wartime action his troops gave him the nickname "Thunderbolt," since he "struck like a thunderbolt" when he took them into combat. As the officer in charge of the experiment that turned Bruce Banner into the HULK, General Ross became obsessed with capturing the Hulk by any means necessary. For a time, he possessed the electrical form of ZZZAX, and he later sacrificed himself to destroy the mutant Nevermind. Restored to life, he has won back his position as Air Force general, and is trying to forge an improved relationship with Bruce Banner. **DW**

Rose, The

FIRST APPEARANCE (JC) Daredevil #131 (March 1976); (RF) Amazing Spider-Man #83 (April 1970) **REAL NAME** Jacob Conover; Richard Fisk **OCCUPATION** (JC) columnist; (RF) crime lord **BASE** (JC) New York City **HEIGHT** (JC) 6 ft; (RF) 6 ft 2 in **WEIGHT** (JC) 210lbs; (RF) 225lbs **EYES** (JC) brown; (RF) brown **FEATHERS** (JC) brown; (RF) blue **SPECIAL POWERS/ABILITIES** (JC & RF) criminal masterminds, manipulators, and strategists.

The first leather-masked Rose was Richard Fisk, the son of criminal KINGPIN. Fisk believed that his father was an honest businessman. When he learned the truth, he tried to ruin his father's empire and became a member of HYDRA. Fisk eventually joined forces with his father and became the Rose but was killed by his mother. The second Rose was a police officer seeking revenge on the Kingpin. The third and current Rose is Jacob Conover, who wrote for the *Daily Bugle*. He was given the identity as a reward for saving the life of crime lord Don Fortunato. Conover was captured by SPIDER-MAN and is currently in prison. **TD**

Roth, Arnold

FIRST APPEARANCE Captain America #270 (May 1982)
REAL NAME Arnold "Arnie" Roth
OCCUPATION Sailor, later publicist, later costume shop manager
BASE New York City
HEIGHT Unrevealed **WEIGHT** Unrevealed **EYES** Blue **HAIR** Grey
SPECIAL POWERS/ABILITIES Possessed the normal human strength of a man of his age who engaged in mild exercise.

Arnold Roth became friends with Steve Rogers when they were growing up in the 1930s. During World War II, Roth served in the US Navy and realized that Captain America was his friend Steve. While Captain America spent years in suspended animation, Roth aged normally. Learning of Roth's friendship with Captain America, Baron Helmut Zemo (*see* Baron Zemo I) imperiled Roth and his life partner, Michael. Later, the Red Skull captured Roth. Captain America and Roth remained friends. Roth worked as the Avengers' publicist and managed Steve Rogers' costume shop before dying from bone cancer. **PS**

Ruiz, "Rigger"

FIRST APPEARANCE The Mighty Thor Vol. 1 #426 (Nov. 1990)
REAL NAME Margarita Allegra "Rigger" Ruiz
OCCUPATION Police officer **BASE** New York City
HEIGHT Unknown **WEIGHT** Unknown
EYES Unknown **HAIR** Black
SPECIAL POWERS/ABILITIES Adept with range of weaponry; she invented "port-a-pulley" for easy navigation of elevator shafts.

Margarita Allegra "Rigger" Ruiz is the armory specialist of Code: Blue, a SWAT team designated to deal with superpowered criminals. Bodybuilder Rigger has come face-to-face with these superhumans on a regular basis and her experiences have been many and varied. The strongest member of Code: Blue, Rigger has rescued hostages from the Wrecking Crew, been driven mad by the Super Villain Dementia, and posed as a slave during a mission to Asgard. During this last assignment, Rigger also flirted with Fandral the Dashing, an Asgardian noble—life is never dull in Code: Blue. **AD**

Russian

FIRST APPEARANCE Punisher Vol. 5 #8 (November 2000)
REAL NAME Unrevealed
OCCUPATION Mercenary **BASE** Mobile
HEIGHT 7 ft 2 in **WEIGHT** 573 lbs
EYES Blue **HAIR** Reddish-blond
SPECIAL POWERS/ABILITIES Post-reconstruction, the Russian possessed enhanced strength and damage resistance.

The mercenary nicknamed "the Russian" accepted a job from crime boss Ma Gnucci to kill the Punisher. After a brutal fight, the Punisher smothered the Russian, later taunting Ma Gnucci by showing her the Russian's severed head. A secret paramilitary agency then resurrected the Russian, giving him an enhanced body with boosted olfactory senses, three hearts, and a toughened skeleton. This new body required regular injections of female hormones. The Russian apparently died when he was caught in the explosion of a nuclear warhead on Grand Nixon Island. **DW**

Ryker, General John

A mendacious individual, General John Ryker was involved in US President Kennedy's assassination, dropped gamma bombs on US troops in the Gulf, and was desperate to learn the secret behind the Hulk. Ryker's obsession with old Greenskin was driven by a need to find a cure for his cancer-ridden wife. However, when she found out what he was doing, Ryker fled. In his drive to understand the Hulk, Ryker tormented Banner and many others. Vagrants from across America were taken to Ryker's research facility where they were subjected to agonising tortures. Realizing that success lay in the mental rather than physical manipulation of his test subjects, Ryker began using his soldiers. He transformed one man—Private Tibbetts—into a corrupted version of the Hulk, codenamed Flux. Definitely driven, certainly insane, he may have disappeared for the time being but Ryker is certain to return. **AD**

A human guinea pig faces a painful death by gamma radiation.

FACTFILE

REAL NAME
General John Ryker

OCCUPATION
Senior General in US Army

BASE
Currently unknown

HEIGHT 6 ft 2 in
WEIGHT 190 lbs
EYES Brown
HAIR Gray

FIRST APPEARANCE
Incredible Hulk vol.3 #14 (May 2000)

POWERS
Brilliant manipulator of others, possesses intuitive understanding of others' emotional vulnerabilities; exceptional strategist, excels at seeing big picture; inveterate liar; psychotic dispassion for the suffering of others.

SHIELD

Helping to keep the peace all around the world

SHIELD

FACTFILE

NOTABLE MEMBERS
NICK FURY (Second director)
CONTESSA VALENTINA
ALLEGRA DI FONTAINE
YELENA BELOVA (Black Widow)
G. W. BRIDGE (fourth director)
SHARON CARTER (Agent 13), fifth director; liaison officer to Captain America.
JESSICA DREW (Spider-Woman)
THADDEUS "DUGAN", (third director)
MARIA HILL (current director)
GABRIEL JONES
AL MACKENZIE (CIA liaison)
ALI MORALES
CLAY QUARTERMAIN
NATASHA ROMANOVA (Black Widow)
JASPER SITWELL
JIMMY WOO

BASE The Helicarrier; mobile

FIRST APPEARANCE
Strange Tales #135 (August 1965)

Nick Fury was one of SHIELD's top operatives.

SHIELD (Supreme Headquarters International Espionage Law-Enforcement Division; later changed to Strategic Hazard Intervention, Espionage and Logistics Directorate) is a counter-terrorism, intelligence, espionage, and peace-keeping organization. SHIELD runs covert as well as military operations, and works with governments and their military forces around the world.

ESSENTIAL STORYLINES
- ***Strange Tales #135*** Nick Fury, who will be the organization's top operative and eventual leader, is recruited by SHIELD.
- ***Strange Tales #158*** HYDRA Island sinks, and Baron Wolfgang Von Strucker, HYDRA'S leader is killed.

SHIELD'S FORMATION

SHIELD was established to counter the threat posed by the technologically advanced neo-fascist subversive organization known as HYDRA. The identity of SHIELD's founders remains classified, as does the identity of its first executive director, who was assassinated by HYDRA operatives. SHIELD's second and longest-serving leader was Nick FURY, a Colonel in the US army, who had also been a top CIA operative. Other important SHIELD members include Timothy "Dum Dum" DUGAN, Valentina Allegro DE FONTAINE, and Jasper Sitwell.

For many years, SHIELD's headquarters was the Helicarrier, a huge flying aircraft carrier that was kept airborne at all times. It carried a squadron of jet fighters and an ICBM. The Helicarrier was destroyed, but SHIELD maintains its many regional headquarters throughout the world. SHIELD also keeps close ties to the Super Hero community and has called upon CAPTAIN AMERICA, the AVENGERS, and the FANTASTIC FOUR for help; other allies have included MOCKINGBIRD, QUASAR, and Anthony Stark (IRON MAN). In addition to battling global terrorist and military threats, SHIELD has saved the world many times from extraterrestrial invasion and infiltration. As well as its human operatives, SHIELD also employs LMDs, Life Model Decoys. These are incredibly lifelike androids which are sent into extremely dangerous situations to help avoid human casualties.

AIM are continually inventing new terror weapons, such as this "Zombie Monster" confronting the Hulk.

SHIELD has a formidable high-tech arsenal at its disposal ready to deploy at trouble spots anywhere in the world.

ALLIES AND ENEMIES

Over the years SHIELD's main adversaries have included HYDRA, AIM, ZODIAC, the Corporation, the YELLOW CLAW, the VIPER, the RED SKULL, CENTURIUS, and DOCTOR DEMONICUS. SHIELD provided intelligence and technical support to the Avengers and the Fantastic Four during the Kree-Skrull War, when a battle of the aliens took place very close to Earth. **MT**

The subversive terrorist organization HYDRA, dedicated to world domination, is one of SHIELD's most dangerous threats.

Sabretooth

SABRETOOTH

FACTFILE

REAL NAME
Victor Creed

OCCUPATION
Assassin

BASE
Mobile

HEIGHT 6 ft 6 in

WEIGHT 275 lbs

EYES Amber

HAIR Blond

FIRST APPEARANCE
Iron Fist Vol. 1 #14 (August 1977)

POWERS

Sabretooth possesses an extended lifespan, thanks to the healing ability that also allows him to recover rapidly from almost any injury. He also possesses enhanced animalistic strength, speed and agility, and razor-sharp claws on each hand.

A vicious, psychotic killer, little is known about the early life of Victor Creed, the mutant called Sabretooth, save that he apparently came from an abusive background. His healing ability having kept him alive and youthful for decades, he first acquired the alias Sabretooth in the 1960s, when he did wetwork for the CIA.

Bitter Feud

Like Wolverine, Sabretooth's abilities were enhanced by the top-secret Weapon X project, and while the two men share much history in common, they are the bitterest of enemies. Sabretooth routinely returns to stalk and defeat Wolverine on the latter's birthday each year. And because of his enmity for Wolverine, Sabretooth has been pulled into the X-Men's orbit time and again, sometimes in partnership with other villain such as Mister Sinister, sometimes on his own. But while there is still some humanity left within Wolverine's heart, Sabretooth's soul is as black as pitch, and he is about as irredeemable an individual as has ever existed. **TB**

The enmity between Sabretooth and Wolverine spans decades. On Wolverine's birthday each year, no matter where he was in the world, Sabretooth would appear to challenge him.

Sabra

FIRST APPEARANCE The Incredible Hulk #250 (August 1980)
REAL NAME Ruth Bat-Seraph **OCCUPATION** Police officer; Israeli government agent **BASE** Jerusalem, Israel
HEIGHT 5 ft 11 in **WEIGHT** 240 lbs **EYES** Brown **HAIR** Black
SPECIAL POWERS/ABILITIES Wrist bracelets equipped with neuronic-frequency stunners that shoot "energy quills." Cape has a device that neutralizes gravity, enabling flight. Superhuman strength.

When Ruth Bat-Seraph's mutant powers emerged in childhood, the Israeli government sent Ruth and her parents to live at a special kibbutz, where she was trained in the use of her powers. She became the first member of the Israeli government's "Super-Agent" program, and was given a cover identity as a policewoman.

Terrorists killed her son, and so have become her particular enemies.

Sabra has also worked for the Paris branch of Professor X's X-Corporation.

The name "Sabra" is the Israeli word for both a native-born Israeli and for a sweet, prickly pear. **PS**

Sage

FIRST APPEARANCE Uncanny X-Men vol. 1 #132 (April 1980)
REAL NAME Unrevealed, goes by "Tessa"
OCCUPATION Member of New Excalibur **BASE** England
HEIGHT 5 ft 7 in **WEIGHT** 135 lbs **EYES** Blue **HAIR** Black
SPECIAL POWERS/ABILITIES Able to remember everything she sees and hears; can "jump start" the mutant abilities of others; possesses limited telepathy.

Born in Eastern Europe, the mysterious woman codenamed Sage rescued an injured Professor X from Afghanistan and became one of his first mutant recruits. Rather than joining the original X-Men team, Sage became a spy within the Hellfire Club, where she worked as an advisor to Black King Sebastian Shaw.

When she tricked the mind-controlling Elias Bogan into losing a wager, a vengeful Bogan scarred her face. Rescued by Storm, Sage joined the X-Men and most recently became a member of New Excalibur. **DW**

SALEM'S SEVEN

FACTFILE

FORMER MEMBERS

BRUTACUS
Enhanced strength

GAZELLE
Superhuman agility and reflexes

HYDRON
Able to blast water from left arm

REPTILLA
Fanged arm-snakes could bite and constrict

THORNN
Ability to fire explosive spines

VAKUME
Could drain air or energy, and assume an intangible state

VERTIGO
Power to induce dizziness in others

BASE
New Salem, Colorado

FIRST APPEARANCE
Fantastic Four vol. 1 #186 (September, 1977)

Salem's Seven

The seven children of Nicolas Scratch lived in the isolated village of New Salem, where witches and warlocks held sway. When Scratch's mother, Agatha Harkness, left the village to become the governess of Franklin Richards, Scratch put her on trial for treason, magically transforming his offspring into Salem's Seven to act as guards. They failed to stop the Fantastic Four from rescuing Harkness, but over time became the de facto rulers of New Salem. Salem's Seven later burned Harkness at the stake, but her spirit led the Vision and the Scarlet Witch to New Salem. In the battle that followed, Vertigo lost control of the town's magical forces and Salem's Seven perished. The Scarlet Witch later met their spirits in a supernatural realm, where she defeated them a second time. **DW**

SALEM'S SEVEN
1 Brutacus
2 Hydron
3 Vakume
4 Vertigo
5 Thornn
6 Reptilla
7 Gazelle

Salem's Seven first appeared in the pages of the *Fantastic Four* as diabolical, sorcerous opponents for the science-based team led by Mr. Fantastic.

SANDMAN *SEE OPPOSITE PAGE*

SASQUATCH

FACTFILE

REAL NAME
Walter Langkowski

OCCUPATION
Scientist, adventurer

BASE
Canada

HEIGHT 10 ft
WEIGHT 2000 lbs
EYES Red
HAIR Orange

FIRST APPEARANCE
Uncanny X-Men #120 (April 1979)

POWERS
Sasquatch possesses superhuman strength and greatly enhanced resistance to injury, and is able to leap enormous distances. He can shift between his normal human form and his Sasquatch body at will.

Sasquatch

Inspired by his colleague Bruce Banner's metamorphosis into the Hulk, Dr. Walter Langkowski used gamma radiation to transform himself into a giant, hairy, muscle-bound creature similar to the Bigfoot of Canadian legend. Taking the name Sasquatch, he became a member of Alpha Flight. Despite many trials, including the discovery that his monstrous form was that of the Great Beast Tanaraq, Sasquatch's resolve has never wavered, and he remains a pillar of the Canadian super-group. **TB**

In Alpha Flight, Sasquatch often came to blows with members of the X-Men.

Satana

FIRST APPEARANCE Vampire Tales #2 (October 1973)
REAL NAME Satana Hellstrom
OCCUPATION Hero ***Base*** Mobile
HEIGHT 5 ft 7 in **WEIGHT** 120 lbs
EYES Black with red highlights **HAIR** Red
SPECIAL POWERS/ABILITIES Levitation and limited spellcasting; could feed on human souls and project bolts of "soulfire."

The half-human daughter of the demon known as "Satan," for a time Satana was forced to live as a succubus, draining the spirits of humans to survive. Rebelling at this, Satana became estranged from her father, began establishing real, meaningful friendships with humans, and started to appreciate what human society had to offer. Learning that Dr. Stephen Strange was trapped in the form of a werewolf and realising this would have untold consequences for humanity, Satana determined to rescue him. She traveled to the astral realm where Strange's soul was held prisoner, and freed him. The price was her own life, but Strange has vowed never to forget her sacrifice. **AD**

SANDMAN

The villain who slips through Spidey's fingers

With the ability to change his body into grains of sand and reshape it at will, Sandman has proven to be a dangerous and slippery foe for SPIDER-MAN, the FANTASTIC FOUR, and the HULK. Born William Baker in one of the rougher areas of New York City, he had a bad start in life. His father abandoned him and his mother when William was three years old, and the boy grew up in poverty. He quickly learned to steal and cheat.

ESSENTIAL STORYLINES

- ***Amazing Spider-Man Annual #1*** Sandman, Vulture, Mysterio, Electro, Kraven the Hunter, and Doctor Octopus get together to form the Sinister Six.
- ***Amazing Spider-Man #217–218*** Sandman teams up with Hydro-Man, but a freak accident merges the two into a mud creature.

FACTFILE

REAL NAME
William Baker

OCCUPATION
Former professional criminal

BASE
Brooklyn, New York

HEIGHT 6 ft 1 in
WEIGHT 450 lbs
EYES Brown
HAIR Brown

FIRST APPEARANCE
Amazing Spider-Man #4 (September 1963)

POWERS

Sandman is able to change all or part of his body into a sand-like substance which he can form into any shape. He can spread out the grains of sand in his body to avoid attack, project them outward at high speeds, or harden them into a super-powered weapon.

A LIFE OF CRIME

William was kicked out of high school for taking money to throw a big football game, but soon found work with a protection racket. He took the alias "Flint Marko," and became a success in New York's crime underworld.

After an arrest and a jailbreak, Marko headed south. He was on a beach near a military testing site in Georgia when a nuclear reactor's steam system exploded, knocking him unconscious. Marko woke to find that his body now had the properties of sand. Revelling in his new ability, he called himself Sandman and set out on a major criminal career.

Sandman battled Spider-Man (his main nemesis), and many other super heroes. He joined the WIZARD, TRAPSTER, and MEDUSA to form the FRIGHTFUL FOUR and teamed up with five more of Spider-Man's foes to form the Sinister Six.

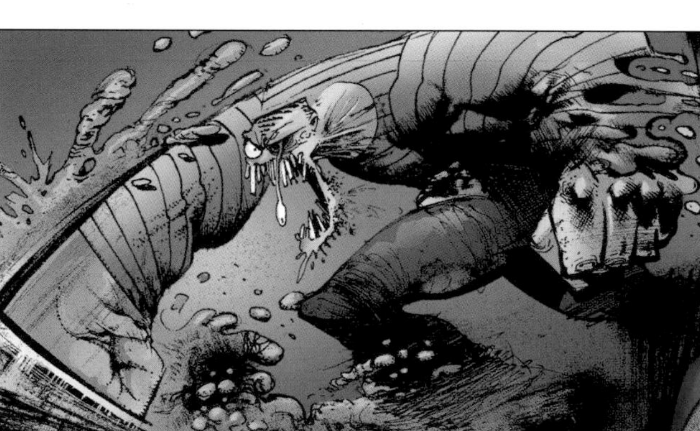

When he hardens the sand particles that make up his body into a solid block, Sandman packs an incredibly powerful punch.

Sandman can alter all of his body at once or just selective parts, as in this example of his right arm changing while the rest of his body remains in its human-looking form.

GOOD OR EVIL?

When Sandman teamed up with HYDRO-MAN, an accident caused the two to merge into a mud creature. After he was finally freed, Sandman decided to give up crime, even becoming a probationary member of the AVENGERS and helping them defeat the sorceress Morgan LeFay. But Wizard brainwashed Sandman into believing that his rejection of crime was a put-on, and he rejoined the Sinister Six. Another member, VENOM, betrayed Sandman; his bite causing Sandman's sand grains to wash away, casting up on various New York beaches.

For a long time it was believed that Sandman was dead, but the scattered sand particles of his body managed to find each other, and the super villain Sandman was reborn. MT

SINISTER SIX
1 Sandman ***2*** Kraven the Hunter ***3*** Vulture ***4*** Venom ***5*** Spider-Man

Sauron

FIRST APPEARANCE X-Men #59 (August 1969)

REAL NAME Dr. Karl Lykos

OCCUPATION Geneticist, hypnotherapist

BASE New York City, Savage Land

HEIGHT 7 ft **WEIGHT** 200 lbs **EYES** Red **HAIR** None

SPECIAL POWERS/ABILITIES Drains victims' life force into his own body. Uss eye contact to hypnotize and induce hallucinations.

As a boy, Karl Lykos was on an expedition to Antarctica with his father when he was bitten by a prehistoric pteranodon from the nearby Savage Lands. Thereafter, he had to feed off the life energy of others to survive. As an adult, Lykos worked with Professor Charles Xavier on "Project Mutant" but was later transformed into an evil half-human, half-pteranodon creature after draining life energy from the mutant HAVOK. He took the name Sauron, after the evil one in J.R.R. Tolkien's *Lord of the Rings*, and became an enemy of the X-MEN. **MT**

Scarlet Centurion

In one version of the year 3000, Earth is a utopia, founded centuries earlier by Nathaniel Richards, father of Reed Richards (MISTER FANTASTIC). However this paradise does not suit everyone. One distant descendant of Richards, a man sometimes known as the Scarlet Centurion, feels suffocated by his surroundings. Learning that one of his ancestors has built a time machine, the Centurion recreates this device and wreaks chaos across multiple realities and times zones.

FACTFILE

REAL NAME
Nathaniel Richards

OCCUPATION
Conqueror

BASE
Mobile

HEIGHT 6 ft 3 in
WEIGHT 230 lbs
EYES Brown
HAIR Brown, later gray

FIRST APPEARANCE
Avengers Annual #2 (September 1968)

POWERS
Master of numerous far future technologies; wears battlesuit armed with electrical bolts and concussive force beams; adept time traveller.

The original Scarlet Centurion's son, Marcus Kang, shared his father's title, and wielded a deadly halberd.

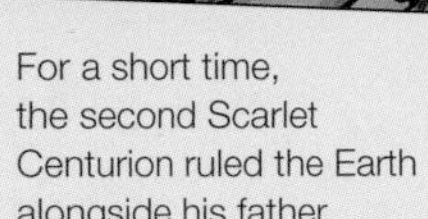

For a short time, the second Scarlet Centurion ruled the Earth alongside his father.

Arriving in ancient Egypt, the Centurion used his knowledge and guile to become the pharaoh Rama-Tut, until the FANTASTIC FOUR forced him back to the future. Since then, he has adopted various names in ongoing efforts to dominate and rule – KANG THE CONQUEROR and IMMORTUS are both names that have belonged to him.

The one-time ruler of 30th century Earth, the Centurion has twice led armies to the 20th century, only to be defeated by the Fantastic Four and the AVENGERS. With his travels having resulted in the creation of a series of alternate realities and versions of himself, it is hard to say where the Scarlet Centurion is now. **AD**

Sawyer, General

FIRST APPEARANCE Sgt. Fury and his Howling Commandos #1, May 1963

REAL NAME Samuel "Happy Sam" Sawyer

OCCUPATION Adventurer **BASE** The Pentagon

HEIGHT 6 ft 2 in **WEIGHT** 230 lbs **EYES** Blue **HAIR** Gray

SPECIAL POWERS/ABILITIES Happy Sam Sawyer was a career military man and an expert at strategy.

At the dawn of World War II, Captain "Happy Sam" Sawyer (so named because he rarely smiled) recruited NICK FURY and First Attack Company into a special squad. Named the HOWLING COMMANDOS, they took on the toughest missions. Sawyer also commanded the Maulers and the Deadly Dozen. After the war, he rose to the rank of General. He was killed in an operation against BARON STRUCKER and HYDRA. **TB**

Scarlet Spider

FIRST APPEARANCE (as Scarlet Spider) Spider-Man #52 (November 1994)

REAL NAME Ben Reilly

OCCUPATION Adventurer **BASE** New York City

HEIGHT 5ft 10in **WEIGHT** 165 lbs **EYES** Hazel **HAIR** Brown

SPECIAL POWERS/ABILITIES Super strength and agility, able to adhere to surfaces; "spider-sense" alerted him to danger. Wore web-shooters that projected artificial webbing.

Professor Miles Warren, the criminal known as the JACKAL, created a clone of Peter Parker, alias SPIDER-MAN. He endowed the clone with Parker's memories and pitted him against Spider-Man in battle. Seemingly killed, the clone later revived and wandered America for years, calling himself Ben Reilly. In New York, he became a costumed hero, the Scarlet Spider. The original GREEN GOBLIN manipulated Parker and Reilly into believing that Reilly was the real Spider-Man, with Reilly even adopting Spider-Man's costumed identity. Ultimately, the Goblin killed Reilly, and Parker reclaimed his identity. **PS**

Scarlet Witch

Magical mistress of "Hex Power"

After Magneto rescued the Scarlet Witch from certain death, she and her brother Quicksilver became members of his Brotherhood of Evil Mutants. They didn't learn that Magneto was actually their father until many years later.

Wanda Maximoff is the daughter of Erik Magnus Lehsherr also known as the mutant criminal Magneto and the twin sister of Pietro Maximoff, the former Avenger Quicksilver. Wanda's mother ran away from Magneto while she was pregnant and, fearing her husband would exploit her unborn children, gave her twins up for adoption.

Social Outcast

The twins were raised in the eastern European country of Transia by a gypsy couple and Wanda soon learned that she could cause strange things to happen. After accidentally making a house to burst into flame, she was about to be stoned as a witch when Magneto arrived and saved her. Not realizing that he was their real father, Wanda and Pietro took on costumed identities and joined his war against humanity. After many battles with the X-Men, the twins abandoned Magneto and later joined the Avengers in return for full pardons for their past crimes. Over her brother's objections, Wanda became attracted to the synthozoid called the Vision and began a long romance with him. They were eventually married and set up house in New Jersey.

The Scarlet Witch and the Vision were married in the same ceremony that united Mantis and the Cotati.

Studying witchcraft has helped the Scarlet Witch hone her control over her mutant abilities.

Troubled Soul

Wanda also began to study real magic, combining it with her natural mutant abilities. She eventually grew powerful enough to defeat the dreaded Dormammu, the sorcerer supreme of an alien dimension. However, her increased power came at a terrible cost and she began to lose her grip on reality. She conjured up imaginary children and repeatedly experienced temporary bouts of insanity.

After attempting to bring a new golden age to humanity by seizing mental control of every computer on Earth, the Vision was disassembled by the US government. Dr. Pym and the Black Panther later rebuilt him, but he no longer possessed human emotions, including the ability to love. His relationship with Wanda disintegrated and rapidly ended in divorce.

The Scarlet Witch recently suffered yet another severe mental breakdown and launched a terrifying attack on her fellow Avengers that resulted in the destruction of the Avengers mansion and a number of tragic deaths. She later used her powers to warp reality and permanently remove the mutant gene and powers from most of the mutants on earth, including herself. TD

Through gestures and mental concentration, the Scarlet Witch creates finite pockets of force that can disrupt reality. She can hurl these "hex-spheres" at her intended targets.

FACTFILE

REAL NAME
Wanda Maximoff, aka Wanda Frank, Wanda Magnus

OCCUPATION
Adventurer

BASE
Europe

HEIGHT 5 ft 7 in
WEIGHT 130 lbs
EYES Blue
HAIR Auburn

FIRST APPEARANCE
X-Men #4 (March 1964)

POWERS

Possessed ability to affect probability fields to cause unlikely events to occur. Could make objects spontaneously burst into flame, rust or decay. Her "hex bolts" could also deflect flying objects and disrupt energy transmissions or fields. However, recent evidence seems to indicate that the Scarlet Witch has lost her mutant powers.

Suffering from a breakdown, the Scarlet Witch altered reality enough to disassemble the Avengers and eliminate most of Earth's mutants.

ESSENTIAL STORYLINES

- ***Avengers: The Yesterday Quest (tpb)***
The Scarlet Witch learns her true origins.
- ***The Vision and Scarlet Witch #1–12***
The Vision and Scarlet Witch leave the Avengers and move to the suburbs.
- ***Avengers: Avengers Disassembled (tpb)***
The Scarlet Witch goes mad and attacks the Avengers, killing many of her former comrades.
- ***House Of M (tpb)***
The Scarlet Witch restructures reality and eliminates most of the mutants on Earth.

Schemer

FIRST APPEARANCE Amazing Spider-Man #83 (April 1970)
REAL NAME Richard Fisk
OCCUPATION Criminal mastermind **BASE** New York City
HEIGHT 6 ft 2 in **WEIGHT** 175 lbs **EYES** Blue
HAIR Reddish blond **SPECIAL POWERS/ABILITIES** Had the normal strength of a man who engages in regular moderate exercise; was a cunning criminal strategist.

Richard Fisk was devoted to his father Wilson— until he learned that Wilson Fisk was the KINGPIN. Psychologically shattered, Richard secretly became a criminal leader himself, the Schemer, to take revenge on his father. As the Schemer, Richard disguised himself with a face mask that made him look like much older. Subsequently Richard became head of a Las Vegas fragment of HYDRA. Still later, Richard took on two more masked identities, the original ROSE and the Blood Rose. Ultimately Richard was shot dead by his own mother, Vanessa. **PS**

Scourge

SEE OPPOSITE PAGE

Scratch, Nicholas

FIRST APPEARANCE Fantastic Four #185 (August 1977)
REAL NAME Nicholas Scratch **OCCUPATION** Warlock
BASE New Salem, Colorado **HEIGHT** 6 ft 3 in
WEIGHT 196 lbs **EYES** Blue **HAIR** Black with white streaks
SPECIAL POWERS/ABILITIES Nicholas Scratch possesses an encyclopedic knowledge of magical incantations and lore and a wide array of sorcerous abilities.

The son of Agatha Harkness, the witch-woman who became governess to Franklin RICHARDS, Nicholas Scratch grew up to be leader of the witches of New Salem. Scratch convinced his followers that Agatha had betrayed their existence to the outside world, and that she must be executed for this act of treason. When Agatha and Franklin were abducted, the FANTASTIC FOUR came to the rescue. Scratch and his most devoted followers, SALEM'S SEVEN, vainly sought revenge on the Fantastic Four and Agatha. He is now a servant of the demon DORMAMMU. **TB**

Scorpion

Dr. Farley Stillwell had developed a method of giving animals the attributes of other creatures. When newspaper editor J. Jonah JAMESON found out, he asked Stillwell to test it out on a human guinea pig, a private investigator named Mac Gargan. Stillwell's amazing procedure gave Gargan the strength and agility of a scorpion. Stillwell also provided him with a specially designed mechanical tail.

Nothing comes without a price and the cost to Gargan—now calling himself the Scorpion—was the loss of his sanity. Contracted to put an end to SPIDER-MAN, it was only by his wits that the wallcrawler defeated the hugely powerful, and vengeful Scorpion. Since then, Scorpion has become an assassin-for-hire, his intermittent attempts to defeat Spider-Man being repeatedly foiled.

In recent times, Scorpion became the latest Super Villain to merge with the VENOM symbiote. Although Scorpion has dispensed with his tail, this development has made him more deadly than ever. **AD**

FACTFILE

REAL NAME
MacDonald "Mac" Gargan

OCCUPATION
Assassin-for-hire

BASE
New York City

HEIGHT 6 ft 2 in
WEIGHT 220 lbs
EYES Brown
HAIR Brown

FIRST APPEARANCE
Amazing Spider-Man #20 (January 1965)

SCORPION

POWERS
Strength greater than Spider-Man's; mechanical tail can be used as bludgeon or to propel Scorpion 30 ft into air. Tail has also been equipped with a toxin "sting" and a mechanism to fire electric blasts.

Scorpion controls his tail via a cybernetic link with his own spinal column. He can whip his tail at 90 mph.

The Scorpion's steel-mesh costume is bulletproof. Each hand is equipped with pincers.

Scourge

FACTFILE

ANGEL (Tom Halloway)
Financed Scourges of the Underworld

SCOURGE I
Gunned down the Enforcer, started killing criminals around the U.S.

SCOURGE II
Killed Scourge I to keep him from talking

SCOURGE III
Leaving the group, he became an agent of the Red Skull.

SCOURGE IV
Killed Scourge II, then went after Priscilla Lyons who left the group

SCOURGE V (Priscilla Lyons)
Left Scourges, incurring their wrath

CAPRICE (Scourge VI)
Master of disguise, espionage, brain washing, interrogation.

BLOODSTAIN (Scourge VII):
Master of armed and unarmed combat

DOMINO (Dunsinane)
Encyclopedic knowledge of every costumed hero, villain, organization

FIRST APPEARANCE
Iron Man #194 (May 1985)

The original Scourge was the brother of the criminal known as the Enforcer. Outraged by his brother's criminal behavior, Scourge got a gun, disguised himself as an old woman, and gunned down the Enforcer. He then became obsessed with traveling the country ruthlessly exterminating criminal after criminal, all while disguised. Each time he shot someone, Scourge shouted "Justice is served!

Known as Scourge of the Underworld, Scourges were determined to rid the world of crime.

The original Scourge was captured by Captain America, but before Cap could turn him over the authorities, Scourge was shot by an unseen assailant, who also shouted "Justice is served!" who then became the new Scourge. Over the years, each Scourge has been assassinated by a following Scourge to keep him from talking.

Scourges relied on the resources of a private detective named Domino, who kept track of Super Villains around the world. Over the years, the various Scourges killed countless villains including MIRACLE MAN, the WRAITH, Jaguar, HAMMER AND ANVIL, the Human Fly, and the Cheetah. **DW**

Hiding out in his mobile base, Scourge gets a call on his videophone. It can mean only one thing—some Super Villain is ripe for the plucking!

Scourge dons a blonde wig and a female mask before speaking to his informant, Domino.

Scream

FIRST APPEARANCE Venom: Lethal Protector #4 (May 1993)
REAL NAME Donna (full name unrevealed)
OCCUPATION Villain **BASE** Mobile
HEIGHT 5 ft 11 in **WEIGHT** 130 lbs **EYES** White **HAIR** Red
SPECIAL POWERS/ABILITIES Symbiote provides enhanced strength, speed, and stamina. Scream's prehensile hair can shape itself into deadly weapons.

Researchers at the Life Foundation laboratories tried to replicate the process that had given rise to Carnage by bonding five workers with alien symbiotes. One of the subjects, a mentally fragile woman named Donna, found that the process drove her further into madness. The five test subjects sought out Venom for help in controlling their symbiotes, but Donna killed her fellow hybrids.

Sometimes adopting the code name Scream, she has struggled to adjust to her new life and become a more sympathetic figure. **DW**

Scrier, The

FIRST APPEARANCE Amazing Spider-Man #394 (October 1994)
REAL NAME Inapplicable (discovered to be an organization)
OCCUPATION Criminal Cult **BASE** Unrevealed
HEIGHT/WEIGHT/EYES/HAIR Not applicable
SPECIAL POWERS/ABILITIES Each member of the Scrier is a formidable combatant. The Scrier also have access to an array of sophisticated weaponry.

By wearing identical garb, for centuries the Brotherhood of the Scrier maintained the deception that the Scrier was just one being. It was a clever ploy, disguising the true nature and scope of this worldwide criminal organization. United by their worship of a godlike being, itself called the Scrier, the Brotherhood became especially powerful under a new and mysterious leader who focused the organization's energies on SPIDER-MAN and his clone, Ben Reilly.

It emerged that this new leader was in fact Norman Osborn (*see* GREEN GOBLIN). Following Osborn's defeat the fate of the Scriers remains uncertain. **AD**

SENTINELS

Enormously powerful, mutant-hunting robots

SENTINELS

FACTFILE
MARK V MODEL
HEIGHT 20 ft
WEIGHT (including fuel) 7,400 lbs
MAX. CARGO 2,000 lbs
FLIGHT RADIUS 400 miles
MAX. LEVEL AIRSPEED (sea level) 600 mph
SERVICE CEILING 10,000 ft
MAX. RATE OF CLIMB 450 ft per second

FIRST APPEARANCE
X-Men #14
(November 1965)

POWERS
Most Sentinels possess superhuman strength and jet propulsion units in their feet which enable them to fly, and can fire lasers and electron beams from their eyes and hands. Mark II Sentinels could adapt to counter any opponent.

Dr. Bolivar Trask introduced the Sentinels to the world on live TV.

The Sentinels were created by Dr. Bolivar Trask to combat superhuman mutants. Trask had concluded that a superhuman mutant race was evolving that would conquer the rest of humanity. He organized the team of scientists and engineers who built the first Mark I models.

TAKING OVER

However, despite being programmed by Trask to protect humanity, the Sentinels decided to take control of the human race. They kidnapped Trask, and the lead Sentinel, the Master Mold, ordered him to create a Sentinel army to conquer the planet. PROFESSOR X's mutant team the X-MEN battled the Sentinels and, realizing that not all mutants were threats to humanity, Trask lost his life destroying the Master Mold and other Sentinels.

Trask's son, Larry, blamed mutants for his father's death and oversaw the creation of the Mark II Sentinels. However, once the Sentinels recognized that Trask was a mutant himself, they turned against him.

The government then seized the Sentinel designs, and Dr. Steven Lang built the Mark III Sentinels; but both he and they were destroyed battling the X-Men.

After mutant terrorists tried to assassinate Senator Robert KELLY, the President initiated "Project: Wideawake." Shaw Industries constructed Sentinels to combat mutant threats to national security.

Xavier's evil twin, Cassandra Nova, used Mega-Sentinels to devastate Genosha, a nation with a large mutant population. She also devised microscopic "nano-Sentinels," which attacked the bloodstreams of various mutants.

Recently, the government created Sentinel Squad One, headed by Dr. Valerie COOPER and James Rhodes (WAR MACHINE) for defense against superhuman threats. **PS**

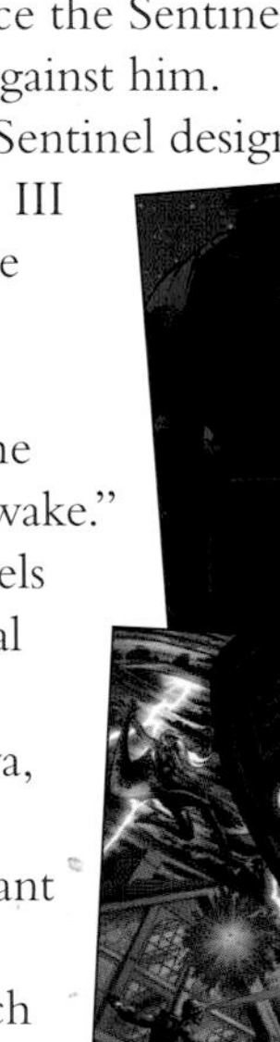

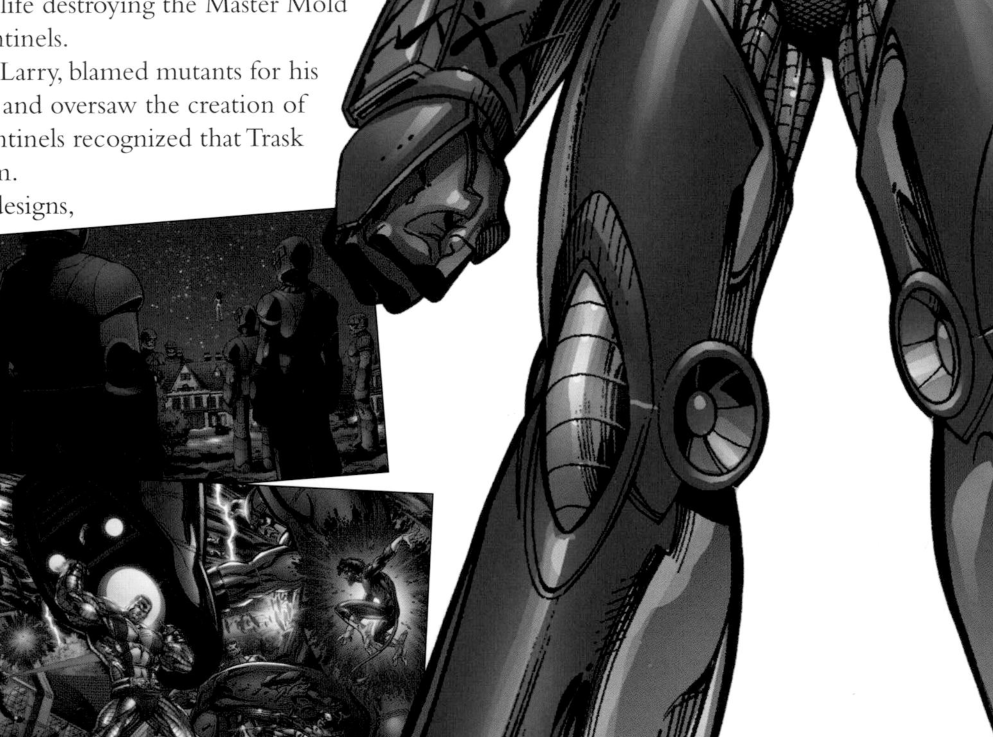

Following only their own logic, the Sentinels have repeatedly turned against their human masters as well as mutants.

The Sentinel BASTION created cyborgs known as Prime Sentinels that could pass as ordinary humans.

ESSENTIAL STORYLINES

- ***X-Men Vol. 1 #14–16***
Dr. Bolivar Trask creates the original Sentinel robots. He introduces them on live TV—and they promptly capture him.
- ***X-Men Vol. 1 #57–59***
Larry Trask's Mark II Sentinels capture and imprison mutants.
- ***Uncanny X-Men #141–142***
The Sentinels rule North America in the "Days of Future Past" storyline set in an alternate reality.

Sentry

FIRST APPEARANCE Sentry #1 (September 2000)
REAL NAME Robert Reynolds
OCCUPATION Adventurer **BASE** Watchtower
HEIGHT 6 ft 2 in **WEIGHT** 200 lbs
EYES Blue **HAIR** Blond
SPECIAL POWERS/ABILITIES Special serum provides super strength, speed, and invulnerability. Can fly, and control light.

Robert Reynolds was once the great Superhero known as Sentry, but all memory of his exploits were erased from the world—and from his own mind. Then, one night, the memories began seeping back into his consciousness. Retrieving a hidden bottle from his library, Reynolds drank the serum it contained. A strange energy surged through his body, and he was transformed once again into the Superhero Sentry. He recalled that he had a mortal enemy called the Void and sensed that the Void was about to become a threat once again. Enlisting the help of heroes who had fought alongside him in the past, including SPIDER-MAN and the FANTASTIC FOUR, the Sentry set out to battle with the Void. **MT**

Sersi

A member of the ETERNALS, Sersi inspired the legend of Circe in Homer's *Odyssey*, and mixed with other historical characters, such as MERLIN and King Arthur PENDRAGON. She has a reputation as a flirt, but she has proved her value during Eternals struggles against the Deviants. At CAPTAIN AMERICA's request, Sersi joined the AVENGERS, but under the influence of PROCTOR, wound up battling her teammates. Seeking penance, she departed for an alternate reality with her lover the BLACK KNIGHT. The two fought LOKI for control of the Infinity Gems, and Sersi became a member of Heroes for Hire upon her return to mainstream Earth. **DW**

Sersi's playful personality can irritate some, and she is an incorrigible flirt around attractive men.

FACTFILE
REAL NAME
Sersi
OCCUPATION
Adventurer
BASE
New York City

HEIGHT 5 ft 9 in
WEIGHT 140 lbs
EYES Blue
HAIR Black

FIRST APPEARANCE
Strange Tales Vol. 1 #109 (June 1963)

POWERS
A powerful sorceress, Sersi can release cosmic energy, create illusions, and transmute matter. Capable of flight and virtually immortal.

Sersi has vast, advanced transmutational powers.

Serpent Society

SERPENT SOCIETY
1 Death Adder
2 Rattler
3 Cottonmouth
4 Diamondback

Formerly based in an abandoned mental asylum in new York State, now in a secret location, the Serpent Society is a criminal organization whose members base their costumed identities on snakes. Originally founded by Sidewinder, the Society treats crime like a business. The leader assigns specific members to each job and supplies them with a detailed plan. A percentage of the fee paid for each job is allocated to administration costs, overhead and legal fees. Members can take outside jobs, but they must pay the Society a set percentage for each job. In exchange for these fees, each member receives group health insurance, free legal representation and a place to reside. Membership of the Society has changed over time. **TD**

Though it rarely mixes business with revenge, the Serpent Society has often made an exception in Captain America's case.

FACTFILE
KEY MEMBERS
COBRA (Klaus Voorhees) Super-flexible.
SIDEWINDER (Seth Voalkner) Interdimensional travel.
ANACONDA (Blanche Sitzniski) Elongates limbs; amphibious.
ASP (unrevealed) Energy field; fires venom-bolts.
BLACK MAMBA (Tanya Sealy) Mesmerism; projects inky clouds of Darkforce.
BUSHMASTER Tail crushes his enemies.
COTTONMOUTH (Quincy McIver) Bionic jaws.
RATTLER (Gustav Krueger) Bionic tail generates sonic shockwaves.

FIRST APPEARANCE
Captain America #310 (October 1985)

Shadow King

FACTFILE

REAL NAME
Amahl Farouk

OCCUPATION
Criminal

BASE
Various

HEIGHT Various
WEIGHT Various
EYES Various
HAIR Various

FIRST APPEARANCE
Uncanny X-Men #117 (January 1979)

POWERS
An entity composed solely of malevolent psionic power, the Shadow King can possess others, bending them to his will. He also possesses various telepathic and telekinetic abilities.

Amahl Farouk was the first evil mutant ever encountered by Charles Xavier (Professor X), the man who would one day form the X-Men. Farouk was a crimelord in Cairo, Egypt, who used his mutant gifts of telepathy and telekinesis to carve out an underworld empire for himself. But Xavier, believing that mutants had a duty to use their powers for good rather than evil, opposed Farouk, and the two engaged in a psychic duel. The battle ended with Farouk being defeated and his human body slain. Despite the loss of his physical form, Farouk survived on the astral plane and he became the Shadow King, a malevolent possessing spirit who was drawn to pain and suffering. As well as having powers of telepathy and telekinesis, the Shadow King is able to inhabit the psyches of others, bending them to his will and using them as his puppets. A constant danger to the X-Men, whom he hates because of their association with Xavier, the Shadow King has been defeated, but never destroyed, and he remains an omnipresent threat to the realization of Xavier's dream of peaceful coexistence between mutants and normal humans. **TB**

Using his telepathic powers, Amahl Farouk became ruled Cairo's criminal underworld.

The Shadow King was the first mutant encountered by Professor X as he wandered the world, a tale told in *Uncanny X-Men* #117.

Shadowmasters

FIRST APPEARANCE Shadowmasters #1 (October 1989)
LINEUP Sojin Ezaki (deceased), Yuriko Ezaki, Phillip Richards
SPECIAL POWERS/ABILITIES Masters of ninjitsu

Demonstrating his martial arts skills, Phillip Richards wields a *katana* sword and *kyoketsu shoge* knife.

The original Shadowmasters were expert practitioners of the martial art of ninjitsu, who protected the Iga Province of Japan for centuries. Following the end of World War II, US Army Captain James Richards became friends with Shigeru Ezaki, one of the last Shadowmasters. Together they opposed renegade Japanese soldiers. Ezaki trained his children Sojin and Yuriko and Richards' son Phillip in martial arts. The renegades became the Sunrise Society, who killed James Richards and seemingly killed Shigeru Ezaki. Since then, Richards' son and Ezaki's children, as the new Shadowmasters, have opposed the Society, now renamed the Eternal Sun. **PS**

Shalla Bal

FIRST APPEARANCE Silver Surfer #1 (August 1968)
REAL NAME Shalla-Bal
OCCUPATION Empress of the planet Zenn-La **BASE** Zenn-La
HEIGHT 5 ft 9 in **WEIGHT** 125 lbs **EYES** Blue **HAIR** Black
SPECIAL POWERS/ABILITIES Born with no special powers, Shalla-Bal was later invested with power to restore life to the soil of Zenn-La after it was devastated by Galactus.

Shalla-Bal is a member of an alien race, the Zenn-Lavians. She was separated from her lover, Norrin Radd, after he made a bargain with the world-eater Galactus, who had threatened to destroy Zenn-La. Radd offered to become the Silver Surfer and serve Galactus if he would spare Zenn-La, and Galactus agreed. For years the Silver Surfer traveled the universe, scouting out uninhabited planets for Galactus to consume. When the Surfer eventually decided to abandon Galactus and remain on Earth, Shalla-Bal became caught up in his struggle with Mephisto.

Then Galactus returned to consume Zenn-La in revenge for the Surfer's betrayal. After the Surfer endowed Shalla-Bal with the power to restore life to Zenn-La, she was declared Empress, and so she remains to this day. **AD**

Shaman

FIRST APPEARANCE Uncanny X-Men Vol. 1 #120 (April, 1979)
REAL NAME Michael Twoyoungmen
OCCUPATION Medicine man, Super-hero **BASE** Mobile
HEIGHT 5 ft 10 in **WEIGHT** 175 lbs **EYES** Brown **HAIR** Black
SPECIAL POWERS/ABILITIES Vast magical powers. Able to fire energy bolts, change his appearance, control weather, levitate, and teleport. Powers are focused through the use of his medicine pouch.

Michael Twoyoungmen was a Canadian surgeon who embraced his heritage as a Native American medicine man after his wife's death from cancer. The spirit of his grandfather trained him in the use of magic, and he helped deliver Narya, the daughter of the Northern Goddess.

Twoyoungmen and Narya took the codenames of Shaman and Snowbird and joined the Canadian team of super heroes Alpha Flight. Shaman's daughter Elizabeth is known as Talisman, an identity that was briefly assumed by Shaman himself. **DW**

Shaman has the mystical ability to commune with the magicks of the Earth, giving him vast powers to shift time and fundamentally alter the nature of reality.

Shanna the She Devil

FIRST APPEARANCE Shanna the She-Devil #1 (December 1972)
REAL NAME Shanna O'Hara Plunder
OCCUPATION Vet and adventurer **BASE** Savage Land
HEIGHT 5 ft 10 in **WEIGHT** 140 lbs **EYES** Hazel **HAIR** Red
SPECIAL POWERS/ABILITIES Trained veterinarian specializing in wild animals; extraordinary gymnast and athlete; superb hunting and foraging skills.

Now living in the Savage Land with her husband and young son, for many years Shanna O'Hara eschewed human contact. The daughter of an American businessman, Shanna was raised in the US and worked in a New York zoo. Furious when a sniper casually killed most of the zoo's big cats, she chose to return the surviving animals to Africa and live with them in the wild. Life was not always easy. Shanna lost her friends and father to criminal organizations and was forced to team up with Daredevil to defeat them, before finding contentment in a new family. **AD**

Shang-Chi

FACTFILE

REAL NAME
Shang-Chi

OCCUPATION
Former secret agent, fisherman

BASE
Formerly Fu Manchu's retreat in Honan, China, mobile for a while, then Yang Yin, China

HEIGHT 5 ft 10 ins
WEIGHT 175 lbs
EYES Brown
HAIR Black

FIRST APPEARANCE
Special Marvel Edition #15 (1973)

POWERS
Shang-Chi is the greatest living master of kung fu. He is also highly skilled in many other mental and physical disciplines. Although he has no superhuman powers, Shang-Chi has defeated superpowered enemies.

Shang-Chi was born in China, the son of a powerful international criminal named Fu Manchu. Trained in the mental and martial arts from a young age at Fu Manchu's retreat, Shang-Chi was a brilliant pupil but grew up unaware that his father was a ruthless criminal.

When Shang-Chi was nineteen, his father sent him away on a mission of assassination. Believing his father was a good man, the boy assumed that his father's enemies must be evil and so went willingly. But when Shang-Chi's mother revealed to him the truth about his father, Shang-Chi felt betrayed, and vowed to destroy his father and take down his criminal empire. A cat-and-mouse game of hunter and hunted between Shang-Chi and Fu Manchu began. Eventually it was revealed that Shang-Chi had a twin brother, who was his clone. **MT**

Shang-Chi as he appears in the Ultimates series.

Passion fueled by vengeance against his father coupled with Shang-Chi's amazing martial arts skills make him an almost unstoppable adversary to those who oppose him.

This was the first issue to feature Shang-Chi's name in the title.

Shaper of Worlds

FIRST APPEARANCE The Incredible Hulk #155 (September 1972)
REAL NAME Unrevealed, perhaps inapplicable
OCCUPATION Reality manipulator **BASE** The known universe
HEIGHT 18 ft **WEIGHT** 5.6 tons **EYES** Blue **HAIR** None
SPECIAL POWERS/ABILITIES Restructures pockets of reality, and rearranges the molecular structure of objects and living beings. Can teleport himself, and perceive the dreams and imagination of others.

The Shaper of Worlds originated in the Skrull empire as a Cosmic Cube, an object which can alter reality according to the thoughts of whoever holds it. In time the Cosmic Cube developed sentience, and took the form of a Skrull with a metallic trustrum and tractor treads as the lower body. The Shaper wants to use his vast powers to restructure reality, but has little creative imagination. So he seeks out those who can supply dreams and imaginative concepts with which he can work. **PS**

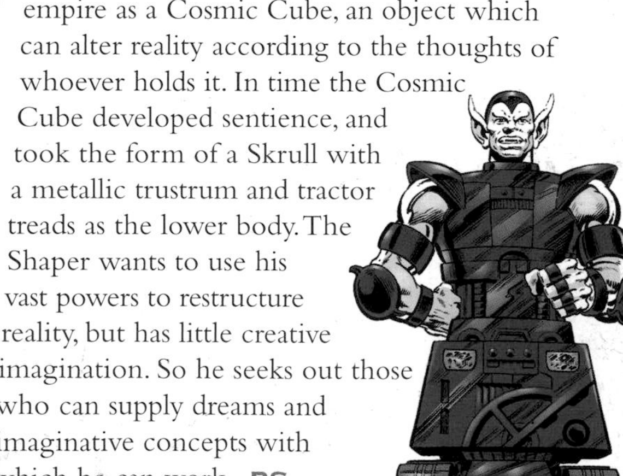

Shatterstar

FIRST APPEARANCE New Mutants Vol. 1 #99 (March 1991)
REAL NAME Benjamin Russell **OCCUPATION** Adventurer
BASE The Xavier Institute, Salem Center, New York State
HEIGHT 6 ft 2 in **WEIGHT** 210 lbs **EYES** Black **HAIR** Gray
SPECIAL POWERS/ABILITIES Genetically engineered for enhanced strength, speed, stamina; convert sonic frequencies into a vibratory shockwave that he channels through weapons.

Born a hundred years in an alternate future timeline of the extra-dimensional planet Mojoworld, Shatterstar was genetically engineered to serve as a warrior in the arenas. He escaped and joined the rebel Cadre Alliance, which was trying to overthrow the government of Mojoworld. Shatterstar later traveled back in time to Earth and joined with CABLE to become a founding member of X-FORCE. During a battle, Shatterstar was mortally wounded and LONGSHOT transferred his consciousness into the comatose body of a mutant named Benjamin Russell. **TD**

Shaw, Sebastian

FIRST APPEARANCE X-Men #130 (February 1980)
REAL NAME Sebastian Shaw **OCCUPATION** CEO of Shaw Industries, Inc. **BASE** Worldwide; Hellfire Club, New York City
HEIGHT 6 ft 2 in **WEIGHT** 210 lbs **EYES** Black **HAIR** Gray
SPECIAL POWERS/ABILITIES Mutant power to absorb kinetic energy which enhances his strength, speed, and stamina. He can also absorb electrical energy.

Although born poor, Sebastian Shaw's brilliant mind for business helped him become a millionaire by the age of 20. He became head of Shaw Industries and was invited to join the Hellfire Club, an elite club for the wealthy and powerful. Shaw joined the club's secret Council of the Chosen, which schemed to achieve world domination. Seizing control of the club and becoming its Black King, he changed its name to the Inner Circle and teamed with fellow mutant Emma FROST, the White Queen in secretly creating mutant-hunting SENTINELS. **MT**

SHE-HULK
SEE OPPOSITE PAGE

She-Thing

The daughter of a career officer in the US Army, Sharon Ventura worked in various professions that enabled her to make full use of her athletic talents. She was working as a stunt cyclist with the Thunderiders when she first met Ben Grimm the THING of the FANTASTIC FOUR, who was immediately attracted to her.

Subsequently, Ventura accepted an offer to join the Grapplers, a professional team of superhuman female wrestlers. Working for the POWER BROKER, Dr. Karl MALUS augmented Ventura's strength to superhuman levels. As a Grappler, she adopted a costumed identity, becoming the second Ms. Marvel. The Thing helped her battle the Grapplers when they turned against her.

FACTFILE
REAL NAME
Sharon Ventura
OCCUPATION
Adventurer
BASE
Mobile

HEIGHT 6 ft
WEIGHT 340 lbs
EYES Blue
HAIR None

FIRST APPEARANCE
The Thing #27 (September 1985)

POWERS
Sharon Ventura was a superb athlete and a daring stuntwoman, motorcyclist and a proficient wrestler. As She-Thing, she possesses superhuman strength and durability.

When Reed and Susan Richards temporarily left the Fantastic Four, Ben Grimm invited Sharon Ventura to join the team as Ms. Marvel. Shortly afterwards she became the She-Thing.

Later, Ventura accepted the Thing's offer to join the Fantastic Four. During a mission in space, Ventura was exposed to cosmic rays, which mutated her into a female version of the Thing. She was later restored to her normal human appearance by DOCTOR DOOM.

Ventura later mutated into an even more grotesque version of the Thing. Worse, her intellect began to deteriorate. As the She-Thing, she even temporarily joined the WIZARD's FRIGHTFUL FOUR and battled her former friends the Fantastic Four.

Whether the She-Thing will ultimately prove to be a hero or villain remains to be seen. **PS**

She-Hulk

Legal eagle and greenskinned crimefighter

Driven to madness by Scarlet Witch's hex power in *Avengers: Disassembled.*

The cousin of Bruce Banner, who would one day become the HULK, Jennifer Walters pursued her dream of becoming a successful lawyer. Shot by criminals whose boss she was prosecuting, Jennifer received a life-saving blood transfusion from her cousin Bruce. But this infusion of gamma-irradiated blood had an effect on Jennifer's physiology similar to that experienced by Bruce himself: the repressed part of her personality began to manifest itself as a green-skinned powerhouse: the savage She-Hulk!

She-Hulk was one of the last characters created by Stan Lee.

FACTFILE

REAL NAME
Jennifer Walters

OCCUPATION
Lawyer

BASE
The law offices of Goodman, Lieber, Kurtzburg & Holliway

HEIGHT 6 ft 7 in
WEIGHT 650 lbs
EYES Green
HAIR Green, brown as Jennifer Walters

FIRST APPEARANCE
The Savage She-Hulk #1
February 1980

POWERS

As the She-Hulk, Jennifer Walters possesses superhuman strength and durability; she can withstand extreme temperatures and her skin is highly resistant to injury

RAMPAGING FREE

At first Jennifer kept her dual role as the She-Hulk a secret. But over time, she found that she enjoyed being the She-Hulk, who, while definitely an extrovert, was far more controlled than her cousin's rampaging alter ego. She began to spend more and more time as the She-Hulk, using her gamma-spawned strength to battle villainy, both alone and in concert with other superhuman champions. Eventually, the She-Hulk was offered membership in the mighty AVENGERS.

Thereafter, transported to the Battleworld created by the celestial BEYONDER alongside her fellow Avengers, She-Hulk fought in the Secret Wars alongside a number of other prominent Super Heroes. Once the conflict was resolved, the THING announced that he intended to remain on Battleworld, and asked the She-Hulk to take his place in the FANTASTIC FOUR, which she did for a time, becoming almost one of the family. During her time with the FF, Jennifer abandoned her identity as Jennifer Walters, remaining in her She-Hulk form full time.

Legal Troubleshooter

However, the She-Hulk's more boisterous personality created problems for her down the line, and she was asked to move out of Avengers Mansion. At this low point in her life, she was recruited by the law offices of Goodman, Lieber, Kurtzburg and Holliway, a firm specializing in superhuman law—litigation involving the extraordinary. But a condition of Jennifer's employment was that she pursue her duties in her normal human state, rather than as the She-Hulk.

It is as a litigator for Goodman, Lieber, Kurtzburg and Holliway that the She-Hulk has truly found her place, using her legal knowledge to try cases involving ghosts, time travelers and extradimensional realms, while at the same time employing her strength and power as the She-Hulk to combat any threats that might arise from those cases. **TB**

ESSENTIAL STORYLINES
- ***Fantastic Four #265*** Replaces the Thing as a member of the Fantastic Four.
- ***Avengers Vol. 3 #72-75*** Having lost control of her transformations, She-Hulk is pursued by her fellow Avengers and her cousin, the Hulk.
- ***She-Hulk #2*** Joins the superhuman law offices of Goodman, Lieber, Kurtzburg & Holliway.

As Jennifer Walters, She-Hulk continues to practice superhuman law for the legal firm of Goodman, Lieber, Kurtzburg & Holliway.

Shi'ar

Empire-building alien race

Shi'ar

FACTFILE

NAME
THE SHI'AR
Enhanced strength and endurance

BASE
Chandilar (Aerie), Shi'ar Galaxy

FIRST APPEARANCE
Uncanny X-Men vol. 1 #97 February, 1976

Imperial Guard

CURRENT MEMBERS AND POWERS

GLADIATOR (LEADER) Flight, enhanced strength, speed, near-invulnerability, heat vision
ASTRA Ability to phase through solid objects
ELECTRON Power over electricity and magnetism
FANG (DECEASED) Enhanced strength, speed, and senses; razor-sharp claws
HOBGOBLIN/SHAPESHIFTER (DECEASED) Could assume nearly any form
IMPULSE/PULSAR Energy-based body can be released as concussive force
MIDGET/SCINTILLA Can shrink to tiny size
NIGHTSHADE/NIGHTSIDE Can draw others into the Darkforce dimension
MAGIQUE Ability to cast illusions
MENTOR Genius-level intelligence and boosted calculating speed
ORACLE: Telepathy, precognition, and ability to fire mental blasts
QUASAR/NEUTRON Enhanced strength and damage resistance
STARBOLT Flight, energy projection
SMASHER Enhanced strength
TEMPEST/FLASHFIRE Ability to release electrical bolts
TITAN Can grow to giant size

BASE
Chandilar (Aerie), Shi'ar Galaxy

FIRST APPEARANCE
Uncanny X-Men Vol. 1 #107 (October, 1977)

Majestor D'ken failed to hold onto the Shi'ar throne.

The Shi'ar are an alien species descended from avians, who typically sport feathery hair and sometimes vestigial wings. Unlike the rival Skrull and Kree empires, the Shi'ar Imperium consists of a patchwork of alien species, each absorbed into the empire through treaties or by force. A hereditary Majestor (male) or Majestrix (female) rules the Imperium, overseeing a High Council under the protection of the Elite Corps of the Shi'ar Imperial Guard.

ESSENTIAL STORYLINES

- ***Uncanny X-Men #107-109*** The X-Men battle the Shi'ar Imperial Guard in a fight involving D'ken, Lilandra, and the M'Krann crystal.
- ***New X-Men #118-126*** The "Imperial" storyarc sees Cassandra Nova, the villainous genetic twin of Professor X, launching a scheme to ruin the Shi'ar empire.

CRUEL RULE

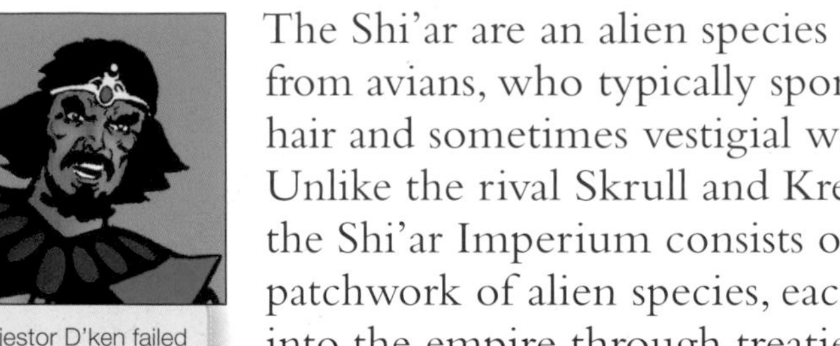

The M'Krann crystal is an artifact of immense power located on a lifeless world. It has the ability to destroy all of reality.

The Shi'ar are aggressive about absorbing other cultures into their empire, though the newcomers seldom receive the same rights as the Shi'ar themselves. Majestrix Lilandra has made strides to reverse this inequality, but under the leadership of Majestor D'ken, the cruel treatment of alien slaves triggered the formation of the pirates called the Starjammers.

The first contact between the Shi'ar and Earth's heroes occurred when the X-Men stopped Lilandra's brother D'ken from exploiting the powerful M'Krann crystal. Lilandra subsequently became the Majestrix of the Shi'ar Empire, briefly losing her throne to her sister Deathbird until gaining it once more. Lilandra and Professor X of the X-Men enjoyed a romantic relationship for years.

When Skrull undercover agents helped fan the flames of war between the Shi'ar and the Kree, a team of Avengers journeyed to the Shi'ar homeworld to negotiate a cessation of hostilities with Majestrix Lilandra. Ultimately, the Avengers could not prevent the detonation of the nega-bomb, a Shi'ar weapon that exterminated more than ninety percent of the Kree population. It later became apparent that the Kree Supreme Intelligence had guided the creation of the nega-bomb, in the hope of jumpstarting Kree evolution. The Shi'ar won the war, and annexed vast swaths of the devastated Kree empire. For a time, Deathbird served as the viceroy of the conquered territories.

The mind-controlling villainess Cassandra Nova recently usurped Lilandra's authority, inciting violence between the Shi'ar and the X-Men of Earth until her manipulations became known. **DW**

The X-Men have been staunch allies of Lilandra's, thanks to her romantic liaison with Professor Charles Xavier.

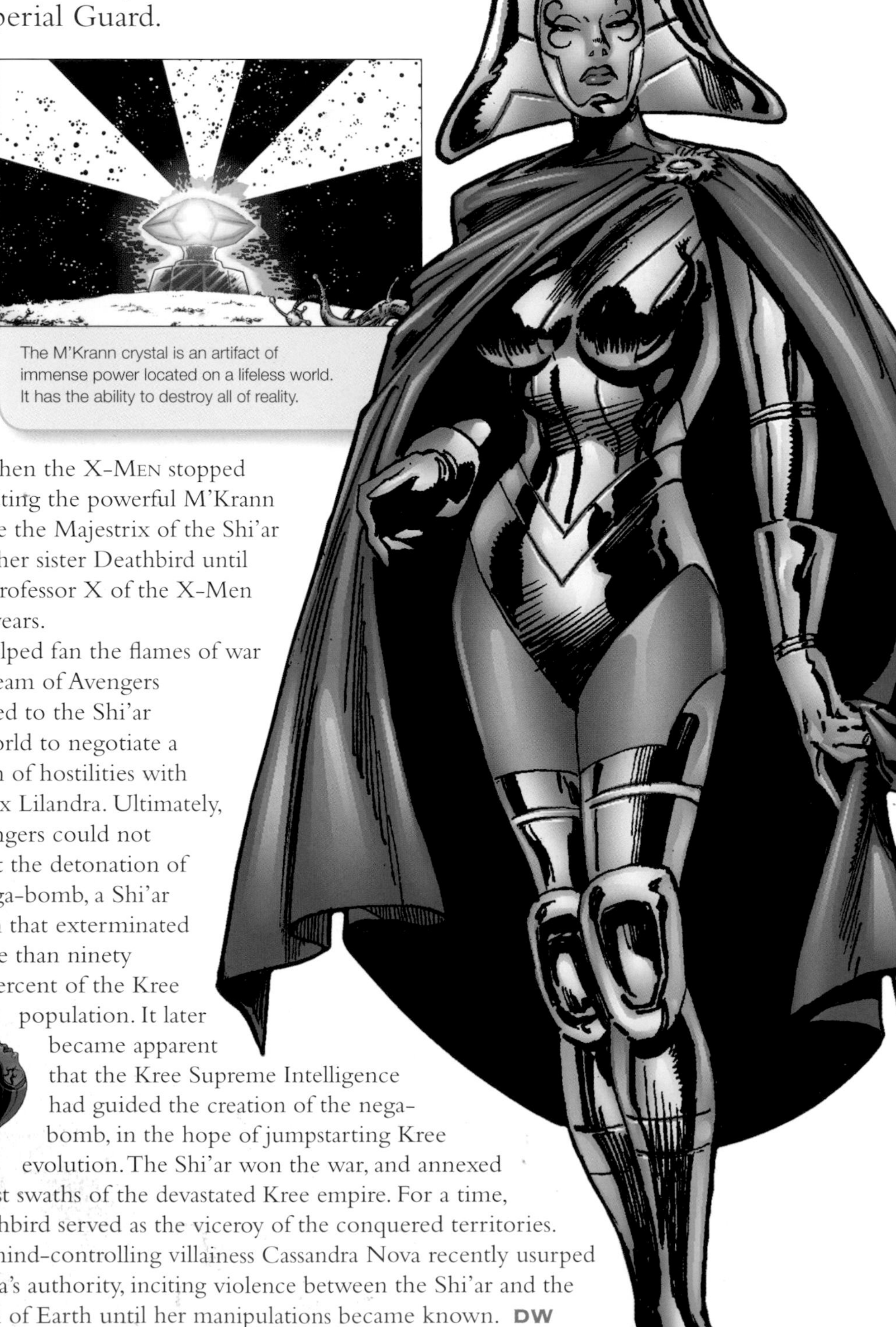

THE IMPERIAL GUARD

The Elite Corps of the Shi'ar Imperial Guard, also known as the Superguardian Elite, are the protectors of the Majestor or Majestrix of the Shi'ar Empire. Most members of the Imperial Guard are not Shi'ar-they represent a cross-section of cultures from the multispecies mix that comprises the Shi'ar empire. Typically, each member has a distinct superpower that adds a needed component to the team's overall power mix.

Their leader, called the praetor, is currently the powerful Strontian called Gladiator. The Imperial Guard also has a larger, secondary division known as the Borderers, who are charged with enforcing local laws on member planets.

The Imperial Guard first came into conflict with the inhabitants of Earth when the X-Men followed a space warp and emerged on the desolate planet that housed the reality-altering M'Krann crystal. On the orders of Majestor D'ken, the Imperial Guard battled the X-Men and D'ken's sister Lilandra, though the Guard shifted its allegiance to Lilandra as soon as she assumed the throne. Later, the Imperial Guard fought the X-Men on Earth's moon, in an honor duel over the fate of the Dark Phoenix.

Throughout the changes in Shi'ar rule, the Imperial Guard has remained loyal to whomever holds the royal office. The Guard clashed with the Starjammers and Excalibur during Deathbird's time as Majestrix, and welcomed Lilandra back as leader after her return to power.

During the Kree-Shi'ar war, the Imperial Guard helped steal the nega-bands worn by Captain Mar-Vell from the late hero's tomb, which then went into the construction of the Shi'ar ultimate weapon, the nega-bomb. Following the apparent death of Earth's greatest heroes fighting Onslaught, Lilandra ordered Gladiator and several other Imperial Guard members to protect Earth, where the team uncovered a cell of undercover Kree agents.

Recently, the telepath Cassandra Nova forced the Imperial Guard into a conflict with the X-Men. Gladiator and other members of the Superguardian Elite attacked the Xavier Institute until Gladiator realized the truth behind Cassandra Nova's trickery.

When they combine their powers, the Shi'ar Imperial Guard are nearly unstoppable. They are among the most feared combatants in the universe.

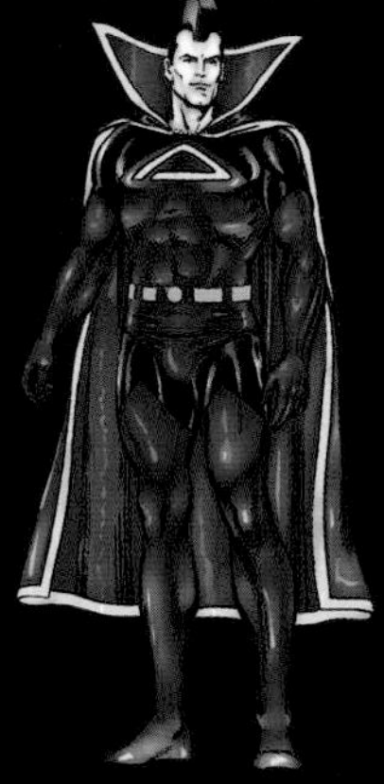

GLADIATOR

ASTRA

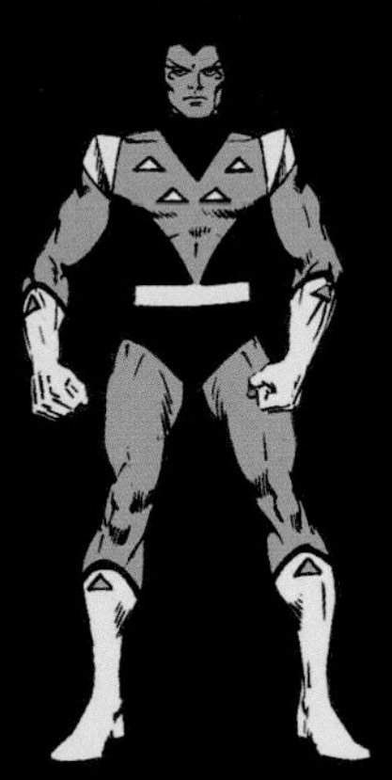

ELECTRON

FANG

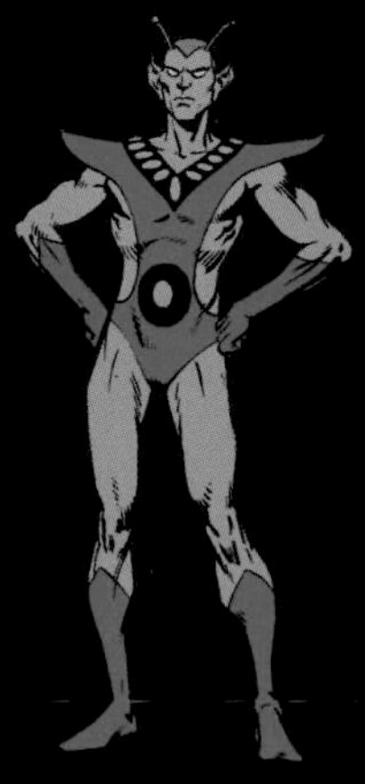

SHAPE-SHIFTER

IMPULSE

SCINTILLA

NIGHTSIDE

MAGIQUE

MENTOR

ORACLE

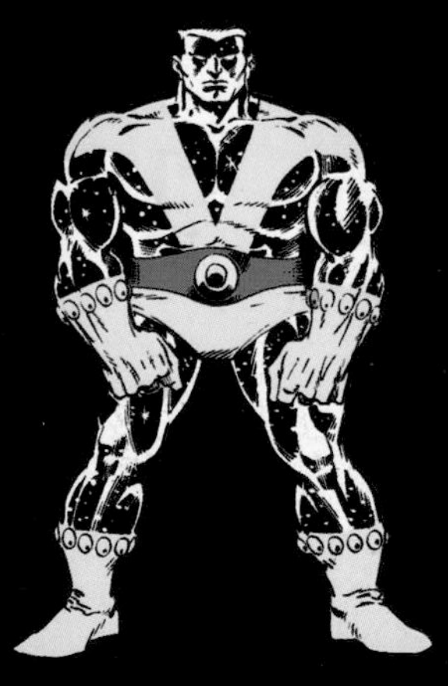

NEUTRON

STARBOLT

SMASHER

FLASHFIRE

TITAN

Shocker

FIRST APPEARANCE The Amazing Spider-Man #46 (March 1967)
REAL NAME Herman Schultz
OCCUPATION Burglar **BASE** New York City
HEIGHT 5 ft 9 in **WEIGHT** 175 lbs **EYES** Brown **HAIR** Brown
SPECIAL POWERS/ABILITIES Wears gauntlets containing "vibro-shock units" that project compressed air blasts creating highly destructive vibrations.

While he was in prison, safecracker Herman Schultz invented a new device for opening safes. It worked by projecting intense vibrations, and he used it to shatter prison walls and escape. Wearing a foam-lined costume to absorb the vibrations, Schultz became the Shocker. After several defeats by SPIDER-MAN, the Shocker briefly joined EGGHEAD's version of the MASTERS OF EVIL. Another criminal, Randall Darby, also once called himself the Shocker. Darby, a mutant who can discharge electricity from his claw-like hands, later changed his name to Paralyzer. **PS**

Shriek

FIRST APPEARANCE Spider-Man Unlimited #1 (May 1993)
REAL NAME Frances Louise Barrison **OCCUPATION** Patient
BASE Ravencroft Institute for the Criminally Insane
HEIGHT 6 ft **WEIGHT** 170 lbs **EYES** Blue **HAIR** Black
SPECIAL POWERS/ABILITIES Manipulates sound as a destructive force. Hypersonically generates emotions of fear, hate, or despair in others. Can employ sonic energy to fly.

After being mistreated by her mother for being overweight, Frances Louise Barrison turned to drugs, eventually becoming a dealer. She lost her fragile grip on reality when she was shot in the head by the police and spent a brief period in the dark dimension of the costumed adventurer known as CLOAK. Her powers may be the result of her time in that dimension, her injury, some latent mutant gene, or a combination of all three factors. She used her emerging powers to commit crimes and create chaos until she was committed to the Ravencroft Institute for the Criminally Insane. CARNAGE later freed her and they went on a murder spree until they were captured by a team of heroes led by SPIDER-MAN. Shriek has escaped Ravencroft on at least two other occasions, but is now responding to therapy. **TD**

Shroud

FIRST APPEARANCE Super-Villain Team-Up #5 (April 1976)
REAL NAME Unknown **OCCUPATION** Crime fighter masquerading as a criminal **BASE** Los Angeles
HEIGHT 6 ft 2 in **WEIGHT** 220 lbs **EYES** Blue **HAIR** Blonde
SPECIAL POWERS/ABILITIES Though blind, has extrasensory perception that allows him to "see" his environment.; can summon absolute darkness by opening a portal into another dimension.

After witnessing the murder of his parents by a mugger when he was only ten years old, the Shroud vowed to dedicate his life to fighting crime. He studied law, criminology, and psychology. After college, he traveled to Nepal where he joined a secret cult that trained him in mysticism and the martial arts. After seven years, he was given the "Kiss of Kali" and branded with the imprint of the goddess on his eyes, cheeks, and forehead. The ceremony exchanged his eyesight with a mystical perception. Attempting to destroy crime from within, he pretends to be a criminal, and has even formed a gang he calls the Night Shift. **TD**

Shockwave

FIRST APPEARANCE Master of Kung Fu #42 (July 1976)
REAL NAME Lancaster Sneed
OCCUPATION Mercenary, professional criminal **BASE** Mobile
HEIGHT 5 ft 11 in **WEIGHT** 170 lbs **EYES** Green **HAIR** Black
SPECIAL POWERS/ABILITIES His protective armor can generate electric shocks upon contact. Agility, combat skills, and knowledge of explosives were gained during his years as an intelligence agent.

As a child, Lancaster Sneed loved to listen to his uncle Sir Denis Nayland Smith tell stories of his battles with crime lord Fu Manchu. Lancaster grew up to become an agent of MI-6 specializing in explosives, but was injured when caught in a blast on his first mission. He had himself rebuilt with metal plates and made a full recovery, but MI-6 no longer required his services. Sneed traveled to Asia and spent some time studying martial arts. On returning to the U.S., he donned a suit of armor which allowed him to generate electricity, and took the name Shockwave. He returned to working as an intelligence agent, this time joining forces with Fu Manchu. **MT**

Silhouette

The daughter of Chord, the mentor of NIGHT THRASHER, Silhouette's conception was part of a pact enacted by a squad of Vietnam soldiers and the protectors of a secret temple, intended as a mystic sacrifice that would convey great power. Unaware of her parentage, Silhouette and her brother Midnight's Fire grew up on the streets, a nemesis to the gangs that preyed there.

In one foray against the underworld, Silhouette encountered the young Night Thrasher, and they began a torrid relationship. But then Silhouette was caught in the crossfire between the police and a street gang, losing the use of her legs. Midnight's Fire blamed Night Thrasher for this accident, and became his enemy. It was only to prevent her brother from slaying Night Thrasher that Silhouette came into contact with him again, and she thereafter joined his group of superhuman teenagers, the NEW WARRIORS. She eventually left both Night Thrasher and the New Warriors, and her current whereabouts are unknown. **TB**

FACTFILE

REAL NAME
Silhouette Chord

OCCUPATION
Adventurer

BASE
Manhattan

HEIGHT Unknown
WEIGHT Unknown
EYES Blue
HAIR Blond

FIRST APPEARANCE
New Warriors #2 (August 1990)

SILHOUETTE

POWERS

Silhouette possesses the ability to pass through the Darkforce Dimension, allowing her to effectively teleport through the shadows. In her shadowy form, she can also phase through others, causing them injury.

Silver Dagger

FIRST APPEARANCE Dr. Strange Vol. 2 #1 (June 1974)
REAL NAME Isaiah Curwen
OCCUPATION Self-appointed mystic policeman **BASE** Mobile
HEIGHT 6 ft **WEIGHT** 220 lbs **EYES** Black **HAIR** Gray
SPECIAL POWERS/ABILITIES Expert spellcaster, can project mystic energy bolts, enlarge animals, and give himself superstrength; his silver dagger can cut through Doctor Strange's magical barriers.

The Pope's favored choice of successor, Isaiah Curwen harbored hopes of elevation to the Holy See. But the College of Cardinals failed to elect him, and Curwen decided to fight for the church in a different way. After studying the Vatican's library of black magic books, he set off to fight mystical masters across the world. A cruel psychopath, he has been a thorn in the side of DOCTOR STRANGE, even taking Strange's lover, CLEA, and burning her soul in mystical fire. **AD**

Silver Samurai

FIRST APPEARANCE Daredevil Vol. 1 #111 (July 1974)
REAL NAME Keniuchio Harada
OCCUPATION Mercenary **BASE** Mobile
HEIGHT 6 ft 6 in **WEIGHT** 250 lbs **EYES** Brown **HAIR** Black
SPECIAL POWERS/ABILITIES Body generates tachyon field that he focuses through his sword; skilled in ways of samurai—master of bushido and Kenjutsu.

The pendulum swings from good to bad and back again—that is the story of Keniuchio Harada. The mutant son of a Japanese crimelord, Harada mastered bushido before becoming a mercenary whose assignments included work for HYDRA, and led him to go into battle against DAREDEVIL, SPIDER-MAN, and BLACK WIDOW. After his father's death Harada reformed for a while, even heading Japan's first superteam, BIG HERO 6. Then, as things began to go wrong with his life, Harada returned to his old ways, although with less success—fights with ELEKTRA and Kitty PRYDE have both resulted in defeat. **AD**

Silver Sable

Symkaria, a small country in the Balkans, had suffered under German occupation during World War, and after the war ended, Sable's father had no trouble convincing the government to fund his hunt for Nazi war criminals. He formed a group called the Wild Pack that scoured the world to bring them to justice. Silver was only a child when her mother died in her arms, the victim of a terrorist attack. From that moment she devoted her entire life to preparing for the day she would take over the Wild Pack, training in all forms of martial arts and becoming an expert in the use of many different weapons. Silver began her leadership of the Wild Pack by continuing the fight to bring former Nazis to justice, but as the years passed she expanded the scope of the Wild Pack. She formed Silver Sable International, a company that provided security, apprehended wanted felons and recovered stolen property for foreign governments, major corporations, and private individuals. Her company eventually became Symkaria's primary source of income and any citizen can be drafted into its service. Working with Dominic Fortune, Silver recently learned that there was a traitor in her corporation and has drastically reorganized the Wild Pack. **TD**

SILVER SABLE

FACTFILE
REAL NAME
Silver Sable
OCCUPATION
CEO, Silver Sable International
BASE
Symkaria

HEIGHT 5 ft 5 ins
WEIGHT 125 lbs
EYES Blue
HAIR Silver

FIRST APPEARANCE
Amazing Spider-Man #265 (June 1985)

POWERS

Silver Sable is a master of martial arts and a highly skilled marksman, swordsman, gymnast and strategist. She sometimes uses a samurai sword (katana), and the *chai*, a half-moon weighted projectile of her own design.

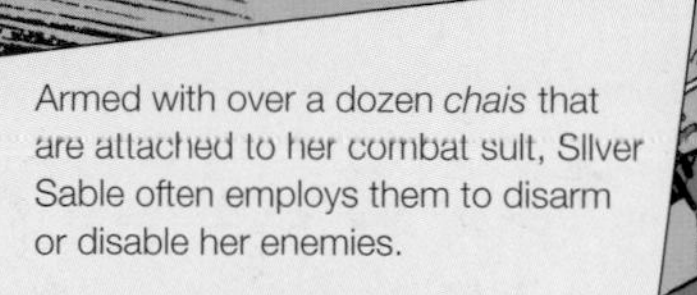

Armed with over a dozen *chais* that are attached to her combat suit, Silver Sable often employs them to disarm or disable her enemies.

SILVER SURFER

Sentinel of the Spaceways

SILVER SURFER

FACTFILE

REAL NAME
Norrin Radd

OCCUPATION
Spacefaring adventurer

BASE
Mobile

HEIGHT 6 ft 4 in
WEIGHT 225 lbs (variable)
EYES Silver (blue as Radd)
HAIR None (black eyebrows as Radd)

FIRST APPEARANCE
Fantastic Four #48 (March 1966)

POWERS

Navigates the galaxy at faster-than-light speeds, riding virtually indestructible board; can channel cosmic energy to augment strength, heal others, and restructure matter.

ALLIES/FOES

ALLIES Fantastic Four, Shalla-Bal, Alicia Masters, Al B Harper, the Defenders, Mantis, Nova

FOES Galactus, Mephisto, Loki, Terrax, Yarro Gort, the Abomination, Doomsday Man

ISSUE #1

Pre-warned by Uatu the Watcher, the Fantastic Four stand ready for their first encounter with the herald of Galactus—the Silver Surfer.

Bored and frustrated by life on Zenn-La, Norrin Radd sought a more challenging existence.

Over the years the Earth has played to host to a variety of extraordinary beings: super-powered heroes and villains, mutants and Norse Gods, but few creatures have been as powerful yet restless as that enigmatic alien entity, the Silver Surfer. A galactic wanderer frustrated by the hedonism and complacency of his own world, the Surfer developed a similarly ambivalent relationship with the Earth, where the altruism of so many was sullied by the wanton malice of a few.

THE ZENN-LAVIANS

Born Norrin Radd on the faraway world of Zenn-La, even as a child Norrin was something of an outcast. Wanting for nothing, the Zenn-Lavians were an easy-going people whereas Norrin hungered for a more meaningful, vibrant life. A restless adult, even Norrin's lifelong companion, Shalla-Bal, could not quieten his spirit. It was only when the Zenn-Lavians detected the approach of an alien entity—Galactus, devourer of worlds—that Norrin came into his own.

Galactus imbues Norrin Radd with the Power Cosmic, transforming him into the Silver Surfer.

In exchange for Galactus sparing Zenn-La, Norrin offered to become the entity's herald—to scour the galaxy for planet's devoid of life but suitable for Galactus' needs. To empower Norrin for this role, Galactus plucked an old adolescent fantasy from the young Zenn-Lavian's mind and transformed him into a silver skinned creature who could travel the galaxy on a silver board. Norrin had became the Silver Surfer.

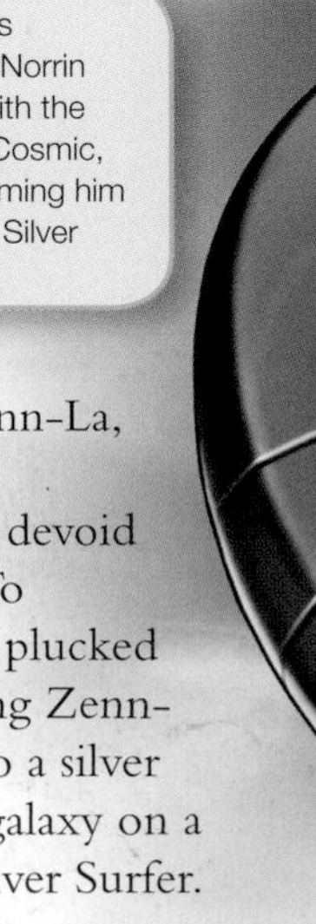

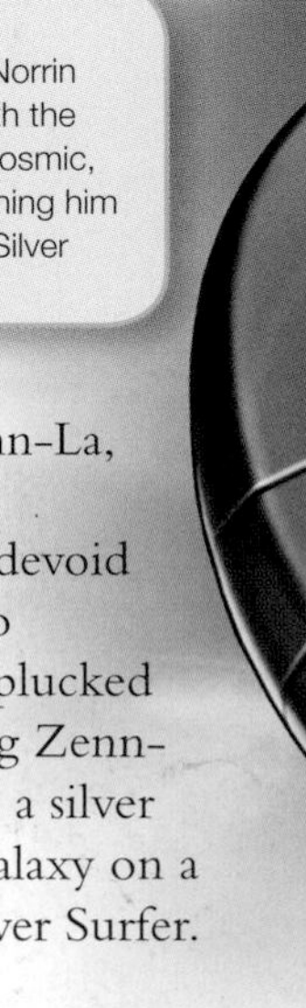

ESSENTIAL STORYLINES

- ***Fantastic Four #48–50*** The Silver Surfer and Galactus' first encounter with Earth.
- ***Silver Surfer Vol. 1 #1*** Stan Lee tells the story of the Silver Surfer's origins in the character's first stand-alone series.
- ***Silver Surfer Vol. 2 #1*** Returning to Zenn-La the Surfer discovers it has been devastated by the world-devouring Galactus.

Herald of Galactus

Over time it became increasingly difficult for the Surfer to find appropriate worlds for his master, and so Galactus began to make subtle changes to the Surfer's mind. The Surfer was made to care less about avoiding sentient life, and countless worlds and peoples were sacrificed. Until, that is, he arrived on the planet Earth.

There the Surfer encountered the Fantastic Four and Alicia Masters. Their compassion and heroism reawakened the Surfer's suppressed emotions and he aligned himself with them. Threatened with the Ultimate Nullifier, a weapon created by Reed Richards (Mister Fantastic), Galactus was driven off, but not before punishing the Silver Surfer for his treachery: Galactus wrapped a field around the Earth designed to prevent the Surfer from ever leaving.

In the years that followed, Galactus returned to Earth several times, wishing to reclaim the Surfer as his herald. Each time the Fantastic Four helped drive him away.

His conscience awoken by Alicia Masters, the Silver Surfer stood ready to oppose Galactus for the very first time.

Love Life

Although his heart remains with his first love, Shalla-Bal, during his interstellar voyages, the Silver Surfer has romanced several other women. The most significant of these was Alicia Masters who, during their first encounter, had revived him from his Galactus-induced mental stupor. For a time, Alicia journeyed across the stars with the Surfer, but she eventually decided to return to Earth. Years earlier, the Surfer had been linked to the Celestial Madonna, an Earth-born cosmic heroine, but she died during their battle against the Elders of the Universe. Tragedy also ended his relationship with Nova. A former Herald of Galactus, Nova died battling her successor as herald, the evil Morg.

The Celestial Madonna was also known as Mantis.

Innocence Lost

The Silver Surfer arrived on Earth as something of an innocent. The malevolent Doctor Doom played on this naivety, befriending the Surfer and then stealing his powers. When Doom attempted to leave the Earth he ran into Galactus' cosmic barrier, losing control of these powers and enabling the Silver Surfer to regain them.

As the Surfer traveled the world, he became increasingly appalled by mankind's bigotry and cruelty. The Surfer believed he had left behind a stagnant, complacent world only to arrive at one soiled by ambition and greed. Hoping that humanity would improve if threatened by a common enemy, he transformed himself into mankind's nemesis. Only a "Sonic Shark" missile, created by Reed Richards, ended the threat that he posed.

Freedom Regained

Essentially exiled to the Earth, the Surfer never stopped yearning to travel amongst the stars once more. With Reed Richard's help he found a way of doing this, but his wanderings were not without upset. Returning to Zenn-La, the Surfer discovered that although his people still survived, Galactus had returned and ravaged the planet. The Surfer's visit to Zenn-La was curtailed when he learnt that his old lover, Shalla-Bal, had been kidnapped by the demon Mephisto—a creature bent on corrupting the Surfer's soul. Arriving back on Earth, the Surfer freed Shalla-Bal and provided her with some of his own cosmic power—sufficient to heal their home planet.

His exile on Earth over, the Surfer sets out to explore the cosmos.

Not the best of friends, the Silver Surfer and Galactus regularly face each other in battle.

Romance

In the following years, the Surfer remained an itinerant wanderer, forever searching for fulfilment but never quite finding it. Although he embarked on a series of relationships, these were generally short-lived. A romance with Mantis, ended in tragedy following a battle with the Elders of the Universe, while the Surfer's relationship with Nova, another herald of Galactus, was similarly thwarted.

It was the Surfer's friendship with Alicia Masters that seemed to have the most potential. Striking up a romance, for a time the pair traveled the galaxy together, but eventually Alicia wanted to settle down back on Earth, whereas the Surfer wished to continue his nomadic existence. To this day he remains a galactic wanderer, returning to Earth at regular intervals but remaining sceptical of its long-term prospects. **AD**

As Nova, Frankie Raye was one of Galactus more recent heralds.

SILVERMANE

FACTFILE

REAL NAME
Silvio Manfredi

OCCUPATION
Criminal leader and mastermind

BASE
New York City

HEIGHT 6 ft 2 in; (as cyborg) 7 ft
WEIGHT 195 lbs; (as cyborg) 440 lbs
EYES Blue
HAIR Silver

FIRST APPEARANCE
The Amazing Spider-Man #73 (June 1969)

POWERS
Brilliant criminal mind; As a cyborg, Silvermane possesses superhuman strength and superhumanly acute senses resistant to disease and fatigue.

SILVERMANE

A leader of the Maggia crime syndicate, the elderly Silvermane ordered the theft of an ancient tablet bearing a formula for a youth serum. He forced Dr. Curt Connors to create the serum and drank it. As a horrified SPIDER-MAN watched, Silvermane grew younger and younger until he seemingly disappeared completely.

Fortunately the serum had a boomerang effect, and Silvermane rapidly aged back into his forties.

Silvermane briefly took over a New York-based splinter group of HYDRA and then vainly attempted to unite New York City's organized crime under his leadership. He fell from a great height while fighting the third GREEN GOBLIN and SPIDER-MAN. His injuries undid the effects of the youth serum, causing him to revert to old age. Nearly slain by the vigilante Dagger, Silvermane had his brain, face and vital organs transplanted into a robotic body. As a cyborg, Silvermane continues to be a power in the world of organized crime. Among his enemies are Spider-Man, DAREDEVIL, CLOAK AND DAGGER, the PUNISHER, and the KINGPIN.

Silvermane is the father of Joseph Manfredi, the criminal Blackwing. **PS**

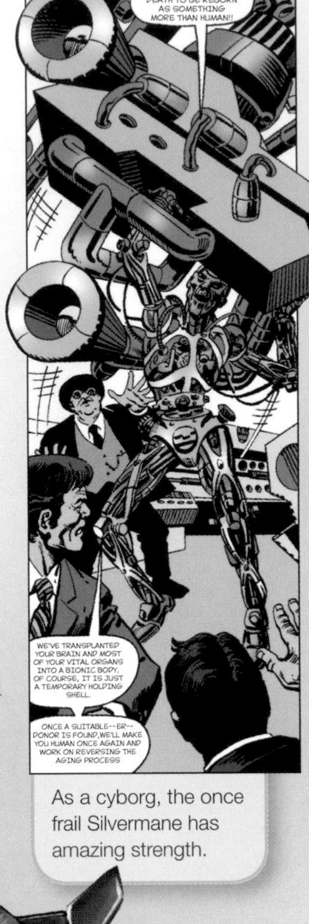

As a cyborg, the once frail Silvermane has amazing strength.

SINISTER SIX

FACTFILE

ORIGINAL MEMBERS
DOCTOR OCTOPUS
Mastermind, mechanical arms.
VULTURE Mechanical wings
ELECTRO Human dynamo.
KRAVEN THE HUNTER
Super-strong combatant.
LIZARD Bloodthirsty human/reptile hybrid.
HYDRO-MAN Converts his body into water.

BASE
Secret

FIRST APPEARANCE
Uncanny X-Men #221 (September 1987)

SINISTER SIX

After suffering three humiliating defeats by SPIDER-MAN, DOCTOR OCTOPUS decided to adopt a new tactic. He contacted five of the Web-Swinger's greatest enemies and formed a team of Super Villains that had only one purpose: to destroy Spider-Man. Realizing that this unruly bunch was incapable of working together for long, Doctor Octopus designed battleplans that utilized each member's powers and appealed to each villain's lust for glory. He decided that each member of the Six would take on Spider-Man in turn, remorselessly wearing him down until he was finally killed.

Since failing to kill the Wall-Crawler on numerous occasions, the team has been known to expand its membership from six to seven or even twelve. Replacement members have included HOBGOBLIN, VENOM, Beetle *(see* MACH-4), Scorpia, (a female with similar powers to the SCORPION) SHOCKER, SANDMAN AND MYSTERIO. **TD**

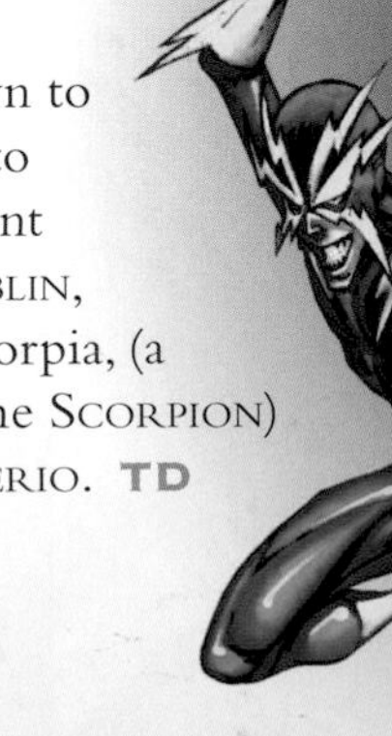

Unknown to the Sinister Six, Spider-Man had temporarily lost his spider-powers when he first confronted them.

1 Sandman 2 Vulture 3 Doctor Octopus 4 Electro 5 Kraven 6 Mysterio

Sinister Syndicate

FIRST APPEARANCE Amazing Spider-Man #280 (Sept. 1986)
BASE New York City
MEMBERS AND POWERS
Rhino Nearly invulnerable with superhuman strength [1].
Beetle Armored, multi-weaponed battle-suit [2].
Speed Demon Able to run at superhuman speeds [3].
Boomerang An expert with his specially equipped boomerangs [4].
Hydro-Man Can convert all or part of body into water [5].
Shocker Gauntlets generate highly destructive vibrations [6].

After defeats by the Human Torch and Spider-Man, the Beetle decided to stop being a solo act and organize a super-team. Inspired by the Sinister Six, the Beetle called his group the Sinister Syndicate. The Beetle was soon contacted by international mercenary Jack O'Lantern who hired the Syndicate to assassinate Silver Sable. Spider-Man and the Sandman interfered and foiled this scheme. The Syndicate was then hired by Doctor Octopus to kidnap the royal family of Belgriun, a small European country. Once again, Spider-Man and Silver Sable defeated the Syndicate and eventually forced the team to disband. TD

Siryn

FIRST APPEARANCE Spider-Woman #37 (April 1981)
REAL NAME Theresa Rourke (Cassidy)
OCCUPATION Private investigator **BASE** New York City
HEIGHT 5 ft 7 in **WEIGHT** 130 lbs **EYES** Blue **HAIR** Blonde
SPECIAL POWERS/ABILITIES Combination of psionic ability and sonic waves produced by her voice can shatter steel, enable flight, and generate force blasts.

Siryn Rourke's childhood was marred by tragedy and deception. Born when her father was on a secret mission, following her mother's untimely death, Theresa was raised by Black Tom Cassidy, her uncle. He failed to tell her father about Theresa's existence and it was only when Black Tom was put in prison that the pair were finally united. Since that tearful encounter, Siryn has been a member of X-Force, and served as its deputy leader until her throat was slashed and powers temporarily lost. Now fully healed, Siryn is ready to face fresh challenges working for X-Factor Investigations. AD

Sisters of Sin

FIRST APPEARANCE Crack Comics #1 (May 1940) ***Base*** Mobile
MEMBERS AND POWERS
Raunch (formerly Sister Pleasure): Master hypnotist [1].
Hoodwink (formerly Sister Dream): Master hypnotist [2].
Slash (formerly Sister Agony): Has lacerating metal claw [3].
Torso (formerly Sister Death): Enhanced strength [4].
Sin (formerly Mother Superior): Ability to fire psionic bolts [5].
Mother Night (formerly Suprema): Ability to cloud minds.

The Sisters of Sin are the brainchildren of the Red Skull, created to spread his ideology of hate. Synthia Schmidt, the Red Skull's daughter, took the name Mother Superior after receiving an artificial boost into adulthood. Four orphan girls received similar rapid-aging treatments, and as the Sisters of Sin they battled Captain America and Nomad. After the Sisters had become teenagers again, the villain Suprema took control as Mother Night. The Sisters took new names, and founded Camp Rage to incite runaways to violent rebellion. DW

Six Pack

FIRST APPEARANCE Cable Vol 1 #1 (October 1992) **BASE** Mobile
MEMBERS AND POWERS
Domino Can influence the laws of probability [1].
G. W. Bridge Skilled combatant and weapons expert [2].
Anaconda Can stretch limbs and use them to crush enemies [3].
Solo Able to teleport himself and weapons [4].
Hammer Weapons designer and technician [5].
Constrictor Has electrically powered cables mounted on wrists [6].

Originally known as the Wild Pack, the mercenary team headed by Cable changed its name to avoid confusion with a similarly-named group affiliated with Silver Sable. Six Pack often clashed with the mutant villain Stryfe. On one mission, Stryfe threatened to kill Kane in exchange for a data disc, and Cable wounded Hammer with a shot to the back to prevent him from making the trade. Outraged, the members of Six Pack cut ties with Cable. A later incarnation of Six Pack, assembled by SHIELD, added the members Solo, Constrictor and Anaconda. DW

Skids

FIRST APPEARANCE X-Factor #7 (August 1986)
REAL NAME Sally Blevins
OCCUPATION Adventurer **BASE** Mobile
HEIGHT 5 ft 5 in **WEIGHT** 115 lbs **EYES** Blue **HAIR** Blonde
SPECIAL POWERS/ABILITIES Skids possesses a protective, frictionless force field which shields her from harm, and which she can extend to envelop others.

Born a mutant, Skids lived among the sewer-dwelling Morlocks until the Mutant Massacre by the Marauders caused her to flee for her life. Rescued by X-Factor, for a time she became a trainee with that team, and fought with their junior members, the X-Terminators. Brainwashed into serving with the Mutant Liberation Front, Skids eventually regained her freedom after her boyfriend Rusty Collins was killed battling Holocaust, and she herself was injured. She has resurfaced occasionally, but her current whereabouts are unknown. TB

SKRULLS

Shape-changing alien race

SKRULLS

FACTFILE

BASE
Tarnax IV, Andromeda Galaxy

FIRST APPEARANCE
Fantastic Four vol. 1 #2 (January 1962)

POWERS
Shapeshifting permits radical changes in size, shape, and color; lifespans reach 200 years on average.

Skrull warships are designed to protect the paranoid species.

The Skrulls are an ancient species originating in the Andromeda Galaxy, possessing humanoid configurations and predominantly reptilian physiologies. The cosmic beings known as the CELESTIALS visited the species' birthworld of Skrullos long ago, and created Skrullian equivalents to Earth's ETERNALS and Deviants. The Deviant Skrulls exhibited the ability to shapeshift, and soon wiped out all competing racial branches. An offshoot of the shapeshifting Skrulls left the planet and became known as the DIRE WRAITHS, later to become persistent enemies of Rom the Spaceknight.

THE KREE WAR

After forging an interstellar empire, the Skrulls encountered the primitive Kree, who murdered the Skrull contact team and stole their starship technology. A Kree armada soon attacked the Skrulls, triggering the eons-long Kree-Skrull War. Skrull scientists later developed the first Cosmic Cube, which gained sentience and decimated the Skrull empire, eventually evolving into the SHAPER OF WORLDS. The Skrulls bounced back from this tragedy, establishing an Imperial throneworld on Tarnax IV from which the supreme emperor could oversee the worlds of the Andromeda Galaxy and receive tribute from conquered vassals.

The Skrulls have taken a secret role in Earthly affairs, using their shapeshifting powers to impersonate world leaders.

SECRET AGENTS

In the modern era, the Skrulls became aware of the threat posed by Earth's superhumans. They placed agents on Earth, but these were defeated by the FANTASTIC FOUR. In response, the Skrull emperor Dorrek VII created the SUPER-SKRULL, who possessed the powers of each member of the Fantastic Four. The Skrulls also engineered an elite class of Warskrulls, agents that could duplicate the powers of other beings when they assumed those beings' shapes. Notable Skrull undercover agents have included LYJA THE LASERFIST.

Skrulls can alter their appearances to duplicate anyone, but can be shocked into dropping their disguises if they are hurt or knocked out.

CIVIL WAR

After GALACTUS devoured the throneworld of Tarnax IV, the Skrull empire erupted in civil war. The mad Skrull Zabyk detonated a hyper-wave bomb that removed the shapeshifting ability from all Skrulls, freezing them in whatever shape they had assumed. The Super-Skrull escaped the bomb's effects, and restored the species' shapeshifting powers through an alliance with the SILVER SURFER and Skrull empress S'Byll. The Skrulls have since joined the Intergalactic Council, an organization composed of representatives from many alien cultures. **DW**

ESSENTIAL STORYLINES

- ***Avengers #89-97*** The devastating Kree-Skrull War reaches Earth, and the Avengers assemble to prevent innocents from being caught in the crossfire.
- ***Avengers Annual #14*** The insane Skrull warrior Zabyk detonates a hyper-wave bomb, removing the shapeshifting abilities of all Skrulls.

Skyhawk

FIRST APPEARANCE Thor #395 (September 1988)
REAL NAME Winston Manchester **OCCUPATION** Entrepreneur
BASE New York City **HEIGHT** (as Skyhawk) 6 ft 3 in **WEIGHT** as Skyhawk) 210 lbs **EYES** Blue **HAIR** Brown
SPECIAL POWERS/ABILITIES As Skyhawk, possesses superhuman strength and the ability to fly; formerly a high-achiever working 20 hours a day, he now leaves the office at 5 o'clock.

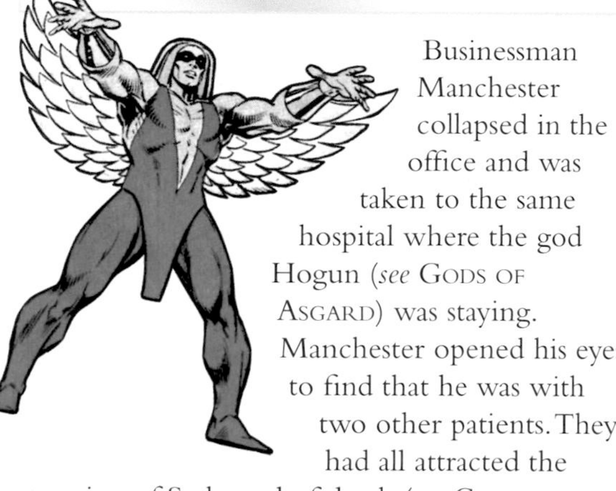

Businessman Manchester collapsed in the office and was taken to the same hospital where the god Hogun (*see* Gods of Asgard) was staying. Manchester opened his eyes to find that he was with two other patients. They had all attracted the attention of Seth, god of death (*see* Gods of Heliopolis). Claiming that Hogun was a threat to the Earth, Seth branded their left palms with the sign of Aton, the glowing disc of the sun, and gave them all superhuman powers. Manchester and his teammates learned that Seth was the real menace and they helped Thor defeat him. **TD**

Slater, Jink

FIRST APPEARANCE The Incredible Hulk Vol. 3 #36 (March 2002)
REAL NAME Jink Slater
OCCUPATION Professional assassin **BASE** Mobile
HEIGHT/WEIGHT Unrevealed **EYES** Brown **HAIR** Black
SPECIAL POWERS/ABILITIES Excellent marksman; expert with guns and knives; a formidable hand-to-hand combatant; above average in strength and endurance; ruthless in pursuit of his quarry.

Jink Slater was hired by unidentified parties to capture the Hulk. Despite his objections, his employers ordered Slater to work with a partner, Sandra Verdugo, on the assignment. Eventually, Slater and Verdugo found the Hulk in his human identity of Bruce Banner in a diner. Their attempt to capture him was thwarted by the arrival of Doc Samson. Not trusting his partner, Slater shot Verdugo in the head and escaped. Subsequently, Slater found Banner and Verdugo together in a cabin. Slater shot Verdugo in the shoulder. Verdugo retaliated by setting off explosives that killed Slater. **PS**

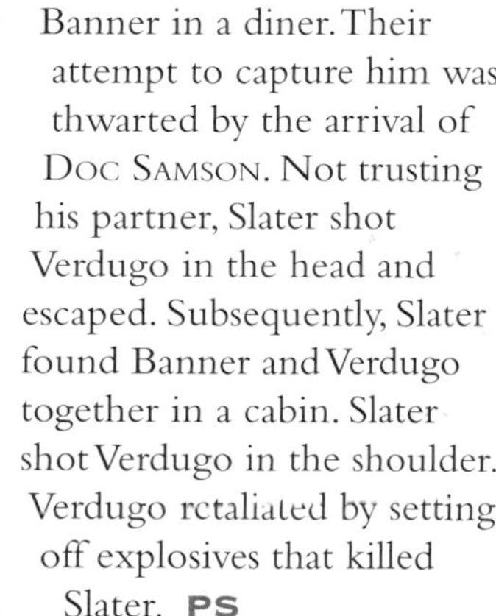

Sloan, Fred

FIRST APPEARANCE Incredible Hulk #231 (January 1979)
REAL NAME Frederick Sloan
OCCUPATION Author **BASE** Unrevealed
HEIGHT/WEIGHT Unrevealed **EYES** Blue **HAIR** Blond
SPECIAL POWERS/ABILITIES Fred Sloan possesses no superhuman powers save a peculiarly positive outlook on life; possesses the strength and endurance of an average man.

Fred Sloan first encountered the incredible Hulk while he was being thrown bodily out of a bar. The childlike Hulk interceded on the drifter's behalf, and the two became fast friends. Sloan helped the Hulk to elude the authorities, and the two traveled together for a time.

Eventually they encountered Woodgod and his band of similar human-animal hybrids known as the Changelings, and Sloan decided to remain with them.

In time, he wrote a book, entitled *Hulk Encounter: A Survivor's Story*, which painted the green behemoth in an unusually positive light. **TB**

Smythe, Alistair

FIRST APPEARANCE Amazing Spider-Man Annual #19 (1985)
REAL NAME Alistair Smythe
OCCUPATION Criminal inventor **BASE** New York City
HEIGHT 6 ft **WEIGHT** 220 lbs **EYES** Brown **HAIR** Brown
SPECIAL POWERS/ABILITIES Ultimate Spider-Slayer armature provides enhanced strength, and features built-in cutting blades and web shooters.

Alistair Smythe grew up hating Spider-Man. His father, Professor Spencer Smythe, built the first robotic Spider-Slayer units, and Alistair continued the Spider-Slayer legacy after his father's death.

Following a stint in the employ of the Kingpin, Alistair constructed ever more deadly Spider-Slayers until an accident left him in a wheelchair. In response, he fashioned a cyborg armature for himself and emerged as the Ultimate Spider-Slayer. Alistair tried to coerce J. Jonah Jameson into helping him, but Jameson knocked him out with a baseball bat. **DW**

Smythe, Professor

FIRST APPEARANCE Amazing Spider-Man Vol. 1 #25 (June 1965)
REAL NAME Spencer Smythe
OCCUPATION Professor, criminal inventor **BASE** New York City
HEIGHT 5 ft 10 in **WEIGHT** 175 lbs **EYES** Gray **HAIR** Gray
SPECIAL POWERS/ABILITIES Genius-level expertise in engineering and robotics.

Professor Spencer Smythe's life was marked by an irrational hatred for Spider-Man. He used his engineering expertise to construct the Spider-Slayer, a Spider-Man hunting robot, and persuaded *Daily Bugle* publisher J. Jonah Jameson to pay for it. He followed up with several improved generations of Spider-Slayers, but the radiation used in their construction gradually poisoned him. He died during a revenge plot hatched against both Spider-Man and Jameson, leaving his son Alistair (*see* Smythe, Alistair) to carry on his work. **DW**

Snarks *see next page*

Snow Queen

FIRST APPEARANCE Wolverine Vol. 2 #24 (May 1990)
REAL NAME Unrevealed
OCCUPATION Assassin **BASE** Unrevealed
HEIGHT/WEIGHT Unknown **EYES** Blue **HAIR** Blond
SPECIAL POWERS/ABILITIES Generates mental static that occludes minds of others; trained in the use of various types of weapons and explosives.

The only known report of the mutant assassin known as Snow Queen relates to a short visit to 1930s Madripoor, where she encountered Wolverine. Employed to kill a barman in the town with a suitcase of explosives, her plan went wrong when a street urchin stole the case. When Wolverine attempted to intervene, the Snow Queen overwhelmed him with her mental powers. It is thought that she died minutes later when the recovered suitcase detonated prematurely. **AD**

Snarks

FACTFILE

REAL NAME
Zn'rx (pronounced "Snarks")

BASE
The planet Snarkworld

HEIGHT 8 ft (average)
WEIGHT 400 lbs (average)
EYES Red
HAIR None (green scales)

FIRST APPEARANCE
Power Pack #1 (August 1984)

POWERS
Snarks are larger, stronger and live longer than human beings. As well as various high-tech weapons (their technology is generally more advanced than Earth's), they have a vicious array of teeth and sharp claws. Like Earth's reptiles they are cold-blooded and so vulnerable to extremes of cold.

A malevolent, warlike, reptilian race, the Zn'rx or "Snarks" are based on a planet in the Milky Way galaxy known on Earth as Snarkworld. The Snarks first came to notice when their ages-long conflict with the horselike Kymellians spilled over to Earth.

The Snarks are perennial enemies of the super-powered children of the Power Pack.

The Queen Mother, Maraud, sent raiding parties to Earth in order to learn the secrets of a new scientific breakthrough discovered by Dr. James Power, and use it as a weapon against their ancient foes. Sent by his people to prevent this from happening, Kymellian champion Aelfyre Whitemane was slain by the Snarks, but not before he passed on his abilities to Dr. Powers' four children. These children, now known as the Power Pack, defeated the Snark menace. Thereafter, the Snarks became obsessed with taking Whitemane's powers for themselves, and repeatedly staged attacks on the Power children, to no avail.

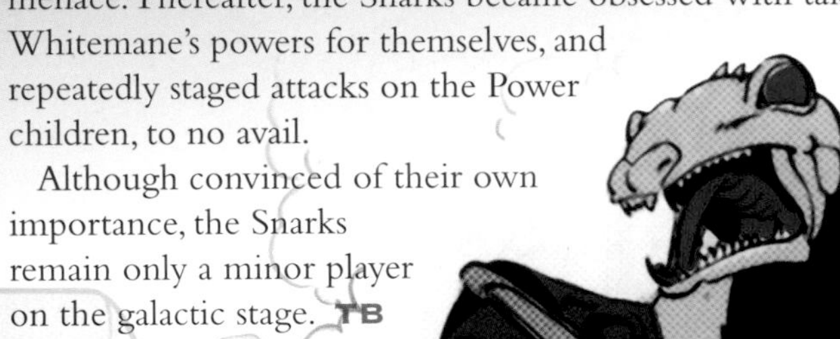

Although convinced of their own importance, the Snarks remain only a minor player on the galactic stage. **TB**

The Snarks were given their name by Aelfyre Whitemane after the monster in the famous poem "The Hunting of the Snark" by Lewis Carroll.

Snowbird *see opposite page*

Solarr

FIRST APPEARANCE Captain America #160 (April 1973)
REAL NAME Silas King **OCCUPATION** Criminal
BASE New York City; Project Pegasus complex
HEIGHT 6 ft **WEIGHT** 210 lbs **EYES** Brown **HAIR** Blond
SPECIAL POWERS/ABILITIES He can absorb, store, and control solar energy, and discharge this energy in the form of powerful heat blasts fired from his hands.

Narcotics smuggler Silas King's van broke down in the Mojave desert. After several days in the desert sun his latent mutant power was released. Adopting the name Solarr, he move used his power to rob banks. He became partners with Klaw and later joined Egghead's Emissaries of Evil. Solarr's criminal endeavors were repeatedly stopped by the Avengers, Captain America, Spider-Man, and the Thing. He was imprisoned for study at the Project: Pegasus energy research center and was killed by the animated corpse of a guard he had burned to death, which had been brought back to life by Bres of the Fomor race. **MT**

Sommers, April

FIRST APPEARANCE Incredible Hulk #208 (February 1977)
REAL NAME April Sommers **OCCUPATION** Model, actress, apartment superintendent **BASE** New York City
HEIGHT 5 ft 8 in **WEIGHT** 123 lbs **EYES** Blue **HAIR** Blonde
SPECIAL POWERS/ABILITIES Possesses the strength, speed and reflexes of an average female who regularly engages in moderate exercise. Extremely personable.

An often-unemployed model and actress, Sommers also supported herself by working as the superintendent of the apartment building where she lived. The job provided her with free rent and a small weekly salary. She once rented a room to Dr. Bruce Banner, completely unaware of the fact that he was secretly the Hulk, and she later helped him get a temporary job at a construction site. Though she was attracted to Bruce at first, her interest quickly waned as he began to act more and more mysteriously. She eventually learned his secret. After asking Bruce to leave, Sommers gave the apartment to his friend Jim Wilson. **TD**

SNOWBIRD

FACTFILE

REAL NAME
Narya

OCCUPATION
Goddess; adventurer

BASE
Canada

HEIGHT 5 ft 10 in
WEIGHT 108 lbs
EYES (Snowbird) White; (Anne McKenzie) blue
HAIR Pale blonde; (in animal form) White

FIRST APPEARANCE
(as Anne McKenzie) Uncanny X-Men #120 (April 1979)

POWERS
Snowbird can assume the form of a human woman or of any animal native to the Canadian Arctic. She has superhuman strength and the ability to fly.

Snowbird

Nelvanna, goddess of the Northern Lights, wished to have a child that was half human, half god, a child that could defend humanity from the mystical Great Beasts. She mated with a human named Richard Easton, and the Native American sorcerer Michael Twoyoungmen raised the infant, named Narya. Narya grew to adulthood within a few years, and James MacDonald Hudson invited her and Twoyoungmen to join Alpha Flight, a team of superhuman operatives he was organizing for the government.

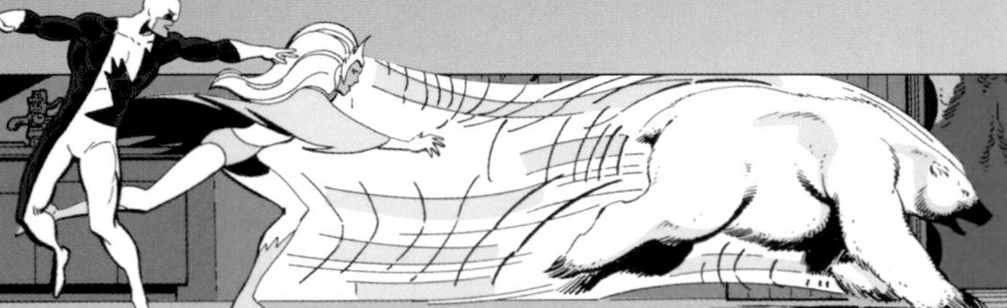

Snowbird can become any animal native to the Canadian Arctic, gaining its abilities. When she takes the form of a creature smaller than herself, like an owl, she becomes a human-sized version of it.

Narya took the name Snowbird, and took the cover identity of Anne McKenzie, an officer in the Canadian Mounties.

Another Alpha Flight member, Walter Langkowski, could transform into a legendary monster called a Sasquatch. Sasquatch fell under the mental control of Tanaraq, one of the Great Beasts. To stop Tanaraq, Snowbird slew Sasquatch's physical body.

Anne McKenzie married a fellow officer in the RCMP, Doug Thompson, and they had a son. Subsequently, a menace called Pestilence took mental possession of Snowbird. Hudson's wife Heather defeated Pestilence by killing Narya's physical form. Langkowski's spirit took over Narya's resurrected body, becoming the new Sasquatch. Snowbird's spirit later gained a new body and returned to Alpha Flight. **PS**

Snowbird can transform herself into a Sasquatch, also known as "Bigfoot". She also gains mass when becoming a larger creature.

Son of Satan

FIRST APPEARANCE Incredible Hulk #231 (January 1979)
REAL NAME Daimon Hellstrom
OCCUPATION Demonologist, occult investigator
BASE San Francisco
HEIGHT 6 ft 1 in **WEIGHT** 180 lbs **EYES** Blue **HAIR** Red
SPECIAL POWERS/ABILITIES Commands considerable supernatural powers and can cast spells to transport himself and others between Earth and mystical dimensions. He can project a fire-like mystical energy called soulfire or hellfire, and can also fire powerful concussive energy blasts.

Daimon Hellstrom is the son of a demon father named Satan and a human mother. Sent to an orphanage after his mother's breakdown, Daimon returned home and discovered her diary, from which he learned the truth about his father. Satan brought Daimon to the demon's netherworld domain, where, using the name Son of Satan, Daimon vowed to battle his father. As Son of Satan he joined the Defenders and eventually defeated his father. **MT**

FACTFILE

KEY MEMBERS

GENERAL CHEN
The first Supreme Serpent; A grossly overambitious individual.

DAN DUNN
Co-leader; talk-show host, white right-winger.

MONTAGUE HALE
Co-leader and black, left-winger.

J.C. PENNYSWORTH
Head of Richmond Enterprises; sponsor of Sons of the Satan

HATE-MONGER
Foments hatred and anger.

RUSSELL DABOIA
Mystic powers.

SKINHEAD
Superhuman neo-Nazi.

BASE California

FIRST APPEARANCE
Avengers Vol. 1 #32 (September 1966)

Serpent Signs can be used to record and leave messages.

Sons of the Serpent

"As the first serpent drove Adam and Eve from Eden, so shall we drive all foreigners from this land." This is the mantra of the Sons of the Serpent—an organization fueled by hatred and sponsored by a few wealthy businessmen. Targeting non-whites, immigrants, and the infirm, the Sons of the Serpent is dedicated to making the US a citadel of white racial supremacy.

During their first bid for power, they took CAPTAIN AMERICA hostage to try to force the AVENGERS into publicly supporting their evil cause. When this failed, the Sons developed further plots aimed at dividing America and black against white, one of which actually culminated in a mind-controlled Captain America fighting against his black partner, the FALCON.

After repeated knock backs, their plans have become increasingly desperate. They have even resorted to crude mysticism, perhaps a sign of their waning influence. AD

The Sons of the Serpent tried to kidnap Captain America.

Little more than a gang of thugs, the Sons of the Serpent will attack any unarmed individual.

FACTFILE

NOTABLE MEMBERS

CRIMSON DYNAMO (5)
In armor, has superhuman strength, durability and can fly.

URSA MAJOR (3)
Transforms into a large bear; retains his intelligence while in bear form.

VANGUARD (8)
Forcefield repels virtually all electromagnetic and kinetic energy. By crossing his hammer and sickle in front of his body, he can redirect energy repelled by his natural force field

DARKSTAR (6)
Manipulates extradimensional energy called the Darkforce.

TITANIUM MAN (Gremlin) (9)
Armor provided superhuman strength, durability flight; fired force blasts from hands.

BASE
The former Soviet Union, now Russia

FIRST APPEARANCE
Incredible Hulk #258 (April 1981)

Soviet Super Soldiers

Created to be the Soviet Union's answer to the AVENGERS, the Soviet Super-Soldiers functioned as that nation's defenders through much of the latter part of the Cold War. But eventually, questioning some of the orders given to them by the State, they rebelled, and began to operate independently. The Russian government later sent their replacement team, the Supreme Soviets, to reclaim the members of the Soviet Super Soldiers and bring them back into line—an attempt that met with failure.

Thereafter, with the fall of communism and the dissolution of the Soviet Union, the surviving members of both the Soviet Super Soldiers and the Supreme Soviet joined forces with other new heroes to become first the People's Protectorate, then the Winter Guard, still dedicated to using their great powers to defend their homeland, no matter who ruled it. TB

SOVIET SUPER SOLDIERS
1 Red Guardian ***2*** Unidentified ***3*** Ursa Major ***4*** Unidentified ***5*** Crimson Dynamo ***6*** Darkstar ***7*** Unidentified ***8*** Vanguard ***9*** Titanium Man (The Gremlin) ***10*** Unidentified ***11*** Unidentified ***12*** Unidentified ***13*** Volvic ***14*** Unidentified

Southern, Candy

FIRST APPEARANCE X-Men #31 (April 1967)
REAL NAME Candace Southern **OCCUPATION** CEO Southern Industries **BASE** New York City, Colorado Rocky Mountains
HEIGHT Unknown **WEIGHT** Unknown **EYES** Blue **HAIR** Black
SPECIAL POWERS/ABILITIES Normal human strength of woman who engaged in regular exercise. Had great leadership abilities.

Archangel Warren Worthington was unable to prevent Candy's murder.

Candace "Candy" Southern began dating Warren Worthington III when they were teenagers. Southern discovered that Worthington was the ANGEL, a member of X-MEN, when his uncle, the original DAZZLER abducted her. Southern and Worthington later shared a home in the Rocky Mountains which became the DEFENDERS' headquarters. Southern was the team's business manager and government liaison. She was killed by Worthington's enemy, Cameron Hodge. Southern's mind was assimilated into the group consciousness of the techno-organic PHALANX. She sacrificed herself to destroy Hodge. **PS**

Speedfreek

FIRST APPEARANCE Incredible Hulk Vol. 2 #388 (December 1991)
REAL NAME Leon Shappe
OCCUPATION Assassin **BASE** Mobile
HEIGHT/WEIGHT Unrevealed **EYES** Brown **HAIR** Brown
SPECIAL POWERS/ABILITIES Combat suit of titanium steel alloy that is virtually indestructible; rocket-powered boots enable flight and travel at 150 mph; uses two long adamantium blades.

A petty criminal and police informant, Leon Shappe would stoop to anything to feed his drug habit. Stealing a sophisticated combat suit from a local inventor, Shappe decided to use it to become an assassin-for-hire known as Speedfreek. His brain addled by drugs, he became a ruthless killer, reveling in his gruesome work. Hired by a gangster to kill a young man at a charity ball, Shappe was defeated by Hulk. They later clashed again and, dodging Speedfreek's slashing blades, the Hulk threw a car battery at him. Speedfreek cut the battery in two, showering himself with acid. He has not been heard of since. **AD**

Speed Demon

FIRST APPEARANCE Amazing Spider-Man Vol. 1 #222 (Nov. 1981)
REAL NAME James Sanders
OCCUPATION Professional criminal **BASE** New York City
HEIGHT 5 ft 11 in **WEIGHT** 175 lbs **EYES** Black **HAIR** Gray
SPECIAL POWERS/ABILITIES A super speedster, able to run at up to 160 mph; also possesses superhuman strength.

Chemist James Sanders received the gift of superspeed and superhuman strength from the GRANDMASTER, who recruited him to serve with the Squadron Sinister. At first Sanders went by the name Whizzer, but changed his identity to Speed Demon to avoid confusion with the 1940s hero. Speed Demon, a frequent foe of SPIDER-MAN, later joined the SINISTER SYNDICATE and the team of reformed criminals known as the THUNDERBOLTS. He is a member of the most recent incarnation of the Thunderbolts, having been added to the roster by BARON VON STRUCKER to work as a spy. **DW**

Space Phantom

FIRST APPEARANCE Avengers #2 (November 1963)
REAL NAME Unknown **OCCUPATION** Agent of Immortus
BASE Limbo **HEIGHT** 6 ft 6 in **WEIGHT** 215 lbs **EYES** Blue
HAIR Red **SPECIAL POWERS/ABILITIES** Space Phantom can change his appearance to look like any living being. If they have superpowers, then he assumes those powers as well. The being whose form is taken is instantly sent to the dimension of Limbo.

Space Phantom is an alien from the planet Phantus, which shifted into the timeless dimension of Limbo when the space-time continuum ruptured. Stranded in Limbo, Space Phantom met IMMORTUS, the master of that realm. Immortus offered to free Space Phantom if he brought him beings to study. When Space Phantom agreed, Immortus gave him the power to assume the form of any being as a way to bring him subjects. When Space Phantom took on the form of another being, it was immediately sent to Limbo for Immortus to examine. On the occasion when Space Phantom tried to send the Thunder God, THOR, into Limbo, he was stopped and sent back into the timeless dimension. **MT**

Speedball

FIRST APPEARANCE Amazing Spider-Man Annual #22 (1988)
REAL NAME Robert Baldwin **OCCUPATION** High-school student
BASE New York City, formerly Springdale, Connecticut
HEIGHT 5 ft 6 in **WEIGHT** 133 lbs **EYES** Blue **HAIR** Blond
SPECIAL POWERS/ABILITIES Personal force-field allows him to absorb all kinetic energy directed at him and reflect it back at a greater velocity, which he often does by bouncing off objects.

While working as an intern at a research laboratory, Robert Baldwin was accidentally bombarded by bubbles of energy from another dimension. A gang of thieves attempted to steal some rare metals from the lab and one of them struck Baldwin with a gun, triggering his new powers. Baldwin subdued the thieves by ricocheting off the walls and ceiling to knock them down. After learning to control his powers, Baldwin took the costumed identity of Speedball (also nicknamed the Masked Marvel) and became a crimefighter in his hometown of Springdale. He later became a founding member of the NEW WARRIORS. **TD**

Sphinx

FIRST APPEARANCE Nova Vol. 3 #6 (October 1999)
REAL NAME Anath-Na Mut
OCCUPATION Wizard **BASE** Mobile flying pyramid
HEIGHT 7 ft 2 in **WEIGHT** 450 lbs **EYES** Red **HAIR** None
SPECIAL POWERS/ABILITIES Enhanced strength; Ka stone permitted immortality, flight, telepathy, energy transference, and the ability to fire concussive beams.

Anath-Na Mut, an ancient Egyptian mutant given further powers by the Caretaker of Arcturus, served in the court of Ramses II until his failure to defeat Moses branded him an exile. He became the immortal Sphinx through the energies of the Ka stone, wandering for five thousand years until absorbing the extraterrestrial Xandar living computer with unwitting help from the hero NOVA. Now nearly omnipotent, the Sphinx met defeat at GALACTUS' hands. Later, Anath-Na Mut returned to life. When he merged with his reincarnated Egyptian lover, Meryet Karim (Sphinx II), the two formed the "Omni-Sphinx." **DW**

Spider-Man

Your friendly neighborhood web-slinger

Spider-Man

FACTFILE

REAL NAME
Peter Benjamin Parker

OCCUPATION
Freelance photographer, science teacher

BASE
New York City

HEIGHT 5 ft 10 in
WEIGHT 170 lbs
EYES Hazel
HAIR Brown

FIRST APPEARANCE
Amazing Fantasy #15 (August 1962)

POWERS

Possesses the proportionate strength, speed, agility and reflexes of a spider. Can cling to any surface and generate organic webbing. Also possesses a "spider-sense" that warns him of danger and can psychically align him with his environment. Invented spider-tracers that he can track across the city with his spider-sense.

ALLIES/FOES

ALLIES Ben and May Parker, Mary Jane Parker, Captain America, The Avengers, the Fantastic Four, the X-Men, Eugene "Flash" Thompson, Betty Brant Leeds.

FOES Chameleon, Vulture, Doctor Octopus, Sandman, Kingpin, Green Goblin, Lizard, Electro, Kraven the Hunter, Black Cat, Venom, Mysterio, Carnage, Scrier, Judas Traveller.

ISSUE #1

While attending a scientific demonstration, Peter Parker was bitten by a spider that had been exposed to radioactivity. Feeling nauseous, the teenager immediately headed home and began to exhibit the most amazing powers—like the ability to stick to walls and crawl up sheer surfaces!

Before gaining his spider-powers, Peter Parker was weaker than most of the kids his age.

Peter Parker's parents died in a plane crash while he was still a child. When they said goodbye at the airport, his parents told him to be a good boy for his Aunt May and Uncle Ben Parker, who later raised him as their own son. Peter always thought of his Uncle Ben as his best friend. Not only did Ben Parker spend quality time with the boy, he had a great sense of humor and many hours telling jokes and pulling gags on Peter who developed a real appreciation for quips and pranks. Peter studied hard in school and became an honor student. Although his teachers praised him, the other students had little use for a know-it-all like puny Parker. The girls thought him too quiet, and the boys considered him a wimp.

ORIGIN OF SPIDER-MAN

On the day his life changed forever, Peter went to a science exhibition by himself where he was bitten by a common house spider that had been exposed to a massive dose of radiation. Within a few hours, Peter discovered that he could stick to walls and had gained other amazing arachnid abilities.

Anxious to cash in on his new powers he designed a distinctive costume that concealed his identity, built a pair of web-shooters and went into showbusiness using the Amazing Spider-Man as his stage name.

One night, after a performance, he was walking toward an elevator when a security guard asked him to stop a fleeing man. However, Peter Parker did nothing and the burglar escaped.

Peter has begun to suspect that his powers may be the result of paranormal forces.

MY FAULT -- ALL MY FAULT! IF ONLY I HAD STOPPED HIM WHEN I COULD HAVE! BUT I DIDN'T -- AND NOW -- UNCLE BEN -- IS DEAD...

A few days later the same thief murdered Peter's Uncle Ben! Filled with remorse, Peter vowed that he would never allow another innocent person to suffer because Spider-Man had failed to act. He had learned, in the hardest possible way, to use his great powers in a responsible manner.

High-School Hero

Spider-Man soon found himself battling criminals such as the Chameleon, the Vulture, Doctor Octopus, the Sandman, Doctor Doom, the Lizard, Electro, Mysterio, the Green Goblin, the Scorpion. and many more. He attempted to join the Fantastic Four and began a feud with the Human Torch.

J. Jonah Jameson, publisher of the *Daily Bugle,* hated masked vigilantes and claimed Spider-Man was a menace to the public. Peter saw an opportunity to exploit Jameson's campaign and began taking pictures of himself as Spider-Man. He was soon supporting himself by selling these pictures to the *Bugle* on a freelance basis.

Peter eventually graduated from Midtown High with the highest scholastic average in the school's history. However, he almost missed the graduation ceremony. While the other seniors were donning caps and gowns, he was busy battling the Molten Man. He won his fight and arrived at the ceremony just in time to learn that he had won a full scholarship to Empire State University.

The Green Goblin murdered Gwen Stacy, Peter's first true love.

College Years And Beyond

While in college, Peter met Mary Jane Watson (his future wife, *see* Parker, Mary Jane), but began to date Gwen Stacy. (Gwen would later die tragically at the hands of the Green Goblin.) Peter became best friends with Harry Osborn and later learned that the Green Goblin was secretly Harry's father Norman. Spider-Man also encountered such villains as Kingpin, the Rhino, the Shocker, Silvermane and the Prowler.

After graduating from college, Peter encountered the acrobatic cat burglar Black Cat (his girlfriend for a while), and the criminals Hydro-Man, Speed Demon and the Hobgoblin. He also battled the unstoppable Juggernaut and cosmically-powered Firelord. He temporarily donned a new black costume that possessed some additional new powers, but later proved to be an alien symbiote. Meanwhile, his relationship with the beautiful model Mary Jane Watson had grown serious and they were married.

Spider-Man tangles with Doctor Octopus above the streets of Manhattan.

Further Developments

After leading a European crime cult for many years, Norman Osborn reentered Peter's life. Peter also met a man called Ezekiel who claimed that Spider-Man's powers were the result of magic and not a radioactive spider. Peter later confronted the Queen, who had the power to control insects and she mutated him into a giant spider. After returning to his human form, Peter learned that his powers and strength had been increased and that he had gained the ability to produce organic webbing. Peter also joined a new Avengers team.

After a battle with the mysterious, super-strong, vampiric villain Morlun, in which Peter appeared to have been killed, Peter temporarily accepted a new armored costume and a job working for Tony Stark (*see* Iron Man). However he has since returned to his traditional look. **TD**

Essential Storylines

- ***Amazing Spider-Man #31–33*** Spider-Man battles the Master Planner in order to obtain a rare serum that can save Aunt May's life.
- ***Amazing Spider-Man: Fearful Symmetry or Kraven's Last Hunt (tpb)*** Kraven the Hunter kidnaps Spider-Man and take his place in a battle against the deadly Vermin.
- ***Amazing Spider-Man: The Saga of the Alien Costume (tpb)*** Spider-Man learns that his new black costume is actually an alien symbiote.
- ***Amazing Spider-Man vs. Venom (tpb)*** Spider-Man meets his match when Venom enters his life.
- ***Amazing Spider-Man: Identity Crisis (tpb)*** When a $5 million bounty is placed on his head for a murder he didn't commit, Spider-Man must adopt four new costumed identities to find the real murderer.
- ***Amazing Spider-Man: Coming Home (tpb)*** Spider-Man meets the man called Ezekiel and learns there may be a lot more to his origin than he ever realized.

The Alien Suit

Along with other heroes, Spider-Man was transported to a planet created by a near-omnipotent being called the Beyonder and forced to fight in a series of "Secret Wars". When his original red and blue costume was torn in battle, the web-spinner tried to repair it, but mistakenly activated a device that released a little black ball. The ball spread across him, duplicating the costume worn by the Julia Carpenter Spider-Woman.

Spider-Man's new suit could instantly mimic any kind of clothing, could carry his camera and spare change, was equipped with its own web-shooters and possessed a seemingly endless supply of webbing. He eventually discovered that the alien suit was a symbiote with a mind of its own. Spider-Man had to enlist the scientific help of Mr. Fantastic to remove it, using soundwaves at a certain frequency.

Rejected by Spidey, the symbiote grafted itself to Eddie Brock to become Venom (top).

Spider-Girl

FIRST APPEARANCE What If? #105 (February 1998)
REAL NAME May "Mayday" Parker
OCCUPATION High-school student **BASE** New York City
HEIGHT 5 ft 5 in **WEIGHT** 112 lbs **EYES** Brown **HAIR** Brown
SPECIAL POWERS/ABILITIES Similar powers of agility, strength, and climbing ability as Spider-Man; uses web-shooters, developed by her father, to travel across the city or trap enemies.

Usually attired in red and blue, Spider-Woman sometimes wears a black costume.

In a possible future, SPIDER-MAN is injured battling the GREEN GOBLIN and retires from crime-fighting. His wife (see PARKER, MARY JANE) gives birth to their first child and Peter Parker becomes a forensic scientist for the NYPD. His daughter May grows up to play high-school basketball. During a game, she exhibits superhuman agility and soon learns of her father's past. Having inherited his powers, May decides to take up the family business as Spider-Girl. She battles new villains, such as Funny Face, Crazy Eight, Dragon Lord, and Killerwatt. She also confronts the sons and daughters of villains that had once challenged her dad like Electra, Raptor and Normie Osborn. Spider-Girl has also aided other Super Heroes like the AVENGERS and the Fantastic Five. **TD**

Like most teenagers, Spider-Girl is never without her cell phone, which snaps into a holder on her web-shooters.

Spider-Man 2099

FIRST APPEARANCE Spider-Man 2099 #1 (November 1992)
REAL NAME Miguel O'Hara
OCCUPATION Genetic engineer, adventurer **BASE** New York City
HEIGHT 5 ft 10 in **WEIGHT** 170 lbs **EYES** Brown **HAIR** Brown
SPECIAL POWERS/ABILITIES Superhuman strength, speed and agility. Can adhere to surfaces and project webbing from spinnerets in forearms. Retractable talons and fangs that secrete poison.

In 2099 A D in an alternate future, Miguel O'Hara, head of genetics for the Alchemax corporation, tried to recreate the powers of the original SPIDER-MAN. His superior, Tyler Stone, controlled him by addicting him to a drug called Rapture. Trying to cure himself, O'Hara underwent his own experimental genetic manipulation process. This was sabotaged by a co-worker, causing O'Hara to develop spider-like powers. He became the Spider-Man of 2099, battling both supercriminals and Alchemax. After his secret identity was exposed he joined the EXILES. **PS**

SPIDER-WOMAN
SEE OPPOSITE PAGE

Spirit of '76

FIRST APPEARANCE The Invaders Vol. 1 #14 (March 1977)
REAL NAME William Nasland
OCCUPATION Costumed adventurer **BASE** Mobile
HEIGHT 6 ft 2 in **WEIGHT** 215 lbs **EYES** Blue **HAIR** Black
SPECIAL POWERS/ABILITIES Top level athlete and formidable hand-to-hand combatant; wore a bullet-proof cape; as Captain America he had a steel shield, which was not indestructible.

Inspired by CAPTAIN AMERICA's World War II exploits, William Nasland became the costumed adventurer, Spirit of '76. After battling Nazi spies in Philadelphia, Nasland moved to Great Britain and joined the Crusaders team of heroes, until its leader was revealed to be a German agent. Nasland continued to contribute to the war effort, partnering Captain America on a mission to Berlin. Following the Cap's apparent demise, Nasland agreed to become a second Captain America but his career as this emblematic figurehead was cut short when he died preventing the assassination of would-be congressman John F. Kennedy. **AD**

Spiral

FIRST APPEARANCE Longshot #1 (September 1985)
REAL NAME "Ricochet" Rita
OCCUPATION Warrior sorceress **BASE** Mobile
HEIGHT 5 ft 10 in **WEIGHT** 150 lbs **EYES** Blue **HAIR** Silver
SPECIAL POWERS/ABILITIES Enhanced strength; spellcasting abilities allow teleportation between dimensions; excellent swordswoman who can wield six weapons at once.

Spiral is a six-armed sorceress who works as an aide to the alien despot MOJO. An actress in her former life, Spiral received genetic alterations in the Mojoverse dimension that reshaped her form and gave her other enhancements, including the ability to manipulate magic. On Earth, Spiral briefly served with the mutant government operatives in FREEDOM FORCE and opened an exclusive cybernetics store, the Body Shoppe, whose customers included LADY DEATHSTRIKE. **DW**

Spitfire

FIRST APPEARANCE The Invaders Vol. 1 #7 (July 1976)
REAL NAME Jacqueline Falsworth Crichton
OCCUPATION Adventurer **BASE** Falsworth Manor, England
HEIGHT 5 ft 4 in **WEIGHT** 110 lbs **EYES** Blue **HAIR** Blonde
SPECIAL POWERS/ABILITIES Spitfire can move at superhuman speed. She can run up to 50 miles per hour and sustain that speed for up to four hours.

During World War II, Jacqueline Falsworth was serving in England's Home Guard, a civil defense group, when she was attacked by the Nazi vampire Baron Blood. She was rescued by the original HUMAN TORCH, an android who gave her a transfusion of his artificial blood. The combination of the vampire bite and the Human Torch's blood gave Falsworth amazing superhuman speed. She adopted the name Spitfire and teamed up with the INVADERS, a group of costumed heroes who battled against the Axis powers during the war. Over time her powers faded, but another transfusion from the Human Torch was able to restore them. **MT**

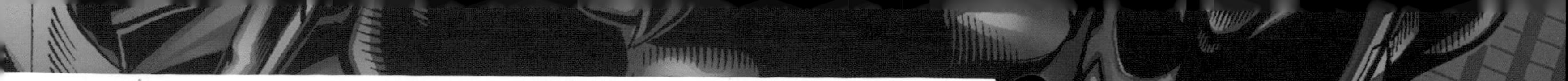

Spider-Woman

Investigator with irresistible powers

Jessica Drew, the original Spider-Woman, was born in the 1920s. Suffering from radiation poisoning, she received an injection of spider serum from her father's research partner—the man who would become the High Evolutionary. Drew remained in a genetic accelerator for decades, finally emerging at the relative age of 14.

COME ON DARLING--REACT! YOU'VE GOT TO REACT!
ALL MY WORK, MY HOPES-- THEY'RE ALL CENTERED ON YOU.

Like many superhumans, Jessica Drew gained her powers as a result of forbidden science.

Going Solo

For several years she lived with the animalistic New Men on Mount Wundagore, before falling in with HYDRA and becoming their assassin, Arachne. Nick Fury of SHIELD convinced her to leave HYDRA, and Drew became a Super Hero in Los Angeles. Calling herself Spider-Woman, Drew believed for a time that she was a spider evolved to human form. She later became a bounty hunter, then a private investigator. Spider-Woman saved the life of Giant-Man (Bill Foster) through a blood transfusion, and lost some of her powers in the process. She then lost all her powers when a villainous Spider-Woman named Charlotte Witter, stole them. Drew then became a mentor to the youngest Spider-Woman, Martha "Mattie" Franklin. Jessica Drew has since regained her former abilities, serving as an agent of SHIELD and as a member of the New Avengers.

Wings let Spider-Woman glide, and she can now fly unassisted.

FACTFILE

REAL NAME
Jessica Drew

OCCUPATION
Adventurer

BASE
Mobile

HEIGHT 5 ft 10 in
WEIGHT 130 lbs
EYES Green
HAIR Brown (dyed black)

FIRST APPEARANCE
Marvel Spotlight vol. 1 #32 (February 1977)

Spider-Woman

POWERS

Enhanced strength, speed, and hearing; flight; superhuman healing factor; emits mood-altering pheromones that attract both sexes; ability to adhere to walls and fire electric "venom blasts."

KEY STORYLINES

- ***The Spider-Woman #1*** The first issue of her original, self-titled series sees Jessica Drew striking out on her own as a hero.
- ***Spider-Woman: Origin #1–6*** This limited series retells Spider-Woman's beginnings, from a HYDRA pawn to a member of the New Avengers.
- ***New Avengers #1*** Jessica Drew returns in her role of Spider-Woman in the New Avengers.

A Second Spider

Julia Carpenter became the second heroic Spider-Woman, making her debut during the Beyonder's Secret Wars. She received her powers from a secret government agency and joined the mutants of Freedom Force, later serving with both the Avengers, West Coast and its spinoff, Force Works. She lost her powers at the hands of Charlotte Witter.

Spider Sense

The third heroic Spider-Woman was Mattie Franklin, the niece of J. Jonah Jameson. She briefly lost her powers to Charlotte Witter, but later re-absorbed the powers of all the other Spider-Women, including Witter. Franklin was the most inexperienced Spider-Woman, and relied on guidance from Jessica Drew to control her powers. DW

Charlotte Witter was the only villainous Spider-Woman. Doctor Octopus bestowed her with powers sufficient to kill Spider-Man. Witter also possessed the ability to drain the powers of the other Spider-Women, but lost them when defeated by Mattie Franklin.

Spymaster

FIRST APPEARANCE Iron Man #33 (January 1971)
REAL NAME Unrevealed
OCCUPATION Industrial spy **BASE** Mobile
HEIGHT 6 ft **WEIGHT** 195 lbs **EYES** Blue **HAIR** Blonde
SPECIAL POWERS/ABILITIES Master of disguise; exceptional hand-to-hand combatant; brilliant saboteur; expert with all kinds of hi-tech weaponry; bulletproof costume; used hoverjet for transport.

Right from his first days as the Iron Man, Tony Stark was dogged by industrial espionage agent, the Spymaster. Initially working with a team of assistants known as the Espionage Elite, Spymaster made repeated efforts to obtain Stark Industries' secrets. Each time he was thwarted, each time he escaped, and each time he sought and found a new employer. Zodiac, SHIELD, and Madame Masque all employed Spymaster but it was Stark's archfoe Justin Hammer who benefited most. Shortly before Spymaster's death at the hands of rival spy the Ghost, he had obtained some old Iron Man blueprints. The Guardsmen built from these were to dog Stark's life for months. AD

St. Lawrence, Col.

FIRST APPEARANCE Incredible Hulk Vol. 2 #446 (October 1996)
REAL NAME Colonel Cary St. Lawrence
OCCUPATION US Army officer **BASE** Mobile
HEIGHT/WEIGHT Unrevealed **EYES** Brown **HAIR** Black
SPECIAL POWERS/ABILITIES Skilled military strategist, highly trained athlete, adept with variety of weaponry.

When she was a cadet at West Point academy, General "Thunderbolt" Ross was dismissive about Cary St. Lawrence's chances of a successful career in the military. Inspired to work even harder to prove him wrong, Cary graduated third in her class.

Assigned to capture the Hulk, Cary proved to be unusually effective in her dealings with the green fiend. At first she favored brute force during her encounters with the creature, but soon came to realize that there was no point in employing strong-arm tactics: after all, the Hulk only got more powerful the angrier he became. She thus began to use more subtle approaches to subdue the creature. Perhaps all the Hulk has ever needed is a woman's touch... AD

Squadron Supreme

In a 12-issue series, the Squadron Supreme explores absolute power.

The Squadron Supreme is a force of superhuman champions inhabiting the Earth of an alternate reality. They have crossed paths with the Avengers many times, including an early team-up to eradicate the evil influence of the serpent-god Set's Serpent Crown.

The Squadron Supreme faced their greatest challenge when the Overmind and Null the Living Darkness conquered their planet. Hyperion escaped to mainstream Earth and recruited the Defenders, who successfully defeated the Overmind. The damage to their world from the Overmind war was so great that the Squadron Supreme implemented the Utopia Program, seizing control of the government and forcibly implementing new methods of policing and social engineering. Nighthawk left the Squadron in protest, and organized the Redeemers to act as a rebel insurgency. The Redeemers forced the Squadron's surrender, and the two groups dismantled the Utopia Program. The Squadron Supreme later became marooned on mainstream Earth, where they adventured alongside Quasar.

The Squadron has now successfully liberated their own world from the grip of various monolithic corporations who were seeking to gain control of the planet. DW

FACTFILE

NOTABLE MEMBERS

HYPERION (leader)
Flight, enhanced strength, super-speed, near-invulnerability, atomic vision .

AMPHIBIAN
Enhanced strength, able to live underwater at ocean depths.

DOCTOR SPECTRUM
Power prism permits flight and the projection of hard-energy objects.

GOLDEN ARCHER
Unsurpassed skill with a bow and arrow.

NIGHTHAWK
Brilliant strategist, top-level combatant.

POWER PRINCESS
Enhanced strength, skilled warrior.

THE WHIZZER
Super-speedster.

BASE Squadron City

FIRST APPEARANCE:
Avengers Vol. 1 #85 (March 1971)

SQUADRON SUPREME
1 Tom Thumb ***2*** Whizzer ***3*** Nuke ***4*** Redstone ***5*** Shape ***6*** Power Princess ***7*** Hyperion ***8*** Lamprey ***9*** Doctor Spectrum ***10*** Firefox ***11*** Arcanna ***12*** Blue Eagle ***13*** Black Archer ***14*** Ape X

Stacy, Gwen

The daughter of Police captain George Stacy, Gwen first became aware of Peter Parker when the two of them enrolled at Empire State University. Although attracted to Parker, Gwen was initially put off by his frequent moodiness and his apparent cowardliness in the face of danger—little realizing that Parker was secretly the Amazing Spider-Man. Eventually, however, she and Peter became a couple, despite competition from her rival, Mary Jane Watson (*see* Parker, Mary Jane). But the Parker-Stacy relationship was an uneasy one—after her father was slain during a battle between Spider-Man and Doctor Octopus, Gwen came to hate Spider-Man, a fact that weighed heavily on Peter's mind. Not long after, Gwen was captured by the Green Goblin and hurled from the top of a bridge. When Spider-Man attempted to save her with his webbing, the sudden shock of deceleration snapped Gwen's neck, causing her death. **TB**

Hurled off of a bridge by the Green Goblin, Gwen Stacy perished without ever learning that her boyfriend Peter Parker was secretly Spider-Man.

Stacy, Gwen

FACTFILE

REAL NAME
Gwendolyn Stacy

OCCUPATION
Student

BASE
Empire State University, New York City

HEIGHT 5 ft 7 in
WEIGHT 130 lbs
EYES Blue
HAIR Blonde

FIRST APPEARANCE
Amazing Spider-Man #31 (December 1965)

POWERS

Gwen Stacy possessed an aptitude for science, but no special powers of any kind.

Stane, Obadiah

Stane, Obadiah

FACTFILE

REAL NAME
Obadiah Stane

OCCUPATION
President and chairman of the board of Stane International

BASE
Stane International headquarters, Long Island, New York

HEIGHT 6 ft 5 in
WEIGHT 230 lbs
EYES Blue
HAIR Bald

FIRST APPEARANCE
Iron Man #163 (October 1982)

POWERS

"Iron Monger" battlesuit amplified his strength to superhuman levels; boot jets enabled flight; projected repulsor rays (force beams) and laser blasts.

Orphaned when his father killed himself in a game of Russian roulette, Obadiah Stane regarded life as a game that he was determined to win. His preferred tactic was to wage psychological warfare against his opponent. Stane became the head of a multinational corporation that produced munitions. Knowing that Anthony Stark, head of Stark International, was a reformed alcoholic, Stane manipulated events to drive Stark back to drinking.

Stane took aim at his adversaries' weaknesses.

Buying up the debts of Stark International, Stane took control of the company, renaming it Stane International, and froze Stark's personal fortune. Stark duly became a drunken derelict.

Eventually Stark stopped drinking and resumed his secret identity as Iron Man. Stane had his scientists create his own armored battlesuit, called the Iron Monger. In the Iron Monger armor, Stane personally battled Iron Man, who defeated him. Removing his helmet, Stane committed suicide by firing a repulsor ray blast at his head. **PS**

Stane's Iron Monger armor was larger than Iron Man's, but he could not defeat him.

Starfox

FIRST APPEARANCE Iron Man vol. 1 #55 (February 1973)
REAL NAME Eros
OCCUPATION Adventurer **BASE** Mobile
HEIGHT 6 ft 1 in **WEIGHT** 190 lbs **EYES** Blue **HAIR** Red
SPECIAL POWERS/ABILITIES Flight; enhanced strength; telekinesis; ability to generate personal force fields; the power to stimulate the brain's pleasure centers.

Eros is an Eternal, raised on the Saturn moon of Titan by his father, Mentor. His buoyant outlook on life is the opposite of that of his older brother, death-worshipping Thanos. For years Eros wandered the Earth in search of sensual pleasure, but returned to Titan when Thanos and the Super-Skrull attacked it. After the death of Captain Mar-Vell, Eros looked after Mar-Vell's son, Genis-Vell (*see* Captain Marvel). Eros eventually joined the Avengers as Starfox. With the Avengers and solo, Starfox helped to foil Thanos's efforts to assemble the Infinity Gauntlet and took part in the Kree-Shi'ar war known as Operation Galactic Storm. Starfox also helped Genis-Vell defeat the alternate-reality being Thanatos and restore Genis-Vell's mind after a bout of insanity. **DW**

Starhawk

FIRST APPEARANCE Defenders #27 (September 1975)
REAL NAME Stakar Vaughn Ogord
OCCUPATION Adventurer **BASE** Arcturus IV
HEIGHT/WEIGHT/EYES/HAIR Unknown
SPECIAL POWERS/ABILITIES Starhawk can fly at light speed and can manipulate cosmic energy. He also has the power of precognition, knowing events that will occur before they happen.

Stakar Vaughn Ogord is the child of the superpowered beings Quasar and Kismet. He is half human and half artificial being.

Born on the planet Vesper, Stakar was kidnapped as an infant and taken to the planet Arcturus IV, where he was adopted by Ogord, a Reaver. Stakar eventually married Ogord's daughter Aleta.

When an accident merged Stakar and Aleta, they became a single being known as Starhawk. Starhawk fled Arcturus IV and joined the Guardians of the Galaxy, the 31st Century Avengers. Possessing precognition, Starhawk relives his life over and over, making changes and adjustments each time. **MT**

Star Stalker

FIRST APPEARANCE (Star Stalker I) Avengers #123 (May 1974), (Star Stalker II) Power Pack #56 (May 1990)
REAL NAME Unrevealed **OCCUPATION** Predator
BASE Planet Vormir in the Kree Galaxy (Greater Magellanic Cloud)
HEIGHT 16 ft 6 in **WEIGHT** Unrevealed **EYES** Black **HAIR** None **SPECIAL POWERS/ABILITIES** Superhuman strength. Could drain planetry energy and travel through outer space without protection.

The original, red Star Stalker was a member of the alien reptilian race of Vorns. He used his tail as a weapon and his mutant powers to form an ionic cocoon to drain energy from other planets. His enemies were the Priests of Pama, a cult of Kree who knew his vulnerability to intense heat. Following the massacre of Priests of Pama living on Earth, the Star Stalker journeyed there to absorb its energies. The Vision slew him with heat beams. The Star Stalker's son, who inherited his father's powers, but had green skin, later menaced Earth. He was apparently destroyed by the superhuman Nova (Frankie Raye). **PS**

Starjammers, The

The Starjammers' leader, Corsair, is quick-witted and skilled with a blade.

Christopher Summers, father of Scott Summers (Cyclops), was abducted by the alien Shi'ar and made a slave within their empire. After his wife died for Emperor D'ken's pleasure, Summers staged a jailbreak with his fellow prisoners Ch'od, Raza, and Hepzibah. The group became the Starjammers, space pirates who fought against the cruel excesses of Shi'ar rule.

The team helped the X-Men defeat D'ken in his bid to possess the M'Krann crystal, and later teamed with the X-Men to rescue D'ken's sister Lilandra from kidnappers. The Starjammers accepted Carol Danvers (*see* Warbird) as a member when she possessed the cosmic power of Binary, and both Lilandra and Professor X traveled with the team during the fight against the royal usurper Deathbird. The Starjammers found themselves caught up in the Kree/Shi'ar war of Operation Galactic Storm, and aided Kree refugees in the aftermath. Their pilot Keeyah joined at this time, assisting the Starjammers against the Uncreated. **DW**

FACTFILE

MEMBERS AND POWERS
CORSAIR (3) (Christopher Summers) Excellent pilot, swordsman, and combatant.
CH'OD (1) Natural strength, tough skin, slashing claws.
HEPZIBAH (2) Feline reflexes, night vision, retractable claws.
RAZA (4) Cyborg strength, vision and reflexes, skilled with bladed weapons.
SIKORSKY Advanced medical knowledge.
KEEYAH Skilled pilot.
BASE Mobile

FIRST APPEARANCE
Uncanny X-Men vol. 1 #104 (April 1977)

Stick

FIRST APPEARANCE Daredevil Vol. 1 #176 (November 1981)
REAL NAME Unrevealed
OCCUPATION Sensei **BASE** Mobile
HEIGHT 5 ft 9 in **WEIGHT** 135 lbs **EYES** Blue **HAIR** White
SPECIAL POWERS/ABILITIES Martial arts expert; "proximity sense" allows him to detect others despite his blindness; some telepathic abilities; an inspirational teacher.

Stick, who earned his name through his skill at wielding a combat staff, was the sensei of an elite warrior school despite being blind. When young Matt Murdock (*see* DAREDEVIL) lost his vision in a toxic waste accident, it was Stick who taught him how to develop his remaining senses to compensate. Stick also trained the assassin ELEKTRA; however he expelled her when she proved unable to control her rage in combat. When the evil ninjas of the HAND attacked Stick and his allies, Stick absorbed the life essences of his attackers into his body; unfortunately the strain of this act killed him. DW

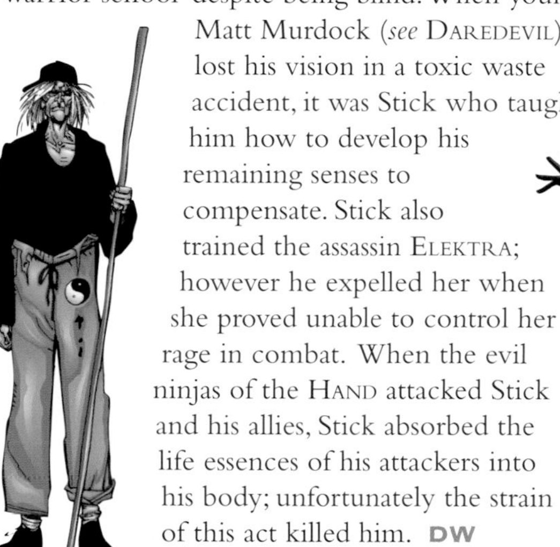

Stinger

FIRST APPEARANCE Spider-Girl #1 (October 1998)
REAL NAME Cassandra Lang **OCCUPATION** Adventurer
BASE New York City (Earth-982) **HEIGHT** 5 ft 5 in
WEIGHT 105 lbs **EYES** Blue **HAIR** Reddish-blonde
SPECIAL POWERS/ABILITIES Synthetic wing implants enable flight; armoured costume protects from harm; possesses ability to shrink to the size of a wasp.

Born in an alternate reality, Stinger is the super-powered pseudonym of Cassandra Lang, the daughter of the second ANT MAN, Scott Lang. Cassandra combined the powers and costume of her father with those of the WASP, and although she may not have been the most powerful of Super Heroes, she demonstrated a natural aptitude for organization and leadership. With a new generation of heroes emerging, Cassandra helped reform the AVENGERS and was in charge of the resurrected superteam when LOKI attempted to rid the world of Super Heroes. AD

Stone, Lt. Marcus

FIRST APPEARANCE Thor Vol. 1 #404 (June 1989)
REAL NAME Marcus Stone
OCCUPATION Police officer **BASE** New York City
HEIGHT 6 ft 2 in **WEIGHT** 225 lbs **EYES** Brown **HAIR** Bald
SPECIAL POWERS/ABILITIES A dedicated and tenacious police officer who never gives up on a case; an expert marksman and highly trained hand-to-hand combatant.

After serving as one of New York's Finest for 25 years, Marcus Stone was ready to retire. His marriage to his childhood sweetheart was in trouble because he kept bringing his police work home with him. Stone knew the time had come to choose between his job and his wife. On what should have been his last day, he stumbled upon a battle between the mighty THOR and Ulik the unconquerable rock troll. After Thor fell, Stone pursued Ulik and managed to arrest him. Having proved that normal cops can handle super-menaces, Stone was later assigned to head up Code: Blue, a special New York City strike-force that takes on Super Villains. TD

Stilt-Man

FIRST APPEARANCE Daredevil #8 (June 1965)
REAL NAME Wilbur Day **OCCUPATION** Criminal
BASE New York City **HEIGHT** 5 ft 10 in (variable)
WEIGHT 185 lbs **EYES** Brown **HAIR** Black
SPECIAL POWERS/ABILITIES Legs of armored costume can extend up to 60 feet in length; costume also contains a formidable array of built-in weaponry..

While working as the assistant to scientist Carl Kaxton, Wilbur Day made off with the inventor's revolutionary new hydraulic ram technology. Adapting the device in an armored costume, Day became the Stilt-Man, and embarked on a life of crime. However, his efforts were regularly foiled by DAREDEVIL. After many defeats, and having become a laughing stock among the criminal element, Day intended giving up his costumed identity, but found himself pulled back into the criminal underworld. Ironically, the only hero over whom the Stilt-Man has repeatedly triumphed is the Amazing SPIDER-MAN, whom he's bested on at least two occasions! TB

Stingray

FIRST APPEARANCE Tales to Astonish Vol. 1 #95 (Sept. 1967)
REAL NAME Walter Newell **OCCUPATION** Adventurer, oceanographer **BASE** Mobile within Atlantic Ocean
HEIGHT 6 ft 3 in **WEIGHT** 200 lbs **EYES** Hazel **HAIR** Brown
SPECIAL POWERS/ABILITIES Costume incorporates built-in rebreathing apparatus and provides enhanced strength, the ability to travel underwater at great speed, and to fire electrical bolts.

The US government gave a seemingly impossible task to oceanographer Walter Newell: bring in NAMOR the Sub-Mariner for questioning. Newell designed a revolutionary submersible suit and actually succeeded in his task, in the process becoming the adventurer Stingray. Subsequent adventures saw him fighting the Atlantean warlord ATTUMA, and becoming a reserve member of the AVENGERS. Newell is part-time Super Hero at best, preferring to concentrate on his scientific research. DW

Stone, Tiberius

FIRST APPEARANCE Iron Man Vol. 3 #37 (February 2001)
REAL NAME Tiberius "Ty" Stone **OCCUPATION** Owner of Viastone, a multinational corporation **BASE** Mobile
HEIGHT 6 ft **WEIGHT** 210 lbs **EYES** Blue **HAIR** Blond
SPECIAL POWERS/ABILITIES Brilliant business strategist; a totally ruthless sociopath, driven by jealousy and revenge.

Ty Stone and Tony Stark were childhood friends, though they often competed when it came to sports, girls, and grades. Their parents were business rivals and Stark's father eventually drove Stone's to the verge of bankruptcy. Still pretending to be Stark's friend, Stone vowed to get revenge. He planted news stories that tarnished Stark's reputation, stole Stark's girlfriend, Rumiko Fujikawa, and attempted to take over Stark Industries. To draw IRON MAN into action, Stone hired the RADIOACTIVE MAN as his bodyguard and faked his own kidnapping. He also tried to trap Stark within a world of virtual reality, but Stark escaped; Stone is now trapped in the prison he intended for his rival. TB

STORM

FACTFILE
REAL NAME
Ororo Munroe
OCCUPATION
Adventurer
BASE
Professor X's School for Gifted Youngsters, Salem Center, New York

HEIGHT 5 ft 11 in
WEIGHT 127 lbs
EYES Blue
HAIR White

FIRST APPEARANCE
Giant-Size X-Men #1 (1975)

POWERS
Mutant ability to manipulate the weather. Storm can control the creation of rain, snow, sleet, fog, hail, and lightning. She can create hurricane-force winds or lower the temperature around her to freezing point and below.

Storm

Ororo Munroe is descended from a long line of African witch-priestesses. Her mother married an American, and Ororo was born in New York City. When the child was six months old, the family moved to Egypt. Five years later, Ororo's parents were killed during an Arab-Israeli conflict. Five-year-old Ororo was buried under the rubble of her home beside her dead mother's body.

The child wandered the streets of Cairo and eventually became a thief and pickpocket. By the age of 12, her amazing mutant power to control the weather began to emerge. She traveled throughout Africa, where she used her abilities to help several tribes, who came to worship her as a goddess.

Professor Charles Xavier (*see* Professor X) came to Africa and convinced Ororo to use her powers to help all of humanity. She soon joined the X-Men under the codename Storm and quickly became one of Professor X's most trusted X-Men. Storm even leads the team when Cyclops is not available. **MT**

Storm leading her fellow X-Men, including Havok, Gambit, Wolverine, Iceman, and Rogue, into battle.

STRANGER, THE

FACTFILE
REAL NAME
Unrevealed
OCCUPATION
Surveyor of Worlds
BASE
The Stranger's own Labworld

HEIGHT Variable
WEIGHT Variable
EYES Black
HAIR White

FIRST APPEARANCE
Uncanny X-Men Vol. 1 #11 (May 1965)

POWERS
Vast strength; wields cosmic power to emit energy blasts, reshape matter, generate force fields, levitate, and change his own size.

Stranger, The

The Stranger is an immeasurably powerful cosmic being, created from the life-energies of a vanished species from the planet Gigantus in the Andromeda Galaxy. The Gigantians built the Stranger to stand against the Overmind, a villainous composite entity fashioned by the Gigantians' traditional enemies, the Eternians.

The Stranger wandered for eons until encountered Earth. Convinced that Earth's superhuman mutants posed a threat to the greater galaxy, the Stranger attempted to destroy the Earth on multiple occasions. The heroism of champions such as the Hulk, won him over, and the Stranger agreed to spare Earth for the immediate future. Later, the Stranger faced and defeated the Overmind, then selected an alternate-dimensional Earth from the New Universe as an object of study for his Labworld. The Stranger remains an unpredictable figure with mysterious motives, and possesses an unrevealed connection to the Living Tribunal. **DW**

Straw Man

FIRST APPEARANCE Dead of Night #11 (August 1975)
REAL NAME Skirra Corvus
OCCUPATION Mystic guardian **BASE** An unnamed magical realm
HEIGHT 5 ft 10 in **WEIGHT** 60 lbs **EYES** Red **HAIR** Yellow
SPECIAL POWERS/ABILITIES Incarnates himself in bodies composed of straw; projects fear; can command crows and local plant life, and has assorted other mystic attributes.

A being indigenous to an extra-dimensional realm bordering that of Earth, the Straw Man can access our universe through a mystic painting that depicts him. The painting's origins are shrouded in mystery; it is coveted by the Cult of Kalumai, who can summon their demonic master and his underlings through it. However the Straw Man considers himself a guardian of the Earth, and has successfully kept Kalumai in check. Recruited by the Dweller-In-Darkness as one of his Fear Lords, the Straw Man refused to go along with the demonic entity's plan to subjugate Earth, and he incarnated himself as Skirra Corvus, a television personality, in whose form he was able to warn DOCTOR STRANGE of the Dweller's plan. TB

Stryfe

Infected with a techno-organic virus that threatened to turn his entire body into organic metal, the infant Nathan Summers was taken nearly two millennia into an alternate future to save his life.

In case he should die, Mother Askani of the Askani Sisterhood arranged for the infant to be cloned. This clone, which was free from the techno-organic virus, was stolen away and raised by the tyrant APOCALYPSE, who gave him the name Stryfe.

The original Nathan grew up to become the hero CABLE, leader of the freedom fighters that battled armies commanded by Stryfe. Both men traveled back to the "mainstream" time period of the X-MEN, where they have continued to bitterly oppose each other. Although his original form was destroyed, Stryfe's consciousness can take over other bodies. PS

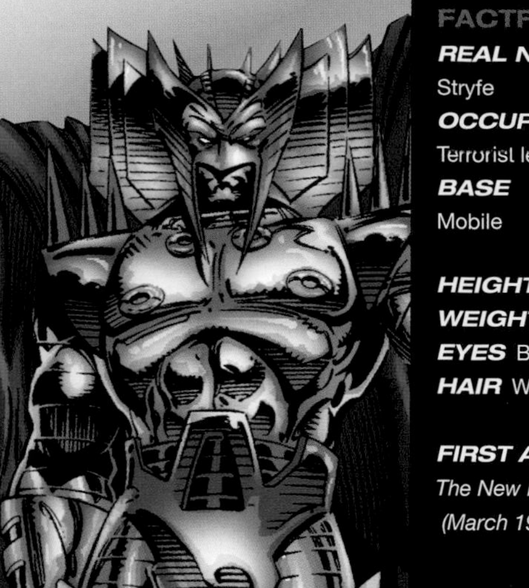

Ironically, since Stryfe is free from the techno-organic virus, he must wear metal armor for protection.

FACTFILE
REAL NAME
Stryfe
OCCUPATION
Terrorist leader
BASE
Mobile

HEIGHT 6 FT 8 IN
WEIGHT 350 lbs
EYES Blue
HAIR White

FIRST APPEARANCE
The New Mutants #87 (March 1990)

POWERS
A mutant possessing superhuman strength and other physical abilities, Stryfe also has vast telepathic and telekinetic powers. Unlike his clone Cable, he does not have to waste any of these powers keeping a techno-organic virus in check.

STRYFE

Strong Guy

FIRST APPEARANCE New Mutants #29 (July 1985)
REAL NAME Guido Carosella **OCCUPATION** Special Enforcer for X-Factor Investigations **BASE** New York City
HEIGHT 7 ft **WEIGHT** 750 lbs **EYES** Blue **HAIR** White
SPECIAL POWERS/ABILITIES Absorbs kinetic energy—failure to release it quickly causes physical distortions and damages heart; kinetic energy enhances strength.

A new recruit to Jamie Madrox's nascent X-FACTOR Investigations, until recently Guido Carosella was enslaved in a Tokyo-based mutant fighting club. Although Guido's mutation causes him constant physical pain, he rarely lets this show— indeed, in his spare time he sometimes moonlights as a stand-up comedian. An occasional bodyguard to rock musician Lila CHENEY, Guido has also served with X-Factor and it was there that Guido first struck up his friendship with Jamie Madrox. AD

Sugar Man

FIRST APPEARANCE Generation Next vol. 1 #2 (April 1995)
REAL NAME Unknown
OCCUPATION Adventurer, former assassin **BASE** Mobile
HEIGHT 6 ft 9 in **WEIGHT** 400 lbs **EYES** White
HAIR Black **SPECIAL POWERS/ABILITIES** Enhanced strength and reflexes; razor-sharp extendible tongue; four arms; advanced regenerative abilities; can control his size and mass.

Sugar Man comes from the alternate future known as the Age of Apocalypse, where he operated the Seattle Core slave camp. When COLOSSUS broke in to the camp to rescue his sister Illyana Rasputin, Sugar Man shrunk down and hid in Colossus's boot, eventually emerging in the mainstream timeline 20 years in the past. From his new vantage point, Sugar Man was able to build up the island nation of Genosha by supplying genetic technology to create a population of mutate slaves. Sugar Man survived the Genosha holocaust, but seemingly died months later at the hands of CALLISTO. DW

SUMMERS, RACHEL

Mutant child from another time

FACTFILE

REAL NAME
Rachel Anne Summers, now Rachel Grey

OCCUPATION
Adventurer

BASE
The Xavier Institute, Salem Center, New York

HEIGHT 5 ft 7 in
WEIGHT 125 lbs
EYES Green
HAIR Red

FIRST APPEARANCE
The Uncanny X-Men #141 (January 1981)

POWERS
Rachel Summers has considerable telepathic and telekinetic abilities. She formerly served as the host of the Phoenix Force, which greatly amplified her psionic powers.

In an alternate future Ahab brainwashed Rachel into serving as his telepathic mutant "hound."

Rachel Summers is the daughter of the Scott Summers (CYCLOPS) and Jean GREY (alias Phoenix) of an alternate timeline known as the "Days of Future Past." In this reality, the US government activated mutant-hunting robot Sentinels after Senator Robert KELLY was assassinated by mutant terrorists. Federal troops attacked PROFESSOR X's mansion, the X-Men's base, and captured Rachel.

PHOENIX

Rachel was brainwashed into becoming a mutant "hound," using her telepathic powers to track down other mutants. Her face was branded with tattoos (which nowadays she uses her powers to conceal). Eventually Rachel rebelled and attacked her master, AHAB. As punishment, she was confined to a mutant concentration camp. By now the Sentinels had taken control of North America. In an effort to change history, Rachel used her powers to send the astral self of her friend Kate PRYDE (a middle-aged version of Kitty) back in time. Kate's spirit journeyed to the "mainstream" reality of the X-Men, where she thwarted Kelly's assassination. After returning to their alternate future, Kate sent Rachel back through time to the "mainstream" reality, where she joined the X-Men. Rachel bonded with the Phoenix Force, enabling her to tap its energies, and adopted the name "Phoenix." Subsequently she became a founding member of Excalibur.

As Phoenix, Rachel could use the cosmic Phoenix Force, though not to the same extent as Jean Grey.

MOTHER ASKANI

Rachel was cast two thousand years hence into an alternate Earth which was ruled by the mutant tyrant Apocalypse. There she founded a group of rebels, the Askani. Decades later, as the elderly Mother Askani, she sent one of her followers back in time to retrieve the infant Nathan Summers. Mother Askani also transported the astral selves of Scott Summers and Jean Grey into new bodies in this alternate future, where they raised Nathan for ten years. Then Mother Askani sent Scott and Jean's astral selves back to their proper time and bodies, before she herself perished. Nathan grew up to become CABLE. After an alteration in the timestream, Rachel was a living teenager once more, though she lost her connection to the Phoenix Force. She was held captive in an alternate future by a being named Gaunt. Cable returned her to the X-Men's time, and she rejoined the team. In honor of her mother, Rachel now calls herself "Rachel Grey" and has adopted Jean's original code name, "Marvel Girl." **PS**

As mother Askani, Rachel created a clone of the infant Cable, called Stryfe.

In honor of Jean Grey, Summers has assumed her mother's identities of Phoenix and Marvel Girl.

ESSENTIAL STORYLINES

- ***New Mutants Vol. 1 #18, Excalibur Vol. 1 #52***
  In her timeline, Rachel witnesses the federal attack on Xavier's mansion and becomes Ahab's "hound."
- ***Uncanny X-Men #184-199***
  Rachel journeys to the "mainstream" timeline, joins the X-Men and becomes the New Phoenix.
- ***Adventures of Cyclops and Phoenix #1-4***
  As the elderly Mother Askani, Rachel brings Scott Summers and Jean Grey to a distant future to raise the young Cable.

Super-Adaptoid

FIRST APPEARANCE Tales Of Suspense #82 (October 1966)
REAL NAME None **OCCUPATION** Super-assassin
BASE Mobile **HEIGHT/WEIGHT/EYES/HAIR** Variable
SPECIAL POWERS/ABILITIES Android that can duplicate the appearance and powers, clothing and weaponry of anyone who passes within 10 ft of the scanning instruments in its eyes. It can mimic a maximum of eight beings at a single time.

Powered by a sliver of the Cosmic Cube, the Adaptoid was created by the subversive organization AIM (Advanced Idea Mechanics) to be the ultimate weapon against superhuman foes. Sent to destroy Captain America, the creature took on a composite appearance and copied the powers of Hawkeye, the Wasp, and Goliath among others. After absorbing the power of Kubik, the living manifestation of the Cosmic Cube, the Adaptoid was drained of all its powers, and destroyed in a battle with the Avengers. The Adaptoid was later reactivated and its current whereabouts are unknown. TD

Sunfire

FIRST APPEARANCE X-Men Vol. 1 #64 (January 1970)
REAL NAME Shiro Yoshida **OCCUPATION** Adventurer
BASE Department H, Canada, (formerly) Tokyo, Japan.
HEIGHT 5 ft 10 in **WEIGHT** 175 lbs **EYES** Brown **HAIR** Black
SPECIAL POWERS/ABILITIES Can project "solar fire" and create super-heated air currents to fly. Has a psionic protective force field. Trained in karate, Japanese Samurai swordsmanship and kendo.

Sunfire's mother was exposed to radiation when the US dropped an atomic bomb on Hiroshima. When his mutant power surfaced, Sunfire vowed vengeance on the US, destroying a monument at the United Nations and clashing with the X-Men. Professor Xavier invited Sunfire to join a new group of X-Men and he did, temporarily. Preferring to go on special missions for Japan, Sunfire was hypnotised by Dr. Demonicus to fight the West Coast Avengers. He was recently recruited by Department H (a branch of the Canadian Ministry of Defense) to their government-sponsored super hero team, Alpha Flight. TD

Sunspot

FIRST APPEARANCE Marvel Graphic Novel #4 (1982)
REAL NAME Roberto da Costa
OCCUPATION Leader of Hellfire Club **BASE** New York City
HEIGHT 5 ft **WEIGHT** 130 lbs **EYES** Brown **HAIR** Black
SPECIAL POWERS/ABILITIES Solar powers provide super-strength, thermal updrafts for flight, projection of heat and light, and concussive blasts of solar energy.

Sunspot grew up as a wealthy corporate heir in Rio de Janeiro, Brazil. As he aged, he manifested the mutant ability to absorb and convert solar energy. In his powered-up form, Sunspot appears as a being of black, crackling force. Sunspot has been associated with several organisations. He is one of the founding members of the New Mutants, and has also served with the Fallen Angels and X-Force. He recently accepted a position as Lord Imperial of the Hellfire Club, in an attempt to legitimize the organization. Reignfire, Sunspot's genetic copy, is a terrorist with the Mutant Liberation Front. DW

Super-Apes

Over time, the savage Super-Apes gained human level intelligence.

Reed Richards wanted to test a new rocket fuel in a ship designed to take the Fantastic Four to the moon. They hoped to get to the moon before the Soviets. But unknown to Reed, a Soviet scientist named Ivan Kragoff had built his own ship, which he hoped would get him to the moon first. Kragoff had trained three apes, a gorilla, a baboon, and a orangutan to help him operate the ship. Aware of the cosmic rays that gave the Fantastic Four their powers, Kragoff intentionally exposed himself and the apes to cosmic rays during their journey to the moon. Kragoff, now calling himself the Red Ghost, and the three apes all gained different super-powered abilities.

Once on the moon, the Super Apes battled the Fantastic Four, but quickly turned against Kragoff who starved them to keep them controlled. As their poweres continued to develop, each of the three Super Apes eventually gained human-level intelligence. The original Apes and Red Ghost have buried their differences and still accompany him on his exploits. MT

SUPER-APES
1 Igor the baboon
2 Miklho the gorilla
3 Peotor the orangutan
4 Red Ghost

FACTFILE
MEMBERS
IGOR
A gorilla
MIKLHO
A baboon
PEOTOR
An orangutan
BASE Mobile

FIRST APPEARANCE
Fantastic Four #13 (April 1963)

SUPER-APES

POWERS

Igor: possesses the ability to shapeshift.

Miklho: possesses super-strength.

Peotor: possesses the ability to control magnetism.

Super-Skrull

SUPER-SKRULL

FACTFILE

REAL NAME
Kl'rt

OCCUPATION
Warrior

BASE
Mobile, usually within the Skrull Empire

HEIGHT 6 ft
WEIGHT 625 lbs
EYES Green
HAIR None

FIRST APPEARANCE
Fantastic Four #18 (September 1963)

POWERS

The Super-Skrull is an extraterrestrial possessing the combined abilities of the Fantastic Four, and the physical malleability common to all Skrulls. He can project hypnotic energy from his eyes.

Super-Skrull can project a beam that briefly paralyzes and makes foes do his will.

After the FANTASTIC FOUR prevented the SKRULLS from conquering Earth, the Skrull Emperor vowed to develop a super-weapon that could destroy them. His scientists created the Super-Skrull, a warrior bionically re-engineered to possess all the powers of the Fantastic Four. The Super-Skrull's first battle ended in failure and he was imprisoned by the Fantastic Four. He eventually escaped, taking on the identity of the Invincible Man and kidnapping Franklin Storm, the father of the Invisible Girl (see INVISIBLE WOMAN) and HUMAN TORCH, but his success was short-lived and the Fantastic Four again defeated him. Temporarily exiled for his repeated failures, the Super-Skrull was drafted back into service during the Kree-Skrull War. He recently battled Genis, the son of the original CAPTAIN MARVEL, when he kidnapped an Earthling who had the ability to warp reality. He planned to use the young woman's talents to aid the Skrull Empire, but she foiled him by wishing her powers away. The Super-Skrull is now hiding on Earth in human guise. TB

Supreme Intelligence

SUPREME INTELLIGENCE

FACTFILE

REAL NAME
Supremor

OCCUPATION
Planetary leader

BASE
Kree-Lar

HEIGHT n/a
WEIGHT n/a
EYES Black with yellow pupils
HAIR Green stalks

FIRST APPEARANCE
Fantastic Four #65 (August 1967)

POWERS

The Supreme Intelligence possesses the combined intellect of the greatest minds in Kree history. In the past, the Supreme Intelligence has projected its consciousness into a powerful artificial body in order to actively engage in battle.

At one point, the Supreme Intelligence wished to add Rick Jones and Mar-Vell to its brain bank.

The Intelligence detonates a nega bomb, to wipe out most of the Kree and kickstart their evolution.

Decades ago, the KREE race learned that their ancient intergalactic enemies, the SKRULLS, had successfully created a cosmic cube. In an effort to maintain parity with them they created the Supreme Intelligence, an aggregate entity made up of the finest minds ever to exist within the Kree empire. Upon their deaths, those brains deemed worthy of being added to the great repository were absorbed into the Supreme Intelligence's make-up, adding their knowledge and experience to its own.

Shortly after its creation, the Supreme Intelligence seized control of the Kree empire, becoming at once its supreme dictator and an object of religious worship. In this capacity, Supremor has guided the destiny of the Kree, ever attempting to overcome the evolutionary dead end that this space-faring race of militaristic conquerors had seemingly reached. TB

Few of the Kree race escape the nega-bomb blast, but those that do will continue to evolve and perpetuate the Kree empire.

Swarm

FIRST APPEARANCE The Champions #14 (July 1977)
REAL NAME Fritz Von Meyer
OCCUPATION Scientist, conqueror **BASE** Mobile
HEIGHT 6 ft 5 in **WEIGHT** Unrevealed **EYES** None **HAIR** None
SPECIAL POWERS/ABILITIES Von Meyer's consciousness can mentally control a mutant queen bee, and through her, vast numbers of mutant bees.

After World War II Nazi scientist Fritz Von Meyer studied bees in South America. He was attacked by a colony of bees whose exposure to radiation had given them unusually high intelligence. Von Meyer's body was consumed, but his consciousness survived and took control of the bees, which swarmed in the configuration of a human body around his skeleton. Thus was created Swarm. Seeking world conquest, Swarm has battled the Champions of Los Angeles, the original Spider-Man, Ben Reilly as Spider-Man, and the Runaways. PS

Switzler, Beverly

FIRST APPEARANCE Howard the Duck #1 (January 1976)
REAL NAME Beverly Switzler
OCCUPATION Former art model and actress
BASE Cleveland, Ohio
HEIGHT/WEIGHT Unrevealed **EYES** Blue **HAIR** Red
SPECIAL POWERS/ABILITIES As an art model, she can stand perfectly still.

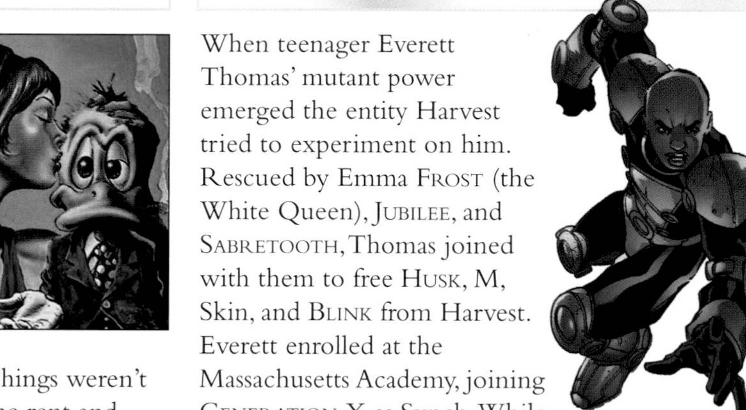

A former art model, Beverly Switzler's life was transformed by an encounter with that extradimensional waterfowl, Howard the Duck. After Howard rescued her from Financial Wizard, Pro-Rata, the pair began a life together in Cleveland, Ohio. Things weren't easy—they had difficulty paying the rent and, despite Howard's desire for the quiet life, they were constantly getting embroiled in the shenanigans of nefarious characters. Doctor Bong proved to be the most intransigent of these. Lusting after Beverly, he eventually forced her to marry him, but when he failed to consummate their relationship she returned to Howard and had the marriage annulled. AD

Synch

FIRST APPEARANCE X-MEN #36 (September 1994)
REAL NAME Everett Thomas
OCCUPATION Student **BASE** Massachusetts Academy
HEIGHT 5 ft 11 in **WEIGHT** 165 lbs **EYES** Brown
HAIR Black (shaved bald)
SPECIAL POWERS/ABILITIES Able to take on the superhuman powers of others while they remain in his immediate vicinity.

When teenager Everett Thomas' mutant power emerged the entity Harvest tried to experiment on him. Rescued by Emma Frost (the White Queen), Jubilee, and Sabretooth, Thomas joined with them to free Husk, M, Skin, and Blink from Harvest. Everett enrolled at the Massachusetts Academy, joining Generation X as Synch. While battling the villain Emplate, who fed off the bone marrow of mutants, Synch became a creature like Emplate himself. He was rescued from Emplate's influence by his teammates. Synch sacrificed his life to save the Generation X students by trying to disarm a bomb planted by Adrienne Frost, elder sister of Emma Frost, at the time Generation X's headmistress. MT

Swordsman

SWORDSMAN

FACTFILE
REAL NAME
Philip Javert
OCCUPATION
Adventurer
BASE
Mobile

HEIGHT 6 ft 4 in
WEIGHT 250 lbs
EYES Blue
HAIR Black

FIRST APPEARANCE
Avengers Vol. 1 #343 (January 1992)

POWERS
The Swordsman was a skilled swordfighter and combatant. An expert in all bladed weapons, he usually carried a set of throwing knives as well as his sword. He was also a superb athlete and excelled in unarmed combat.

The original Swordsman, Jacques DuQuesne, left his job in a circus to pursue a life of crime. He joined the Avengers as an agent of the evil Mandarin, but came to admire the team and refused to help destroy them. The Swordsman died saving Mantis from Kang the Conqueror.

Philip Javert was the second Swordsman. From an alternate universe, he was the dimensional counterpart of Jacques DuQuesne. Betrayed by the Avengers from his own timeline, Javert initially battled this world's Avengers but then joined them as the new Swordsman. Later, he and Magdalene left for another dimension.

A third Swordsman came from the Counter-Earth created by Franklin Richards in the Heroes Reborn incident. The fourth Swordsman (Andreas Von Strucker) served in the Thunderbolts. DW

Jacques DuQuesne dies in Mantis's arms.

The identity of the Swordsman has become a legacy, passing between characters but always retaining a swashbuckling skill with a blade.

MARVEL IN THE 2000s

In the new millennium, Marvel focused on story arcs that could be collected into trade paperbacks. *Maximum Security*, a new Captain Marvel series and *Ultimate Spider-Man* were published in 2000. *X-Treme X-Men*, *Exiles*, *Blink* and *Citizen V* all came out in 2001. "'Nuff Said", an event that crossed over every Marvel title, three *The Call of Duty* limited series, *The Infinity Abyss, Marville, The Order*, *The Ultimates* and *X-Statix* were all major launches in 2002. Story arcs like "Unthinkable" and "Authoritative Action" rocked the Fantastic Four and new titles like *Emma Frost*, *Marvel 1602*, *Runaways* and *Sentinel* debuted in 2003. "Ragnarok" and "Avengers Disassembled" brought both Thor and the Avengers to dramatic conclusions, and titles like *Astonishing X-Men* and *New X-Men*, took their place in 2004. *New Avengers*, *Young Avengers* and *Araña* became monthly series and *Drax the Destroyer*, *GLA*(Great Lakes Avengers), *Last Hero Standing* and *Machine Teen* all had limited runs in 2005. Generation M, Marvel Zombies, Nextwave, New Excalibur, Ares and multi-title crossovers like "I ♥ Marvel," "Annihilation" and "Civil War" all looked like big successes in 2006.

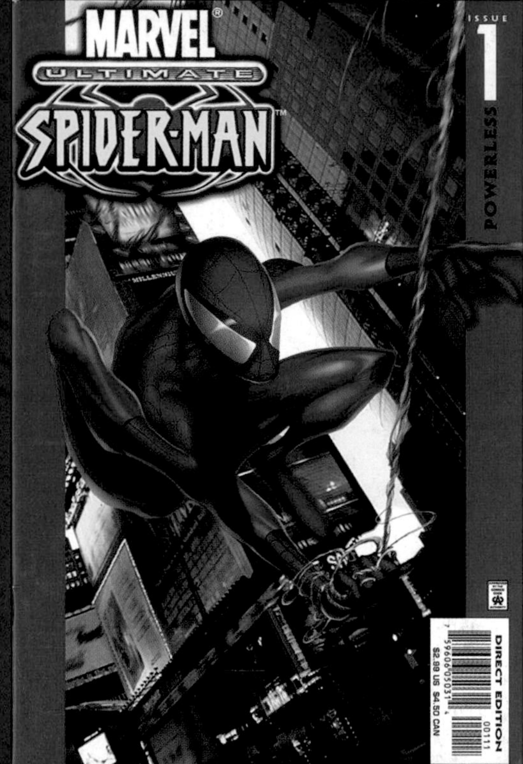

ULTIMATE SPIDER-MAN #1 (2000)

An alternate universe updates the origin and adds new twists to the origin of Spider-Man and a host of other familiar characters.

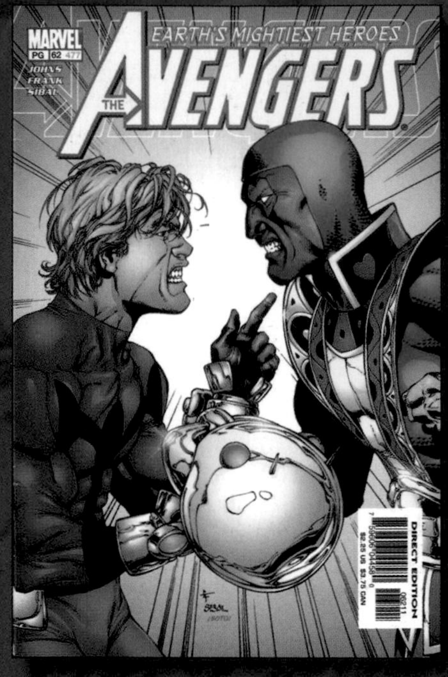

AVENGERS VOL. 3 #62 (2002)

As his personal biochemistry grows more unstable, Jack of Hearts lashes out at Scott Lang and accuses him of riding on the original Ant-Man's coattails.

FANTASTIC FOUR # 500 (2003)

Believing that it will take more than science to defeat his greatest enemies, Doctor Doom employs demonic sorcery against the world's greatest super team.

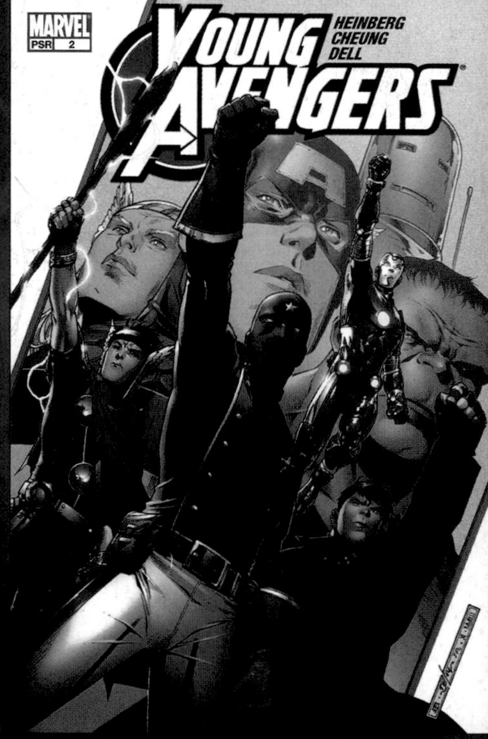

YOUNG AVENGERS #2 (2005)

Upon learning that he's destined to grow up to become the time-traveling despot called Kang, a teenager travels to the past and forms a new super-team to save him from fate.

NEW AVENGERS #1 (2005)

After disbanding months ago, a new team of Avengers spontaneously draws together when an army of super-villains stake a massive jail break in a multi-title crossover called "Breakout."

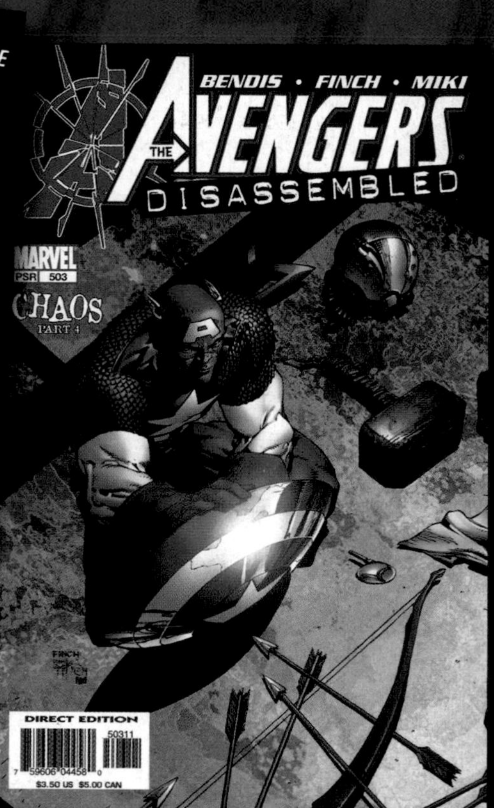

AVENGERS #503 (2004)

After Jack of Hearts, Ant-Man, Vision, and Hawkeye have fallen in battle, the surviving Avengers suddenly realize that there is a traitor in their midst and they all unite against the Scarlet Witch.

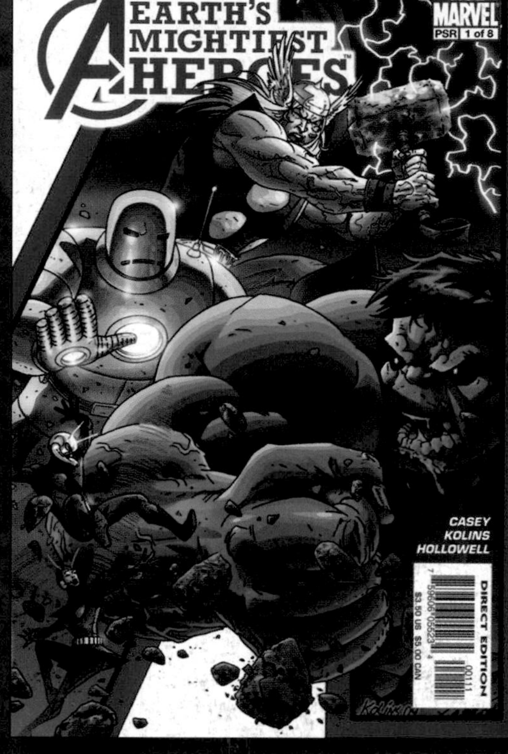

AVENGERS: EARTH'S MIGHTIEST HEROES #2 (2005)

A look into the early, pivotal period of the Marvel Universe, when five heroes, Iron Man, Thor, Giant-Man, the Wasp and the Hulk banded together to fight the foes no single hero could overcome!

HOUSE OF M #1(2005)

Having suffered a nervous breakdown which disassembled the Avengers, the Scarlet Witch uses her abilities to restructure reality so that Magneto now rules the Earth.

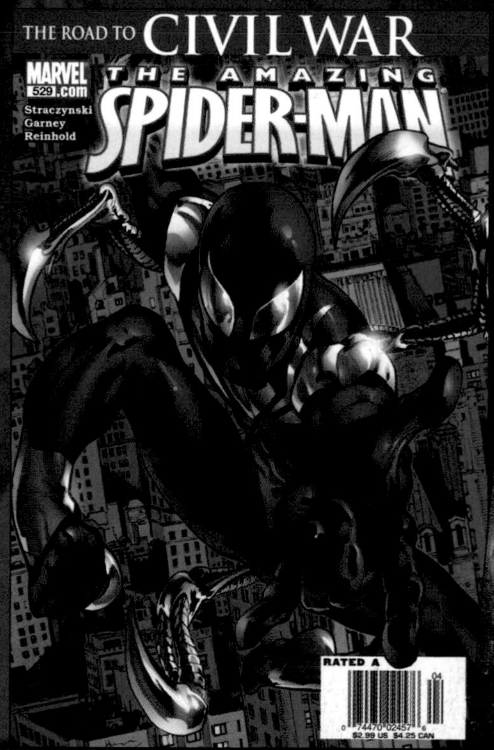

AMAZING SPIDER-MAN #529 (2006)

As the government decides to register all superheroes, Spider-Man begins working for Tony Stark.

ANNIHILATION PROLOGUE (2006)

When an unstoppable menace threatens the spaceways, Drax the Destroyer, Nova, Ronan the Accuser and the Super-Skrull unite against it.

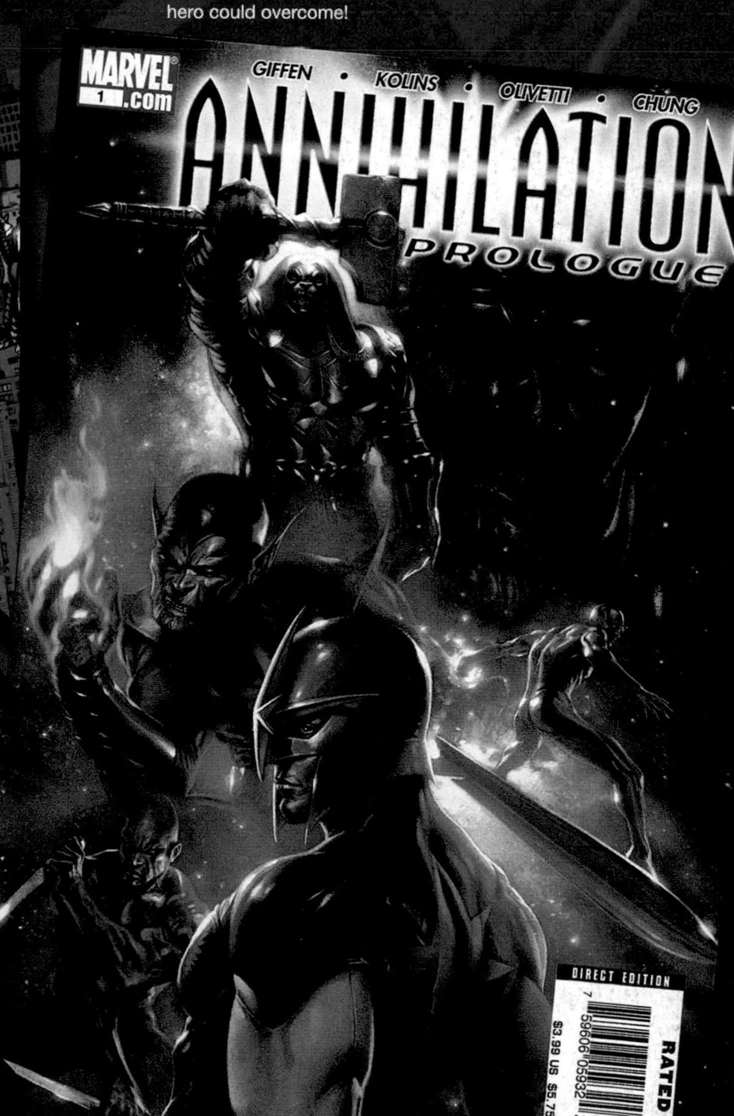

Taine, Sydney

FIRST APPEARANCE Nightside #1 (December 2001)
REAL NAME Sydney Taine
OCCUPATION Police detective **BASE** New York City
HEIGHT/WEIGHT/EYES Unrevealed **HAIR** Black and gray
SPECIAL POWERS/ABILITIES Skilled in a variety of martial arts, including capoeira; adept in various forms of weapons combat; no known superpowers.

Sydney Taine is the only detective in the NYPD trusted by the Others, individuals that appear human but who are driven by sinister thirsts and passions. While investigating the death of three crime bosses, Sydney, partnered by Ape Largo, uncovered a plot by the Others to obtain the Three Lost Treasures of Tao. Defeating them with cunning and fighting prowess, Sydney returned the stolen treasures to Suzuki Shosan, her former teacher. Sydney may be a member of the Players, a powerful alien race. **AD**

Talbot, Colonel Glenn

FIRST APPEARANCE Tales to Astonish #61 (November 1964)
REAL NAME Glenn Talbot
OCCUPATION Major, later Colonel in U.S. Air Force; head of security, Desert Base; later adjutant to General T. E. "Thunderbolt" Ross; later commanding officer, Gamma Base
BASE Desert Base, New Mexico; later Gamma Base, New Mexico
HEIGHT 6 ft 1 in **WEIGHT** 215 lbs **EYES** Blue **HAIR** Brown
SPECIAL POWERS/ABILITIES Normal human strength.

Glenn Talbot finally married Betty Ross, but she never stopped loving his adversary Bruce Banner, alias the Hulk.

General Thaddeus E. "Thunderbolt" Ross installed Major Glenn Talbot as security head of Desert Base, New Mexico, to investigate Dr. Bruce Banner. Talbot became Banner's rival for the love of Ross's daughter, Betty. He eventually learned that Banner was the monstrous Hulk. For years Talbot aided General Ross in attempts to capture or kill the Hulk. Betty married Talbot, but she later divorced him, realizing she still loved Banner. Promoted to colonel, Talbot was finally killed by an electrical overload while attacking the Hulk. **PS**

Talbot, Major Matt

FIRST APPEARANCE Incredible Hulk #436 (December 1995)
REAL NAME William M. "Matt" Talbot
OCCUPATION U.S. Air Force Major
BASE Mobile
HEIGHT 6 ft **WEIGHT** 210 lbs
EYES Blue **HAIR** Brown
SPECIAL POWERS/ABILITIES None.

Major William M. "Matt" Talbot is the nephew of Colonel Glenn Talbot. Matt Talbot is furious at his uncle's wife Betty for dumping his uncle in favor of the HULK.

Matt went to Betty's house and appeared to rescue her from a berserk soldier, but then he slapped her and called her names for hurting his uncle. Out of control, Talbot shot Betty in each leg. When the Hulk came to rescue Betty, he was hit by Talbot's plasma blasts, but it turned out that the gun Talbot used contained stun pellets that soon wore off. Talbot escaped having exacted some measure of revenge for his uncle's broken heart. **MT**

Talisman

FIRST APPEARANCE Alpha Flight #5 (December 1983)
REAL NAME Elizabeth Twoyoungmen
OCCUPATION Student **BASE** Canada
HEIGHT 5 ft 10 in **WEIGHT** 175 lbs **EYES** Blue **HAIR** Black
SPECIAL POWERS/ABILITIES Has natural mystical abilities and can control magical energy; when wearing the "circlet," she can command spirits and manipulate mystical energies.

The latest in a long line of North American shamans, Elizabeth Twoyoungmen was transformed into the long prophesied Talisman when she place a "circlet of enchantment" on her forehead. She later went on to join ALPHA FLIGHT.

For years, Elizabeth had been estranged from her father Michael Twoyoungmen, who was the SHAMAN. The circlet gradually corrupted Elizabeth and caused father and daughter to grow apart once more. Finally, Michael was forced to take the circlet as his own in order to defeat the mystical creature Pestilence. Elizabeth has since regained her sense of self, and her difficulties with her father have been resolved. **TB**

Tanaka, Kenjiro

FIRST APPEARANCE Quasar #5 (December 1989)
REAL NAME Kenjiro Tanaka
OCCUPATION Former SHIELD agent
BASE New York City
HEIGHT 5 ft 10 in **WEIGHT** 160 lbs **EYES** Black **HAIR** Black
SPECIAL POWERS/ABILITIES None; received combat training from SHIELD

Kenjiro "Ken" Tanaka attended SHIELD academy alongside Wendell Vaughn, who later became the cosmic hero QUASAR. After graduation, Tanaka took an undercover position within International Data Integration and Control (IDIC) and became its director of design. He eventually left IDIC to join his former classmate at Vaughn Security Systems. Tanaka discovered the link between Wendell Vaughn and Quasar but agreed to keep the secret safe. He now heads up Vaughn Security Systems while Quasar is away saving the galaxy. DW

Tana Nile

FIRST APPEARANCE Thor #129 (June 1966)
REAL NAME Tana Nile
OCCUPATION Colonizer of Rigel **BASE** Rigel-3
HEIGHT 5 ft 4 in **WEIGHT** 110 lbs **EYES** Blue **HAIR** Black
SPECIAL POWERS/ABILITIES Can increase her density at will, giving her superhuman strength and durability; using her mind thrust, she can control the actions of another being.

One of the Colonizers of the Rigellian Empire, Tana Nile first visited Earth for the purpose of annexing it for her people. Opposed by the mighty THOR, she was able to overwhelm the Thunder God. But eventually, Thor earned Earth's freedom—much to Tana's disappointment. Later, Tana took up residence on Earth for a time and accompanied Thor and his fellow gods on a number of adventures. She helped locate a suitable substitute world for the Rigellian seat of government after the destruction of Rigel-3. Most recently, Tana accompanied the group of young mutants and misfits called the Daydreamers on a series of psychedelic journeys. TB

Tarantula

A criminal used the name Tarantula during the days of the Old West, but the first modern Tarantula, Anton Miguel Rodriguez, was a brutal revolutionary from the small South American country of Delvadia. Government officials gave him a costume and a variant of the super-soldier formula that altered his physiology. They intended to make him a symbol of their country akin to CAPTAIN AMERICA.

Delvadian leaders made the Tarantula a national symbol during a time of uprising.

The Tarantula became a professional criminal and assassin. After various exploits, he traveled to New York, where he planned to rob passengers on a boat on the Hudson River and hold them ransom. SPIDER-MAN and the PUNISHER thwarted his plans. He later mutated into a humanoid spider due to treatments related to Roxxon Oil. Unable to bear his transformation into a giant spider, Tarantula killed himself in a police standoff. His daughter donned the Tarantula costume and teamed up with the daughter of Batroc the Leaper before dying at the hands of the TASKMASTER.

Rodriguez voluntarily served the Delvadian government, grateful for a chance to fight.

Captain Luis Alvarez of Delvadia became the second official Tarantula, promoted by the Delvadian government to replace Rodriguez. He turned out to be as brutal and ruthless as his predecessor. While on a mission to the United States to execute Delvadians who had fled the country, he came into conflict with SPIDER-MAN. Alvarez was exiled from his country and later died when the armed vigilante team the Jury executed him as part of an initiation rite. DW

FACTFILE
REAL NAME
Luis Alvarez
OCCUPATION
Government assassin
BASE
Delvadia, South America

HEIGHT 6 ft 1 in
WEIGHT 185 lbs
EYES Brown
HAIR Black

FIRST APPEARANCE
Web of Spider-Man vol. 1 #36 (March 1988)

POWERS
Enhanced reflexes and combat abilities; increased strength; retractable boot-spikes deliver drugs or poisons that kill or paralyze.

Enhanced reflexes and military training allow the Tarantula to make surgical stabs with his venomous boot-spikes.

Taskmaster

FIRST APPEARANCE Avengers #195 (May 1980)
REAL NAME Unknown
OCCUPATION Mercenary, teacher **BASE** Mobile
HEIGHT 6 ft 2 in **WEIGHT** 220 lbs **EYES /HAIR** Not known
SPECIAL POWERS/ABILITIES Can copy other people's movements, regardless of complexity, after watching them once.

The Taskmaster can mimic anyone's movements, be they a cowboy wielding a lasso, an American Football quarterback, or a Super Hero. The Taskmaster committed several grand larcenies before establishing a series of academies to train professional criminals. When the AVENGERS realized he was effectively operating a criminal production line, they began closing his academies down. He suffered a brief spell in prison, during which he trained a new CAPTAIN AMERICA—John Walker (*see* US AGENT). Since escaping incarceration, the Taskmaster has turned to mercenary work, realizing that it is more lucrative. **DW**

Tatterdemalion

FIRST APPEARANCE Werewolf By Night #9 (September 1973)
REAL NAME Arnold Pattonroth (alias Michael Wyatt)
OCCUPATION Tap-dancer, actor **BASE** Los Angeles
HEIGHT 5 ft 9 in **WEIGHT** 165 lbs **EYES** Blue **HAIR** Brown
SPECIAL POWERS/ABILITIES Enhanced strength, speed; gloves treated with a solvent that dissolves paper and fabric; Kevlar body armor; cloak contains chloroform capsules; indestructible scarf.

A dancer working under the name Michael Wyatt, Pattonroth was robbed of his life's savings by Las Vegas mobsters. He joined an army of derelicts on the streets of Los Angeles and declared war on the rich by destroying their money and possessions. Defeated by the WEREWOLF and SPIDER-MAN, Pattonroth moved back to Las Vegas and attacked the criminals who had stolen from him. He later returned to LA and was recruited into the Night Shift, a criminal organization run by the SHROUD. **TD**

Taurus

FIRST APPEARANCE The Avengers #72 (January 1970)
REAL NAME Cornelius Van Lunt
OCCUPATION Criminal mastermind **BASE** New York City
HEIGHT 6 ft 2 in **WEIGHT** 260 lbs **EYES** Brown **HAIR** Black
SPECIAL POWERS/ABILITIES Utilized Star-Blazer handgun, which fired blasts of stellar energy

Fascinated by astrology, multimillionaire businessman Cornelius Van Lunt secretly founded the criminal organization ZODIAC in order to achieve political and economic domination of the world. Each of Zodiac's 12 leaders was named after his or her astrological sign and was based in a different American city: Van Lunt became Taurus, based in New York. Both in his true identity and as Taurus, Van Lunt clashed with the AVENGERS. Van Lunt ended up battling MOON KNIGHT aboard a plane and died when it crashed. There have since been various other versions of the Zodiac organization, each with its own Taurus. **PS**

Techno

FIRST APPEARANCE Strange Tales #141 (February 1966)
REAL NAME Paul Norbert Ebersol
OCCUPATION Criminal inventor **BASE** Mobile
HEIGHT/WEIGHT Variable **EYES** Red **HAIR** None
SPECIAL POWERS/ABILITIES Prodigiously inventive scientist; robot body is able to transform its limbs into blast cannons or convert itself into a space station.

Paul Ebersol's grasp of technology borders on the miraculous. He began his criminal career executing technologically assisted crimes just for the intellectual challenge. Ebersol could transfer his consciousness to other vessels, and when his own body was badly hurt he installed himself in one of his own robots—Tech-Pac. Although still remembered for his attempt to conquer the Earth with BARON ZEMO, Ebersol has made some efforts to reform, joining the government-backed REDEEMERS and helping to save a dying CABLE. It is unclear what destiny has in store for him. **AD**

Teen Brigade

The Teen Brigade was a group of teenaged shortwave radio enthusiasts, founded by Rick JONES to keep tabs on the HULK. By relaying possible sightings to the other members of their volunteer network, the group could often pin down the Hulk's current location. It was the Teen Brigade's call for help that assembled the AVENGERS for the very first time, and the Teen Brigade later helped the newly-revived CAPTAIN AMERICA track down a suspect who had turned the Avengers to stone. The group acted as a precursor of sorts to Captain America's "Stars and Stripes" computer hotline network.

A second grouping of the Teen Brigade helped Rick Jones bring Bruce Banner and Betty Ross to the site of the original detonation site that turned Banner into the Hulk. The Corruptor derailed their mission, but he quickly met defeat and the Teen Brigade escaped without injury. **DW**

FACTFILE
MEMBERS
RICK JONES (founder), **CANDY**; **RIDER**, **SPECS**, **WHEELS**, plus other unnamed volunteers.
BASE
Mobile

FIRST APPEARANCE
Incredible Hulk Vol. 1 #6 (March 1963)

The Teen Brigade used short-wave radios and Internet-enabled computers to keep in touch with each other.

Temugin

FIRST APPEARANCE Iron Man #53 (June 2002)
REAL NAME Temugin
OCCUPATION Criminal leader **BASE** China
HEIGHT/WEIGHT Unrevealed **EYES** Brown **HAIR** None
SPECIAL POWERS/ABILITIES Supreme martial artist; harnesses the power of his Chi to perform feats of incredible strength, speed and agility; possesses the Mandarin's ten rings of power.

The illegitimate son of the criminal mastermind known to the world as the MANDARIN, Temugin was raised in a remote monastery, where he was trained virtually from birth in the secrets of unlocking the inner power of one's own Chi, or spiritual life-force. Although he had little contact with his father during his upbringing, when Temugin received a package containing the Mandarin's ten rings of power (each of which endowed the wearer with a different ability) along with his dead hands, he learned that the Mandarin had been killed in battle with Iron Man, and he felt honor-bound to avenge his death.

Reluctantly taking over the reins of the Mandarin's criminal empire, Temugin has clashed with Iron Man on a number of occasions, but has not yet discharged this honor-debt. TB

Terminus

FIRST APPEARANCE Fantastic Four Vol. 1 #269 (August 1984)
REAL NAME Terminus **OCCUPATION** Destroyer of worlds
BASE Mobile **HEIGHT** 150 ft **WEIGHT** unrevealed
EYES Inapplicable **HAIR** None
SPECIAL POWERS/ABILITIES Immeasurable strength, nearly indestructible; can regenerate body parts; carries a lance that fires atomic energy

Terminus is an intelligent creation made from living metal, grown by the alien Terminex in a failed attempt to protect them from the CELESTIALS. A continuum of Termini exist, from Stage 1 metallic microbes to the Stage 4 behemoths represented by Terminus. Taking revenge on planets that the Celestials had spared, Terminus claimed Earth for his own but met defeat at the hands of the FANTASTIC FOUR. The Deviant called Jorro wore the Terminus armor and destroyed the Savage Land. Terminus defeated a duplicate and emerged as the Stage 5 "Ulterminus," only to be vanquished by THOR. DW

Terrax

FIRST APPEARANCE Fantastic Four #211 (October 1979)
REAL NAME Tyros
OCCUPATION Interstellar traveller **BASE** Mobile
HEIGHT 6 ft 6 in **WEIGHT** 2,750 lbs **EYES** Gray **HAIR** None
SPECIAL POWERS/ABILITIES Body covered with supple, rocky shell; animates rock and commands it to do his bidding; lifted Manhattan into orbit around Earth.

GALACTUS the world-devourer was looking for a new herald who would have fewer qualms than the SILVER SURFER about finding worlds to satisfy his insatiable hunger. For a time, he thought that Tyros, a tyrannical ruler from the planet Birj, would be a suitable candidate. Galactus was wrong. Despite being provided with new improved powers, Tyros, rechristened Terrax, remained a restless, rebellious soul. It was not long before he had betrayed his overbearing master.

Terrax traveled to Earth, where he held the whole of Manhattan hostage. A happier creature nowadays, Terrax has been freed from Galactus and idles away his time travelling among the stars. AD

Terror

FIRST APPEARANCE Daredevil #305 (June 1992)
REAL NAME Unknown (possibly Shreck) **OCCUPATION** Criminal
BASE San Francisco **HEIGHT** 6 ft 2 in **WEIGHT** 170 lbs
EYES Variable **HAIR** None
SPECIAL POWERS/ABILITIES Able to replace parts of his body with those of humans or animals, gaining the powers of those body parts, as well as their "memories." If Terror takes a body part from a superhuman being he gains that being's power. Removes limbs or other parts by generating a special acid that allows him both to tear off a body part and to bond it to his own. Expert with firearms.

At some point in the distant past, the virtually indestructible being now known as Terror battled a green bear-shaped demon. The only way to defeat the demon was to sacrifice his own form, but in doing so he took on the form of the dead demon. He also gained the demon's power to bond the limbs of others to his body. His body is now made up of a collection of dead or decaying body parts. Now his associate Boneyard helps him collect body parts. He was also befriended by a half-human, half-demon being named Hellfire. Terror formed Terror Inc., an assassination bureau. MT

The spikes on Terror's face came from a demon. He can remove them and use them as weapons or regrow them.

Thanos

FIRST APPEARANCE Iron Man #55 (February 1973)
REAL NAME Thanos
OCCUPATION Conqueror **BASE** Sanctuary III
HEIGHT 6 ft 7 in **WEIGHT** 985 lbs **EYES** Red **HAIR** None
SPECIAL POWERS/ABILITIES Synthesizes ambient cosmic energy for use in a variety of ways, from increasing strength to firing energy blasts; also possesses a personal force-field and other devices.

Born on the Eternal colony on Titan, Saturn's moon, young Thanos was ostracized because of his hideous mutant nature. Morose and withdrawn, Thanos became obsessed with DEATH, not merely as a concept but as an actual entity. He gathered an army of intergalactic mercenaries and set out to conquer and destroy. Now infamous as the Mad Titan, Thanos's exploits include eradicating half of the lifeforms in the universe with the Infinity Gauntlet. But in every instance, Thanos' own weaknesses of character have enabled heroic opponents to thwart his schemes. **TB**

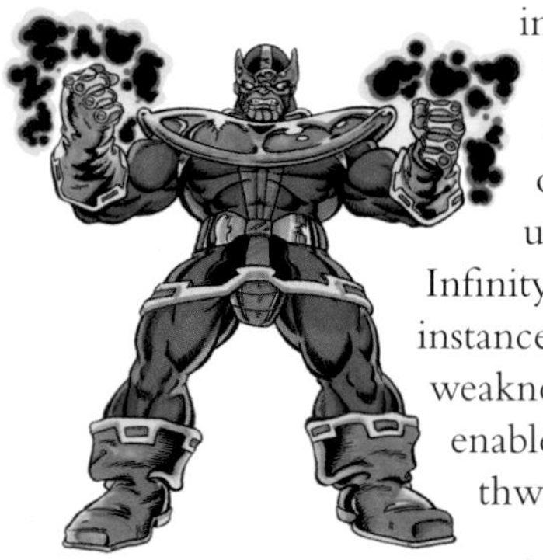

Thena

FIRST APPEARANCE The Eternals Vol. 1 #5 (November 1976)
REAL NAME Azura, changed by royal decree to Thena
OCCUPATION Warrior, scholar **BASE** Olympia, Greece
HEIGHT 5 ft 10 in **WEIGHT** 160 lbs **EYES** Blue **HAIR** Blonde
SPECIAL POWERS/ABILITIES Superhuman strength; mental control over body gives virtual immortality; sionic abilities include flight through levitation; projects cosmic energy from eyes or hands.

Thena is the daughter of Zuras, ruler of the superhuman race called the ETERNALS, and his wife Cybele. As part of a pact between the Eternals and the Olympian gods, Zuras renamed Azura "Thena" after the goddess Athena. Thousands of years ago, Thena met KRO, a member of another offshoot of humanity, the Deviants. Thena and Kro became attracted to each other, and they had twin children, known as Donald and Deborah Ritter. Upon the demise of Zuras, Thena succeeded him as Prime Eternal, but she subsequently lost this position to another Eternal, IKARIS. **PS**

THING, THE *SEE OPPOSITE PAGE*

3-D Man

FIRST APPEARANCE Marvel Premiere #35 (April 1977)
REAL NAME Charles "Chuck " Chandler
OCCUPATION Test pilot, adventurer **BASE** None
HEIGHT 6 ft 2 in **WEIGHT** 200 lbs **EYES** Blue **HAIR** Blond
SPECIAL POWERS/ABILITIES Strength, stamina, agility and speed three times that of a normal human; a brilliant pilot with the ability to sense the presence of alien Skrulls.

The year was 1958. Kidnapped by SKRULLS, Chuck Chandler escaped from their ship causing it to explode. He crash-landed in his XF-13 plane and, as he clambered from the wreckage, Skrull radiation imprinted his essence onto the glasses worn by his brother, Hal. By concentrating hard while wearing these spectacles, Hal could resurrect his brother as 3-D Man; however, side effects caused Hal to put his glasses to one side. Some years later Hal embarked on a successful quest to bring his brother back permanently. Chuck had not aged a single day and began his life anew. **AD**

Thompson, Eugene "Flash"

FACTFILE
REAL NAME
Eugene Thompson
OCCUPATION
Unemployed
BASE
New York City

HEIGHT 6 ft 2 in
WEIGHT 185 lbs
EYES Blue
HAIR Reddish-blond

FIRST APPEARANCE
Amazing Fantasy Vol. 1 #15 (August 1962)

POWERS
Formerly a gifted athlete, nicknamed "Flash" because of his speed. He was a star of Midtown High's football and baseball teams.

Eugene Thompson's athletic prowess made him a football hero at Midtown High School, helping him overcome the insecurities of having a father—Harry, an alcoholic cop—who regularly beat him. At Midtown, Flash dated Liz Allan (later Liz OSBORN), the most popular girl in the school. He looked down on bookish Peter Parker, and was also jealous of him, fearing that Liz was attracted to Peter. Ironically, Flash was a big fan of SPIDER-MAN. Flash went on to attend Empire State University with Parker and, in time, the two became friends.

Thompson later joined the military and served in South-East Asia. He later had an affair with Betty Brant LEEDS, the wife of *Daily Bugle* reporter Ned Leeds, which led to him being framed as the criminal HOBGOBLIN.

Depressed, Thompson sank into alcoholism. Norman Osborn (the GREEN GOBLIN) offered him a job at his company Oscorp, but only as part of his scheme to hurt anyone who was friends with Peter Parker. Osborn forced Thompson to drink whiskey and arranged for Thompson's car to crash into Midtown High, where Parker was working as a teacher.

This accident left Thompson in a coma, and Liz Osborn arranged for his full-time care. **DW**

A natural athlete in school, Flash found it difficult to achieve similar levels of popularity later in life.

Thing, The

Big-hearted tough guy of the Fantastic Four

The radiation shields on Reed Richards' spaceship failed and pilot, Ben Grimm was bombarded with cosmic rays.

Ben Grimm, alias The Thing is a, hot-headed member of the FANTASTIC FOUR, using his abilities to fight evil, almost as often as he does battle with himself. Ben grew up in New York City in poverty. Like his older brother, Daniel, he got involved with a street gang (*see* YANCY STREET GANG). After his parents died, Ben was taken in by his uncle Jake, a doctor, who helped set the boy on the right track. Ben ended up going to Empire State University on a football scholarship. His first-year roommate was brilliant science student Reed Richards, who became Ben's best friend.

FACTFILE

REAL NAME
Benjamin Jacob Grimm

OCCUPATION
Adventurer, former test pilot, wrestler

BASE
New York City

HEIGHT 6 ft
WEIGHT 500 lbs
EYES Blue
HAIR (human form) Brown; (the Thing) None

FIRST APPEARANCE
Fantastic Four #1 (November 1961)

POWERS
Superhuman strength, endurance, and durability. He can lift 85 tons, absorb the blast of an armor-piercing bazooka shell, withstand temperature extremes, and needs no suit to survive in space or in the ocean depths.

Alicia Masters is Ben's true love, she loves him for himself and cares nothing for his monstrous appearance.

A Grimm Tale

When Reed told Ben of his plan to one day build a starship, Ben jokingly said that he would pilot the ship.

After college, Ben joined the US Air Force and became an excellent pilot and astronaut. Reed's starship reached the test stage but the Federal government threatened to cut off funding, Reed decided to stage a test flight. Ben agreed to pilot the ship, though he worried that shields weren't strong enough.

Reed and Ben blasted into space along with Reed's fiancée, Susan Storm, and Sue's brother Johnny. In space, the foursome was bombarded with high levels of cosmic radiation.

The Thing battles a team of monsters led by Groot, who is able to manipulate trees and his own wood-like body.

ESSENTIAL STORYLINES
- ***Fantastic Four #1*** An accident in space changes pilot Ben Grimm into the orange-colored-rock-encrusted the Thing.
- ***Fantastic Four #8*** The Thing meets Alicia Masters and a long love affair begins.
- ***Fantastic Four #310*** Having quit the Fantastic Four, the Thing decides to join the West Coast Avengers, when he mutates into an even more grotesque creature, and sets off for Monster Island to find Mole Man.

Let the Clobberin' Begin!

The crew were altered on a genetic level and gained unusual powers. Ben's skin turned orange and rocky, and his strength grew tremendously, earning him the nickname the Thing. Reed convinced the others that they should use their powers to help humanity as the Fantastic Four. Ben would sometimes revert back to his human form unexpectedly, but neither he nor Reed could control this change.

Ben's life changed when he fell in love with blind sculptress Alicia MASTERS. Returning from exile after being transported to distant Battleworld by the BEYONDER, Ben discovered that in his absence, Johnny Storm and Alicia Masters had become lovers. Enraged, the Thing quit the Fantastic Four, but after a stint with the West Coast AVENGERS and self-imposed exile on the MOLE MAN's Monster Island, he returned to the FF. MT

THOR

The Asgardian God of Thunder

THOR

FACTFILE

REAL NAME
Thor Odinson (alias Donald Blake, Eric Masterson, Jake Olson)

OCCUPATION
God of Thunder

BASE
Asgard

HEIGHT 6 ft 6 in
WEIGHT 640 lbs
EYES Blue
HAIR Blond

FIRST APPEARANCE
Journey Into Mystery Vol. 1 #83 (August 1962)

POWERS

Enhanced strength, near-invulnerability, longevity, and vast magical abilities provided by the Odinforce. Wields the unbreakable hammer of Mjolnir which can open interdimensional portals, permit flight, channel storms, and fire energy blasts.

ALLIES/FOES

ALLIES The Avengers, Beta Ray Thor, Sif, Warriors Three

FOES Loki, Surtur, the Enchantress, the Absorbing Man

ISSUE #1

In *Journey into Mystery*, Thor leads a double life as the Thunder God and the mortal man Donald Blake. Later, Thor dropped the Blake identity.

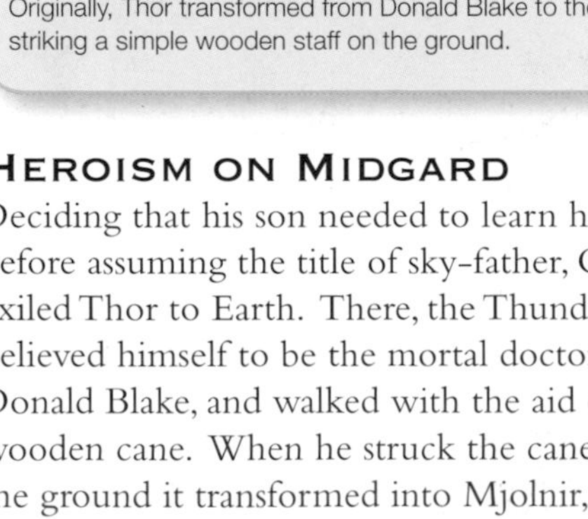

Thor could transport himself to Midgard via Asgard's rainbow bridge, or by using the powers of his hammer Mjolnir.

Thor was the God of Thunder, the beloved champion of Asgard and a figure of worship among the ancient Norse. He loved his people so much that he triggered their destruction in the end battle of Ragnarok, finally breaking a repeating cycle of futility. Thor was born to Odin, the ruler (sky-father) of Asgard, and Gaea, the mother goddess of Earth (a place known to the Asgardians as Midgard).

EARLY LIFE

Groomed from an early age to assume his father's throne, Thor grew up with his best friend Balder and his first love, Sif. But Thor's half-brother Loki hated him, and schemed to become ruler of Asgard himself. When Thor proved himself worthy of carrying the uru hammer Mjolnir, he took up the identity as the Thunder God.

Thor mingled with his Earthly worshippers throughout the 9th century, leading Vikings into battle. He later abandoned his followers after several of them butchered a Christian monastery. Over the succeeding centuries he spent most of his time in Asgard, venturing to Earth to battle Loki in the Old West and mistakenly becoming a pawn of the Nazis during World War II.

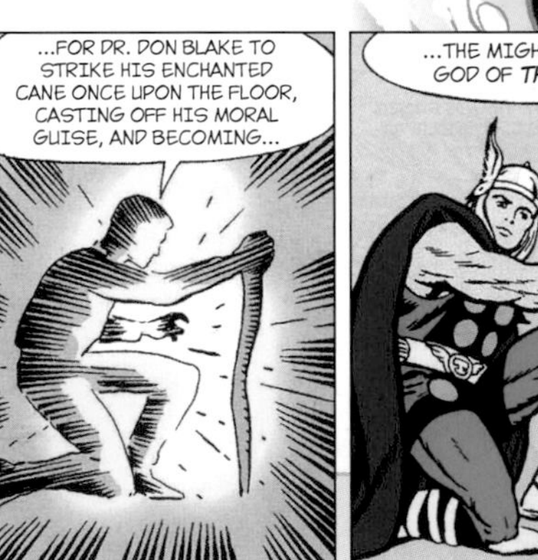

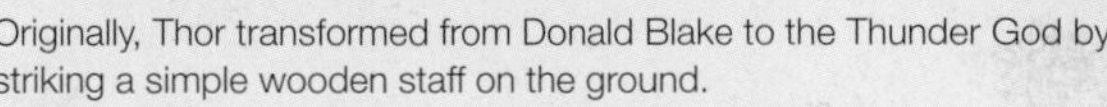

Originally, Thor transformed from Donald Blake to the Thunder God by striking a simple wooden staff on the ground.

HEROISM ON MIDGARD

Deciding that his son needed to learn humility before assuming the title of sky-father, Odin exiled Thor to Earth. There, the Thunder God believed himself to be the mortal doctor Donald Blake, and walked with the aid of a wooden cane. When he struck the cane on the ground it transformed into Mjolnir, and Thor regained his powers and all memories of

As one of the core members of the Avengers, Thor defeated the robot Ultron and crushed countless other threats to humanity.

STORMY TIMES

A second incarnation of the Thunder God appeared when Thor merged his spirit with Earth architect Eric Masterson. Thor entered temporary exile for apparently killing Loki, and Masterson carried on, posing as Thor while wielding the hammer of Mjolnir. Masterson later received the identity of Thunderstrike, before perishing in battle against the Egyptian god Seth and overcoming a curse laid upon Masterson by the weapon of Bloodaxe. Thor subsequently assumed the civilian identity of dead EMS worker Jake Olson, though he soon gave this up and let a resurrected Olson continue his life. Eric Masterson's son, Kevin, later took up the role of Thunderstrike in a possible future timeline also inhabited by Spider-Girl.

Thor and Thunderstrike unite their mystical hammers to unleash even greater power. Thor, who considered Eric Masterson one of the most noble mortals he had ever encountered, greatly mourned his death.

his life on Asgard. For years, he lived a dual identity as both Thor and Blake, battling super-powered threats such as the Radioactive Man and the Absorbing Man. Loki sought to entrap Thor by drawing him into conflict with the Hulk, but only succeeded in uniting a group of heroes that would become the Avengers. Thor became a founding member of the Avengers, and fought alongside such heroes as Captain America, Iron Man, and the Olympian half-god Hercules.

Few beings ever bested Thor in combat, but the alien Beta Ray Bill defeated the Thunder God and proved worthy of wielding the hammer of Mjolnir. An impressed Odin forged a new hammer, Stormbreaker, for Bill to wield. Thor finally gave up his Donald Blake alter ego at this time, briefly trying out a new identity as construction worker Sigurd Jarlson. New trials continued to vex Thor—his father Odin seemingly perished in combat against the fire demon Surtur, and Thor refused the throne, the honor instead passing to Balder. Thor suffered unimaginable torment when a curse rendered him incapable of death. Combat wounds nearly disintegrated his body until the enchantment was reversed.

RAGNAROK

The events that led to the end of Asgard began with the true death of Odin, slain in battle with Surtur. Thor took up the mantle of rulership and became empowered with the mystical Odinforce. Wishing to take a more direct role over earthly affairs, Thor moved Asgard to a location on Earth and transformed the planet into a dictatorship that endured for two hundred years. At last realizing the error of his actions, he unwound the previous two centuries through time travel. Loki enlisted Surtur to forge new weapons comparable in power to Mjolnir. With such tools at his disposal, he rallied his followers and conquered Asgard. Thor, realizing that Loki's actions presaged the final conflagration of Ragnarok, followed the Odinforce on a spiritual journey. The Thunder God uncovered the truth of the Ragnarok cycle—its endless loop of creation and rebirth had been orchestrated by the godlike Those Who Sit Above in Shadow for their amusement.

Ragnarok, the twilight of the gods, spelled an end to all of the five races of the dimension of Asgard.

Unwilling to endure his people's dishonor throughout yet another meaningless cycle, Thor severed the tapestry that wove the reality of Asgard's dimension, wiping himself and all of Asgard from existence.

Will Thor return? In the past, Ragnarok had been a self-perpetuating cycle, and the circumstances of Asgard's return could spring from the same processes that restored it in the past. But these thoughts are speculation. For now, Thor sleeps the sleep of the gods. **DW**

Beta Ray Bill proved he was able to fight alongside the Asgardians, and became Beta Ray Thor.

ESSENTIAL STORYLINES

- ***The Mighty Thor #337***
Beta Ray Bill explodes into action as a rival, and later an ally, of the Thunder God.
- ***Thor: Son of Asgard #1–12***
This limited series explores the early adventures of a young Balder the Brave, Sif, and Thor.
- ***The Mighty Thor #582–588***
It's Ragnarok, the Asgardian apocalypse, and the long-running series comes to an end with the total destruction of Asgard and all who live there.

Thunderball

FIRST APPEARANCE Defenders #17 (November 1974)
REAL NAME Dr. Eliot Franklin
OCCUPATION Physicist, engineer, criminal **BASE** New York City
HEIGHT 6 ft 6 in **WEIGHT** (normal) 225 lbs, (with superhuman powers) 350 lbs **EYES** Brown **HAIR** Black
SPECIAL POWERS/ABILITIES Possesses superhuman strength and durability; wields virtually indestructible wrecking ball.

A physicist turned criminal, Dr. Eliot Franklin was in prison when he met Dirk Garthwaite, alias the Wrecker, who had lost his superhuman powers. Garthwaite and Franklin broke out of prison along with two fellow convicts, Henry Camp and Brian Philip Calusky. All four men were holding onto the Wrecker's enchanted crowbar when it was struck by lightning. As a result, the Wrecker's superhuman powers were divided among the four, who became known as the Wrecking Crew. Franklin took the name Thunderball. Although he has operated alone, he most often appears as a member of the Wrecking Crew. PS

Thunderbird

FIRST APPEARANCE Giant-Size X-Men #1 (1975)
REAL NAME John Proudstar
OCCUPATION X-Man (deceased) **BASE** New York City/Mobile/New York State
HEIGHT 6ft 1in **WEIGHT** 225 lbs **EYES** Brown **HAIR** Black
SPECIAL POWERS/ABILITIES Super strength and stamina; can run at 35mph for long periods; leathery skin protects him from harm.

Eager to emulate his warrior ancestors, Native American John Proudstar joined the American Marines as an under-age cadet and served with distinction. John's mutant powers emerged relatively late when, at the age of 20, he wrestled a rampaging bison with his bare hands. He joined the X-Men after being sought out by Professor X, but died on only his second mission: jumping onto a criminal's escape plane, he was killed when the aircraft blew up. John's brother, James, eventually followed in his footsteps but it was a long time before he forgave Professor X. AD

Thunderbolts

The Thunderbolts came into conflict with Captain America.

The Thunderbolts were formed by Baron Zemo, from the members of his Masters of Evil team of Super Villains, when it appeared that both the Avengers and the Fantastic Four had died as a result of their battle with Onslaught. With the world hurting from the loss of these great heroes, Zemo plotted to give the Super Villains new identities and introduce them to the world as a team of Super Heroes called the Thunderbolts.

The Thunderbolts were so successful in their guise of Super Heroes that many in the group began to think of themselves as heroes rather than villains. They battled evil Super Villains such as the Wrecking Crew, the Circus of Crime, and a new version of the Masters of Evil. When the Avengers and the Fantastic Four returned, the true identities of the Thunderbolts were revealed by Zemo, to make them dependent on him, in an attempt to ensure their loyalty. MT

FACTFILE

NOTABLE MEMBERS

CITIZEN V (BARON ZEMO)
Team leader
TECHNO (THE FIXER)
Varies her molecular density
MACH-1 (BEETLE)
Wears a suit that enables him to fly, fire weapons, and resist attack
SONGBIRD (SCREAMING MIMI)
Can transform the sound of her voice into physical forms
ATLAS (GOLIATH)
Can increase his size and mass
METEORITE (MOONSTONE)
Superhuman strength and invulnerability
JOLT
Exceptional strength, speed, agility
CHARCOAL
Can change his body into charcoal, creating flames or diamonds
HAWKEYE Expert archer

BASE Mobile

FIRST APPEARANCE
The Incredible Hulk #449 (January 1997)

THUNDERBOLTS
1 Blizzard ***2*** Songbird ***3*** Joystick
4 Charcoal ***5*** Beetle ***6*** Atlas
7 Speed Demon ***8*** Radioactive Man

Thunderstrike

Divorced and with sole custody of his young son, Eric Masterson was an architect who was working at a building site where Thor, under a secret identity, was also employed. Thor was attacked by the Mongoose, and during the battle Eric was injured by falling girders. He was left with a permanent limp. After becoming friends with Thor, Eric was wounded again, this time mortally, and Odin merged him with the thunder god to save his life. Thereafter, Masterson would assume the form of Thor whenever the hero was needed on Earth. When Thor seemingly slew his brother Loki and was banished from this plane of reality, Eric took his place as Thor II. Eventually the real Thor returned, and Eric was given his own enchanted mace and became Thunderstrike. Thunderstrike eventually sacrificed himself to save Thor. In one possible future, Eric Masterson's son, Kevin, decides to attend art school in New York City. When he visits Avengers Mansion, he is given his father's enchanted mace and eventually merges with it. Taking on his father's name, Kevin joins the Avengers of his timeline. TD

The original Thunderstrike is one of many Avengers who died in the line of duty.

Like his father, Kevin Masterson can physically transform into Thunderstrike through intense concentration.

FACTFILE

REAL NAME
Eric Masterson (father), Kevin Masterson (son)

OCCUPATION
Architect (father), college student (son)

BASE
New York City

HEIGHT 6 ft 6 in (father), 6 ft (son)
WEIGHT 640 lbs (father), 585 lbs (son)
EYES Blue
HAIR Blond

FIRST APPEARANCE
Thor #391 (father)
Thor #392 (son)
Thor #432 (father as Thunderstrike)
What If #105 (son as Thunderstrike)

POWERS
(Father) Super-strong, owns enchanted uru mace that projects concussive blasts of mystical energy. Flies by throwing mace and gripping its strap. (Son) Super-strong; projects concussive blasts of mystical energy, which can be used to propel him through the air.

Thundra

FIRST APPEARANCE Fantastic Four Vol. 1 #129 (December 1972)
REAL NAME Thundra
OCCUPATION Warrior
BASE United Sisterhood Republic of North America
HEIGHT 7ft 2in **WEIGHT** 350 lbs **EYES** Green **HAIR** Red
SPECIAL POWERS/ABILITIES Enhanced strength, endurance, reflexes, and damage resistance; skilled at wielding a chain.

In an alternate future timeline, the 23rd century is led by a matriarchy where men are raised as servants or breeding stock. Thundra, born into the United Sisterhood Republic of North America, became one of its finest warriors. When men from a branching timeline invaded her own, Thundra journeyed to the modern era where she befriended the Thing. While in the modern era, she worked for a time as an operative of Roxxon Oil, where she led a team in infiltrating government energy research facility Project Pegasus. She later returned to rule the variant future timeline of Femizonia. Thundra is now the consort of her onetime enemy Arkon of Polemachus, and recently lost her right eye during an internal rebellion. DW

Tiger Shark

FIRST APPEARANCE Sub-Mariner #5 (September 1968)
REAL NAME Todd Arliss
OCCUPATION Amphibious criminal **BASE** The deep blue sea
HEIGHT 6 ft 1 in **WEIGHT** 450 lbs **EYES** Gray **HAIR** Brown
SPECIAL POWERS/ABILITIES Amphibious—able to withstand great water pressure and swim at up to 60mph; also possesses superhuman strength.

His genes spliced with those of Namor the Sub-Mariner and a tiger shark, Todd Arliss, former Olympic-level swimmer, became a superpowered amphibian. Namor was angered by his forced involvement in the process, and he and Tiger Shark became vengeful foes. When Tiger Shark's powers began to fade, he kidnapped Namor's father, Leonard MacKenzie, and blackmailed Namor into donating more powers. Chaos ensued during the transfer process and Tiger Shark ended up killing MacKenzie with a lead pipe. He remains at large, more deadly than ever—it seems his fate is bound up with Namor's. AD

Tigra

FIRST APPEARANCE The Cat #1 (November 1972)
REAL NAME Greer Grant Nelson
OCCUPATION Adventurer **BASE** New York City
HEIGHT 5ft 10in **WEIGHT** 180 lbs **EYES** Green
HAIR (human form) black, (cat form) orange fur with black stripes
SPECIAL POWERS/ABILITIES Enhanced strength, slashing claws, and heightened senses of smell, hearing, and vision.

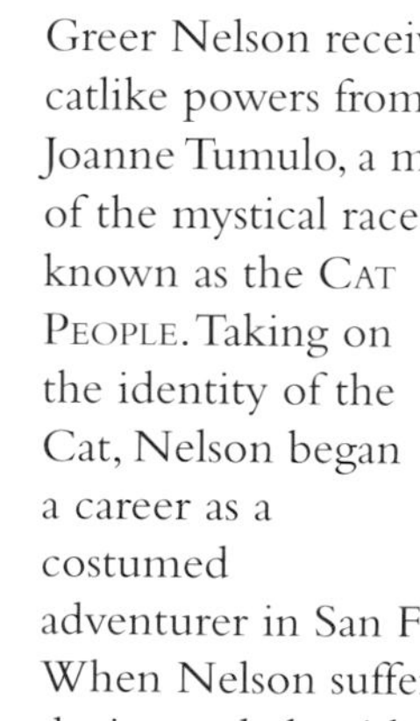
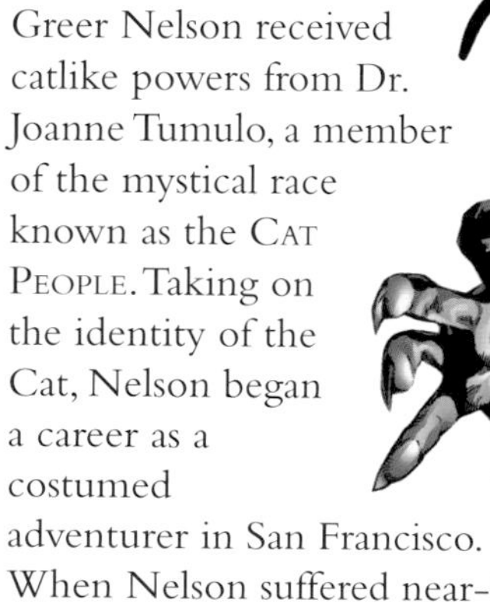

Greer Nelson received catlike powers from Dr. Joanne Tumulo, a member of the mystical race known as the Cat People. Taking on the identity of the Cat, Nelson began a career as a costumed adventurer in San Francisco. When Nelson suffered near-fatal injuries during a clash with HYDRA, the Cat People saved her life, imbuing her body with a cat-soul. She became her their legendary champion, Tigra, and proved her worth as a member of the West Coast Avengers while struggling to keep her feline instincts in check. In her identity as Greer Nelson, she has recently become a New York City police officer. DW

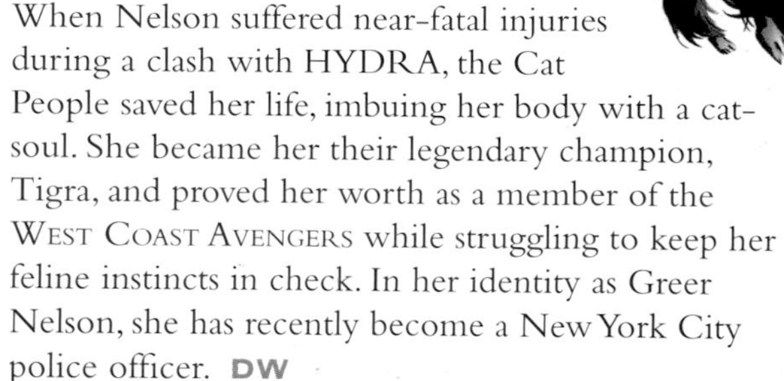

Time Keepers, The

FIRST APPEARANCE Thor Vol. 1 #282 (April 1979)
BASE Citadel at the End of Time
MEMBERS AND POWERS
Ast, Vort, Zanth All Time Keepers possess nearly unlimited powers of time-manipulation, including time travel and the ability to rapidly age or devolve people and things.

The Time Keepers are guardians of the timestream, created by He Who Remains (the final chairman of the Time Variance Authority) at the end of time to replace his flawed agents, the Time Twisters. The Time Keepers sought to preserve their existence at all costs, which led them to enlist Immortus to destroy the meddling Avengers and powerful "nexus beings" such as the Scarlet Witch. Kang, with help from Rick Jones, seemingly wiped out the Time Keepers after they attempted to eliminate a host of alternate realities. DW

Tinkerer, The

FIRST APPEARANCE Amazing Spider-Man Vol. 1 #2 (May 1963)
REAL NAME Phineas Mason
OCCUPATION Criminal inventor **BASE** New York City
HEIGHT 5 ft 8 in **WEIGHT** 175 lbs **EYES** Gray **HAIR** White
SPECIAL POWERS/ABILITIES Genius-level ability to create sophisticated gadgets and deadly weapons from everyday pieces of machinery or scrap metal.

Phineas Mason, the "Terrible Tinkerer," is unparalleled in his ability to create and repair machinery, and long ago became the premiere gadget-maker for the criminal underworld. Among the Tinkerer's works are Diamondback's throwing diamonds and the Scorpion's tail.

The Tinkerer's son, Rick Mason, became known as the Agent during his work for SHIELD, but died at the hands of criminals released from prison by Judge Hart. Furious with Hart, the Tinkerer shot and killed him, but later used his resources to restore Hart to life. DW

Titania

Davida DeVito, alias Titania, was the leader of the original Grapplers, a team of female professional wrestlers. Titania and her teammates were hired by the Roxxon Oil company to sabotage the government's Project: Pegasus. They were defeated and sent to prison. After her release, Titania's strength was enhanced to superhuman levels by the Power Broker. She continued to lead an expanded Grapplers team. However, Titania was assassinated by a new Grappler called Golddigger, who appears to have been working with the vigilante Scourge.

Mary "Skeeter" MacPherran lived in a Denver suburb that was transported by the Beyonder to his "Battleworld." There Doctor Doom gave her super-strength to serve in his army of criminals during the first "Secret War." This new Titania and her teammate, "Crusher" Creel, the Absorbing Man, grew attracted to one another. After returning to Earth, Titania sometimes operated on her own and had a personal feud with the She-Hulk. Titania also served as a member of the Masters of Evil and the Frightful Four. Titania and the Absorbing Man were married. Creel stayed with Titania when she contracted cancer. After her cure, Titania and Creel seemed to reform. They later separated. PS

Doctor Doom turned Skeeter MacPherran, the second Titania, into one of the strongest women on Earth.

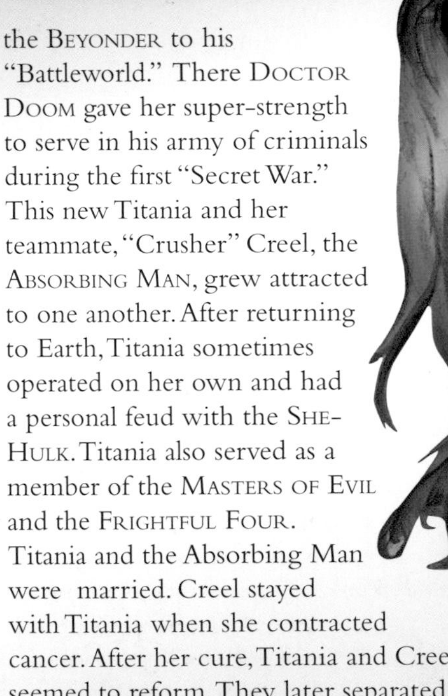

The Super Hero Titania hates most is She-Hulk. She-Hulk and the Avengers even invaded Titania's wedding to fight the villains who were wedding guests!

FACTFILE

REAL NAME
(I) Davida DeVito (II) Mary "Skeeter" MacPherran

OCCUPATION
(I) Professional wrestler, criminal (II) Criminal

BASE
(I) Mobile, later Los Angeles (II) Formerly a suburb of Denver, Colorado, later New York City

HEIGHT (I) 6 ft 1 in (II) 6 ft 6 in
WEIGHT (I) 194 lbs (II) 545 lbs
EYES (I) Blue (II) Blue
HAIR (I) Black (II) Red-blonde

FIRST APPEARANCE
(I) Marvel Two-in-One #54 (August 1979) (II) Marvel Super Heroes Secret Wars #3 (July 1984)

POWERS
(I) Possessed superhuman strength—able to lift about 2 tons; skilled wrestler and hand-to-hand combatant.
(II) Possesses superhuman strength—able to lift about 90 tons; superhuman stamina and durability. Resistant to heat, cold, injury, and disease.

Titanium Man

FIRST APPEARANCE Tales of Suspense Vol. 1 #69 (Sept. 1965)
REAL NAME Boris Bullski **OCCUPATION** Former Russian champion **BASE** Moibile **HEIGHT** (without armor) 7 ft 1 in
WEIGHT (without armor) 475 lbs **EYES** Blue **HAIR** Black
SPECIAL POWERS/ABILITIES Unusual strength proportionate to his giant size; armor provided flight, enhanced strength, near-invulnerability, and the ability to fire energy blasts from hands.

Russian inventor Boris Bullski devised the Titanium Man armor in order to crush Iron Man and win favor with his superiors. As Titanium Man, Bullski lost to Iron Man in a televised slugfest of East vs. West. A second Titanium Man, the mutant known as the Gremlin, died when his armor exploded. Boris Bullski later returned as an agent of AIM, but died in battle with Iron Man. A new Titanium Man recently appeared, failing in his bid to sabotage Tony Stark's mission to destroy a comet that was on course for Earth. **DW**

Topaz

FIRST APPEARANCE Werewolf By Night #13 (January 1974)
REAL NAME Unrevealed; possibly Topaz
OCCUPATION Sorceress **BASE** New York City
HEIGHT 5 ft 3 in **WEIGHT** 100 lbs **EYES** Brown **HAIR** Black
SPECIAL POWERS/ABILITIES A trained sorceress with a multitude of mystic spells at her command, primarily empathy-based in nature.

Branded a witch after she made a flower bloom in the desert as a child, Topaz was incarcerated in a prison camp, where she was adopted and trained in the mystic arts by Taboo. Topaz served as the familiar for Taboo's sorcery until, in pursuit of Jack Russell, the Werewolf By Night, Topaz turned against her mentor rather than allow Russell and his friends to come to harm. It has been prophesied that, one day Topaz will be capable of wiping away the evils of the world. Topaz recently joined forces with Jennifer Kale and Satana as the Witches to recover the stolen Tome of Zhered-Na. **TB**

Trainer, Dr. Seward

FIRST APPEARANCE Peter Parker: Spider-Man Vol. 1 #54 (January 1995) **REAL NAME** Seward Trainer
OCCUPATION Geneticist **BASE** New York City
HEIGHT 5 ft 10 in **WEIGHT** 200 lbs **EYES** Brown **HAIR** Brown
SPECIAL POWERS/ABILITIES A genius in the fields of biology and genetic engineering.

So brilliant that he was once employed by the High Evolutionary, geneticist Seward Trainer gave in to Green Goblin Norman Osborn's blackmailing and participated in a plot to crush Spider-Man Peter Parker's morale. By tampering with the Jackal's research, Trainer made it appear that Parker was a clone. Dr. Trainer became a father figure to the real clone, Ben Reilly (Scarlet Spider), but died at the hands of the villain Gaunt before he could confess his role in the scheme. His daughter Carolyn Trainer briefly took the identity of Doctor Octopus II. **DW**

Tombstone

FIRST APPEARANCE Web of Spider-Man #36 (March 1988)
REAL NAME Lonnie Thompson Lincoln
OCCUPATION Professional hitman **BASE** Mobile
HEIGHT 6 ft 7 in **WEIGHT** Unknown **EYES** Pink **HAIR** White
SPECIAL POWERS/ABILITIES Enhanced strength, speed, stamina, and reflexes; skilled hand-to-hand fighter and assassin.

Lonnie Lincoln was born an African-American albino. He grew up in Harlem, New York City with Joe "Robbie" Robertson, whom he coerced into keeping quiet regarding a murder that Lincoln had committed. Lincoln became an assassin for mob figures such as the Kingpin, and gained superhuman powers after exposure to an experimental gas. Following a stint with the Sinister Twelve, Tombstone served a prison term in the Cage and received a heart bypass operation. He escaped, and remains at large. **DW**

Torpedo

FIRST APPEARANCE Daredevil Vol. 1 #126 (October 1975)
REAL NAME Brock Jones
OCCUPATION Crimefighter **BASE** Clairton, West Virginia
HEIGHT 6ft **WEIGHT** 200 lbs **EYES** Blue **HAIR** Blond
SPECIAL POWERS/ABILITIES Battlesuit provides damage resistance; turbojets at wrists and ankles add power to punches; suit also generate shockwaves, and permits supersonic flight.

Inventor Michael Stivak became the first Torpedo when his uncle, Senator Eugene Stivak, convinced him to build a battlesuit. In truth, Senator Stivak had been prodded to do so by the extraterrestrial Dire Wraiths, who wanted to a weapon capable of defeating their enemy Rom the Spaceknight. After the younger Stivak's death, Brock Jones fought crime while wearing the costume and fended off Senator Stivak's efforts to retrieve it. He died in his adopted hometown of Clairton, West Virginia while battling the Dire Wraiths. **DW**

Trapster

FIRST APPEARANCE Strange Tales #104 (January 1963)
REAL NAME Peter Petruski
OCCUPATION Criminal **BASE** New York City
HEIGHT 5 ft 10 in **WEIGHT** 160 lbs **EYES** Brown **HAIR** Brown
SPECIAL POWERS/ABILITIES Carries assorted weapons at all times, most of them applications of his paste-formula.

Chemist Peter Petruski happened upon a formula for a super-strong, quick-hardening adhesive. He constructed a special handgun that could project it without clogging, and set out to make his name among the criminal fraternity as Paste-Pot Pete. However, not even a name-change to the Trapster and an alliance with the Wizard, the Sandman, and Medusa as the Frightful Four has brought him the respect he craves. Something of a laughing stock because of his first villainous alias and his choice of weapon, the Trapster nonetheless remains a persistent threat—no matter how often heroes like the Fantastic Four or Spider-Man defeat him, he always comes back for more. **TB**

Traveller, Judas

FIRST APPEARANCE Web of Spider-Man #117 (October 1994)
REAL NAME Dr. Judas Traveller
OCCUPATION Adventurer **BASE** Currently unknown
HEIGHT 6 ft 7 in **WEIGHT** 245 lbs **EYES** Blue (pupils turn red when he uses his powers) **HAIR** White
SPECIAL POWERS/ABILITIES Possesses limited psionic powers and the mutant ability to alter people's perceptions of reality.

Famous criminal psychologist Dr. Judas Traveller was lecturing in Europe when he became aware of the Brotherhood of SCRIERS, a secret criminal organization. The Scriers sent an assassin to inject Traveller with a fatal drug. Instead of killing him, the drug triggered Traveller's mutant abilities and he suffered a nervous breakdown. The Scriers supervised his recovery and assigned four agents—Mr. Nacth, Medea, Boone, Chakra and a Scrier—to watch over him 24 hours a day. After SPIDER-MAN freed him from the Scriers' control, Traveller went into hiding. **TD**

Triathlon

FIRST APPEARANCE Avengers Vol. 3 #8 (September 1998)
REAL NAME Delroy Garrett Jr.
OCCUPATION Adventurer **BASE** New York City
HEIGHT 6 ft 3 in **WEIGHT** 200 lbs **EYES** Brown **HAIR** Brown
SPECIAL POWERS/ABILITIES Possesses physical attributes of strength, speed and agility that are three times greater than the peak of human potential; can run fast enough to dodge bullets.

An Olympic sprinter brought low and disgraced by a steroid scandal, Delroy Garrett Jr. joined a philosophical movement known as the Triune Understanding, hoping to realize his latent potential. Jonathan Tremont, leader of the Triune Understanding, merged Garrett Jr. with the cosmic energy shard of the 3-D MAN and gave his new recruit virtually superhuman abilities. As the hero Triathlon, Garrett Jr. joined the AVENGERS. During a fight against the Triple-Evil, he temporarily gained cosmic powers when he absorbed three cosmic energy shards. **DW**

Triton

FIRST APPEARANCE Fantastic Four #45 (December 1965)
REAL NAME Unrevealed
OCCUPATION Scout **BASE** Washington, D.C.
HEIGHT 6 ft 1 in **WEIGHT** 210 lbs **EYES** Green **HAIR** None
SPECIAL POWERS/ABILITIES Can breathe underwater but cannot survive on land without special equipment. Has superhuman strength and other physical adaptations for undersea living.

Triton is a member of the royal family of the INHUMANS, a genetic offshoot of the human race. The son of the Inhuman priest and philosopher Mander and his biologist mother Azur, Triton was exposed to mutagenic Terrigen mist when a year old. The resulting mutations adapted him to live and breathe underwater. Along with other members of the royal family, Triton was banished when MAXIMUS first usurped the throne. While in exile, Triton first encountered and fought the FANTASTIC FOUR. Since then, however, Triton has become the ally of the Fantastic Four and Prince NAMOR. **PS**

Turbo

TURBO

FACTFILE
REAL NAME
Michiko "Mickey" Musashi
OCCUPATION
Adventurer, journalist
BASE
Mobile

HEIGHT 5 ft 7 in
WEIGHT 125 lbs
EYES Brown
HAIR Black

FIRST APPEARANCE
New Warriors #28 (October 1992)

POWERS
Turbo's suit is fitted with jet turbines. It allows Turbo to fly faster than a commercial jet, and the powerful turbines on her wrists allow her to deliver turbine-powered hyper-punches. The suit can also fire energy bursts, and its visor has telescopic sights.

Mickey Musashi never wanted to be a hero. In fact the journalism student thought that being a Super Hero was a ridiculous notion...until she came across the Turbo suit. This remarkable piece of equipment was created by a human scientist under the orders of the DIRE WRAITHS. When the suit's inventor learned that the suit was to be used for evil purposes, he gave it to a man named Brock Jones, who donned it to fight crime as the hero TORPEDO.

Eventually, the Wraiths found and killed Brock Jones, and the suit passed to Brock's cousin Mike Jeffries, who shared it with Musashi. As it turned out, the suit worked better for her than for Jeffries and she reluctantly became the hero known as Turbo.

While teamed with the NEW WARRIORS team, Turbo battled the Dire Wraiths, as well as the criminal team known as Heavy Mettle.

Retiring from battling evil as Turbo, Musashi pursued her journalism career. More significantly, Musashi set up a group named Excelsior with the express purpose of dissuading super-powered teenagers from choosing to risk their lives as heroes. **MT**

Turbo's wrist turbines pack a powerful punch, delivering as much force as a jet engine.

Turner D. Century

FIRST APPEARANCE Spider-Woman #33 (December 1980)
REAL NAME Clifford F. Michaels
OCCUPATION Former vigilante and reformer
BASE New York City, Mobile, New York State
HEIGHT 6 ft 1 in **WEIGHT** 185 lbs **EYES** Blue **HAIR** Black
SPECIAL POWERS/ABILITIES Extensive engineering expertise; carries umbrella that doubles as flame-thrower; rides flying bike.

Adopted as a child by multi-millionaire Morgan MacNeil Hardy, Clifford Michaels had a sheltered upbringing where he learnt all about America's declining morals. As an adult Clifford ventured into San Francisco and railed against lax morality as Turner D. Century. Clifford's impact was negligible and he became increasingly militant, burning buildings and killing iniquitous individuals. During a clash with Spider-Woman his surrogate father died in a fire. Before Clifford could make recompense he was killed by the Scourge. **TB**

Typhoid Mary

FIRST APPEARANCE Daredevil Vol. 1 #254 (May 1988)
REAL NAME Mary (last name possibly Mezinis or Walker)
OCCUPATION Criminal **BASE** New York City
HEIGHT 5 ft 10 in **WEIGHT** 140 lbs **EYES** Brown **HAIR** Brown
SPECIAL POWERS/ABILITIES Telekinesis, pyrokinesis, and also limited hypnotic ability; a skilled hand-to-hand combatant and expert with various bladed weapons.

Childhood abuse caused Mary to develop a disassociative identity disorder, giving her three distinct personalities: timid Mary, lustful Typhoid, and vicious Bloody Mary. Through therapy, a fourth personality has sometimes emerged that is a stable combination of all three. Typhoid Mary worked as an assassin for the Kingpin, and played a cruel game with Daredevil by charming him as Mary and tormenting him as Typhoid. Many times she has attempted to leave her criminal past behind her, but her Typhoid identity always reasserts itself. She recently escaped from the Raft prison. **DW**

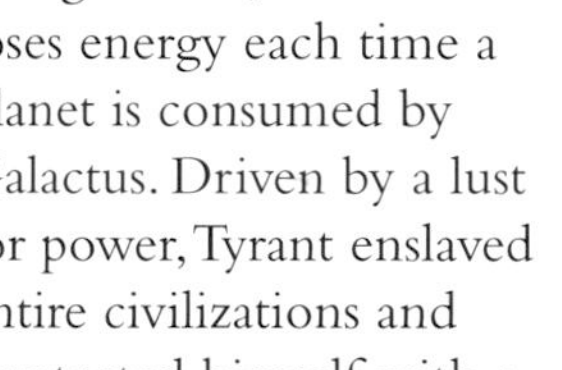

Tyrant

FIRST APPEARANCE Silver Surfer Vol. 3 #81 (June 1993)
REAL NAME Unrevealed
OCCUPATION Conqueror of Worlds
BASE Star-Traveling Fortress
HEIGHT 29 ft **WEIGHT** 20 tons **EYES** Red **HAIR** None
SPECIAL POWERS/ABILITIES Virtually unlimited cosmic power on a par with Galactus.

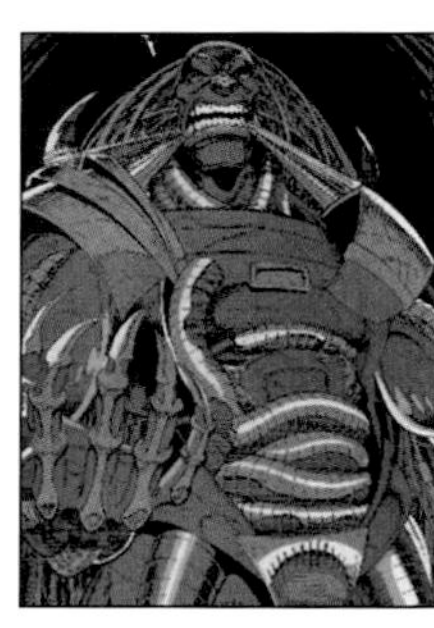

Created by Galactus billions of years ago, Tyrant draws his power from living worlds, and thus loses energy each time a planet is consumed by Galactus. Driven by a lust for power, Tyrant enslaved entire civilizations and protected himself with a robot army. Among the few who successfully opposed him were the women warriors of the Spinsterhood. In the modern era, Tyrant nearly succeeded in killing Galactus until Galactus' herald Morg unleashed the unstoppable energies of the Ultimate Nullifier. Tyrant and Galactus both vanished, though Galactus has since returned. **DW**

Tyrannus gulps a goblet of the Fountain of Youth.

Tyrannus

Romulus Augustulus, better known as Tyrannus, served as the last emperor of the Roman Empire, until his defeat by the forces of King Arthur Pendragon in the 6th century. Merlin the Magician banished Tyrannus by teleporting him to the underground world of Subterranea. There the would-be despot discovered the Fountain of Youth and ruled the Subterraneans, who took the name Tyrannoids.

In the modern era, Tyrannus launched a war against the Mole Man for control of Subterranea, and became a frequent foe of the Hulk. He incurred the green giant's wrath by accidentally kidnapping his girlfriend, Betty Ross (see Banner, Betty).

Tyrannus journeyed to the fabled city of El Dorado and used the city's Sacred Flame of Life in a bid to take over the world. Reduced to a disembodied spirit after a failed attempt to merge with the Flame of Life, Tyrannus briefly inhabited the Abomination before winning back his original body. Tyrannus allied with the Avengers to defeat the Deviant army that had invaded Subterranea, but the Tyrannoids later turned on their master. His current fate is unknown. **DW**

TYRANNUS

FACTFILE
REAL NAME
Romulus Augustulus
OCCUPATION
Would-be conqueror
BASE
Subterranea

HEIGHT 6 ft 2 in
WEIGHT 225 lbs
EYES Light brown
HAIR Blond

FIRST APPEARANCE
Incredible Hulk Vol. 1 #5 (January 1963)

POWERS
Psychic powers including mind-control, telepathy, and the ability to drain life energy. The Fountain of Youth provides Tyrannus with immortality, giving him plenty of time for devising ways to conquer the surface world.

Tyrannus's planned invasion of the surface world was smashed by Hulk.

UATU THE WATCHER

Self-appointed observers of the universe, the WATCHERS vowed never to interfere in the affairs of others. As the Watcher responsible for Earth and its solar system, Uatu has broken this rule several times since encountering the FANTASTIC FOUR. His most significant intervention in human affairs came just before Earth's first visit from GALACTUS and the SILVER SURFER, when he warned the Fantastic Four of the impending alien threat. Cautioned for his repeated interference, Uatu was stripped of his role as Watcher but he has since been reinstated. **AD**

FACTFILE
REAL NAME
Uatu
OCCUPATION
Observer
BASE
Mobile; New York State

HEIGHT Variable
WEIGHT Variable
EYES No visible irises
HAIR None

FIRST APPEARANCE
Fantastic Four #13 (April 1963)

UATU THE WATCHER

POWERS
Virtually immortal; has superhuman intelligence, is telepathic and can teleport from Earth to the Moon.

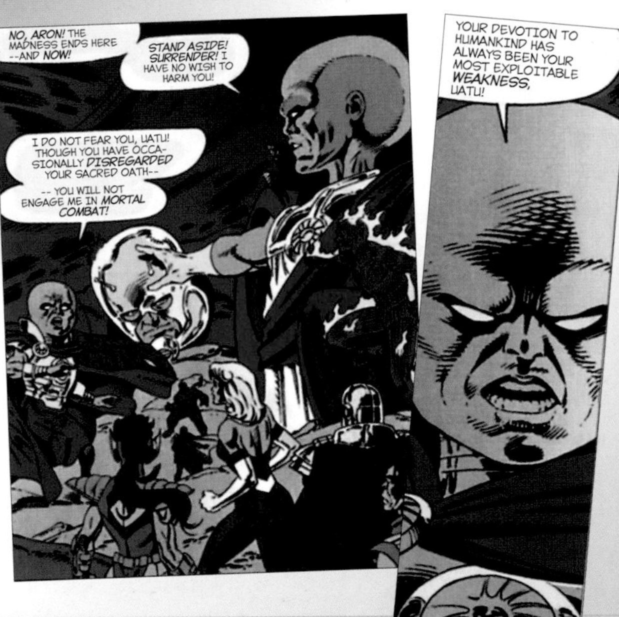

Uatu stepped in to prevent Aron, the Rogue Watcher from destroying the Fantastic Four heroes and turning the Milky Way into his own personal fiefdom.

U-FOES

U-FOES

FACTFILE
KEY MEMBERS
IRONCLAD
Enhanced strength, iron-hard skin, can increase his mass
VAPOR
Transforms into various gases
VECTOR
Can repel objects away from him at great speed
X-RAY
Flight, can project hard radiation, impervious to physical damage while in energy form
BASE
Brooklyn, New York; Stark Tower New York

FIRST APPEARANCE
Incredible Hulk Vol. 2 #254 (December 1980)

Hoping to duplicate the process by which the FANTASTIC FOUR had gained their powers, millionaire Simon Utrecht enlisted rocket pilot Mike Steel, engineer Jimmy Darnell, and technical specialist Ann Darnell to accompany him into space. The experiment worked, and the cosmic radiation they were exposed to gave each a unique power: Steel became a metal-coated being, Jimmy gained control over radiation, his sister Ann converted into a gaseous state, and Utrecht himself discovered that he could repel objects. As IRONCLAD, VAPOR, X-Ray, and Vector, the four new superhumans formed a group they called the U-Foes. They first unleashed their powers on Bruce Banner, whom they blamed for grounding their test flight prematurely, but were unable to control their new powers and lost badly once Banner transformed into the HULK. Over time, the U-Foes became more disciplined and, after honing their powers, found work as professional mercenaries. Their employers have included the LEADER and the Master of the World. **DW**

Using their abilities to find employment as mercenaries, the U-Foes have clashed with Spider-Man and others in their quest for money and power.

CHARACTER KEY
1 Vector
2 Ironclad
3 X-Ray
4 Vapor

Ultron

Robot with an evil mind of its own

Henry Pym built Ultron as a robotic servant and programmed his creation with his own brain patterns. But Ultron immediately rebelled against his maker, escaping to plot the extermination of all humanity. Engineering a succession of upgraded bodies for himself, he finally emerged as Ultron-5 to fight Pym's teammates in the Avengers.

FACTFILE
REAL NAME
Ultron
OCCUPATION
Would-be world conqueror
BASE
Mobile
HEIGHT 6 ft
WEIGHT 535 lbs
EYES Glowing red
HAIR None

FIRST APPEARANCE
Avengers Vol. 1 #54 (July 1968)

POWERS
Enhanced strength, near-invulnerability, energy projection; and flight; uses encephalo-ray to hypnotize others or put them into a coma.

Ultron assembled a team of Masters of Evil to combat the Avengers.

Bodyhopping

By posing as the villainous Crimson Cowl, Ultron assembled a second grouping of the Masters of Evil. He then created the android Vision, using a duplicate body from the original Human Torch and brainwave patterns from Wonder Man. Ironically, just like Ultron himself, the Vision rebelled against his creator and defected to the Avengers, setting the pattern for most of Ultron's subsequent creations.

Ultron incorporated indestructible adamantium into his frame beginning with the Ultron-6 body. Ultron-7 was a gargantuan construct, while Ultron-8 was responsible for creating his robotic "wife," Jocasta.

Ultron-9 perished in a vat of molten adamantium, and Machine Man deactivated Ultron-10. Ultron-11 participated in the Beyonder's Secret Wars. Ultron-12, initially a member of the Lethal Legion, repented and tried to atone for his criminal past until destroyed by Ultron-11. During the Acts of Vengeance conspiracy, Doctor Doom programmed Ultron-13 with all previous personalities running simultaneously, making it easy for Daredevil to beat the addled robot. Ultron-14 created a new mate called Alkhema, though the two robots could not agree on their differing approaches to genocide.

The Vision and Ultron had a shared history, but still found themselves to be bitter enemies.

Multiplying Machines

Ultron-15 built hundreds of duplicates and conquered the eastern European country of Slorenia, meeting defeat when Henry Pym exposed him to metal-disintegrating vibranium. Hidden "Ultron Imperative" programming within Alkhema led to Ultron's return, and, after a battle, Ultron affixed his decapitated head to a suit of Iron Man's armor. Several Ultron robots appeared during the Avengers Disassembled event, though these may have been projections by the Scarlet Witch. One of Ultron's old plots recently came to light when the teenager Victor Mancha learned of his cybernetic origins as Ultron's pawn for infiltrating the Avengers. **DW**

Ultron created Jocasta as a mate, but she betrayed him and aided the Avengers.

ESSENTIAL STORYLINES

- ***Avengers Vol. 3 #19-22***
In the story "Ultron Unlimited," the robot tyrant annihilates a tiny European nation with an army of duplicates.
- ***Runaways Vol. 2 #1-6***
Ultron is revealed as the creator of a teenage cyborg, leading to a battle with the Runaways in the story arc "True Believers."

U-Man

FIRST APPEARANCE Invaders Vol. 1 #3 (November 1975)
REAL NAME Meranno
OCCUPATION Warrior; former scientist **BASE** Mobile
HEIGHT 7 ft **WEIGHT** 450 lbs **EYES** Blue **HAIR** Gray
SPECIAL POWERS/ABILITIES Enhanced strength and stamina, able to breathe both air and water, can swim at high speed; devious scientific mind.

The Atlantean Meranno allied himself with Nazi Germany in the late 1930s, betraying his people by orchestrating an attack that crippled the Atlantean fleet. NAMOR banished the traitor, and Meranno used Nazi science to augment his strength.

As U-Man, he became a member of the Super-Axis team and frequently battled Namor, CAPTAIN AMERICA, and the other INVADERS throughout World War II. In the modern era, U-Man has been an ally of the Atlantean warlord ATTUMA. **DW**

Unicorn

FIRST APPEARANCE Tales of Suspense #56 (August 1964)
REAL NAME Milos Masaryk
OCCUPATION Intelligence agent, later criminal **BASE** Mobile
HEIGHT 6 ft 2 in **WEIGHT** 220 lbs **EYES** Blue **HAIR** Red
SPECIAL POWERS/ABILITIES Possesses superhuman strength and durability; wears helmet with "power horn" that can project concussive energy blasts, lasers, and microwaves; wears rocket belt permitting flight.

A Czech-born operative for Russian intelligence, Milos Masaryk was assigned to guard Professor Anton Vanko's laboratory. Vanko invented the harness, helmet, and "power horn" that Masaryk wore as the Unicorn. While spying on Stark Industries, the Unicorn first battled his longtime enemy IRON MAN. The Unicorn underwent treatment that endowed him with superhuman strength but caused rapid cellular deterioration. His sanity deteriorated as well, and he seemingly committed suicide by walking into the sea. **PS**

The Unicorn takes his name from his helmet's "power horn."

Umar

Stepping into the void left by the defeat of her brother Dormammu, Umar often attempted to bring about Doctor Strange's downfall.

The sister of the dread DORMAMMU and a member of the mystical Faltine race, Umar was exiled along with her brother from their home dimension, and sought sanctuary within the Dark Dimension. But Dormammu, who had magically altered himself so as to become a being of pure energy, eventually conquered the Dark Dimension, and banished Umar, whom he saw as the only threat to his power base. But with Dormammu's defeat at the hands of DOCTOR STRANGE, Umar was released from imprisonment, and herself battled Strange, both in order to avenge her brother and in order to expand her power base. In the years that have followed, Umar has remained a constant threat to Doctor Strange and to Earth, whether allied with Dormammu or on her own, and despite the fact that her daughter, CLEA, has become Strange's disciple in the mystic arts. **TB**

FACTFILE
REAL NAME
Umar
OCCUPATION
Sorceress
BASE
Dark Dimension

HEIGHT Unknown
WEIGHT Unknown
EYES Black
HAIR Black

FIRST APPEARANCE
Strange Tales #150 (November 1966)

POWERS
Umar possesses extensive mystic knowledge, which allows her to cast powerful spells for a variety of purposes.

Umar invokes the power of the Lamp of Lucifer in order to learn her brother's defeat—and how to avoid meeting a similar fate herself.

Over the years, Umar has often allied herself with her brother Dormammu in her attempts to gain power.

Union Jack

FACTFILE
REAL NAME
Joseph Chapman
OCCUPATION
Adventurer
BASE
Great Britain

HEIGHT 6 ft
WEIGHT 195 lbs
EYES Brown
HAIR Light brown

FIRST APPEARANCE
Captain America Vol. 1 #253 (January 1980)

POWERS
Enhanced strength and speed; wears a bulletproof costume, carries a variety of guns, and a silver dagger.

The original Union Jack, Lord James Falsworth, fought for the British during World War I as a member of the heroic team Freedom's Five. After an injury, he was succeeded as Union Jack by his son, Brian (formerly known as the Destroyer), while his daughter Jacqueline went on to become SPITFIRE. Both heroes joined the World War II-era INVADERS, where they fought alongside CAPTAIN AMERICA and NAMOR the Sub-Mariner; Brian also founded the heroic post-war V-Battalion.

The third Union Jack is Joey Chapman, who took up the mantle when Spitfire's son, Kenneth Crichton, refused to follow in his uncle's footsteps. Chapman joined the Knights of Pendragon and received superhuman abilities through possession of the Pendragon spirit. As Union Jack, Chapman has served with the most recent Invaders team. **DW**

Union Jack is a member of the New Invaders. The team's proactive role in ending world threats puts them at odds with traditional heroes, including Captain America's Avengers.

Unus the Untouchable

FIRST APPEARANCE X-Men #8 (November 1964)
REAL NAME Angelo Unuscione
OCCUPATION Professional criminal **BASE** Mobile
HEIGHT 6 ft 1 in **WEIGHT** 220 lbs **EYES** Blue **HAIR** Black
SPECIAL POWERS/ABILITIES Generates an impenetrable force-field around body; redoubtable hand-to-hand combatant.

Unus was invited to join the BROTHERHOOD OF EVIL MUTANTS if he could defeat an X-Man. Fighting BEAST, Unus was beaten when his opponent employed a device to magnify Unus' force-field out of his control. As a criminal in partnership with the BLOB, Unus again lost control of his force-fields. Unable to breathe, he collapsed and was thought to have died until Quicksilver discovered him in the ruins of the decimated island of Genosha (*see* GENOSHANS). **AD**

Upstarts

FIRST APPEARANCE Uncanny X-Men Vol. 1 #281 (October 1991)
FORMER MEMBERS AND POWERS
Gamesmaster Telepath who reads billions of minds simultaneously [1].
Siena Blaze Controlled the Earth's electromagnetic field [2].
Shinobi Shaw Can change his body from rock-solid to intangible [3].
Fabian Cortez Could overload the abilities of other mutants [4].
Trevor Fitzroy Drained victims' life energy to control time [5].
Andrea and Andreas von Strucker (Fenris Twins) Could project energy blasts when in contact with one another [6] and [7].
Graydon Creed Wore strength-boosting battle armor [8].

Looking for a new challenge, the GAMESMASTER gathered a group of young humans and mutants to compete in a murderous game. The contestants, who called themselves the Upstarts, earned points if they killed powerful targets such as members of the X-MEN, the NEW MUTANTS, or the HELLFIRE CLUB. The Upstarts launched a number of high-profile hits during their short career, and often fought each other. Eventually many members died, and the survivors, bored with the sport, disbanded. **DW**

Urich, Ben

FIRST APPEARANCE Daredevil #153 (July 1978)
REAL NAME Benjamin Urich
OCCUPATION Reporter for the *Daily Bugle*
BASE New York City
HEIGHT 5 ft 9 in **WEIGHT** 140 lbs **EYES** Brown **HAIR** Gray
SPECIAL POWERS/ABILITIES None; a skilled and responsible investigative journalist.

Ben Urich started his journalism career as a copy boy at the *Daily Bugle*. He worked his way up to become a reporter. Urich began gathering information about DAREDEVIL, and soon learned the hero's true identity and personal history. He thought about publishing an article revealing all of this to the public, but then realized that such an article would destroy Daredevil. So he burned all his notes and files and told Daredevil what he knew. The two became friends, and Daredevil's secret remained safe. **MT**

U.S. Agent

FIRST APPEARANCE Captain America #323 (November 1986)
REAL NAME John F. Walker **OCCUPATION** adventurer; government agent **BASE** Washington, DC
HEIGHT 6 ft 4 in **WEIGHT** 270 lbs **EYES** Blue **HAIR** Blond
SPECIAL POWERS/ABILITIES Superhuman strength and stamina; carries a shield made of Vibranium, which can absorb the vibrations from concussive forces directed against it.

Walker's older brother was a soldier who died in the Vietnam War, and Walker joined the military to honor his memory. After completing his service, he heard that the POWER BROKER had developed a process to give normal people superhuman strength. Walker duly became the Super-Patriot.

When the COMMISSION ON SUPERHUMAN ACTIVITIES forced Steve Rogers to give up being CAPTAIN AMERICA, it assigned Walker to replace him. Rogers later reclaimed his mantle, and Walker became the U.S. Agent. He was assigned to the West Coast AVENGERS and stayed on the team until it renamed itself FORCE WORKS. He also led a team called the Jury against the THUNDERBOLTS and was later drafted to lead the government's new INVADERS team. **TD**

VALKYRIE

FACTFILE

REAL NAME
Brunnhilde

OCCUPATION
Adventurer, former Chooser of the Slain

BASE
Asgard

HEIGHT 6 ft 3 ins
WEIGHT 475 lbs
EYES Blue
HAIR Blonde

FIRST APPEARANCE
Avengers vol. 1 #87 (April 1971)

POWERS

Valkyrie has enhanced strength, longevity, and stamina; can perceive the onset of death, can teleport to the realm of the dead.

VALKYRIE

Wielding a mystical sword, Valkyrie deflects an energy attack.

Odin, ruler of Asgard, made Brunnhilde the leader of the Valkyrior, giving her the task of selecting worthy warriors from among the slain and bringing them to Valhalla. Brunnhilde fulfilled her role ably until the villainous ENCHANTRESS trapped her spirit within a crystal and kept it there for centuries, using it to invest herself and others of her choosing with Valkyrie powers. As well as stealing her powers, in modern times the Enchantress also assumed Brunnhilde's form to deceive the AVENGERS. She gave the powers of Valkyrie to the socialite Samantha Parrington, and later to Barbara Norriss, intending to use them as her pawns. However, Brunnhilde eventually succeeded in restoring her consciousness into Norriss' body, and soon won back her original body.

The Defenders were Valkyrie's extended family. As a core member, she helped the team fight off countless threats to the planet.

As Valkyrie, Brunnhilde joined the DEFENDERS and seemingly sacrificed her life to defeat the evil entity known as the DRAGON OF THE MOON. She later returned by inhabiting new host bodies, but perished in the events surrounding THOR's unleashing of Ragnarok. The Samantha Parrington version of Valkyrie has regained her powers, and has continued her adventuring career. **DW**

VAMP

FIRST APPEARANCE Captain America #217 (January 1978)
REAL NAME Unrevealed
OCCUPATION Secret agent **BASE** Mobile
HEIGHT 5 ft 2 in **WEIGHT** 125 lbs **EYES** Blue **HAIR** Black
SPECIAL POWERS/ABILITIES A trained secret agent, the Vamp wore an absorbo-belt that allowed her to duplicate the strength and physical skills of anyone around her.

Due to her excellent fighting skills, the woman known as the Vamp was selected to become one of the first Super-Agents of SHIELD. Unfortunately, the Vamp was a double-agent, secretly working for the criminal Corporation, and assigned to infiltrate SHIELD. She had also been subjected to a genetic modification, which allowed her to transform into a psionically-powered creature called Animus.

Eventually, the Vamp's true loyalties were exposed and she was incarcerated. She subsequently became yet another victim of the notorious serial killer of Super Villains the SCOURGE OF THE UNDERWORLD. **TD**

VANGUARD

FIRST APPEARANCE Iron Man #109 (April 1978)
REAL NAME Nicolai Krylenko
OCCUPATION Adventurer **BASE** Belarus
HEIGHT 6 ft 3 in **WEIGHT** 230 lbs **EYES** Blue **HAIR** Red
SPECIAL POWERS/ABILITIES Generates force-field that repels most energy directed at him; also uses hammer and sickle to redirect the repelled energy.

Born in the Soviet Union, Nicolai Krylenko lived a life that was marked by deception and duplicity right from the start. Born with mutant powers, he and his twin sister Laynia were adopted by the state after their mother died in childbirth. Their father, a nuclear physicist, was told they were stillborn. Raised by the Soviet machine to be a counterweight to the increasingly prolific US mutants, Nicolai and Laynia became members of the state sponsored super-team, the Super-Soldiers. Inevitably, they learnt the truth about their background and since then Nicolai has pursued more semi-autonomous roles. He is currently a member of super-team, the Winter Guard. **AD**

Van Helsing, Rachel

FIRST APPEARANCE Tomb of Dracula #3 (July 1972)
REAL NAME Rachel Van Helsing
OCCUPATION Vampire slayer **BASE** London, England
HEIGHT 5 ft 8 in **WEIGHT** 135 lbs **EYES** Blue **HAIR** Blonde
SPECIAL POWERS/ABILITIES Expert vampire slayer whose preferred weapon was the crossbow; was also a parapsychologist and anthropologist.

Rachel Van Helsing was the descendant of Dr. Abraham Van Helsing, the 19th century nemesis of Dracula. As a child she saw Dracula murder her parents to get back at Dr. Van Helsing. Rachel was raised by another of Dracula's enemies, Quincy Harker. She became the most formidable member of his band of vampire slayers, frequently battling Dracula. After a troubled romance with her teammate FRANK DRAKE, Rachel moved to New York State, where Dracula finally turned her into a vampiress. On her request, Wolverine impaled her through the heart, and she died peacefully. **PS**

Vapor

FIRST APPEARANCE The Incredible Hulk #254 (December 1980)
REAL NAME Ann Darnell **OCCUPATION** Life support technologist turned criminal **BASE** Mobile
HEIGHT 5 ft 6 in **WEIGHT** (in human form) 122 lbs
EYES (in human form) Green, (as Vapor) White **HAIR** Auburn
SPECIAL POWERS/ABILITIES Can transform herself into any kind of gas; can resume her original human form for brief periods only.

Intent on acquiring superhuman powers the same way that the FANTASTIC FOUR did, millionaire industrialist Simon Utrecht financed the construction of his own spaceship. His crew consisted of Ann Darnell, her brother Jimmy, and pilot Mike Steel. As they had intended, their spaceship, lacking radiation shielding, was bombarded by cosmic rays. This radiation reacted with gases to convert Ann Darnell's body into a gaseous state. Her three companions also gained super-powers and the quartet became known as the U-FOES. They are longstanding enemies of the HULK, and have also worked for other criminals, including the LEADER and the Master. **PS**

Varua

FIRST APPEARANCE (unnamed) Thor Vol. I #300
REAL NAME Mira **OCCUPATION** Pupil of the Celestials
BASE Celestial Mothership, previously Ruk Island
HEIGHT/WEIGHT/EYES Unrevealed **HAIR** Brown
SPECIAL POWERS/ABILITIES Posesses telepathy, teleportation, flight, and ability to generate the Blue Flame, which changes her and others into the Uni-Mind, a psionic entity.

Born in 1405 on Ruk Island, Mira began life as a priestess. In 1419 she was recruited into the YOUNG GODS by the godesses of Earth's pantheons. Mira was taken to train in combat under Katos on the Celestial Mothership where she became Varua. After the Sea Witch had a prophetic dream, the CELESTIALS granted the Young Gods 3 days on earth to investigate evil threats. Varua was held captive by the Deviants who used a brain mine to make her help them reawaken GHAUR. Varua was forced by Ghaur to create a Uni-Mind with other prisoners to give its power to him. This was cut open by the BLACK KNIGHT, which set everyone free. Varua departed with Delta Force. **ED**

Vanisher

FIRST APPEARANCE Uncanny X-Men Vol. 1 #2 (November 1963)
REAL NAME Unknown
OCCUPATION Professional criminal **BASE** New York City
HEIGHT 5 ft 5 in **WEIGHT** 175 lbs
EYES Green **HAIR** None
SPECIAL POWERS/ABILITIES Mutant ability to teleport himself and others by accessing the Darkforce dimension

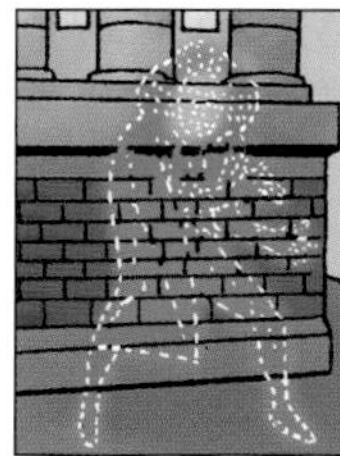

The mysterious Vanisher built a criminal organization around his ability to commit crimes using teleportation. He tried to extort money from the US government by stealing defense plans until foiled by the original X-MEN. The Vanisher acted as the mentor to a gang of teenage runaways known as the Fallen Angels. The being called Darkling later took control of the Vanisher and set him against the NEW WARRIORS. The Vanisher subsequently joined a new team of ENFORCERS. **DW**

Varnae

FIRST APPEARANCE Bizarre Adventures #33 (December, 1982)
REAL NAME Varnae
OCCUPATION Lord of Earth's Vampires **BASE** Mobile
HEIGHT 10 ft **WEIGHT** 475 lbs **EYES** Red **HAIR** Green
SPECIAL POWERS/ABILITIES Near-immortality, enhanced strength, ability to grow in size and become a wolf, a bat, or a cloud of mist; can telepathically influence and vampirize others.

Varnae became the first vampire in the days of ancient Atlantis, when the Darkholders who worshipped the Elder God CHTHON subjected him to anti-death experimentations. Over the millennia Varnae battled the Catholic Church's Montesi lineage, to prevent them from discovering the Montesi Formula that would destroy all vampires. In the year 1459, Varnae died and passed his title as Lord of the Vampires to Dracula. Through sorcerous incantations, Varnae returned in the modern era, and battled enemies including DOCTOR STRANGE and BLADE. Varnae is also responsible for reversing the effects of the Montesi Formula, which had temporarily eradicated Earth's vampires. **DW**

Vengeance

FIRST APPEARANCE Ghost Rider Vol. 2 #21 (December 1976)
REAL NAME Michael Badilino **OCCUPATION** Detective
BASE New York City **HEIGHT** (Badilino) 5 ft 10 ins, (Vengeance) 6 ft 6 ins **WEIGHT** (Badilino) 195 lbs, (Vengeance) 235 lbs
EYES Green **HAIR** Black
SPECIAL POWERS/ABILITIES Can project cold fire that causes others physical pain; his penance stare causes mental anguish.

MEPHISTO tricked the GHOST RIDER into blasting detective Michael Badilino's father with hellfire. Unaware of Mephisto's involvement, Badilino made a deal with him to gain mystical powers and destroy the Ghost Rider. Now known as Vengeance, he learned the truth, made peace with the Ghost Rider, and joined the Midnight Sons to battle demons like Mephisto. Vengeance was captured by Badilino's old enemy Anthony Hellgate, and though freed by the Ghost Rider he was never the same. Vengeance eventually appeared to destroy himself in a huge explosion, but seemingly returned to help Ghost Rider battle the demon known as Blackheart. **TB**

Venom

FACTFILE

REAL NAME
Edward Charles "Eddie" Brock

OCCUPATION
Former journalist, later vigilante

BASE
New York City

HEIGHT 6 ft 3 in
WEIGHT 260 lbs
EYES Blue
HAIR Reddish-blond

FIRST APPEARANCE
The Amazing Spider-Man #298 (March 1988)

POWERS
Venom possesses superhuman strength, speed, and agility. Like Spider-Man, his hands and feet can adhere to most surfaces. Can project web-like substance from his "costume."

The symbiote flowed over Eddie Brock, viewing the suicidal journalist as a kindred spirit.

While SPIDER-MAN was on the BEYONDER's "Battleworld," he acquired a black costume, which turned out to be an alien being that bonded itself to him. Spider-Man rejected this alien symbiote, which then latched onto an ex-*Daily Globe* columnist Eddie Brock. He had wrecked his career by identifying the wrong man as a murderer known as the Sin-Eater—an error revealed by Spider-Man. Brock also had cancer and had resolved to kill himself. When the symbiote bonded with Brock the cancer went into remission. As Venom, Brock became one of Spider-Man's deadliest rivals and foes.

When Brock's cancer returned, he sold the symbiote to crime boss Don Fortunato, who gave it to his son Angelo. As a second Venom, Angelo attacked Spider-Man, but the symbiote deserted him in mid-battle, and Angelo fell to his death. The symbiote then bonded with Spider-Man's enemy Mac Gargan, the SCORPION, who became the third Venom. PS

Venom saw himself as a protector of the innocent. However, he would kill criminals outright.

Driven by a shared hatred of Spider-Man, the composite creature Venom made repeated attempts to kill him.

Verdugo, Sandra

FIRST APPEARANCE Incredible Hulk vol. 3, #36 (March 2002)
REAL NAME Sandra Verdugo
OCCUPATION Mercenary, Home Base operative **BASE** Mobile
HEIGHT 5 ft 8 in **WEIGHT** 122 lbs **EYES** Black **HAIR** Black
SPECIAL POWERS/ABILITIES Recipient of H-Section Programming: is able to recover from most injuries and revive from death; brilliant markswoman, athlete and hand-to-hand combatant.

A one-time member of the US Special Forces, Sandra Verdugo worked as a mercenary before becoming pregnant by DOC SAMSON. When Sandra's eight-year-old son was kidnapped, the clandestine organisation Home Base offered her a deal. Home Base would retrieve her son if Sandra would agree to become one of their operatives. Her mission would be to capture the HULK.

Sandra agreed but it wasn't long before she turned on her new employers. With the help of Doc Samson and the Hulk, Sandra was reunited with her son just before Home Base's headquarters were destroyed. Mother and child are thought to have perished in the conflagration. AD

Vermin

FIRST APPEARANCE Captain America #272 (August 1982)
REAL NAME Unknown
OCCUPATION Unknown **BASE** Mobile
HEIGHT 6ft **WEIGHT** 220 lbs **EYES** Red **HAIR** Brown
SPECIAL POWERS/ABILITIES Superhuman strength and speed. Teeth and nails can cut through soft metals. Greatly enhanced sense of smell. Can command rats to attack an enemy.

The being now called Vermin grew up on the streets of New York City where he was found by Baron Helmut Zemo, the son of a Nazi scientist, and Arnim Zola, a Nazi geneticist. These two changed Vermin so that he resembled a rat, and gained rat-like abilities. He was then sent out to kill Zemo and Zola's longtime enemy, CAPTAIN AMERICA. Vermin sent a pack of rats to attack the hero, who managed to survive and captured him. Vermin escaped and was taken to Zemo's base in Mexico, but later returned to New York, where he was eventually captured by Captain America and SPIDER-MAN and taken to a high security mental institution. MT

Vernard, Kristoff

FIRST APPEARANCE Fantastic Four Vol. 1 #247 (October 1982)
REAL NAME Kristoff Vernard
OCCUPATION Kristoff Vernard **BASE** Latveria
HEIGHT 4 ft 11 in, (in suit) 6ft 7in **WEIGHT** 103 lbs, (in suit) 293 lbs **EYES** Brown **HAIR** Brown
SPECIAL POWERS/ABILITIES Enhanced strength; damage resistance; ability to generate force fields or fire concussion beams.

Kristoff Vernard is believed by some to be the biological son of Nathaniel Richards, making him the half-brother of Reed Richards (Mister Fantastic). After the death of Kristoff's mother in Latveria, Doctor Doom discovered the boy and groomed him as his heir. When Doom appeared to have died, his Doombots brainwashed Kristoff into believing that he was Doom. Kristoff donned an armored suit and attacked the Fantastic Four, though his enemies eventually helped restore his true identity. Kristoff later teamed up with Nathaniel Richards to reclaim Latveria from usurpers. DW

Vibraxas

FIRST APPEARANCE Fantastic Four Vol. 1 #390 (July 1994)
REAL NAME N'Kano
OCCUPATION Adventurer **BASE** Mobile
HEIGHT 5 ft 10 in **WEIGHT** 165 lbs
EYES Brown **HAIR** Brown
SPECIAL POWERS/ABILITIES Can generate intense vibratory force.

The young Wakandan N'Kano gained his powers when an experimental Vibrasurge project backfired, seemingly killing his mother. Taken in by the Black Panther, he traveled to America and became a member of the Fantastic Force under the name Vibraxas. When he accidentally murdered a gang member, Vibraxas went back to Wakanda to stand trial, but he was exonerated. After the Fantastic Force disbanded, Vibraxas found love with Queen Divine Justice, a member of the "Dora Milaje" who serve the Wakandan king as bodyguards and wives-in-training. DW

Vindicator

FIRST APPEARANCE Uncanny X-Men #139 (November 1980)
REAL NAME Heather McNeil Hudson
OCCUPATION Member of Alpha Flight
BASE Tamarind Island, British Columbia, Canada
HEIGHT 5 ft 5 in **WEIGHT** 120 lbs **EYES** Green **HAIR** Red
SPECIAL POWERS/ABILITIES Thermal-energy battlesuit provides ability to fly, generate force fields and fire concussive blasts.

Heather McNeil Hudson and her husband James Hudson helped found the Canadian Super Hero group Alpha Flight. James took leadership of Alpha Flight as the costumed hero Guardian, and Heather did the same after his apparent death. As the new leader of Alpha Flight, Heather called herself Vindicator and wore a modified version of her husband's battlesuit. She and James later had a baby girl and left on a mission to deep space. Recent manipulations of the timestream have created copies of the original Alpha Flight members, including Heather, who are active on Earth. DW

Viper

The original Viper used lethal poison-tipped throwing darts to carve out a criminal career.

Her face scarred at some point in her nebulous past, the woman who would one day be known as Viper began her career as a member of the international terrorist organization called Hydra. After the leadership of Hydra was captured by Nick Fury and SHIELD, she assumed command of the remnants of the organization and, as Madame Hydra, excelled at creating panic and terror until Captain America brought her down. Madame Hydra later resurfaced in Virginia, where she murdered Jordan Stryke, a costumed criminal known as Viper, as he was being escorted by US marshals to Washington DC to testify about his criminal connections. She stole his costume and, assuming his name, took command of the Serpent Squad he had assembled. Under the new Viper's leadership, the Serpent Squad became a terrorist unit. Since then, both alone or in concert with allies such as the Silver Samurai, Baron Strucker and the Red Skull, Viper has continued to hatch plans resulting in chaos and anarchy. Although she has declared her intention for world domination, Viper has been known to launch attacks where there is no obvious advantage to be gained. Though her injured face has long since healed, the scars in her psyche run deep, and whatever unknown demons plague her constantly drive Viper to acts dedicated to the destruction of world governments and innocent people. TB

FACTFILE
REAL NAME
Unrevealed
OCCUPATION
Terrorist
BASE
Mobile

HEIGHT 5 ft 9 ins
WEIGHT Unknown
EYES Green
HAIR Black with green highlights

FIRST APPEARANCE
Captain America #110 (February 1969)

VIPER

POWERS
Viper is a superb strategist and a trained terrorist with extensive knowledge of weaponry, tactics, and fighting styles. She is skilled in a number of martial arts and an expert in the use of various weapons, including whips.

Virgo

FIRST APPEARANCE Avengers #72 (January 1970)
REAL NAME Elaine McLaughlin
OCCUPATION Professional criminal
BASE Denver, Colorado
HEIGHT 5 ft 6 in **WEIGHT** 125 lbs **EYES** Green **HAIR** Red
SPECIAL POWERS/ABILITIES Sharp criminal mind; good organizer; a skilled hand-to-hand combatant.

Gang boss Virgo was recruited to be a member of Cornelius Van Lunt's Zodiac crime cartel, in which each member would adopt the guise of a different sign of the zodiac, and control a territory in a different American city. Zodiac was equipped with state-of-the-art weaponry and their ultimate goal was global domination. However, their bid for power was foiled by the combined forces of SHIELD and the Avengers. Later, a rogue Zodiac faction led by former Cartel member Scorpio and using androids to represent the twelve zodiological symbols targeted the original Zodiac leaders for death. In the end, Virgo was slain by her robot counterpart. TB

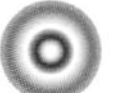

Vision *SEE OPPOSITE PAGE*

Von Doom, Cynthia

FIRST APPEARANCE Astonishing Tales #8 (October 1971)
REAL NAME Cynthia von Doom
OCCUPATION Sorceress **BASE** Astral plane
HEIGHT 5 ft 8 in **WEIGHT** 150 lbs **EYES** Brown **HAIR** Brown
SPECIAL POWERS/ABILITIES Knowledge of magic allowed her to contact demons; however she often unleashed foces that it was beyond her abilities to control.

Cynthia von Doom was a sorceress who belonged to a group of Latverian gypsies called the Zefiro. She married Werner von Doom, a healer. Their son Victor grew up to become Doctor Doom. Cynthia summoned the demon Mephisto, who offered her great power so she could overthrow Latveria's ruthless king and give her people a homeland. She unleashed terrible magic but could not control it. One of the king's guards killed her, and her soul joined Mephisto in Hell. After Cynthia's death, young Victor found his mother's trunk of magic paraphernalia. Every year since he has tried to summon her back from Mephisto's realm. AD

Vulture

Adrian Toomes gained self-esteem from criminality. A founder of B&T Electronics with his friend Gregory Bestman, Toomes had just completed his electromagnetic harness—which enabled him to fly—when he discovered his partner had been defrauding the company. Desperate for revenge Toomes destroyed the company's factory and found a substantial cache of money. He then embarked upon a life of crime, throughout which he has been continually dogged by Spider-Man.

FACTFILE
REAL NAME
Adrian Toomes
OCCUPATION
Inventor; criminal
BASE
Staten Island

HEIGHT 5 ft 11 in
WEIGHT 175 lbs
EYES Hazel
HAIR None

FIRST APPEARANCE
Amazing Spider-Man Vol. 1 #2 (May 1963)

POWERS
Electromagnetic harness worn beneath costume enables the Vulture to fly at speeds of up to 95 mph. It also augments his strength, agility, and endurance to superhuman levels.

For a short time, two Vultures soared the skies of Manhattan.

While Toomes was in prison, his cellmate, Blackie Drago, discovered the location of Toomes' spare Vulture suit. Finding it difficult to use, Drago also suffered defeat at Spider-Man's hands, before being beaten by Toomes, who had escaped incarceration. Since then, Toomes' criminal shenanigans have continued to be interspersed with battles with the wallcrawler. Although now an old man, Toomes' hatred of Spider-Man is likely to keep him alive for years to come. AD

VISION

Synthozoid with a human heart

Ultron forced Horton to help him build the Vision. Horton then programmed the Vision for independent thoughts.

The synthozoid who would become the Vision was programmed with the brain patterns of WONDER MAN, who was believed to be deceased at the time. The synthozoid was created by ULTRON, the AVENGERS' robotic archenemy, with the help of Professor Phineas T. Horton, the scientist responsible for the original Human Torch.

FACTFILE

REAL NAME
Inapplicable

OCCUPATION
Adventurer

BASE
New York City

HEIGHT 6 ft 3 in
WEIGHT 300 lbs; however weight may vary from nothing to 90 tons.
EYES Gold
HAIR None

FIRST APPEARANCE
Avengers #57
(October 1968)

POWERS
Superhuman strength, endurance; jewel on brow discharges blasts of solar energy. He can make all or part of body hard as diamond. He can decrease his mass to become a wraith. He can partially materialize within another person, causing extreme pain.

EMOTIONAL SIGNALS

Ultron immediately sent the Vision to lure the Avengers into a death trap. Like Wonder Man before him, the Vision grew to admire the Avengers and couldn't betray them. He broke free of Ultron's control and helped the Avengers defeat him. The grateful heroes rewarded the Vision by inviting him to join the team. He was so shaken by the gesture that he actually shed a tear. The Vision's human emotions began to surface over time and he slowly realized that he was falling in love with Wanda Maximoff, the SCARLET WITCH. When she returned his feelings, they were married and took a leave of absence from the Avengers, settling in Leonia, New Jersey.

ESSENTIAL STORYLINES
- ***Giant-Size Avengers #4*** The Vision and Scarlet Witch are married.
- ***The Vision and Scarlet Witch #1–12*** The Vision and Scarlet Witch leave the Avengers and move to the suburbs.
- ***Avengers #251-254*** The Vision attempts to take over every computer on Earth.
- ***West Coast Avengers #42–45*** The government kidnaps and disassembles the Vision.

A MATTER OF TRUST

The Vision later returned to action to aid the Avengers against ANNIHILUS, and was severely injured. STARFOX attempted to cure him by linking him with ISACC, a massive computer complex that controlled the moon of Saturn called Titan. ISACC tapped into a control crystal left in the Vision by Ultron and used it to alter the android's way of thinking. When the Vision was elected chairmen of the Avengers, he decided to bring a new golden age to humanity by taking control of every computer on Earth. However, the other Avengers convinced him to abandon his ambitious plan. Believing he could no longer be trusted, the government kidnapped and disassembled the Vision.

The Avengers were the only true family the Vision ever knew.

Infected by a virus, the Vision's body was completely liquefied.

VICTIM OF MADNESS

He was rescued by the West Coast Avengers and rebuilt by Dr. PYM and the BLACK PANTHER, but he had lost all his human emotions and could no longer return the Scarlet Witch's love. Their marriage eventually ended in divorce. The Vision's android body was later destroyed when the Scarlet Witch when mad and disassembled the Avengers. A version of the Vision was recently revived when his programming was integrated into the neuro-kinetic armor of the YOUNG AVENGER known as Iron Lad. TD

War

FIRST APPEARANCE X-Factor #11 (December 1986)
REAL NAME Abraham Lincoln Kieros **OCCUPATION** Former Horseman of Apocalypse **BASE** Unknown
HEIGHT 6 ft 6 in **WEIGHT** 270 lbs **EYES** Blue **HAIR** Brown
SPECIAL POWERS/ABILITIES As the Horseman of the Apocalypse War, Abraham could shatter objects just by concentrating on them and clapping his hands.

Vietnam war veteran Abraham Kieros was forced to live out his days in an iron lung. When APOCALYPSE offered to heal Abraham if he became one of his Four Horsemen, Abraham seized the opportunity. As the Horseman War, Abraham helped the group to win their first victory over X-FACTOR, but after that they suffered repeated defeats. Eventually, Apocalypse disbanded the group and Abraham returned to his paralyzed state. He would have remained in this condition if ARCHANGEL, another former Horseman, had not healed him. Abraham is now determined to make the most of this new life. The role of War has since been filled by the HULK, DEATHBIRD, and Gazer. **AD**

War Machine

As a pilot, Jim was prepared for flight-equipped armor.

While serving with the US Marines in Southeast Asia, helicopter pilot James Rhodes encountered Tony Stark, who had just escaped from a warlord by using a suit of powered armor. Rhodes became Tony Stark's pilot, and took the role of Iron Man during one of Stark's bouts with alcoholism.

During a period when Stark was believed dead, Rhodes became CEO of Stark Industries. He later wore a variant version of the Iron Man armor as the heroic War Machine, and briefly changed his armor to an alien construct called the Eidolon Warwear. After the events known as the Crossing, Rhodes temporarily gave up his career to start a salvage company. He returned to fight mercenary Parnell Jacobs, who became a new, villainous War Machine. **DW**

Befitting its name, the War Machine armor is packed with offensive weaponry.

FACTFILE
REAL NAME
James Rupert Rhodes
OCCUPATION
Adventurer
BASE
Mobile

HEIGHT 6 ft 1 in
WEIGHT 210 lbs
EYES Brown
HAIR Brown

FIRST APPEARANCE
Iron Man Vol. 1 #118 (January 1979)

WAR MACHINE

POWERS
Armor provides flight, enhanced strength, damage resistance, and the ability to project destructive energy.

Warbird

Carol Danvers served with US Air Force intelligence and NASA, before exposure to Kree technology gave her superhuman powers. As the hero Ms. Marvel, she joined the AVENGERS. The villain IMMORTUS kidnapped her, took her to the Limbo dimension, brainwashed, and impregnated her. She escaped to Earth, but lost her powers and memories to the absorbing mutant ROGUE. Ms. Marvel worked with the X-MEN until she received cosmic power in genetic experiments conducted by the alien BROOD. As Binary, she joined the galaxy-hopping STARJAMMERS. After her return home and a slight dip in power levels, she took the identity of Warbird.

Danvers resigned from the Avengers when problems with alcoholism came to light, and sought treatment for her addiction. She became the superhuman liaison for US Homeland Security and, after the events of House of M, she took the codename Ms. Marvel once more. **DW**

FACTFILE
REAL NAME
Carol Danvers
OCCUPATION
Adventurer
BASE
New York City

HEIGHT 5 ft 11 in
WEIGHT 124 lbs
EYES Blue
HAIR Blonde

FIRST APPEARANCE
Marvel Super-Heroes Vol. 1 #13 (March 1968)

WARBIRD

POWERS
Warbird possessed the ability to fly, enhanced strength, damage resistance, and could absorb and rechannel energy.

Carol Danvers, now known as Ms. Marvel, is a member of the New Avengers.

WARLOCK

Genetically created life form

At first Adam Warlock was known simply as "Him."

Adam Warlock was the genetic creation of a maverick group of scientists known as the ENCLAVE. He was the prototype for what they hoped would be an invincible army, with which they planned to conquer the world. While forming in his cocoon, Warlock overheard his creators' plans. When he hatched, he rebelled against them, destroyed their base, and used his cosmic power to take off into space.

ESSENTIAL STORYLINES

- ***The Infinity Abyss Miniseries*** While living in one of his self-generated cocoons, Warlock is revived to battle six clones of Thanos.
- ***Warlock Miniseries*** The Enclave create another Warlock to rule the Earth, but he turns out to be an illusion in the mind of Janie, placed there by the real Adam Warlock to teach her compassion.

FACTFILE

REAL NAME
Adam Warlock

OCCUPATION
Avenger, Savior of Worlds

BASE
Counter-Earth

HEIGHT 6 ft 2 in
WEIGHT 240 lbs
EYES White
HAIR Blond

FIRST APPEARANCE
Fantastic Four #66 (September 1967)

POWERS
Body can trap cosmic energy which enhances his strength, endurance, and healing powers; also uses this energy to reduce gravity enabling him to fly; projects energy blasts from his hands.

When he emerged from his developmental cocoon, Warlock refused to go along with the plans his creators had for him, rebelling against them.

Adam Warlock has golden colored skin.

HIGH EVOLUTIONARY

At this point, drifting through space, Warlock met the HIGH EVOLUTIONARY, a human who had learned how to control evolution, who was creating an artificial world called "Counter-Earth." He was hoping to create a planet free from evil, but the creature MAN-BEAST brought evil to this pure world.

The High Evolutionary gave Warlock the Soul Gem, which could draw souls into another dimension, and Warlock battled Man-Beast. In the end, however, Warlock was unable to defeat evil on Counter-Earth, and left to fight the good fight elsewhere in the universe.

THE MAGUS

In his travels, Warlock encountered the MAGUS, the power-crazed leader of the Universal Church of Truth, an armed militia trying to spread their religious empire throughout the universe. This Church destroyed the populations of planets that refused to convert. To his horror, Warlock discovered that the Magus was actually an alternate future version of himself.

Warlock subsequently battled the Titan THANOS, who mortally wounded him. Warlock's soul retreated into the Soul Gem, where it lived peacefully for many years until he emerged to battle Thanos once more. MT

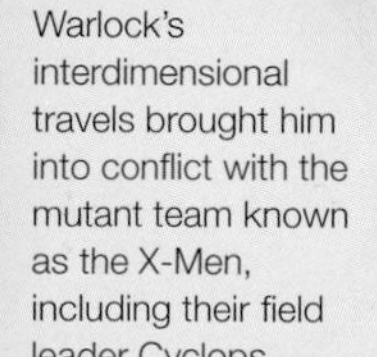

Warlock's interdimensional travels brought him into conflict with the mutant team known as the X-Men, including their field leader Cyclops.

Pip the Troll, Adam Warlock's friend, helped him battle the Titan Thanos.

Warriors Three

WARRIORS THREE

FACTFILE

MEMBERS AND POWERS

FANDRAL
Enhanced strength, master swordsman.

HOGUN
Enhanced strength, superb hand-to-hand combatant

VOLSTAGG
Enhanced strength and endurance, ability to consume vast quantities of drink

BASE Asgard

FIRST APPEARANCE:
Journey into Mystery Vol. 1 #119 (August 1965)

The Warriors Three were champions of Asgard, although their reckless exploits also brought them notoriety. Fandral was dashing, as quick with a blade as he was with his wit. Taciturn Hogun, nicknamed the Grim, came from a faraway land in Asgard's dimension and wielded a mace in battle. Volstagg was the heart of the band, though his boisterous nature often got the others into trouble.

The Three often fought at the side of the thunder god THOR, helping put down threats from LOKI and going on quests, such as the retrieval of apples from the world-tree Yggdrasil or securing a magic pig from Dionysus of Olympus. When Thor triggered Ragnarok (*see* GODS OF ASGARD), Asgard was wiped from existence, with the Warriors Three presumably among the casualties. **DW**

WARRIORS THREE
1 Hogan
2 Volstagg
3 Fandral

In adventures that spanned the dimensional planes, Fandral, Hogun, and Volstagg bested gods.

WASP ***SEE OPPOSITE PAGE***

Watchers, The

WATCHERS

FACTFILE

NOTABLE MEMBERS

THE ONE
(the leader of the Watchers),
IKOR, EMNU, UATU, ECCE,
ARON (the renegade watcher)

BASE
The Watchers' homeworld is unknown, but believed to be in a galaxy other than the Milky Way.

FIRST APPEARANCE
Tales of Suspense #53 (May 1964)

POWERS
All Watchers possess vast mental and physical powers, and the ability to manipulate energy. They are telepathic, can alter their appearance using their mental powers, and teleport through space at hyper-light speeds.

The Watchers are an ancient race of extraterrestrials who, eons ago, took upon themselves the task of observing the planets, peoples, and phenomena of the universe, without taking an active part in the affairs of the peoples under observation.

The Watchers adopted their policy of passive observation after a disastrous experiment. A group of Watchers, including UATU THE WATCHER who eventually came to observe Earth, once gave the knowledge of atomic power to the inhabitants of the planet Prosilicus, believing this would advance the race technologically.

However the Prosilicans used the knowledge to create nuclear weapons and waged war on their own planet, and against others. After this, the Watchers vowed to only passively observe, never to interfere. Uatu, however, met Reed Richards and came to look kindly on the FANTASTIC FOUR. He has helped the team numerous times, especially during their conflicts with the world-eater GALACTUS. **MT**

The Watchers have all sworn a sacred oath not to interfere in a planet's affairs.

Watson, Anna May

FIRST APPEARANCE Amazing Spider-Man #15 (August 1964)
REAL NAME Anna May Watson
OCCUPATION Retired **BASE** Florida
HEIGHT 5 ft 8 in **WEIGHT** 180 lbs **EYES** Blue **HAIR** White
SPECIAL POWERS/ABILITIES A kind and loving heart.

The aunt of Mary Jane Watson (*see* PARKER, MARY JANE), in her youth Anna Watson shared many of the same hopes and dreams as her young niece. As a young woman harboring hopes of an acting career, she moved to California and married. Sadly, her acting dream came to nought and her marriage collapsed following an affair. Returning to New York, Anna looked after Mary Jane following her parents' separation and the two became close. The nextdoor neighbour and best friend of May PARKER, Anna helped pair off Peter Parker (*see* SPIDER-MAN) and Mary Jane, but has now moved to Florida to enjoy her twilight years. **AD**

Wasp

Buzziest hero of the Avengers team

Janet Van Dyne was with her scientist father Vernon when he visited Dr. Henry Pym to ask him to collaborate on a project to use an energy beam to detect signals from extraterrestrial civilizations. Pym declined, but was attracted to Janet, who reminded him of his late wife Maria. Van Dyne proceeded with his experiment. However, a criminal from the Kosmosian race tracked Van Dyne's beam to Earth and murdered him.

Pym implanted cells in Janet that would enable her to grow antennae to communicate with insects. The antennae cells died early in her career.

FACTFILE

REAL NAME
Janet Van Dyne

OCCUPATION
Adventurer, fashion designer

BASE
Avengers Mansion, New York City; Cresskill, New Jersey; later Oxford, England

HEIGHT 5 ft 4 in
WEIGHT 110 lbs
EYES Blue
HAIR Auburn

FIRST APPEARANCE
Tales to Astonish #44 (June 1963)

POWERS
Ability to shrink in size down to a half inch in height. When the Wasp is 4 ft. 2 in. or less in height, wings appear from her body, enabling her to fly. Can discharge bioelectric force bolts from her hands.

The fun-loving Wasp enjoyed teasing her partner Henry Pym, here in Giant-Man mode.

Pym Particles

The Wasp's bioelectric "stings" can inflict pain on even superhumanly strong foes.

Janet told Pym she was determined to bring her father's killer to justice. Impressed, Pym revealed his dual identity as Ant-Man and offered to endow her with superhuman abilities and make her his crimefighting partner. Janet agreed and became the Wasp. Pym taught her to use gas containing subatomic "Pym particles" to shrink herself and regain normal size. He also implanted cells beneath her shoulderblades that enabled her to grow wings at insect size. Ant-Man and the Wasp duly defeated the "creature from Kosmos." Pym and Janet also fell in love. It was Pym who suggested that he, the Wasp, the Hulk, Iron Man, and Thor band together, and Janet who suggested the name "The Avengers."

A Stormy Marriage

Pym adopted other costumed identities, Giant-Man and Goliath, and then an alternate, aggressive personality named Yellowjacket. Realizing that he was still Pym, Janet married him anyway, and he soon regained his true personality. Pym later had a nervous breakdown, and he and Janet were divorced; however time healed the rift and the became friends, and eventually lovers, once more.

Over the years the Wasp's powers have altered. She can now change size by mental command, and vary in size anywhere between insect size and her normal height. Whereas she formerly used weapons called "wasp's stings," she can now project bioelectricity from her hands.

The Wasp has served with great distinction as chairman of the Avengers. A wealthy heiress, she has also led a second career as a fashion designer. **PS**

Janet Van Dyne briefly used her size-changing powers to grow to gigantic size, but soon went back to fighting evil as the Wasp.

ESSENTIAL STORYLINES
- ***Avengers #59–60*** Janet Van Dyne marries Henry Pym in his new Yellowjacket identity.
- ***Avengers #214–219*** Janet Van Dyne divorces Henry Pym and becomes Avengers chairman.
- ***Avengers #270–277*** In her final mission as chairman, Wasp leads Avengers in thwarting Masters of Evil's takeover of Avengers Mansion.

Weapon X

FACTFILE

NOTABLE MEMBERS

WOLVERINE Mutant healing factor, enhanced senses, adamantium-bonded skeleton, retractable claws.

SABRETOOTH Similar powers to Wolverine.

MAVERICK/AGENT ZERO Absorbs and discharge energy; age suppressant.

SILVER FOX Artificial healing factor and age suppressant.

DEADPOOL Artificial healing factor, enhanced reflexes, teleportation device.

MARROW Bone growth; agility; recuperative powers.

MESMERO Hypnosis.

SAURON Drains life force from others; transforms into pterosaur.

CHAMBER Blasts of psionic energy from chest furnace.

BASE Weapon X facility, Alberta, Canada

FIRST APPEARANCE
Marvel Comics Presents Vol. 1 #72 (March 1991)

In 1945, a liberated concentration camp unearthed the genetics research of MISTER SINISTER, giving birth to the US government's Weapon Plus program. The government's previous Super-Soldier project (which produced CAPTAIN AMERICA) retrospectively became Weapon I. Weapons II and III used animal subjects, Weapons IV, V, and VI experimented on ethnic minorities, and Weapons VII, VIII, and IX relied on mutants. In the 1960s, Weapon X (conducted in conjunction with the Canadian government's Department K) produced memory-wiped operatives including WOLVERINE and SABRETOOTH, and used Shiva robots to eliminate rogue agents. Wolverine escaped and became a member of the X-MEN.

Weapon X eventually disbanded, but Weapon Plus continued under the leadership of John Sublime, who took the program up to Weapon XV. Sublime reopened Weapon X, recruiting mutants as field operatives and executing surplus mutants in the Neverland concentration camp. Wolverine teamed with AGENT ZERO and Fantomex (a product of Weapon XIII) to investigate the program, but found that it had seemingly gone underground. **DW**

WEAPON X
1 Sauron ***2*** Brent Jackson, Director
3 Wild Child ***4*** Aurora

Wendigo

FACTFILE

REAL NAME
Various

OCCUPATION
Forest creature

BASE
Mobile in Canadian wilderness

HEIGHT 9 ft 7 in
WEIGHT 1,800 lbs
EYES Red
HAIR White

FIRST APPEARANCE
Incredible Hulk Vol. 2 #162 (April 1973)

POWERS Mystically enhanced strength, stamina, and reflexes; nearly indestructible, slashing claws on hands and feet.

An ancient curse dooms anyone who consumes human flesh in the Canadian wilderness to become a Wendigo, a savage and near-mindless being covered with shaggy white fur. The hunter Paul Cartier became one of the earliest Wendigos, after resorting to cannibalism to survive in a snowed-in cave. Cartier tried to transfer the curse to the HULK, but his hunting companion Georges Baptiste voluntarily became the new Wendigo.

Many more Wendigos have since appeared, including fur trapper François Lartigue and cryptozoologist Michael Fleet. The Canadian government, apparently hoping to exploit the creature's superhuman attributes, employed a Wendigo operative codenamed Yeti as part of its Weapon PRIME program. During its time with Weapon PRIME, Yeti attacked CABLE'S X-FORCE as well as the hero NORTHSTAR. Most recently, the sorcerer Mauvais assumed the identity of a Wendigo, and was dragged into the otherdimensional realm of the Great Beasts after a fight with WOLVERINE. **DW**

Wendigo uses his mystically powered strength to go toe-to-toe with superpowered opponents.

WEREWOLF

FACTFILE

REAL NAME
Jacob Russoff, later changed to Jack Russell

OCCUPATION
Adventurer

BASE
Los Angeles, California

HEIGHT 5 ft 10 in
WEIGHT 200 lbs
EYES Blue; (as Werewolf) Red
HAIR Red, (as Werewolf) Brown

FIRST APPEARANCE
Marvel Spotlight #2 (February 1972)

POWERS
Superhuman strength, agility, reflexes, stamina, and senses.

WEREWOLF

Jack Russell's ancestor, Grigori Russoff, had the misfortune to be bitten by a female werewolf in 1795 in his home country of Transylvania. The curse eventually afflicted Jack. When he turned 18, Jack was transformed into a mindless, savage werewolf during the three nights of the full moon.

The mystical, extradimensional beings known as "The Three Who Are All" gave Jack the power to change into a werewolf at will, while retaining his human mind. He used this ability as a crimefighter. However, on the nights of the full moon, he still changes into a werewolf involuntarily and his mind becomes that of the beast. On those nights, he protects others by locking himself away in an escape-proof room.

In his career as a crimefighter, Werewolf has crossed paths with SPIDER-WOMAN, MOON KNIGHT, TIGRA and others. Once, while on the rampage as a werewolf, Jack Russell was subdued by the West Coast AVENGERS. **MT**

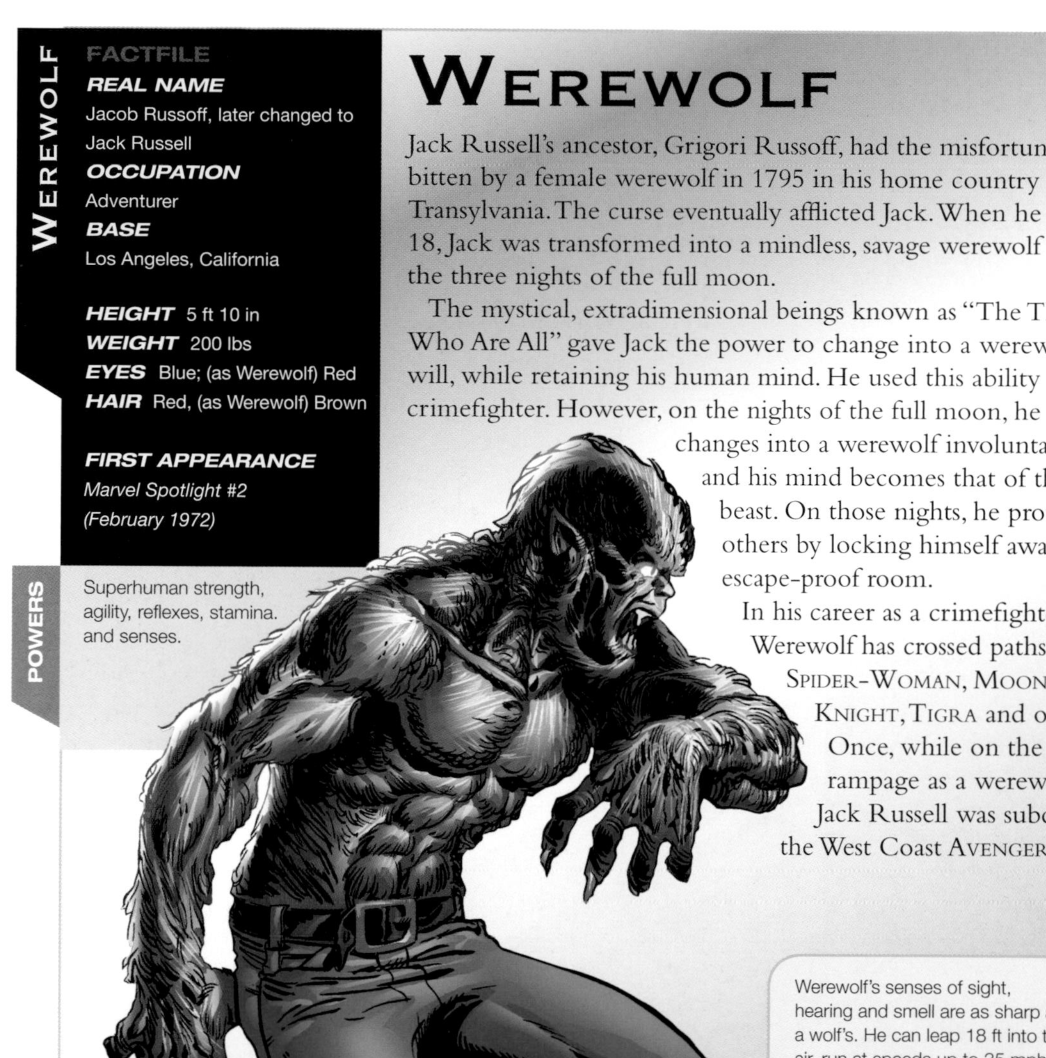

Werewolf's senses of sight, hearing and smell are as sharp as a wolf's. He can leap 18 ft into the air, run at speeds up to 35 mph, and is immune to normal injury.

WHITEMANE

FIRST APPEARANCE Power Pack #1 (August 1984)
REAL NAME Aelfyre Whitemane
OCCUPATION Scientist **BASE** His sentient starship, Friday
HEIGHT 6 ft **WEIGHT** 320 lbs **EYES** Pink **HAIR** White
SPECIAL POWERS/ABILITIES Like all Kymellians, Whitemane was born with the potential to project energy, teleport, and fly. These powers required much practise and training to master.

Aelfyre Whitemane, nicknamed "Whitey" was a scientist of the Kymellian race. He discovered that Dr. James POWER was working on a matter/antimatter converter. Whitey knew the dangers of this device, which had destroyed his homeworld. His message back home was intercepted by the Z'nrx (*see* SNARKS), who wanted to use Dr. Power's invention as a weapon. They shot down Whitey's starship. Near death, the Kymellian transferred his powers to Dr. Power's children, who became the POWER PACK. **MT**

WHITEOUT

FIRST APPEARANCE Uncanny X-Men #249 (October 1989)
REAL NAME Unknown
OCCUPATION Unknown **BASE** The Savage Land
HEIGHT 5 ft 11 in **WEIGHT** 144 lbs
EYES White **HAIR** Unknown
SPECIAL POWERS/ABILITIES Creates flash of brilliant light which has the potential to blind anyone she chooses.

A native of the Savage Land, situated somewhere in Antarctica, little is known about the creature known as Whiteout. She was briefly a member of ZALADANE's Savage Land mutants, and it is thought that her first and only mission with this group involved an attack on the X-MEN in Chile, where that mutant team was searching for their lost team-mate, POLARIS.

Subsequently, Whiteout was a member of Superia's Femizons and their effort to put women in charge of the world. Her appearances since have been both sporadic and fleeting. **AD**

WHIRLWIND

FIRST APPEARANCE Tales to Astonish #50 (December 1963)
REAL NAME David Cannon
OCCUPATION Criminal **BASE** New York State
HEIGHT 6 ft 1 in **WEIGHT** 220 lbs **EYES** Blue **HAIR** Brown
SPECIAL POWERS/ABILITIES Able to revolve at amazingly high speed, rendering himself untouchable; throws wrist blades while spinning, to deadly effect; never becomes dizzy.

David Cannon's career has had almost as many twists and turns as his alter ego: during his life he has been a petty criminal, a circus performer, an ice-skater, a wrestler, and a MASTER OF EVIL. Before he was Whirlwind he called himself the Human Top. His criminal career has been marked by encounters with Dr. Henry PYM and the WASP, with whom he developed something of a love-hate relationship. **AD**

WHITMAN

FIRST APPEARANCE Amazing Spider-Man vol. 1 #196 (September 1979) **REAL NAME** Debra Whitman
OCCUPATION Former secretary at Empire State University
BASE The Midwest
HEIGHT 5 ft 6 in **WEIGHT** 120 lbs **EYES** Green **HAIR** Blonde
SPECIAL POWERS/ABILITIES None; only the strength of a woman of her age and weight who indulges in moderate exercise.

Debra Whitman met Peter Parker while both were students at Empire State University. Whitman worked as a teaching assistant and as the secretary to the dean, Morris Sloan. Debra and Peter began dating, but the romance fell foul of Debra's growing obsession that her boyfriend might be the notorious SPIDER-MAN.

Hoping to calm her down, Peter revealed the truth of his dual identity, but she refused to believe him. Debra eventually moved to the Midwest with her friend Biff Rifkin. **DW**

White Tiger

FIRST APPEARANCE Deadly Hands of Kung Fu #19 (December 1975)
REAL NAME Hector Ayala
OCCUPATION Student **BASE** New York City
HEIGHT *ft *in **WEIGHT** *** lbs **EYES** **** **HAIR** ****
SPECIAL POWERS/ABILITIES Amulet gave him enhanced strength and agility, and an innate understanding of the martial arts.

Student Hector Ayala discovered amulets once worn by the Sons of the Tiger that granted him superhuman strength, speed, agility, and martial arts skills. As the White Tiger, Hector fought crime in his poverty-stricken neighborhood, but he was badly injured during Gideon Mace's campaign to wipe out Super Heroes and retired his costumed identity for years. On Hector's first night back as the White Tiger he was mistaken for a criminal. He ended up shot dead. His amulets have been passed on to his niece, Federal Agent Del Toro, who seems poised to become a new incarnation of the White Tiger. **TB**

White Wolf

FIRST APPEARANCE Black Panther vol. 3 #4 (February 1999)
REAL NAME Hunter **OCCUPATION** Leader of the Hatut Zeraze
BASE Wakanda, later mobile
HEIGHT 6ft 2in **WEIGHT** 210 lbs **EYES** Blue **HAIR** Black
SPECIAL POWERS/ABILITIES A formidable hand-to-hand combatant and master spy. His costume is made of vibranium microweave fabric, protecting him from physical impact.

When his parents died in a plane crash in Wakanda, Africa, Hunter, a Caucasian, was adopted by Wakanda's king, T'Chaka. Later T'Chaka fathered an heir, T'Challa, and Hunter lost his status as the king's favored son, developing a jealous hatred of T'Challa. Hunter was made the leader of the Hatut Zeraze ("Dogs of War"), who served as the Wakandan secret police. But when T'Challa became king, he disbanded the Hatut Zeraze, objecting to their brutality. Hunter and his men left Wakanda and became mercenaries. T'Challa and Hunter became enemies as the Black Panther and the White Wolf. **PS**

Whizzer

Bitten by a poisonous snake as a child, Bob Frank's scientist father gave him a transfusion of mongoose blood in an attempt to save his life. This transfusion sparked Bob's latent mutant abilities, and granted him superspeed. Reaching manhood, Bob became the Whizzer, and set out to battle crime and the Axis powers. During the World War II, the Whizzer was a member of the Liberty Legion, where he met Miss America, his future wife and then the Invaders. After the war, both the Whizzer and Miss America served in the All-Winners Squad; they then retired from the heroic life to raise children.

Tragically, Miss America died in childbirth, and the Whizzer's son was a horrifically mutated radioactive mutant known as Nuklo.

The Whizzer briefly came out of retirement to fight with the Avengers.

FACTFILE
REAL NAME
Robert Frank
OCCUPATION
Adventurer
BASE
New York City

HEIGHT 5 ft 10 in
WEIGHT 180 lbs
EYES Brown
HAIR Brown, later gray

FIRST APPEARANCE
Giant-Size Avengers #1 (August 1974)

POWERS
The Whizzer possessed superhuman speed, which allowed him to run at several hundred miles per hour.

The Whizzer was so fast he could become a human whirlwind by running around in circles.

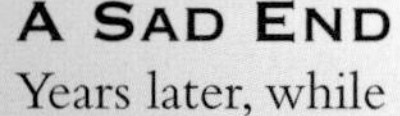

A Sad End

Years later, while trying to cure his son's condition, the Whizzer was attacked and suffered a fatal heart attack. The Whizzer should not be confused with the member of the Squadron Sinister, who now operates as Speed Demon, nor with the member of the other-Earth Squadron Supreme. **TB**

The rigors of a super-heroic life proved too much for the Whizzer at his advanced age.

Wild Thing

FIRST APPEARANCE J2 #5 (February 1999)
REAL NAME Rina Logun **OCCUPATION** High-school student
BASE Saddle River, New Jersey
HEIGHT 5 ft 2 in **WEIGHT** 98 lbs **EYES** Brown **HAIR** Black
SPECIAL POWERS/ABILITIES Superhuman strength, speed, agility, and a healing power giving immunity from poisons, gases, or drugs; psychic claws can cut through virtually any substance.

In a possible future, the former assassin Elektra marries Wolverine of the X-Men and has a daughter. Named Rina, she inherits many of her father's physical powers and also possesses the mutant ability to generate psychic claws. Ignoring her parents' objections, Rina hones her powers and becomes Wild Thing. When J2, son of the original Juggernaut, reveals himself to the public, she hunts him down and challenges him to a fight, which Wolverine breaks up. Rina later joins with Spider-Girl and the Avengers to prevent the god Loki from ending the age of heroes. **TD**

Will O'the Wisp

Jackson Arvad's boss at the Brand Corporation, James Melvin, was constantly driving the scientist to devise new technologies. A lab accident led to Jackson becoming trapped in an electro-magnetic field and Melvin left him to die. However, Jackson clung to life, despite a number of set-backs, and found that he could now manipulate all the molecules in his body. He initially had some difficulty controlling his mutation, but when he finally overcame these problems, he brought both Melvin and the Brand Corporation down. **AD**

FACTFILE
REAL NAME
Jackson Arvad
OCCUPATION
Scientist; adventurer
BASE
Mobile

HEIGHT 6 ft 1 in
WEIGHT 195 lbs
EYES White
HAIR Blond

FIRST APPEARANCE
Amazing Spider-Man #235 (December 1982)

POWERS
Controls sub-atomic particles in his body to become intangible, fly, and increase strength; uses limited telepathic ability to compel others to do his will.

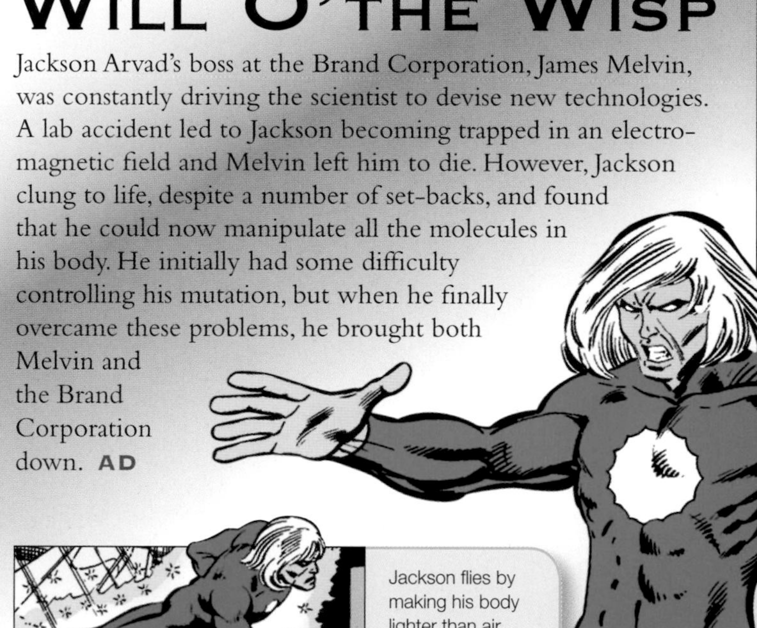

Jackson flies by making his body lighter than air and projecting excess molecules behind him.

Wild Child

FIRST APPEARANCE Alpha Flight #1 (August 1983)
REAL NAME Kyle Gibney
OCCUPATION None **BASE** Mobile
HEIGHT 5ft 8in **WEIGHT** 152 lbs **EYES** Green-blue **HAIR** Blond
SPECIAL POWERS/ABILITIES Superb hand-to-hand combatant; has superhuman senses and claw-like fingernails; can see in the dark.

A traumatic and abusive childhood turned Kyle Gibney, or Wild Child, into a desperately unstable and unhappy adult. After he was thrown out by his parents when his feral mutation manifested, a clandestine organisation found him and sought to exaggerate his bestial nature. Unable to control his animal urges, Wild Child began to drift and although he has had help from various individuals and organisations he has repeatedly reverted to his bestial nature. Alpha Flight and Omega Flight, Wolverine and Aurora, Weapon X and Department H—they have all taken an interest in Wild Child, but he remains a deeply unsettled individual. **AD**

Wilson, Jim

FIRST APPEARANCE Incredible Hulk #131 (September 1970)
REAL NAME Jim Wilson
OCCUPATION Former thief **BASE** Mobile
HEIGHT 6 ft **WEIGHT** 200 lbs **EYES** Brown **HAIR** Black
SPECIAL POWERS/ABILITIES No superhuman powers, but a loyal friend despite—or because of—his tough upbringing.

Growing up as tough street kid no one ever gave Jim Wilson a break. So it was perhaps no surprise that he was destined to become friends with that well-known outsider the Hulk. Jim was homeless and starving when he snatched a woman's purse. However, he became overcome with guilt and left the purse where the woman could find it. Jim was hiding out in an abandoned tenement when he encountered the Hulk and offered him his last candy bar. Wilson agreed to help the Hulk find Banner and avoid the army, and the Hulk's sense of loyalty to Wilson grew. Sadly, a few years later, Jim Wilson would die from AIDS. **MT**

Windshear

FIRST APPEARANCE Alpha Flight Vol. 1 #95 (April 1991)
REAL NAME Colin Ashworth Hume
OCCUPATION Adventurer **BASE** England
HEIGHT 6 ft **WEIGHT** 183 lbs **EYES** Brown **HAIR** Brown
SPECIAL POWERS/ABILITIES Mutant ability to create solid molecules of air and project them as force waves; can transform liquid into gas; Roxxon armor enables him to fly.

A former operative of Roxxon Oil, Windshear used his air-shaping abilities to further Roxxon's corrupt schemes. Roxxon supplied him with a battlesuit that enabled him to fly; the suit was also fitted with a radio receiver and a retractable plexiglass visor. In time, Windshear became disillusioned with Roxxon, and joined the Canadian superteam Alpha Flight to fight on the side of heroism.

When the Canadian government temporarily disbanded Alpha Flight, Windshear used the opportunity to retire from adventuring. He returned to his native England and opened a curio shop selling his own hard-air constructs. **DW**

Wind Warrior

FIRST APPEARANCE Thor Vol. 1 #395 (September 1988)
REAL NAME Pamela Shaw **OCCUPATION** Adventurer
BASE New York City **HEIGHT** (Shaw) 5 ft, 2 in; (Wind Warrior) 5 ft 11 in **WEIGHT** (Shaw) 135 lbs; (Wind Warrior) 143 lbs
EYES Blue **HAIR** (Shaw) Auburn; (Wind Warrior) Unknown
SPECIAL POWERS/ABILITIES Enhanced strength; flies by controlling wind updrafts; transforms herself into a living whirlwind.

Pamela Shaw was driven to despair after her child died and her husband left her, and was hospitalized following a failed suicide attempt. There, the death god Seth (see Gods of Heliopolis) transformed her and two other patients into superhumans so he could set them against the Asgardian champion Hogun the Grim (a member of the Warriors Three). As Wind Warrior, Shaw joined Earth Lord and Skyhawk to form a team they called Earth Force. Later, learning of Seth's malevolent intentions, Earth Force turned on its creator and the members became independent agents. **DW**

Wing

FIRST APPEARANCE Marvel Premiere #19 (November 1974)
REAL NAME Colleen Wing
OCCUPATION Private detective **BASE** New York City
HEIGHT 5 ft 9 in **WEIGHT** 135 lbs **EYES** Blue **HAIR** Brown
SPECIAL POWERS/ABILITIES Excellent swordswoman and martial arts expert, also a very fine detective.

The partner of ex-police officer Misty Knight, Colleen Wing is one half of Nightwing Restorations Ltd, a private detective agency. Half Japanese, Colleen was raised in Japan and trained as a samurai warrior. Meeting Misty soon after arriving in New York, Colleen became her main support when Misty lost her right arm in the line of duty. Colleen suggested they go into business together. Nightwing Restorations is now an established organization, but how it will fare against its new rival, X-Factor Investigations, is yet to be seen. **AD**

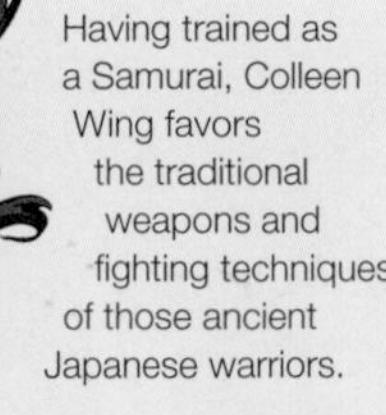

Having trained as a Samurai, Colleen Wing favors the traditional weapons and fighting techniques of those ancient Japanese warriors.

Wingfoot

FIRST APPEARANCE Fantastic Four #50 (May 1966)
REAL NAME Wyatt Wingfoot **OCCUPATION** Adventurer
BASE Fantastic Four HQ, Keewazi Reservation, Oklahoma
HEIGHT 6 ft 5 in **WEIGHT** 269 lbs **EYES** Brown **HAIR** Black
SPECIAL POWERS/ABILITIES No superhuman powers, but extremely skilled in hand-to-hand combat; also a brilliant horseman, tracker, motorcyclist, and trainer of animals.

In addition to his excellent combat skills and his great ability to work with animals, Wyatt Wingfoot is also an expert motorcyclist.

Wyatt Wingfoot is a member of the Keewazi tribe of Native Americans. Born on a reservation in Oklahoma, Wingfoot went to Metro College near New York City, where Johnny Storm, the Human Torch, was his roommate. The two became close friends, and soon Wingfoot was accompanying the Fantastic Four on their adventures proving to be a valuable ally.

Wingfoot eventually went to live with the Fantastic Four and began a romance with Jennifer Walters, the She-Hulk. However, when oil was discovered on the Keewazi reservation, he returned home to help his people manage their newfound resource and ensure they were not exploited by multinational oil companies. **MT**

Wisdom, Peter

FIRST APPEARANCE Excalibur Vol. 1 #86 (February 1995)
REAL NAME Peter Wisdom
OCCUPATION Adventurer **BASE** United Kingdom
HEIGHT 5 ft 9 in **WEIGHT** 140 lbs **EYES** Hazel **HAIR** Black
SPECIAL POWERS/ABILITIES Possesses the mutant power to create intense heat in the form of "hot knives," which he then projects from his hands.

Peter Wisdom was a special operative for Black Air, a British government organization that investigated paranormal phenomena. He discovered that Black Air was secretly working with the London branch of the Hellfire Club, procuring extraterrestrial weaponry and performing genetic experiments on humans. As a result, Wisdom turned against Black Air and joined the Super Hero team Excalibur.

Wisdom eventually left Excalibur and took over the team of young mutants known as X-Force. Wisdom was seemingly shot dead during an X-Force mission. However, he turned up alive and joined a new, second British-based Excalibur team. **PS**

Wiz Kid

FIRST APPEARANCE X-Terminators #1 (October 1988)
REAL NAME Takashi "Taki" Matsuya
OCCUPATION Student **BASE** New York City
HEIGHT 4 ft 7 in **WEIGHT** 87 lbs **EYES** Brown **HAIR** Black
SPECIAL POWERS/ABILITIES Mutant ability to technoform machinery: able to mold objects into any configuration that his imagination can conceive.

The accident that killed his parents, left Takashi Matsuya (Taki to his friends) wheelchairbound and depressed. Taki focused his attentions on building highly sophisticated devices; when his ability to technoform objects manifested, his engineering abilities became even more prodigious. Captured by N'ASTIRH, Taki agreed to create a bridge between the Limbo dimension and Earth. However, when he realized the devastation being caused, Taki helped to foil N'astirh's plan. Taki has since returned to school. **AD**

Wizard

FIRST APPEARANCE Strange Tales #102 (November 1962)
REAL NAME Bentley Whitman
OCCUPATION Criminal **BASE** New York City
HEIGHT 5 ft 8 in **WEIGHT** 150 lbs **EYES** Hazel **HAIR** Brown
SPECIAL POWERS/ABILITIES Costume features an anti-gravity disk that enables him to fly, and "wonder gloves," which give him heightened strength and a protective force field.

Once an inventor and escapologist who lived up to his stage name the Wizard, Bentley Whitman was furious that his fame was being eclipsed by the new Super Heroes, especially Johnny Storm, the HUMAN TORCH. Determined to regain mass acclaim, the Wizard turned to villainy, and tried to destroy the Torch and his sister, Invisible Girl (*see* INVISIBLE WOMAN).

After several defeats, the Wizard organized a sinister counterpart to the FANTASTIC FOUR comprised of himself, the TRAPSTER, the SANDMAN and MEDUSA. This team, known as the FRIGHTFUL FOUR, has challenged the heroic FF on numerous occasions, and come perhaps the closest to destroying them. **TB**

Wolfsbane

Born in Scotland, the orphaned Rahne Sinclair was raised by a fanatical minister, Reverend Craig. At puberty, her mutant power to transform into a wolf emerged. Believing she was possessed by the devil, Reverend Craig led a mob in pursuit of Rahne, who fled in wolf form. Shot by one of the mob, Rahne transformed back to human form. Geneticist Dr. Moira MACTAGGERT rescued Rahne, and made Rahne her ward.

Rahne joined the NEW MUTANTS, organized by MacTaggert's colleague PROFESSOR X, remaining with the team after Cable reorganized it into X-FORCE. Sinclair eventually joined the second version of X-FACTOR. After X-Force collapsed, Sinclair lived with MacTaggert at her Muir Island base.

After MacTaggert's death, Sinclair taught at the Xavier Institute. She now works for Jamie Madrox's X-Factor Investigations. **PS**

FACTFILE
REAL NAME
Rahne Sinclair
OCCUPATION
Adventurer
BASE
Mutant Town, New York City

HEIGHT (lupine form) Up to 12 ft standing on hind legs
WEIGHT (lupine form) Up to 1,050 lbs
EYES Blue-green
HAIR Reddish-brown

FIRST APPEARANCE
Marvel Graphic Novel #4: The New Mutants (1982)

WOLFSBANE

POWERS
Mutant ability to transform herself into a wolf while retaining most of her human intellect, or into a transitional form which combines human and lupine aspects. Has more acute senses in lupine form.

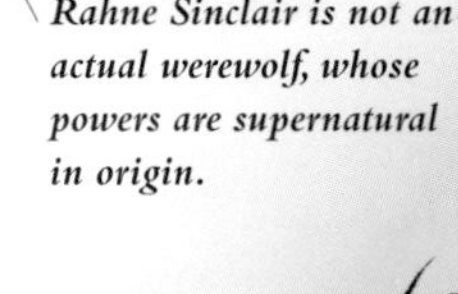

Rahne Sinclair is not an actual werewolf, whose powers are supernatural in origin.

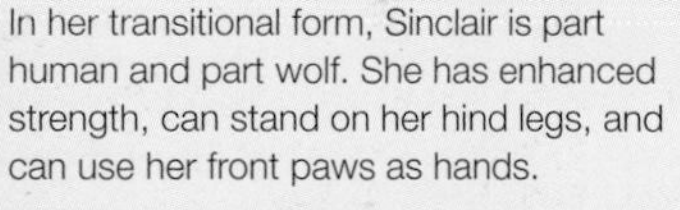

In her transitional form, Sinclair is part human and part wolf. She has enhanced strength, can stand on her hind legs, and can use her front paws as hands.

WOLVERINE

The best there is at what he does—but what he does isn't pretty!

WOLVERINE

FACTFILE
REAL NAME
James Howlett; often goes by Logan
OCCUPATION
Adventurer
BASE
The Xavier Academy, Salem Center, Westchester, New York

HEIGHT 5 ft 3 in
WEIGHT 195 lbs
EYES Brown
HAIR Black

FIRST APPEARANCE
Incredible Hulk #180 (October 1974)

POWERS
Wolverine possesses a "healing factor" that allows him to recover from almost any injury in seconds. His skeleton has been laced with the unbreakable metal Adamantium, which makes his bones unshatterable. Wolverine also possesses three foot-long adamantium claws that retract from either hand, capable of slicing through almost any substance known to man.

ALLIES/FOES
ALLIES X-Men, New Avengers, Nick Fury.

FOES Sabretooth, Omega Red, Silver Samura.

ISSUE #1
After a successful limited series in 1982, Wolverine was awarded his own ongoing title in November, 1988, a series devoted to his solo adventures apart from his fellow X-Men. The title has been published ever since.

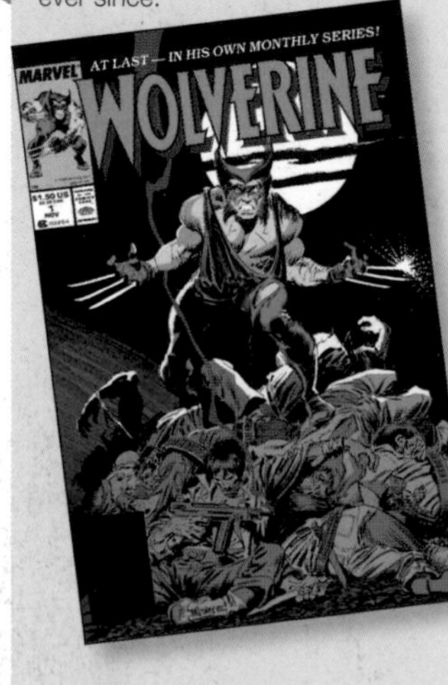

Childhood traumas were repressed by a mutant healing factor.

Born at the turn of the century, James Howlett, the man who would one day become known and feared as Wolverine, was a sickly child. But he was also born a mutant, gifted with the remarkable ability to heal virtually instantaneously from almost any wound. He also had razor-sharp claws made of bone, a fact he first became aware of when, during a domestic dispute, he accidentally unsheathed his claws for the first time, killing his assailant.

ESSENTIAL STORYLINES
- ***Origin #1–6***
The secret beginnings of Wolverine are revealed for the first time.
- ***Wolverine Limited Series #1–4***
Wolverine must wage a war of honor in Japan to protect the woman he loves, and to prove that he is more man than beast.
- ***Wolverine vol. 2 #21–34***
Brainwashed by Hydra, Wolverine is sent to kill the greatest Super Heroes in the Marvel Universe.

THE WANDERER

Forced by his nature to leave behind the pampered world in which he grew up, Howlett began a life of wandering, moving from place to place. His own healing factor acted upon his mind to suppress the traumatic memories of his childhood, leaving him a man without a past. Over the years, he took on a succession of menial jobs, building up his strength and stamina, and losing himself in the repetitiveness of simple work. By this point, he had adopted the name Logan, after the groundskeeper at the Howlett estate, who might have been his real father. But both the man and the estate were long lost among the indistinct memories buried deep within his mind.

A haunted figure, Logan spent much of his youth wandering the world.

Logan lived the life of a drifter, moving from one adventure to another, learning all there was to know about fighting along the way. He fought in both world wars, spent time in Japan, and made his home-away-from-home in the tiny city of Madripoor, a haven for smugglers and pirates. His miraculous healing factor prolonged his natural lifespan, making him appear far younger than he truly was. For a time, he operated as a secret agent for the Canadian government, a vocation and association that would come to have dire ramifications.

A secret project of the Canadian government was attempting to create a more perfect breed of operative, a super-soldier along the lines of the

Wolverine's claws have been reinforced with adamantium

With an unbreakable adamantium skeleton, retractable razor-sharp claws, and a healing factor that also prolongs his lifespan, Wolverine is an almost unbeatable opponent.

Selected as a subject for enhancement due to his incredible healing factor, the mysterious forces behind the Canadian Weapon X project laced Logan's skeleton and claws with the unbreakable metal, adamantium.

famous Captain America. Kidnapped off the streets and used as a guinea pig, Logan, now referred to as Weapon X, was subjected to unimaginable pain and tortures as his captors attempted to mold him to their liking. Realizing that Logan's healing factor would allow him to survive procedures which would kill any ordinary man, the scientists of the Weapon X project laced his skeleton with a nearly-unbreakable metal alloy known as adamantium. They also attempted to control his mind through brainwashing, which only served to scramble Logan's memories even further.

But eventually, they could contain Logan no longer. Reduced to a bestial state, more animal than man, Logan broke free, annihilated the Weapon X project and all of its personnel, and fled into the Canadian wilderness. He lived there for many years, hunting small game to survive. But a chance meeting with James MacDonald Hudson and his wife Heather put Logan on the road to humanity. They took the beast-man back into their homes, and nursed him back to health.

Hudson himself was a scientist doing work for the Canadian government, where he has developed a battlesuit that he hoped would make him a hero on a par with the newly-revealed American group, the Fantastic Four.

A New Name

Attempting to put together an equivalent team of Super Heroes in the service of the Canadian government, Hudson brought Logan into Alpha Flight, where he was given the codename Wolverine. Hudson had intended Wolverine to be the leader of this new strike force, but all that changed when a man in a wheelchair entered the scene.

The man was Professor Charles Xavier (Professor X), the mutant telepath who had founded the clandestine team of mutant Super Heroes called the X-Men.

Wolverine leaped at the chance to join Professor Charles Xavier's mutant team of X-Men.

Recognizing Wolverine's mutant nature, Professor X offered him a place among others of his kind. Desiring to escape the rules and regulations of life as a government operative, Wolverine accepted Xavier's offer, coming to live in his School for Gifted Youngsters, which doubled as the X-Men's headquarters.

At last Wolverine had found his place in the world. While his savage nature initially alienated him from his fellow mutants, he found friendship among them, and came to be one of the strongest believers in Professor X's dream of co-existence between mutants and normal humans—though this belief was tinged with a healthy cynicism. Although he continually struggles with the darker, animalistic side of himself, Wolverine has found honor, and truly regained his humanity as an X-Man.

Recently, as a result of the world-altering adventure known as House of M, Wolverine regained all of his memories of his past. Where this newly-recovered knowledge will take him in his life's journey remains to be seen. **TB**

As a result of the reality-altering powers of the Scarlet Witch, Wolverine gained possession of all of his lost memories. This knowledge remained with Logan even after the world returned to its normal state.

Wonder Man

The virtually immortal hero

WONDER MAN

FACTFILE

REAL NAME
Simon Williams

OCCUPATION
Adventurer

BASE
New York City

HEIGHT 6 ft 2 in
WEIGHT 380 lbs
EYES Red
HAIR Gray

FIRST APPEARANCE
Avengers vol. 1 #9 (October 1964)

POWERS
Body composed of ionic energy, which provides enhanced strength, stamina, flight, longevity, virtual invulnerability, and freedom from the need to eat or even breathe. Wonder Man is virtually immortal because his ionic body reforms whatever injuries he receives.

Wonder Man's body is now composed entirely of ionic energy.

Born the wealthy inheritor of a family business, Simon Williams ran the company into near-bankruptcy and embezzled funds to invest with the criminal MAGGIA. Nursing a grudge toward the competing Stark Industries and its champion, IRON MAN, Williams underwent ionic energy treatments from BARON ZEMO and the original MASTERS OF EVIL. As Wonder Man, he infiltrated the AVENGERS, but refused to follow through on Zemo's scheme to destroy the team and perished after aiding his Avengers teammates. The homicidal robot ULTRON later copied Wonder Man's brain patterns to help program the android VISION.

ESSENTIAL STORYLINES
- ***Avengers Vol. 1 #9*** Wonder Man makes his debut as a villain, attempting to infiltrate the Avengers while secretly working for the Masters of Evil.
- ***Wonder Man #1–29*** Wonder Man gets his own series in the early 1990s, which runs for 29 issues.
- ***West Coast Avengers #2*** Wonder Man joins the West Coast Avengers, where he falls in love with teammate the Scarlet Witch.

Wonder Man has adventured throughout known space and encountered thousands of alien cultures.

BACK TO LIFE

Believed dead, Wonder Man hibernated in an ionic coma until restored, in a zombie-like state, by his unstable brother Eric, the GRIM REAPER. The resurrected Wonder Man returned to the Avengers, befriending the BEAST and forging a close bond with the Vision, whom he viewed as a brother due to their shared brain patterns. Wonder Man became a part time actor and stuntman, and also helped to establish the WEST COAST AVENGERS. At this time he realized he loved the SCARLET WITCH, who had since married the Vision.

After the Vision's dismemberment and reassembly, Wonder Man refused to allow his brain patterns to be copied a second time, driving a wedge between him and the Scarlet Witch. Nevertheless, as time went by, the two began a romance, and Wonder Man pursued a successful acting career in Hollywood movies.

SECOND CHANCES

After the West Coast Avengers disbanded, Wonder Man joined Iron Man's spinoff crew, FORCE WORKS. On the team's first mission, KREE agents apparently killed Wonder Man. However, the hero lived on as a disembodied being of ionic energy, occasionally materializing in a semi-corporeal state through the powers of the Scarlet Witch. The Grim Reaper attempted to exploit this spectral Wonder Man by assembling a new LEGION OF THE UNLIVING to attack he Avengers.

Eventually, Wonder Man successfully reconstituted himself, and he has since established the non-profit Second Chances Foundation, and struck up a romance with Carol Danvers (see WARBIRD). **DW**

Wonder Man and his teammates in the West Coast Avengers restrain a rebuilt Vision.

Wong

FACTFILE

REAL NAME
Wong

OCCUPATION
Manservant

BASE
Dr Strange's Sanctum Sanctorum, Bleeker Street, Greenwich Village, New York City

HEIGHT 5 ft 8 in
WEIGHT 140 lbs
EYES Brown
HAIR Blond; Wong currently shaves his head

FIRST APPEARANCE
Strange Tales #110 (July 1963)

POWERS
Wong is an expert martial artist, although he has not actively practiced his skills in several years. He is a highly efficient manservant with a variety of homemaking skills, and utterly loyal to Doctor Strange.

The youngest surviving member of a bloodline whose members served the mystical ANCIENT ONE, Wong was offered into service of the master mage at the time of his birth. He was tutored and became skilled in those arts which would make him of value to the Ancient One, including a deep study of the martial arts of Kamar-Taj.

When Wong became an adult, the Ancient One dispatched him to the United States, so that he could become the manservant of the Ancient One's former disciple, DOCTOR STRANGE.

Since that time, Wong has been a faithful retainer to Strange, dealing with all the trivial earthly matters that would otherwise distract the master sorcerer from his noble mission: defending the Earth from mystic peril. **TB**

Wong journeyed from a remote Tibetan monastery to New York's Greenwich Village to serve Doctor Strange.

As well as possessing some minor mystical skills, Wong is an excellent cook.

Wrecker

FIRST APPEARANCE Thor #148 (January 1968)
REAL NAME Dirk Garthwaite
OCCUPATION Criminal **BASE** Mobile
HEIGHT 6 ft 3 in **WEIGHT** 320 lbs **EYES** Blue **HAIR** Brown
SPECIAL POWERS/ABILITIES Superhuman strength and invulnerability; mental link to his enchanted crowbar allows him to transfer his powers into the crowbar, and then back to himself.

Wrecker was violent criminal who used a crowbar to demolish the scenes of his crimes thereby hindering investigation. When he was accidentally given magic powers by KARNILLA, the Norn Queen, Wrecker went on a rampage that attracted the attention of THOR. Placed in prison by the Asgardian automaton named Destroyer, Wrecker escaped with three other inmates who took on the costumed identities of THUNDERBALL, Bulldozer, and Piledriver, collectively known as the Wrecking Crew. This foursome later joined BARON ZEMO's MASTERS OF EVIL. **MT**

Wraith

FIRST APPEARANCE Marvel Team-Up #48 (August 1976)
REAL NAME Brian DeWolff **OCCUPATION** Vigilante crimefighter
BASE New York City **HEIGHT** 5 ft 11 in **WEIGHT** 190 lbs
EYES Blue **HAIR** Reddish-blond
SPECIAL POWERS/ABILITIES Able to affect the minds of others, controlling them, casting illusions, or rendering himself invisible; also able to evade Spider-Man's "spider-sense."

Woodgod

FIRST APPEARANCE Marvel Premiere #31 (August 1976)
REAL NAME Woodgod
OCCUPATION Lawgiver of the Changelings
BASE The Rocky Mountains, Colorado
HEIGHT 6 ft 3 in **WEIGHT** 265 lbs
EYES Red **HAIR** Reddish-brown
SPECIAL POWERS/ABILITIES Woodgod possesses superhuman strength and an immunity to nerve gas.

Woodgod is a genetically engineered being, created by scientists David and Ellen Pace. Combining human and animal genetic material, the Paces created Woodgod, who resembles the half-human, half-goat Satyr of Greek myth. The townsfolk of Liberty, near the Pace's farm in New Mexico, convinced themselves that Woodgod was a dangerous monster. They tried to kill the creature using a canister of a deadly nerve gas invented by David Pace. Woodgod proved to be immune to the gas, but the Paces were both killed. The Grief-stricken Woodgod discovered the Paces' notes and created a race of half-human, half-animal beings, which he called Changelings. The Changelings found a secret home away from humanity in the Colorado Rockies. Woodgod dreams that one day the Changelings will be able to come out of hiding and live in harmony with the human race. **MT**

Responding to an incident, police officer Brian DeWolff was crippled when a bullet lodged in his spine. In his effort to heal his son, Phillip DeWolff transformed him into a superpowered, flesh-and-blood automaton that only he could control. Turning his son into a vigilante named the Wraith, Phillip's control of Brian came to an end following the intervention of SPIDER-MAN and IRON FIST. Free at last, Brian continued his career as a costumed crimefighter, until slain by the SCOURGE. **AD**

X-Cutioner

FIRST APPEARANCE X-Men Annual #1 (1970)
REAL NAME Carl Denti
OCCUPATION Vigilante; former FBI agent **BASE** Washington, DC
HEIGHT 6 ft 1 in **WEIGHT** 210 lbs **EYES** Brown **HAIR** Brown
SPECIAL POWERS/ABILITIES Possesses neuro-stun gauntlet, psi-lance, laser sword, teleporter, cloaking field, phasing unit, grappling claws, propulsion boots and a genetic scanner. Shi'ar battle-armor enhances strength to almost superhuman levels.

Special Agent Denti had been partnered with Fred Duncan, who had secretly aided Professor X on many occasions. Duncan often stored equipment and weaponry that the X-Men had confiscated from alien races and other super-menaces. After Duncan was murdered by unknown parties, Denti vowed revenge. He discovered Duncan's connections to the X-Men and used the impounded weaponry to hunt down mutants who had not been convicted for their crimes. He crossed paths with the X-Men, and also assisted the Punisher on occasion. After Denti gave up his hunt, he was briefly replaced by a second X-Cutioner who was an alternate reality version of Gambit, but later died in action.

X-Corps

FIRST APPEARANCE Uncanny X-Men #401 (January 2002)
BASE Paris, France
MEMBERS AND POWERS
Blob Superhuman size and strength; can create a gravity field that makes him immovable [2]. **Avalanche** Generates destructive vibrations from his hands [2]. **Banshee** Projects sonic screech [3]. **Husk** Biomorph: sheds skin to reveal transformed body beneath [4]. **Jubilee II** Projects "fireworks" from her fingers [5].

Following the death of his lover, Moira MacTaggert, and the collapse of the Massachusetts Academy where he was headmaster, Sean Cassidy lost his way. Establishing X-Corps, a paramilitary operation, Sean sought to enforce good behaviour between mutants. After releasing a number of criminal mutants from jail, he imprisoned the telepathic mutant, Mastermind and used her to control these mutants' activities. It wasn't long before the organization began to collapse, a process accelerated by the shapechanger Mystique who brought X-Corps to its knees, by freeing Mastermind and stabbing Sean in the throat. AD

X-Factor

X-FACTOR I
1 Archangel ***2*** Iceman
3 Marvel Girl ***4*** Cyclops
5 Beast

The name X-Factor has been used by a succession of mutant teams over the years. Originally, it was an alias adopted by the original X-Men, who decided to go undercover as mutant hunters so as to be able to secretly recruit and train young mutants. Eventually, they abandoned this deception, but kept the name until they rejoined the X-Men proper. After that, the X-Factor title was adopted by the team of government-sanctioned mutants led by Havok, who maintained it through several line-up shifts and changes of mission statement. Most recently, the name was appropriated by Jaime Madrox, one of the former members of Havok's X-Factor, as the name of his Mutant Town detective agency. TB

FACTFILE
MEMBERS AND POWERS
MADROX
Creates duplicates of himself.
STRONG GUY
Transforms kinetic energy directed against himself into strength.
SIRYN
Vocal chords can create sonic blasts.
M
Super-strength, durability and flight.
RICTOR
Currently powerless; formerly could creates seismic shifts in the Earth.
BUTTERFLY
Instinctively understands causality, and creates a desired effect through a small action.
WOLFSBANE
Can transform into a wolflike creature.
BASE
Mutant Town, New York City

FIRST APPEARANCE
X-Factor #1 (June 2002)

X-Factor II

The second X-Factor team's headquarters was in a high-tech facility located in the Blue Ridge Mountains in Virginia.

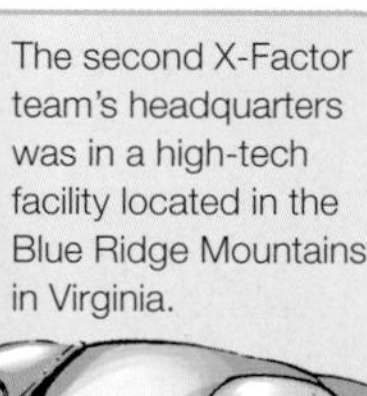

X-FACTOR II
1 Wolfsbane ***2*** Polaris
3 Multiple Man, with two duplicates
4 Strong Guy ***5*** Havok

Cable, founder and mentor of X-Force.

X-Force

Professor X founded a young mutant team, the New Mutants, for training. After Xavier had journeyed into outer space and a new headmaster, Magneto, had come and gone, Cable became the team's mentor. He trained his young charges to become soldiers against mutant threats and renamed the team X-Force. The initial roster included Boom Boom (later Meltdown) and Cannonball, Feral, Shatterstar, Warpath, and the shapeshifter Copycat, who posed as Cable's ally Domino. The real Domino later joined X-Force, as did Bedlam, Caliban, Moonstar, Rictor, Siryn, and Sunspot.

After Cable left, former British intelligence agent Peter Wisdom briefly took over as leader, turning the team into an even more aggressive commando squad. X-Force then disbanded.

Two other teams have been called X-Force. The first, predating Cable's group, consisted of members of the US armed forces who underwent artificial mutation. A third group briefly usurped the name "X-Force" before adopting the more original name X-Statix. **PS**

X-FORCE
1 Bedlam *2* Domino *3* Cannonball *4* Danielle Moonstar *5* Warpath (Proudstar) *6* Meltdown (Boom Boom) *7* Sunspot *8* Siryn

X-Force

FACTFILE

NOTABLE MEMBERS

BEDLAM (Jesse Aaronson)
Can disrupt electronic devices.

DOMINO
Can alter luck in her favor, formidable combatant.

CANNONBALL
Can propel himself through the air by releasing energy

DANIELLE MOONSTAR
Could create images from the minds of others

WARPATH (Proudstar)
Superhuman strength, speed, and durability.

MELTDOWN (Boom Boom)
Creates explosive energy balls.

SUNSPOT
Absorbs solar energy for superhuman strength

SIRYN Sonic scream

BASE
Various

FIRST APPEARANCE
X-Force #1
(August 1991)

X-Man

Even on the alternate Earth known as the Age of Apocalypse, Mister Sinister is as obsessed with the progeny of Jean Grey and Scott Summers (*see* Cyclops) as the Mister Sinister of Earth-616. After obtaining genetic material from these two individuals, he created their child artificially, naming him Nathan Grey. By greatly accelerating the child's growth and development Sinister intended to use Nathan's mutant powers to fight Apocalypse.

Ultimately, the Age of Apocalypse timeline was doomed. After killing Sinister—an act which gave him no pleasure—Nate managed to escape to the mainstream Earth. Following his arrival he made it his goal to prevent this Earth from suffering the same dystopian fate. Although initially at odds with the X-Men, he eventually joined the team, before becoming a shaman and dedicating himself to healing and guiding others. Sadly, Nate's life was to end prematurely when he sacrificed himself to protect his adopted home reality. **AD**

When moved to anger, X-Man's psionic fury was almost unstoppable.

X-Man

FACTFILE

REAL NAME
Nathan "Nate" Grey

OCCUPATION
Shaman

BASE
Mobile

HEIGHT 5 ft 9 in
WEIGHT 171 lbs
EYES Blue
HAIR Brown

FIRST APPEARANCE
X-Man #1
(March 1995)

POWERS
A telepath of vast power; able to read and control minds, project his astral form across the world, and create complex psionic illusions, and "psionic spikes." Also possessed considerable telikinetic powers, allowing him to move heavy objects at will.

X-Men

Earth's mightiest team

X-MEN

FACTFILE

MEMBERS AND POWERS

PROFESSOR X (Charles Xavier)
Telepathy
CYCLOPS (Scott Summers)
Optic power beams
PHOENIX (Marvel Girl I, Jean Grey)
Telepathy, telekinesis
ARCHANGEL (Angel, Warren Worthington III)
Wings enabling flight
BEAST (Henry McCoy)
Superhuman strength and agility
ICEMAN (Bobby Drake)
Generates intense cold
COLOSSUS (Peter Rasputin)
Turns to "organic steel"
NIGHTCRAWLER (Kurt Wagner)
Teleportation
ROGUE (Real name unrevealed)
Absorbs memories and abilities
SHADOWCAT (Kitty Pryde)
"Phases" through solid objects
STORM (Ororo Munroe)
Controls weather
WOLVERINE (Logan)
Adamantium skeleton and claws

BASE The Xavier Institute, Salem Center, New York State

FIRST APPEARANCE
X-Men #1 (September 1963)

ALLIES/FOES

ALLIES The New Mutants, Excalibur, X-Factor, Generation X, the Fantastic Four, the Avengers, Spider-Man, Doctor Strange

FOES Magneto, the Juggernaut, the Sentinels, Apocalypse, Mister Sinister, Mystique, Brotherhood of Evil Mutants, the Hellfire Club, the Brood

ISSUE #1

Professor X trains his X-Men and the team are confronted with arch-enemy Magneto.

The X-Men are a team of superhuman mutants that was founded by Professor Charles Xavier (Professor X), who is not only a mutant himself, but is also one of the world's leading authorities on mutation. In founding the X-Men, Xavier had two principal purposes. First, he sought to find young mutants and to train them in utilizing their superhuman powers. Second, Xavier intended the X-Men to serve as a combat team to defend "ordinary" humans against attack by other mutants. Further, Xavier recognizes that "normal" humans tend to fear and distrust the mutants who are appearing in their midst, and that therefore mutants often suffer persecution.

XAVIER'S DREAM

In founding the X-Men, Xavier created a community of mutants living together on his estate. Xavier is a visionary who hopes to help bring about peaceful coexistence between mutants and the rest of the human race. The X-Men are dedicated to this goal, which they call "Xavier's dream." Xavier has explained that he named the team "X-Men" after the "extra" powers that his mutant students possess. (Of course, "X" is also the first letter of Xavier's last name.) As a young man, Xavier battled another mutant telepath, Amahl Farouk, alias the Shadow King, in Egypt. This encounter made him aware of the need to protect humanity from malevolent mutants.

Road to Recovery

Xavier subsequently lost the use of his legs in a clash with an alien who called himself Lucifer. Deeply depressed, Xavier led a reclusive existence at his family mansion. However, he began treating a ten-year-old girl named Jean Grey whose mutant powers had emerged prematurely.

Years later, the FBI initiated an investigation of mutants, headed by agent Fred Duncan. Xavier met

THE X-MEN
1 Storm **2** Banshee **3** Angel
4 Sunfire **5** Iceman **6** Havok
7 Polaris **8** Marvel Girl (Jean Grey)
9 Colossus **10** Nightcrawler
11 Wolverine **12** Cyclops
13 Thunderbird

ESSENTIAL STORYLINES

- ***Giant-Size X-Men #1***
  Charles Xavier forms a new international team of X-Men.
- ***The Uncanny X-Men #129–137***
  "The Dark Phoenix Saga": the X-Men try to stop the mad Phoenix (Jean Grey) from wreaking havoc through the cosmos and save her from insanity.
- ***The Uncanny X-Men #141–142***
  "Days of Future Past": present day X-Men try to prevent a future America ruled by Sentinels.

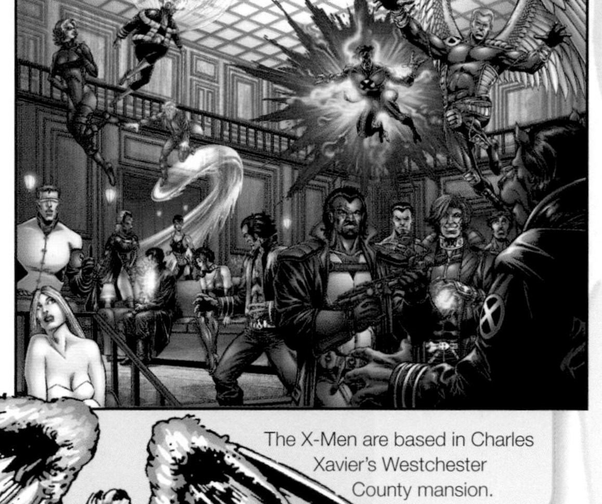

The X-Men are based in Charles Xavier's Westchester County mansion.

with Duncan and volunteered to locate young mutants and train them in managing their potentially dangerous abilities. Duncan agreed to the plan and pledged to keep Xavier's work with mutants secret. Xavier soon recruited five adolescent mutants to his school, giving each of them codenames: Cyclops, Iceman, the Angel (*see* Archangel), the Beast, and Marvel Girl (the teenage Jean Grey). All five were enrolled at Professor Xavier's School for Gifted Youngsters, a private school based in Xavier's mansion, in the town of Salem Center in New York City's Westchester County.

There Xavier educated them in conventional academic subjects, while secretly teaching them how to utilize their mutant abilities.

The next member of the X-Men, who served only briefly, was the Mimic, who was not a mutant but had the ability to imitate mutant powers. During a period when Xavier was in seclusion, he was impersonated by the Changeling, a shapeshifting mutant who died heroically. The mutants Havok and Lorna Dane, later known as Polaris, joined the team subsequently.

New Recruits

Most of the X-Men became trapped on the island of Krakoa, which proved to be a gigantic mutant organism. Xavier then recruited a new team of X-Men from various countries. The new members included the Banshee, from Ireland; Colossus, from Russia; Nightcrawler, from Germany; Storm, from equatorial Africa; Sunfire, from Japan; Thunderbird, a Native American; and Wolverine, from Canada.

Led by Cyclops, the new recruits rescued the X-Men from Krakoa. After their return, the senior X-Men left the team, except for Cyclops, who remained as deputy leader. Sunfire quit, and Thunderbird was killed during the new X-Men's second mission.

Over subsequent years, many other members have joined the X-Men, including Kitty Pryde, alias Shadowcat; Rogue; Rachel Summers, known both as the second Phoenix and the current Marvel Girl; Psylocke; the Dazzler; and Longshot. During a temporary reformation, even the X-Men's archfoe Magneto even joined the team.

Xavier formed a new international team of X-Men after the immense mutant Krakoa the Living Island captured the original team.

After forming their own group, X-Factor, the five founding X-Men returned to their original team. Xavier's school was renamed the Xavier Institute. Further new members included Forge, Jubilee, Gambit, Bishop, Revanche, Cannonball, Joseph (a clone of Magneto), Dr. Cecilia Reyes, Marrow and Maggott.

Storm organized a short-lived spinoff team called the X-Treme X-Men, which included, among others, Sage, the third Thunderbird, Lifeguard and Slipstream. Most of these members later joined the main X-Men team.

Open Secret

Recent new X-Men members have included Cable, Chamber, Husk, Northstar, Stacy X, the traitor Xorn, and former X-Men foes Emma Frost (The White Queen), and the Juggernaut. Ever since Charles Xavier's evil twin sister Cassandra Nova exposed him as a mutant, the Xavier Institute has been known to the general public as the base of the X-Men.

The Institute has considerably increased its student body, and senior X-Men act as teachers. The Institute and the X-Men also now openly work on behalf of mutant rights. **PS**

CEREBRO

Cerebro is a machine invented by Professor Charles Xavier to locate mutants possessing superhuman abilities. Cerebro accomplishes this by detecting psionic energy emitted by the minds of superhuman mutants. Cerebro operates best when it is linked to the mind of a telepath, such as Xavier or Jean Grey, through a headset. Xavier utilized an early version of Cerebro, called Cyberno, to locate Scott Summers, who became Cyclops. On combining with the Sentinel Bastion's nanotechnology, Cerebro became sentient. It posed a menace until Xavier destroyed it. Since then Xavier has created an advanced version, called Cerebra.

Among the X-Men's adversaries are Sabretooth (left, fighting Wolverine), the insect-like alien Brood (battling Cyclops), and their leading nemesis Magneto (top right, attacking Bishop).

FACTFILE

MEMBERS AND POWERS

XI'AN CHI XAN
With his left hand he disintegrates matter, with his right hand he heals injuries.

CEREBRA
Detects mutants with her mind.

KRYSTALIN
Creates crystals from thin air.

MEANSTREAK
Travels at superhuman speeds.

METALHEAD
Touches any metal and assumes its properties.

SKULLFIRE
Absorbed energy makes his skeleton glow.

BLOODHAWK
Transmutes body to develop red skin and bat-like wings.

BASE
The Savage Land, Antarctica

FIRST APPEARANCE
X-Men 2099 #1 (October 1993)

The X-Men 2099 were initially based in the mountains of New Mexico.

X-Men 2099

In an alternate future, the Earth is ruled by malevolent, self-serving corporations and mutants have been outlawed— forced underground.
In the year 2099, one mutant dedicated himself to overthrowing this oppressive world order. Gathering some of the surviving mutants together to form a new band of X-Men, the almost messianic Xi'an Chi Xan (also known as the Desert Ghost) began challenging this status quo.

Initially based at a mountain fortress in New Mexico that had once belonged to an enemy named Master Zhao, these X-Men were to become the protectors of Halo City in California, which had been declared a safe haven for mutants. However, when an approaching Phalanx planetoid caused severe flooding, mutants and humans were forced to flee to the Savage Land, in the Antarctic. Following the Phalanx's defeat, humanity is now in a position to rebuild. With humans and mutants now united together, the future is, once again, full of possibilities. **AD**

X-MEN 2099
1 Bloodhawk ***2*** Krystalin ***3*** Desert Ghost ***4*** Skullfire ***5*** Metalhead ***6*** Cerebra ***7*** Meanstreak

FACTFILE

MEMBERS AND POWERS

HENRIETTA HUNTER Empathic powers, could resurrect herself.

VIVISECTOR Could shapeshift into wolflike form.

EL GUAPO Could levitate while riding a skateboard.

DEAD GIRL Can return to life, can become intangible and communicate with the dead.

VENUS DEE MILO Body composed of pure energy, could self-teleport and project energy blasts.

DOOP Self-levitation

ANARCHIST Acidic sweat generated energy bolts.

MISTER SENSITIVE (Orphan) Self-levitation, superhuman speed, heightened senses.

PHAT Could increase the size of any part of his body

BASE Mobile

FIRST APPEARANCE
(as X-Force) *X-Force #116 (May 2001);* (as X-Statix) *X-Statix #1 (September 2002)*

Mr. Sensitive and Venus were lovers until both died on their final mission.

X-Statix

Rather than hide their mutant abilities from a bigoted humanity, the members of X-Statix took a completely opposite approach. They used their mutant powers to become rich and famous. The team was known as X-Force, having stolen the name from another mutant band.

The members of this new X-Force battled criminals to protect the public. But their adventures were telecast as a reality show, and members became celebrities. They paid for their success with their lives. During one show, most of the team, including the leader Zeitgeist, were massacred. Only the Anarchist, the teleporter U-Go Girl, and Doop survived.

Guy Smith, alias the Orphan and Mister Sensitive, became the leader of the team. Other recruits included Bloke, Dead Girl, El Guapo, Phat, Saint Anna, the Spike, Venus Dee Milo, and the Vivisector. Smith was succeeded as leader by the Anarchist and mutant pop star Henrietta Hunter. To avoid potential legal action, the group changed its name to X-Statix. The team continued to suffer fatalities, and the roster was completely wiped out on X-Statix's final mission. **PS**

X-STATIX
1 Henrietta Hunter ***2*** Vivisector ***3*** El Guapo ***4*** Dead Girl ***5*** Venus Dee Milo ***6*** Doop ***7*** Anarchist ***8*** Mister Sensitive ***9*** Phat

CHARACTER KEY
1 Angry Eagle
2 Simian
3 Spanner
4 Torque
5 Jubilee

X-People

The X-People inhabit an alternate future in which the Earth's superhuman population is dominated by a new generation of champions. In this reality, the X-Men have been recast as the X-People. Under the leadership of an adult Jubilee, the team upholds the principles of Professor X, who envisioned the peaceful coexistence of humans and mutants.

The new faces making up the roster of the X-People include the winged Angry Eagle, the gymnastic Simian, shapeshifting Spanner, and superfast Torque. Former members included the speedster Bluestreak, and an aging Cyclops, who still maintains connections to the team. The X-People battled J2 (son of Juggernaut) when the villainess Enthralla used her hypnotic abilities to coerce them into violence. Later, the X-People trained Wild Thing (daughter of Wolverine), but she declined the team's offer of membership. **DW**

FACTFILE

CURRENT MEMBERS AND POWERS

JUBILEE (leader)
Generates explosive energy bursts.

ANGRY EAGLE
Flight, enhanced eyesight.

SIMIAN
Enhanced agility, talented acrobat.

SPANNER
Can elongate limbs and change shape.

TORQUE
A super-speedster.

BASE
Mobile

FIRST APPEARANCE
J2 Vol. 1 #1 (October 1998)

Xandu

FIRST APPEARANCE Amazing Spider-Man Annual #2 (1965)
REAL NAME Unknown
OCCUPATION Sorceror **BASE** New York City
HEIGHT/WEIGHT Unrevealed **EYES** Blue **HAIR** White
SPECIAL POWERS/ABILITIES Xandu possesses numerous abilities derived from his sorcery, most notably a hypnotic gaze that makes other people do his bidding.

A would-be master sorcerer into whose possession half of the mystic Wand of Watomb fell, Xandu desired the power that would be his if he could unite both halves of this magical talisman. Recruiting several toughs at the waterfront and casting a spell that turned them into robots, Xandu sent them to recover the other half of the wand from Dr. Strange. But Strange gained an unexpected ally when Spider-Man stumbled on the robbery, and together they defeated Xandu's agents. Strange caused Xandu to forget all of his magical knowledge, but this didn't prevent the renegade sorcerer from returning again and again to challenge the two heroes. **TB**

XSE, The

FIRST APPEARANCE Uncanny X-Men Vol. 1 #282 (November 1991)
NOTABLE MEMBERS AND POWERS
Bishop Can absorb and release any form of energy
Randall (deceased) Immune to radiation, skilled combatant
Malcolm (deceased) Could distinguish between humans and mutants
Shard (deceased) Can absorb light and emit it as shockwaves
Hecate Projects a null-light field that causes others to see their fears

In an alternate future in which Earth's population rose up against their oppressors, the Sentinels, a mutant police force was formed to ensure peace between mutants and humans. This group, founded by the mutant Hecate, called itself Xavier's Security Enforcers in tribute to the idealism of the X-Men's Professor X. The XSE eventually arrived in our world's current reality while pursuing renegade member Trevor Fitzroy. A traitorous splinter group, Xavier's Underground Enforcers, included Greystone (1), Archer (2), and Fixx (3). **DW**

Xemnu

FIRST APPEARANCE Journey into Mystery #62 (November 1960)
REAL NAME Xemnu **OCCUPATION** Former ruler **BASE** Mobile
HEIGHT 11 ft **WEIGHT** 1,100 lbs **EYES** Red
HAIR Reddish-brown; moe recently white
SPECIAL POWERS/ABILITIES Consciousness able to survive without body for indefinite periods; psionically manipulate individuals through vast hypnotic abilities.

Although he cuts a lonely, tragic figure, Xemnu the Titan remains a very real threat to mankind. The one-time ruler of his native world, Xemnu left there to travel the galaxy. Upon returning home he discovered it had been ravaged by plague, and his people were dead. Having felt most at home on Earth, Xemnu returned there and made several attempts to transform its citizens into members of his own race. He was repeatedly rebuffed, the Hulk, Dr Strange and the Thing all taking turns to defeat him. Xemnu looks set to be the last of his kind. **AD**

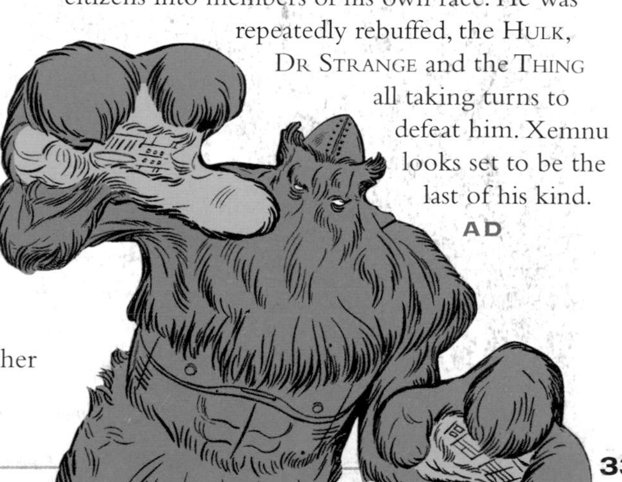

Yama, Jimmy

FIRST APPEARANCE Spider-Girl Vol. 1 #1 (October 1998)
REAL NAME Jimmy Yama
OCCUPATION High-school student **BASE** New York City
HEIGHT 5 ft 5 in **WEIGHT** 145 lbs **EYES** Brown **HAIR** Black
SPECIAL POWERS/ABILITIES Jimmy is an ordinary teenager with no special powers.

In a future timeline populated by a second generation of Earth's heroes, Jimmy Yama is a Midtown High School student and friend to May Parker (Spider-Girl). Yama's nemesis is Midtown bully Moose Mansfield. When Yama lashed out at Moose and inadvertently injured him, he stood trial for punitive damages until Moose's parents dropped the case.

Yama has tried several times to establish a romantic relationship with May, but his efforts have been hindered by his shyness. **DW**

Yancy Street Gang

FIRST APPEARANCE Fantastic Four vol. 1 #6 (September 1962)
BASE Yancy Street, on the Lower East Side of Manhattan

Based around the tough neighborhood of Manhattan's Lower East Side, the Yancy Street Gang was at one time led by Daniel Grimm, the wayward older brother of Ben Grimm, fated to transform into the Thing. Daniel was killed during a rumble between the Yancy gang and a rival street gang, and Ben eventually replaced his brother as the leader. But when Ben moved out west after the death of his mother, the Yancy Gang took it as a betrayal.

After Ben was transformed into the Thing and became one of the Fantastic Four, the Yancy Street Gang made it their mission to heckle and bedevil their former member. Some pranks attributed to the Yancy Street Gang were actually perpetrated by the Human Torch—and there is every indication that, beneath their seeming dislike of the Thing, the Gang actually admires their former leader and the Fantastic Four. **TB**

The Gang have often got their kicks by teasing and tormenting the Thing.

Yashida

FIRST APPEARANCE X-Men #118 (February 1979)
REAL NAME Mariko Yashida
OCCUPATION Head of Clan Yashida **BASE** Japan
HEIGHT 5 ft **WEIGHT** 100 lbs **EYES** Brown **HAIR** Black
SPECIAL POWERS/ABILITIES An exceptional businesswoman; had the normal fitness of a woman of her age and weight, but no special powers.

For many years, Mariko Yashida was the love of Wolverine's life. Meeting her during a mission to Japan, their relationship blossomed in New York, and they remained in contact even after her forced marriage to a brutal criminal associate of her father. The deaths of Mariko's husband and her father presented them with the opportunity for marriage, but Mariko wanted to wait—she had inherited the family business and wished to sever its criminal links first. In the end, the pair never wed—when she was poisoned by an assassin, Wolverine was forced to kill Mariko in order to end her terrible suffering. **AD**

Yellow Claw

FIRST APPEARANCE Yellow Claw #1 (October 1956)
REAL NAME Unrevealed **OCCUPATION** Conqueror
BASE Various hidden bases around the world
HEIGHT 6 ft 2 in **WEIGHT** 210 lbs **EYES** Brown **HAIR** Bald
SPECIAL POWERS/ABILITIES Knowledge of biochemistry, genetics, robotics, and sorcery (can reanimate the dead); can mentally create illusions in the minds of others.

Born in China in the 19th century, the Yellow Claw has long been determined to conquer the world. Through elixirs he has created, the Yellow Claw has extended his lifespan into the present. Early schemes to conquer America were repeatedly thwarted by FBI agent Jimmy Woo, with whom his grandniece Suwan was in love. In more recent times, SHIELD Director Nick Fury battled a "Yellow Claw" that was actually a robot created by Doctor Doom. However, the real Yellow Claw reemerged, and has clashed with Fury, Captain America, the Avengers, and other heroes. **PS**

Yellowjacket II

FIRST APPEARANCE Avengers Vol. 1 #264 (February 1986)
REAL NAME Rita DeMara
OCCUPATION Adventurer; former criminal **BASE** Mobile
HEIGHT 5 ft 5 in **WEIGHT** 115 lbs **EYES** Blue **HAIR** Blonde
SPECIAL POWERS/ABILITIES Battlesuit provided flight, the ability to shrink via Pym particles, and gloves that fired "disruptor sting" blasts of electricity.

Rita DeMara adopted the identity of Yellowjacket after stealing Hank Pym's original battlesuit from Avengers Mansion. She embarked on a life of crime as the second Yellowjacket, joining the Masters of Evil until eventually turning against that group.

Her efforts to go straight earned her reserve member status in the Avengers, and a place with the Guardians of the Galaxy. Yellowjacket II tragically died at the hands of Iron Man, who at the time was under the mental control of Immortus. **DW**

Young Avengers

In a possible alternate future, a young robotics student named Nathaniel Richards is saved from death in the year 3016 by his future self. Nathaniel also learns that he is destined to grow up to become Kang the Conqueror. Horrified, the 16-year-old flees to modern-day Earth, hoping to circumvent his fate by securing help from the Avengers, Kang's greatest enemies.

Unfortunately, Nathaniel arrives soon after the Scarlet Witch has disassembled the current team. He breaks into Stark Industries (*see* Iron Man) and uploads the central processing unit of the recently destroyed android the Vision, finding a failsafe program that pinpoints the next generation of super-powered youths. Calling himself Iron Lad, Nathaniel quickly recruits them and trains them for a battle with Kang.

When Captain America and Iron Man learn of this new team, they try to convince the teenagers to disband before they get hurt, but Kang arrives and demands the return of Iron Lad so that destiny could fulfil its preordained course. Otherwise Kang would not exist! In the resulting battle, Kang is killed and Iron Lad must accept his destiny in order to prevent the destruction of the current timeline. TD

YOUNG AVENGERS
1 Wiccan
2 Stature
3 Hulkling
4 The Patriot
5 Kate Bishop

After leading the team against Mr. Hyde (left), Patriot admitted he had taken a mutant growth hormone to increase his physical powers.

FACTFILE
MEMBERS AND POWERS
IRON LAD (Nathaniel Richards)
Scientific genius with a suit of psychokinetic armor that responds to his thoughts.
WICCAN, formerly Asgardian (Billy Kaplan)
Projects mystical energy.
KATE BISHOP
Olympic-level athlete and weapons-master.
STATURE (Cassie Lang)
Size-changing abilities.
HULKLING (Teddy Altman)
shapeshifter with healing factor.
PATRIOT (Eli Bradley)
Enhanced speed and agility.
BASE
Formerly Avengers Mansion, New York City

FIRST APPEARANCE
Young Avengers #1 (February 2005)

Young Gods

The finest examples of humanity, the Young Gods were chosen by Gaea, the spirit of the Earth, and the combined heads of the various pantheons of Earthly gods to be presented to the space-faring Celestials at the time of their Fourth Host, as an example of the potential of mankind. Gathered over a thousand-year period, endowed with their godlike powers and kept in a state of stasis until they were needed, the Young Gods did impress the Celestials as to the worthiness of the species they had created years before, and ensured the survival of the Earth. Thereafter, the Young Gods vanished into outer space with the Celestials. They have seldom been seen since. TB

THE YOUNG GODS
1 Moonstalker
2 Calculus
3 Caduceus
4 Genii
5 Daydreamer
6 Splice
7 Varua
8 Highnote
9 Mindslinger
10 Sea Witch
11 Brightsword
12 Harvest

FACTFILE
MEMBERS AND POWERS
BRIGHTSWORD
Wields an energy sword.
CADUCEUS
Possesses a healing touch.
CALCULUS
Predicts future, reads minds.
DAYDREAMER
Creates images in others' minds.
GENII
Brings inanimate objects to life.
HARVEST
Command over plant life.
HIGHNOTE
Generates blasts of sonic energy.
MINDSLINGER
Transforms into other objects.
MOONSTALKER
Superhumanly swift.
SEA WITCH
Controls all forms of water.
SPLICE
Can reshape matter.
VARUA
Telepathy, teleportation, flight; can unite the Young Gods into the Uni-Mind

FIRST APPEARANCE
Thor # 202 (August 1972)

Yukio

FIRST APPEARANCE Wolverine vol. 1 #1 (September 1982)
REAL NAME Yukio (full name unrevealed)
OCCUPATION Adventurer, former assassin **BASE** Mobile
HEIGHT 5 ft 9 in **WEIGHT** 130 lbs **EYES** Brown **HAIR** Black
SPECIAL POWERS/ABILITIES Highly skilled athlete, martial artist, and knife-thrower.

Yukio started out as a thief, running capers with Gambit, before becoming an assassin in the service of Japanese underworld kingpin Lord Shingen of Clan Yashida. Her employer sent her after Wolverine; however, she eventually befriended him and his X-Men teammates, particularly Storm. Wolverine grew to trust Yukio so much that he left his foster daughter Amiko in her care. Yukio and Amiko were later attacked by Omega Red and Lady Deathstrike. During the fight, Yukio suffered crippling injuries from which she has only recently recovered.
DW

Zabu

FIRST APPEARANCE X-Men #10 (March 1965)
REAL NAME Zabu **OCCUPATION** Companion to Ka-Zar
BASE The Savage Land, Antarctica
HEIGHT/WEIGHT Unrevealed **EYES** Green **HAIR** Orange
SPECIAL POWERS/ABILITIES Has two long, sharp, saber-like teeth that he uses as weapons; possesses great strength and agility, and is unusually intelligent for a saber-tooth tiger.

Zabu is the last known saber-tooth tiger on Earth. The dominant predators during the Ice Age, saber-tooths still survived in the Savage Land, until nearly all of them were exterminated by Savage Land natives. When Maa-Gor and his Swamp Men slew Zabu's mate, the infuriated tiger hunted them down. Zabu attacked Maa-Gor just as he was about to kill Kevin Plunder, the orphaned son of an explorer. In the ensuing struggle, Kevin shot Maa-Gor, wounding him, and thereby saving Zabu's life.

Ever since, Zabu and Kevin have been loyal companions, and Kevin is known today as the jungle lord KA-ZAR, which means "Son of the Tiger." **PS**

Zaran

FIRST APPEARANCE Master of Kung Fu #77 (June 1979)
REAL NAME Maximillian Zaran
OCCUPATION Mercenary **BASE** Mobile
HEIGHT 6 ft 1 in **WEIGHT** 235 lbs **EYES** Blue **HAIR** Red
SPECIAL POWERS/ABILITIES Skilled with a wide range of ancient weapons, including nunchakus, shurikens, maces, bows and arrows, staffs, and knives; he can also fire a gun.

A former British MI6 agent and now a mercenary, Maximillian Zaran's career has been chequered to say the least. After defecting from the British secret service, Zaran worked for Fah Lo Suee, Fu Manchu's daughter, but she cut his contract short. For a time his own apprentice usurped Zaran's identity, but this situation has since been resolved and Zaran is now a member of BATROC'S Brigade. The Brigade undertook an assignment for MAELSTROM, during which Zaran was responsible for killing Grasshopper, mere seconds after the man-sized insect joined the GREAT LAKES AVENGERS. **AD**

Z'Nox

FIRST APPEARANCE X-Men #65 (February 1970)
BASE Z'nox, Huz'deyr solar system, Andromeda galaxy
SPECIAL POWERS/ABILITIES Villainous race boasts highly sophisticated technology and are able to move their homeworld through space.

Although unable to subvert the SKRULL dominance of their home galaxy Andromeda, the warlike Z'nox were a highly sophisticated and deadly race of world conquerors. When PROFESSOR X learned that a Z'nox invasion force was heading towards Earth, he went into complete seclusion, leaving the mutant shapeshifter the CHANGELING to stand in for him. As the fleet approached, Xavier combined his mind with those of the X-MEN and the Earth's entire population to psionically repel the attack. **AD**

ZODIAC *SEE OPPOSITE PAGE*

Zaladane

FIRST APPEARANCE Astonishing Tales Vol. 1 #1 (December 1970)
REAL NAME Zala Dane (allegedly)
OCCUPATION High priestess **BASE** The Savage Land
HEIGHT 5 ft 9 in **WEIGHT** 125 lbs **EYES** Blue **HAIR** Black
SPECIAL POWERS/ABILITIES Zaladane is a sorceress who possesses assorted spell-based abilities.

The High Priestess of Garrok, Zaladane led believers against the other tribes of the Savage Land in a bid for power. Zaladane' sorcery transformed Kirk Marston into the avatar of Garrok on Earth, and she supported him as his second in command. After her bid to conquer the Savage Land had been foiled, Zaladane's mutates abducted Lorna Dane, the X-Man known as POLARIS. Posing as Lorna's long-lost sister, Zaladane succeeded in transferring Polaris' magnetic abilities to herself, albeit temporarily. Thereafter, in a failed bid to control all of the magnetic forces on Earth, Zaladane ran afoul of MAGNETO, who overwhelmed her with his own superior magnetic might, and left her for dead. **TB**

Zarathos

FIRST APPEARANCE Marvel Spotlight Vol. 1 #5 (August 1972)
REAL NAME Zarathos **OCCUPATION** The Spirit of Vengeance
BASE The netherworld dimension of Mephisto
HEIGHT 20 ft **WEIGHT** 225 lbs **EYES/HAIR** Not applicable
SPECIAL POWERS/ABILITIES Virtually immortal demon; uses magic to enhance strength, height, weight. Can employ levitation and project magical blasts of concussive force. Can project cold fire that sears the souls of his enemies.

Zarathos is a demon who journeyed to Earth before the Dawn of Man. He slumbered until a sorcerer awoke him and offered to trade souls for his aid. MEPHISTO, lord of the underworld, grew jealous of a cult that grew around Zarathos and enslaved him, sending him to possess humans in the causes of sin, corruption, and vengeance. In recent years, Zarathos became bound to stunt motorcyclist Johnny Blaze and later to bike messenger Danny Ketch, transforming both of them into the demonic GHOST RIDER. **TD**

Zola, Armin

FIRST APPEARANCE Captain America Vol. 1 #208 (April 1977)
REAL NAME Arnim Zola **OCCUPATION** Criminal biochemist
BASE Weisshorn Mountain, Switzerland
HEIGHT 5 ft 10 in **WEIGHT** 200 lbs
EYES Brown **HAIR** None
SPECIAL POWERS/ABILITIES Brilliant geneticist; can mentally project his intelligence into any of his creations.

During the late 1930s, Swiss geneticist Arnim Zola discovered a tome of Deviant science and learned how to create artificial life. He built himself a new body, with a brain inside its chest, a holographically-projected face, and an "ESP box" for a head. Zola became a valued member of Hitler's Third Reich, preserving Hitler's consciousness after his death in the form of the Hate-Monger. Zola's creations have included Primus and Doughboy, as well as bio-plastoids that can impersonate any being. A frequent foe of CAPTAIN AMERICA, Zola is also responsible for resurrecting the RED SKULL into a copy of Captain America's own body. **DW**

ZODIAC

FACTFILE

MEMBERS AND POWERS

ARIES
Shoots fire from his horns.

AQUARIUS
Carries a gun that fires blasts of electricity.

CANCER
Superhuman strength, ability to create and control torrents of water.

CAPRICORN
Superhuman leaping and climbing abilities

GEMINI
Can split into two bodies, can grow to huge size and strength, can project energy.

LEO
Superhuman strength and leaping ability.

LIBRA
Can fly, can become intangible

PISCES
Can easily maneuver underwater

SAGITTARIUS
Advanced archery skills

SCORPIO
Wields the powerful Zodiac Key

TAURUS
Superhuman strength

VIRGO
Highly skilled in creating and using machines

BASE Mobile

FIRST APPEARANCE
(in shadow) Defenders #49 (July 1977); (fully seen) Defenders #50 (August 1977)

ZODIAC
1 Aquarius ***2*** Virgo ***3*** Gemini ***4*** Aries ***5*** Leo ***6*** Capricorn ***7*** Sagittarius ***8*** Libra ***9*** Taurus ***10*** Pisces ***11*** Cancer

Zodiac is a criminal organization, made up of intelligent androids. Each member of Zodiac is based on a zodiac sign. There was also another organization called Zodiac made up of 12 human criminals. The original human Zodiac was formed by Cornelius van Lunt and intended to rule humanity. Eventually they were all killed battling the android Zodiac. The second (android) Zodiac was formed when Jacob Fury (Scorpio from the original human Zodiac and brother of Nick Fury) gained possession of the powerful Zodiac Key. The Key unlocked Fury's potential for evil. Fury became the android Scorpio and with 11 other androids, each representing a sign of the Zodiac, he began a battle against Earth's greatest heroes.

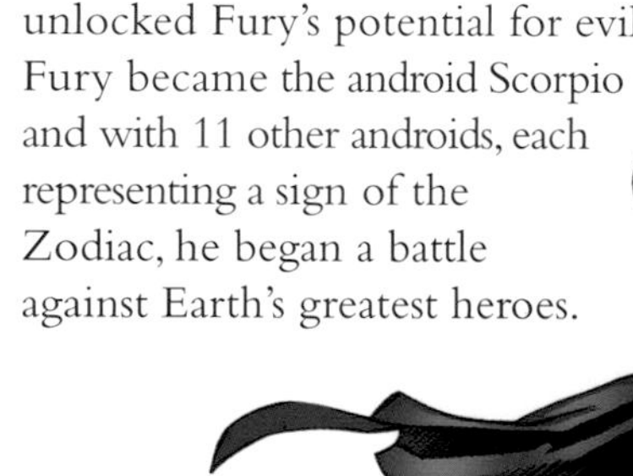

ZODIAC ATTACK

The battle raged on, and in time, the DEFENDERS joined the fight to stop Zodiac. Eventually, the AVENGERS defeated the android Zodiac. Some were destroyed and others were taken into custody, (though these Zodiac soon escaped).

During a clash with the West Coast AVENGERS, Scorpio used the Zodiac Key to transport them all to the dimension of the Brotherhood, where the Zodiac androids fell inert. **MT**

Scorpio wields the Zodiac Key, which can fire energy bolts and teleport people and objects from one dimension to another. It was sent to Earth by the Brotherhood, a cult from another dimension that believes that the Key's existence depends on constant conflict between good and evil.

ZOMBIE

FIRST APPEARANCE Tales of the Zombie #1 (August 1973)
REAL NAME Simon William Garth
OCCUPATION Former businessman **BASE** New Orleans
HEIGHT 6 ft 2 in **WEIGHT** 220 lbs
EYES White **HAIR** Black
SPECIAL POWERS/ABILITIES Superhuman strength and regenerative ability.

A ruthless businessman named Simon Garth treated his employees with contempt. Eventually, his gardener, Gyps, became so upset that he killed Garth and resurrected him as a zombie. For two years the zombified Garth wandered the Earth, initially controlled by Gyps and later by one despicable individual after another. However the love of a good woman restored Garth to life for a short spell, enabling him to put his affairs in order. Although he then became a zombie once more, a benevolent voodoo priest intervened to help Garth end his undead existence. **AD**

ZZZAX

FIRST APPEARANCE Incredible Hulk #166 (August 1973)
REAL NAME Inapplicable **OCCUPATION** Purveyor of destruction
BASE Mobile **HEIGHT** Variable (max. 40 ft)
WEIGHT Negligible **EYES /HAIR** Inapplicable
SPECIAL POWERS/ABILITIES Unlimited electricity-manipulating powers including flight, super strength, and the ability to fire electrical bolts of concussive force.

Zzzax is a living electromagnetic field, formed by a bizarre accident that took place at a Consolidated Edison nuclear power plant. By absorbing the electromagnetic brainwave energies of its victims, Zzzax gained a limited degree of sentience and fashioned itself into a crude humanoid form. Zzzax can grow in size by draining energy from its surroundings, a tactic that it has employed when battling its most frequent foe, the HULK.

For a time, the consciousness of the irascible General "Thunderbolt" ROSS inhabited the form of Zzzax. Recently, Zzzax escaped from captivity after ELECTRO sprang a horde of Super Villains from the Raft jail. **DW**

INDEX

*Entries in **bold** signify that a character has his, her or its own entry.*

D

N

O

P

Q

R

S